Hospitality Financial Accounting

Hospitality Financial Accounting

Jerry J. Weygandt *Ph.D., C.P.A.*
Arthur Andersen Alumni Professor of Accounting
University of Wisconsin

Donald E. Kieso *Ph.D., C.P.A.*
KPMG Peat Marwick
Emeritus Professor of Accounting
Northern Illinois University

Paul D. Kimmel *Ph.D., C.P.A.*
Associate Professor of Accounting
University of Wisconsin—Milwaukee

Agnes L. DeFranco *Ed.D., C.H.E., C.H.A.E.*
Associate Professor of Hospitality
University of Houston

WILEY
JOHN WILEY & SONS, INC.

The specimen financial statements (the Appendix) are printed with permission of Hilton Hotels Corporation.

The information and trademarks offered herein are the property of Hilton Hotels Corporation.

Hilton is a registered trademark of Hilton Hotels Corporation. All rights reserved. Used with permission.

This book is printed on acid-free paper. ♾

Published by John Wiley & Sons, Inc., Hoboken, New Jersey
Published simultaneously in Canada

Library of Congress Cataloging-in-Publication Data:
Hospitality financial accounting / Jerry J. Weygandt ... [et al.]
p. cm.
Includes bibliographical references and index.
ISBN 0-471-27055-5 (cloth)
1. Hospitality industry—Accounting I. Weygandt, Jerry J.

HF5686.H75H66 2003
657′.836—dc21 2003049737

Printed in the United States of America

10 9 8 7 6 5 4 3 2 1

TO THE INSTRUCTOR

With this text, we seek to create a book about the hospitality business that makes the subject clear and fascinating to beginning students. That is our passion: to provide a link between hospitality financial accounting principles, student learning, and the real world.

STUDENT EMPOWERMENT AND SUCCESS

In our effort to create an effective text, we surveyed the market and talked personally to instructors. We heard again and again that the biggest challenges students face are to become motivated to learn how to study and to manage their tasks. We were gratified to learn that our general accounting texts have helped empower students to meet these challenges and have been rated highest in customer satisfaction by both instructors and students.

We have responded to these challenges by making the pedagogical framework of *Hospitality Financial Accounting* strong and the presentation clear. We want to give hospitality students the tools and the motivation they need to succeed in subsequent accounting courses and in their future hospitality careers.

GOALS AND FEATURES OF THIS EDITION

This first edition of *Hospitality Financial Accounting* provides an opportunity to offer to the hospitality discipline a textbook that has set high standards for quality. Reviewers of *Hospitality Financial Accounting* comment positively on the writing style, the use of real-world examples, pedagogical features, and the fact that the textbook is not only about accounting but about business as well.

The primary purpose in creating a financial accounting textbook specifically for hospitality students was to maintain these successful features and improve on them.

- We've carefully evaluated all topics regarding their suitability for and relevance to the beginning hospitality accounting course. Topics beyond the scope of the first hospitality accounting course are not included. Features and topics relevant to today's Internet and e-business environment are included.
- A student's textbook should be as pedagogically effective as possible. *The Navigator*, our guide to the learning process in the book, has been well received and has proven effective for students seeking to improve their study skills. *Action Plans*, which accompany mini-demonstrations ("Do It") and Demonstration Problems in each chapter, help students develop their problem-solving skills.
- The book involves the student in the learning process and ensures that the student understands the *why* as well as the *how*. The message is consistent with the Accounting Education Change Commission recommendations, which encourage an emphasis on communication skills, critical thinking and decision-making skills, ethics, international accounting, and real-world emphasis.
- This book includes user-oriented material. Our reasons were twofold: (1) to accomplish the objectives of the Accounting Education Change Commission, and (2) to demonstrate the relevance of accounting to hospitality students. Most of the user material is in the *Exercises* section of the end-of-chapter material. These learning activities are designed to develop many skills that will be of use to students in other courses and in life after college, including financial statement analysis skills and the ability to use the Internet. In addition, to give students the opportunity to follow an extended real-world example, we have integrated references to the Hilton Hotels financial statements throughout the book, including Review It questions, ratio presentations, and end-of-chapter assignments.

HIGHLIGHTS IN EACH CHAPTER

CHAPTER 1 *Hospitality Accounting in Action*

- Feature Story on Conrad Hilton and related "A Look Back" exercise with solution
- Complete definitions of financial and managerial accounting
- An Accounting in Action (AIA) e-Business Insight on the impact of Internet use in the hospitality industry

CHAPTER 2 *Accounting Principles*

- Feature Story on revenue and expense recognition and reporting
- Detailed coverage of the Uniform System of Accounts and Financial Reporting
- AIA Business Insights on expense reporting for casinos and profit margin expectations in hospitality businesses

CHAPTER 3 *The Recording Process*

- Information on electronic data processing in the preparation of managerial reports

CHAPTER 4 *Adjusting the Accounts*

- Discussion of accrual-basis versus cash-basis accounting at the beginning of the chapter
- An AIA e-Business Insight on revenue from a Web-site ad space

CHAPTER 5 *Completion of the Accounting Cycle*

- Feature Story on Rhino's Foods, Inc. about educating employees on the financial health of the company as a motivational tool
- An AIA e-Business Insight on the monthly billing of a private club

CHAPTER 6 *Subsidiary Ledgers and Special Journals*

- Feature Story on the different managerial opportunities in the hospitality industry
- Detailed discussion of the various journals in accounting

CHAPTER 7 *Accounting for Merchandising Operations in Hospitality*

- Feature Story on how foodservice companies set prices while maintaining a profitable margin
- Emphasis on a simplified coverage of the perpetual inventory system
- Information on how to use a worksheet

CHAPTER 8 *The Statement of Cash Flows*

- Feature Story "Cash Is King" emphasizing the importance of cash to the success of a hospitality company

- Detailed discussion of the direct and indirect methods of the statement of cash flows

CHAPTER 9 Payroll

- Feature Story on the importance of service in the hospitality industry and the impact of labor cost wages to the success of a company
- A Technology in Action focuses on payroll fraud and how to avoid it
- Important information on the Fair Labor Standards Act
- Complete coverage on Tipped Employees and Tips Credit, an important accounting function for service-based industries

CHAPTER 10 Inventories, Cost Calculations, and Internal Controls

- Detailed analysis of food and beverage cost calculations and inventories in foodservice operations
- An illustration of the effects of inventory errors on two years' income statements
- A Technology in Action on the importance of controls in saving money

CHAPTER 11 Accounting for Receivables and Payables

- A discussion of credit policies and the importance of the use of credit in the hospitality industry

CHAPTER 12 Long-Term and Intangible Assets

- Feature Story highlighting Homestead Resort and its preparation for the 2002 Winter Olympics
- Full coverage of the four depreciation methods
- Discussion of MACRS

CHAPTER 13 Sole Proprietorships, Partnerships, and Corporations

- Full discussion of the formation of sole proprietorships, partnerships, and corporations, including S-corporations

APPENDIX Specimen Financial Statements

- Hilton Hotels Corporation

PEDAGOGICAL FRAMEWORK

Hospitality Financial Accounting provides tools to help students learn accounting concepts and procedures and apply them to the real world. It places increased emphasis on the processes students undergo as they learn.

Learning How to Use the Text

- A **Student Owner's Manual** begins the text to help students understand the value of the text's learning aids and how to use them.
- Chapter 1 contains **notes** that explain each learning aid the first time it appears.
- Finally, **The Navigator** pulls all the learning aids together into a learning system designed to guide students through each chapter and help them succeed in learning the material. It consists of (1) a checklist at the beginning of the chapter, which outlines text features and study skills they will need, and (2) a series of check boxes that prompt students to use the learning aids in the chapter and set priorities as they study. At the end of the chapter, students are reminded to return to The Navigator to check off their completed work. An example of The Navigator is above.

THE NAVIGATOR ✓

- Understand *Concepts for Review* ❑
- Read *Feature Story* ❑
- Scan *Study Objectives* ❑
- Read *Preview* ❑
- Read text and answer *Before You Go On* *p.* 40 ❑ *p.* 47 ❑ *p.* 64 ❑
- Work *Demonstration Problem* ❑
- Review *Summary of Study Objectives* ❑
- Complete *Assignments* ❑

Understanding the Context

- **Concepts for Review,** listed at the beginning of each chapter, identify concepts that will apply in the chapter to come. In this way, students see the relevance to the current chapter of concepts covered earlier.
- The **Feature Story** helps students picture how the chapter topic relates to the real world of accounting and business. It serves as a running example in the chapter and is the topic of a series of review questions call **A Look Back at Our Feature Story,** toward the end of the chapter.
- **Study Objectives** form a learning framework throughout the text, with each objective repeated in the margin at the appropriate place in the main body of the chapter and again in the **Summary**. Further, end-of-chapter assignment materials are linked to the Study Objectives.
- A chapter **Preview** links the chapter-opening Feature Story to the major topics of the chapter. First, an introductory paragraph explains how the Feature Story relates to the topic to be discussed, and then a graphic outline of the chapter provides a "visual road map" useful for seeing the big picture, as well as the connections between subtopics.

Learning the Material

- **Financial statements** appear regularly throughout the book. Often, numbers or categories are highlighted in colored type to draw attention to key information.
- **Key ratios,** using data from **Hilton Hotels Corporation 2001 Annual Report,** are examined in appropriate spots throughout the text. Integration of ratios enables students to see in a single presentation two important pieces of information about financial data: how they are presented in financial statements and how users of financial information analyze them.

- **The Accounting Equation** appears in the margin next to key journal entries throughout the text. This feature reinforces the students' understanding of the impacts of an accounting transaction on the financial statements.
- **Key terms** and concepts are printed in blue where they are first explained in the text and are defined again in the end-of-chapter glossary.
- **Helpful Hints** boxes help clarify concepts being discussed.
- **Accounting in Action** boxes give students insight into how real companies use accounting in practice. The AIA boxes, some of which are highlighted with striking photographs, cover business, ethics, and international issues. Of particular interest are the **e-Business Insight** boxes reporting on how business technology is expanding the service provided by accountants.
- **Technology in Action** boxes show how users of accounting information use computers.
- **Color illustrations** visually reinforce important concepts of the text.
- **Infographics**, a special type of illustration, help students visualize and apply accounting concepts to the real world. They provide entertaining and memorable visual reminders of key concepts.
- Marginal **Alternative Terminology** notes present synonymous terms, since terminology may differ in the business world.
- **Before You Go On** sections occur at the end of each key topic and often consist of two parts:
  - * ***Review It*** questions serve as a learning check by asking students to stop and answer questions about the material covered. ***Review It*** questions marked with the *Hilton* icon (see right) send students to find information in the Hilton Hotels 2001 Annual Report (excerpted in the Appendix at the end of the text). These exercises help cement students' understanding of how topics covered in the chapter are reported in real-world financial statements. Answers appear at the end of the chapter.
  - * A mini-demonstration problem, in a section called ***Do It***, gives immediate practice of the material just covered and is keyed to homework exercises. An ***Action Plan*** lists the steps necessary to complete the task, and a ***Solution*** is provided to help students understand the reasoning involved in reaching an answer.
  - * The last **Before You Go On** exercise in the chapter takes students back for a critical look at the chapter-opening Feature Story.
- Marginal **International Notes** introduce international issues and problems in accounting.
- Marginal **Ethics Notes** help sensitize students to the real-world ethical dilemmas of accounting and business.

Putting It Together

- **Demonstration Problems** give students the opportunity to refer to a detailed solution to a representative problem as they do homework assignments. ***Action Plans*** list strategies to assist students in understanding similar types of problems.
- The **Summary of Study Objectives** relates the study objectives to the key points of the chapter. It gives students another opportunity to review, as well as to see how all the key topics within the chapter are related.
- The **Glossary** defines all the key terms and concepts introduced in the chapter.

Developing Skills Through Practice

- **Exercises** build students' confidence and test their basic skills. Some take a little longer to complete and present more of a challenge. Several exercises stress the application of the concepts presented in the chapter. Each exercise is keyed to one or more study objective.

Expanding and Applying Knowledge

One or two exercises in each chapter offer a wealth of resources to help instructors and students pull together the learning for the chapter. These exercises offer projects for those instructors who want to broaden the learning experience by bringing in more real-world decision-making and critical-thinking activities. The exercises are described below:

- A **Financial Reporting Problem** directs students to study various aspects of the financial statements in Hilton's 2001 Annual Report, which is excerpted in the Appendix at the end of the text.
- **Exploring the Web** exercises guide students to Internet Web sites where they can find and analyze information to the chapter topic.
- The **Group Decision Case** helps build decision-making skills by analyzing accounting information in a less-structured situation. These cases require evaluation of a manager's decision or lead to a decision among alternative courses of action. As group activities, they promote teamwork.
- **Ethics Cases** describe typical ethical dilemmas and ask students to analyze situations, identify the stakeholders and the ethical issues involved, and decide on appropriate courses of action.

SUPPLEMENTARY MATERIALS AND TEACHING AIDS

Hospitality Financial Accounting features a full line of teaching and learning resources developed and revised to help you create a more dynamic and innovative learning environment.

Student success is a major theme of the supplements package. These resources—including print and Internet-based materials—also take an *active learning approach* to help build students' skills and analytical abilities.

- **Web site at www.wiley.com/college.** Recognizing that the Internet is a valuable resource for students and instructors, we have developed a Web site at www.wiley.com/college to provide a variety of additional resources.

Instructor's Resources

For the instructor, we have designed a support package to help you maximize your teaching effectiveness.

Instructor's Manual. The **Instructor's Manual** is a comprehensive resource guide designed to assist professors in preparing lectures and assignments, including sample syllabi for the hospitality financial accounting course, evaluating homework assignments, and preparing quizzes and exams. (Also available at www.wiley.com/college.) Each chapter contains the following information:

- Chapter Review and Lecture Outline: **Chapter reviews** cover the significant topics and points contained in each chapter. Teaching tips and references to text materials are in the **enhanced lecture outlines**. Further, a twenty-minute quiz in the form of ten true/false and five multiple-choice questions (with solutions) is provided.
- **Solutions:** These are detailed solutions to all exercises in the textbook. Suggested answers to the questions found on the Web site are also included. Each chapter includes a table to identify the difficulty level and estimated completion time of each exercise.
- **Test Bank:** The test bank allows instructors to tailor examinations according to study objectives and content. Each chapter includes exercises as well as multiple-choice, matching, and true/false questions.

PowerPoint Presentation Material. The PowerPoint lecture aid contains a combination of key concepts, illustrations, and problems from the textbook for use in the classroom. Easily customizable for classroom use, the presentations are designed according to the organization of the material in the textbook to reinforce hospitality financial accounting principles visually and graphically. (Available at www.wiley.com/college.)

Student Active Learning Aids

In addition to innovative pedagogy included in the text, we offer a number of valuable learning aids for students. These are intended to enhance true understanding so that students will be able to apply hospitality financial accounting concepts.

Working Papers. **Working Papers** are accounting forms for all end-of-chapter exercises. A convenient resource for organizing and completing homework assignments, they demonstrate how to correctly set up solution formats and are directly tied to textbook assignments.

Excel Working Papers. Available on CD-ROM, these Excel-formatted forms can be used for end-of-chapter exercises. The **Excel Working Papers** provide students with the option of printing forms and completing them manually, or entering data electronically and then printing out a completed form. By entering data electronically, students can paste homework to a new file and e-mail the worksheet to their instructor.

Self-Study Questions. These online practice tests enable students to check their understanding of important concepts. Located at www.wiley.com/college, the **self-study questions** are keyed to the study objectives and students can go back and review sections of the chapter in which they find they need further work. The quizzes are graded to give students immediate feedback.

Questions. These questions, located at www.wiley.com/college, provide a full online review of chapter content and help students prepare for class discussions and testing situations. Students answer the questions online and then their work is e-mailed directly to their instructor. Instructors can find the answers to these questions in the Instructor's Manual and with the online instructor resources.

ACKNOWLEDGMENTS

During the course of development of *Hospitality Financial Accounting* I benefited greatly from manuscript reviewers. The constructive suggestions and innovative ideas of the reviewers and the creativity and accuracy of the ancillary author are greatly appreciated.

Reviewers

I thank these reviewers of *Hospitality Financial Accounting* for their excellent suggestions in shaping the content of this text and its proposal:

Richard F. Ghiselli, Purdue University
Yang H. Huo, Roosevelt University
Ronald L. Jordan, University of Houston
Lee M. Kreul, Purdue University
Stephen M. Lebruto, University of Central Florida
Patricia McCaughey, Endicott College
Kevin W. Poirier, Johnson & Wales University
Richard Savich, California State Polytechnic University, Pomona
Don St. Hilaire, California State Polytechnic University, Pomona
Darrell Van Loenen, University of Wisconsin–Stout

In addition, the reviewers and focus group participants of the original *Financial Accounting, Fourth Edition*, provided excellent feedback to help us write this text:

Sheila Ammons, Austin Community College
David Carr, Austin Community College
Andy Chen, Northeast Illinois University
Edward J. Corcoran, Community College of Philadelphia
Jeff Edwards, Portland Community College
Doug Laufer, Metropolitan State College of Denver
James Lukawitz, University of Memphis
Janice Mardon, Green River Community College
John Marts, University of North Carolina–Wilmington
Kathy S. Moffeit, Southwest Texas State University
Carla Rich, Pensacola Junior College
Patricia Robinson, Johnson & Wales University

Ancillary Author

The input of the ancillary author in her thoroughness and accuracy has created a valuable package of materials to support this text:

Tanya Venegas, University of Houston

Publications

We would like to thank the Hilton Hotels Corporation for permitting the use of its 2001 Annual Report.

A Final Note of Thanks

I would also like to convey my sincere thank-you to Jerry Weygandt, Don Kieso, and Paul Kimmel, the authors of the original text. They have graciously given me their trust and the most wonderful opportunity to adapt their book for use in the hospitality industry. Last but not least, thanks to Julie Kerr, a wonderful friend and editor, who makes this project a pleasure.

Agnes DeFranco
University of Houston
Houston, Texas

HOW TO USE THE STUDY AIDS IN THIS BOOK

THE RECORDING PROCESS

THE NAVIGATOR ✓

- Understand *Concepts for Review* ❑
- Read *Feature Story* ❑
- Scan *Study Objectives* ❑
- Read *Preview* ❑
- Read text and answer *Before You Go On* *p. 81* ❑ *p. 85* ❑ *p. 97* ❑ *p. 99* ❑
- Work *Demonstration Problem* ❑
- Review *Summary of Study Objectives* ❑
- Complete *Assignments* ❑

The Navigator is a learning system designed to guide you through each chapter and help you succeed in learning the material. It consists of (1) a checklist at the beginning of the chapter, which outlines text features and study skills you will need, and (2) a series of check boxes that prompt you to use the learning aids in the chapter and set priorities as you study.

CONCEPTS FOR REVIEW

Before studying this chapter, you should know or, if necessary, review:

a. What are assets, liabilities, stockholders' equity, retained earnings, dividends, revenues, and expenses. (Ch. 1, pp. 11–12)

b. Why assets equal liabilities plus stockholders' equity. (Ch. 1, p. 11)

c. What transactions are and how they affect the basic accounting equation. (Ch. 1, pp. 14–20)

THE NAVIGATOR

The **Feature Story** helps you picture how the chapter topic relates to the real world of accounting and business. Throughout the chapter, references to the Feature Story will help you put new ideas in context, organize them, and remember them. The problem called **A Look Back at Our Feature Story** toward the end of the chapter helps you pull together the ideas learned in the chapter. Many Feature Stories end with the **URL** of the company cited in the story.

Concepts for Review, listed at the beginning of each chapter, are the accounting concepts you learned in previous chapters that you will need to know in order to understand the topics you are about to learn. Page references are provided if you need to review before reading the chapter.

FEATURE STORY

No Such Thing as a Perfect World

When she got a job doing the accounting for **Forster's Restaurants**, Tanis Anderson had almost finished her business administration degree at Simon Fraser University. But even after Tanis completed her degree requirements, her education still continued—this time, in the real world.

Tanis's responsibilities include paying the bills, tracking food and labor costs, and managing the payroll for **The Mug and Musket**, a popular destination restaurant in Surrey, British Columbia. "My title is Director of Finance," she laughs, "but really that means I take care of whatever needs doing!"

The use of judgment is a big part of the job. As Tanis says, "I learned all the fundamentals in my business classes, but school prepares you for a perfect world, and there is no such thing."

She feels fortunate that her boss understands her job is a learning experience as well as a responsibility. "Sometimes he's let me do something he knew perfectly well was a mistake so I can learn something through experience," she admits.

To help others gain the benefits of her real-world learning, Tanis is always happy to help students in the area who want to use Forster's as the subject of a project or report. "It's the least I can do," she says.

THE NAVIGATOR

Study Objectives at the beginning of each chapter give you a framework for learning the specific concepts and procedures covered in the chapter. Each study objective reappears in the margin at the point where the concept is discussed. Finally, you can review all the study objectives in the **Summary** at the end of the chapter.

STUDY OBJECTIVES

After studying this chapter, you should be able to

1. Explain what an account is and how it helps in the recording process.
2. Define debits and credits and explain how they are used to record business transactions.
3. Identify the basic steps in the recording process.
4. Explain what a journal is and how it helps in the recording process.
5. Explain what a ledger is and how it helps in the recording process.
6. Explain what posting is and how it helps in the recording process.
7. Prepare a trial balance and explain its purposes.
8. Identify the advantages of manual and computerized accounting systems.

THE NAVIGATOR

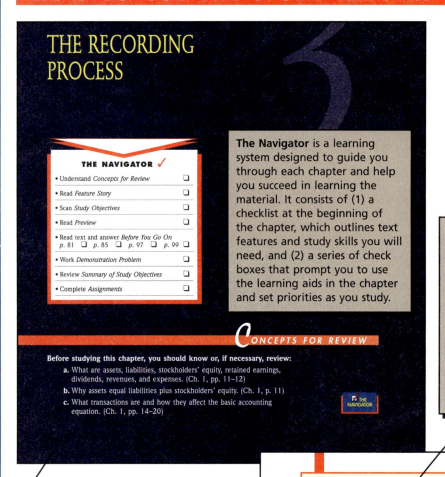

The **Preview** begins by linking the Feature Story with the major topics of the chapter. It is followed by a graphic outline of major topics and subtopics that will be discussed. This narrative and visual preview gives you a mental framework upon which to arrange the new information you are learning.

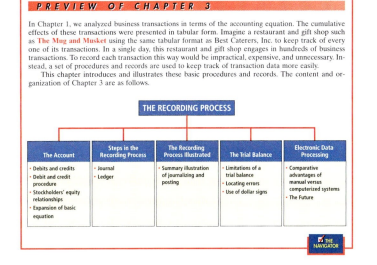

PREVIEW OF CHAPTER 3

In Chapter 1, we analyzed business transactions in terms of the accounting equation. The cumulative effects of these transactions were presented in tabular form. Imagine a restaurant and gift shop such as **The Mug and Musket** using the same tabular format as Best Caterers, Inc. to keep track of every one of its transactions. In a single day, this restaurant and gift shop engages in hundreds of business transactions. To record each transaction this way would be impractical, expensive, and unnecessary. Instead, a set of procedures and records are used to keep track of transaction data more easily.

This chapter introduces and illustrates these basic procedures and records. The content and organization of Chapter 3 are as follows.

THE RECORDING PROCESS

- **The Account**
  - Debits and credits
  - Debit and credit procedure
  - Stockholders' equity relationships
  - Expansion of basic equation
- **Steps in the Recording Process**
  - Journal
  - Ledger
- **The Recording Process Illustrated**
  - Summary illustration of journalizing and posting
- **The Trial Balance**
  - Limitations of a trial balance
  - Locating errors
  - Use of dollar signs
- **Electronic Data Processing**
  - Comparative advantages of manual versus computerized systems
  - The Future

THE NAVIGATOR

STUDY OBJECTIVE 1

Explain what an account is and how it helps in the recording process.

THE ACCOUNT

An **account** is an individual accounting record of increases and decreases in a specific asset, liability, or stockholders' equity item. For example, Best Caterers, Inc. (the company discussed in Chapter 1) would have separate accounts for Cash, Accounts Receivable, Accounts Payable, Service Revenue, Salaries Expense, and so on. In its simplest form, an account consists of three parts: (1) the title of the account, (2) a left or debit side, and (3) a right or credit side. Because the alignment of these parts of an account resembles the letter T, it is referred to as a **T account**. The basic form of an account is shown in Illustration 3-1.

Illustration 3-1
Basic form of account

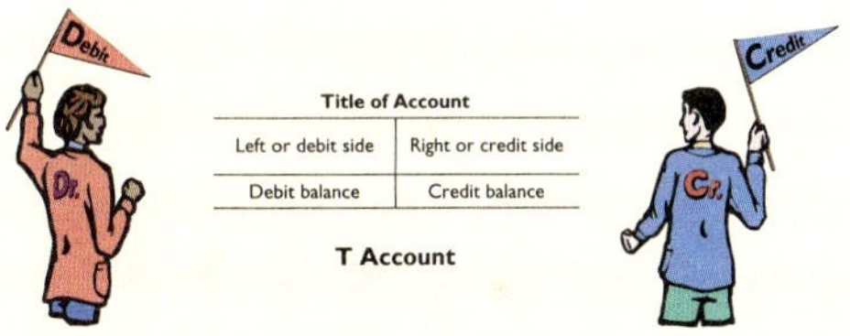

76

Steps in the Recording Process 83

in the ledger. The sequence of events in the recording process is shown in Illustration 3-13.

The basic steps in the recording process occur repeatedly. The analysis of transactions was illustrated in Chapter 1. Further examples will be given in this and later chapters. The other steps in the recording process are explained in the next sections.

Technology in Action examples show how computer technology is used in accounting and business.

TECHNOLOGY IN ACTION

Computerized and manual accounting systems basically parallel one another. Most of the procedures are handled by electronic circuitry in computerized systems. They seem to occur invisibly. But, to fully comprehend how computerized systems operate, you need to understand manual approaches for processing accounting data.

Technology in Action boxes show how computers are used by accountants and by users of accounting information.

THE JOURNAL

Transactions are initially recorded in chronological order in a **journal** before being transferred to the accounts. Thus, the journal is referred to as the book of original entry. For each transaction the journal shows the debit and credit effects on specific accounts. Companies may use various kinds of journals, but every company has the most basic form of journal, a **general journal**. Typically, a general journal has spaces for dates, account titles and explanations, references, and two amount columns. Whenever we use the term journal in this textbook without a modifying adjective, we mean the general journal.

STUDY OBJECTIVE 4

Explain what a journal is and how it helps in the recording process.

Study Objectives reappear in the margins at the point where the topic is discussed. End-of-chapter assignments are keyed to study objectives.

The journal makes several significant contributions to the recording process:

1. It discloses in one place the complete effects of a transaction.
2. It provides a chronological record of transactions.
3. It helps to prevent or locate errors because the debit and credit amounts for each entry can be readily compared.

Key terms and concepts are printed in blue where they are first explained in the text, and they are defined again in the end-of-chapter glossary.

Entering transaction data in the journal is known as **journalizing**. Separate journal entries are made for each transaction. A complete entry consists of (1) the date of the transaction, (2) the accounts and amounts to be debited and credited, and (3) a brief explanation of the transaction.

Illustration 3-14 shows the technique of journalizing, using the first two transactions of Best Caterers, Inc. These transactions were: September 1, stockholders invested $15,000 cash in the corporation in exchange for shares of stock, and com-

Accounting in Action boxes give you more glimpses into the real world of business. These high-interest boxes are classified by three types of issues—business, ethics, and international—each identified by its own icon. New in this edition, **e-Business Insights** describe how e-business technology is expanding the services provided by accountants.

The Recording Process Illustrated 95

ACCOUNTING IN ACTION *Business Insight*

E-business is having a tremendous impact on how companies share information within the company, and with people outside the company, such as suppliers, creditors, and investors. A new type of software, Extensible Markup Language (XML), is enabling the creation of a universal way to exchange data.

An organization called XBRL.org is using XML to develop an internally accepted framework called the Extensible Business Reporting Model (XBRL). The organization comprises representatives from industry, accounting firms, investment houses, bankers, regulators, and others. The goal of this organization is to establish a framework that "the global business information supply chain will use to create, exchange, and analyze financial reporting information including, but not limited to, regulatory filings such as annual and quarterly financial statements, general ledger information, and audit schedules."

SOURCE: www.XBRL.org.

Infographics, a special type of illustration, pictorially link concepts to the real world and provide visual reminders of key concepts.

that has legal title to the goods. Legal title is determined by the terms of sale, as shown in Illustration 10-1 and described below.

1. **FOB (free on board) shipping point:** Ownership of the goods passes to the buyer when the public carrier accepts the goods from the seller.
2. **FOB destination:** Legal title to the goods remains with the seller until the goods reach the buyer.

Illustration 10-1
Terms of sale

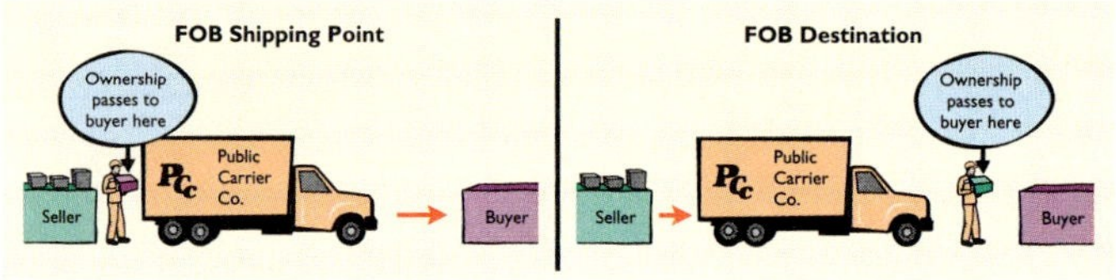

Color illustrations visually reinforce important concepts and therefore often contain material that may appear on exams.

to stockholders. The distribution of cash or other assets to stockholders is called a **dividend**. Dividends reduce retained earnings. However, dividends are not an expense of a corporation. A corporation first determines its revenues and expenses and then computes net income or **net loss**. At this point, a corporation may decide to distribute a dividend.

In summary, the principal sources (increases) of stockholders' equity are (1) investments by stockholders and (2) revenues from business operations. In contrast, reductions (decreases) in stockholders' equity are a result of (1) expenses and (2) dividends. These relationships are shown in Illustration 1-6.

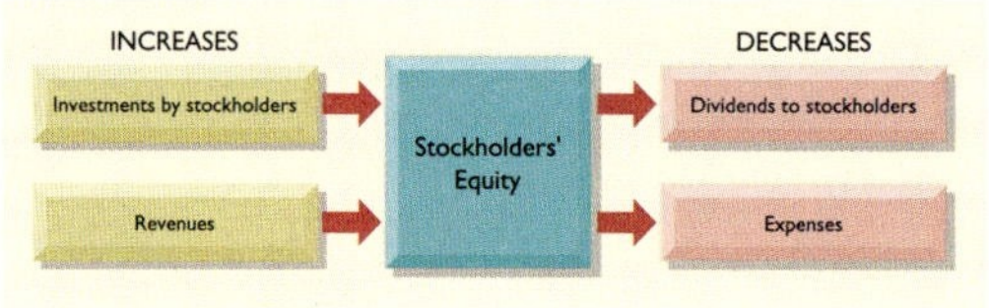

Illustration 1-6
Increases and decreases in stockholders' equity

Before You Go On sections follow each key topic. ***Review It*** questions prompt you to stop and review the key points you have just studied. If you cannot answer these questions, you should go back and read the section again.

Review It questions marked with the Hilton icon ask you to find information in Hilton's 2001 Annual Report, which is excerpted in the Appendix at the end of the text.

Brief ***Do It*** exercises ask you to put your newly acquired knowledge to work. They outline an ***Action Plan*** necessary to complete the exercise, and the accompanying ***Solution*** helps you see how the problem should be solved. (The ***Do It*** exercises are keyed to similar homework exercises.)

BEFORE YOU GO ON...

REVIEW IT

1. Why is ethics a fundamental business concept?
2. What are generally accepted accounting principles? Give an example.
3. Explain the monetary unit and the economic entity assumptions.
4. The accounting equation is: Assets = Liabilities + Stockholders' Equity. Replacing the words in that equation with dollar amounts, what is **Hilton's** accounting equation at December 31, 2001? (The answer to this question is provided on page 32.)
5. What are assets, liabilities, and stockholders' equity?

Review It questions marked with this icon require that you use **Hilton's** 2001 Annual Report.

Hilton

DO IT

Classify the following items as issuance of stock (I), dividends (D), revenues (R), or expenses (E). Then indicate whether the following items increase or decrease stockholders' equity: (1) rent expense, (2) service revenue, (3) dividends, and (4) salaries expense.

Do It exercises give you immediate practice of the material just covered.

ACTION PLAN

- Review the rules for changes in stockholders' equity: Investments and revenues increase stockholders' equity. Expenses and dividends decrease stockholders' equity.
- Understand the sources of revenue: the sale of merchandise, performance of services, rental of property, and lending of money.
- Understand what causes expenses: the consumption of assets or services.
- Recognize that dividends are distributions of cash or other assets to stockholders.

SOLUTION

1. Rent expense is classified as an expense (E); it decreases stockholders' equity.
2. Service revenue is classified as revenue (R); it increases stockholders' equity.
3. Dividends is classified as dividends (D); it decreases stockholders' equity.
4. Salaries expense is classified as an expense (E); it decreases stockholders' equity.

Related exercise material: 1-1, 1-2, 1-3, 1-4, 1-5, 1-6, 1-7, and 1-8.

THE NAVIGATOR

revenue to another company. For example, the $200 accrual of fees by Premier is an accrued expense to the client that received the service.

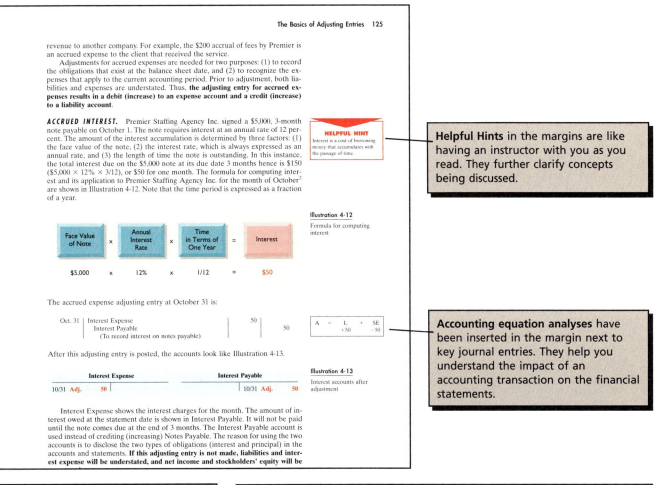

Adjustments for accrued expenses are needed for two purposes: (1) to record the obligations that exist at the balance sheet date, and (2) to recognize the expenses that apply to the current accounting period. Prior to adjustment, both liabilities and expenses are understated. Thus, **the adjusting entry for accrued expenses results in a debit (increase) to an expense account and a credit (increase) to a liability account.**

ACCRUED INTEREST. Premier Staffing Agency Inc. signed a $5,000, 3-month note payable on October 1. The note requires interest at an annual rate of 12 percent. The amount of the interest accumulation is determined by three factors: (1) the face value of the note, (2) the interest rate, which is always expressed as an annual rate, and (3) the length of time the note is outstanding. In this instance, the total interest due on the $5,000 note at its due date 3 months hence is $150 ($5,000 × 12% × 3/12), or $50 for one month. The formula for computing interest and its application to Premier Staffing Agency Inc. for the month of October[2] are shown in Illustration 4-12. Note that the time period is expressed as a fraction of a year.

HELPFUL HINT
Interest is a cost of borrowing money that accumulates with the passage of time.

Helpful Hints in the margins are like having an instructor with you as you read. They further clarify concepts being discussed.

Illustration 4-12
Formula for computing interest

Face Value of Note	×	Annual Interest Rate	×	Time in Terms of One Year	=	Interest
$5,000	×	12%	×	1/12	=	$50

The accrued expense adjusting entry at October 31 is:

Oct. 31	Interest Expense	50	
	Interest Payable		50
	(To record interest on notes payable)		

A	=	L	+	SE
		+50		−50

Accounting equation analyses have been inserted in the margin next to key journal entries. They help you understand the impact of an accounting transaction on the financial statements.

After this adjusting entry is posted, the accounts look like Illustration 4-13.

Illustration 4-13
Interest accounts after adjustment

Interest Expense		Interest Payable	
10/31 Adj. 50			10/31 Adj. 50

Interest Expense shows the interest charges for the month. The amount of interest owed at the statement date is shown in Interest Payable. It will not be paid until the note comes due at the end of 3 months. The Interest Payable account is used instead of crediting (increasing) Notes Payable. The reason for using the two accounts is to disclose the two types of obligations (interest and principal) in the accounts and statements. **If this adjusting entry is not made, liabilities and interest expense will be understated, and net income and stockholders' equity will be**

Financial statements appear throughout the book. Often, numbers or categories are highlighted in colored type to draw your attention to key information.

of liquidity. That is, they are listed in the order in which they are expected to be converted into cash. This arrangement is illustrated in Illustration 5-18 in the presentation of **UAL, Inc. (United Airlines).**

Illustration 5-18
Current assets section

UAL, INC. (UNITED AIRLINES)
Balance Sheet (partial)
(in millions)

Current assets	
Cash	$ 310
Short-term investments	379
Receivables	1,284
Aircraft fuel, spare parts, and supplies	340
Prepaid expenses	368
Other current assets	254
Total current assets	$2,935

Many of the last **Before You Go On** exercises take you back for a critical look at the chapter-opening Feature Story.

BEFORE YOU GO ON . . .

REVIEW IT

1. What are the income statement, retained earnings statement, balance sheet, and statement of cash flows?
2. How are the financial statements interrelated?

A LOOK BACK AT OUR FEATURE STORY

Refer back to the Feature Story about Hilton at the beginning of the chapter, and answer the following questions.

1. If you were interested in investing in Hilton, what would the balance sheet and income statement tell you?
2. Would you request audited financial statements? Explain.
3. Will the financial statements show the market value of the company? Explain.

SOLUTION

1. The balance sheet reports the assets, liabilities, and stockholders' equity of the company. The income statement presents the revenues and expenses and resulting net income (or net loss) for a specific period of time. The balance sheet is like a snapshot of the company's financial condition at a point in time. The income statement indicates the profitability of the company. Also, the sources of the company's revenues and its expenses are provided in the income statement.
2. You should request **audited** financial statements—statements that a CPA has examined and expressed an opinion as to the fairness of presentation. You should not make decisions without having audited financial statements.
3. The financial statements will not show the market value of the company. One important principle of accounting is the cost principle, which states that assets should be recorded at cost. Cost has an important advantage over other valuations: it is reliable.

THE NAVIGATOR

A Look Back exercises refer to the chapter-opening Feature Story. These exercises help you analyze that real-world situation in terms of the accounting topic of the chapter.

Demonstration Problem 25

DEMONSTRATION PROBLEM

Hospitality Legal Services, Inc., which provides contract services for caterers and their clients, was incorporated on July 1, 2004. During the first month of operations, the following transactions occurred.

1. Stockholders invested $10,000 in cash in exchange for shares of stock.
2. Paid $800 for July rent on office space.
3. Purchased office equipment on account, $3,000.
4. Provided legal services to clients for cash, $1,500 (use Service Revenue).
5. Borrowed $700 cash from a bank on a note payable.
6. Performed legal services for client on account, $2,000.
7. Paid monthly expenses: salaries $500; utilities $300; and telephone $100.

Instructions

(a) Prepare a tabular summary of the transactions.

(b) Prepare the income statement, retained earnings statement, and balance sheet at July 31 for Hospitality Legal Services, Inc.

Demonstration Problems are a final review of the chapter. The **Action Plan** gives tips about how to approach the problem, and the **Solution** demonstrates both the form and content of complete answers.

ACTION PLAN

- Remember that assets must equal liabilities and stockholders' equity after each transaction.
- Investments and revenues increase stockholders' equity.
- Dividends and expenses decrease stockholders' equity.
- The income statement shows revenues and expenses for a period of time.
- The retained earnings statement shows the changes in retained earnings for a period of time.
- The balance sheet reports assets, liabilities, and stockholders' equity at a specific date.

SOLUTION TO DEMONSTRATION PROBLEM

(a)

	Assets			= Liabilities		+ Stockholders' Equity		
Transaction	Cash	+ Accounts Receivable	+ Equipment	= Notes Payable	+ Accounts Payable	+ Common Stock	+ Retained Earnings	
(1)	+$10,000					+$10,000		
(2)	−800						−$800	Rent Expense
	9,200					10,000	−800	
(3)			+$3,000		+$3,000			
	9,200		3,000		3,000	10,000	−800	
(4)	+1,500						+1,500	Service Revenue
	10,700		3,000		3,000	10,000	700	
(5)	+700			+$700				
	11,400		3,000	700	3,000	10,000	700	
(6)		+$2,000					+2,000	Service Revenue
	+11,400	2,000	3,000	700	3,000	10,000	2,700	
(7)	−900						−500	Salaries Expense
							−300	Utilities Expense
							−100	Telephone Expense
	$10,500	$2,000	$3,000	$700	$3,000	$10,000	$1,800	
	$15,500			$15,500				

(b)

HOSPITALITY LEGAL SERVICES, INC.
Income Statement
For the Month Ended July 31, 2004

Revenues		
Service revenue		$3,500
Expenses		
Rent expense	$800	
Salaries expense	500	
Utilities expense	300	
Telephone expense	100	
Total expenses		1,700
Net income		$1,800

Demonstration Problems review the chapter material. These sample problems provide you with ***Action Plans*** that list the strategies needed to solve the problem and with ***Solutions***.

The **Summary of Study Objectives** relates the study objectives to the key points in the chapter. It gives you another opportunity to review as well as to see how all the key topics within the chapter are related.

SUMMARY OF STUDY OBJECTIVES

1. ***Explain the meaning of generally accepted accounting principles and identify the key items of the conceptual framework.*** Generally accepted accounting principles are a set of rules and practices that are recognized as a general guide for financial reporting purposes. Generally accepted means that these principles must have "substantial authoritative support." The key items of the conceptual framework are: (1) objectives of financial reporting; (2) qualitative characteristics of accounting information; (3) elements of financial statements; and (4) operating guidelines (assumptions, principles, and constraints).

2. ***Describe the basic objectives of financial reporting.*** The basic objectives of financial reporting are to provide information that is (1) useful to those making investment and credit decisions; (2) helpful in assessing future cash flows; and (3) helpful in identifying economic resources (assets), the claims to those resources (liabilities), and the changes in those resources and claims.

3. ***Discuss the qualitative characteristics of accounting information and elements of financial statements.*** To be judged useful, information should possess the following qualitative characteristics: relevance, reliability, comparability, and consistency. The elements of financial statements are a set of definitions that can be used to describe the basic terms used in accounting.

4. ***Identify the basic assumptions used by accountants.*** The major assumptions are: monetary unit, economic entity, time period, and going concern.

5. ***Identify the basic principles of accounting.*** The major principles are revenue recognition, matching, full disclosure, and cost.

6. ***Identify the two constraints in accounting.*** The major constraints are materiality and conservatism.

7. ***Understand and analyze classified financial statements.*** We presented classified balance sheets and classified (multiple-step) income statements in Chapters 4 and 5, respectively. Two new items added to the classified income statement in this chapter are income taxes and earnings per share. Three items used to analyze the balance sheet are the current ratio, working capital, and debt to total assets. Earnings per share, profit margin percentage (return on sales), return on assets, and return on common stockholders' equity are used to analyze profitability.

8. ***Explain the accounting principles used in international operations.*** There are few recognized worldwide accounting standards. The International Accounting Standards Committee (IASC), of which the United States is a member, is working to obtain conformity in international accounting practices.

9. ***Identify the various systems of accounting procedures used in the hospitality industry.*** There are currently three systems: The Uniform System of Accounts for the Lodging Industry, The Uniform System of Accounts for Restaurants, and The Uniform System of Financial Reporting for Clubs. Each has a long history, and their purpose is to provide users of financial information with comparable data and meaningful analyses.

10. ***Understand accounting and financial management in a hotel.*** Proper accounting and financial management of a hotel is crucial to its success. The chief accounting officer is known as the controller. The controller is part of the hotel's executive committee, which includes the general manager and all department heads. The controller interacts with all the department heads, assisting and consulting with them on all financial matters so each department head makes sound decisions.

11. ***Understand accounting and financial management in a foodservice operation and a club.*** The controller of a foodservice operation focuses on food, beverage, and labor costs. Food and beverage cost analyses are of particular importance due to the amount of money spent and the perishable nature of the products. The club industry is unique in that its customers are all members of the club. Members pay dues to the club and in return have a decision-making role in club operations. Members also spend money on food and beverage, merchandising, and others amenities. Therefore, a club controller must account for revenues by looking at different cost centers such as golf, tennis, spa, and food and beverages to provide solid information for management.

THE NAVIGATOR

104 CHAPTER 3 The Recording Process

credits after posting. A trial balance also uncovers errors in journalizing and posting and is useful in preparing financial statements.

8. ***Identify the advantages of both the manual and computerized accounting systems.*** A manual accounting system is advantageous when one is learning accounting. Learning the system manually provides users with a better comprehension of accounting and its logic. A computerized system does have the advantages of speed, efficiency, accuracy, and timeliness of information. However, the data compiled are only as good and as accurate as the data being entered. Thus, manual and computerized accounting systems do complement each other.

THE NAVIGATOR

GLOSSARY

Account A record of increases and decreases in specific asset, liability, or stockholders' equity items (p. 76).

Application Solutions Providers Companies that provide application solutions directly to the end-users in the industry. The end-users purchase application solutions via the Internet rather than the software (p. 100).

Chart of accounts A list of accounts and the account numbers that identify their location in the ledger (p. 88).

Common stock Issued in exchange for the owners' investment paid in to the corporation (p. 79).

Compound entry A journal entry that involves three or more accounts (p. 84).

Credit The right side of an account (p. 77).

Debit The left side of an account (p. 77).

Dividend A distribution by a corporation to its stockholders on a pro rata (equal) basis (p. 79).

Double-entry system A system that records in appropriate accounts the dual effect of each transaction (p. 77).

General journal The most basic form of journal (p. 83).

General ledger A ledger that contains all asset, liability, and stockholders' equity accounts (p. 85).

Journal An accounting record in which transactions are initially recorded in chronological order (p. 83).

Journalizing The entering of transaction data in the journal (p. 83).

Ledger The entire group of accounts maintained by a company (p. 85).

Posting The procedure of transferring journal entries to the ledger accounts (p. 87).

Retained earnings Net income that is retained in the business (p. 79).

Simple entry A journal entry that involves only two accounts (p. 84).

T account The basic form of an account (p. 76).

Three-column form of account A form with columns for debit, credit, and balance amounts in an account (p. 86).

Trial balance A list of accounts and their balances at a given time (p. 97).

The **Glossary** defines all the key terms and concepts introduced in the chapter. Page references help you find any terms you need to study further.

EXERCISES

Indicate debit and credit effects and normal balance. (SO 2)

3-1 For each of the following accounts indicate (a) the effect of a debit or a credit on the account and (b) the normal balance.

1. Accounts Payable
2. Advertising Expense
3. Service Revenue
4. Accounts Receivable
5. Common Stock
6. Dividends

Identify accounts to be debited and credited. (SO 2)

3-2 Transactions for Doris Wang Company for the month of June are presented below. Identify the accounts to be debited and credited for each transaction, and journalize the transactions.

June 1 Doris Wang invests $12,000 cash in exchange for shares of common stock in a small printing corporation.
2 Buys equipment on account for $7,500.
3 Pays $800 to landlord for June rent.
12 Bills B. J. Chang $400 for printing work done.

Indicate basic and debit–credit analysis. (SO 4)

3-3 Jim Carrey Corporation has the following transactions during August of the current year. Indicate (a) the basic analysis and (b) the debit–credit analysis illustrated on pages 90–93 of the text. Journalize the transactions.

Aug. 1 Opens an office as a financial advisor, investing $15,000 in cash in exchange for common stock.
4 Pays insurance in advance for 6 months, $2,100.
16 Receives $1,000 from clients for services rendered.
27 Pays secretary $900 salary.

Exercises range in difficulty, helping you focus on one study objective at a time. This will help you build confidence in your basic skills and knowledge to use the material learned in the chapter. More difficult exercises help you pull together several concepts from the chapter.

Group Decision Cases require teams of students to evaluate a manager's decision or choose from among alternative courses of action. They help prepare you for the business world by giving you practice in solving problems with colleagues.

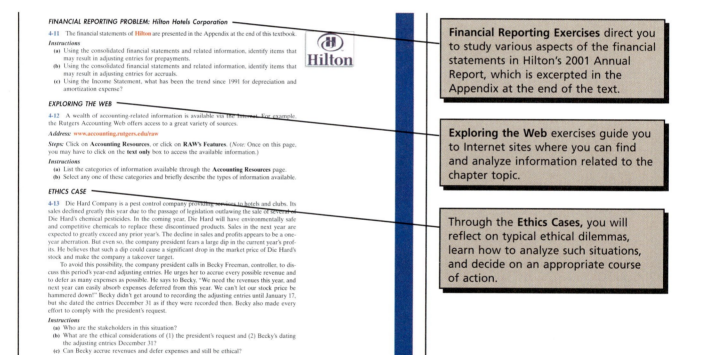

Exercises 197

GROUP DECISION CASE

6-12 Ehlert & Ramos is a wholesaler of small restaurant appliances and parts. Ehlert & Ramos is operated by two owners, Bill Ehlert and Denise Ramos. In addition, the company has one employee, a repair specialist, who is on a fixed salary. Revenues are earned through the sale of appliances to retailers (approximately 75% of total revenues), appliance parts to do-it-yourselfers (10%), and the repair of appliances brought to the store (15%). Appliance sales are made on both a credit and cash basis. Customers are billed on prenumbered sales invoices. Credit terms are always net/30 days. All parts sales and repair work are cash only.

Merchandise is purchased on account from the manufacturers of both the appliances and the parts. Practically all suppliers offer cash discounts for prompt payments, and it is company policy to take all discounts. Most cash payments are made by check. Checks are most frequently issued to suppliers, to trucking companies for freight on merchandise purchases, and to newspapers, radio, and TV stations for advertising. All advertising bills are paid as received. Bill and Denise each make a monthly drawing in cash for personal living expenses. The salaried repairman is paid twice monthly. Ehlert & Ramos currently has a manual accounting system.

Instructions

With the class divided into groups, answer the following.

(a) Identify the special journals that Ehlert & Ramos should have in its manual system. List the column headings appropriate for each of the special journals.

(b) What control and subsidiary accounts should be included in Ehlert & Ramos's manual system? Why?

FINANCIAL REPORTING PROBLEM: Hilton Hotels Corporation

4-11 The financial statements of Hilton are presented in the Appendix at the end of this textbook.

Instructions

(a) Using the consolidated financial statements and related information, identify items that may result in adjusting entries for prepayments.

(b) Using the consolidated financial statements and related information, identify items that may result in adjusting entries for accruals.

(c) Using the Income Statement, what has been the trend since 1991 for depreciation and amortization expense?

EXPLORING THE WEB

4-12 A wealth of accounting-related information is available via the Internet. For example, the Rutgers Accounting Web offers access to a great variety of sources.

Address: **www.accounting.rutgers.edu/raw**

Steps: Click on **Accounting Resources**, or click on **RAW's Features**. (*Note:* Once on this page, you may have to click on the **text only** box to access the available information.)

Instructions

(a) List the categories of information available through the **Accounting Resources** page.

(b) Select any one of these categories and briefly describe the types of information available.

ETHICS CASE

4-13 Die Hard Company is a pest control company providing services to hotels and clubs. Its sales declined greatly this year due to the passage of legislation outlawing the sale of several of Die Hard's chemical pesticides. In the coming year, Die Hard will have environmentally safe and competitive chemicals to replace these discontinued products. Sales in the next year are expected to greatly exceed any prior year's. The decline in sales and profits appears to be a one-year aberration. But even so, the company president fears a large dip in the current year's profits. He believes that such a dip could cause a significant drop in the market price of Die Hard's stock and make the company a takeover target.

To avoid this possibility, the company president calls in Becky Freeman, controller, to discuss this period's year-end adjusting entries. He urges her to accrue every possible revenue and to defer as many expenses as possible. He says to Becky, "We need the revenues this year, and next year can easily absorb expenses deferred from this year. We can't let our stock price be hammered down!" Becky didn't get around to recording the adjusting entries until January 17, but she dated the entries December 31 as if they were recorded then. Becky also made every effort to comply with the president's request.

Instructions

(a) Who are the stakeholders in this situation?

(b) What are the ethical considerations of (1) the president's request and (2) Becky's dating the adjusting entries December 31?

(c) Can Becky accrue revenues and defer expenses and still be ethical?

Financial Reporting Exercises direct you to study various aspects of the financial statements in Hilton's 2001 Annual Report, which is excerpted in the Appendix at the end of the text.

Exploring the Web exercises guide you to Internet sites where you can find and analyze information related to the chapter topic.

Through the **Ethics Cases,** you will reflect on typical ethical dilemmas, learn how to analyze such situations, and decide on an appropriate course of action.

Answers to *Review It* Questions based on the Hilton's financial statements provide feedback to your search for information in the Hilton Annual Report.

Answer to Hilton Review It Question 4, p. 122

2001 depreciation and amortization expense is $391 million; 2000 depreciation and amortization expense is $382 million.

Remember to go back to the Navigator box on the chapter-opening page and check off your completed work.

After you complete your homework assignments, it's a good idea to go back to **The Navigator** checklist at the start of the chapter to see if you have used all the study aids of the chapter.

BRIEF CONTENTS

DETAILED CONTENTS

HOSPITALITY ACCOUNTING IN ACTION

THE NAVIGATOR ✓

- Understand *Concepts for Review* ❑
- Read *Feature Story* ❑
- Scan *Study Objectives* ❑
- Read *Preview* ❑
- Read text and answer *Before You Go On* *p. 7* ❑ *p. 13* ❑ *p. 20* ❑ *p. 24* ❑
- Work *Demonstration Problem* ❑
- Review *Summary of Study Objectives* ❑
- Complete *Assignments* ❑

The Navigator is a learning system designed to prompt you to use the learning aids in the chapter and set priorities as you study.

CONCEPTS FOR REVIEW

Before studying this chapter, you should know or, if necessary, review:

a. How to use the study aids in this book. (Student Owner's Manual, pages x–xvi)

b. The nature of the special student supplements that accompany this textbook. (Student Owner's Manual, page viii)

Concepts for Review highlight concepts from your earlier reading that you need to understand before starting the new chapter.

THE NAVIGATOR

The **Feature Story** helps you picture how the chapter topic relates to the real world of accounting and business. You will find references to the story throughout the chapter.

Feature Story

From a Bank to a Hotel

The child of a Norwegian immigrant father and a German-American mother, Conrad N. Hilton had a strong belief in the American Dream. His philosophy and strength were derived from his faith in God, his belief in the brotherhood of man, his patriotic confidence in his country, and his conviction that there is a natural law that obliges all humankind to help those who are suffering, distressed, or destitute.

Hilton arrived in Cisco, Texas, in 1919 intending to buy a local bank. Instead he bought the Mobley Hotel, believing that he could utilize some of the hotel-keeping experience he had gained with his family in New Mexico. He constructed his first hotel, the Dallas Hilton, which opened on August 2, 1925.

Hilton successfully adapted to the economy of the American Great Depression in the 1930s. He expanded his empire by purchasing other hotels throughout the United States, including the Sir Francis Drake in San Francisco; The Plaza in New York; the Waldorf-Astoria Hotel in New York; the Stevens, currently known as the Chicago Hilton & Towers; and the Palmer House in Chicago. Internationally, Hilton developed his business by building hotels in such exotic locales as San Juan, Madrid, Istanbul, Havana, Berlin, and Cairo.

Although things do not always go as planned, and a bank instead became a hotel empire, lack of planning is often a recipe for disaster. Hilton did not become one of the largest hotel companies in the world without careful planning. **Hilton Hotels'** managers are constantly working to increase revenues and minimize costs. Careful consideration must be given to many types of decisions: what new products to provide, where to build the next hotel, how to finance current operations and expansion, where to locate, and whether to buy or lease properties.

The information needed for these decisions is provided by the company's accounting system. In addition, the company must report its results to the investors and creditors who provide it with the funds it needs to operate. A company communicates its past performances and its plans for the future in its annual report. A copy of the **Hilton Hotels Corporation's** 2001 Annual Report accompanies this text. In this book, you will learn how the accounting information in the annual report was determined, as well as how to use such information to make business decisions of all sorts.

Source: www.hrm.uh.edu/organizations/hallofhonor/cnhbiolong.pdf

THE NAVIGATOR

Study Objectives

After studying this chapter, you should be able to

Study Objectives give you a framework for learning the specific concepts covered in the chapter.

1. Explain what accounting is.
2. Identify the users and uses of accounting.
3. Understand why ethics is a fundamental business concept.
4. Explain the meaning of generally accepted accounting principles and the cost principle.
5. Explain the meaning of the monetary unit assumption and the economic entity assumption.
6. State the basic accounting equation, and explain the meaning of assets, liabilities, and stockholders' equity.
7. Analyze the effects of business transactions on the basic accounting equation.
8. Understand what the four financial statements are and how they are prepared.

THE NAVIGATOR

PREVIEW OF CHAPTER 1

The opening story about **Hilton Hotels Corporation** highlights the importance of having good financial information to make effective business decisions. Whatever one's pursuits or occupation, the need for financial information is inescapable. You cannot earn a living, spend money, buy on credit, make an investment, or pay taxes without receiving, using, or providing financial information. Good decision making depends on good information.

The purpose of this chapter is to show you that accounting is the system used to provide useful financial information. The content and organization of Chapter 1 are as follows.

ACCOUNTING IN ACTION

What Is Accounting?	The Building Blocks of Accounting	Using the Building Blocks	Financial Statements
• Who uses accounting data • Brief history of accounting • Bookkeeping and accounting • Accounting and you	• Ethics—a fundamental business concept • Generally accepted accounting principles • Assumptions • Basic accounting equation	• Transaction analysis • Summary of transactions	• Income statement • Retained earnings statement • Balance sheet • Statement of cash flows

THE NAVIGATOR

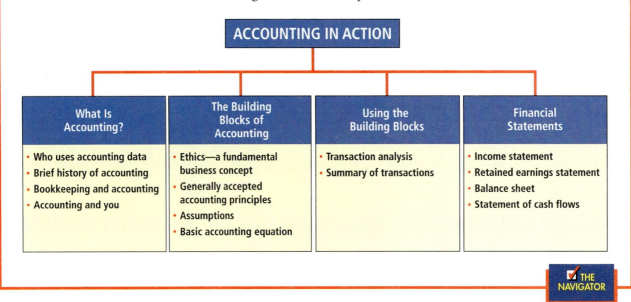

The **Preview** describes and outlines the major topics and subtopics you will see in the chapter.

WHAT IS ACCOUNTING?

STUDY OBJECTIVE 1

Explain what accounting is.

Essential terms are printed in blue when they first appear, and are defined in the end-of-chapter glossary.

Accounting is an information system that **identifies, records**, and **communicates** the economic events of an organization to interested users. Let's take a closer look at these three activities.

1. **Identifying** economic events involves selecting the **economic activities relevant to a particular organization**. The sale of goods and services by the **Hilton Hotels Corporation**, the providing of services by **Disney**, the payment of wages by **The Club Corporation of America**, and the collection of ticket and broadcast money and the payment of expenses by major league sports teams are examples of economic events.
2. Once identified, economic events are **recorded** to provide a history of the organization's financial activities. Recording consists of keeping a **systematic, chronological diary of events**, measured in dollars and cents. In recording, economic events are also classified and summarized.
3. The identifying and recording activities are of little use unless the information is **communicated** to interested users. Financial information is communicated through **accounting reports**, the most common of which are called **financial statements**. To make the reported financial information meaningful, account-

ants report the recorded data in a standardized way. Information resulting from similar transactions is accumulated and totaled. For example, all sales transactions of the **Hilton Hotels Corporation** are accumulated over a certain period of time and reported as one amount in the company's financial statements. Such data are said to be reported **in the aggregate**. By presenting the recorded data in the aggregate, the accounting process simplifies a multitude of transactions and makes a series of activities understandable and meaningful.

References throughout the chapter tie the accounting concepts you are learning to the story that opened the chapter.

A vital element in communicating economic events is the accountant's ability to **analyze** and **interpret** the reported information. Analysis involves the use of ratios, percentages, graphs, and charts to highlight significant financial trends and relationships. Interpretation involves **explaining the uses, meaning, and limitations of reported data**. The Appendix at the end of this textbook illustrates the financial statements and accompanying notes and graphs from the **Hilton Hotels Corporation.** We refer to these statements at various places throughout the text. At this point, they probably strike you as complex and confusing. By the end of this course, you'll be surprised at your ability to understand and interpret them.

The accounting process is summarized in Illustration 1-1.

Illustration 1-1

Accounting process

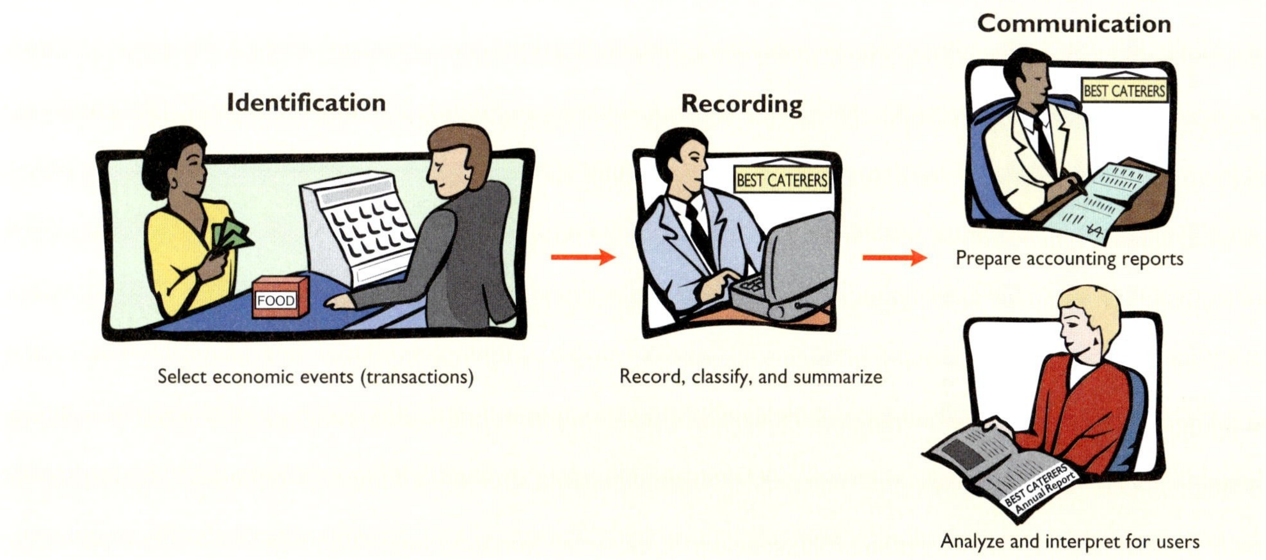

Accounting should consider the needs of the users of financial information. Therefore, you should know who these users are and something about their information needs.

WHO USES ACCOUNTING DATA

Because it communicates financial information, accounting is often called *the language of business.* The information that a user of financial information needs depends on the kinds of decisions that the user makes. The differences in the decisions divide the users of financial information into two broad groups: internal users and external users.

STUDY OBJECTIVE 2

Identify the users and uses of accounting.

Internal Users

Internal users of accounting information are managers who plan, organize, and run a business. These include **foodservice managers, housekeeping supervisors, rooms division managers, and others**. In running a business, managers must answer many important questions, as shown in Illustration 1-2.

Illustration 1-2

Questions asked by internal users

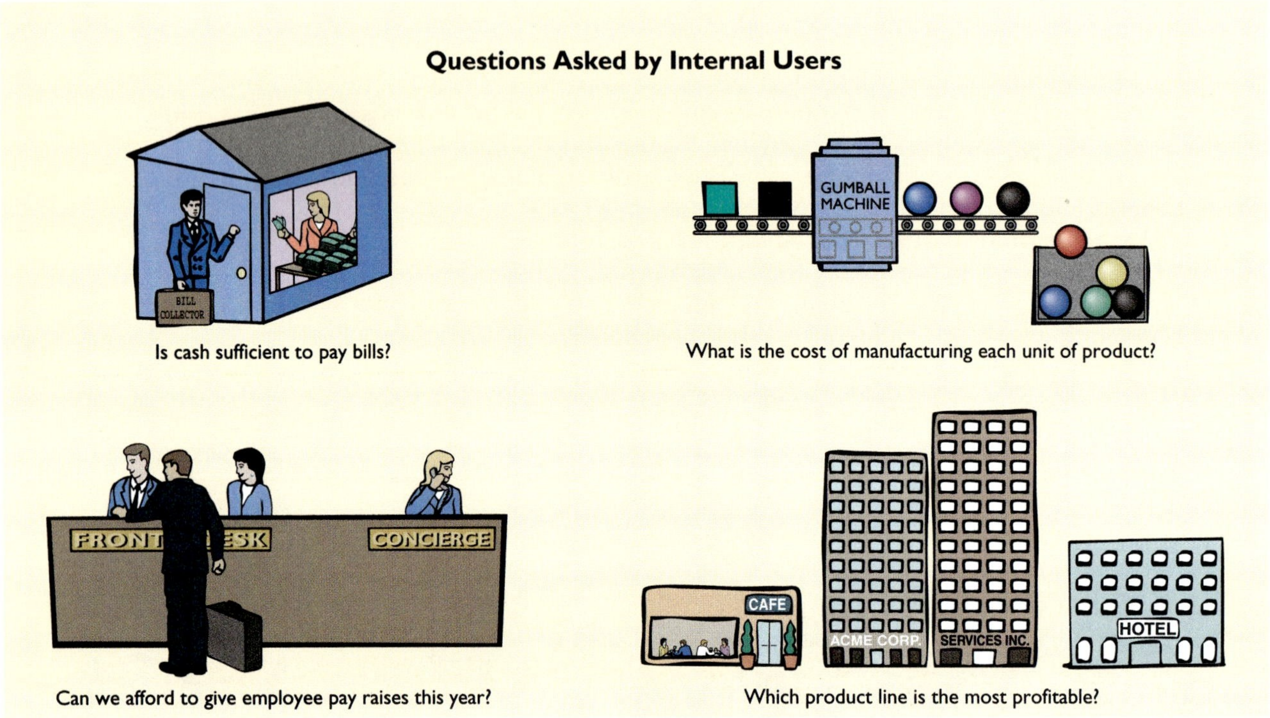
Questions Asked by Internal Users
BILL COLLECTOR
Is cash sufficient to pay bills?
GUMBALL MACHINE
What is the cost of manufacturing each unit of product?
CONCIERGE
Can we afford to give employee pay raises this year?
CAFE
ACME CORP.
SERVICES INC.
HOTEL
Which product line is the most profitable?

To answer these and other questions, users need detailed information on a timely basis. For internal users, accounting provides **internal reports**. Examples are financial comparisons of operating alternatives, projections of income from new sales campaigns, and forecasts of cash needs for the next year. In addition, summarized financial information is presented in the form of financial statements.

External Users

There are several types of **external users** of accounting information. **Investors** (owners) use accounting information to make decisions to buy, hold, or sell stock. **Creditors** such as suppliers and bankers use accounting information to evaluate the risks of granting credit or lending money. Some questions that may be asked by investors and creditors about a company are shown in Illustration 1-3.

The information needs and questions of other external users vary considerably. **Taxing authorities**, such as the Internal Revenue Service, want to know whether the company complies with the tax laws. **Regulatory agencies**, such as the Securities and Exchange Commission and the Federal Trade Commission, want to know whether the company is operating within prescribed rules. **Customers** are interested in whether a company will continue to honor product warranties and support its product lines. **Labor unions** want to know whether the owners can pay increased wages and benefits. **Economic planners** use accounting information to forecast economic activity.

HELPFUL HINT

The IRS requires businesses to retain records that can be audited. Also, the Foreign Corrupt Practices Act requires public companies to keep records.

Illustration 1-3

Questions asked by external users

Questions Asked by External Users

Is the company earning satisfactory income?

How does the company compare in size and profitability with competitors?

Will the company be able to pay its debts as they come due?

ACCOUNTING IN ACTION *International Insight*

In 1999, the number of berths (built-in beds on a cruise ship) provided by the cruise line industry in the North American market was more than 154,000 units. However, a cruise line is not simply a floating hotel. With all the amenities it has to offer, including spas, 24-hour foodservice, tennis courts, and casinos, cruises are closely scrutinized by the National Transportation Safety Board, Federal Maritime Commission, and the U.S. Coast Guard. The growth of this industry has resulted in increased regulations and greater capacity of new ships. This has created additional issues for the accounting personnel in the cruise line industry and the public accounting firms that service them. For example, ships need to be dry-docked for maintenance. If the next dry dock is estimated to be $2 million and is scheduled to be done in twenty months, then the accounting personnel should accrue $100,000 per month on the books. Therefore, the full $2 million will be recognized as a prepaid asset to be recorded at the time of dry docking.

SOURCE: Mitchell R. Less and Scott A. Mager (1999), "A Cruise Ship Is Not Just a Floating Hotel," *Bottomline*, 14(3), 15–20.

Accounting in Action examples illustrate important and interesting accounting situations in business.

BRIEF HISTORY OF ACCOUNTING

The **origins of accounting** are generally attributed to the work of Luca Pacioli, an Italian Renaissance mathematician. Pacioli was a close friend and tutor to Leonardo da Vinci and a contemporary of Christopher Columbus. In his text *Summa de Arithmetica, Geometria, Proportione et Proportionalite,* Pacioli described a system to ensure that financial information was recorded efficiently and accurately.

With the advent of the **Industrial Age** in the nineteenth century and, later, the emergence of large corporations, a separation of the owners from the managers of businesses took place. As a result, the need to report the financial status of the enterprise became more important, to ensure that managers acted in accord with owners' wishes. Also, transactions between businesses became more complex, making it necessary to improve approaches for reporting financial information.

E-Business Insights provide examples of how e-business technology has influenced accounting and financial reporting.

Our economy has now evolved into a post-industrial age—**the information age**—in which many "products" are information services. The computer has been the driver of the information age.

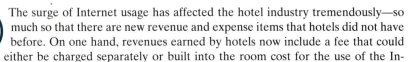

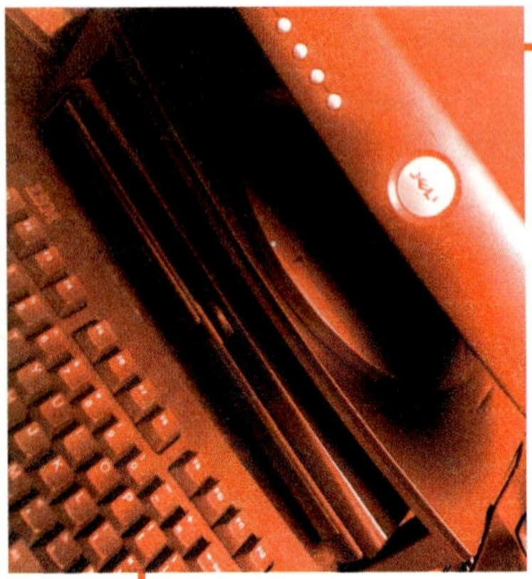

ACCOUNTING IN ACTION e-Business Insight

The surge of Internet usage has affected the hotel industry tremendously—so much so that there are new revenue and expense items that hotels did not have before. On one hand, revenues earned by hotels now include a fee that could either be charged separately or built into the room cost for the use of the Internet, business center usage, and banquet facilities, which are associated with convention services and presentations. Other revenues also include rental and installation of equipment, computers, ethernet cards, hubs, patch cables, and even the set-up of mini-LAN systems. Expenses, on the other hand, include the cost of leasing lines, Internet provider fees, telephone charges, equipment leases, and wages and salary of hotel and contract personnel, to name a few.

SOURCE: Henry A. Weeks, "Internet Revenue and Expense," *Bottomline*, 15(4) (2000), 73–74.

DISTINGUISHING BETWEEN BOOKKEEPING AND ACCOUNTING

Many individuals mistakenly consider bookkeeping and accounting to be the same. This confusion is understandable because the accounting process **includes the bookkeeping function**. However, accounting also includes much more. **Bookkeeping usually involves only the recording of economic events**. It is therefore just one part of the accounting process. In total, **accounting involves the entire process of identifying, recording, and communicating economic events**.

Accounting may be further divided into financial accounting and managerial accounting. **Financial accounting** is the field of accounting that provides economic and financial information for investors, creditors, and other external users. **Managerial accounting** provides economic and financial information for managers and other internal users. Financial accounting is covered in this textbook.

ACCOUNTING AND YOU

One question frequently asked by students of accounting is, "How will the study of accounting help me?" It should help you a great deal, because a working knowledge of accounting is desirable for virtually every field of endeavor. Some examples of how accounting is used in other careers include:

General management: Imagine running a theme park, a major resort, a school, a foodservice facility, a **McDonald's** franchise. All general managers need to understand accounting data in order to make wise business decisions.

Marketing: A marketing specialist develops strategies to help the sales force be successful. But making a sale is meaningless unless it is a profitable sale. Marketing people must be sensitive to costs and benefits, which accounting helps them quantify and understand.

Finance: Do you want to be a controller, a chief financial officer, a food and beverage controller, a purchasing analyst? These fields rely heavily on accounting. In all of them you will regularly examine and analyze financial statements. In fact, it is difficult to get a good job in a finance function without two or three courses in accounting.

Real estate: Have you ever considered hotel properties as real estate? When you decide to buy or sell properties, you will need to understand finance and real estate. Many hospitality programs, especially at the Master's degree level, offer courses in real estate. Can the buyer afford to make the payments to the bank? Does the cash flow from an industrial property justify the purchase price? What are the tax benefits of the purchase? All these are questions that need answers.

Accounting is useful even for occupations you might think completely unrelated. If you become a doctor, a lawyer, a social worker, a teacher, an engineer, an architect, or an entrepreneur—you name it—a working knowledge of accounting is relevant. You will need to understand financial reports in any enterprise you are associated with.

ACCOUNTING IN ACTION *Business Insight*

Help Wanted: Forensic CPAs

Tom Taylor's job at the **FBI** has changed. He used to pack a .357 magnum; now he wields a no. 2 pencil and a notebook computer. Taylor, age 37, for two years an FBI agent, is a forensic accountant, somebody who sniffs through company books to ferret out white-collar crime. Demand for this service has surged in the past few years. In one recent year, a recruiter for San Diego's **Robert Half International**, a headhunting firm, had requests for more than 1,000 such snoops.

Qualifications: A CPA with FBI, IRS, or similar government experience. Interestingly, despite its macho image, the FBI has long hired mostly accountants and lawyers as agents.

BEFORE YOU GO ON...

Before You Go On questions at the end of major text sections offer an opportunity to stop and reexamine the key points you have studied.

REVIEW IT

1. What is accounting?
2. What is meant by analysis and interpretation?
3. Who uses accounting information? Identify specific internal and external users of accounting information.
4. To whom are the origins of accounting generally attributed?
5. What is the difference between bookkeeping and accounting?
6. How can you use your accounting knowledge?

THE NAVIGATOR

THE BUILDING BLOCKS OF ACCOUNTING

Every profession develops a body of theory consisting of principles, assumptions, and standards. Accounting is no exception. Just as a doctor follows certain standards in treating a patient's illness, an accountant follows certain standards in reporting financial information. For these standards to work, a fundamental business concept is followed—ethical behavior.

ETHICS—A FUNDAMENTAL BUSINESS CONCEPT

STUDY OBJECTIVE 3

Understand why ethics is a fundamental business concept.

Wherever you make your career—whether in accounting, marketing, hotel or foodservice management, finance, or elsewhere—your actions will affect other people and organizations. The standards of conduct by which one's actions are judged as right or wrong, honest or dishonest, fair or not fair, are **ethics**. Imagine trying to carry on a business or invest money if you could not depend on the individuals you deal with to be honest. If managers, customers, investors, co-workers, and creditors all consistently lied, effective communication and economic activity would be impossible. Information would have no credibility.

Fortunately, most individuals in business are ethical. Their actions are both legal and responsible, and they consider the organization's interests in their decision making. However, sometimes public officials and business executives act unethically. For example, the **Enron** board waived Enron's code of ethics where an executive created questionable partnerships; a trader with **Salomon Brothers** improperly overbid in auctions of U.S. Treasury bonds; **World Com** continued acquiring companies including MCI, MFS, and UUNET, until the 75 acquisitions were unable to function well together.

To sensitize you to ethical situations and to give you practice at solving ethical dilemmas, we have included in the book three types of ethics materials in certain chapters: (1) marginal notes that provide helpful hints for developing ethical sensitivity, (2) Ethics in Accounting boxes that highlight ethics situations and issues, and (3) at the end of the chapter, an ethics case simulating a business situation. In the process of analyzing these ethics cases and your own ethical experiences, you should apply the three steps outlined in Illustration 1-4.

Illustration 1-4

Steps in analyzing ethics cases

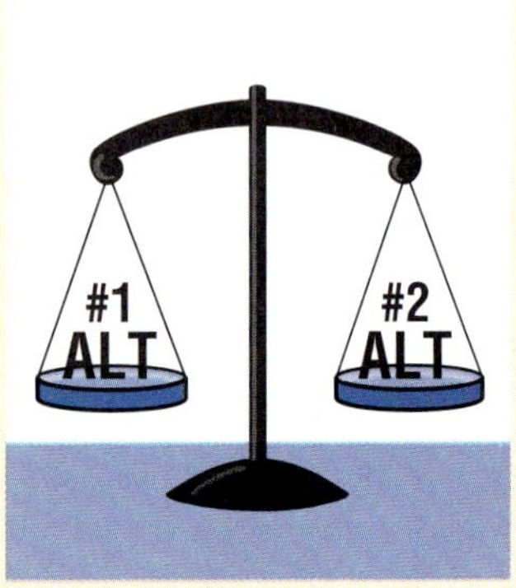

Solving an Ethical Dilemma

1. Recognize an ethical situation and the ethical issues involved.	2. Identify and analyze the principal elements in the situation.	3. Identify the alternatives, and weigh the impact of each alternative on various stakeholders.
Use your personal ethics to identify ethical situations and issues. Some businesses and professional organizations provide written codes of ethics for guidance in some business situations.	Identify the *stakeholders*—persons or groups who may be harmed or benefited. Ask the question: What are the responsibilities and obligations of the parties involved?	Select the most ethical alternative, considering all the consequences. Sometimes there will be one right answer. Other situations involve more than one right solution; these situations require an evaluation of each and a selection of the best alternative.

GENERALLY ACCEPTED ACCOUNTING PRINCIPLES

STUDY OBJECTIVE 4

Explain the meaning of generally accepted accounting principles and the cost principle.

The accounting profession has developed standards that are generally accepted and universally practiced. This common set of standards is called **generally accepted accounting principles (GAAP)**. These standards indicate how to report economic events.

Two organizations are primarily responsible for establishing generally accepted accounting principles. The first is the **Financial Accounting Standards Board (FASB)**. This private organization establishes broad reporting standards of general applicability as well as specific accounting rules. The second standards-setting group is the Securities and Exchange Commission (SEC). The SEC is a governmental agency that requires companies to file financial reports following generally accepted accounting principles. In situations where no principles exist, the SEC often mandates that certain guidelines be used. In general, the FASB and the SEC work hand in hand to assure that timely and useful accounting principles are developed.

INTERNATIONAL NOTE

The standards-setting processes in Canada, Mexico, and the United States are similar in most respects. All three have relatively open deliberations on new rules, and they support efforts to follow international standards. The use of similar accounting principles within North America has implications for the success of the North American Free Trade Agreement (NAFTA).

One important principle is the cost principle, which states that assets should be recorded at their cost. **Cost is the value exchanged at the time something is acquired.** If you buy a house today, the cost is the amount you pay for it, say $200,000. If you sell the house in two years for $230,000, the sales price is its **market value**—the value determined by the market for homes at that time. At the time of acquisition, cost and fair market value are the same. In subsequent periods, cost and fair market value may vary, **but the cost amount continues to be used in the accounting records.**

To see the importance of the cost principle, consider the following example. At one time, Greyhound Corporation had 128 bus stations nationwide that cost approximately $200 million. The current market value of the stations is now close to $1 billion. But, until the bus stations are actually sold, estimates of their market values are subjective—they are informed estimates. So, under the cost principle, the bus stations are recorded and reported at $200 million, not $1 billion.

As the Greyhound example indicates, cost has an important advantage over other valuations: Cost is **reliable**. The values exchanged at the time something is acquired generally can be **objectively measured** and can be **verified**. Critics argue that cost is often not relevant and that market values provide more useful information. Despite this shortcoming, cost continues to be used in the financial statements because of its reliability.

ALTERNATIVE TERMINOLOGY
The cost principle is often referred to as the *historical cost principle*.

ASSUMPTIONS

STUDY OBJECTIVE 5

Explain the meaning of the monetary unit assumption and the economic entity assumption.

In developing generally accepted accounting principles, certain basic assumptions are made. These assumptions provide a foundation for the accounting process. Two main assumptions are the monetary unit assumption and the economic entity assumption.

Monetary Unit Assumption

The monetary unit assumption requires that only transaction data that can be expressed in terms of money be included in the accounting records. This assumption enables accounting to quantify (measure) economic events. The monetary unit assumption is vital to applying the cost principle discussed earlier. This assumption does prevent some relevant information from being included in the accounting records. For example, the health of the owner, the quality of service, and the morale of employees would not be included because they cannot be quantified in terms of money.

An important part of the monetary unit assumption is the added assumption that the unit of measure remains sufficiently constant over time. However, the assumption of a stable monetary unit has been challenged because of the significant decline in the purchasing power of the dollar. For example, what used to cost $1.00 in 1960 costs more than $4.00 in 2004. In such situations, adding, subtracting, or comparing 1960 dollars with 2004 dollars is highly questionable. The profession has recognized this problem and encourages companies to disclose the effects of changing prices.

Economic Entity Assumption

An economic entity can be any organization or unit in society. It may be a business enterprise (such as Marriott International, Inc.), a governmental unit (the state of Ohio), a municipality (Seattle), a school district (St. Louis District 48), or a church (Southern Baptist). The **economic entity assumption** requires that the activities of the entity be kept separate and distinct from the activities of its owner and all other economic entities. To illustrate, Sally Rider, owner of Sally's Boutique, should keep her personal living costs separate from the expenses of the boutique. **Disney's Parks and Resorts** and its Studio Entertainment are segregated into separate economic entities for accounting purposes.

ACCOUNTING IN ACTION *Ethics Insight*

A 400-seat independently owned restaurant in Irvine, California, was cited for alleged minimum-wage violations and failure to itemize payroll deductions on 395 incidents during a one-year auditing period. In addition, the restaurant had not provided workers' compensation insurance for 28 employees and owed $170,106 in back wages and overtime. The Labor Standards Enforcement Division slapped a fine of more than $300,000 on the owners.

SOURCE: "400-Seat-Operator Hit with $300K in Fines, Vows Appeal," *Nation's Restaurant News*, 34(7) (February, 14, 2000), 40.

We will generally discuss the economic entity assumption in relation to a business enterprise, which may be organized as a proprietorship, partnership, or corporation.

HELPFUL HINT
Approximately 70 percent of U.S. companies are proprietorships; however, they account for only 6.5 percent of gross revenues. Corporations are approximately 19 percent of all companies, but account for 90 percent of the revenues. Obviously, proprietorships, though numerous, tend to be small.

PROPRIETORSHIP. A business owned by one person is generally a **proprietorship**. The owner is often the manager/operator of the business. Small service-type businesses (travel agencies, beauty salons, and interior decorators), farms, and small retail stores (cigar specialty shops, ice-cream parlors, and sandwich shops) are often sole proprietorships. **Usually only a relatively small amount of money (capital) is necessary to start in business as a proprietorship. The owner (proprietor) receives any profits, suffers any losses, and is personally liable for all debts of the business.** There is no legal distinction between the business as an economic unit and the owner, but the accounting records of the business activities are kept separate from the personal records and activities of the owner.

PARTNERSHIP. A business owned by two or more persons associated as partners is a **partnership**. In most respects a partnership is like a proprietorship except that more than one owner is involved. Typically a partnership agreement (written or oral) sets forth such terms as initial investment, duties of each partner, division of net income (or net loss), and settlement to be made upon death or withdrawal of a partner. Each partner generally has unlimited personal liability for the debts of the partnership. **Like a proprietorship, for accounting purposes the partnership affairs must be kept separate from the personal activities of the partners.** Partnerships are often used to organize retail and service-type businesses, including professional practices (lawyers, architects, and certified public accountants) who work especially with the hospitality industry, providing much needed services.

CORPORATION. A business organized as a separate legal entity under state corporation law and having ownership divided into transferable shares of stock is a **corporation**. The holders of the shares (stockholders) enjoy **limited liability**; that is, they are not personally liable for the debts of the corporate entity. **Stockholders may transfer all or part of their shares to other investors at any time** (i.e., sell their shares). The ease with which ownership can change adds to the attractiveness of investing in a corporation. Because ownership can be transferred without dissolving the corporation, the corporation **enjoys an unlimited life**.

Although the combined number of proprietorships and partnerships in the United States is more than four times the number of corporations, the revenue produced by corporations is nine times greater. Most of the largest hospitality enterprises in the United States—for example, **Hilton Hotels**, **Starwood**, **Marriott**, and the **Walt Disney Company**—are corporations.

BASIC ACCOUNTING EQUATION

STUDY OBJECTIVE 6

State the basic accounting equation, and explain the meaning of assets, liabilities, and stockholders' equity.

Other essential building blocks of accounting are the categories into which economic events are classified. The two basic elements of a business are what it owns and what it owes. **Assets** are the resources owned by a business. For example, the 2001 year-end figures showed **Marriott** having total assets of approximately $9,107 million. Liabilities and stockholders' equity are the rights or claims against these resources. Thus, a company such as **Marriott** that has $9,107 million of assets also has $9,107 million of claims against those assets. Claims of those to whom money is owed (creditors) are called **liabilities**. Claims of owners are called **stockholders' equity**. For example, **Marriott** has liabilities of $5,629 million and stockholders' equity of $3,487 million. This relationship of assets, liabilities, and stockholders' equity can be expressed as an equation as shown in Illustration 1-5.

Illustration 1-5

The basic accounting equation

Assets = Liabilities + Stockholders' Equity

This relationship is referred to as the **basic accounting equation**. Assets must equal the sum of liabilities and stockholders' equity. Because creditors' claims must be paid before ownership claims if a business is liquidated, liabilities are shown before stockholders' equity in the basic accounting equation.

The accounting equation applies to all **economic entities** regardless of size, nature of business, or form of business organization. It applies to a small proprietorship such as a corner delicatessen as well as to a giant corporation such as **Carlson Companies Inc.,** which owns various hotel brands and also **TGI Friday's**. The equation provides the **underlying framework** for recording and summarizing the economic events of a business enterprise.

Let's look in more detail at the categories in the basic accounting equation.

Assets

As noted above, **assets** are resources owned by a business. They are used in carrying out such activities as production, consumption, and exchange. The common characteristic possessed by all assets is the capacity to provide future services or benefits. In a business enterprise, that service potential or future economic benefit eventually results in cash inflows (receipts) to the enterprise.

For example, the enterprise Campus Pizza owns a delivery truck that provides economic benefits from its use in delivering pizzas. Other assets of Campus Pizza are tables, chairs, jukebox, cash register, oven, mugs and silverware, and, of course, cash.

Liabilities

Liabilities are claims against assets. That is, **liabilities are existing debts and obligations**. For example, businesses of all sizes usually borrow money and purchase merchandise on credit. Campus Pizza, for instance, purchases cheese, sausage, flour, and beverages on credit from suppliers. These obligations are called **accounts**

payable. Campus Pizza also has a **note payable** to First National Bank for the money borrowed to purchase the delivery truck. Campus Pizza may also have **wages payable** to employees and **sales and real estate taxes payable** to the local government. All of these persons or entities to whom Campus Pizza owes money are its **creditors**.

Most claims of creditors attach to the entity's **total assets** rather than to the specific assets provided by the creditor. Creditors may legally force the liquidation of a business that does not pay its debts. In that case, the law requires that creditor claims be paid before ownership claims.

Stockholders' Equity

The ownership claim on total assets is known as **stockholders' equity**. It is equal to total assets minus total liabilities. Here is why: The assets of a business are supplied or claimed by either creditors or stockholders. To determine what belongs to stockholders, we therefore subtract creditors' claims—the liabilities—from assets. The remainder—stockholders' equity—is the stockholders' claim on the assets of the business. It is often referred to as **residual equity** (that is, the equity "left over" after creditors' claims are satisfied). The stockholders' equity section of a corporation's balance sheet consists of (1) paid-in (contributed) capital and (2) retained earnings (earned capital).

PAID-IN CAPITAL. **Paid-in capital** is the term used to describe the total amount paid in by stockholders. The principal source of paid-in capital is the investment of cash and other assets in the corporation by stockholders in exchange for capital stock. Corporations may issue several classes of stock, but the stock representing ownership interest is common stock.

RETAINED EARNINGS. The **retained earnings** section of the balance sheet is determined by three items: revenues, expenses, and dividends.

Revenues. **Revenues** are the gross increases in stockholders' equity resulting from business activities entered into for the purpose of earning income. Generally, revenues result from the sale of merchandise, the performance of services, the rental of property, and the lending of money.

Revenues usually result in an increase in an asset. They may arise from different sources and are identified by various names depending on the nature of the business. Campus Pizza, for instance, has two categories of sales revenues—pizza sales and beverage sales. Other titles for and sources of revenue common to many businesses are: sales, fees, services, commissions, interest, dividends, royalties, and rent.

HELPFUL HINT
The effect of revenues is positive—an increase in stockholders' equity coupled with an increase in assets or a decrease in liabilities.

Expenses. **Expenses** are the decreases in stockholders' equity that result from operating the business. They are the cost of assets consumed or services used in the process of earning revenue. Expenses represent actual or expected cash outflows (payments). Like revenues, expenses take many forms and are identified by various names depending on the type of asset consumed or service used. For example, Campus Pizza recognizes the following types of expenses: cost of ingredients (meat, flour, cheese, tomato paste, mushrooms, etc.); cost of beverages; wages expense; utilities expense (electric, gas, and water expense); telephone expense; delivery expense (gasoline, repairs, licenses, etc.); supplies expense (napkins, detergents, aprons, etc.); rent expense; interest expense; and property tax expense. When revenues exceed expenses, **net income** results. When expenses exceed revenues, a **net loss** results.

HELPFUL HINT
The effect of expenses is negative—a decrease in stockholders' equity coupled with a decrease in assets or an increase in liabilities.

Dividends. When a company is successful, it generates net income. **Net income** represents an increase in net assets which are then available to distribute to stockholders. The distribution of cash or other assets to stockholders is called a **dividend**. Dividends reduce retained earnings. However, dividends are not an expense of a corporation. A corporation first determines its revenues and expenses and then computes net income or **net loss**. At this point, a corporation may decide to distribute a dividend.

In summary, the principal sources (increases) of stockholders' equity are (1) investments by stockholders and (2) revenues from business operations. In contrast, reductions (decreases) in stockholders' equity are a result of (1) expenses and (2) dividends. These relationships are shown in Illustration 1-6.

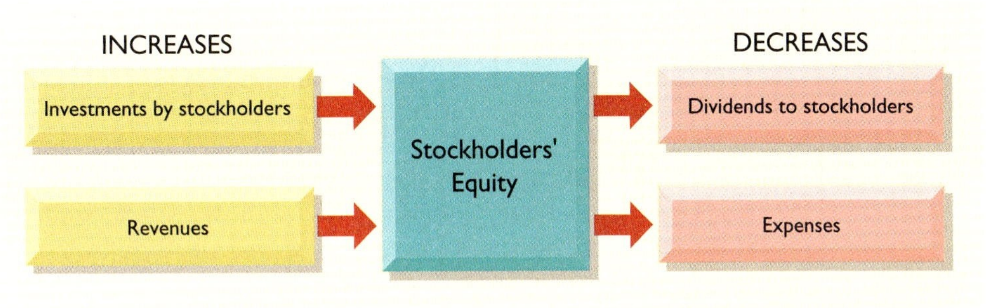

Illustration 1-6

Increases and decreases in stockholders' equity

BEFORE YOU GO ON...

REVIEW IT

1. Why is ethics a fundamental business concept?
2. What are generally accepted accounting principles? Give an example.
3. Explain the monetary unit and the economic entity assumptions.
4. The accounting equation is: Assets = Liabilities + Stockholders' Equity. Replacing the words in that equation with dollar amounts, what is **Hilton's** accounting equation at December 31, 2001? (The answer to this question is provided on page 32.)
5. What are assets, liabilities, and stockholders' equity?

Review It questions marked with this icon require that you use **Hilton's** 2001 Annual Report.

Hilton

DO IT

Classify the following items as issuance of stock (I), dividends (D), revenues (R), or expenses (E). Then indicate whether the following items increase or decrease stockholders' equity: (1) rent expense, (2) service revenue, (3) dividends, and (4) salaries expense.

Do It exercises give you immediate practice of the material just covered.

ACTION PLAN

- Review the rules for changes in stockholders' equity: Investments and revenues increase stockholders' equity. Expenses and dividends decrease stockholders' equity.
- Understand the sources of revenue: the sale of merchandise, performance of services, rental of property, and lending of money.
- Understand what causes expenses: the consumption of assets or services.
- Recognize that dividends are distributions of cash or other assets to stockholders.

SOLUTION

1. Rent expense is classified as an expense (E); it decreases stockholders' equity.
2. Service revenue is classified as revenue (R); it increases stockholders' equity.
3. Dividends is classified as dividends (D); it decreases stockholders' equity.
4. Salaries expense is classified as an expense (E); it decreases stockholders' equity.

Related exercise material: 1-1, 1-2, 1-3, 1-4, 1-5, 1-6, 1-7, and 1-8.

THE NAVIGATOR

USING THE BUILDING BLOCKS

STUDY OBJECTIVE 7

Analyze the effects of business transactions on the basic accounting equation.

Transactions (often referred to as business transactions) are the economic events of an enterprise that are recorded. Transactions may be identified as external or internal. **External transactions involve economic events between the company and some outside enterprise.** For example, Campus Pizza's purchase of cooking equipment from a supplier, payment of monthly rent to the landlord, and sale of pizzas to customers are external transactions. **Internal transactions are economic events that occur entirely within one company.** The use of cooking and cleaning supplies illustrates internal transactions for Campus Pizza.

A company may carry on many activities that do not in themselves represent business transactions. Hiring employees, answering the telephone, talking with customers, and placing orders for merchandise are examples. Some of these activities, however, may lead to business transactions: Employees will earn wages, and merchandise will be delivered by suppliers. Each event must be analyzed to find out if it has an effect on the components of the basic accounting equation. If it does, it will be recorded in the accounting process. Illustration 1-7 demonstrates the transaction identification process.

Illustration 1-7

Transaction identification process

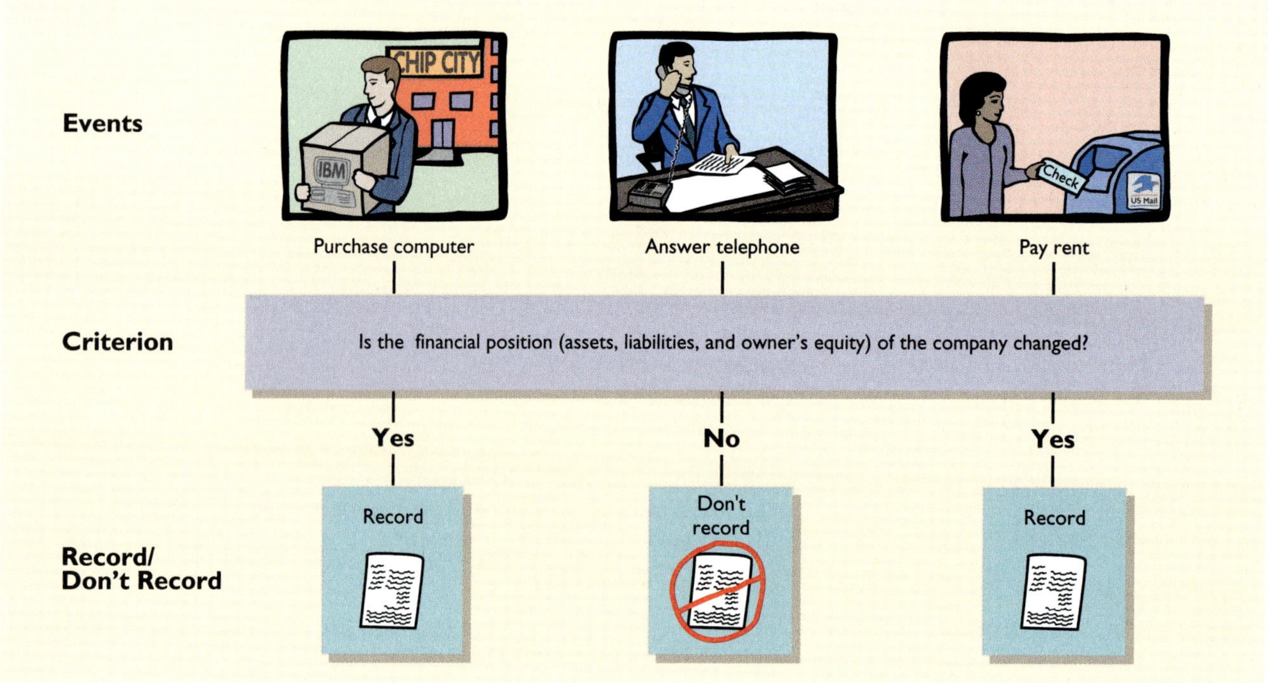

The equality of the basic equation must be preserved. Therefore, each transaction must have a dual effect on the equation. For example, if an asset is increased, it must be offset by one or more of the following:

1. Decrease in another asset
2. Increase in a specific liability
3. Increase in owner's/stockholders' equity

It follows that two or more items could be affected when an asset is increased. For example, as one asset is increased $10,000, another asset could decrease $6,000 and a specific liability could increase $4,000. Note also that any change in an individual liability or ownership claim is subject to similar analysis.

TRANSACTION ANALYSIS

The following examples are business transactions for a new computer programming business during its first month of operations. You will want to study these transactions until you are sure you understand them. They are not difficult, but they are important to your success in this course. The ability to analyze transactions in terms of the basic accounting equation is essential for an understanding of accounting.

Transaction (1). Investment by Stockholders

Ray and Barbara Neal decide to open a catering service that they incorporate as Best Caterers, Inc. They invest $15,000 cash in the business in exchange for $15,000 of common stock. The common stock indicates the ownership interest that the Neals have in Best Caterers, Inc. The transaction results in an equal increase in both assets and stockholders' equity. In this case, there is an increase in the asset Cash of $15,000, and an increase in Common Stock of $15,000.

The effect of this transaction on the basic equation is shown below. Recorded to the right of Common Stock is the reason why stockholders' equity changed (i.e., investment).

	Assets	=	**Liabilities**	+	**Stockholders' Equity**	
	Cash	=			Common Stock	
(1)	**+$15,000**	=			**+$15,000**	**Investment**

Observe that the equality of the basic equation has been maintained. Note also that the source of the increase in stockholders' equity is indicated, to make clear that the increase is an investment rather than revenue from operations. Why does this matter? Because investments by stockholders do not represent revenues; they are excluded in determining net income. Therefore, it is necessary to make clear that the increase is an investment rather than revenue from operations. Additional investments (i.e., investments made by stockholders after the corporation has been initially formed) have the same effect on stockholders' equity as the initial investment.

Transaction (2). Purchase of Equipment for Cash

Best Caterers, Inc. purchases computer equipment for $7,000 cash. This transaction results in an equal increase and decrease in total assets, though the composition of assets is changed: Cash is decreased $7,000, and the asset Equipment is increased $7,000. The specific effect of this transaction and the cumulative effect of the first two transactions are:

		Assets			=	**Liabilities**	+	**Stockholders' Equity**
		Cash	+	Equipment	=			Common Stock
	Old Bal.	$15,000						$15,000
(2)		**−7,000**		**+$ 7,000**				
	New Bal.	$ 8,000	+	$ 7,000	=			$15,000
		$15,000						

Observe that total assets are still $15,000 and stockholders' equity also remains at $15,000, the amount of the original investment.

Transaction (3). Purchase of Supplies on Credit

Best Caterers, Inc. purchases for $1,600 from Acme Supply Company various supplies expected to last several months. Acme agrees to allow Best Caterers to pay this bill next month, in October. This transaction is often referred to as a purchase on account or a credit purchase. Assets are increased by the transaction because of the expected future benefits of using the paper and supplies, and liabilities are increased by the amount due Acme Company. The asset Supplies is increased $1,600, and the liability Accounts Payable is increased by the same amount. The effect on the equation is:

		Assets					=	Liabilities	+	Stockholders' Equity
		Cash	+	Supplies	+	Equipment	=	Accounts Payable	+	Common Stock
	Old Bal.	$8,000				$7,000				$15,000
(3)				+$1,600				+$1,600		
	New Bal.	$8,000	+	$1,600	+	$7,000	=	$1,600	+	$15,000
				$16,600					$16,600	

Total assets are now $16,600. This total is matched by a $1,600 creditor's claim and a $15,000 stockholders' claim.

Transaction (4). Services Rendered for Cash

Best Caterers, Inc. receives $1,200 cash from customers for catering services it has provided. This transaction represents Best Caterers' principal revenue-producing activity. Recall that **revenue increases stockholders' equity**. Both assets and stockholders' equity are, therefore, increased. In this transaction, Cash is increased $1,200, and Retained Earnings is increased $1,200. The new balances in the equation are:

		Assets					=	Liabilities	+	Stockholders' Equity			
		Cash	+	Supplies	+	Equipment	=	Accounts Payable	+	Common Stock	+	Retained Earnings	
	Old Bal.	$8,000		$1,600		$7,000		$1,600		$15,000			
(4)		+1,200										+1,200	Service Revenue
	New Bal.	$9,200	+	$1,600	+	$7,000	=	$1,600	+	$15,000	+	$1,200	
				$17,800						$17,800			

The two sides of the equation balance at $17,800. Note that stockholders' equity is increased when revenues are earned. The source of the increase in stockholders' equity is indicated as Service Revenue. Service revenue is included in determining Best Caterers, Inc's. net income.

Transaction (5). Purchase of Advertising on Credit

Best Caterers, Inc. receives a bill for $250 from the *Daily News* for advertising the opening of its business but postpones payment of the bill until a later date. This transaction results in an increase in liabilities and a decrease in stockholders' equity. The specific items involved are Accounts Payable and Retained Earnings. The effect on the equation is:

	Assets			=	Liabilities	+	Stockholders' Equity			
	Cash	+ Supplies	+ Equipment	=	Accounts Payable	+	Common Stock	+	Retained Earnings	
Old Bal.	$9,200	$1,600	$7,000		$1,600		$15,000		$1,200	
(5)					+250				−250	Advertising Expense
New Bal.	$9,200	+ $1,600	+ $7,000	=	$1,850	+	$15,000	+	$ 950	
		$17,800					$17,800			

The two sides of the equation still balance at $17,800. Observe that Retained Earnings is decreased when the expense is incurred, and the specific cause of the decrease (Advertising Expense) is noted. Expenses do not have to be paid in cash at the time they are incurred. When payment is made at a later date, the liability Accounts Payable will be decreased and the asset Cash will be decreased [see Transaction (8)]. The cost of advertising is considered an expense, as opposed to an asset, because the benefits have been used. This expense is included in determining net income.

Transaction (6). Services Rendered for Cash and Credit

Best Caterers, Inc. provides catering services of $3,500 for customers. Cash of $1,500 is received from customers, and the balance of $2,000 is billed to customers on account. This transaction results in an equal increase in assets and stockholders' equity. Three specific items are affected: Cash is increased $1,500; Accounts Receivable is increased $2,000; and Retained Earnings is increased $3,500. The new balances are as follows:

	Assets				=	Liabilities	+	Stockholders' Equity			
	Cash	+ Accounts Receivable	+ Supplies	+ Equipment	=	Accounts Payable	+	Common Stock	+	Retained Earnings	
Old Bal.	$ 9,200		$1,600	$7,000		$1,850		$15,000		$ 950	
(6)	+1,500	+$2,000								+3,500	Service Revenue
New Bal.	$10,700	+ $2,000	+ $1,600	+ $7,000	=	$1,850	+	$15,000	+	$4,450	
			$21,300					$21,300			

Why increase Retained Earnings by $3,500 when only $1,500 has been collected? Because the inflow of assets resulting from the earning of revenues does not have to be in the form of cash. Remember that stockholders' equity is increased when revenues are earned; in Best Caterers' case revenues are earned when the service is provided. When collections on account are received at a later date, Cash will be increased and Accounts Receivable will be decreased [see Transaction (9)].

Transaction (7). Payment of Expenses

Expenses paid in cash for September are store rent $600, salaries of employees $900, and utilities $200. These payments result in an equal decrease in assets and stockholders' equity. Cash is decreased $1,700 and Retained Earnings is decreased by the same amount. The effect of these payments on the equation is:

	Assets				=	Liabilities +	Stockholders' Equity		
	Cash	+ Accounts Receivable	+ Supplies	+ Equipment	=	Accounts Payable	+ Common Stock	+ Retained Earnings	
Old Bal.	$10,700	$2,000	$1,600	$7,000		$1,850	$15,000	$4,450	
(7)	−1,700							−600	Rent Expense
								−900	Salaries Expense
								−200	Utilities Expense
New Bal.	$ 9,000 +	$2,000 +	$1,600 +	$7,000	=	$1,850	+ $15,000	+ $2,750	
	$19,600					$19,600			

The two sides of the equation now balance at $19,600. Three lines are required in the analysis to indicate the different types of expenses that have been incurred.

Transaction (8). Payment of Accounts Payable

Best Caterers, Inc. pays its *Daily News* advertising bill of $250 in cash. Remember that the bill was previously recorded [in Transaction (5)] as an increase in Accounts Payable and a decrease in Retained Earnings. Thus, this payment "on account" decreases the asset Cash by $250 and also decreases the liability Accounts Payable by $250. The effect of this transaction on the equation is:

	Assets				=	Liabilities +	Stockholders' Equity	
	Cash	+ Accounts Receivable	+ Supplies	+ Equipment	=	Accounts Payable	+ Common Stock	+ Retained Earnings
Old Bal.	$9,000	$2,000	$1,600	$7,000		$1,850	$15,000	$2,750
(8)	−250					−250		
New Bal.	$8,750 +	$2,000 +	$1,600 +	$7,000	=	$1,600	+ $15,000	+ $2,750
	$19,350					$19,350		

Observe that the payment of a liability related to an expense that has previously been incurred does not affect stockholders' equity. The expense was recorded in Transaction (5) and should not be recorded again. Neither Common Stock nor Retained Earnings changes as a result of this transaction.

Transaction (9). Receipt of Cash on Account

The sum of $600 in cash is received from customers who have previously been billed for services [in Transaction (6)]. This transaction does not change total assets, but it changes the composition of those assets. Cash is increased $600 and Accounts Receivable is decreased $600. The new balances are:

	Assets				=	Liabilities +	Stockholders' Equity	
	Cash	+ Accounts Receivable	+ Supplies	+ Equipment	=	Accounts Payable	+ Common Stock	+ Retained Earnings
Old Bal.	$8,750	$2,000	$1,600	$7,000		$1,600	$15,000	$2,750
(9)	+600	−600						
New Bal.	$9,350 +	$1,400 +	$1,600 +	$7,000	=	$1,600	+ $15,000	+ $2,750
	$19,350					$19,350		

Note that a collection on account for services previously billed and recorded does not affect stockholders' equity. Revenue was already recorded in Transaction (6) and should not be recorded again.

Transaction (10). Dividends

The corporation pays a dividend of $1,300 in cash to Ray and Barbara Neal, the stockholders of Best Caterers, Inc. This transaction results in an equal decrease in assets and stockholders' equity. Both Cash and Retained Earnings are decreased $1,300, as shown below.

	Assets				=	Liabilities	+	Stockholders' Equity		
	Cash	+ Receivable	+ Supplies	+ Equipment	=	Accounts Payable	+	Common Stock	+ Retained Earnings	
Old Bal.	$9,350	$1,400	$1,600	$7,000		$1,600		$15,000	$2,750	
(10)	−1,300								−1,300	Dividends
New Bal.	$8,050 +	$1,400 +	$1,600 +	$7,000	=	$1,600	+	$15,000 +	$1,450	
	$18,050					$18,050				

Note that the dividend reduces retained earnings, which is part of stockholders' equity. Dividends are not expenses. Like stockholders' investments, dividends are excluded in determining net income.

SUMMARY OF TRANSACTIONS

The transactions of Best Caterers, Inc. are summarized in Illustration 1-8. The transaction number, the specific effects of the transaction, and the balances

Illustration 1-8

Tabular summary of Best Caterers, Inc. transactions

	Assets				=	Liabilities	+	Stockholders' Equity		
Transaction	Cash	+ Accounts Receivable	+ Supplies	+ Equipment	=	Accounts Payable	+	Common Stock	+ Retained Earnings	
(1)	+$15,000				=		+	$15,000		Investment
(2)	−7,000			+$7,000						
	8,000		+	7,000	=			15,000		
(3)			+$1,600			+$1,600				
	8,000		+ 1,600 +	7,000	=	1,600	+	15,000		
(4)	+1,200								+1,200	Service Revenue
	9,200		+ 1,600 +	7,000	=	1,600	+	15,000 +	1,200	
(5)						+250			−250	Advert. Expense
	9,200		+ 1,600 +	7,000	=	1,850	+	15,000 +	950	
(6)	+1,500	+$2,000							+3,500	Service Revenue
	10,700 +	2,000 +	1,600 +	7,000	=	1,850	+	15,000 +	4,450	
(7)	−1,700								−600	Rent Expense
									−900	Salaries Expense
									−200	Utilities Expense
	9,000 +	2,000 +	1,600 +	7,000	=	1,850	+	15,000 +	2,750	
(8)	−250					−250				
	8,750 +	2,000 +	1,600 +	7,000	=	1,600	+	15,000 +	2,750	
(9)	+600	−600								
	9,350 +	1,400 +	1,600 +	7,000	=	1,600	+	15,000 +	2,750	
(10)	−1,300								−1,300	Dividends
	$ 8,050 +	$1,400 +	$1,600 +	$7,000	=	$1,600	+	$15,000 +	$1,450	
	$18,050					$18,050				

after each transaction are indicated. The illustration demonstrates a number of significant facts:

1. Each transaction must be analyzed in terms of its effect on
   (a) the three components of the basic accounting equation.
   (b) specific types (kinds) of items within each component.
2. The two sides of the equation must always be equal.
3. The causes of each change in the stockholders' claim on assets must be indicated in the Common Stock and Retained Earnings columns.

There! You made it through transaction analysis. If you feel a bit shaky on any of the transactions, it would probably be a good idea at this point to get up, take a short break, and come back again for a 10- to 15-minute review of the transactions, to make sure you understand them before you go on to the next section.

BEFORE YOU GO ON...

REVIEW IT

1. What is an example of an external transaction? What is an example of an internal transaction?
2. If an asset increases, what are the three possible effects on the basic accounting equation?

DO IT

A tabular analysis of the transactions made by Roberta Mendez & Co., a decorating consulting firm, for the month of August is shown below. Each increase and decrease in stockholders' equity is explained.

	Assets			=	Liabilities	+	Stockholders' Equity			
	Cash	+	Office Equipment	=	Accounts Payable	+	Common Stock	+	Retained Earnings	
1.	+25,000						+25,000			Investment
2.			+7,000		+7,000					
3.	+8,000								+8,000	Service Revenue
4.	−850								−850	Rent Expense

Describe each transaction that occurred for the month.

ACTION PLAN

- Analyze the tabular analysis to determine the nature and effect of each transaction.
- Keep the accounting equation always in balance.
- Remember that a change in an asset will require a change in another asset, a liability, or in stockholders' equity.

SOLUTION

1. Stockholders purchased additional shares of stock for $25,000 cash.
2. The company purchased $7,000 of office equipment on credit.
3. The company received $8,000 of cash in exchange for services performed.
4. The company paid $850 for this month's rent.

Related exercise material: 1-4, 1-5, 1-7, 1-8, and 1-9.

THE NAVIGATOR

FINANCIAL STATEMENTS

After transactions are identified, recorded, and summarized, four financial statements are prepared from the summarized accounting data:

STUDY OBJECTIVE 8

Understand what the four financial statements are and how they are prepared.

1. An **income statement** presents the revenues and expenses and resulting net income or net loss of a company for a specific period of time.
2. A **retained earnings statement** summarizes the changes in retained earnings for a specific period of time.
3. A **balance sheet** reports the assets, liabilities, and stockholders' equity of a business enterprise at a specific date.
4. A **statement of cash flows** summarizes information concerning the cash inflows (receipts) and outflows (payments) for a specific period of time.

Each statement provides management, stockholders, and other interested parties with relevant financial data.

The financial statements of Best Caterers, Inc. and their interrelationships are shown in Illustration 1-9 (page 22). The statements are interrelated: **(1) Net income of $2,750 shown on the income statement is added to the beginning balance of retained earnings in the retained earnings statement. (2) Retained earnings of $1,450 at the end of the reporting period shown in the retained earnings statement is reported on the balance sheet. (3) Cash of $8,050 on the balance sheet is reported on the statement of cash flows.**

HELPFUL HINT
The income statement, retained earnings statement, and statement of cash flows are all for a *period* of time, whereas the balance sheet is for a *point* in time.

Also, every set of financial statements is accompanied by explanatory notes and supporting schedules that are an integral part of the statements. Examples of these notes and schedules are illustrated in later chapters of this textbook.

Be sure to carefully examine the format and content of each statement. The essential features of each are briefly described in the following sections.

HELPFUL HINT
There is only one group of notes for the whole set of financial statements, rather than separate sets of notes for each financial statement.

INCOME STATEMENT

The primary focus of the income statement is to report the success or profitability of the company's operations over a specific period of time. For example, Best Caterers' income statement is dated "For the Month Ended September 30, 2004." It is prepared from the data appearing in the retained earnings column of Illustration 1-8. The heading of the statement identifies the company, the type of statement, and the time period covered by the statement.

ALTERNATIVE TERMINOLOGY
The income statement is sometimes referred to as the *statement of operations*, *earnings statement*, or *profit and loss statement*.

On the income statement, revenues are listed first, followed by expenses. Finally net income (or net loss) is determined. Although practice varies, we have chosen in our illustrations and homework solutions to list expenses in order of magnitude. Alternative formats for the income statement will be considered in later chapters.

Note that investment and dividend transactions between the stockholders and the business are not included in the measurement of net income. For example, the cash dividend from Best Caterers, Inc. was not regarded as a business expense, as explained earlier. This type of transaction is considered a reduction of retained earnings which causes a decrease in stockholders' equity.

RETAINED EARNINGS STATEMENT

Best Caterers, Inc.'s retained earnings statement reports the changes in retained earnings for a specific period of time. The time period is the same as that covered by the income statement ("For the Month Ended September 30, 2004"). Data for the preparation of the retained earnings statement are obtained from the retained earnings column of the tabular summary (Illustration 1-8) and from the income statement in Illustration 1-9.

Illustration 1-9

Financial statements and their interrelationships

HELPFUL HINT

The heading of each statement identifies the company, the type of statement, and the specific date or time period covered by the statement.

HELPFUL HINT

The four financial statements are prepared in the sequence shown for the following reasons: Net income is computed first and is needed to determine the ending balance in retained earnings. The ending balance in retained earnings is needed in preparing the balance sheet. The cash shown on the balance sheet is needed in preparing the statement of cash flows.

HELPFUL HINT

Note that final sums are double-underlined, and negative amounts are presented in parentheses.

BEST CATERERS, INC.
Income Statement
For the Month Ended September 30, 2004

Revenues		
Service revenue		$4,700
Expenses		
Salaries expense	$900	
Rent expense	600	
Advertising expense	250	
Utilities expense	200	
Total expenses		1,950
Net income		$2,750

(1)

BEST CATERERS, INC.
Retained Earnings Statement
For the Month Ended September 30, 2004

Retained earnings, September 1	$ 0
Add: Net income	2,750
	2,750
Less: Dividends	1,300
Retained earnings, September 30	$1,450

(2)

BEST CATERERS, INC.
Balance Sheet
September 30, 2004

Assets

Cash		$ 8,050
Accounts receivable		1,400
Supplies		1,600
Equipment		7,000
Total assets		$18,050

Liabilities and Stockholders' Equity

Liabilities		
Accounts payable		$ 1,600
Stockholders' equity		
Common stock	$15,000	
Retained earnings	1,450	16,450
Total liabilities and stockholders' equity		$18,050

(3)

BEST CATERERS, INC.
Statement of Cash Flows
For the Month Ended September 30, 2004

Cash flows from operating activities		
Cash receipts from revenues		$ 3,300
Cash payments for expenses		(1,950)
Net cash provided by operating activities		1,350
Cash flows from investing activities		
Purchase of equipment		(7,000)
Cash flows from financing activities		
Sale of common stock	$15,000	
Payment of cash dividends	(1,300)	13,700
Net increase in cash		8,050
Cash at the beginning of the period		0
Cash at the end of the period		$ 8,050

The beginning retained earnings amount is shown on the first line of the statement. Then, net income and dividends are identified. The retained earnings ending balance is the final amount on the statement. The information provided by this statement indicates the reasons why retained earnings increased or decreased during the period. If there is a net loss, it is deducted with dividends in the retained earnings statement.

BALANCE SHEET

Best Caterers, Inc.'s balance sheet reports the assets, liabilities, and stockholders' equity at a specific date (September 30, 2004). The balance sheet is prepared from the column headings and the month-end data shown in the last line of the tabular summary (Illustration 1-8).

Observe that the assets are listed at the top, followed by liabilities and stockholders' equity. Total assets must equal total liabilities and stockholders' equity. In the Best Caterers illustration, only one liability, accounts payable, is reported on the balance sheet. In most cases, there will be more than one liability. When two or more liabilities are involved, a customary way of listing is shown in Illustration 1-10.

Illustration 1-10

Presentation of liabilities

Liabilities	
Notes payable	$10,000
Accounts payable	63,000
Salaries payable	18,000
Total liabilities	$91,000

The balance sheet is like a snapshot of the company's financial condition at a specific moment in time (usually the month-end or year-end).

ACCOUNTING IN ACTION *Business Insight*

Why do companies choose the particular year-ends that they do? Not every company uses December 31 as the accounting year-end. Many companies choose to end their accounting year when inventory or operations are at a low. This is advantageous because compiling accounting information requires much time and effort by managers, so they would rather do it when they aren't as busy operating the business. Also, inventory is easier and less costly to count when it is low. Some companies whose year-ends differ from December 31 are **Delta Air Lines**, June 30; **Walt Disney Productions**, September 30; **Kmart Corp.**, January 31; and **Dunkin Donuts, Inc.**, October 31.

STATEMENT OF CASH FLOWS

The primary purpose of a statement of cash flows is to provide financial information about the cash receipts and cash payments of an enterprise for a specific period of time. **The statement of cash flows reports (1) the cash effects of a company's operations during a period, (2) its investing transactions, (3) its financing transactions, (4) the net increase or decrease in cash during the period, and (5) the cash amount at the end of the period.**

HELPFUL HINT
Investing activities pertain to investments made by the company, not investments made by the stockholders.

Reporting the sources, uses, and net increase or decrease in cash is useful because investors, creditors, and others want to know what is happening to a company's most liquid resource. The statement of cash flows, therefore, provides answers to the following simple but important questions:

HELPFUL HINT
The cash at the end of the period reported in the statement of cash flows equals the cash reported in the balance sheet.

1. Where did the cash come from during the period?
2. What was the cash used for during the period?
3. What was the change in the cash balance during the period?

A statement of cash flows for Best Caterers, Inc. is provided in Illustration 1-9.

As shown in the statement, cash increased $8,050 during the period: Net cash flow provided from operating activities increased cash $1,350. Cash flow from investing transactions decreased cash $7,000. And cash flow from financing transactions increased cash $13,700. At this time, you need not be concerned with how these amounts are determined. Chapter 6 will examine in detail how the statement is prepared.

BEFORE YOU GO ON...

REVIEW IT

1. What are the income statement, retained earnings statement, balance sheet, and statement of cash flows?
2. How are the financial statements interrelated?

A LOOK BACK AT OUR FEATURE STORY

A Look Back exercises refer to the chapter-opening Feature Story. These exercises help you analyze that real-world situation in terms of the accounting topic of the chapter.

Refer back to the Feature Story about **Hilton** at the beginning of the chapter, and answer the following questions.

1. If you were interested in investing in **Hilton**, what would the balance sheet and income statement tell you?
2. Would you request audited financial statements? Explain.
3. Will the financial statements show the market value of the company? Explain.

SOLUTION

1. The balance sheet reports the assets, liabilities, and stockholders' equity of the company. The income statement presents the revenues and expenses and resulting net income (or net loss) for a specific period of time. The balance sheet is like a snapshot of the company's financial condition at a point in time. The income statement indicates the profitability of the company. Also, the sources of the company's revenues and its expenses are provided in the income statement.
2. You should request **audited** financial statements—statements that a CPA has examined and expressed an opinion as to the fairness of presentation. You should not make decisions without having audited financial statements.
3. The financial statements will not show the market value of the company. One important principle of accounting is the cost principle, which states that assets should be recorded at cost. Cost has an important advantage over other valuations: it is reliable.

THE NAVIGATOR

DEMONSTRATION PROBLEM

Hospitality Legal Services, Inc., which provides contract services for caterers and their clients, was incorporated on July 1, 2004. During the first month of operations, the following transactions occurred.

1. Stockholders invested $10,000 in cash in exchange for shares of stock.
2. Paid $800 for July rent on office space.
3. Purchased office equipment on account, $3,000.
4. Provided legal services to clients for cash, $1,500 (use Service Revenue).
5. Borrowed $700 cash from a bank on a note payable.
6. Performed legal services for client on account, $2,000.
7. Paid monthly expenses: salaries $500; utilities $300; and telephone $100.

Instructions

(a) Prepare a tabular summary of the transactions.

(b) Prepare the income statement, retained earnings statement, and balance sheet at July 31 for Hospitality Legal Services, Inc.

Demonstration Problems are a final review of the chapter. The **Action Plan** gives tips about how to approach the problem, and the **Solution** demonstrates both the form and content of complete answers.

ACTION PLAN

- Remember that assets must equal liabilities and stockholders' equity after each transaction.
- Investments and revenues increase stockholders' equity.
- Dividends and expenses decrease stockholders' equity.
- The income statement shows revenues and expenses for a period of time.
- The retained earnings statement shows the changes in retained earnings for a period of time.
- The balance sheet reports assets, liabilities, and stockholders' equity at a specific date.

SOLUTION TO DEMONSTRATION PROBLEM

(a)

	Assets			=	Liabilities		+ Stockholders' Equity		
Transaction	**Cash**	**+ Accounts Receivable**	**+ Equipment**	**=**	**Notes Payable**	**+ Accounts Payable**	**+ Common Stock**	**+ Retained Earnings**	
(1)	+$10,000						+$10,000		
(2)	−800							−$800	Rent Expense
	9,200			=			10,000 +	−800	
(3)			+$3,000			+$3,000			
	9,200	+	3,000	=		3,000 +	10,000 +	−800	
(4)	+1,500							+1,500	Service Revenue
	10,700	+	3,000	=		3,000 +	10,000 +	700	
(5)	+700				+$700				
	11,400	+	3,000	=	700 +	3,000 +	10,000 +	700	
(6)		+$2,000						+2,000	Service Revenue
	+11,400 +	2,000 +	3,000	=	700 +	3,000 +	10,000 +	2,700	
(7)	−900							−500	Salaries Expense
								−300	Utilities Expense
								−100	Telephone Expense
	$10,500 +	$2,000 +	$3,000	=	$700 +	$3,000 +	$10,000 +	$1,800	
	$15,500				$15,500				

(b)

HOSPITALITY LEGAL SERVICES, INC.
Income Statement
For the Month Ended July 31, 2004

Revenues		
Service revenue		$3,500
Expenses		
Rent expense	$800	
Salaries expense	500	
Utilities expense	300	
Telephone expense	100	
Total expenses		1,700
Net income		$1,800

This would be a good time to return to the **Student Owner's Manual** at the beginning of the book (or look at it for the first time if you skipped it before) to read about the various types of assignment materials that appear at the end of each chapter. Knowing the purpose of the different assignments will help you appreciate what each contributes to your accounting skills and competencies.

HOSPITALITY LEGAL SERVICES, INC.
Retained Earnings Statement
For the Month Ended July 31, 2004

Retained earnings, July 1	$ -0-
Add: Net income	1,800
Retained earnings, July 31	$1,800

HOSPITALITY LEGAL SERVICES, INC.
Balance Sheet
July 31, 2004

Assets		
Cash		$10,500
Accounts receivable		2,000
Equipment		3,000
Total assets		$15,500
Liabilities and Stockholders' Equity		
Liabilities		
Notes payable		$ 700
Accounts payable		3,000
Total liabilities		3,700
Stockholders' equity		
Common stock	$10,000	
Retained earnings	1,800	11,800
Total liabilities and stockholders' equity		$15,500

THE NAVIGATOR

SUMMARY OF STUDY OBJECTIVES

1. *Explain what accounting is.* Accounting is an information system that identifies, records, and communicates the economic events of an organization to interested users.

2. *Identify the users and uses of accounting.* (a) Management uses accounting information in planning, controlling, and evaluating business operations. (b) Investors (owners) decide whether to buy, hold, or sell their financial interests on the basis of accounting data. (c) Creditors (suppliers and bankers) evaluate the risks of granting credit or lending money on the basis of accounting information. Other groups that use accounting information are taxing authorities, regulatory agencies, customers, labor unions, and economic planners.

3. *Understand why ethics is a fundamental business concept.* Ethics are the standards of conduct by which actions are judged as right or wrong. If you cannot depend on the honesty of the individuals you deal with, effective communication and economic activity would be impossible, and information would have no credibility.

4. *Explain the meaning of generally accepted accounting principles and the cost principle.* Generally accepted accounting principles are a common set of standards used by accountants. The cost principle states that assets should be recorded at their cost.

5. *Explain the meaning of the monetary unit assumption and the economic entity assumption.* The monetary unit assumption requires that only transaction data capable of being expressed in terms of money be included in the accounting records. The economic entity assumption requires that the activities of each economic entity be kept separate from the activities of its owners and other economic entities.

6. *State the basic accounting equation, and explain the meaning of assets, liabilities, and stockholders' equity.* The basic accounting equation is:

$$\text{Assets} = \text{Liabilities} + \text{Stockholders' Equity}$$

Assets are resources owned by a business. Liabilities are creditorship claims on total assets. Stockholders' equity is the ownership claim on total assets.

7. *Analyze the effects of business transactions on the basic accounting equation.* Each business transaction must have a dual effect on the accounting equation. For example, if an individual asset is increased, there must be a corresponding (1) decrease in another asset, or (2) increase in a specific liability, or (3) increase in stockholders' equity.

8. *Understand what the four financial statements are and how they are prepared.* An income statement presents the revenues and expenses of a company for a specified period of time. A retained earnings statement summarizes the changes in retained earnings that have occurred for a specific period of time. A balance sheet reports the assets, liabilities, and stockholders' equity of a business at a specific date. A statement of cash flows summarizes information about the cash inflows (receipts) and outflows (payments) for a specific period of time.

THE NAVIGATOR

GLOSSARY

Accounting The information system that identifies, records, and communicates the economic events of an organization to interested users (p. 2).

Assets Resources owned by a business (p. 11).

Balance sheet A financial statement that reports the assets, liabilities, and stockholders' equity at a specific date (p. 21).

Basic accounting equation Assets = Liabilities + Stockholders' Equity (p. 11).

Bookkeeping A part of accounting that involves only the recording of economic events (p. 6).

Corporation A business organized as a separate legal entity under state corporation law having ownership divided into transferable shares of stock (p. 10).

Cost principle An accounting principle that states that assets should be recorded at their cost (p. 9).

Dividend A distribution by a corporation to its stockholders on a pro rata (equal) basis (p. 12).

Economic entity assumption An assumption that requires that the activities of the entity be kept separate and distinct from the activities of its owners and all other economic entities (p. 10).

Ethics The standards of conduct by which one's actions are judged as right or wrong, honest or dishonest, fair or not fair (p. 8).

Expenses The cost of assets consumed or services used in the process of earning revenue (p. 12).

Financial accounting The field of accounting that provides economic and financial information for investors, creditors, and other external users (p. 6).

Financial Accounting Standards Board (FASB) A private organization that establishes generally accepted accounting principles (p. 8).

Generally accepted accounting principles (GAAP) Common standards that indicate how to report economic events (p. 8).

Income statement A financial statement that presents the revenues and expenses and resulting net income or net loss of a company for a specific period of time (p. 21).

Liabilities Creditorship claims on total assets (p. 11).

Managerial accounting The field of accounting that provides economic and financial information for managers and other internal users (p. 6).

Monetary unit assumption An assumption stating that only transaction data that can be expressed in terms of money be included in the accounting records (p. 9).

Net income The amount by which revenues exceed expenses (p. 12).

Net loss The amount by which expenses exceed revenues (p. 12).

Partnership An association of two or more persons to carry on as co-owners of a business for profit (p. 10).

Proprietorship A business owned by one person (p. 10).

Retained earnings statement A financial statement that summarizes the changes in retained earnings for a specific period of time (p. 21).

Revenues The gross increase in stockholders' equity resulting from business activities entered into for the purpose of earning income (p. 12).

Securities and Exchange Commission (SEC) A governmental agency that requires companies to file financial reports in accordance with generally accepted accounting principles (p. 9).

Statement of cash flows A financial statement that provides information about the cash inflows (receipts) and cash outflows (payments) of an entity for a specific period of time (p. 21).

Stockholders' equity The ownership claim on total assets of a corporation (p. 12).

Transactions The economic events of the enterprise that are recorded by accountants (p. 14).

APPENDIX *The Accounting Profession*

What would you do if you join the accounting profession? You probably would work in one of three major fields—public accounting, private accounting, or not-for-profit accounting.

STUDY OBJECTIVE 9

Identify the three major fields of the accounting profession and potential accounting careers.

PUBLIC ACCOUNTING

In **public accounting**, you would offer expert service to the general public in much the same way that a doctor serves patients and a lawyer serves clients. A major portion of public accounting practice involves **auditing**. In this area, a **certified public accountant** (CPA) examines the financial statements of companies and expresses an opinion as to the fairness of presentation. When the presentation is fair, users consider the statements to be **reliable**. For example, **Hilton** investors and creditors would demand audited financial statements before extending it financing.

Taxation is another major area of public accounting. The work performed by tax specialists includes tax advice and planning, preparing tax returns, and representing clients before governmental agencies such as the Internal Revenue Service.

A third area in public accounting is **management consulting**. It ranges from installing basic accounting systems to helping companies determine whether they should use the space shuttle for high-tech research and development projects.

PRIVATE ACCOUNTING

Instead of working in public accounting, you might choose to be an employee of a business enterprise. In **private (or managerial) accounting**, you would be involved in one of the following activities.

1. **General accounting**—recording daily transactions and preparing financial statements and related information.
2. **Cost accounting**—determining the cost of producing specific products.
3. **Budgeting**—assisting management in quantifying goals concerning revenues, costs of goods sold, and operating expenses.
4. **Accounting information systems**—designing both manual and computerized data processing systems.
5. **Tax accounting**—preparing tax returns and engaging in tax planning for the company.
6. **Internal auditing**—reviewing the company's operations to determine compliance with management policies and evaluating the efficiency of operations.

You can see that within a specific company, private accountants perform as wide a variety of duties as the public accountant.

Illustration 1A-1 presents the general career paths in public and private accounting.

NOT-FOR-PROFIT ACCOUNTING

Like businesses that exist to make a profit, not-for-profit organizations also need sound financial reporting and control. Donors to such organizations as the **Coca-Cola Foundation**, the **Conrad N. Hilton Foundation**, and the **Red Cross** want information about how well the organization has met its objectives and whether continued support is justified. Hospitals, colleges, and universities must make decisions about the allocation of funds. Local, state, and federal governmental units provide financial information to legislators, citizens, employees, and creditors. At the federal level, the largest employers of accountants are the **Internal Revenue Service**, the **General Accounting Office**, the **Federal Bureau of Investigation**, and the **Securities and Exchange Commission**.

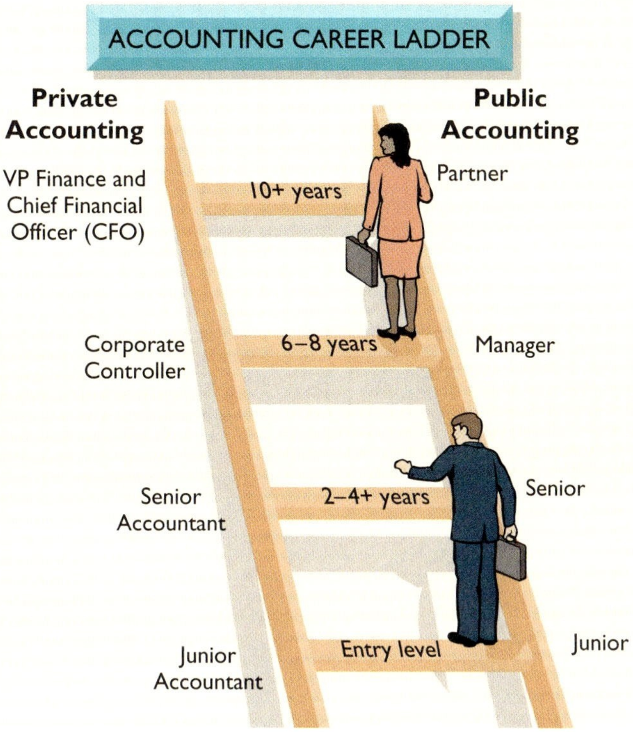

Illustration 1A-1

Career paths in public and private accounting

Summary of Study Objective for Appendix

9. *Identify the three major fields of the accounting profession and potential accounting careers.* The accounting profession comprises three major fields: public accounting, private accounting, and not-for-profit accounting. In public accounting one may pursue a career in auditing, taxation, or management consulting. In private or managerial accounting, one may pursue a career in cost accounting, budgeting, general accounting, accounting information systems, tax accounting, or internal auditing. In not-for-profit accounting one may pursue a career at hospitals, universities, and foundations, or in local, state, and federal governmental units.

Glossary for Appendix

Auditing The examination of financial statements by a certified public accountant in order to express an opinion as to the fairness of presentation (p. 28).

Management consulting An area of public accounting involving financial planning and control and the development of accounting and computer systems (p. 28).

Private (or managerial) accounting An area of accounting within a company that involves such activities as cost accounting, budgeting, and accounting information systems (p. 28).

Public accounting An area of accounting in which the accountant offers expert service to the general public (p. 28).

Taxation An area of public accounting involving tax advice, tax planning, and preparation of tax returns (p. 28).

Exercises

1-1 Presented below is the basic accounting equation. Determine the missing amounts.

Use basic accounting equation. (SO 6)

	Assets	=	Liabilities	+	Stockholders' Equity
(a)	$90,000		$50,000		?
(b)	?		$45,000		$85,000
(c)	$97,000		?		$62,000

Use basic accounting equation. (SO 6)

1-2 Given the accounting equation, answer each of the following questions.

1. The liabilities of Leno Health Drinks are $90,000, and the stockholders' equity is $280,000. What is the amount of Leno's total assets?
2. The total assets of Letterman Pizza are $210,000, and its stockholders' equity is $90,000. What is the amount of its total liabilities?
3. The total assets of Conan Salads Co. are $900,000, and its liabilities are equal to one half of its total assets. What is the amount of Conan Salads' stockholders' equity?

Use basic accounting equation. (SO 6)

1-3 At the beginning of the year, Italian Pasta Company had total assets of $850,000 and total liabilities of $500,000. Answer the following questions.

1. If total assets increased $150,000 during the year and total liabilities decreased $80,000, what is the amount of stockholders' equity at the end of the year?
2. During the year, total liabilities increased $100,000 and stockholders' equity decreased $50,000. What is the amount of total assets at the end of the year?
3. If total assets decreased $90,000 and stockholders' equity increased $130,000 during the year, what is the amount of total liabilities at the end of the year?

Determine effect of transactions on basic accounting equation. (SO 7)

1-4 Presented below are three business transactions. On a sheet of paper, list the letters (a), (b), (c) with columns for assets, liabilities, and stockholders' equity. For each column, indicate whether the transactions increased (+), decreased (−), or had no effect (NE) on assets, liabilities, and stockholders' equity.

(a) Purchased supplies on account.
(b) Received cash for providing a service.
(c) Expenses paid in cash.
(d) Invested cash in the business.
(e) Paid cash dividend.
(f) Received cash from a customer who had previously been billed for services provided.

Classify various items. (SO 6, 7)

1-5 Classify each of the following items as asset (A), liability (L), revenue (R), or expense (E).

____**(a)** Advertising expense	____**(e)** Cash
____**(b)** Commission revenue	____**(f)** Rent revenue
____**(c)** Insurance expense	____**(g)** Utilities expense
____**(d)** Office equipment	____**(h)** Accounts payable

Classify accounts as assets, liabilities, or stockholders' equity. (SO 6)

1-6 Pressing Cleaners has the following balance sheet items.

Accounts payable	Accounts receivable
Cash	Notes payable
Cleaning equipment	Salaries payable
Cleaning supplies	Common stock

Instructions

Classify each item as an asset, liability, or stockholders' equity.

Analyze the effect of transactions. (SO 6, 7)

1-7 Selected transactions for Green Acres Catering Company are listed below.

1. Made cash investment to start business.
2. Paid monthly rent.
3. Purchased equipment on account.
4. Billed customers for services performed.
5. Paid dividends.
6. Received cash from customers billed in (4).
7. Incurred advertising expense on account.
8. Purchased additional equipment for cash.
9. Received cash from customers when service was rendered.

Instructions

List the numbers of the above transactions and describe the effect of each transaction on assets, liabilities, and stockholders' equity. For example, the first answer is: (1) Increase in assets and increase in stockholders' equity.

Analyze the effect of transactions on assets, liabilities, and stockholders' equity. (SO 6, 7)

1-8 Blaskowski Foodservices entered into the following transactions during May 2004.

1. Purchased kitchen equipment for $22,000 from Wheeler Appliances on account.
2. Paid $5,000 cash for May rent on storage space.
3. Received $15,000 cash from customers for contracts billed in April.
4. Provided services to Bilder Construction Company for $10,000 cash.

5. Paid Southern States Power Co. $11,000 cash for energy usage in May.
6. Stockholders invested an additional $32,000 in the business.
7. Paid Wheeler Appliances for the terminals purchased in (1) above.
8. Incurred advertising expense for May of $2,000 on account.

Instructions

Indicate with the appropriate letter whether each of the transactions above results in

(a) an increase in assets and a decrease in assets.
(b) an increase in assets and an increase in stockholders' equity.
(c) an increase in assets and an increase in liabilities.
(d) a decrease in assets and a decrease in stockholders' equity.
(e) a decrease in assets and a decrease in liabilities.
(f) an increase in liabilities and a decrease in stockholders' equity.
(g) an increase in stockholders' equity and a decrease in liabilities.

Analyze transactions and compute net income. (SO 6, 7)

1-9 On April 1, Crossroads Travel Agency, Inc. was established. The following transactions were completed during the month.

1. Stockholders invested $20,000 cash, receiving common stock in exchange.
2. Paid $800 cash for April office rent.
3. Purchased office equipment for $2,500 cash.
4. Incurred $300 of advertising costs in the *Chicago Tribune,* on account.
5. Paid $750 cash for office supplies.
6. Earned $12,000 for services rendered: Cash of $3,000 is received from customers, and the balance of $9,000 is billed to customers on account.
7. Paid $500 cash dividend.
8. Paid *Chicago Tribune* amount due in transaction (4).
9. Paid employees' salaries $1,500.
10. Cash of $7,000 is received from customers who have previously been billed in transaction (6).

Instructions

(a) Prepare a tabular analysis of the transactions using the following column headings: Cash, Accounts Receivable, Supplies, Office Equipment, Accounts Payable, Common Stock, and Retained Earnings.
(b) From an analysis of the Retained Earnings column, compute the net income or net loss for April.

Analyze transactions and prepare income statement, balance sheet, and retained earnings statement. (SO 6, 7, 8)

1-10 Jennifer Lopez Cheesecake Corporation was formed on July 1, 2004. On July 31, the balance sheet showed Cash $5,000, Accounts Receivable $1,900, Supplies $500, Office Equipment $5,000, Accounts Payable $4,200, Common Stock $7,500, and Retained Earnings $700. During August the following transactions occurred.

1. Collected $1,600 of accounts receivable.
2. Paid $2,700 cash on accounts payable.
3. Earned revenues of $8,400, of which $3,000 is collected in cash and the balance is due in September.
4. Purchased additional office equipment for $1,000, paying $250 in cash and the balance on account.
5. Paid salaries $1,500, rent for August $1,100, and advertising expenses $350.
6. Paid dividends of $750.
7. Received $1,000 from Standard Federal Bank—money borrowed on a note payable.
8. Incurred utility expenses for month on account $300.

Instructions

(a) Prepare a tabular analysis of the August transactions beginning with July 31 balances. The column heading should be as follows: Cash + Accounts Receivable + Supplies + Office Equipment = Notes Payable + Accounts Payable + Common Stock + Retained Earnings.
(b) Prepare an income statement for August, a retained earnings statement for August, and a balance sheet at August 31.

FINANCIAL REPORTING PROBLEM: Hilton Hotels Corporation

1-11 The actual financial statements of **Hilton Hotels**, as presented in the company's 2001 Annual Report, are contained in the Appendix (at the back of the textbook).

Instructions
Refer to **Hilton's** financial statements and answer the following questions.

(a) What were Hilton's total assets at December 31, 2001? At December 31, 2000?
(b) How much cash (and cash equivalents) did Hilton have on December 31, 2001?
(c) What amount of accounts payable did Hilton report on December 31, 2001? On December 31, 2000?
(d) What was Hilton's total revenue in 2000? In 2001?
(e) What is the amount of the change in Hilton's net income from 2000 to 2001?

EXPLORING THE WEB

1-12 This exercise will familiarize you with skill requirements, job descriptions, and salaries for accounting careers.

Address: **www.careers-in-accounting.com**

Instructions
Go to the site shown above. Answer the following questions.

(a) What are the three broad areas of accounting (from "Skills and Talents")?
(b) List eight skills required in accounting.
(c) How do the three accounting areas differ in terms of these eight required skills?
(d) Explain one of the key job functions in accounting.
(e) Based on the *Smart Money* survey, what is the salary range for a junior staff accountant with Deloitte & Touche?

Answer to Hilton Review It Question 4, p. 13

Hilton's accounting equation is:

Assets	=	Liabilities	+	Stockholders' Equity
\$8,785,000	=	\$7,002,000	+	\$1,783,000

Remember to go back to the Navigator box on the chapter-opening page and check off your completed work.

2

ACCOUNTING PRINCIPLES

THE NAVIGATOR ✓

- Understand *Concepts for Review* ❑
- Read *Feature Story* ❑
- Scan *Study Objectives* ❑
- Read *Preview* ❑
- Read text and answer *Before You Go On*
  p. 40 ❑ *p.* 47 ❑ *p.* 64 ❑
- Work *Demonstration Problems* ❑
- Review *Summary of Study Objectives* ❑
- Complete *Assignments* ❑

CONCEPTS FOR REVIEW

Before studying this chapter, you should know or, if necessary, review:

a. The two organizations primarily responsible for setting accounting standards. (Ch. 1, pp. 8–9)

b. The monetary unit assumption and the economic entity assumption. (Ch. 1, pp. 9–10)

c. The cost principle. (Ch. 1, p. 9)

THE NAVIGATOR

FEATURE STORY

Certainly Worth Investigating!

It is often difficult to determine in what period some revenues and expenses should be reported. There are rules that give guidance, but occasionally these rules are overlooked, misinterpreted, or even intentionally ignored. Consider the following examples.

- **Reliant Energy**, a provider of electricity and energy services to wholesale and retail markets, restated their revenues down by 10 percent for the first quarter of 2001. This came one week after the company admitted to using bogus trades to overstate revenues.

- **Merck**, one of the giants in pharmaceuticals, withdrew an initial public offering of Medco Health Solutions, its pharmacy benefits management unit, at a total price of about $46 million when it found out that Medco booked $14 billion in revenues that it never collected.

- **Adelphia Communications**, once a leading cable TV firm, booked marketing support payments it received from Motorola Inc. and Scientific-Atlanta Inc. incorrectly in order to overstate its EBITDA (earnings before interest, tax, depreciation, and amortization) by almost $95 million.

Often in cases such as these, the company's shareholders sue the company because of the decline in the stock price due to the disclosure of the misinformation. In light of this eventuality, why might management want to report revenues or expenses in the wrong period? Company managers are under intense pressure to report higher earnings every year. If actual performance falls short of expectations, management might be tempted to bend the rules.

One analyst suggests that investors and auditors should be suspicious of sharp increases in monthly sales at the end of each quarter or big jumps in fourth-quarter sales. Such events don't always mean management is cheating, but they are certainly worth investigating.

THE NAVIGATOR

STUDY OBJECTIVES

After studying this chapter, you should be able to

1. Explain the meaning of generally accepted accounting principles and identify the key items of the conceptual framework.
2. Describe the basic objectives of financial reporting.
3. Discuss the qualitative characteristics of accounting information and elements of financial statements.
4. Identify the basic assumptions used by accountants.
5. Identify the basic principles of accounting.
6. Identify the two constraints in accounting.
7. Understand and analyze classified financial statements.
8. Explain the accounting principles used in international operations.
9. Identify the various systems of accounting procedures used in the hospitality industry.
10. Understand accounting and financial management in a hotel.
11. Understand accounting and financial management in a foodservice operation and a club.

THE NAVIGATOR

PREVIEW OF CHAPTER 2

As indicated in the Feature Story, it is important that general guidelines be available to resolve accounting issues. Without these basic guidelines, each enterprise would have to develop its own set of accounting practices. If this happened, we would have to become familiar with every company's peculiar accounting and reporting rules in order to understand their financial statements. It would be difficult, if not impossible, to compare the financial statements of different companies. This chapter explores the basic accounting principles used in developing specific accounting guidelines. The Uniform Systems of Accounts used in hospitality accounting reporting is also discussed.

The content and organization of Chapter 2 are as follows:

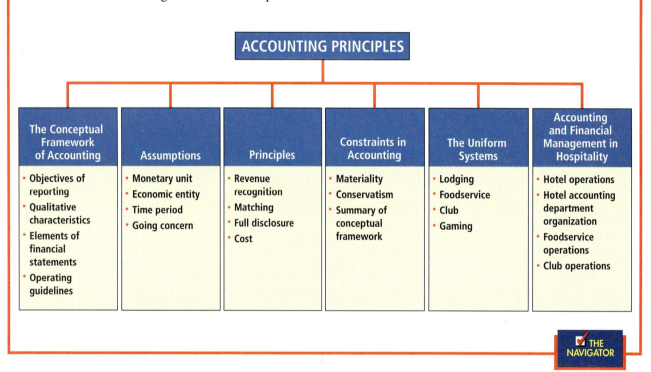

ACCOUNTING PRINCIPLES

- **The Conceptual Framework of Accounting**
  - Objectives of reporting
  - Qualitative characteristics
  - Elements of financial statements
  - Operating guidelines
- **Assumptions**
  - Monetary unit
  - Economic entity
  - Time period
  - Going concern
- **Principles**
  - Revenue recognition
  - Matching
  - Full disclosure
  - Cost
- **Constraints in Accounting**
  - Materiality
  - Conservatism
  - Summary of conceptual framework
- **The Uniform Systems**
  - Lodging
  - Foodservice
  - Club
  - Gaming
- **Accounting and Financial Management in Hospitality**
  - Hotel operations
  - Hotel accounting department organization
  - Foodservice operations
  - Club operations

THE NAVIGATOR

THE CONCEPTUAL FRAMEWORK OF ACCOUNTING

STUDY OBJECTIVE 1

Explain the meaning of generally accepted accounting principles and identify the key items of the conceptual framework.

What you have learned up to this point in the book is a process that leads to the preparation of financial reports about a company. These are the company's financial statements. This area of accounting is called **financial accounting**. The accounting profession has established a set of standards and rules that are recognized as a general guide for financial reporting. This recognized set of standards is called **generally accepted accounting principles (GAAP)**. *Generally accepted* means that these principles must have "substantial authoritative support." Such support usually comes from two standard-setting bodies: the Financial Accounting Standards Board (FASB) and the Securities and Exchange Commission (SEC).[1]

[1]The SEC is an agency of the U.S. government that was established in 1933 to administer laws and regulations relating to the exchange of securities and the publication of financial information by U.S. businesses. The agency has the authority to mandate generally accepted accounting principles for companies under its jurisdiction. However, throughout its history, the SEC has been willing to accept the principles set forth by the FASB and similar bodies.

Since the early 1970s the business and governmental communities have given the FASB the responsibility for developing accounting principles in this country. This is an ongoing process; accounting principles change to reflect changes in the business environment and in the needs of users of accounting information.

Prior to the establishment of the FASB, accounting principles were developed on a problem-by-problem basis. Rule-making bodies developed accounting rules and methods to solve specific problems. Critics charged that the problem-by-problem approach led over time to inconsistent rules and practices. No clearly developed conceptual framework of accounting existed to refer to in solving new problems.

HELPFUL HINT
Accounting principles are affected by economic and political conditions that change over time. As a result, accounting principles are not cut into stone like the periodic table in chemistry or a formula in math.

In response to these criticisms, the FASB developed a **conceptual framework**. It serves as the basis for resolving accounting and reporting problems. The FASB spent considerable time and effort on this project. The Board views its conceptual framework as ". . . a constitution, a coherent system of interrelated objectives and fundamentals."[2]

The FASB's conceptual framework consists of four items:

1. Objectives of financial reporting
2. Qualitative characteristics of accounting information
3. Elements of financial statements
4. Operating guidelines (assumptions, principles, and constraints)

We will discuss these items on the following pages.

ACCOUNTING IN ACTION *International Insight*

Different political and cultural influences affect the accounting that occurs in foreign countries. For example, in Sweden, accounting is considered an instrument to be used to shape fiscal policy. In Europe generally, more emphasis is given to social reporting (more information on employment statistics, health of workers, and so on) than in the United States. European labor organizations are strong and demand that type of information from management.

OBJECTIVES OF FINANCIAL REPORTING

STUDY OBJECTIVE 2
Describe the basic objectives of financial reporting.

The FASB began to work on the conceptual framework by looking at the objectives of financial reporting. Determining these objectives required answers to such basic questions as: Who uses financial statements? Why? What information do they need? How knowledgeable about business and accounting are financial statement users? How should financial information be reported so that it is best understood?

In answering these questions, the FASB concluded that financial reporting should have three objectives:

1. The information is useful to those making investment and credit decisions.
2. The financial reports are helpful in assessing future cash flows.
3. The economic resources (assets), the claims to those resources (liabilities), and the changes in those resources and claims are clearly identified.

The FASB then undertook to describe the characteristics that make accounting information useful.

[2]"Conceptual Framework for Financial Accounting and Reporting: Elements of Financial Statements and Their Measurement," *FASB Discussion Memorandum* (Stamford, Conn.: 1976), p. 1.

QUALITATIVE CHARACTERISTICS OF ACCOUNTING INFORMATION

STUDY OBJECTIVE 3

Discuss the qualitative characteristics of accounting information and elements of financial statements.

How does a company like the **Club Corporation of America** decide on the amount of financial information to disclose? In what format should its financial information be presented? How should assets, liabilities, revenues, and expenses be measured? The FASB concluded that the overriding criterion for such accounting choices is **decision usefulness**. The accounting practice selected should be the one that generates the most useful financial information for making a decision. To be useful, information should possess the following qualitative characteristics: relevance, reliability, comparability, and consistency.

Relevance

Accounting information has **relevance** if it makes a difference in a decision. Relevant information has either predictive or feedback value or both. **Predictive value** helps users forecast future events. For example, when **Four Seasons Hotels & Resorts** issues financial statements, the information in them is considered relevant because it provides a basis for predicting future earnings. **Feedback value** confirms or corrects prior expectations. When **Four Seasons** issues financial statements, it confirms or corrects prior expectations about the financial health of the company.

HELPFUL HINT
What makes accounting information relevant? Answer: Relevant accounting information provides feedback, serves as a basis for predictions, and is timely (current).

In addition, accounting information has relevance if it is **timely**. It must be available to decision makers before it loses its capacity to influence decisions. If **Four Seasons** reported its financial information only every five years, the information would be of limited use in decision making.

Reliability

Reliability of information means that the information is free of error and bias. In short, it can be depended on. To be reliable, accounting information must be **verifiable**: We must be able to prove that it is free of error and bias. It also must be a **faithful representation** of what it purports to be: It must be factual. If the **Felcor Lodging Trust** balance sheet reports assets of $8 billion when it had assets of $51 billion, then the statement is not a faithful representation. Finally, accounting information must be **neutral**: It cannot be selected, prepared, or presented to favor one set of interested users over another. To ensure reliability, certified public accountants audit financial statements.

HELPFUL HINT
What makes accounting information reliable? Answer: Reliable accounting information is free of error and bias, is factual, verifiable, and neutral.

Comparability

Accounting information about an enterprise is most useful when it can be compared with accounting information about other enterprises. **Comparability** results when different companies use the same accounting principles. For example, **Accor** and **Adam's Mark** use the cost principle in reporting plant assets on the balance sheet. Also, each company uses the revenue recognition and matching principles in determining its net income.

Conceptually, comparability should also extend to the methods used by companies in complying with an accounting principle. Accounting methods include the FIFO and LIFO methods of inventory costing, and various depreciation methods. At this point, comparability of methods is not required, even for companies in the same industry. Thus, **LaQuinta Inns and Suites** and **Choice Hotels International** may use different inventory costing and depreciation methods in their financial statements. The only accounting requirement is that each company **must disclose** the accounting methods used. From the disclosures, the external user can determine whether the financial information is comparable.

Consistency

Consistency means that a company uses the same accounting principles and methods from year to year. If a company selects FIFO as the inventory costing method in the first year of operations, it is expected to use FIFO in succeeding years. When financial information has been reported on a consistent basis, the financial statements permit meaningful analysis of trends within a company.

A company *can* change to a new method of accounting. To do so, management must justify that the new method results in more meaningful financial information. In the year in which the change occurs, the change must be disclosed in the notes to the financial statements. Such disclosure makes users of the financial statements aware of the lack of consistency.

ACCOUNTING IN ACTION *Business Insight*

There is a classic story that professors often tell students about a company looking for an accountant. The company approached the first accountant and asked: "What do you believe our net income will be this year?" The accountant said, "Four million dollars." The company asked the second accountant the same question, and the answer was, "What would you like it to be?" Guess who got the job?

The reason we tell the story here is that, because accounting principles offer flexibility, it is important that a consistent treatment be provided from period to period. Otherwise it would be very difficult to interpret financial statements. Perhaps *no* alternative methods should be permitted in accounting. What do you think?

	YTD	%	SEPT. 02
NUMBER OF ROOMS	86		86
THIS MTHS AVAI. OF ROOMS	8077		2224
ROOMS SOLD	4630		1298
PERCNT. OF OCCUPANCY	57.3%	57.3%	58.4%
NET AVERAGE ROOM RATE	85.73		82.03
REVENUE			
ROOMS	396,923	26.9%	106,470
FOOD	753,794	51.1%	196,152
BEVERAGES	62,743	4.3%	15,000
GIFT SHOP	23,045	1.6%	7,699
PUBLIC ROOM RENTALS	118,081	8.0%	34,103
AUDIO & VIDEO	40,604	2.8%	10,051
TELEPHONE	4,608		1,748
GARAGE	62,217		20,489
COPY, FAX	12,305		3,800
VALET, DECRTN, PIANO ETC	1,653		559
OTHER INCOME - TOTAL	80,783	5.5%	26,595
TOTAL NET INCOME	1,475,972	100.0%	- 396,070

The qualitative characteristics of accounting information are summarized in Illustration 2-1.

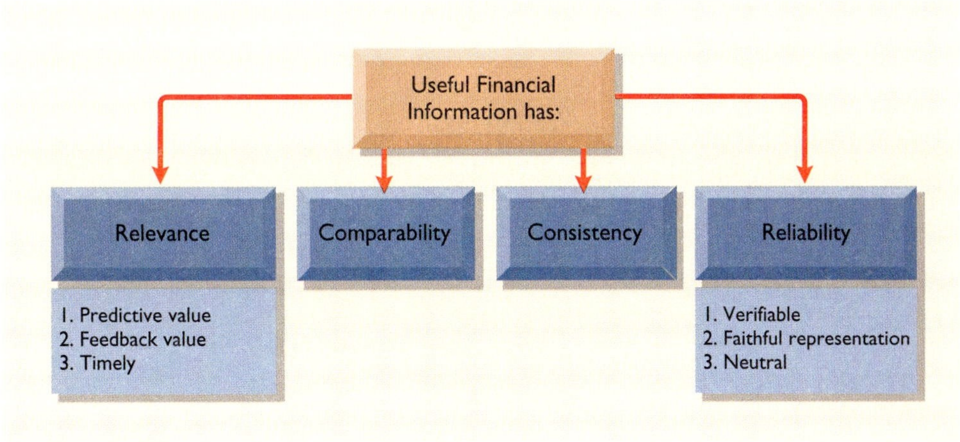

Illustration 2-1

Qualitative characteristics of accounting information

ELEMENTS OF FINANCIAL STATEMENTS

An important part of the accounting conceptual framework is a set of definitions that describe the basic terms used in accounting. The FASB refers to this set of definitions as the **elements of financial statements**. They include such terms as *assets*, *liabilities*, *equity*, *revenues*, and *expenses*.

Because these elements are so important, it is crucial that they be precisely defined and universally applied. Finding the appropriate definition for many of these elements is not easy. For example, should the value of a company's employees be reported as an asset on a balance sheet? Should the death of the company's president be reported as a loss? A good set of definitions should provide answers to these types of questions. Because you have already encountered most of these definitions in earlier chapters, they are not repeated here.

OPERATING GUIDELINES

The objectives of financial reporting, the qualitative characteristics of accounting information, and the elements of financial statements are very broad. Because practicing accountants must solve practical problems, more detailed guidelines are needed. In its conceptual framework, the FASB recognized the need for operating guidelines. We classify these guidelines as assumptions, principles, and constraints. These guidelines are well established and accepted in accounting.

Assumptions provide a foundation for the accounting process. **Principles** are specific rules that indicate how economic events should be reported in the accounting process. **Constraints** on the accounting process allow for a relaxation of the principles under certain circumstances. Illustration 2-2 provides a roadmap of the operating guidelines of accounting. These guidelines (some of which you know from earlier chapters) are discussed in more detail in the following sections.

Illustration 2-2

The operating guidelines of accounting

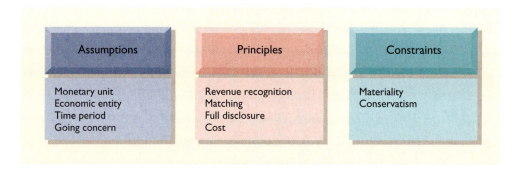

Assumptions	Principles	Constraints
Monetary unit Economic entity Time period Going concern	Revenue recognition Matching Full disclosure Cost	Materiality Conservatism

BEFORE YOU GO ON...

REVIEW IT

1. What are generally accepted accounting principles?
2. What is stated about generally accepted accounting principles in the Report of Independent Public Accountants for **Hilton**? The answer to this question appears on page 73.
3. What are the basic objectives of financial information?
4. What are the qualitative characteristics that make accounting information useful? Identify two elements of the financial statements.

THE NAVIGATOR

STUDY OBJECTIVE 4

Identify the basic assumptions used by accountants.

ASSUMPTIONS

As noted above, assumptions provide a foundation for the accounting process. Below are definitions of four basic accounting assumptions.

MONETARY UNIT ASSUMPTION

The **monetary unit assumption** states that only transaction data that can be expressed in terms of money be included in the accounting records. For example, the value of a company president is not reported in a company's financial records because it cannot be expressed easily in dollars.

An important corollary to the monetary unit assumption is the assumption that the unit of measure remains relatively constant over time. This point will be discussed in more detail later in this chapter.

ECONOMIC ENTITY ASSUMPTION

The **economic entity assumption** states that the activities of the entity be kept separate and distinct from the activities of the owners and of all other economic entities. For example, it is assumed that the activities of **Peabody Hotel Group** can be distinguished from those of other computer companies such as **Cendant**, **Forte Hotels**, and **John Q. Hammons Hotels**.

INTERNATIONAL NOTE

In an action that sent shock waves through the French business community, the CEO of Alcatel-Alsthom was taken into custody for an apparent violation of the economic entity assumption. Allegedly, the executive improperly used company funds to install an expensive security system in his home.

TIME PERIOD ASSUMPTION

The **time period assumption** states that the economic life of a business can be divided into artificial time periods. Thus, it is assumed that the activities of business enterprises such as **MeriStar Hotels and Resorts**, **Ameri Suites**, **Carlson Hospitality**, or any enterprise can be subdivided into months, quarters, or a year for meaningful financial reporting purposes.

GOING CONCERN ASSUMPTION

The **going concern assumption** assumes that the enterprise will continue in operation long enough to carry out its existing objectives. In spite of numerous business failures, companies have a fairly high continuance rate. It has proved useful to adopt a going concern assumption for accounting purposes.

The accounting implications of this assumption are critical. If a going concern assumption is not used, then plant assets should be stated at their liquidation value (selling price less cost of disposal)—not at their cost. In that case, depreciation and amortization of these assets would not be needed. Each period, these assets would simply be reported at their liquidation value. Also, without this assumption, the current–noncurrent classification of assets and liabilities would not matter. Labeling anything as long-term would be difficult to justify.

Acceptance of the going concern assumption gives credibility to the cost principle. Only when liquidation appears imminent is the going concern assumption inapplicable. In that case, assets would be better stated at liquidation value than at cost.

These basic accounting assumptions are illustrated graphically in Illustration 2-3 on the next page.

HELPFUL HINT

(1) Which accounting assumption assumes that an enterprise will remain in business long enough to recover the cost of its assets? (2) Which accounting assumption is justification for the cost principle?
Answers: (1) and (2) Going concern assumption.

PRINCIPLES

STUDY OBJECTIVE 5

Identify the basic principles of accounting.

On the basis of the fundamental assumptions of accounting, the accounting profession has developed principles that dictate how economic events should be recorded and reported. In Chapter 1 we discussed the cost principle and we will also discuss the revenue recognition and matching principles in Chapter 4. Here we now examine a number of reporting issues related to these principles. In addition, we introduce another principle, the full disclosure principle.

Illustration 2-3

Assumptions used in accounting

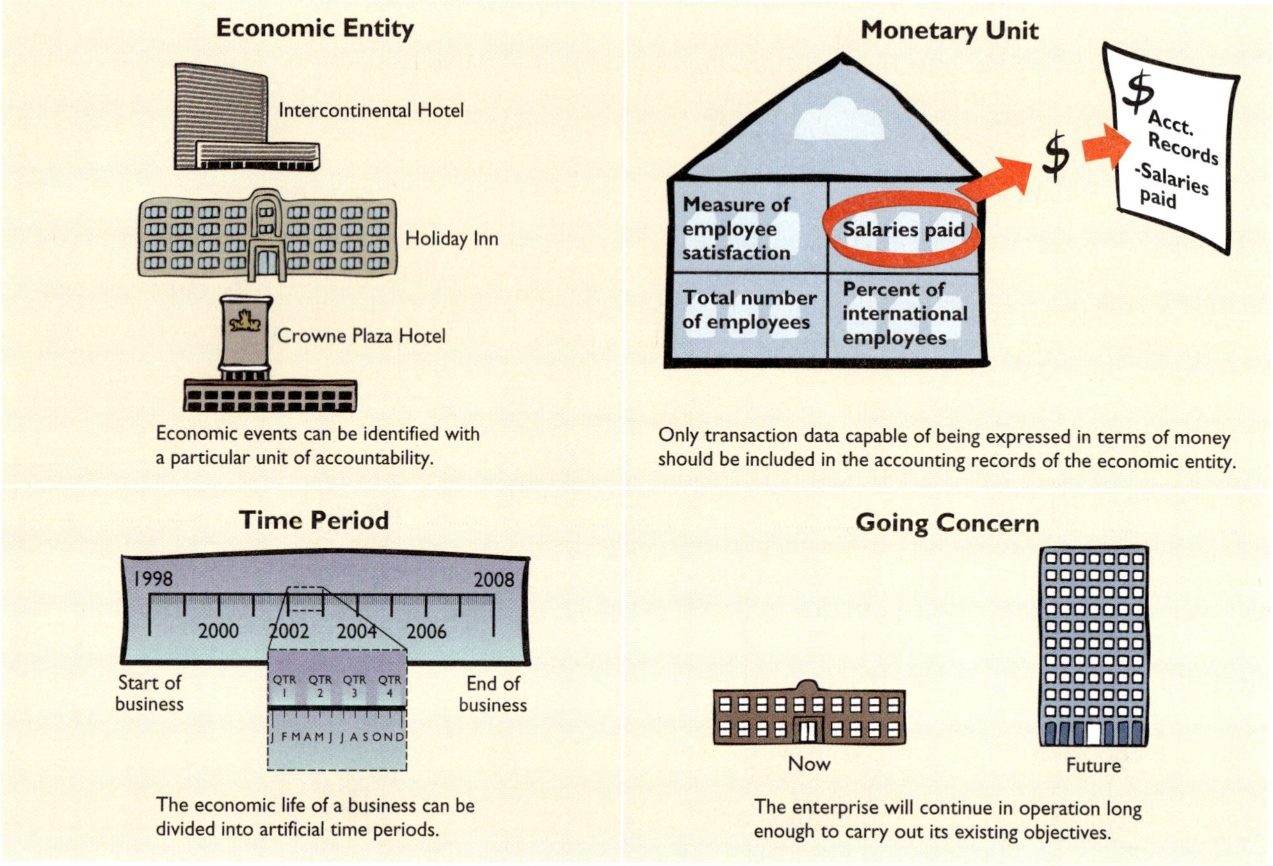
Economic Entity
Intercontinental Hotel
Holiday Inn
Crowne Plaza Hotel
Economic events can be identified with a particular unit of accountability.
Monetary Unit
Measure of employee satisfaction
Salaries paid
Total number of employees
Percent of international employees
$
$ Acct. Records -Salaries paid
Only transaction data capable of being expressed in terms of money should be included in the accounting records of the economic entity.
Time Period
1998
2008
2000
2002
2004
2006
Start of business
End of business
QTR 1 QTR 2 QTR 3 QTR 4
J F M A M J J A S O N D
The economic life of a business can be divided into artificial time periods.
Going Concern
Now
Future
The enterprise will continue in operation long enough to carry out its existing objectives.

REVENUE RECOGNITION PRINCIPLE

> **HELPFUL HINT**
> Revenue should be recognized in the accounting period in which it is earned. This may not be the period in which the related cash is received. In a retail establishment, the point of sale is often the critical point in the process of earning revenue.

The **revenue recognition principle** dictates that revenue should be recognized in the accounting period in which it is earned. But applying this general principle in practice can be difficult. Some companies improperly recognize revenue on goods that have not been shipped to customers. Similarly, until recently, financial institutions immediately recorded a large portion of their loan fees as revenue rather than spreading those fees over the life of the loan.

When a sale is involved, revenue is recognized at the point of sale. This **sales basis** involves an exchange transaction between the seller and buyer. The sales price is an objective measure of the amount of revenue realized. However, two exceptions to the sales basis for revenue recognition have become generally accepted—the percentage-of-completion method and the installment method. These methods are left for more advanced courses.

MATCHING PRINCIPLE (EXPENSE RECOGNITION)

Expense recognition is traditionally tied to revenue recognition: "Let the expense follow the revenue." As you will learn in Chapter 4, this practice is referred to as the **matching principle**. It dictates that expenses be matched with revenues in the period in which efforts are made to generate revenues. Expenses are not recognized when cash is paid, or when the work is performed, or when the product is produced. Rather, they are recognized when the labor (service) or the product actually makes its contribution to revenue.

But, it is sometimes difficult to determine the accounting period in which the expense contributed to revenues. Several approaches have therefore been devised for matching expenses and revenues on the income statement.

To understand these approaches, you need to understand the nature of expenses. Costs are the source of expenses. Costs that will generate revenues only in the current accounting period are expensed immediately. They are reported as **operating expenses** in the income statement. Examples include costs for advertising, sales salaries, and repairs. These expenses are often called **expired costs.**

Costs that will generate revenues in future accounting periods are recognized as assets. Examples include merchandise inventory, prepaid expenses, and plant assets. These costs represent **unexpired costs**. Unexpired costs become expenses in two ways:

1. **Cost of goods sold.** Costs carried as merchandise inventory become expenses when the inventory is sold. They are expensed as cost of goods sold in the period when the sale occurs. Thus, there is a direct matching of expenses with revenues.
2. **Operating expenses.** Other unexpired costs become operating expenses through use or consumption (as in the case of store supplies) or through the passage of time (as in the case of prepaid insurance). The costs of plant assets and other long-lived resources are expensed through rational and systematic allocation methods—periodic depreciation or amortization. Operating expenses contribute to the revenues for the period, but their association with revenues is less direct than for cost of goods sold.

These points about expense recognition are illustrated in Illustration 2-4.

HELPFUL HINT

Costs become expenses when they are charged against revenue.

ETHICS NOTE

Many appear to do it, but few like to discuss it: It's earnings management, and it's a clear violation of the revenue recognition and matching principles. Banks sometimes time the sale of investments or the expensing of bad debts to accomplish earnings objectives. Prominent companies have been accused of matching one-time gains with one-time charge-offs so that current-period earnings are not so high that they can't be surpassed next period.

Illustration 2-4

Expense recognition pattern

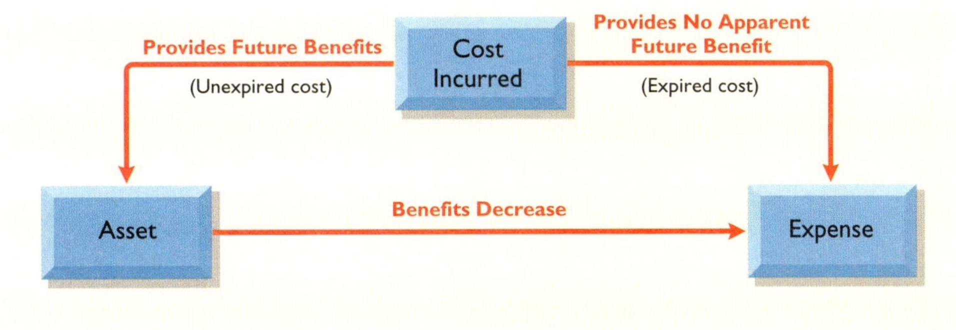

ACCOUNTING IN ACTION *Business Insight*

Implementing expense recognition guidelines can be difficult. Consider, for example, **Harold's Club** (a gambling casino) in Reno, Nevada. How should it report expenses related to the payoff of its progressive slot machines? Progressive slot machines, which generally have no ceiling on their jackpots, provide a lucky winner with all the money that many losers had previously put in. Payoffs tend to be huge, but infrequent. At Harold's, the progressive slots pay off on average every $4\frac{1}{2}$ months.

The basic accounting question is: Can Harold's deduct the millions of dollars sitting in its progressive slot machines from the revenue recognized at the end of the accounting period? One might argue that no, you cannot deduct the money until the "winning handle pull." However, a winning handle pull might not occur for many months or even years. Although an estimate would have to be used, the better answer is to match these costs with the revenue recognized, assuming that an average $4\frac{1}{2}$ months' payout is well documented. Obviously, the matching principle can be difficult to apply in practice.

FULL DISCLOSURE PRINCIPLE

The **full disclosure principle** requires that circumstances and events that make a difference to financial statement users be disclosed. For example, most accountants would agree that hospitality companies should disclose any liability suits pending against them. Interested parties would want to be made aware of this contingent loss. Similarly, it is generally agreed that companies should disclose the major provisions of employee pension plans and long-term lease contracts.

Compliance with the full disclosure principle occurs through the data in the financial statements and the information in the notes that accompany the statements. The first note in most cases is a **summary of significant accounting policies**. It includes, among others, the methods used for inventory costing, depreciation of plant assets, and amortization of intangible assets.

Deciding how much disclosure is enough can be difficult. Accountants could disclose every financial event that occurs and every contingency that exists. But the benefits of providing additional information in some cases may be less than the costs of doing so. Many companies complain of an accounting standards overload. They also object to requirements that force them to disclose confidential information. Determining where to draw the line on disclosure is not easy.

One thing is certain: financial statements were much simpler years ago. In 1930, **General Electric** had no notes to its financial statements. Today it has more than twenty pages of notes! Why this change? A major reason is that the objectives of financial statements have changed. In the past, information was generally presented on what the business had done. Today, the objectives of financial reporting are more future-oriented. The goal is to provide information that makes it possible to predict the amounts, timing, and uncertainty of future cash flows.

ACCOUNTING IN ACTION e Business Insight

Some accountants are reconsidering the current means of financial reporting. They propose a database concept of financial reporting. In such a system, all the information from transactions would be stored in a computerized database to be accessed by various user groups. The main benefit of such a system is the ability to tailor the information requested to the needs of each user.

What makes this idea controversial? Discussion currently revolves around access and aggregation issues. Questions abound: "Who should be allowed to make inquiries of the system?" "What is the lowest/smallest level of information to be provided?" "Will such a system necessarily improve on the current means of disclosure?" Such questions must be answered before database financial accounting can be implemented on a large scale.

COST PRINCIPLE

The **cost principle** dictates that assets be recorded at their cost. Cost is used because it is both relevant and reliable. Cost is **relevant** because it represents the price paid, the assets sacrificed, or the commitment made at date of acquisition. Cost is **reliable** because it is objectively measurable, factual, and verifiable. It is the result of an exchange transaction. Cost is the basis used in preparing financial statements.

The relevance of the cost principle, however, has come under criticism. After acquisition, the argument goes, the cost of an asset is not equivalent to market value or current value. Also, as the purchasing power of the dollar changes, so does the meaning associated with the dollar used as the basis of measurement.

Consider the classic story about the individual who went to sleep and woke up 10 years later. Hurrying to a telephone, he called his broker and asked what his formerly modest stock portfolio was worth. He was told that he was a multimillionaire. His **Starwood** stock was worth $5 million, and his **Hilton** stock was up to $10 million. Elated, he was about to inquire about his other holdings, when the telephone operator cut in with "Your time is up. Please deposit $100,000 for the next three minutes."[3]

Despite the inevitability of changing prices due to inflation, the accounting profession still follows the stable monetary unit assumption in preparing the primary financial statements. While admitting that some changes in prices do occur, the profession believes the unit of measure—the dollar—has remained sufficiently constant over time to provide meaningful financial information. *Sometimes, the disclosure of price-level adjusted data is in the form of supplemental information that accompanies the financial statements.*

The basic principles of accounting are summarized in Illustration 2-5.

HELPFUL HINT
Are you a winner or loser when you hold cash in a period of inflation? Answer: A loser, because the value of the cash declines as inflation climbs.

Illustration 2-5
Basic principles used in accounting

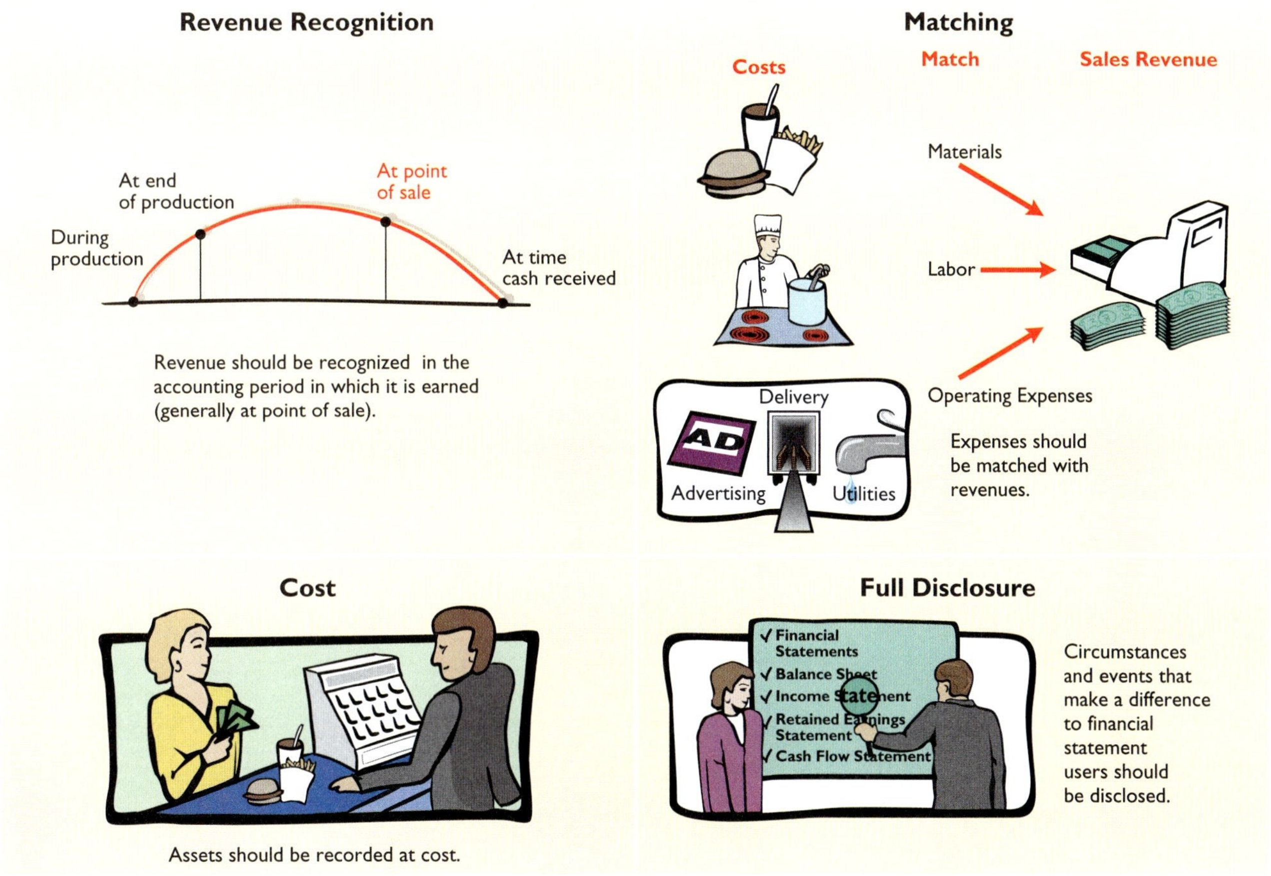

CONSTRAINTS IN ACCOUNTING

STUDY OBJECTIVE 6
Identify the two constraints in accounting.

Constraints permit a company to modify generally accepted accounting principles without reducing the usefulness of the reported information. The constraints are materiality and conservatism.

---

[3]Adapted from *Barron's* (January 28, 1980), p. 27.

MATERIALITY

Materiality relates to an item's impact on a firm's overall financial condition and operations. An item is **material** when it is likely to influence the decision of a reasonably prudent investor or creditor. It is immaterial if its inclusion or omission has no impact on a decision maker. In short, if the item does not make a difference in decision making, GAAP does not have to be followed. To determine the materiality of an amount, the accountant usually compares it with such items as total assets, total liabilities, and net income.

To illustrate how the materiality constraint is applied, assume that Rodriguez Co. purchases a number of low-cost plant assets, such as wastepaper baskets. Although the proper accounting would appear to be to depreciate these wastepaper baskets over their useful life, they are usually expensed immediately. This practice is justified because these costs are considered immaterial. Establishing depreciation schedules for these assets is costly and time consuming and will not make a material difference on total assets and net income. Another application of the materiality constraint would be the expensing of small tools. Some companies expense any plant assets under a specified dollar amount.

CONSERVATISM

HELPFUL HINT
In other words, if two methods are otherwise equally appropriate, choose the one that will least likely overstate assets and income.

The **conservatism** constraint dictates that when in doubt, choose the method that will be least likely to overstate assets and income. *It does not mean understating assets or income.* Conservatism provides a reasonable guide in difficult situations: Do not overstate assets and income.

A common application of the conservatism constraint is the use of the lower of cost or market method for inventories. As Chapter 10 will show, inventories are reported at market value if market value is below cost. This practice results in a higher cost of goods sold and lower net income. In addition, inventory on the balance sheet is stated at a lower amount.

Other examples of conservatism in accounting are the use of the last-in, first-out (LIFO) method for inventory valuation when prices are rising and the use of accelerated depreciation methods for plant assets. Both these methods result in lower asset-carrying values and lower net income than alternative methods.

The two constraints in accounting are graphically depicted in Illustration 2-6.

Illustration 2-6
Constraints in accounting

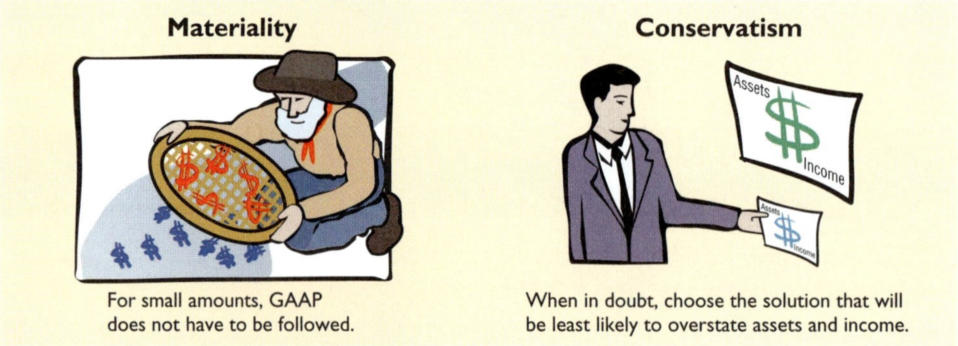

SUMMARY OF CONCEPTUAL FRAMEWORK

As we have seen, the conceptual framework for developing sound reporting practices starts with a set of objectives for financial reporting. It follows with the description of qualities that make information useful. In addition, elements of financial statements are defined. More detailed operating guidelines are then provided. These guidelines take the form of assumptions and principles.

The conceptual framework also recognizes that constraints exist on the reporting environment. The conceptual framework is illustrated graphically in Illustration 2-7.

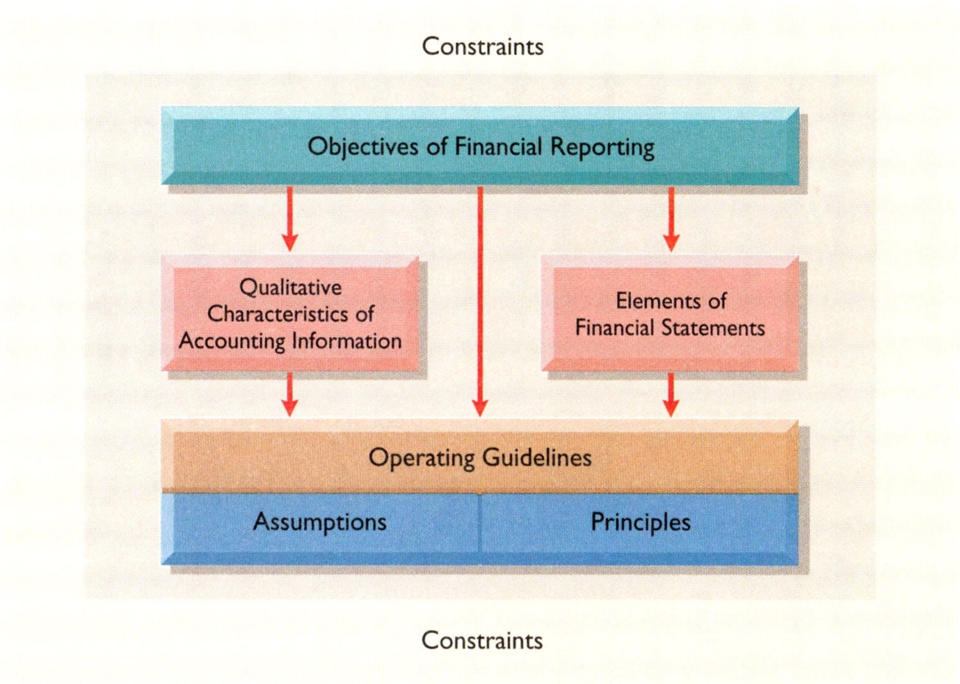

Illustration 2-7
Conceptual framework

BEFORE YOU GO ON...

REVIEW IT

1. What are the monetary unit assumption, the economic entity assumption, the time period assumption, and the going concern assumption?
2. What are the revenue recognition principle, the matching principle, the full disclosure principle, and the cost principle?
3. What are the materiality constraint and the conservatism constraint?

THE NAVIGATOR

STATEMENT PRESENTATION AND ANALYSIS

STUDY OBJECTIVE 7
Understand and analyze classified financial statements.

Financial statements play an important role in attempting to meet the objectives of financial reporting. "Bottom line" information such as total assets and net income are useful to investors, but these single numbers lack sufficient detail for serious analysis. Investors and creditors generally find the parts of a financial statement more useful than the whole. Proper classification within the financial statements is therefore extremely important.

CLASSIFIED BALANCE SHEET

The balance sheet is composed of three major elements: assets, liabilities, and stockholders' equity. Additional segregation within these groups, however, is considered useful to financial statement readers. As will be explained in Chapter 5, the accounts are generally classified as shown in Illustration 2-8.

Illustration 2-8

Standard classification of balance sheet

Assets	Liabilities and Stockholders' Equity
Current assets	Current liabilities
Long-term investments	Long-term liabilities
Property, plant, and equipment	Stockholders' equity
Intangible assets	

If the form of organization is a proprietorship, the term "Owner's equity" instead of Stockholders' equity is used to describe that section of the balance sheet. An account called Capital is reported in the owner's equity section of the balance sheet for a proprietorship. **Capital** is the owner's investment in the business.

To illustrate, assume that Sally Field invests $90,000 on July 10, 2004, to start up Birthday Balloons. The company's balance sheet immediately after the investment looks like Illustration 2-9.

Illustration 2-9

Proprietorship balance sheet

BIRTHDAY BALLOONS
Balance Sheet
July 10, 2004

Cash	$90,000	Sally Field, Capital	$90,000

Because Sally Field owns the business and has chosen not to incorporate, common stock is not issued and net income (net loss) belongs to her. Therefore, common stock and retained earnings accounts are not needed. Instead, her capital account is increased by investments and by net income. It is decreased by withdrawals of assets for personal use and by net losses. The capital account represents Sally Field's claim to the net assets (assets less liabilities) of the company.

If the form of organization is a partnership, each partner has a separate capital account, and the owners' equity section shows the capital accounts of all the partners. For example, assume that A. Teller and B. Penn form a partnership on December 11, 2004, at which time Teller and Penn each invest $60,000. The balance sheet immediately after their investments looks like Illustration 2-10.

HELPFUL HINT
Note "Owners' equity" instead of "Owner's equity" is used for a partnership to indicate multiple owners.

Illustration 2-10

Partnership balance sheet

TELLER AND PENN
Balance Sheet
December 11, 2004

Cash	$120,000	A. Teller, Capital	$ 60,000
		B. Penn, Capital	60,000
			$120,000

CLASSIFIED INCOME STATEMENT

Chapter 7 presented a multiple-step income statement for Sellers Health Foods. The multiple-step income statement included the following.

Sales revenue section—Presents the sales, discounts, allowances, and other related information to arrive at the net amount of sales revenue.

Cost of goods sold—Indicates the cost of goods sold to produce sales.

Operating expenses—Provides information on both selling and administrative expenses.

Other revenues and gains—Indicates revenues earned or gains resulting from nonoperating transactions.

Other expenses and losses—Indicates expenses or losses incurred from nonoperating transactions.

Two additional items are income tax expense and earnings per share.

Income Tax Expense

Income taxes must be paid and therefore reported for a corporation because a corporation is a legal entity separate and distinct from its owners. Proprietorships and partnerships are not separate legal entities; owners are therefore taxed directly on their business income. Stockholders are taxed only on the dividends they receive.

Corporate **income taxes** (or **income tax expense**) are reported in a separate section of the income statement, before net income. The condensed income statement for Hallmark Hotel Brokerage in Illustration 2-11 shows a typical presentation. Note that Income before income taxes is reported before Income tax expense.

Hallmark Hotel Brokerage
Income Statement
For the Year Ended December 31, 2004

Sales	$800,000
Cost of goods sold	600,000
Gross profit	200,000
Operating expenses	50,000
Income from operations	150,000
Other revenues and gains	10,000
Other expenses and losses	4,000
Income before income taxes	**156,000**
Income tax expense	**46,800**
Net income	$109,200

Illustration 2-11

Income statement with income taxes

HELPFUL HINT

Corporations may also use the single-step form of income statements discussed in Chapter 7.

Income tax expense and the related liability for income taxes payable are recorded as part of the adjusting process, preceding financial statement preparation. Using the data above for Hallmark Hotel Brokerage, the adjusting entry for income tax expense at December 31, 2004, would be as follows.

Income tax expense	46,800	
Income taxes payable		46,800
(To record income taxes for 2004)		

A	=	L	+	SE
		+46,800		−46,800

Earnings Per Share

Earnings per share data are frequently reported in the financial press and are widely used by stockholders and potential investors in evaluating the profitability of a company. Investors, especially, attempt to link earnings per share to the market price per share.[4] **Earnings per share (EPS)** indicates the net income earned by each share of outstanding common stock. Thus, **earnings per share is reported only for common stock**. Illustration 2-12 gives the formula for computing earnings per share when there has been no change in outstanding shares during the year.

Illustration 2-12

Earnings per share formula—no change in outstanding shares

Net Income	÷	Number of Common Shares Outstanding	=	Earnings per Share

For example, Hallmark Hotel Brokerage (Illustration 2-11) has net income of \$109,200. Assuming that it has 54,600 shares of common stock outstanding for the year, earnings per share are \$2 (\$109,200 ÷ 54,600).[5]

Because of the importance of earnings per share, most companies are required to report it on the face of the income statement. Generally this amount is simply reported below net income on the statement. For Hallmark Hotel Brokerage the presentation would be as in Illustration 2-13.

Illustration 2-13

Basic earnings per share disclosure

HALLMARK HOTEL BROKERAGE
Income Statement (partial)
For the Year Ended December 31, 2004

Net income	\$109,200
Earnings per share	**\$2.00**

ANALYZING FINANCIAL STATEMENTS

The financial statements should provide financial information that is useful for helping make sound investment and credit decisions. Illustration 2-14 shows the condensed balance sheet and income statement of Blue Ribbon Meats, for 2004.

Illustration 2-14

Financial statements—Blue Ribbon Meats, Inc.

BLUE RIBBON MEATS, INC.
Balance Sheet
December 31, 2004

Assets		**Liabilities and Stockholders' Equity**	
Current assets	\$156,000	Current liabilities	\$ 70,000
Plant and equipment (net)	74,000	Long-term liabilities	114,000
Intangible assets	14,000	Stockholders' equity	60,000
Total assets	\$244,000	Total liabilities and stockholders' equity	\$244,000

[4]The ratio of the market price per share to the earnings per share is referred to as the *price-earnings ratio*. This ratio is reported in the *Wall Street Journal* and other newspapers for common stocks listed on major stock exchanges.

[5]Whenever the number of outstanding shares changes during the year, the calculation of EPS becomes more complicated.

BLUE RIBBON MEATS, INC. Income Statement For the Year Ended December 31, 2004	
Net sales	$430,000
Cost of sales	295,000
Gross profit	135,000
Selling and administrative expenses	109,000
Income from operations	26,000
Other expenses and losses	5,000
Income before income taxes	21,000
Income tax expense	7,000
Net income	$ 14,000
Earnings per share	$0.35

Illustration 2-14

Financial statements—Blue Ribbon Meats, Inc., *Continued*

In analyzing and interpreting financial statement information, three major characteristics are generally evaluated: **liquidity, profitability**, and **solvency**. A **short-term debt holder**, for example, is primarily interested in the ability of a borrower to pay obligations when they become due. The liquidity of the borrower in such a case is extremely important in assessing the safety of a loan. A **long-term debt holder**, however, looks to indicators such as profitability and solvency that point to the firm's ability to survive over a long period of time. Long-term debt holders analyze earnings per share, the relationship of income to total assets invested, and the amount of debt in relation to total assets to determine whether money should be lent and at what interest rate. Similarly, **stockholders** are interested in the profitability and solvency of a company when assessing the likelihood of dividends and the growth potential of the common stock.

Liquidity

What is Blue Ribbon Meats' ability to pay its maturing obligations and meet unexpected needs for cash? The relationship between current assets and current liabilities is critical to helping answer this question. These relationships are expressed as a ratio, called the **current ratio**, and as a dollar amount, called **working capital**.

CURRENT RATIO. The **current ratio** is current assets divided by current liabilities. For Blue Ribbon Meats, Inc., the ratio is 2.23:1, computed in Illustration 2-15.

Current Assets ÷ Current Liabilities = Current Ratio

$156,000 ÷ $70,000 = 2.23:1

Illustration 2-15

Current ratio formula and computation

This ratio means that current assets are more than two times greater than current liabilities. Bankers, other creditors, and agencies such as **Dun & Bradstreet** use this ratio to determine whether the company is a good credit risk. Traditionally, a ratio of 2:1 is considered to be the standard for a good credit rating. Today, however, many sound companies have current ratios of less than 2:1. Hotel and restaurant companies normally have a 0.8:1 to 1.2:1 current ratio. With its 2.23:1 ratio,

Blue Ribbon Meats' short-term debt-paying ability appears to be very favorable.

From the foregoing, you might at first assume that the higher the current ratio, the better. This is not necessarily true. A very high current ratio may indicate that the company is holding more current assets than it currently needs in the business. It is possible, therefore, that the excess resources might be directed to more profitable investment opportunities.

WORKING CAPITAL. The excess of current assets over current liabilities is called **working capital**. For Blue Ribbon Meats, Inc., working capital is $86,000, as shown in Illustration 2-16.

Illustration 2-16

Working capital formula and computation

Current Assets	–	Current Liabilities	=	Working Capital
$156,000	–	$70,000	=	$86,000

The amount of working capital provides some indication of the company's ability to meet its existing current obligations. A large amount of working capital generally means a company can meet its current liabilities as they fall due and, if desired, pay dividends. Although no set standards exist for the level of working capital a company should maintain, the general adequacy of a company's working capital is often determined by comparing data from prior periods and from similar companies of comparable size. Blue Ribbon Meats' working capital appears adequate.

Profitability

Profitability ratios measure the income or operating success of an enterprise for a given period of time. Income, or the lack of it, affects the company's ability to obtain debt or equity financing and the company's ability to grow.

PROFIT MARGIN PERCENTAGE. One important ratio used to measure profitability is the **profit margin percentage** (or rate of return on sales). It measures the percentage of each dollar of sales that results in net income. It is calculated by dividing net income by net sales for the period. Blue Ribbon Meats, Inc.'s profit margin percentage is 3.3 percent, computed in Illustration 2-17.

Illustration 2-17

Profit margin formula and computation

Net Income	÷	Net Sales	=	Profit Margin Percentage
$14,000	÷	$430,000	=	3.3%

This ratio seems low. Much, however, depends on the type of industry. High-volume retailers, such as grocery stores (**Safeway** or **Kroger**) or discount stores (**Wal-Mart** or **Target**), generally have a low profit margin. They make a small profit on each sale but have many sales.

ACCOUNTING IN ACTION *Business Insight*

The type of industry can make a difference in the profit margin percentage investors and creditors expect. Profit margins among service companies—from airlines and banks to telecommunications companies and utilities—have traditionally been lower than those among manufacturers. **Starwood Hotels & Resorts Worldwide Inc.,** for example, showed a profit margin percentage of 3.8 percent in 2001, which is average for a hotel company. **Choice Hotels International, Inc.**'s profit margin percentage was 4.2 percent, and **LaQuinta** posted a loss. **Morton's Restaurant Group Inc.,** which will be compared to the foodservice group, reported a 0.4 percent profit margin for 2001. For the same period, **McDonald's Corp.** posted an 11 percent profit, while **Brinker International, Inc.** was more at the average rate of 4.9 percent. Before using a ratio like the profit margin percentage to evaluate company performance, you need to know what is reasonable performance for the industry.

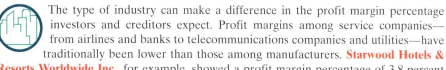

RETURN ON ASSETS. In making an investment, an investor wants to know what rate of return to expect and what risks are associated with that rate of return. The greater the risk, the higher the rate of return the investor will demand on the investment.

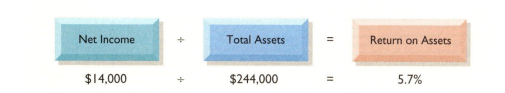

One overall measure of profitability of a company is its rate of **return on assets**. It is calculated by dividing net income by total assets.[6] Blue Ribbon Meats, Inc.'s rate of return is 5.7 percent, computed in Illustration 2-18.

Illustration 2-18

Return on assets formula and computation

Net Income	÷	Total Assets	=	Return on Assets
$14,000	÷	$244,000	=	5.7%

The rate of return on assets is relatively low, which suggests that Blue Ribbon Meats might not be using its assets effectively.

RETURN ON COMMON STOCKHOLDERS' EQUITY. Another widely used rate that measures profitability from the common stockholders' viewpoint is **return on common stockholders' equity**. This rate shows the percentage of net income earned for each dollar of owners' investment. It is calculated by dividing net income by common stockholders' equity. In Blue Ribbon Meats, Inc.'s case, the rate of return is 23.3 percent (or 23.3 cents per dollar), computed in Illustration 2-19.

Illustration 2-19

Return on common stockholders' equity formula and computation

Net Income	÷	Common Equity	=	Return on Common Stockholders' Equity
$14,000	÷	$60,000	=	23.3%

[6] For simplicity, the rate of return calculations are based on end-of-year total amounts. The more conceptually correct *average* total assets and *average* common stockholders' equity are used in later chapters.

Blue Ribbon Meats' return on common stockholders' equity is quite good. The reason for this high rate of return is that Blue Ribbon Meats' assets are earning a return higher than the borrowing costs the company incurs.

Solvency

Solvency measures the ability of an enterprise to survive over a long period of time. Long-term debt holders and stockholders are interested in a company's ability to pay periodic interest and to repay the face value of the debt at maturity.

DEBT TO TOTAL ASSETS. One useful measure of solvency is the **debt to total assets ratio**. It measures the percentage of total assets that creditors, as opposed to stockholders, provide. It is calculated by dividing total debt (liabilities) by total assets, normally expressed as a percentage. Blue Ribbon Meats, Inc.'s debt to total assets ratio is 75.4 percent, computed in Illustration 2-20.

Illustration 2-20

Debt to total assets formula and computation

Total Debt	÷	Total Assets	=	Debt to Total Assets Ratio
$184,000	÷	$244,000	=	75.4%

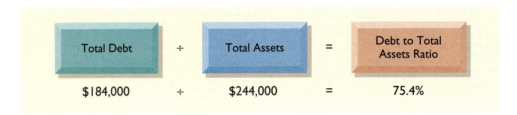

Debt to total assets of 75.4 percent means that Blue Ribbon Meats' creditors have provided approximately three-quarters of its total assets. The higher the percentage of debt to total assets, the greater the risk that the company may be unable to meet its maturing obligations. The lower the percentage, the greater the "buffer" available to creditors should the company become insolvent. In Blue Ribbon Meats' case, unless earnings are positive and very stable, the company may have too much debt.

These percentage and ratio relationships are often used in comparison with (1) expected results, (2) prior year results, and (3) published results of other companies in the same line of business. Conclusions based on a single year's results are hazardous at best.

FINANCIAL STATEMENT PRESENTATION—AN INTERNATIONAL PERSPECTIVE

STUDY OBJECTIVE 8

Explain the accounting principles used in international operations.

World markets are becoming increasingly intertwined. Foreigners use American computers, eat American breakfast cereals, read American magazines, listen to American rock music, watch American movies and TV shows, and drink American soda. Americans drive Japanese cars, wear Italian shoes and Scottish woolens, drink Brazilian coffee and Indian tea, eat Swiss chocolate bars, sit on Danish furniture, and use Arabian oil. The variety and volume of exported and imported goods indicates the extensive involvement of U.S. business in international trade. Many U.S. companies consider the world their market.

Firms that conduct operations in more than one country through subsidiaries, divisions, or branches in foreign countries are referred to as **multinational corporations (MNCs)**. The accounting for such corporations is complicated because foreign currencies are involved. These international transactions must be translated into U.S. dollars.

Differences in Standards

In the new global economy many investment and credit decisions require the analysis of foreign financial statements. Unfortunately, accounting standards are not uniform from country to country. This lack of uniformity results from differences in legal systems, in processes for developing accounting standards, in governmental requirements, and in economic environments.

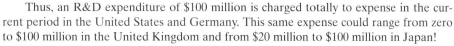

ACCOUNTING IN ACTION *International Insight*

Research and development costs are an example of different international accounting standards. Compare how four countries account for research and development (R&D):

Country	Accounting Treatment
United States	Expenditures are expensed.
United Kingdom	Certain expenditures may be capitalized.
Germany	Expenditures are expensed.
Japan	Expenditures may be capitalized and amortized over 5 years.

Thus, an R&D expenditure of $100 million is charged totally to expense in the current period in the United States and Germany. This same expense could range from zero to $100 million in the United Kingdom and from $20 million to $100 million in Japan!

Do you believe that accounting principles should be comparable across countries?

Uniformity in Standards

Efforts to obtain uniformity in international accounting practices are taking place. In 1973 the **International Accounting Standards Committee (IASC)** was formed by agreement of accounting organizations in the United States, the United Kingdom, Canada, Australia, France, Germany, Japan, Mexico, and the Netherlands. Its purpose is to formulate international accounting standards and to promote their acceptance worldwide.

To date, numerous standards have been issued for IASC members to introduce to their respective countries. But, the IASC has no enforcement powers, so these standards are by no means universally applied. They are, though, generally followed by the multinational companies that are audited by international public accounting firms. The foundation has been laid for progress toward greater uniformity in international accounting.

THE UNIFORM SYSTEMS OF ACCOUNTS AND FINANCIAL REPORTING

STUDY OBJECTIVE 9

Identify the various systems of accounting procedures used in the hospitality industry.

Although FASB sets the rules for public accounting that must be abided by the accounting profession, the hospitality industry also sets procedures and guidelines for its various segments to ensure comparability, accountability, and meaningful usage of accounting data. For new operators, these systems even act as turnkey accounting systems. This means the system has everything included and is ready to be used in operations. The three most used and well-known systems in the industry are for the lodging, foodservice, and club areas. There is currently one under development for the gaming industry.

Why are such industry-specific systems needed? If every industry follows FASB's rules, shouldn't they then have the correct accounting information? In theory, yes. However, the rules for FASB are written for the entire accounting profession. Hospitality has accounts other industries do not, and vice versa. For instance, a restaurant will not have a depletion account for an oil rig, but a restaurant does need an accumulation depreciation account for furniture, fixtures, and equipment. Even within the hospitality industry there are differences. A hotel is different from a club and a club is different from a theme park. Hotels have rooms revenues, country clubs have membership dues, and theme parks have admissions fees. There are recommended procedures to categorize certain expenses or naming of accounts. The accounting information provided is more useful not just for the companies themselves but also for investors, creditors, and even employees.

LODGING INDUSTRY

The **Uniform System of Accounts for the Lodging Industry** is currently in its ninth edition. Of the three systems, this is the oldest. It was first developed by the Hotel Association of New York in 1926 and was known as the Uniform System of Accounts for Hotels. From the 1930s to the 1970s, when most hotels were smaller and motor hotels (motels) were popular, there were actually two systems: the Uniform System of Accounts for Hotels and the Uniform System of Accounts for Smaller Hotels. There was also an expense dictionary where expenditures were categorized under specific accounts so that accountants and controllers could follow the allocation trail.

The ninth edition evolved with industry trends and combines all three books into a seamless system of accounts for the entire lodging industry. The **Hospitality Financial and Technology Professionals (HFTP)** is working with the American Hotel and Lodging Association on the next edition.

FOODSERVICE INDUSTRY

The **Uniform System of Accounts for Restaurants**, first published in 1927, is currently in its seventh edition. It provides sample statements, analyses blueprints, classification of accounts, and an expense dictionary. The aim of this publication, like that of the lodging and club industries, is to assist operators to interpret financial results in a more meaningful manner.

CLUB INDUSTRY

The club industry is a self-regulating industry. With its owners also being its members, accountability is of utmost importance. The **Club Managers Association of America (CMAA)** was formed in 1927 and published the Proposed Uniform System of Accounts for City Clubs in 1942. It was not until 1954 that the first Uniform System of Accounts for Clubs was published. The current fifth edition is known as the **Uniform System of Financial Reporting for Clubs.**

Similar to the hotel industry, the club industry has seen tremendous growth, especially in real estate developments. Many new residential developments also include a club, fully equipped with all amenities and services, including one, and perhaps two, golf courses for its residents.

GAMING INDUSTRY

You may feel that if any industry needs a system, the casino industry should be the first one to have a set of procedures because there are such large amounts of money involved. However, the first edition of this system is still under development. Two reasons contribute to the late birth. First, both Nevada and New Jersey have strict laws governing the operations of casinos, including how money transactions should be documented. Many states with legalized gaming have adopted the rules of Nevada and New Jersey. In addition, casinos have been using parts of the system from the lodging industry. In the current ninth edition of the system of the lodging industry, there are also sections dedicated to the casino industry, suggesting statement presentation formats and guidelines.

ACCOUNTING AND FINANCIAL MANAGEMENT IN HOSPITALITY

HOTEL OPERATIONS

STUDY OBJECTIVE 10

Understand accounting and financial management in a hotel.

Operating a hotel is like being in charge of a small city. The hotel business is full of exciting moments, surprises, heartwarming stories, and also some tough workdays. If you can imagine a mayor taking care of a city, well, that is what a general manager has to do for his or her hotel. The general manager needs to have the hotel properly staffed, with the right equipment and supplies, so guests can have a wonderful experience. *Hospitality* is not just the name that encompasses the industry but is also the key word to success.

While the feature story about Conrad N. Hilton in Chapter 1 emphasizes the need for hospitality, planning and controls through prudent and ethical financial management are equally important. The role of financial management in a hotel is crucial to its success. Reduced to the simplest terms, when the money is not there, the hotel cannot open. The hotel industry really offers a fascinating career. Visit the **American Hotel and Lodging Association (AH&LA)** Web site (www.ahla.com) for more information about the hotel industry from national to local levels.

Interactions with All Departments

A typical hotel is divided into departments. The bigger the hotel, the more departments it has. Most hotels have a front office that takes care of reservations and registration. There is also a housekeeping department and an engineering and maintenance department. If the hotel is a full-service property, it will have a food and beverage department, which may include restaurant, banquet, and in-room dining. Smaller properties may have their human resources and accounting functions centralized at a regional office. An accounting department at a 1,600-room convention property may have forty to fifty employees. Illustration 2-21 shows a sample organization chart for a full-service hotel.

Regardless of how many departments and how many employees, you can see the big picture. In the hotel business, it takes teamwork to provide the ultimate quality service and product to the guests. Five hundred convention attendees staying with the hotel expect to have their rooms ready for check-in and meeting rooms available for work. They will also expect their coffee and meal breaks served on time and the banquet room decorated with their association's banner and other materials. The group's convention organizer is not going to talk to the housekeeper, the restaurant manager, the banquet captain, or the front office separately regarding their needs. This organizer will have one point of contact with the hotel sales and catering office and this hotel manager will need to interact with all departments to communicate the pertinent information. Thus, all departments need to interact and make decisions accordingly.

The General Manager and the Executive Committee

As mentioned, the **general manager** is like the mayor of the city. He or she will work closely with the members of the **executive committee** to manage the hotel.

The executive committee is made up of all the department heads. This group comes together for meetings to make decisions and ensure all information is relayed correctly.

The **controller**, the department head of the accounting department, is a member of the executive committee. Just like the general manager, the controller has to work not only with the employees in the accounting and business office, but also with all department heads. At times, while certain department heads may not need to have constant communication with one another, the controller, as the head financial management person, is required to do so.

Controllers need to know how every department performs and whether each department is making or losing money. They can do so from a simple analysis of the departmental income statement. They can then consult with department heads to point out any concerns that are shown on the financial records. This allows departments to take appropriate actions to ensure the success of the hotel. In the career ladder of a hotel, it is highly possible that a controller can one day become the general manager.

The Casino Hotel

Financial management is important in any hotel. However, it is doubly important in a casino hotel. Think of all the cash that passes through a casino on a daily basis. We are talking about thousands to millions of dollars. The exchange of cash for playing chips, the emptying of cash at slot machines and the table games, the issuing of credit to guests, even the counting of coins and paper money, has set procedures regulated by the hotels and by the law. Therefore, besides taking care of all the billing, cash, and payables of a regular hotel, the accounting functions in a casino hotel include managing all other revenue centers from all the games. This makes a controller's function more interesting and challenging.

Illustration 2-21

Departmental structure in the hotel and lodging industry: (a) departments of a limited-service hotel; (b) departments of a full-service hotel (under 500 rooms); (c) departments of a full-service hotel (over 500 rooms). *Source:* Alan Stutts, *Hotel and Lodging Management: An Introduction* (New York: Wiley, 2001). This material is used by permission of John Wiley & Sons, Inc.

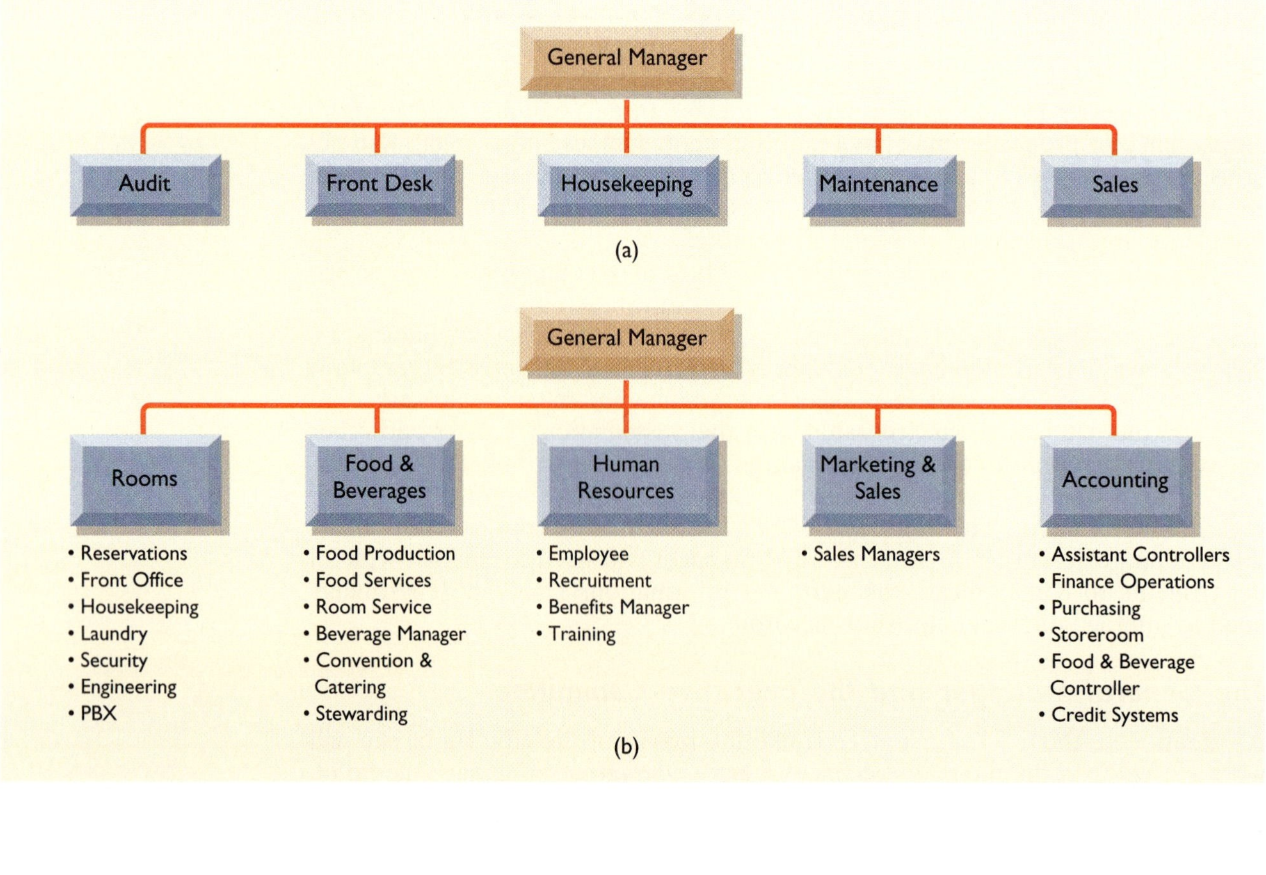

Illustration 2-21

Continued

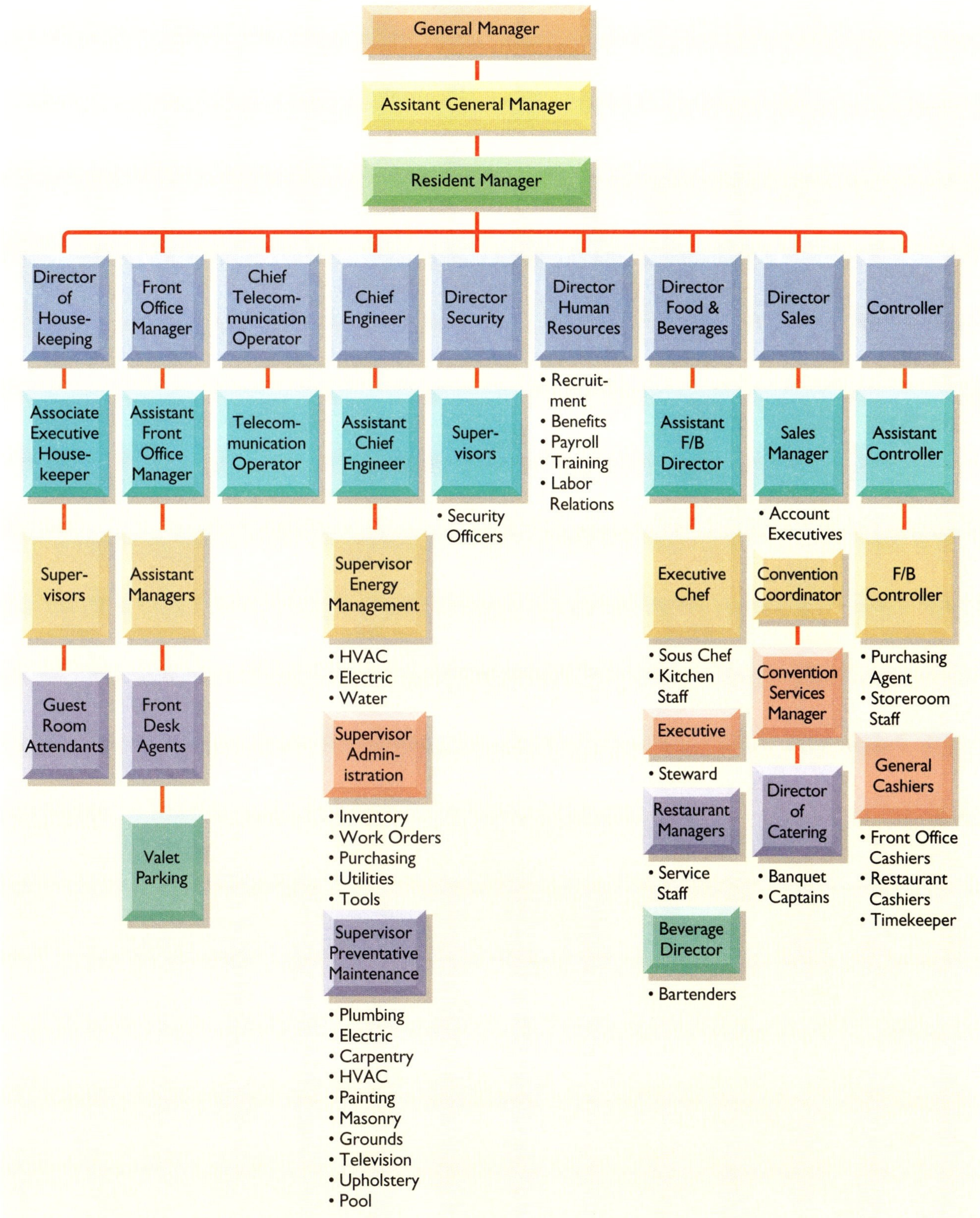

(c)

HOTEL ACCOUNTING DEPARTMENT ORGANIZATION

There are many users of accounting and financial information. It takes quite a bit of work to make sure that records are kept properly for all parties. Illustration 2-22 is an organizational chart of a large hotel's accounting department. This organization depends on the size of the hotel. Some hotels may not have a need for an assistant controller; some of the other functions may not exist in a hotel, such as a food and beverage department. For most limited-service hotels, the general manager may assume the function of the controller, or that function will be centralized at a district or regional office. Following is a short description of some of the accounting functions in a hotel.

Accounts Payable

A key area in accounting, accounts payable ensures that all bills are paid on time and all discounts are taken minimizing the costs of the hotel. Accounts payable

Illustration 2-22

An organization chart of a large hotel accounting department

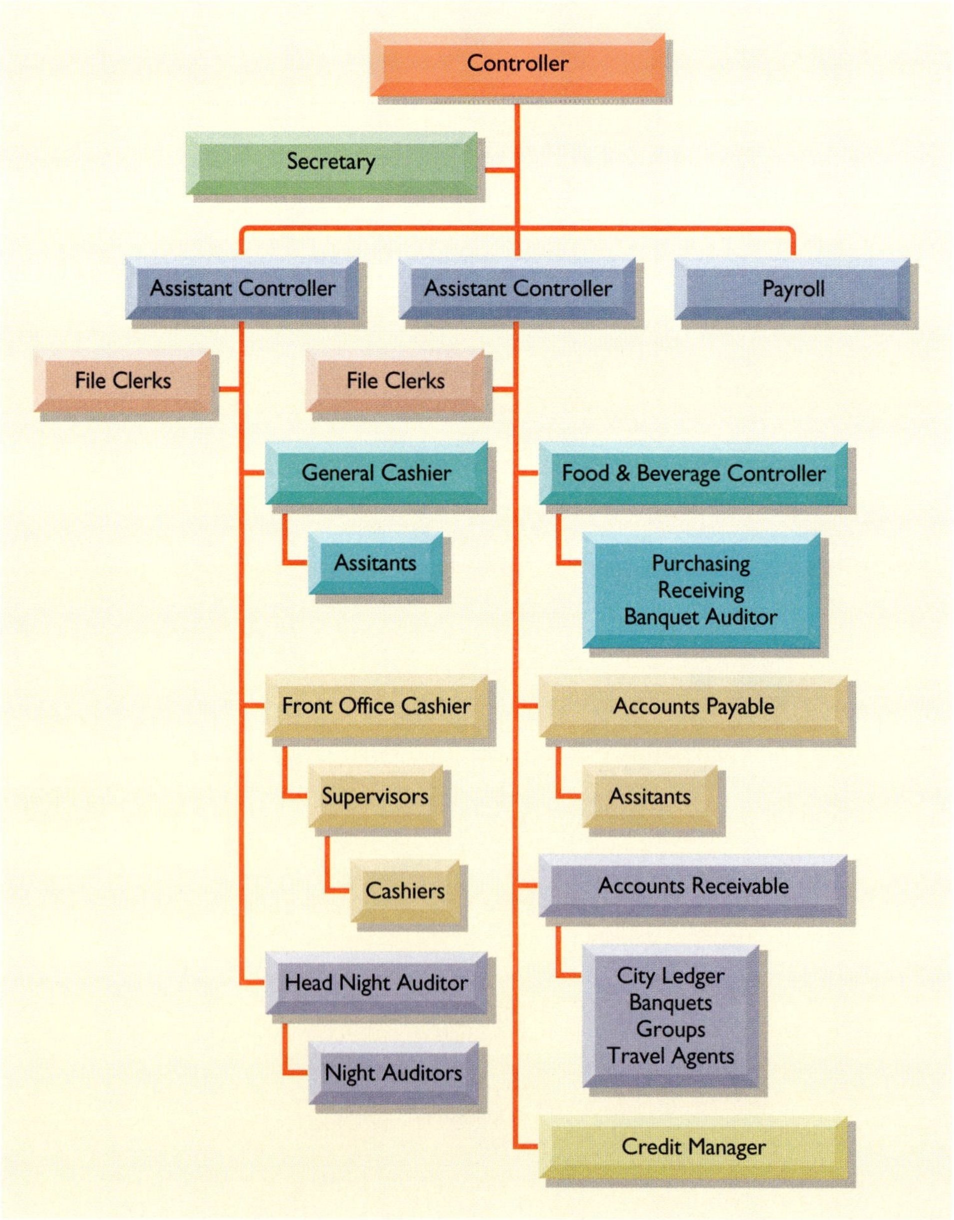

clerks work closely with the purchasing department to verify that all invoices to be paid are indeed invoices of the hotel.

Assistant Controller

In a big hotel, you may see one, or a few, assistant controllers. In smaller hotels, there may not be any. The controller divides the various functions to be performed so that the workload will be even. For example, one assistant might be responsible for daily transactions while another works on special projects, budgets, analyses, and the like.

Guest and City Ledgers

A hotel keeps two ledgers: the guest ledger is associated with the guests staying at the hotel while the city ledger contains all other billings. It is important that the accounting department has a person in accounts receivable working with the city ledger so the hotel is able to bill and collect revenues due.

Night Audit

Night auditors get their name because of the hours they work. At the end of the day after most hotel guests have retired, these auditors begin recording charges to guests' accounts and verifying the revenue for the hotel. However, with computers and various technologies, the hotel industry can post charges instantaneously. Some hotels have actually changed the night auditors to become day auditors.

Banquet Auditor

Besides revenues charged to guest rooms, a large hotel earns the bulk of its food and beverage revenues through banquets. The banquet auditor's function is to verify the correct revenue for billing. This individual works closely with the banquet staff, the sales office staff, and the accounts receivable clerks.

Credit

A big hotel may have its own credit manager whose function is to check and grant credit. In today's business world, many transactions are done on credit rather than cash or cashier checks. It is, therefore, the credit manager's responsibility to conduct such investigations to be sure that a person or company is creditworthy.

Food and Beverage Controller

This is a fun and challenging position, as it has both accounting and food and beverage components. While performing all analyses of food cost percentage, yields on meat, and menu costings, the food and beverage controller also works with the chef to design new menu items, taste new products, and even be a mystery diner to taste-test the menus in other foodservice establishments.

Front-Office Cashiers

The duties of a front-office cashier are often incorporated with the front-office personnel. When guests check out, it is the duty of these cashiers to charge the guests the correct amount and secure a form of payment.

General Cashier

Pause for a minute and think how many cash banks there are in a large hotel: a few at the front office, at least one in the restaurant, at least one in the gift shop, and so on. The general cashier is the person who is in charge of all the cash banks in the hotel. He or she also makes all deposits of checks and credit card receipts.

Operations Analyst

This is a nice position to have in a hotel. An operation analyst performs analyses to help managers operate the hotel more effectively. From guests' statistics to revenue trends, the operations analyst does it all. However, not all hotels are able to afford an analyst on the payroll. If this is the case, an assistant controller often performs these duties. For smaller hotels where there is not an accounting office on the property, this function is done at the regional level.

Payroll

Payroll employees calculate the pay rate with the hours worked to do the payroll so paychecks are released on time. Payroll functions also include filing all payroll taxes and tip credits for tipped employees, as well as keeping track of vacation, sick pay, and other payroll-related deductions.

Systems Manager

A systems manager is not depicted in Illustration 2-22. Since the various accounting functions cover the entire hotel operation, the systems manager or systems analyst, whose job is to take care of all technology issues, is normally founded within the accounting department. In a smaller hotel, the controller or an assistant controller may take on this responsibility. Normally, this position is found at a regional or corporate level and systems analysts will be dispatched to assist the property when needed.

FOODSERVICE OPERATIONS

STUDY OBJECTIVE 11

Understand accounting and financial management in a foodservice operation and a club.

The controller of an independent restaurant or a foodservice operation is similar to that of a food and beverage controller at a hotel. The difference is that the foodservice controller concentrates on only the food and beverage side, whereas a hotel controller oversees various departments of a hotel. Therefore, besides labor cost and overhead items, accounting and financial management in the foodservice business is focused on yield analysis, food and beverage cost control, and the purchasing function.

Purchasing and Yield Analysis

Foodservice operations purchase food, beverages, and other items on a day-to-day basis. In the case of food and beverage, because products are perishable, buying the right amount of food, at the right quality, at the right time, reduces the amount of cash tied in inventory. The extra cash then provides more liquidity to the business.

When buying food and beverage, yield is important. A good-quality piece of beef may have less trimmings, yielding the foodservice operation more meat products to be sold. A can of tomatoes may just look like another can. But if the controller performs a "can-cutting" and compares the two brands, he or she might discover that one is better than the other and the cost difference might work to the advantage of the operation.

Food and Beverage Cost Analysis

In general, for a restaurant or operation that sells alcoholic beverages (liquor, beer, and wine), it is not unusual to have 15 to 30 percent of its total sales derived from beverages. This means 70 to 85 percent of the sales are made from food items. For smaller restaurants and quick-service operations that do not sell alcoholic beverages, all revenue comes from food sales. Therefore, the accounting department spends a lot of time tracking food costs. This is especially important because foodservice operations use products where prices often fluctuate.

Restaurants and operations that sell alcoholic beverages will also track beverage costs and perform various analyses. Do not think for a minute that because beverage sales are only 15 percent of total sales they are not important. First, the restaurant business is a "penny" business. One needs to watch for any penny that is earned or spent; otherwise, the profit margin can easily disappear if the business is not managed wisely. More important, the markup of beverages is very high. A bottle of wine that can be purchased retail for $15 can be sold at the restaurant from $40 to $60, depending on the type of restaurant.

Thus, careful cost analysis provides foodservice operators with useful information for product purchasing and pricing to maximize profits, while offering guests the products they prefer and enjoy. For those who are interested in the restaurant segment, please visit the **National Restaurant Association** Web site at www.restaurant.org.

CLUB OPERATIONS

The club segment of the hospitality industry in North America is substantial. In every major city there are many country clubs. But clubs are not just country clubs. They also include city clubs, yacht clubs, racquet clubs, tennis clubs, other athletic clubs, military clubs, and university clubs. These private clubs are membership-only operations. In 2001, The Club Managers Association of America reported more than 11,000 private clubs in the United States. Since these clubs are restrictive of clientele, the way business is carried out and, thus, the way accounting is performed is quite different from the foodservice and hotel segments of the hospitality industry.

Membership Accounting

While hotels have rooms, food, beverage, and other miscellaneous revenues, and restaurants have food, beverage, and other revenues, clubs have all of these and a unique revenue category—membership dues. Membership dues from country clubs often make up to 50 percent of a club's revenue, while food and beverage percentage is about 35 percent, with other revenues of 15 percent or so rounding up the 100 percent. These other revenues can include athletic fees for guests, golf greens fees for guests, and sales of merchandise in pro shops and gift stores. In city clubs, food and beverage revenues often exceed that of membership, as golf membership is normally not provided in a city club environment. Membership revenues are the main source of funds needed for a club to run its operations.

Golf, Tennis, and Spas

Golf, tennis, and spas are three of the major athletic packages included in many club dues. Depending on the type of club, the initiation fees can run from $10,000 to easily more than $100,000. In certain clubs, you need to be invited and sponsored by existing members before you are put on a waiting list to join. There are also various levels of membership. A full membership will entitle the member to play golf, tennis, and use the athletic and spa facilities, while a social membership will permit the member to use only the food and beverage outlets.

The club accounting department needs to treat each of these outlets as a cost center, just like a restaurant in a hotel or a gift shop, determining the profit and loss of each area. This gives management the needed information to make sound operating decisions.

BEFORE YOU GO ON...

REVIEW IT

1. What is the major difference in the equity section of the balance sheet between a corporation and proprietorship?
2. Where are income tax expense and earnings per share reported on the income statement? How is earnings per share computed?
3. How are the current ratio, working capital, profit margin percentage, return on assets, return on common stockholders' equity, and debt to total assets computed?
4. Explain how these ratios are useful in financial statement analysis.
5. What is the purpose of the International Accounting Standards Committee?
6. What are the three accounting guidelines publications for the hotel, restaurant, and club segments of the industry?
7. Identify and briefly explain the various positions available in an accounting department in a hotel operation.
8. Identify at least three areas in a club accounting operations which differ from that of a hotel operation.

A LOOK BACK AT OUR FEATURE STORY

Refer back to the Feature Story at the beginning of the chapter and the following situations.

1. **Medco's** initial public offering to sell its stocks was stopped by Merck. It reported $14 billion of revenues from co-payments made by patients. Such co-payments went to drug retailers and others, rather than Medco. Is the concept of revenue recognition violated in this situation? Explain.
2. **Adelphia Communications** booked marketing support payments by Motorola and Scientific-Atlanta as sales. Adelphia would pay these companies an extra amount for decoders sold and in turn, these companies will return to Adelphia such amounts as marketing support payments. Since sales were increased, so was the EBITDA.

SOLUTION

1. The revenue recognition principle dictates that revenue should be recognized in the accounting period in which it is earned. Revenue is generally recognized at the point of sale. Medco violated the revenue recognition principle because it never earned such revenues.
2. During the stock market bubble in 1999, EBITDA became the measurment of a company's financial health. The higher the EBITDA, the higher the earnings, and thus the stock price. Higher stock prices mean easier access to capital and a stronger financial picture—on paper. This also encourages Wall Street analysts to forecast increasing EBITDA for the future. So, Adelphia was able to boost its earnings on paper until the scheme fell apart.

THE NAVIGATOR

DEMONSTRATION PROBLEM 1

Presented below are a number of operational guidelines and practices that have developed over time.

Instructions

Identify the accounting assumption, accounting principle, or reporting constraint that most appropriately justifies these procedures and practices. Use only one item per description.

(a) The first note, "Summary of Significant Accounting Policies," presents information on the subclassification of plant assets and discusses the company's depreciation methods.

(b) The local hamburger restaurant expenses all spatulas, french fry baskets, and other cooking utensils when purchased.

(c) Retailers recognize revenue at the point of sale.

(d) Green-Grow Landcape, Inc. includes an estimate of warranty expense in the year in which it sells its lawn mowers, which carry a 2-year warranty.

(e) Companies present sufficient financial information so that creditors and reasonably prudent investors will not be misled.

(f) Companies listed on U.S. stock exchanges report audited financial information annually and report unaudited information quarterly.

(g) Beach Resorts, Inc. does not record the 2004 value of $1.5 million for a piece of beachfront property it purchased in 1989 for $500,000.

(h) Restaurant Supplies, Inc. takes a $32,000 loss on a number of older ovens in its inventory; it paid the manufacturer $107,000 for them but can sell them for only $75,000.

(i) **Frito Lay** is a wholly owned subsidiary of **PepsiCo, Inc.**, and Frito Lay's operating results and financial condition are included in the consolidated financial statements of PepsiCo. (Do not use full disclosure.)

ACTION PLAN

Remember that:

- The four principles are cost, revenue recognition, matching, and full disclosure.
- The two constraints are materiality and conservatism.
- Full disclosure relates generally to the item; materiality to the amount.

SOLUTION TO DEMONSTRATION PROBLEM 1

(a) Full disclosure principle
(b) Materiality constraint
(c) Revenue recognition principle
(d) Matching principle
(e) Full disclosure principle
(f) Time period assumption
(g) Cost principle
(h) Conservatism constraint
(i) Economic entity assumption

THE NAVIGATOR

DEMONSTRATION PROBLEM 2

Presented below is financial information related to Notting Hill Hotel Corporation for the year 2004. All balances are ending balances unless stated otherwise.

Accounts payable	$ 868,000
Accounts receivable	700,000
Accumulated depreciation—equipment	100,000
Administrative expenses	280,000
Bonds payable	1,600,000
Cash	800,000
Common stock	500,000
Cost of goods sold	1,600,000
Dividends	60,000
Equipment	1,100,000
Income tax expense	83,000
Interest expense	60,000
Interest revenue	120,000
Inventories	500,000
Loss on the sale of equipment	35,000
Marketable (trading) securities	400,000
Net sales	2,400,000
Notes payable (short-term)	800,000
Other long-term debt	387,000
Patents and other intangibles	900,000
Prepaid expenses	200,000
Retained earnings (January 1, 2004)	80,000
Selling expenses	220,000
Taxes payable	83,000

Notting Hill Hotel Corporation had 88,000 shares of common stock outstanding for the entire year.

ACTION PLAN

- Remember that income tax expense is reported immediately after "Income before income taxes" for both a multiple-step and single-step income statement.
- Report earnings per share on both a multiple-step and a single-step income statement.
- Disclose net income and dividends on a retained earnings statement.
- Refer to Chapter 5, p. 166, for an example of a classified balance sheet.

Instructions

(a) Prepare a multiple-step income statement.

(b) Prepare a single-step income statement.

(c) Prepare a retained earnings statement.

(d) Prepare a classified balance sheet.

(e) Compute the following balance sheet relationships.
 (1) Current ratio
 (2) The amount of working capital
 (3) Debt to total assets ratio
 What insights do these relationships provide to the reader of the financial statements?

(f) Compute three measures of profitability from the income statement and balance sheet information. What insights do these relationships provide to the reader of the financial statements?

SOLUTION TO DEMONSTRATION PROBLEM 2

(a) Multiple-step income statement

NOTTING HILL HOTEL CORPORATION
Income Statement
For the Year Ended December 31, 2004

Net sales		$2,400,000
Cost of goods sold		1,600,000
Gross profit		800,000
Selling expenses	$220,000	
Administrative expenses	280,000	500,000
Income from operations		300,000
Other revenues and gains		
Interest revenue		120,000
Other expenses and losses		
Loss on sale of equipment	35,000	
Interest expense	60,000	95,000
Income before income taxes		325,000
Income tax expense		83,000
Net income		$ 242,000
Earnings per share		$2.75

(b) Single-step income statement

NOTTING HILL HOTEL CORPORATION
Income Statement
For the Year Ended December 31, 2004

Revenues		
Net sales		$2,400,000
Interest revenue		120,000
Total revenues		2,520,000
Expenses		
Cost of goods sold	$1,600,000	
Selling expenses	220,000	
Administrative expenses	280,000	
Interest expense	60,000	
Loss on the sale of equipment	35,000	2,195,000
Income before income taxes		325,000
Income tax expense		83,000
Net income		$ 242,000
Earnings per share		$2.75

(c) Retained earnings statement

NOTTING HILL HOTEL CORPORATION
Retained Earnings Statement
For the Year Ended December 31, 2004

Retained earnings, January 1	$ 80,000
Add: Net income	242,000
	322,000
Less: Dividends	60,000
Retained earnings, December 31	$262,000

(d) Classified balance sheet

NOTTING HILL HOTEL CORPORATION
Balance Sheet
December 31, 2004

Current assets		
Cash		$ 800,000
Marketable (trading) securities		400,000
Accounts receivable		700,000
Inventories		500,000
Prepaid expenses		200,000
Total current assets		2,600,000
Property, plant, and equipment		
Equipment	$1,100,000	
Less: Accumulated depreciation	100,000	1,000,000
Intangible assets		
Patents and other intangible assets		900,000
Total assets		$4,500,000
Current liabilities		
Notes payable		$ 800,000
Accounts payable		868,000
Taxes payable		83,000
Total current liabilities		1,751,000
Long-term liabilities		
Bonds payable	$1,600,000	
Other long-term debt	387,000	1,987,000
Total liabilities		3,738,000
Stockholders' equity		
Common stock	500,000	
Retained earnings	262,000	762,000
Total liabilities and stockholders' equity		$4,500,000

(e) Balance sheet relationships

(1) Current ratio $= \dfrac{\text{Current assets}}{\text{Current liabilities}} = \dfrac{\$2,600,000}{\$1,751,000} = 1.48{:}1$

(2) Working capital = Current assets − Current liabilities

Current assets	$2,600,000
Current liabilities	1,751,000
Working capital	$ 849,000

(3) Debt to total assets $= \dfrac{\text{Debt}}{\text{Total assets}} = \dfrac{\$3,738,000}{\$4,500,000} = 83.07\%$

Notting Hill's liquidity and solvency are of mixed quality. The current ratio is satisfactory, with its working capital healthy (i.e. current assets well in excess of current liabilities). However, its debt to total assets, at well over 80 percent, is too high. Given the company's relatively low profitability (see next page), its creditors might be concerned.

(f) Profitability relationships

$$\text{Profit margin percentage} = \frac{\text{Net income}}{\text{Net sales}} = \frac{\$242{,}000}{\$2{,}400{,}000} = 10.08\%$$

$$\text{Return on assets} = \frac{\text{Net income}}{\text{Total assets}} = \frac{\$242{,}000}{\$4{,}500{,}000} = 5.38\%$$

$$\begin{array}{c}\text{Return on common}\\ \text{stockholders' equity}\end{array} = \frac{\text{Net income}}{\text{Common stockholders' equity}} = \frac{\$242{,}000}{\$762{,}000} = 31.76\%$$

The profit margin percentage (return on sales) for Notting Hill seems adequate. Given the company's large asset base, however, it should probably generate a higher profit. The company's overall financial picture, then, could be better.

THE NAVIGATOR

SUMMARY OF STUDY OBJECTIVES

1. ***Explain the meaning of generally accepted accounting principles and identify the key items of the conceptual framework.*** Generally accepted accounting principles are a set of rules and practices that are recognized as a general guide for financial reporting purposes. Generally accepted means that these principles must have "substantial authoritative support." The key items of the conceptual framework are: (1) objectives of financial reporting; (2) qualitative characteristics of accounting information; (3) elements of financial statements; and (4) operating guidelines (assumptions, principles, and constraints).

2. ***Describe the basic objectives of financial reporting.*** The basic objectives of financial reporting are to provide information that is (1) useful to those making investment and credit decisions; (2) helpful in assessing future cash flows; and (3) helpful in identifying economic resources (assets), the claims to those resources (liabilities), and the changes in those resources and claims.

3. ***Discuss the qualitative characteristics of accounting information and elements of financial statements.*** To be judged useful, information should possess the following qualitative characteristics: relevance, reliability, comparability, and consistency. The elements of financial statements are a set of definitions that can be used to describe the basic terms used in accounting.

4. ***Identify the basic assumptions used by accountants.*** The major assumptions are: monetary unit, economic entity, time period, and going concern.

5. ***Identify the basic principles of accounting.*** The major principles are revenue recognition, matching, full disclosure, and cost.

6. ***Identify the two constraints in accounting.*** The major constraints are materiality and conservatism.

7. ***Understand and analyze classified financial statements.*** We presented the classified balance sheets and classified income statement in this chapter. In particular, income taxes and earnings per share are highlighted and discussed. Three items used to analyze the balance sheet are the current ratio, working capital, and debt to total assets. Earnings per share, profit margin percentage (return on sales), return on assets, and return on common stockholders' equity are used to analyze profitability.

8. ***Explain the accounting principles used in international operations.*** There are few recognized worldwide accounting standards. The International Accounting Standards Committee (IASC), of which the United States is a member, is working to obtain conformity in international accounting practices.

9. ***Identify the various systems of accounting procedures used in the hospitality industry.*** There are currently three systems: The Uniform System of Accounts for the Lodging Industry, The Uniform System of Accounts for Restaurants, and The Uniform System of Financial Reporting for Clubs. Each has a long history, and their purpose is to provide users of financial information with comparable data and meaningful analyses.

10. ***Understand accounting and financial management in a hotel.*** Proper accounting and financial management of a hotel is crucial to its success. The chief accounting officer is known as the controller. The controller is part of the hotel's executive committee, which includes the general manager and all department heads. The controller interacts with all the department heads, assisting and consulting with them on all financial matters so each department head makes sound decisions.

11. ***Understand accounting and financial management in a foodservice operation and a club.*** The controller of a foodservice operation focuses on food, beverage, and labor costs. Food and beverage cost analyses are of particular importance due to the amount of money spent and the perishable nature of the products. The club industry is unique in that its customers are all members of the club. Members pay dues to the club and in return have a decision-making role in club operations. Members also spend money on food and beverage, merchandising, and other amenities. Therefore, a club controller must account for revenues by looking at different cost centers such as golf, tennis, spa, and food and beverages to provide solid information for management.

THE NAVIGATOR

Glossary

American Hotel and Lodging Association (AH&LA) A trade association whose members are mostly hotels and lodging properties in the United States (p. 57).

Club Managers Association of America (CMAA) A trade association whose members are mostly club managers in the United States (p. 56).

Comparability Ability to compare accounting information of different companies because they use the same accounting principles (p. 38).

Conceptual framework A coherent system of interrelated objectives and fundamentals that can lead to consistent standards (p. 37).

Conservatism The approach of choosing an accounting method when in doubt that will least likely overstate assets and net income (p. 46).

Consistency Use of the same accounting principles and methods from year to year within a company (p. 39).

Controller The department head of the accounting department who has to work with not only the employees in the accounting and business office, but with all department heads (p. 58).

Cost principle Accounting principle that assets should be recorded at their historical cost (p. 44).

Current ratio A measure that expresses the relationship of current assets to current liabilities by dividing current assets by current liabilities (p. 51).

Debt to total assets ratio Solvency measure that indicates the percentage of total assets provided by creditors; calculated as total debt divided by total assets (p. 54).

Earnings per share (EPS) The net income earned by each share of outstanding common stock (p. 50).

Economic entity assumption Accounting assumption that economic events can be identified with a particular unit of accountability (p. 41).

Elements of financial statements Definitions of basic terms used in accounting (p. 39).

Executive committee The executive committee is made up of all the department heads of a hotel. This group comes together for meetings to make decisions and ensure all information is relayed correctly (p. 58).

Full disclosure principle Accounting principle that circumstances and events that make a difference to financial statement users should be disclosed (p. 44).

General manager This person is the manager of the entire hotel. He or she manages the hotel through the various department heads (p. 57).

Generally accepted accounting principles (GAAP) A set of rules and practices, having substantial authoritative support, that are recognized as a general guide for financial reporting purposes (p. 36).

Going concern assumption The assumption that the enterprise will continue in operation long enough to carry out its existing objectives and commitments (p. 41).

Hospitality Financial and Technology Professionals (HFTP) A membership-based organization for financial and technology professionals. Its aim is to provide continuing education, resources, certifications, information sharing, and networking opportunities for its membership. It also produces the HITEC trade show; the largest technology trade show for the hospitality industry worldwide (p. 56).

International Accounting Standards Committee (IASC) An accounting organization whose purpose is to formulate and publish international accounting standards and to promote their acceptance worldwide (p. 55).

Matching principle Accounting principle that expenses should be matched with revenues in the period when efforts are expended to generate revenues (p. 42).

Materiality The constraint of determining if an item is important enough to likely influence the decision of a reasonably prudent investor or creditor (p. 46).

Monetary unit assumption Accounting assumption that only transaction data capable of being expressed in monetary terms should be included in accounting records (p. 41).

National Restaurant Association (NRA) A trade association whose members are mostly restaurateurs and restaurant corporations in the United States (p. 63).

Profit margin percentage Profitability measure that indicates the percentage of each dollar of sales that results in net income; calculated as net income divided by net sales. Also called *rate of return on sales* (p. 52).

Relevance The quality of information that indicates the information makes a difference in a decision (p. 38).

Reliability The quality of information that gives assurance that it is free of error and bias (p. 38).

Return on assets An overall measure of a company's profitability; calculated as net income divided by total assets (p. 53).

Return on common stockholders' equity Profitability measure that shows the rate of net income earned for each dollar of owners' investment; calculated as net income divided by common stockholders' equity (p. 53).

Revenue recognition principle Accounting principle that revenue should be recognized in the accounting period in which it is earned (generally at the point of sale) (p. 42).

Time period assumption Accounting assumption that the economic life of a business can be divided into artificial time periods (p. 41).

The Uniform System of Accounts for the Lodging Industry A system of accounting guidelines and procedures developed for the use of hotel and lodging properties (p. 56).

The Uniform System of Accounts for Restaurants A system of accounting guidelines and procedures developed for the use of hotel and lodging properties (p. 56).

The Uniform System of Financial Reporting for Clubs A system of accounting guidelines and procedures developed for the use of various types of clubs (p. 56).

Working capital The excess of current assets over current liabilities (p. 52).

EXERCISES

Identify generally accepted accounting principles. (SO 1)

2-1 Indicate whether each of the following statements is true or false.

(a) ____ *Generally accepted* means that these principles must have "substantial authoritative support."

(b) ____ Substantial authoritative support for GAAP usually comes from two standard-setting bodies: the FASB and the IRS.

(c) ____ GAAP is a set of rules and practices established by the accounting profession to serve as a general guide for financial reporting purposes.

Identify items included in conceptual framework. (SO 1)

2-2 Indicate which of the following items is(are) included in the FASB's conceptual framework. (Use "Yes" or "No" to answer this question.)

(a) ____ Analysis of financial statement ratios.

(b) ____ Objectives of financial reporting.

(c) ____ Qualitative characteristics of accounting information.

Identify objectives of financial reporting. (SO 2)

2-3 According to the FASB's conceptual framework, which of the following are objectives of financial reporting? (Use "Yes" or "No" to answer this question.)

(a) ____ Provide information that is helpful in assessing past cash flows and stock prices.

(b) ____ Provide information that is useful to those making investment and credit decisions.

(c) ____ Provide information that identifies the economic resources (assets), the claims to those resources (liabilities), and the changes in those resources and claims.

Identify operating guidelines. (SO 4, 5, 6)

2-4 Presented below are four concepts discussed in this chapter.

1. Time period assumption
2. Cost principle
3. Full disclosure principle
4. Conservatism

Match these concepts to the following accounting practices. Each number can be used only once.

(a) ____ Recording inventory at its purchase price.

(b) ____ Using notes and supplementary schedules in the financial statements.

(c) ____ Preparing financial statements on an annual basis.

(d) ____ Using the lower of cost or market method for inventory valuation.

Identify the assumption, principle, or constraint that has been violated. (SO 4, 5, 6)

2-5 A number of accounting reporting situations are described below.

1. Cuneo Company recognizes revenue at the end of the production cycle, but before sale. The price of the product, as well as the amount that can be sold, is not certain.
2. In preparing its financial statements, Diane Torres Company omitted information concerning its method of accounting for inventories.
3. Jan Way Corp. charges the entire premium on a two-year insurance policy to the first year.
4. Holloway Hospital Supply Corporation reports only current assets and current liabilities on its balance sheet. Property, plant, and equipment and bonds payable are reported as current assets and current liabilities, respectively. Liquidation of the company is unlikely.
5. Bagley Inc. is carrying inventory at its current market value of $100,000. Inventory had an original cost of $110,000.
6. Karen Allman Company is in its fifth year of operation and has yet to issue financial statements. (Do not use full disclosure principle.)
7. Jana Kingston Co. has inventory on hand that cost $400,000. Kingston Co. reports inventory on its balance sheet at its current market value of $425,000.
8. Susan Elbe, president of the Classic Music Company, bought a computer for her personal use. She paid for the computer by using company funds and debited the "Computers" account.

Instructions

For each of the above, list the assumption, principle, or constraint that has been violated, if any. List only one term for each case.

Identify the assumption, principle, or constraint that has been violated and prepare correct entries. (SO 4, 5, 6)

2-6 Presented below are some business transactions that occurred during 2004 for Sammy Sosa Company.

(a) Merchandise inventory with a cost of $208,000 is reported at its market value of $260,000. The following entry was made.

Merchandise Inventory	52,000	
Gain		52,000

(b) Equipment worth $60,000 was acquired at a cost of $46,000 from a company that had water damage in a flood. The following entry was made.

Equipment	60,000	
Cash		46,000
Gain		14,000

(c) The president of Sammy Sosa Company, Charles Brieschke, purchased a truck for personal use and charged it to his expense account. The following entry was made.

Travel Expense	18,000	
Cash		18,000

(d) An electric pencil sharpener costing $50 is being depreciated over 5 years. The following entry was made.

Depreciation Expense—Pencil Sharpener	10	
Accumulated Depreciation—Pencil Sharpener		10

Instructions

In each of the situations above, identify the assumption, principle, or constraint that has been violated, if any. Discuss the appropriateness of the journal entries, and give the correct journal entry, if necessary.

2-7 Presented below are the assumptions, principles, and constraints discussed in this chapter.

Identify accounting assumptions, principles, and constraints. (SO 4, 5, 6)

1. Economic entity assumption
2. Going concern assumption
3. Monetary unit assumption
4. Time period assumption
5. Cost principle
6. Matching principle
7. Full disclosure principle
8. Revenue recognition principle
9. Materiality
10. Conservatism

Instructions

Identify by number the accounting assumption, principle, or constraint that describes each situation below. Do not use a number more than once.

(a) Explains why plant assets are not reported at liquidation value. (Do not use historical cost principle.)
(b) Indicates that personal and business record keeping should be separately maintained.
(c) Ensures that all relevant financial information is reported.
(d) Assumes that the dollar is the "measuring stick" used to report on financial performance.
(e) Requires that the operational guidelines be followed for all significant items.
(f) Separates financial information into time periods for reporting purpose.
(g) Requires recognition of expenses in the same period as related revenues.
(h) Indicates that market value changes subsequent to purchase are not recorded in the accounts.

2-8 Presented below are the assumptions, principles, and constraints used in this chapter.

Identify accounting assumptions, principles, and constraints. (SO 4, 5, 6)

1. Economic entity assumption
2. Going concern assumption
3. Monetary unit assumption
4. Time period assumption
5. Full disclosure principle
6. Revenue recognition principle
7. Matching principle
8. Cost principle
9. Materiality
10. Conservatism

Identify by number the accounting assumption, principle, or constraint that matches each description below. Do not use a number more than once.

(a) Repair tools are expensed when purchased. (Do not use conservatism.)
(b) Allocates expenses to revenues in proper period.
(c) Assumes that the dollar is the measuring stick used to report financial information.
(d) Separates financial information into time periods for reporting purposes.
(e) Market value changes subsequent to purchase are not recorded in the accounts. (Do not use revenue recognition principle.)

(f) Indicates that personal and business record keeping should be separately maintained.
(g) Ensures that all relevant financial information is reported.
(h) Lower of cost or market is used to value inventories.

Analyze transactions to identify accounting principle or assumption violated, and prepare correct entries.
(SO 4, 5)

2-9 Dye and Zaur are accountants for SuperResorts. They disagree over the following transactions that occurred during the calendar year 2004.

1. Dye suggests that equipment should be reported on the balance sheet at its liquidation value, which is $15,000 less than its cost.
2. SuperResorts bought a custom-made piece of equipment for $24,000. This equipment has a useful life of 6 years. SuperResorts depreciates equipment using the straight-line method. "Since the equipment is custom-made, it will have no resale value. Therefore, it shouldn't be depreciated but instead should be expensed immediately," argues Dye. "Besides, it provides for lower net income."
3. Depreciation for the year was $18,000. Since net income is expected to be lower this year, Dye suggests deferring depreciation to a year when there is more net income.
4. Land costing $60,000 was appraised at $90,000. Dye suggests the following journal entry.

Land	30,000	
Gain on Appreciation of Land		30,000

5. SuperResorts purchased equipment for $30,000 at a going-out-of-business sale. The equipment was worth $45,000. Dye believes that the following entry should be made.

Equipment	45,000	
Cash		30,000
Gain		15,000

Zaur disagrees with Dye on each of the above situations.

Instructions

For each transaction, indicate why Zaur disagrees. Identify the accounting principle or assumption that Dye would be violating if his suggestions were used. Prepare the correct journal entry for each transaction, if any.

Determine the appropriateness of journal entries in terms of generally accepted accounting principles or assumptions.
(SO 4, 5)

2-10 Presented below are a number of business transactions that occurred during the current year for Chavez, Inc.

1. Because the general level of prices increased during the current year, Chavez, Inc. determined that there was a $10,000 understatement of depreciation expense on its equipment and decided to record it in its accounts. The following entry was made.

Depreciation Expense	10,000	
Accumulated Depreciation		10,000

2. Because of a "flood sale," equipment obviously worth $250,000 was acquired at a cost of $150,000. The following entry was made.

Equipment	250,000	
Cash		150,000
Gain on Purchase of Equipment		100,000

3. The president of Chavez, Inc. used his expense account to purchase a new Saab 9000 solely for personal use. The following entry was made.

Miscellaneous Expense	34,000	
Cash		34,000

4. An order for $30,000 has been received from a customer for products on hand. This order is to be shipped on January 9 next year. The following entry was made.

Accounts Receivable	30,000	
Sales		30,000

5. Materials were purchased on March 31 for $65,000. This amount was entered in the Inventory account. On December 31, the materials would have cost $85,000, so the following entry was made.

Inventory	20,000	
Gain on Inventories		20,000

Instructions

In each situation, discuss the appropriateness of the journal entries in terms of generally accepted accounting principles.

EXPLORING THE WEB

2-11 The **Financial Accounting Standards Board (FASB)** is a private organization established to improve accounting standards and financial reporting. The FASB conducts extensive research before issuing a "Statement of Financial Accounting Standards," which represents an authoritative expression of generally accepted accounting principles.

Address: **www.accounting.rutgers.edu/raw**

Steps

1. Choose **FASB**.
2. Choose **FASB Facts**.

Instructions

Answer the following questions.

(a) What is the mission of the FASB?
(b) How are topics added to the FASB technical agenda?
(c) What characteristics make the FASB's procedures an "open" decision-making process?

ETHICS CASE

2-12 When the Financial Accounting Standards Board issues new standards, the required implementation date is usually 12 months or more from the date of issuance, with early implementation encouraged. Richard Keith, accountant at Manchester Corporation, discusses with his financial vice president the need for early implementation of a recently issued standard that would result in a much fairer presentation of the company's financial condition and earnings. When the financial vice president determines that early implementation of the standard will adversely affect reported net income for the year, he strongly discourages Richard from implementing the standard until it is required.

Instructions

(a) Who are the stakeholders in this situation?
(b) What, if any, are the ethical considerations in this situation?
(c) What does Richard have to gain by advocating early implementation? Who might be affected by the decision against early implementation?

Answer to Hilton Review It Question 2, p. 40

The Report of Independent Public Accountants indicates that **Hilton's** financial statements (balance sheet, statement of operations, shareholders' investment, and cash flows) are presented fairly, in accordance with generally accepted accounting principles.

Hilton™

Remember to go back to the Navigator box on the chapter-opening page and check off your completed work.

3

THE RECORDING PROCESS

THE NAVIGATOR ✓

- Understand *Concepts for Review* ❑
- Read *Feature Story* ❑
- Scan *Study Objectives* ❑
- Read *Preview* ❑
- Read text and answer *Before You Go On* *p.* 81 ❑ *p.* 85 ❑ *p.* 97 ❑ *p.* 99 ❑
- Work *Demonstration Problem* ❑
- Review *Summary of Study Objectives* ❑
- Complete *Assignments* ❑

CONCEPTS FOR REVIEW

Before studying this chapter, you should know or, if necessary, review:

a. What are assets, liabilities, stockholders' equity, retained earnings, dividends, revenues, and expenses. (Ch. 1, pp. 11–12)

b. Why assets equal liabilities plus stockholders' equity. (Ch. 1, p. 11)

c. What transactions are and how they affect the basic accounting equation. (Ch. 1, pp. 14–20)

THE NAVIGATOR

FEATURE STORY

No Such Thing as a Perfect World

When she got a job doing the accounting for **Forster's Restaurants**, Tanis Anderson had almost finished her business administration degree at Simon Fraser University. But even after Tanis completed her degree requirements, her education still continued—this time, in the real world.

Tanis's responsibilities include paying the bills, tracking food and labor costs, and managing the payroll for **The Mug and Musket**, a popular destination restaurant in Surrey, British Columbia. "My title is Director of Finance," she laughs, "but really that means I take care of whatever needs doing!"

The use of judgment is a big part of the job. As Tanis says, "I learned all the fundamentals in my business classes, but school prepares you for a perfect world, and there is no such thing."

She feels fortunate that her boss understands her job is a learning experience as well as a responsibility. "Sometimes he's let me do something he knew perfectly well was a mistake so I can learn something through experience," she admits.

To help others gain the benefits of her real-world learning, Tanis is always happy to help students in the area who want to use Forster's as the subject of a project or report. "It's the least I can do," she says.

THE NAVIGATOR

STUDY OBJECTIVES

After studying this chapter, you should be able to

1. Explain what an account is and how it helps in the recording process.
2. Define debits and credits and explain how they are used to record business transactions.
3. Identify the basic steps in the recording process.
4. Explain what a journal is and how it helps in the recording process.
5. Explain what a ledger is and how it helps in the recording process.
6. Explain what posting is and how it helps in the recording process.
7. Prepare a trial balance and explain its purposes.
8. Identify the advantages of manual and computerized accounting systems.

THE NAVIGATOR

PREVIEW OF CHAPTER 3

In Chapter 1, we analyzed business transactions in terms of the accounting equation. The cumulative effects of these transactions were presented in tabular form. Imagine a restaurant and gift shop such as **The Mug and Musket** using the same tabular format as Best Caterers, Inc. to keep track of every one of its transactions. In a single day, this restaurant and gift shop engages in hundreds of business transactions. To record each transaction this way would be impractical, expensive, and unnecessary. Instead, a set of procedures and records are used to keep track of transaction data more easily.

This chapter introduces and illustrates these basic procedures and records. The content and organization of Chapter 3 are as follows.

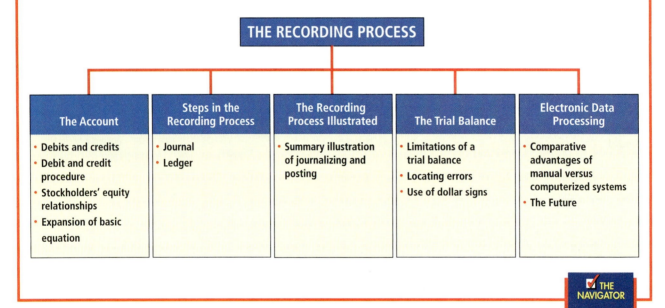

THE RECORDING PROCESS

- **The Account**
  - Debits and credits
  - Debit and credit procedure
  - Stockholders' equity relationships
  - Expansion of basic equation
- **Steps in the Recording Process**
  - Journal
  - Ledger
- **The Recording Process Illustrated**
  - Summary illustration of journalizing and posting
- **The Trial Balance**
  - Limitations of a trial balance
  - Locating errors
  - Use of dollar signs
- **Electronic Data Processing**
  - Comparative advantages of manual versus computerized systems
  - The Future

THE NAVIGATOR

STUDY OBJECTIVE 1

Explain what an account is and how it helps in the recording process.

THE ACCOUNT

An **account** is an individual accounting record of increases and decreases in a specific asset, liability, or stockholders' equity item. For example, Best Caterers, Inc. (the company discussed in Chapter 1) would have separate accounts for Cash, Accounts Receivable, Accounts Payable, Service Revenue, Salaries Expense, and so on. In its simplest form, an account consists of three parts: (1) the title of the account, (2) a left or debit side, and (3) a right or credit side. Because the alignment of these parts of an account resembles the letter T, it is referred to as a **T account**. The basic form of an account is shown in Illustration 3-1.

Illustration 3-1

Basic form of account

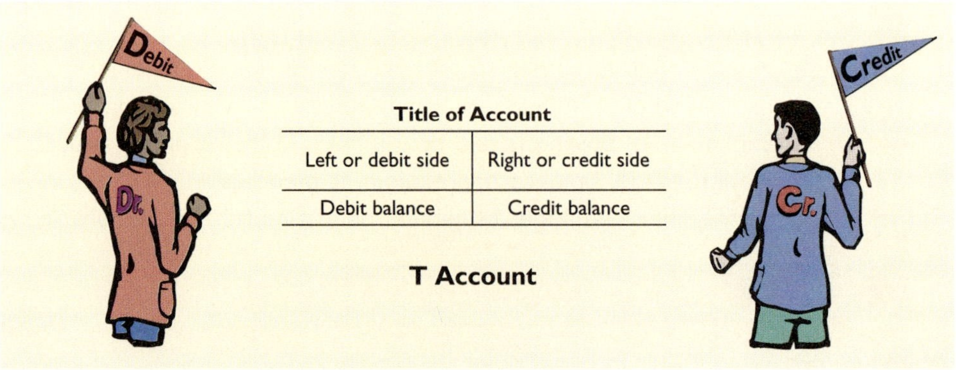

The T account is a standard shorthand in accounting that helps make clear the effects of transactions on individual accounts. We will use it often throughout this book to explain basic accounting relationships. (Note that when we are referring to a specific account, we capitalize its name.)

DEBITS AND CREDITS

STUDY OBJECTIVE 2

Define debits and credits and explain how they are used to record business transactions.

The term **debit** means left, and **credit** means right. They are commonly abbreviated as Dr. for debit and Cr. for credit.[1] These terms are directional signals: They indicate on which side of a T account a number will be recorded. Entering an amount on the left side of an account is called **debiting** the account; making an entry on the right side is **crediting** the account.

The procedure of having debits on the left and credits on the right is an accounting custom, or rule (like the custom of driving on the right-hand side of the road in the United States). *This rule applies to all accounts.* When the totals of the two sides are compared, an account will have a **debit balance** if the total of the debit amounts exceeds the credits. An account will have a **credit balance** if the credit amounts exceed the debits.

The recording of debits and credits in an account is shown in Illustration 3-2 for the cash transactions of Best Caterers, Inc. The data are taken from the cash column of the tabular summary in Illustration 1-9.

Illustration 3-2

Tabular summary compared to account form

Tabular Summary

Cash
$15,000
−7,000
1,200
1,500
−1,700
−250
600
−1,300
$ 8,050

Account Form

Cash			
(Debits)	15,000	**(Credits)**	7,000
	1,200		1,700
	1,500		250
	600		1,300
Balance **(Debit)**	8,050		

HELPFUL HINT
At this point, don't think about increases and decreases in relation to debits and credits. As you'll soon learn, the effects of debits and credits depend on the type of account involved.

In the tabular summary every positive item represents a receipt of cash; every negative amount represents a payment of cash. Notice that in the account form the increases in cash are recorded as debits, and the decreases in cash are recorded as credits. Having increases on one side and decreases on the other helps in determining the total of each side of the account as well as the overall balance in the account. The account balance, a debit of $8,050, indicates that Best Caterers, Inc. has had $8,050 more increases than decreases in cash.

DEBIT AND CREDIT PROCEDURES

HELPFUL HINT
Debits must equal credits for each transaction.

In Chapter 1 you learned the effect of a transaction on the basic accounting equation. Remember that each transaction must affect two or more accounts to keep the basic accounting equation in balance. In other words, for each transaction **debits must equal credits** in the accounts. The equality of debits and credits provides the basis for the **double-entry system** of recording transactions.

Under the double-entry system the dual (two-sided) effect of each transaction is recorded in appropriate accounts. This universally used system provides a logical method for recording transactions. It also offers a means of proving the

[1]These terms and their abbreviations come from the Latin words *debere* (Dr.) and *credere* (Cr.).

accuracy of the recorded amounts. If every transaction is recorded with equal debits and credits, then the sum of all the debits to the accounts must equal the sum of all the credits.

The double-entry system for determining the equality of the accounting equation is much more efficient than the plus/minus procedure used in Chapter 1. There, it was necessary after each transaction to compare total assets with total liabilities and stockholders' equity to determine the equality of the two sides of the accounting equation.

Assets and Liabilities

We know that both sides of the basic equation (Assets = Liabilities + Stockholders' Equity) must be equal. It follows that increases and decreases in assets and liabilities must be recorded opposite from each other. In Illustration 3-2, increases in cash—an asset—were entered on the left side, and decreases in cash were entered on the right side. Therefore, increases in liabilities must be entered on the right or credit side, and decreases in liabilities must be entered on the left or debit side. The effects that debits and credits have on assets and liabilities are summarized in Illustration 3-3.

Illustration 3-3

Debit and credit effects—assets and liabilities

Debits	Credits
Increase assets	Decrease assets
Decrease liabilities	Increase liabilities

HELPFUL HINT
The normal balance for an account is always the same as the increase side.

Debits to a specific asset account should exceed the credits to that account. Credits to a liability account should exceed debits to that account. The **normal balance** of an account is on the side where an increase in the account is recorded. Thus, asset accounts normally show debit balances, and liability accounts normally show credit balances. Illustration 3-4 shows how the normal balances can be diagrammed.

Illustration 3-4

Normal balances—assets and liabilities

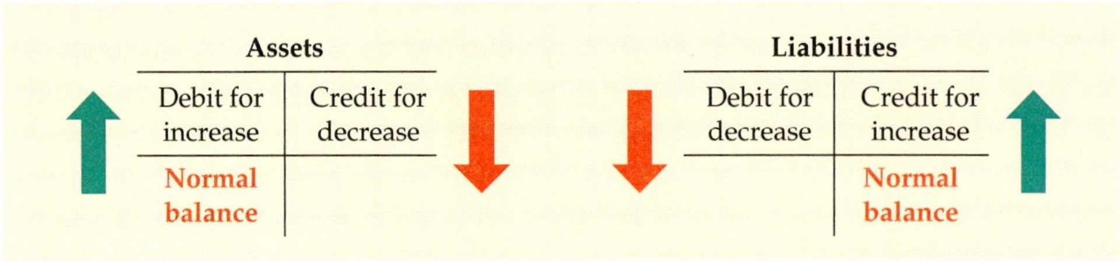

Knowing the normal balance in an account may help you trace errors. For example, a credit balance in an asset account such as Land or a debit balance in a liability account such as Wages Payable would indicate recording errors. Occasionally, an abnormal balance may be correct. The Cash account, for example, will have a credit balance when a company has overdrawn its bank balance (i.e., written a "bad" check).

Stockholders' Equity

As indicated in Chapter 1, there are five subdivisions of stockholders' equity: common stock, retained earnings, dividends, revenues, and expenses. In a double-entry system, accounts are kept for each of these subdivisions, as explained below.

COMMON STOCK. **Common stock** is issued in exchange for the owners' investment paid into the corporation. The Common Stock account is increased by credits and decreased by debits. When cash is invested in the business in exchange for shares of the corporation's stock, Cash is debited and Common Stock is credited.

The rules of debit and credit for the Common Stock account are stated in Illustration 3-5.

Debits	Credits
Decrease common stock	Increase common stock

Illustration 3-5

Debit and credit effect—common stock

The normal balance in this account may be diagrammed as follows.

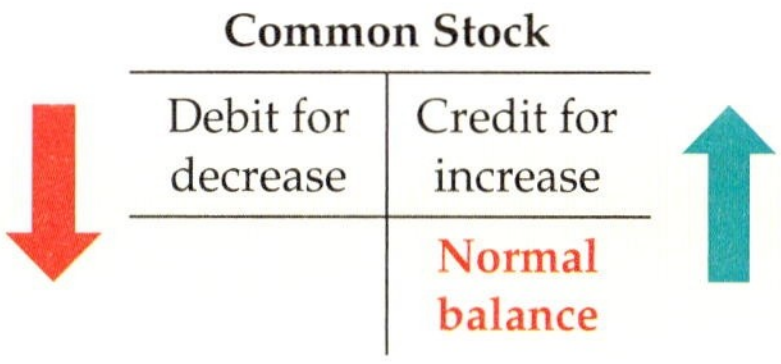

Illustration 3-6

Normal balance—common stock

HELPFUL HINT
The rules for debit and credit and the normal balance of common stock are the same as for liabilities.

RETAINED EARNINGS. **Retained earnings** is net income that is retained in the business. It represents the portion of stockholders' equity that has been accumulated through the profitable operation of the business. Retained earnings is increased by credits (net income) and decreased by debits (dividends or net losses), as shown in Illustration 3-7.

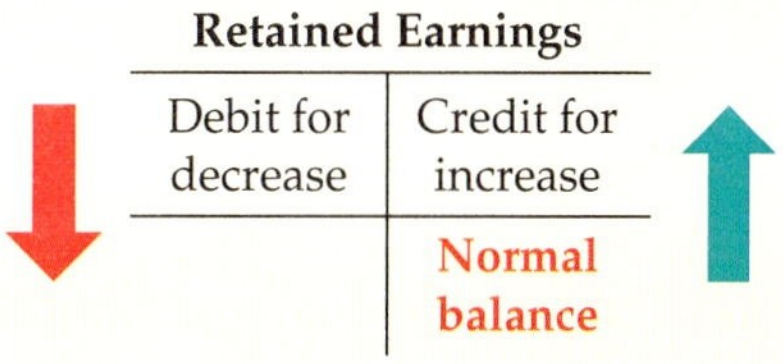

Illustration 3-7

Debit and credit effect and normal balance—retained earnings

DIVIDENDS. A **dividend** is a distribution by a corporation to its stockholders on a pro rata (equal) basis. The most common form of a distribution is a **cash dividend**. Dividends can be declared (authorized) only by the board of directors. They are a reduction of the stockholders' claims on retained earnings. The Dividends account is increased by debits and decreased by credits, with a normal debit balance as shown in Illustration 3-8.

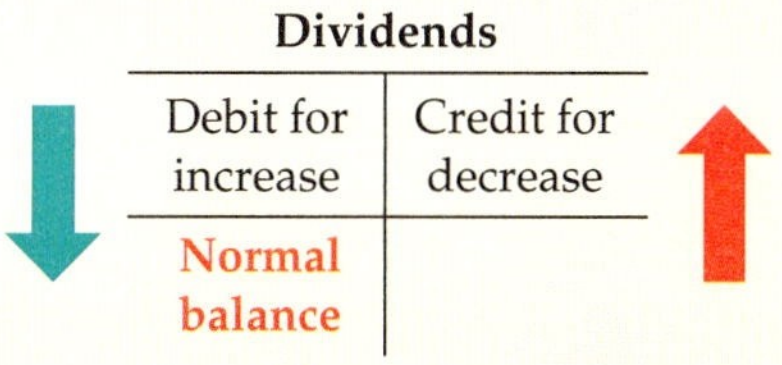

Illustration 3-8

Debit and credit effect and normal balance—dividends

Revenues and Expenses

> **HELPFUL HINT**
> Because revenues increase stockholders' equity, a revenue account has the same debit and credit rules as does the common stock account. Conversely, expenses have the opposite effect.

Remember that the ultimate purpose of earning revenues is to benefit the stockholders of the business. When revenues are earned, stockholders' equity is increased. Revenues are a subdivision of stockholders' equity that provides information as to *why* stockholders' equity increased. Revenue accounts are increased by credits and decreased by debits. Accordingly, **the effect of debits and credits on revenue accounts is identical to their effect on stockholders' equity**.

Expenses have the opposite effect: expenses decrease stockholders' equity. Since expenses are the negative factor in computing net income, and revenues are the positive factor, it is logical that the increase and decrease sides of expense accounts should be the reverse of revenue accounts. Thus, expense accounts are increased by debits and decreased by credits.

The effect of debits and credits on revenues and expenses may be stated as follows.

Illustration 3-9
Debit and credit effects—revenues and expenses

Debits	Credits
Decrease revenues	Increase revenues
Increase expenses	Decrease expenses

Credits to revenue accounts should exceed the debits, and debits to expense accounts should exceed credits. Thus, revenue accounts normally show credit balances, and expense accounts normally show debit balances. Illustration 3-10 diagrams the normal balances.

Illustration 3-10
Normal balances—revenues and expenses

ACCOUNTING IN ACTION *Business Insight*

The Chicago Cubs baseball team has the following major revenue and expense accounts.

Revenues	Expenses
Admissions (ticket sales)	Players' salaries
Concessions	Administrative salaries
Television and radio	Travel
Advertising	Ballpark maintenance

STOCKHOLDERS' EQUITY RELATIONSHIPS

As indicated in Chapter 1, common stock and retained earnings are reported in the stockholders' equity section of the balance sheet. Dividends are reported on the retained earnings statement. Revenues and expenses are reported on the income statement. Dividends, revenues, and expenses are eventually transferred to retained earnings at the end of the period. As a result, a change in any one of these three items affects stockholders' equity. The relationships related to stockholders' equity are shown in Illustration 3-11.

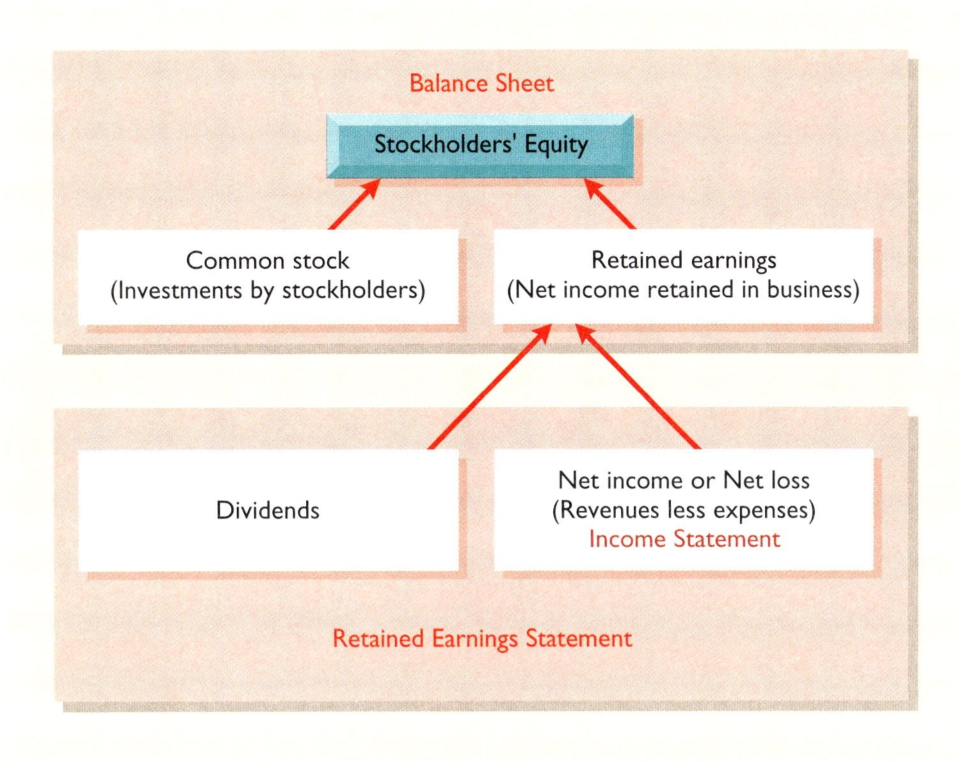

Illustration 3-11

Stockholders' equity relationships

EXPANSION OF THE BASIC EQUATION

You have already learned the basic accounting equation. Illustration 3-12 expands this equation to show the accounts that compose stockholders' equity. In addition, the debit/credit rules and effects on each type of account are illustrated. Study this diagram carefully. It will help you understand the fundamentals of the double-entry system. Like the basic equation, the expanded basic equation must be in balance (total debits equal total credits).

Illustration 3-12

Expanded basic equation and debit/credit rules and effects

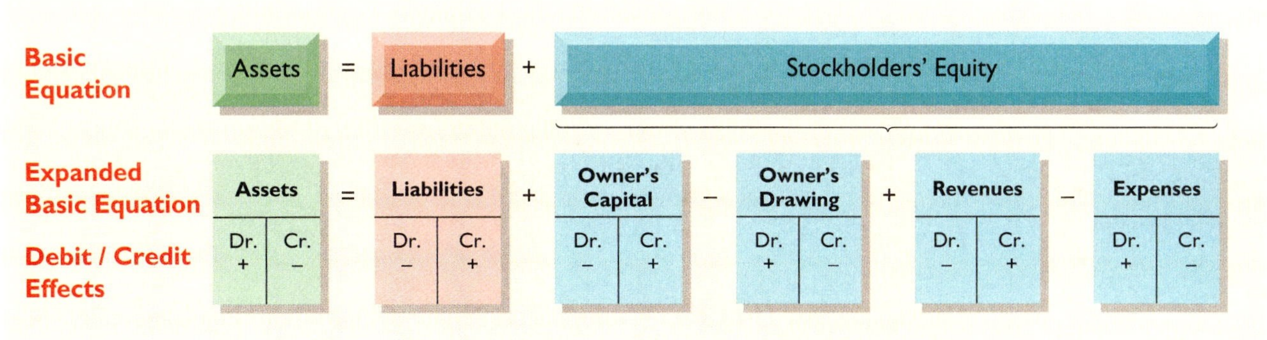

BEFORE YOU GO ON...

REVIEW IT

1. What do the terms *debit* and *credit* mean?
2. What are the debit and credit effects on assets, liabilities, and stockholders' equity?
3. What are the debit and credit effects on revenues, expenses, and dividends?
4. What are the normal balances for **Hilton's** Cash, Accounts Payable, and Interest Expense accounts? The answers to this question are provided on page 108.

DO IT

Kate Browne, president of Raisin Buns, Inc. has just rented space in a shopping mall in which she will open and operate a beauty salon. Long before opening day and before purchasing equipment, hiring assistants, and remodeling the space, Kate has been advised to set up a double-entry set of accounting records in which to record all of her business transactions.

Identify the balance sheet accounts that Raisin Buns, Inc. will likely need to record the transactions needed to establish and open the business. Also, indicate whether the normal balance of each account is a debit or a credit.

ACTION PLAN

- Determine the types of accounts needed: Kate will need asset accounts for each type of asset she invests in the business, and liability accounts for any debts she incurs.
- Understand the types of stockholders' equity accounts: Only Common Stock will be needed when Kate begins the business. Other stockholders' equity accounts will be needed later.

SOLUTION: Raisin Buns, Inc. would likely need the following accounts to record the transactions needed to ready the beauty salon for opening day: Cash (debit balance); Equipment (debit balance); Supplies (debit balance); Accounts Payable (credit balance); Notes Payable (credit balance), if the business borrows money; and Common Stock (credit balance).

Related exercise material: 3-1 and 3-2.

THE NAVIGATOR

STEPS IN THE RECORDING PROCESS

STUDY OBJECTIVE 3

Identify the basic steps in the recording process.

In practically every business, there are three basic steps in the recording process:

1. Analyze each transaction for its effects on the accounts.
2. Enter the transaction information in a journal (book of original entry).
3. Transfer the journal information to the appropriate accounts in the ledger (book of accounts).

Although it is possible to enter transaction information directly into the accounts without using a journal, few businesses do so.

The sequence of events in the recording process begins with the transaction. Evidence of the transaction is provided by a **business document**, such as a sales slip, a check, a bill, or a cash register tape. This evidence is analyzed to determine the effects of the transaction on specific accounts. The transaction is then entered in the journal. Finally, the journal entry is transferred to the designated accounts

Illustration 3-13

The recording process

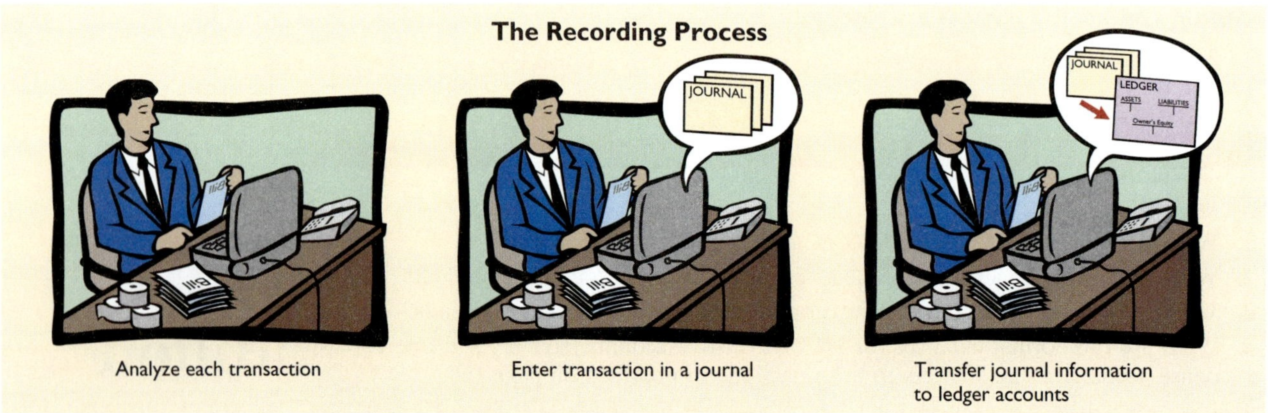

in the ledger. The sequence of events in the recording process is shown in Illustration 3-13.

The basic steps in the recording process occur repeatedly. The analysis of transactions was illustrated in Chapter 1. Further examples will be given in this and later chapters. The other steps in the recording process are explained in the next sections.

Technology in Action examples show how computer technology is used in accounting and business.

TECHNOLOGY IN ACTION

Computerized and manual accounting systems basically parallel one another. Most of the procedures are handled by electronic circuitry in computerized systems. They seem to occur invisibly. But, to fully comprehend how computerized systems operate, you need to understand manual approaches for processing accounting data.

THE JOURNAL

Transactions are initially recorded in chronological order in a **journal** before being transferred to the accounts. Thus, the journal is referred to as the book of original entry. For each transaction the journal shows the debit and credit effects on specific accounts. Companies may use various kinds of journals, but every company has the most basic form of journal, a **general journal**. Typically, a general journal has spaces for dates, account titles and explanations, references, and two amount columns. Whenever we use the term journal in this textbook without a modifying adjective, we mean the general journal.

STUDY OBJECTIVE 4

Explain what a journal is and how it helps in the recording process.

The journal makes several significant contributions to the recording process:

1. It discloses in one place the complete effects of a transaction.
2. It provides a chronological record of transactions.
3. It helps to prevent or locate errors because the debit and credit amounts for each entry can be readily compared.

Entering transaction data in the journal is known as **journalizing**. Separate journal entries are made for each transaction. A complete entry consists of (1) the date of the transaction, (2) the accounts and amounts to be debited and credited, and (3) a brief explanation of the transaction.

Illustration 3-14 shows the technique of journalizing, using the first two transactions of Best Caterers, Inc. These transactions were: September 1, stockholders invested $15,000 cash in the corporation in exchange for shares of stock, and computer equipment was purchased for $7,000 cash. The number J1 indicates that these two entries are recorded on the first page of the general journal.

Illustration 3-14

Technique of journalizing

GENERAL JOURNAL — J1

Date	Account Titles and Explanation	Ref.	Debit	Credit
2002				
Sept. 1	Cash		15,000	
	Common Stock			15,000
	(Issued shares of stock for cash)			
1	Computer Equipment		7,000	
	Cash			7,000
	(Purchased equipment for cash)			

The standard form and content of journal entries are as follows:

- The date of the transaction is entered in the Date column. The date recorded should include the year, month, and day of the transaction.
- The debit account title (that is, the account to be debited) is entered first at the extreme left margin of the column headed "Account Titles and Explanation," and the amount of the debit is recorded in the Debit column.
- The credit account title (i.e., the account to be credited) is indented and entered on the next line in the column headed "Account Titles and Explanation," and the amount of the credit is recorded in the Credit column.
- A brief explanation of the transaction is given on the line below the credit account title.
- A space is left between journal entries. The blank space separates individual journal entries and makes the entire journal easier to read.
- The column titled Ref. (which stands for reference) is left blank when the journal entry is made. This column is used later when the journal entries are transferred to the ledger accounts. At that time, the ledger account number is placed in the Reference column to indicate where the amount in the journal entry was transferred.

It is important to use correct and specific account titles in journalizing. Since most accounts appear later in the financial statements, wrong account titles lead to incorrect financial statements. Some flexibility exists initially in selecting account titles. The main criterion is that each title must appropriately describe the content of the account. For example, the account title used for the cost of delivery trucks may be Delivery Equipment, Delivery Trucks, or Trucks. Once a company chooses the specific title to use, all later transactions involving the account should be recorded under that account title.[2]

If an entry involves only two accounts, one debit and one credit, it is considered a **simple entry**. Some transactions, however, require more than two accounts in journalizing. When three or more accounts are required in one journal entry, the entry is referred to as a **compound entry**. To illustrate, assume that on July 1, Butler Special Events purchases a delivery truck costing $14,000 by paying $8,000 cash and the balance on account (to be paid later). The compound entry is shown in Illustration 3-15.

Illustration 3-15

Compound journal entry

GENERAL JOURNAL — J1

Date		Account Titles and Explanation	Ref.	Debit	Credit
2004					
July	1	Delivery Equipment		14,000	
		Cash			8,000
		Accounts Payable			6,000
		(Purchased truck for cash with balance on account)			

HELPFUL HINT

Assume you find this compound entry:

Wages Expense	700	
Cash		1,200
Rent Expense	400	
(Paid cash for wages and rent)		

Is the entry correct? No. It is incorrect in form because both debits should be listed before the credit. It is incorrect in content because the debit amounts do not equal the credit amount.

In a compound entry, the total debit and credit amounts must be equal. Also, the standard format requires that all debits be listed before the credits.

[2] In homework problems, when specific account titles are given, they should be used. When account titles are not given, you may select account titles that identify the nature and content of each account. The account titles used in journalizing should not contain explanations such as Cash Paid or Cash Received.

BEFORE YOU GO ON...

REVIEW IT

1. What is the sequence of the steps in the recording process?
2. What contribution does the journal make to the recording process?
3. What is the standard form and content of a journal entry made in the general journal?

DO IT

In establishing her beauty salon, Raisin Buns, Inc., Kate Browne as president and sole stockholder engaged in the following activities.

1. Opened a bank account in the name of Raisin Buns, Inc. and deposited $20,000 of her own money in this account in exchange for shares of common stock.
2. Purchased equipment on account (to be paid in 30 days) for a total cost of $4,800.
3. Interviewed three applicants for the position of stylists.

In what form (type of record) should Raisin Buns, Inc. record these three activities? Prepare the entries to record the transactions.

ACTION PLAN

- Understand which activities need to be recorded and which do not. Any that have economic effects should be recorded in a journal.
- Analyze the effects of transactions on asset, liability, and stockholders' equity accounts.

SOLUTION: Each transaction that is recorded is entered in the general journal. The three activities would be recorded as follows.

1. Cash	20,000	
Common Stock		20,000
(Issued shares of stock for cash)		
2. Equipment	4,800	
Acounts Payable		4,800
(Purchased equipment on account)		
3. No entry because no transaction has occurred		

Related exercise material: 3-3 and 3-7.

THE NAVIGATOR

THE LEDGER

STUDY OBJECTIVE 5

Explain what a ledger is and how it helps in the recording process.

The entire group of accounts maintained by a company is called the **ledger**. The ledger keeps in one place all the information about changes in specific account balances.

Companies may use various kinds of ledgers, but every company has a general ledger. A **general ledger** contains all the assets, liabilities, and stockholders' equity accounts, as shown in Illustration 3-16.

Illustration 3-16

The general ledger

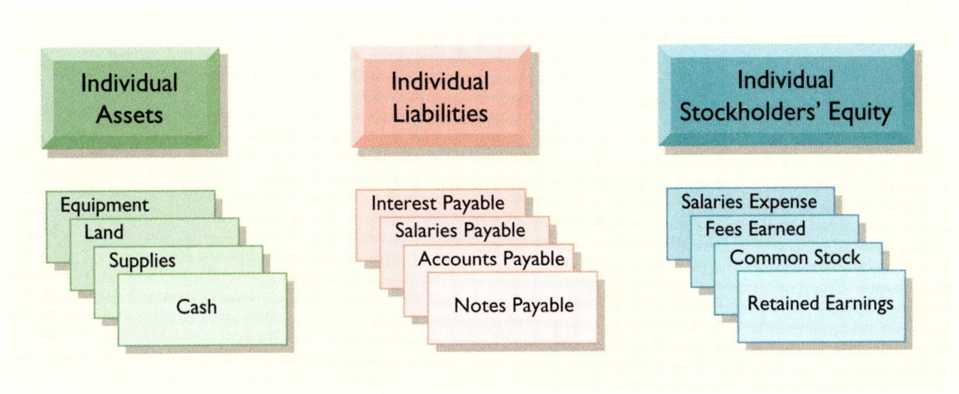

A business can use a looseleaf binder or card file for the ledger. Each account is kept on a separate sheet or card. Whenever the term *ledger* is used in this textbook without a modifying adjective, it means the general ledger.

The ledger should be arranged in the order in which accounts are presented in the financial statements, beginning with the balance sheet accounts. First in order are the asset accounts, followed by liability accounts, stockholders' equity accounts, revenues, and expenses. Each account is numbered for easier identification.

The ledger provides management with the balances in various accounts. For example, the Cash account shows the amount of cash that is available to meet current obligations. Amounts due from customers can be found by examining Accounts Receivable, and amounts owed to creditors can be found by examining Accounts Payable.

ACCOUNTING IN ACTION *Business Insight*

In his autobiography Sam Walton described the double-entry accounting system he began the **Wal-Mart** empire with: "We kept a little pigeonhole on the wall for the cash receipts and paperwork of each [Wal-Mart] store. I had a blue binder ledger book for each store. When we added a store, we added a pigeonhole. We did this at least up to twenty stores. Then once a month, the bookkeeper and I would enter the merchandise, enter the sales, enter the cash, and balance it."

SOURCE: Sam Walton, *Made in America* (New York: Doubleday, 1992), p. 53.

Standard Form of Account

The simple T-account form used in accounting textbooks is often useful for illustration purposes. However, in practice, the account forms used in ledgers are much more structured. A widely used form is shown in Illustration 3-17, using assumed data from a cash account.

Illustration 3-17

Three-column form of account

CASH					No. 101
Date	**Explanation**	**Ref.**	**Debit**	**Credit**	**Balance**
2004					
June 1			25,000		25,000
2				8,000	17,000
3			4,200		21,200
9			7,500		28,700
17				11,700	17,000
20				250	16,750
30				7,300	9,450

This form is often called the **three-column form of account** because it has three money columns—debit, credit, and balance. The balance in the account is determined after each transaction. Note that the explanation space and reference columns are used to provide special information about the transaction.

Posting

STUDY OBJECTIVE 6

Explain what posting is and how it helps in the recording process.

The procedure of transferring journal entries to the ledger accounts is called **posting**. Posting involves the following steps.

1. In the ledger, enter in the appropriate columns of the account(s) debited the date, journal page, and debit amount shown in the journal.
2. In the reference column of the journal, write the account number to which the debit amount was posted.
3. In the ledger, enter in the appropriate columns of the account(s) credited the date, journal page, and credit amount shown in the journal.
4. In the reference column of the journal, write the account number to which the credit amount was posted.

These four steps are diagrammed in Illustration 3-18 using the first journal entry of Best Caterers, Inc. The boxed numbers indicate the sequence of the steps.

Illustration 3-18

Posting a journal entry

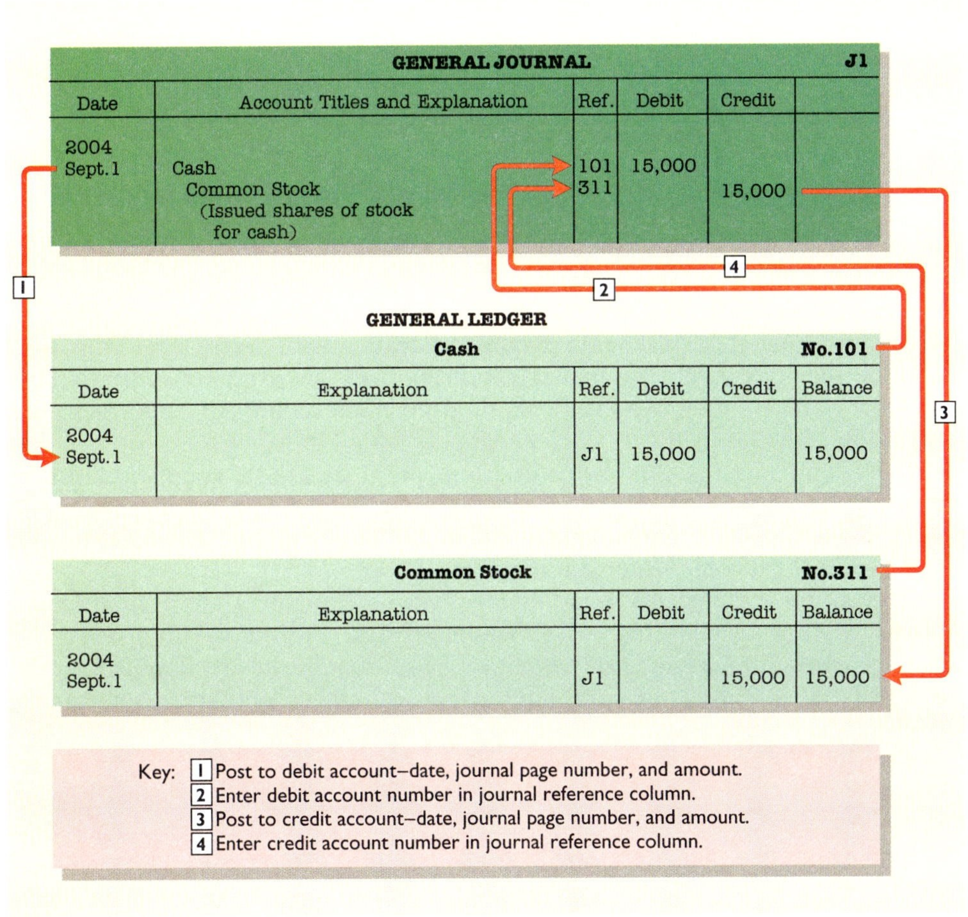

Posting should be performed in chronological order. That is, all the debits and credits of one journal entry should be posted before proceeding to the next journal entry. Postings should be made on a timely basis to ensure that the ledger is up to date.[3]

HELPFUL HINT

How can one tell whether all postings have been completed? Answer: Scan the reference column of the journal to see whether there are any blanks opposite account titles. If there are no blanks, all postings have been made.

[3] In homework problems, it will be permissible to journalize all transactions before posting any of the journal entries.

The reference column *in the journal* serves several purposes. The numbers in this column indicate the entries that have been posted. After the last entry has been posted, this column should be scanned to see that all postings have been made.

The reference column *of a ledger account* indicates the journal page from which the transaction was posted. The explanation space of the ledger account is used infrequently because an explanation already appears in the journal. It generally is used only when detailed analysis of account activity is required.

TECHNOLOGY IN ACTION

Determining what to record is the most critical (and for most businesses the most expensive) point in the accounting process. In computerized systems, after this phase is completed, the input and all further processing just boil down to merging files and generating reports. Programmers and management information system types with good accounting backgrounds (such as they should gain from a good principles textbook) are better able to develop effective computerized systems.

Chart of Accounts

The number and type of accounts used differ for each enterprise. The number of accounts depends on the amount of detail desired by management. For example, the management of one company may want one account for all types of utility expense. Another may keep separate expense accounts for each type of utility, such as gas, electricity, and water. Similarly, a small corporation like Best Caterers, Inc. will have fewer accounts than a corporate giant like **General Mills**. Best Caterers, Inc. may be able to manage and report its activities in twenty to thirty accounts, while **General Mills** requires thousands of accounts to keep track of its worldwide activities.

Most companies have a **chart of accounts** that lists the accounts and the account numbers that identify their location in the ledger. The numbering system used to identify the accounts usually starts with the balance sheet accounts and follows with the income statement accounts.

In this and the next two chapters, we will be explaining the accounting for Premier Staffing Agency Inc. (a service enterprise). Accounts 101–199 indicate asset accounts; 200–299 indicate liabilities; 300–350 indicate stockholders' equity accounts; 400–499, revenues; 601–799, expenses; 800–899, other revenues; and 900–999, other expenses.

The chart of accounts for Premier Staffing Agency Inc. is shown in Illustration 3-19. Accounts shown in red are used in this chapter; accounts shown in black are explained in later chapters.

You will notice that there are gaps in the numbering system of the chart of accounts for Premier Staffing Agency Inc. Gaps are left to permit the insertion of new accounts as needed during the life of the business.

Illustration 3-19

Chart of accounts for Premier Staffing Agency Inc.

CHART OF ACCOUNTS
Premier Staffing Agency Inc.

Assets	Stockholders' Equity
101 Cash	**311 Common Stock**
112 Accounts Receivable	320 Retained Earnings
129 Supplies	**332 Dividends**
130 Prepaid Insurance	350 Income Summary
157 Office Equipment	
158 Accumulated Depreciation—Office Equipment	**Revenues**
	400 Service Revenue
Liabilities	**Expenses**
200 Notes Payable	611 Advertising Supplies Expense
201 Accounts Payable	711 Depreciation Expense
209 Unearned Revenue	722 Insurance Expense
212 Salaries Payable	**726 Salaries Expense**
230 Interest Payable	**729 Rent Expense**
	905 Interest Expense

THE RECORDING PROCESS ILLUSTRATED

Illustrations 3-20 through 3-29 show the basic steps in the recording process, using the October transactions of the Premier Staffing Agency Inc. Its accounting period is a month. A basic analysis and a debit–credit analysis precede the journalizing and posting of each transaction. For simplicity, the T-account form is used in the illustrations instead of the standard account form.

Study the transaction analyses in Illustrations 3-20 through 3-29 carefully. **The purpose of transaction analysis is first to identify the type of account involved, and then to determine whether a debit or a credit to the account is required.** You should always perform this type of analysis before preparing a journal entry. Doing so will help you understand the journal entries discussed in this chapter as well as more complex journal entries to be described in later chapters.

Keep in mind that every journal entry affects one or more of the following items: assets, liabilities, stockholders' equity, revenues, or expenses. By becoming skilled at transaction analysis, you will be able to recognize quickly the impact of any transaction on these five items.

Illustration 3-20

Investment of cash by stockholders

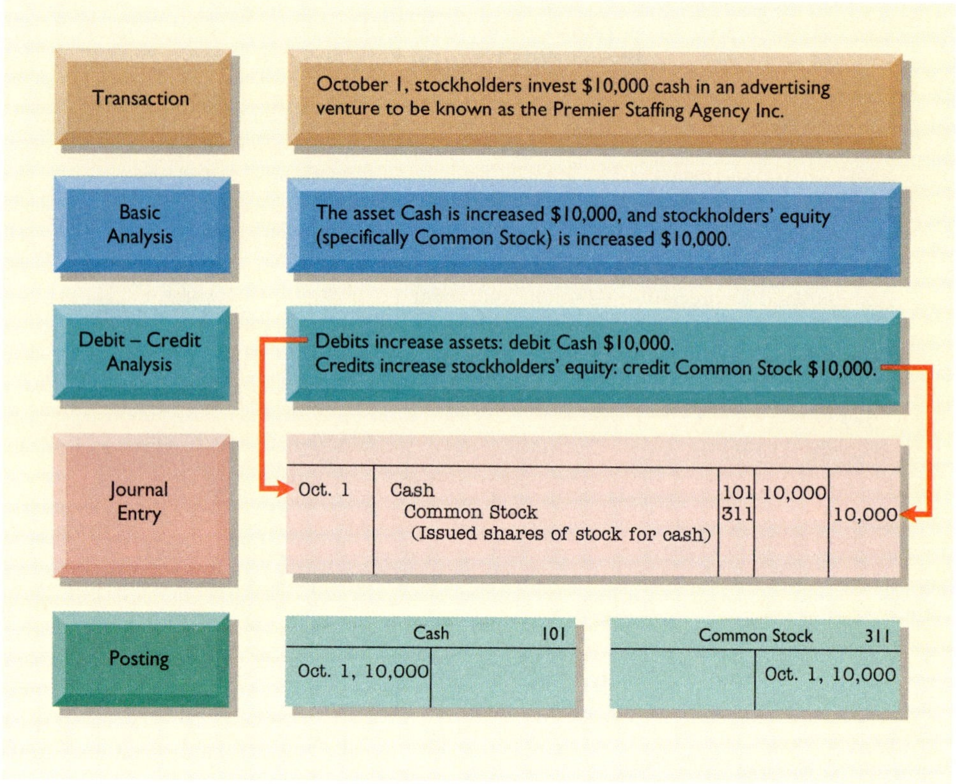

HELPFUL HINT

To correctly record a transaction, you must carefully analyze the event and translate that analysis into debit and credit language.
First: Determine what type of account is involved.
Second: Determine what items increased or decreased and by how much.
Third: Translate the increases and decreases into debits and credits.

Illustration 3-21

Purchase of office equipment

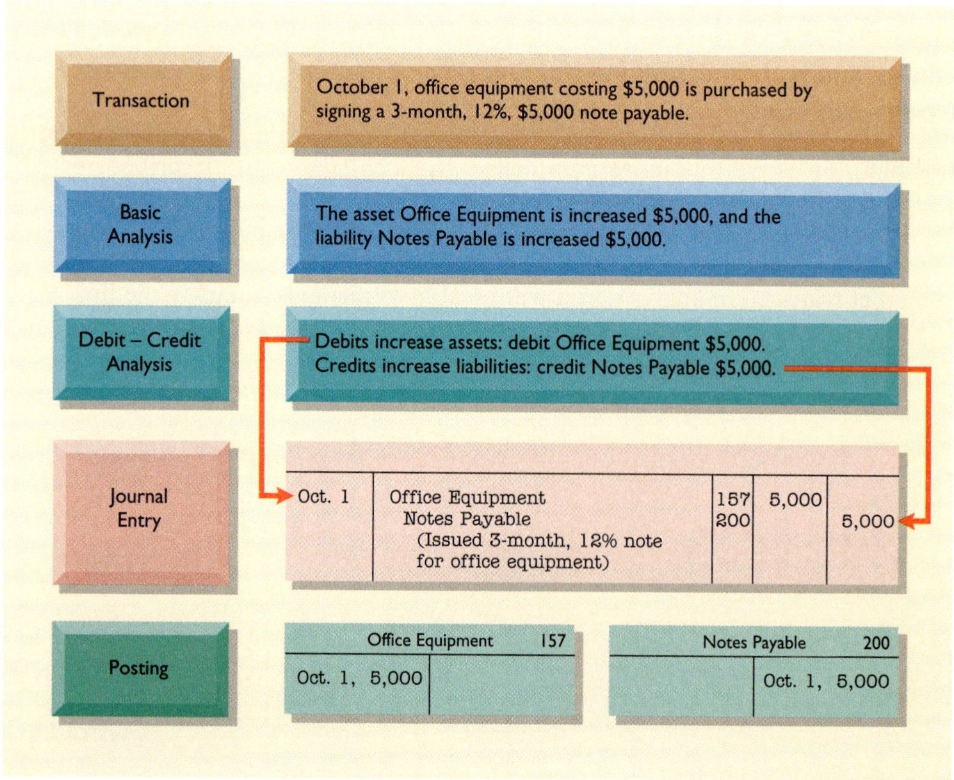

Illustration 3-22

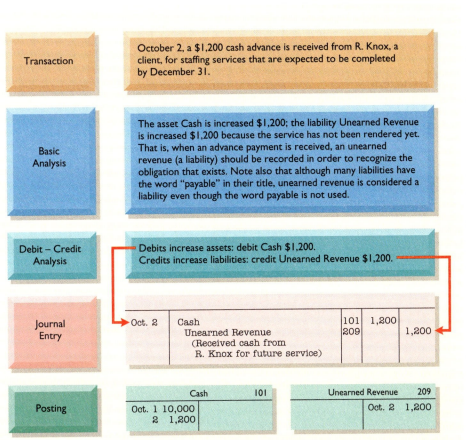

Receipt of cash for future service

Transaction

October 2, a $1,200 cash advance is received from R. Knox, a client, for staffing services that are expected to be completed by December 31.

Basic Analysis

The asset Cash is increased $1,200; the liability Unearned Revenue is increased $1,200 because the service has not been rendered yet. That is, when an advance payment is received, an unearned revenue (a liability) should be recorded in order to recognize the obligation that exists. Note also that although many liabilities have the word "payable" in their title, unearned revenue is considered a liability even though the word payable is not used.

Debit – Credit Analysis

Debits increase assets: debit Cash $1,200.
Credits increase liabilities: credit Unearned Revenue $1,200.

Journal Entry

Oct. 2	Cash	101	1,200	
	Unearned Revenue	209		1,200
	(Received cash from R. Knox for future service)			

Posting

Cash		101
Oct. 1	10,000	
2	1,200	

Unearned Revenue		209
	Oct. 2	1,200

HELPFUL HINT

When the revenue is earned, the Unearned Revenue account is debited (decreased), and a revenue account is credited (increased).

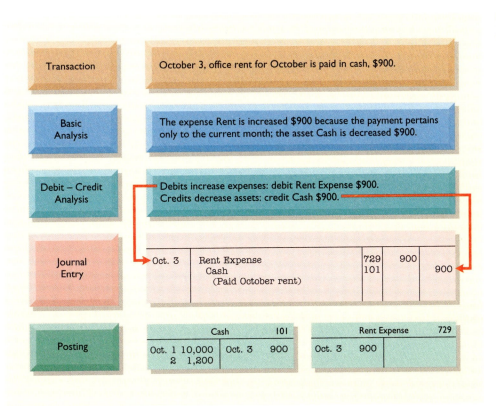

Illustration 3-23

Payment of monthly rent

Transaction

October 3, office rent for October is paid in cash, $900.

Basic Analysis

The expense Rent is increased $900 because the payment pertains only to the current month; the asset Cash is decreased $900.

Debit – Credit Analysis

Debits increase expenses: debit Rent Expense $900.
Credits decrease assets: credit Cash $900.

Journal Entry

Oct. 3	Rent Expense	729	900	
	Cash	101		900
	(Paid October rent)			

Posting

Cash			101
Oct. 1	10,000	Oct. 3	900
2	1,200		

Rent Expense		729
Oct. 3	900	

Illustration 3-24

Payment for insurance

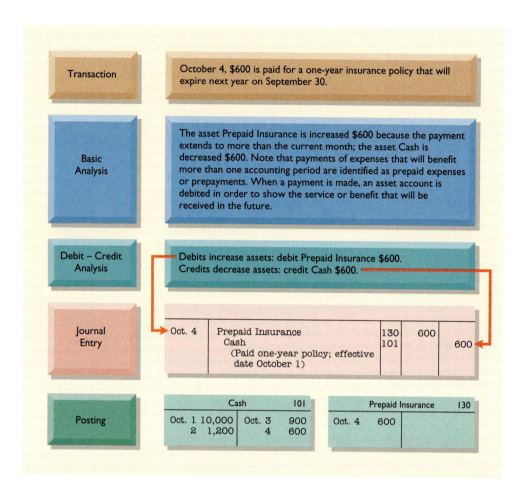

Transaction

October 4, $600 is paid for a one-year insurance policy that will expire next year on September 30.

Basic Analysis

The asset Prepaid Insurance is increased $600 because the payment extends to more than the current month; the asset Cash is decreased $600. Note that payments of expenses that will benefit more than one accounting period are identified as prepaid expenses or prepayments. When a payment is made, an asset account is debited in order to show the service or benefit that will be received in the future.

Debit – Credit Analysis

Debits increase assets: debit Prepaid Insurance $600.
Credits decrease assets: credit Cash $600.

Journal Entry

Oct. 4	Prepaid Insurance	130	600	
	Cash	101		600
	(Paid one-year policy; effective date October 1)			

Posting

Cash			101
Oct. 1	10,000	Oct. 3	900
2	1,200	4	600

Prepaid Insurance			130
Oct. 4	600		

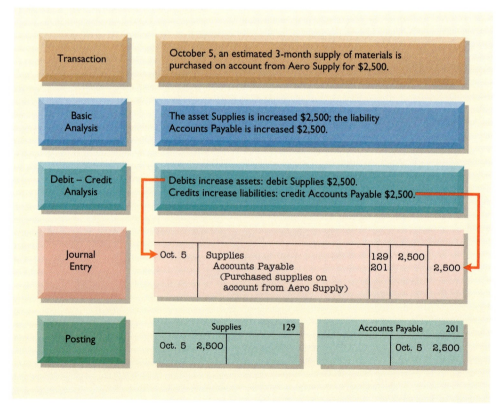

Illustration 3-25

Purchase of supplies on credit

Transaction

October 5, an estimated 3-month supply of materials is purchased on account from Aero Supply for $2,500.

Basic Analysis

The asset Supplies is increased $2,500; the liability Accounts Payable is increased $2,500.

Debit – Credit Analysis

Debits increase assets: debit Supplies $2,500.
Credits increase liabilities: credit Accounts Payable $2,500.

Journal Entry

Oct. 5	Supplies	129	2,500	
	Accounts Payable	201		2,500
	(Purchased supplies on account from Aero Supply)			

Posting

Supplies			129
Oct. 5	2,500		

Accounts Payable			201
		Oct. 5	2,500

Illustration 3-26

Hiring of employees

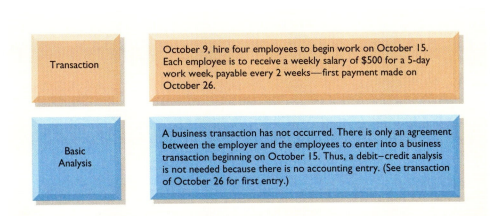

Transaction	October 9, hire four employees to begin work on October 15. Each employee is to receive a weekly salary of $500 for a 5-day work week, payable every 2 weeks—first payment made on October 26.
Basic Analysis	A business transaction has not occurred. There is only an agreement between the employer and the employees to enter into a business transaction beginning on October 15. Thus, a debit–credit analysis is not needed because there is no accounting entry. (See transaction of October 26 for first entry.)

Illustration 3-27

Declaration and payment of dividend by corporation

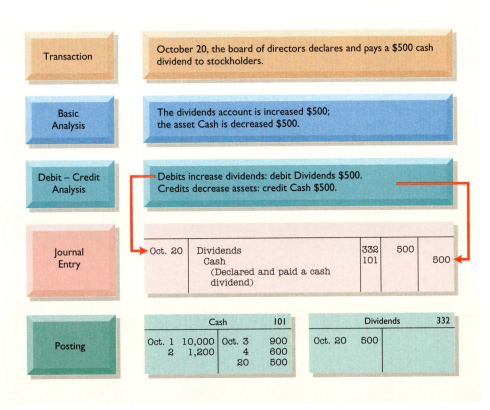

Transaction	October 20, the board of directors declares and pays a $500 cash dividend to stockholders.
Basic Analysis	The dividends account is increased $500; the asset Cash is decreased $500.
Debit – Credit Analysis	Debits increase dividends: debit Dividends $500. Credits decrease assets: credit Cash $500.

Journal Entry

Oct. 20	Dividends	332	500	
	Cash	101		500
	(Declared and paid a cash dividend)			

Posting

Cash			101
Oct. 1	10,000	Oct. 3	900
2	1,200	4	600
		20	500

Dividends			332
Oct. 20	500		

Illustration 3-28

Payment of salaries

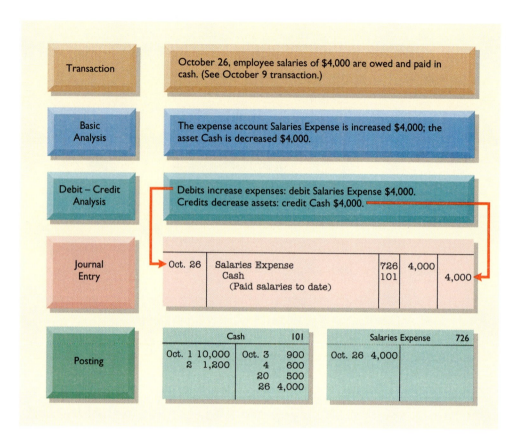

Transaction: October 26, employee salaries of $4,000 are owed and paid in cash. (See October 9 transaction.)

Basic Analysis: The expense account Salaries Expense is increased $4,000; the asset Cash is decreased $4,000.

Debit – Credit Analysis: Debits increase expenses: debit Salaries Expense $4,000. Credits decrease assets: credit Cash $4,000.

Journal Entry

Oct. 26	Salaries Expense	726	4,000	
	Cash	101		4,000
	(Paid salaries to date)			

Posting

Cash			101
Oct. 1	10,000	Oct. 3	900
2	1,200	4	600
		20	500
		26	4,000

Salaries Expense			726
Oct. 26	4,000		

Illustration 3-29

Receipt of cash for services provided

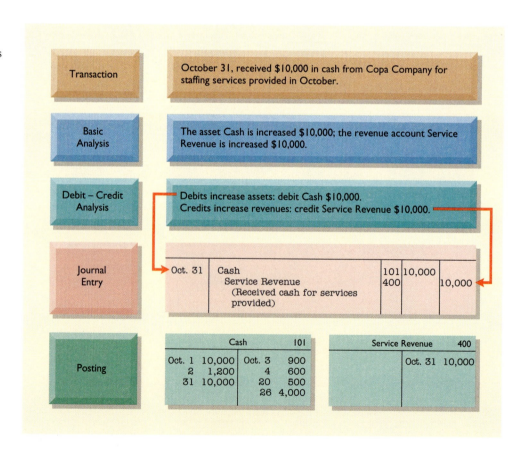

Transaction: October 31, received $10,000 in cash from Copa Company for staffing services provided in October.

Basic Analysis: The asset Cash is increased $10,000; the revenue account Service Revenue is increased $10,000.

Debit – Credit Analysis: Debits increase assets: debit Cash $10,000. Credits increase revenues: credit Service Revenue $10,000.

Journal Entry

Oct. 31	Cash	101	10,000	
	Service Revenue	400		10,000
	(Received cash for services provided)			

Posting

Cash			101
Oct. 1	10,000	Oct. 3	900
2	1,200	4	600
31	10,000	20	500
		26	4,000

Service Revenue			400
		Oct. 31	10,000

ACCOUNTING IN ACTION *e* Business Insight

E-business is having a tremendous impact on how companies share information within the company, and with people outside the company, such as suppliers, creditors, and investors. A new type of software, Extensible Markup Language (XML), is enabling the creation of a universal way to exchange data.

An organization called XBRL.org is using XML to develop an internally accepted framework called the Extensible Business Reporting Language (XBRL). The organization comprises representatives from industry, accounting firms, investment houses, bankers, regulators, and others. The goal of this organization is to establish a framework that "the global business information supply chain will use to create, exchange, and analyze financial reporting information including, but not limited to, regulatory filings such as annual and quarterly financial statements, general ledger information, and audit schedules."

SOURCE: www.XBRL.org.

The journal for Premier Staffing Agency Inc. for October is shown in Illustration 3-30. The ledger is shown in Illustration 3-31, on page 96, with all balances in color.

Illustration 3-30

General journal entries

GENERAL JOURNAL — **PAGE J1**

Date	Account Titles and Explanation	Ref.	Debit	Credit
2004				
Oct. 1	Cash	101	10,000	
	Common Stock	311		10,000
	(Issued shares of stock for cash)			
1	Office Equipment	157	5,000	
	Notes Payable	200		5,000
	(Issued 3-month, 12% note for office equipment)			
2	Cash	101	1,200	
	Unearned Revenue	209		1,200
	(Received cash from R. Knox for future services)			
3	Rent Expense	729	900	
	Cash	101		900
	(Paid October rent)			
4	Prepaid Insurance	130	600	
	Cash	101		600
	(Paid one-year policy; effective date October 1)			
5	Supplies	129	2,500	
	Accounts Payable	201		2,500
	(Purchased supplies on account from Aero Supply)			

Illustration 3-30
Continued

GENERAL JOURNAL **PAGE J1**

Date	Account Titles and Explanation	Ref.	Debit	Credit
20	Dividends	332	500	
	Cash	101		500
	(Declared and paid a cash dividend)			
26	Salaries Expense	726	4,000	
	Cash	101		4,000
	(Paid salaries to date)			
31	Cash	101	10,000	
	Service Revenue	400		10,000
	(Received cash for services provided)			

Illustration 3-31
General ledger

GENERAL LEDGER

Cash No. 101

Date	Explanation	Ref.	Debit	Credit	Balance
2004					
Oct. 1		J1	10,000		10,000
2		J1	1,200		11,200
3		J1		900	10,300
4		J1		600	9,700
20		J1		500	9,200
26		J1		4,000	5,200
31		J1	10,000		15,200

Supplies No. 129

Date	Explanation	Ref.	Debit	Credit	Balance
2004					
Oct. 5		J1	2,500		2,500

Prepaid Insurance No. 130

Date	Explanation	Ref.	Debit	Credit	Balance
2004					
Oct. 4		J1	600		600

Office Equipment No. 157

Date	Explanation	Ref.	Debit	Credit	Balance
2004					
Oct. 1		J1	5,000		5,000

Notes Payable No. 200

Date	Explanation	Ref.	Debit	Credit	Balance
2004					
Oct. 1		J1		5,000	5,000

Accounts Payable No. 201

Date	Explanation	Ref.	Debit	Credit	Balance
2004					
Oct. 5		J1		2,500	2,500

Unearned Revenue No. 209

Date	Explanation	Ref.	Debit	Credit	Balance
2004					
Oct. 2		J1		1,200	1,200

Common Stock No. 311

Date	Explanation	Ref.	Debit	Credit	Balance
2004					
Oct. 1		J1		10,000	10,000

Dividends No. 332

Date	Explanation	Ref.	Debit	Credit	Balance
2004					
Oct. 20		J1	500		500

Service Revenue No. 400

Date	Explanation	Ref.	Debit	Credit	Balance
2004					
Oct. 31		J1		10,000	10,000

Salaries Expense No. 726

Date	Explanation	Ref.	Debit	Credit	Balance
2004					
Oct. 26		J1	4,000		4,000

Rent Expense No. 729

Date	Explanation	Ref.	Debit	Credit	Balance
2004					
Oct. 3		J1	900		900

BEFORE YOU GO ON...

REVIEW IT

1. How does journalizing differ from posting?
2. What is the purpose of (a) the ledger and (b) a chart of accounts?

DO IT

Raisin Buns, Inc. recorded the following transactions in a general journal during the month of March.

Cash	2,280	
Service Revenue		2,280
Wages Expense	400	
Cash		400
Utilities Expense	92	
Cash		92

Post these entries to the Cash account of the general ledger to determine the ending balance in cash. The beginning balance in cash on March 1 was $600.

ACTION PLAN

- Recall that posting involves transferring the journalized debits and credits to specific accounts in the ledger.
- Determine the ending balance by netting the total debits and credits.

SOLUTION

Cash

3/1	600	400
	2,280	92
3/31 Bal.	2,388	

Related exercise material: 3-4 and 3-6.

THE NAVIGATOR

THE TRIAL BALANCE

STUDY OBJECTIVE 7

Prepare a trial balance and explain its purposes.

A **trial balance** is a list of accounts and their balances at a given time. Customarily, a trial balance is prepared at the end of an accounting period. The accounts are listed in the order in which they appear in the ledger; debit balances are listed in the left column and credit balances in the right column.

The primary purpose of a trial balance is to prove (check) that the debits equal the credits after posting. In other words, the sum of the debit account balances in the trial balance should equal the sum of the credit account balances. **If the debits and credits do not agree, the trial balance can be used to uncover errors in journalizing and posting. In addition, it is useful in the preparation of financial statements,** as will be explained in the next two chapters.

There are three steps for preparing a trial balance:

1. List the account titles and their balances.
2. Total the debit and credit columns.
3. Prove the equality of the two columns.

The trial balance prepared from Premier Staffing's ledger is shown in Illustration 3-32.

Illustration 3-32

A trial balance

PREMIER STAFFING AGENCY INC.
Trial Balance
October 31, 2004

	Debit	Credit
Cash	$15,200	
Supplies	2,500	
Prepaid Insurance	600	
Office Equipment	5,000	
Notes Payable		$ 5,000
Accounts Payable		2,500
Unearned Revenue		1,200
Common Stock		10,000
Dividends	500	
Service Revenue		10,000
Salaries Expense	4,000	
Rent Expense	900	
	$28,700	**$28,700**

HELPFUL HINT
To sum a column of figures is sometimes referred to as *to foot* the column. The column is then said to be *footed.*

HELPFUL HINT
A trial balance is so named because it is a test to see if the sum of the debit balances equals the sum of the credit balances.

Note that the total debits ($28,700) equal the total credits ($28,700). Account numbers are sometimes shown to the left of the account titles in the trial balance.

A trial balance is a necessary checkpoint for uncovering certain types of errors before you proceed to other steps in the accounting process. For example, if only the debit portion of a journal entry has been posted, the trial balance would bring this error to light.

LIMITATIONS OF A TRIAL BALANCE

A trial balance does not guarantee freedom from recording errors, however. **It does not prove that all transactions have been recorded or that the ledger is correct.** Numerous errors may exist even though the trial balance columns agree. For example, the trial balance may balance even when (1) a transaction is not journalized, (2) a correct journal entry is not posted, (3) a journal entry is posted twice, (4) incorrect accounts are used in journalizing or posting, or (5) offsetting errors are made in recording the amount of a transaction. In other words, as long as equal debits and credits are posted, even to the wrong account or in the wrong amount, the total debits will equal the total credits.

ETHICS NOTE
Auditors are required to differentiate *errors* from *irregularities* when evaluating the accounting system. An error is the result of an unintentional mistake; as such, it is neither ethical nor unethical. An irregularity, on the other hand, is an intentional misstatement, which is viewed as unethical.

LOCATING ERRORS

The procedure for preparing a trial balance is relatively simple. However, if the trial balance does not balance, locating an error in a manual system can be time consuming, tedious, and frustrating. Errors generally result from mathematical mistakes, incorrect postings, or simply transcribing data incorrectly.

What do you do if you are faced with a trial balance that does not balance? First determine the amount of the difference between the two columns of the trial balance. After this amount is known, the following steps are often helpful:

1. If the error is $1, $10, $100, or $1,000, re-add the trial balance columns and recompute the account balances.
2. If the error is divisible by 2, scan the trial balance to see whether a balance equal to half the error has been entered in the wrong column.
3. If the error is divisible by 9, retrace the account balances on the trial balance to see whether they are incorrectly copied from the ledger. For example, if a balance was $12 and it was listed as $21, a $9 error has been made. Reversing the order of numbers is called a transposition error.

4. If the error is not divisible by 2 or 9 (for example, $365), scan the ledger to see whether an account balance of $365 has been omitted from the trial balance, and scan the journal to see whether a $365 posting has been omitted.

TECHNOLOGY IN ACTION

In a computerized system, the trial balance is often only one column (no debit or credit columns), and the accounts have plus and minus signs associated with them. The final balance therefore is zero. Any errors that develop in a computerized system will undoubtedly involve the initial recording rather than some error in the posting or preparation of a trial balance.

USE OF DOLLAR SIGNS

Note that dollar signs do not appear in the journals or ledgers. Dollar signs are usually used only in the trial balance and the financial statements. Generally, a dollar sign is shown only for the first item in the column and for the total of that column. A single line is placed under the column of figures to be added or subtracted; the total amount is double underlined to indicate the final sum.

HELPFUL HINT
We have avoided the use of cents in the text to save you time and effort.

BEFORE YOU GO ON...

REVIEW IT

1. What is a trial balance and what is its primary purpose?
2. How is a trial balance prepared?
3. What are the limitations of a trial balance?

ELECTRONIC DATA PROCESSING

In accounting offices, calculators, eighteen-column pads, and tapes have moved aside for spreadsheet programs and software applications. In a theme park restaurant, cash registers gave way to point-of-sales systems, which total sales figures and produce managerial reports. In a hotel, the manual folio system was replaced by property management system, and many night audit functions are now performed during the business day. The use of the Internet brings yet another dimension to the hospitality industry.

COMPARATIVE ADVANTAGES OF MANUAL VERSUS COMPUTERIZED SYSTEMS

Are computerized systems better? Well, it depends. With regard to speed, the computerized system wins. In today's business world there is a need to act daily, not monthly, making speed and efficiency the name of the game. However, in accounting there is a need for both the manual and computerized system.

Comprehension and Usage

To really understand accounting and use it effectively, you need to learn it manually first. You need to know the steps involved in the accounting cycle—accounts, types, normal balances, and debits and credits—before determining if an event is a business transaction. Only then do you begin the recording process. First come the journal and the ledger, then the trial balance, and later the adjustments. With a good knowledge of the ins and outs of a manual system, if you make a mistake somewhere, it is quite easy to backtrack and make corrections. If you only know how to enter numbers to input data and do not know why and how the numbers are being compiled, a $10 mistake can easily be compounded into a $200 mistake on the books.

Speed and Efficiency

A computerized system obviously has the advantage over the manual system in this regard. A touch of a few buttons and a short amount of time are all that is needed to generate reports that otherwise take hours. When you enter a debit and a credit into an accounting software, the balances are posted directly into the appropriate accounts in the general ledger. The data are then added and subtracted and a new balance is calculated. This balance is automatically transferred to the correct line item on a trial balance. This all happens in a matter of seconds.

Accuracy

Humans do make errors. If a computer system is programmed correctly, there should not be any errors in the output. The time needed to detect and correct errors can be saved if the system is in full operation. However, if a human error occurs in data entry, the results will still be incorrect.

Timeliness of Information

One advantage of a computerized system is having updated information at your fingertips. As soon as data are entered, the new and updated information is available. Once raw data are gathered, analyzing them is a matter of programming in spreadsheet formulas. A lot of time is saved and information, therefore, is timely. No longer will a manager have to wait two weeks after a month-end closing to find out how much profit and loss were realized in the past month.

A LOOK INTO THE FUTURE

Computerization and technology hold vast potential for the hospitality industry. Personal computers are more efficient than ever, and personal data assistants are part of a businessperson's wardrobe. Touch screens now replace bulky point-of-sales systems in foodservice outlets. Handheld ordering devices for servers are here already. Billing and invoices for a group's hotel stay can be sent via e-mail directly from the property management system. **Application solutions providers (ASPs)** are the fastest growing segment of the technology industry. These firms are targeting the club industry as they provide all technical system components at a secure remote site. Thus, club managers can concentrate their time on membership and operations issues while qualified personnel monitor the technology. Club managers no longer need to worry about shopping for systems, training, hardware and software installation, incremental upgrades, connectivity, and access issues. ASPs are also looking into the hotel industry. Some companies, such as **Meristar Hotels and Resorts**, are their own ASP, providing the remote control and data storing and crunching functions for their general managers.

Technology also touches the restaurant industry. In 1996, **Long John Silver's** revamped its accounting procedures to use computerization in all general ledger, accounts payable and receivable, asset management, store-level reporting, and activity management. Small chain restaurants such as **Pasta Pomodoro** in San Francisco have begun using the Internet for purchasing and business analysis. Let's face it, technology and accounting data go hand in hand.

A LOOK BACK AT OUR FEATURE STORY

Refer back to the Feature Story about **The Mug and Musket** at the beginning of the chapter, and answer the following questions.

1. What accounting entries would Tanis likely make to record (a) the receipt of cash from a customer in payment of their bill, (b) payment of a utility bill, and (c) payment of wages for the waiters?
2. How did Tanis's job as Director of Finance help in her studies as she finished her business administration degree?

SOLUTION

1. Tanis would likely make the following entries.

   (a) Cash
   Food Sales Revenue
   (Receipt of payment for foodservices)

   (b) Utility Expense
   Cash
   (Payment of electric bill)

   (c) Salaries (or Wages) Expense
   Cash
   (Paid waiters' wages)

2. As a result of her accounting position, Tanis was able to relate the subject matter as well as much of the assignment material in her business courses to a real-world context. From her job, she knew how bills were paid, how supplies were determined, and how employees were hired, managed, evaluated, and paid.

THE NAVIGATOR

DEMONSTRATION PROBLEM

Bob Sample and other student investors opened the Campus Laundromat Inc. on September 1, 2004. During the first month of operations the following transactions occurred.

Sept.	1	Stockholders invested $20,000 cash in the business.
	2	Paid $1,000 cash for store rent for the month of September.
	3	Purchased washers and dryers for $25,000, paying $10,000 in cash and signing a $15,000, 6-month, 12% note payable.
	4	Paid $1,200 for one-year accident insurance policy.
	10	Received bill from the *Daily News* for advertising the opening of the laundromat $200.
	20	Declared and paid a cash dividend to stockholders $700.
	30	Determined that cash receipts for laundry fees for the month were $6,200.

The chart of accounts for the company is the same as for Premier Staffing Agency Inc. except for the following: No. 154 Laundry Equipment and No. 610 Advertising Expense.

Instructions

(a) Journalize the September transactions. (Use J1 for the journal page number.)

(b) Open ledger accounts and post the September transactions.

(c) Prepare a trial balance at September 30, 2004.

ACTION PLAN

- Make separate journal entries for each transaction.
- In journalizing, make sure debits equal credits.
- In journalizing, use specific account titles taken from the chart of accounts.
- Provide appropriate description of journal entry.
- Arrange ledger in statement order, beginning with the balance sheet accounts.
- Post in chronological order.
- Use numbers in the reference column to indicate the amount has been posted.
- In the trial balance, list accounts in the order in which they appear in the ledger.
- List debit balances in the left column, and credit balances in the right column.

SOLUTION TO DEMONSTRATION PROBLEM

(a) **GENERAL JOURNAL** **J1**

Date	Account Titles and Explanation	Ref.	Debit	Credit
2004				
Sept. 1	Cash	101	20,000	
	Common Stock	311		20,000
	(Stockholders invested cash in business)			
2	Rent Expense	729	1,000	
	Cash	101		1,000
	(Paid September rent)			
3	Laundry Equipment	154	25,000	
	Cash	101		10,000
	Notes Payable	200		15,000
	(Purchased laundry equipment for cash and 6-month, 12% note payable)			
4	Prepaid Insurance	130	1,200	
	Cash	101		1,200
	(Paid one-year insurance policy)			
10	Advertising Expense	610	200	
	Accounts Payable	201		200
	(Received bill from *Daily News* for advertising)			
20	Dividends	332	700	
	Cash	101		700
	(Declared and paid a cash dividend)			
30	Cash	101	6,200	
	Service Revenue	400		6,200
	(Received cash for laundry fees earned)			

(b) **GENERAL LEDGER**

Cash **No. 101**

Date	Explanation	Ref.	Debit	Credit	Balance
2004					
Sept. 1		J1	20,000		20,000
2		J1		1,000	19,000
3		J1		10,000	9,000
4		J1		1,200	7,800
20		J1		700	7,100
30		J1	6,200		13,300

Prepaid Insurance **No. 130**

Date	Explanation	Ref.	Debit	Credit	Balance
2004					
Sept. 4		J1	1,200		1,200

Laundry Equipment **No. 154**

Date	Explanation	Ref.	Debit	Credit	Balance
2004					
Sept. 3		J1	25,000		25,000

Notes Payable **No. 200**

Date	Explanation	Ref.	Debit	Credit	Balance
2004					
Sept. 3		J1		15,000	15,000

Accounts Payable **No. 201**

Date	Explanation	Ref.	Debit	Credit	Balance
2004					
Sept. 10		J1		200	200

Accounts Payable **No. 201**

Date	Explanation	Ref.	Debit	Credit	Balance
2004					
Sept. 10		J1		200	200

Common Stock **No. 311**

Date	Explanation	Ref.	Debit	Credit	Balance
2004					
Sept. 1		J1		20,000	20,000

Dividends **No. 332**

Date	Explanation	Ref.	Debit	Credit	Balance
2004					
Sept. 1		J1	700		700

Service Revenue **No. 400**

Date	Explanation	Ref.	Debit	Credit	Balance
2004					
Sept. 30		J1		6,200	6,200

Advertising Expense **No. 610**

Date	Explanation	Ref.	Debit	Credit	Balance
2004					
Sept. 10		J1	200		200

Rent Expense **No. 729**

Date	Explanation	Ref.	Debit	Credit	Balance
2004					
Sept. 2		J1	1,000		1,000

(c)

CAMPUS LAUNDROMAT INC.
Trial Balance
September 30, 2004

	Debit	Credit
Cash	$13,300	
Prepaid Insurance	1,200	
Laundry Equipment	25,000	
Notes Payable		$15,000
Accounts Payable		200
Common Stock		20,000
Dividends	700	
Service Revenue		6,200
Advertising Expense	200	
Rent Expense	1,000	
	$41,400	$41,400

THE NAVIGATOR

SUMMARY OF STUDY OBJECTIVES

1. ***Explain what an account is and how it helps in the recording process.*** An account is a record of increases and decreases in specific asset, liability, and stockholders' equity items.

2. ***Define debits and credits and explain how they are used to record business transactions.*** The terms debit and credit are synonymous with left and right. Assets, dividends, and expenses are increased by debits and decreased by credits. Liabilities, common stock, retained earnings, and revenues are increased by credits and decreased by debits.

3. ***Identify the basic steps in the recording process.*** The basic steps in the recording process are (a) analyze each transaction in terms of its effects on the accounts, (b) enter the transaction information in a journal, (c) transfer the journal information to the appropriate accounts in the ledger.

4. ***Explain what a journal is and how it helps in the recording process.*** The initial accounting record of a transaction is entered in a journal before the data are entered in the accounts. A journal (a) discloses in one place the complete effects of a transaction, (b) provides a chronological record of transactions, and (c) prevents or locates errors because the debit and credit amounts for each entry can be readily compared.

5. ***Explain what a ledger is and how it helps in the recording process.*** The entire group of accounts maintained by a company is referred to as the ledger. The ledger keeps in one place all the information about changes in specific account balances.

6. ***Explain what posting is and how it helps in the recording process.*** Posting is the procedure of transferring journal entries to the ledger accounts. This phase of the recording process accumulates the effects of journalized transactions in the individual accounts.

7. ***Prepare a trial balance and explain its purposes.*** A trial balance is a list of accounts and their balances at a given time. Its primary purpose is to prove the equality of debits and credits after posting. A trial balance also uncovers errors in journalizing and posting and is useful in preparing financial statements.

8. ***Identify the advantages of both the manual and computerized accounting systems.*** A manual accounting system is advantageous when one is learning accounting. Learning the system manually provides users with a better comprehension of accounting and its logic. A computerized system does have the advantages of speed, efficiency, accuracy, and timeliness of information. However, the data compiled are only as good and as accurate as the data being entered. Thus, manual and computerized accounting systems do complement each other.

THE NAVIGATOR

GLOSSARY

Account A record of increases and decreases in specific asset, liability, or stockholders' equity items (p. 76).

Application Solutions Providers Companies that provide application solutions directly to the end-users in the industry. The end-users purchase application solutions via the Internet rather than the software (p. 100).

Chart of accounts A list of accounts and the account numbers that identify their location in the ledger (p. 88).

Common stock Issued in exchange for the owners' investment paid in to the corporation (p. 79).

Compound entry A journal entry that involves three or more accounts (p. 84).

Credit The right side of an account (p. 77).

Debit The left side of an account (p. 77).

Dividend A distribution by a corporation to its stockholders on a pro rata (equal) basis (p. 79).

Double-entry system A system that records in appropriate accounts the dual effect of each transaction (p. 77).

General journal The most basic form of journal (p. 83).

General ledger A ledger that contains all asset, liability, and stockholders' equity accounts (p. 85).

Journal An accounting record in which transactions are initially recorded in chronological order (p. 83).

Journalizing The entering of transaction data in the journal (p. 83).

Ledger The entire group of accounts maintained by a company (p. 85).

Posting The procedure of transferring journal entries to the ledger accounts (p. 87).

Retained earnings Net income that is retained in the business (p. 79).

Simple entry A journal entry that involves only two accounts (p. 84).

T account The basic form of an account (p. 76).

Three-column form of account A form with columns for debit, credit, and balance amounts in an account (p. 86).

Trial balance A list of accounts and their balances at a given time (p. 97).

EXERCISES

Indicate debit and credit effects and normal balance. (SO 2)

3-1 For each of the following accounts indicate (a) the effect of a debit or a credit on the account and (b) the normal balance.

1. Accounts Payable
2. Advertising Expense
3. Service Revenue
4. Accounts Receivable
5. Common Stock
6. Dividends

Identify accounts to be debited and credited. (SO 2)

3-2 Transactions for Doris Wang Company for the month of June are presented below. Identify the accounts to be debited and credited for each transaction, and journalize the transactions.

June 1 Doris Wang invests $12,000 cash in exchange for shares of common stock in a small printing corporation.
2 Buys equipment on account for $7,500.
3 Pays $800 to landlord for June rent.
12 Bills B. J. Chang $400 for printing work done.

Indicate basic and debit–credit analysis. (SO 4)

3-3 Jim Carrey Corporation has the following transactions during August of the current year. Indicate (a) the basic analysis and (b) the debit–credit analysis illustrated on pages 90–93 of the text. Journalize the transactions.

Aug. 1 Opens an office as a financial advisor, investing $15,000 in cash in exchange for common stock.
4 Pays insurance in advance for 6 months, $2,100.
16 Receives $1,000 from clients for services rendered.
27 Pays secretary $900 salary.

3-4 Selected transactions for Fernholz Company are presented in journal form below. Post the transactions to T accounts.

Post journal entries to T accounts.
(SO 6)

J1

Date	Account Titles and Explanation	Ref.	Debit	Credit
May 5	Accounts Receivable		6,800	
	Service Revenue			6,800
12	Cash		4,100	
	Accounts Receivable			4,100
15	Cash		3,000	
	Service Revenue			3,000

3-5 An inexperienced bookkeeper prepared the following trial balance that does not balance. Prepare a correct trial balance, assuming all account balances are normal.

Prepare a correct trial balance.
(SO 7)

ARMARO COMPANY
Trial Balance
December 31, 2004

	Debit	Credit
Cash	$31,600	
Prepaid Insurance		$ 3,900
Accounts Payable		7,500
Unearned Fees	5,800	
Common Stock		20,000
Dividends		5,000
Service Revenue		29,200
Salaries Expense	19,000	
Rent Expense		3,000
	$56,400	$68,600

3-6 Selected transactions from the journal of Tiger Woods Inc., investment brokerage firm, are presented below.

Post journal entries and prepare a trial balance.
(SO 6, 7)

Date	Account Titles and Explanation	Ref.	Debit	Credit
Aug. 1	Cash		9,600	
	Common Stock			9,600
	(Investment of cash for stock)			
10	Cash		2,800	
	Service Revenue			2,800
	(Received cash for services provided)			
12	Office Equipment		4,500	
	Cash			2,000
	Notes Payable			2,500
	(Purchased office equipment for cash and notes payable)			
25	Accounts Receivable		1,650	
	Service Revenue			1,650
	(Billed for services provided)			
31	Cash		1,200	
	Accounts Receivable			1,200
	(Receipt of cash on account)			

Instructions

(a) Post the transactions to T accounts.

(b) Prepare a trial balance at August 31, 2004.

Journalize transactions from account data, and prepare a trial balance.
(SO 4, 7)

3-7 The T accounts below summarize the ledger of Quick Response Catering Corporation at the end of the first month of operations:

Cash			No. 101
4/1	10,000	4/15	450
4/12	600	4/25	1,100
4/29	900		
4/30	600		

Unearned Revenue			No. 209
		4/30	600

Accounts Receivable			No. 112
4/7	3,200	4/29	900

Common Stock			No. 311
		4/1	10,000

Supplies			No. 126
4/4	1,800		

Service Revenue			No. 400
		4/7	3,200
		4/12	600

Accounts Payable			No. 201
4/25	1,100	4/4	1,800

Salaries Expense			No. 726
4/15	450		

Instructions

(a) Prepare the complete general journal entries (including explanations) from which the postings to Cash were made.
(b) Prepare a trial balance at April 30, 2004.

Journalize a series of transactions.
(SO 2, 4)

3-8 Evergreen Park Corp. was started on April 1 by Susan and Bill Helms. The following selected events and transactions occurred during April.

Apr. 1 Invested $100,000 cash in the business in exchange for common stock.
4 Purchased land costing $35,000 for cash.
8 Incurred advertising expense of $2,100 on account.
11 Paid salaries to employees $1,200.
12 Hired park manager at a salary of $4,500 per month, effective May 1.
13 Paid $1,800 for a one-year insurance policy.
17 Declared and paid a $900 cash dividend.
20 Received $7,200 in cash for admission fees.
25 Sold 100 coupon books for $30 each. Each book contains six coupons that entitle the holder to one admission to the park.
30 Received $6,200 in cash admission fees.
30 Paid $900 on account for advertising incurred on April 8.

Evergreen uses the following accounts: Cash; Prepaid Insurance; Land; Accounts Payable; Unearned Admissions; Common Stock; Dividends; Admission Revenue; Advertising Expense; and Salaries Expense.

Instructions

Journalize the April transactions.

Journalize transactions, post, and prepare a trial balance.
(SO 2, 4, 6, 7)

3-9 Lauren Kim-Bae is a licensed incorporated CPA. During the first month of operations of the business, the following events and transactions occurred.

May 1 Invested $39,000 cash in exchange for common stock.
2 Hired a secretary-receptionist at a salary of $1,800 per month.
3 Purchased $900 of supplies on account from Frost Supply Company.
7 Paid office rent of $1,200 for the month.
11 Completed a tax assignment and billed client $1,700 for services rendered.
12 Received $5,000 advance on a management consulting engagement.
17 Received cash of $1,500 for services completed for Mutter Company.
31 Paid secretary-receptionist $1,800 salary for the month.
31 Paid 40% of balance due Frost Supply Company.

The company uses the following chart of accounts: No. 101 Cash, No. 112 Accounts Receivable, No. 126 Supplies, No. 201 Accounts Payable, No. 205 Unearned Revenue, No. 311 Common Stock, No. 400 Service Revenue, No. 726 Salaries Expense, and No. 729 Rent Expense.

Instructions

(a) Journalize the transactions.
(b) Post to the ledger accounts.
(c) Prepare a trial balance on May 31, 2004.

Journalize transactions, post, and prepare a trial balance. (SO 2, 4, 6, 7)

3-10 JarJar Theater Inc. opened on April 1. All facilities were completed on March 31. At this time, the ledger showed: No. 101 Cash $10,000; No. 140 Land $10,000; No. 145 Buildings (concession stand, projection room, ticket booth, and screen) $8,000; No. 157 Equipment $6,000; No. 201 Accounts Payable $2,000; No. 275 Mortgage Payable $9,000; and No. 311 Common Stock $23,000. During April, the following events and transactions occurred.

Apr.	2	Paid film rental of $1,000 on first movie.
	3	Ordered two additional films at $500 each.
	9	Received $2,100 cash from admissions.
	10	Made $3,000 payment on mortgage and $500 on accounts payable.
	11	Hired Tim Rowe to operate concession stand. Tim Rowe to pay JarJar Theater 16 percent of gross receipts payable monthly.
	12	Paid advertising expenses $600.
	20	Received one of the films ordered on April 3 and was billed $500. The film will be shown in April.
	25	Received $4,600 cash from admissions.
	29	Paid salaries $1,900.
	30	Received statement from Tim Rowe showing gross receipts of $1,500 and the balance due to JarJar Theater of $240 for April. Tim Rowe paid one-half of the balance due and will remit the remainder on May 5.
	30	Prepaid $800 rental on special film to be run in May.

In addition to the accounts identified above, the chart of accounts shows: No. 112 Accounts Receivable, No. 136 Prepaid Rentals, No. 405 Admission Revenue, No. 406 Concession Revenue, No. 610 Advertising Expense, No. 632 Film Rental Expense, and No. 726 Salaries Expense.

Instructions

(a) Enter the beginning balances in the ledger as of April 1. Insert a check mark (✓) in the reference column of the ledger for the beginning balance.
(b) Journalize the April transactions.
(c) Post the April journal entries to the ledger. Assume that all entries are posted from page 1 of the journal.
(d) Prepare a trial balance on April 30, 2004.

FINANCIAL REPORTING PROBLEM: Hilton Hotels Corporation

3-11 The financial statements of **Hilton** are presented in the Appendix. The statements contain the following selected accounts, stated in millions of dollars, for 2001.

Accounts Payable	$ 533	Income Taxes Payable	$ 4
Accounts Receivable	291	Interest Expense	385
Property, Plant, and Equipment	3,911	Inventory	148

Instructions

(a) Answer the following questions:
  (1) What is the increase and decrease side for each account?
  (2) What is the normal balance for each account?

(b) Identify the probable other account in the transaction and the effect on that account when:
  (1) Accounts Receivable is decreased.
  (2) Accounts Payable is decreased.
  (3) Inventory is increased.

(c) Identify the other account(s) that ordinarily would be involved when:
  (1) Interest Expense is increased.
  (2) Property, Plant, and Equipment is increased.

EXPLORING THE WEB

3-12 Much information about specific companies is available on the World Wide Web. This information includes basic descriptions of the company's location, activities, industry, financial health, and financial performance.

Address: **http://biz.yahoo.com/i**

Steps

1. Type in a company name, or use an index to find company name.
2. Choose **Profile**. Perform instructions (a)–(c) below.
3. Click on the company's specific industry to identify competitors. Perform instructions (d)–(g) below.

Instructions

Answer the following questions.

(a) What was the company's net income?
(b) What was the company's total sales?
(c) What is the company's industry?
(d) What are the names of four of the company's competitors?
(e) Choose one of these competitors.
(f) What is this competitor's name? What were its sales? What was its net income?
(g) Which of these two companies is larger by size of sales? Which one reported higher net income?

Answer to Hilton Review It Question 4, p. 81

Cash—debit; Accounts Payable—credit; Interest Expense–debit.

Remember to go back to the Navigator box on the chapter-opening page and check off your completed work.

ADJUSTING THE ACCOUNTS

4

THE NAVIGATOR ✓

- Understand *Concepts for Review* ❑
- Read *Feature Story* ❑
- Scan *Study Objectives* ❑
- Read *Preview* ❑
- Read text and answer *Before You Go On* *p.* 115 ❑ *p.* 122 ❑ *p.* 127 ❑ *p.* 132 ❑
- Work *Demonstration Problem* ❑
- Review *Summary of Study Objectives* ❑
- Complete *Assignments* ❑

CONCEPTS FOR REVIEW

Before studying this chapter, you should know or, if necessary, review:

a. What a double-entry system is. (Ch. 3, p. 77)

b. How to increase or decrease assets, liabilities, and stockholders' equity using debit and credit procedures. (Ch. 3, pp. 75–80)

c. How to journalize a transaction. (Ch. 3, pp. 83–84)

d. How to post a transaction. (Ch. 3, pp. 87–88)

e. How to prepare a trial balance. (Ch. 3, pp. 97–98)

THE NAVIGATOR

FEATURE STORY

Timing Is Everything

In Chapter 1 you learned a neat little formula: Net income = Revenues − Expenses. And in Chapter 3 you learned some nice, orderly rules for recording corporate revenue and expense transactions. Guess what? Things are not really that nice and neat. In fact, it is often difficult to determine in what time period some revenues and expenses should be reported. And, in measuring net income, timing is everything.

There are rules that give guidance on these issues. But occasionally these rules are overlooked, misinterpreted, or even intentionally ignored. Consider the following examples.

- **Lake Swan Resort** pays its general property insurance on a six-month basis. The total of $18,000 for a six month period, or $3,000 per month, is paid on May 30 for June to November. The entire amount of $18,000 is recorded as an expense for the month of May since it is paid on May 30. Thus, the company has a loss of $7,533 for that month.
- **Juneau Country Club** gives its member an option to pay the entire year's membership with a 5 percent discount. Dues that are received in December 2003 for the year 2004 are all entered at December 2003 as dues income.
- **Cuisine-on-the-Go** receives a 50 percent deposit for a Christmas party in October in the amount of $7,525. When the accountant records the transaction, it is entered as catering income for the month of October.
- **Hospitality Purveyors** has its annual convention in Houston. One event is an off-site event to NASA Johnson Space Center for a tour. Coach buses are contracted for this outing with Luxury Coach, Inc. A check of $3,685 is written to Luxury in May for their services to be provided in September. Luxury records the $3,685 as income for the month of May.

In each case, accrual accounting concepts were violated. That is, revenues or expenses were not recorded in the proper period, which has a substantial impact on reported income. Their timing is off!

THE NAVIGATOR

STUDY OBJECTIVES

After studying this chapter, you should be able to

1. Explain the time period assumption.
2. Explain the accrual basis of accounting.
3. Explain why adjusting entries are needed.
4. Identify the major types of adjusting entries.
5. Prepare adjusting entries for prepayments.
6. Prepare adjusting entries for accruals.
7. Describe the nature and purpose of an adjusted trial balance.
8. Prepare adjusting entries for the alternative treatment of prepayments.

THE NAVIGATOR

PREVIEW OF CHAPTER 4

In Chapter 3 we examined the recording process through the preparation of the trial balance. Before we will be ready to prepare financial statements from the trial balance, additional steps need to be taken. The timing mismatch between revenues and expenses of the four companies mentioned in our Feature Story illustrates the types of situations that make these additional steps necessary. For example, long-lived assets purchased or constructed in prior accounting years are being used to produce goods and provide services in the current year. What portion of these assets' costs, if any, should be recognized as an expense of the current period? Before financial statements can be prepared, this and other questions relating to the recognition of revenues and expenses must be answered. With the answers in hand, we can then adjust the relevant account balances.

The content and organization of Chapter 4 are as follows.

ADJUSTING THE ACCOUNTS

Timing Issues	The Basics of Adjusting Entries	The Adjusted Trial Balance and Financial Statements
• Time period assumption • Fiscal and calendar years • Accrual- vs. cash-basis accounting • Recognizing revenues and expenses	• Types of adjusting entries • Adjusting entries for prepayments • Adjusting entries for accruals • Summary	• Preparing the adjusted trial balance • Preparing financial statements

THE NAVIGATOR

TIMING ISSUES

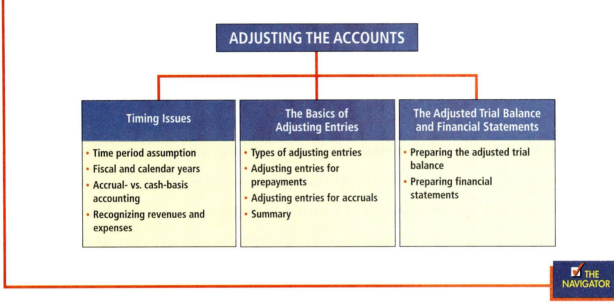

STUDY OBJECTIVE 1

Explain the time period assumption.

No adjustments would be necessary if we could wait to prepare financial statements until a company ended its operations. At that point, we could easily determine its final balance sheet and the amount of lifetime income it earned. The following anecdote illustrates one way to compute lifetime income.

> A grocery store owner from the old country kept his accounts payable on a spindle, accounts receivable on a note pad, and cash in a cigar box. His daughter, having just passed the CPA exam, chided the father: "I don't understand how you can run your business this way. How do you know what your profits are?"
>
> "Well," the father replied, "when I got off the boat forty years ago, I had nothing but the pants I was wearing. Today your brother is a doctor, your sister is a college professor, and you are a CPA. Your mother and I have a nice car, a well-furnished house, and a lake home. We have a good business, and everything is paid for. So, you add all that together, subtract the pants, and there's your profit."

SELECTING AN ACCOUNTING TIME PERIOD

Although the old grocer may be correct in his evaluation, it is impractical to wait so long for the results of operations. All entities, from the corner grocery, to a global company like **Kellogg**, to your college or university, find it desirable and necessary to report the results of their activities more frequently. For example, management usually wants monthly financial statements, and the Internal Revenue Service requires all businesses to file annual tax returns. Therefore, **accountants divide the economic life of a business into artificial time periods**. This convenient assumption is referred to as the **time period assumption**.

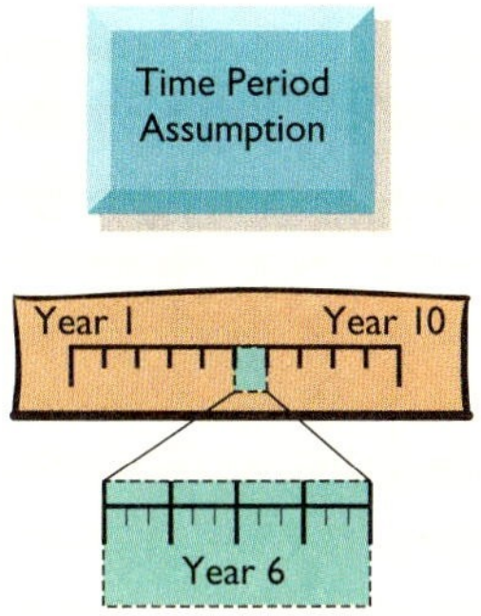

Many business transactions affect more than one of these arbitrary time periods. For example, Farmer Brown's milking machine bought in 1998 and the airplanes purchased by **Delta Air Lines** five years ago are still in use today. Therefore we must determine the relevance of each business transaction to specific accounting periods. Doing so may involve subjective judgments and estimates.

ALTERNATIVE TERMINOLOGY
The time period assumption is also called the *periodicity assumption*.

FISCAL AND CALENDAR YEARS

Both small and large companies prepare financial statements periodically in order to assess their financial condition and results of operations. Accounting time periods are generally *a month*, *a quarter*, or *a year*. Monthly and quarterly time periods are called **interim periods**. Most large companies are required to prepare both quarterly and annual financial statements.

An accounting time period that is one year in length is referred to as a **fiscal year**. A fiscal year usually begins with the first day of a month and ends twelve months later on the last day of a month. The accounting period used by most businesses coincides with the **calendar year** (January 1 to December 31). Companies whose fiscal year differs from the calendar year include **Delta Air Lines**, June 30; **Walt Disney Productions**, September 30; and **CKE Restaurants, Inc.**, January 31. Sometimes a company's year-end will vary from year to year. For example, **Marriott International, Inc.** fiscal year ends on the Friday closest to December 31, which was January 3 in 2003 and January 2 in 2004.

ACCRUAL- VS. CASH-BASIS ACCOUNTING

STUDY OBJECTIVE 2
Explain the accrual basis of accounting.

What you will learn in this chapter is **accrual-basis accounting**. Under the accrual basis, transactions that change a company's financial statements are recorded **in the periods in which the events occur**. For example, using the accrual basis to determine net income means recognizing revenues when earned (rather than when the cash is received). It also means recognizing expenses when incurred (rather than when paid). Information presented on an accrual basis reveals relationships likely to be important in predicting future results. Under accrual accounting, revenues are recognized when services are performed, so trends in revenues are thus more meaningful for decision making.

An alternative to the accrual basis is the cash basis. Under **cash-basis accounting**, revenue is recorded when cash is received, and an expense is recorded when cash is paid. The cash basis often leads to misleading financial statements. It fails to record revenue that has been earned but for which the cash has not been received. Also, expenses are not matched with earned revenues. **Cash-basis accounting is not in accordance with generally accepted accounting principles (GAAP).**

INTERNATIONAL NOTE
Although different accounting standards are often used in other major industrialized countries, accrual-basis accounting is also followed by all these countries.

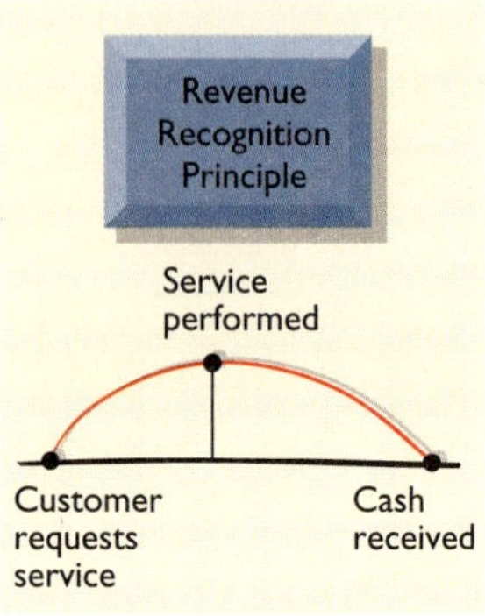

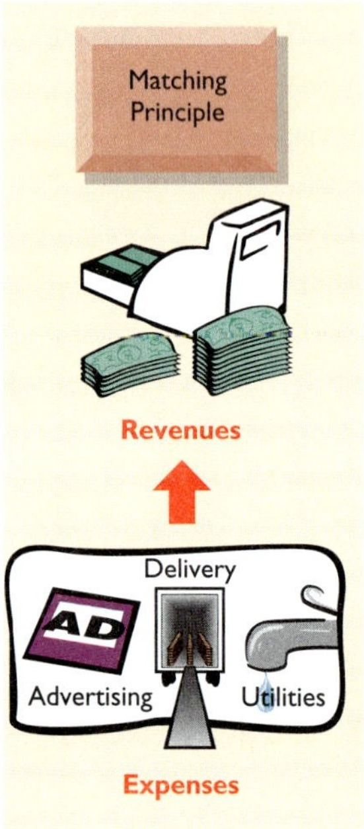

Most companies use accrual-basis accounting. Individuals and some small companies use cash-basis accounting. The cash basis is justified for small businesses because they often have few receivables and payables. Accountants are sometimes asked to convert cash-basis records to the accrual basis. As you might expect, extensive adjusting entries are required for this task.

RECOGNIZING REVENUES AND EXPENSES

Determining the amount of revenues and expenses to be reported in a given accounting period can be difficult. To help in this task, accountants have developed two principles as part of generally accepted accounting principles (GAAP): the revenue recognition principle and the matching principle.

The **revenue recognition principle** dictates that revenue be recognized in the accounting period in which it is earned. **In a service enterprise, revenue is considered to be earned at the time the service is performed.** To illustrate, assume that a dry cleaning business cleans banquet and bed linens on June 30 but hotels do not claim and pay for their cleaning until the first week of July. Under the revenue recognition principle, revenue is earned in June when the service is performed, rather than in July when the cash is received. At June 30, the dry cleaner would report a receivable on its balance sheet and revenue in its income statement for the service performed.

Accountants follow the approach of "let expenses follow revenues." That is, expense recognition is tied to revenue recognition. In the preceding example, this principle means that the salary expense incurred in performing the cleaning service on June 30 should be reported in the income statement for the same period in which the service revenue is recognized. The critical issue in expense recognition is when the expense makes its contribution to revenue. This may or may not be the same period in which the expense is paid. If the salary incurred on June 30 is not paid until July, the dry cleaner would report salaries payable on its June 30 balance sheet. The practice of expense recognition is referred to as the **matching principle** because it dictates that efforts (expenses) be matched with accomplishments (revenues).

ACCOUNTING IN ACTION *Business Insight*

Suppose you are a filmmaker like George Lucas and spend $11 million to produce a film such as *Star Wars.* Over what period should the cost be expensed? It should be expensed over the economic life of the film. But what is its economic life? The filmmaker must estimate how much revenue will be earned from box office sales, video sales, television, and games and toys—a period that could be less than a year or more than twenty years, as is the case for Twentieth Century Fox's *Star Wars.* Originally released in 1977, and rereleased in 1997, domestic revenues total nearly $500 million for *Star Wars* and continue to grow. This situation demonstrates the difficulty of properly matching expenses to revenues.

SOURCE: Star Trek Newsletter, 22.

Once the economic life of a business has been divided into artificial time periods, the revenue recognition and matching principles can be applied. This one assumption and two principles thus provide guidelines as to when revenues and expenses should be reported. These relationships are shown in Illustration 4-1.

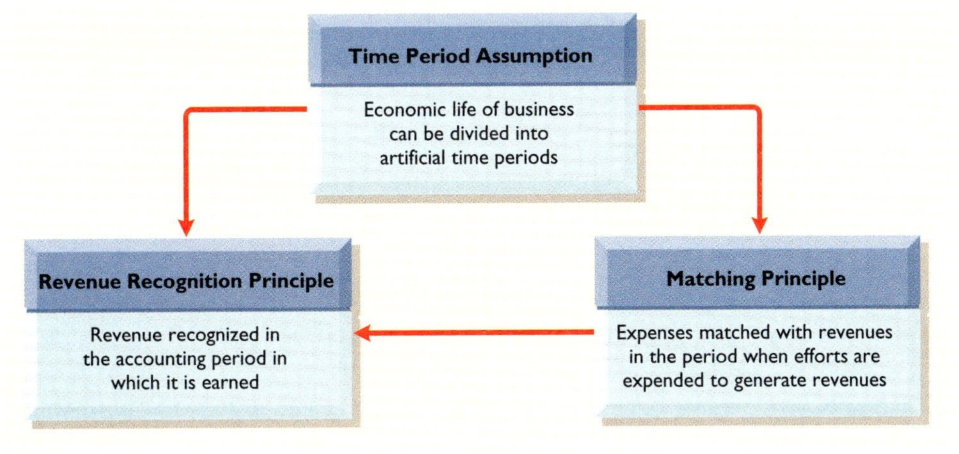

Illustration 4-1
GAAP relationships in revenue and expense recognition

BEFORE YOU GO ON...

REVIEW IT

1. What is the relevance of the time period assumption to accounting?
2. What are the revenue recognition and matching principles?

THE NAVIGATOR

THE BASICS OF ADJUSTING ENTRIES

STUDY OBJECTIVE 3
Explain why adjusting entries are needed.

In order for revenues to be recorded in the period in which they are earned, and for expenses to be recognized in the period in which they are incurred, adjusting entries are made at the end of the accounting period. In short, **adjusting entries** are needed to ensure that the revenue recognition and matching principles are followed.

Adjusting entries make it possible to report on the balance sheet the appropriate assets, liabilities, and stockholders' equity at the statement date and to report on the income statement the proper net income (or loss) for the period. However, the trial balance—the first pulling together of the transaction data—may not contain up-to-date and complete data. This is true for the following reasons.

1. Some events are not journalized daily because it is inexpedient to do so. Examples are the consumption of supplies and the earning of wages by employees.
2. Some costs are not journalized during the accounting period because they expire with the passage of time rather than through recurring daily transactions. Examples are equipment deterioration, and rent and insurance.
3. Some items may be unrecorded. An example is a utility service bill that will not be received until the next accounting period.

Adjusting entries are required every time financial statements are prepared. The starting point is an analysis of each account in the trial balance to determine whether it is complete and up to date. The analysis requires a thorough understanding of the company's operations and the interrelationship of accounts. Preparing adjusting entries is often an involved process. The company may need to make inventory counts of supplies and repair parts. It may need to prepare supporting

HELPFUL HINT
Adjusting entries are needed to enable financial statements to be in conformity with GAAP.

schedules of insurance policies, rental agreements, and other contractual commitments. Adjustments are often prepared after the balance sheet date. However, the adjusting entries are dated as of the balance sheet date.

STUDY OBJECTIVE 4

Identify the major types of adjusting entries.

TYPES OF ADJUSTING ENTRIES

Adjusting entries can be classified as either prepayments or accruals. Each of these classes has two subcategories as shown in Illustration 4-2.

Illustration 4-2

Categories of adjusting entries

Prepayments

1. **Prepaid expenses.** Expenses paid in cash and recorded as assets before they are used or consumed.
2. **Unearned revenues.** Cash received and recorded as liabilities before revenue is earned.

Accruals

1. **Accrued revenues.** Revenues earned but not yet received in cash or recorded.
2. **Accrued expenses.** Expenses incurred but not yet paid in cash or recorded.

Specific examples and explanations of each type of adjustment are given on the following pages. Each example is based on the October 31 trial balance of Premier Staffing Agency Inc. from Chapter 3, reproduced in Illustration 4-3.

Illustration 4-3

Trial balance

PREMIER STAFFING AGENCY INC.
Trial Balance
October 31, 2004

	Debit	Credit
Cash	$15,200	
Supplies	2,500	
Prepaid Insurance	600	
Office Equipment	5,000	
Notes Payable		$ 5,000
Accounts Payable		2,500
Unearned Revenue		1,200
Common Stock		10,000
Retained Earnings		–0–
Dividends	500	
Service Revenue		10,000
Salaries Expense	4,000	
Rent Expense	900	
	$28,700	$28,700

We assume that Premier Staffing uses an accounting period of one month. Thus, monthly adjusting entries will be made. The entries will be dated October 31.

STUDY OBJECTIVE 5

Prepare adjusting entries for prepayments.

ADJUSTING ENTRIES FOR PREPAYMENTS

As indicated earlier, prepayments are either prepaid expenses or unearned revenues. Adjusting entries for prepayments are required to record the portion of the prepayment that represents the **expense incurred** or the **revenue earned** in the current accounting period.

If an adjustment is needed for prepayments, the asset and liability are overstated and the related expense and revenue are understated before the adjustment. For example, in the trial balance, the balance in the asset Supplies shows only supplies purchased. This balance is overstated; a related expense account, Supplies Expense, is understated because the cost of supplies used has not been recognized. Thus the adjusting entry for prepayments will **decrease a balance sheet account** (Supplies) and **increase an income statement account** (Supplies Expense). The effects of adjusting entries for prepayments are graphically depicted in Illustration 4-4.

HELPFUL HINT
Remember that credits decrease assets and increase revenues. Debits increase expenses and decrease liabilities.

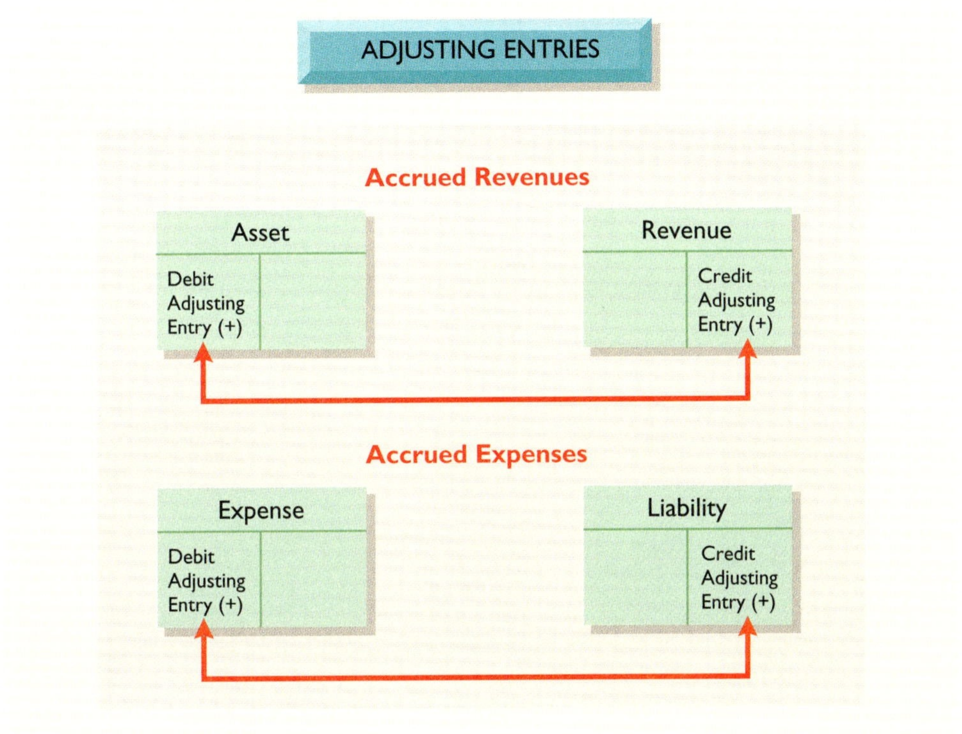

Illustration 4-4

Adjusting entries for prepayments

Prepaid Expenses

As stated on the previous page, expenses paid in cash and recorded as assets before they are used or consumed are called **prepaid expenses**. When a cost is prepaid, an asset account is debited to show the service or benefit that will be received in the future. Prepayments often occur in regard to insurance, supplies, advertising, and rent. In addition, prepayments are made when buildings and equipment are purchased.

Prepaid expenses expire either with the passage of time (e.g., rent and insurance) or through use and consumption (e.g., supplies). The expiration of these costs does not require daily journal entries, which would be unnecessary and impractical. Instead, it is customary to postpone recognizing cost expirations until financial statements are prepared. At each statement date, adjusting entries are made for two purposes: (1) to record the expenses that apply to the current accounting period, and (2) to show the unexpired costs in the asset accounts.

Prior to adjustment, assets are overstated and expenses are understated. **Thus, the prepaid expense adjusting entry results in a debit (increase) to an expense account and a credit (decrease) to an asset account.**

SUPPLIES. Businesses use various types of supplies. For example, a CPA firm will have office supplies such as stationery, envelopes, and accounting paper. Supplies are generally debited to an asset account when they are acquired. In the course of operations, supplies are depleted, but recognition of supplies used is deferred until the adjustment process. At that point, a physical inventory (count) of supplies is taken. The difference between the balance in the Supplies (asset) account and the cost of supplies on hand represents the supplies used (expense) for the period.

Premier Staffing Agency Inc. purchased supplies costing $2,500 on October 5. A debit (increase) was made to the asset Supplies. This account shows a balance of $2,500 in the October 31 trial balance. An inventory count at the close of business on October 31 reveals that $1,000 of supplies are still on hand. Thus, the cost of supplies used is $1,500 ($2,500 − $1,000), and the following adjusting entry is made.

Equation analyses summarize the effects of the transaction on the accounting equation.

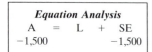

Equation Analysis

A	=	L	+	SE
−1,500				−1,500

Oct. 31	Supplies Expense	1,500	
	Supplies		1,500
	(To record supplies used)		

After the adjusting entry is posted, the two supplies accounts look like Illustration 4-5.

Illustration 4-5

Supplies accounts after adjustment

Supplies			
10/5	2,500	10/31 **Adj.**	**1,500**
10/31 Bal.	1,000		

Supplies Expense			
10/31 **Adj.**	**1,500**		

The asset account Supplies now shows a balance of $1,000, which is the cost of supplies on hand at the statement date. In addition, Supplies Expense shows a balance of $1,500, which equals the cost of supplies used in October. **If the adjusting entry is not made, October expenses will be understated and net income overstated by $1,500. Also, both assets and stockholders' equity will be overstated by $1,500 on the October 31 balance sheet.**

ACCOUNTING IN ACTION *Business Insight*

The costs of product advertising are sometimes considered prepayments. As a manager for **Procter & Gamble** noted, "If we run a long ad campaign for soap and bleach, we sometimes report the costs as prepayments if we think we'll receive sales benefits from the campaign down the road." It is a judgment call whether these costs should be prepayments or expenses in the current period. It is difficult to develop guidelines consistent with the matching principle because situations vary widely across companies. Outlays for advertising can be substantial. Recent big advertising spenders in 2002: **Sears, Roebuck and Co.** spent $58 million, **Nike** $1.03 billion, and **McDonald's** $647.6 million.

INSURANCE. Most companies have fire and theft insurance on merchandise and equipment, personal liability insurance for accidents suffered by customers, and automobile insurance on company cars and trucks. The cost of insurance protection is determined by the payment of insurance premiums. The minimum term of coverage is usually one year, but three- to five-year terms are available and offer lower annual premiums. Insurance premiums normally are charged to the asset account Prepaid Insurance when paid. At the financial statement date it is necessary to debit (increase) Insurance Expense and credit (decrease) Prepaid Insurance for the cost that has expired during the period.

On October 4, Premier Staffing Agency Inc. paid $600 for a one-year fire insurance policy. The effective date of coverage was October 1. The premium was charged to Prepaid Insurance when it was paid, and this account shows a balance of $600 in the October 31 trial balance. Analysis reveals that $50 ($600 ÷ 12) of insurance expires each month. Thus, the following adjusting entry is made.

Insurance

Oct. 4

Insurance purchased; record asset

Insurance Policy			
Oct $50	Nov $50	Dec $50	Jan $50
Feb $50	March $50	April $50	May $50
June $50	July $50	Aug $50	Sept $50
I YEAR $600			

Oct. 31

Insurance expired; record insurance expense

Oct. 31	Insurance Expense	50	
	Prepaid Insurance		50
	(To record insurance expired)		

After the adjusting entry is posted, the accounts look like Illustration 4-6.

Illustration 4-6

Insurance accounts after adjustment

Prepaid Insurance				Insurance Expense	
10/4	600	10/31 Adj.	50	10/31 Adj. 50	
10/31 Bal.	550				

The asset Prepaid Insurance shows a balance of $550. This amount represents the unexpired cost for the remaining eleven months of coverage. The $50 balance in Insurance Expense is equal to the insurance cost that has expired in October. **If this adjustment is not made, October expenses will be understated by $50 and net income overstated by $50. Also, both assets and stockholders' equity will be overstated by $50 on the October 31 balance sheet.**

DEPRECIATION. A business enterprise typically owns productive facilities such as buildings, equipment, and vehicles. Because these assets provide service for a number of years, each is recorded as an asset, rather than an expense, in the year it is acquired. As explained in Chapter 1, such assets are recorded at cost, as required by the cost principle. The term of service is referred to as the **useful life**.

According to the matching principle, a portion of the cost of a long-lived asset should be reported as an expense during each period of the asset's useful life. **Depreciation** is the allocation of the cost of an asset to expense over its useful life in a rational and systematic manner.

Depreciation

Oct. 1

Office equipment purchased; record asset

Office Equipment			
Oct $40	Nov $40	Dec $40	Jan $40
Feb $40	March $40	April $40	May $40
June $40	July $40	Aug $40	Sept $40
Depreciation = $480/year			

Oct. 31

Depreciation recognized; record depreciation expense

Need for Depreciation Adjustment. From an accounting standpoint, acquiring productive facilities is viewed essentially as a long-term prepayment for services. The need for periodic adjusting entries for depreciation is, therefore, the same as that for other prepaid expenses: to recognize the cost that has expired (expense) during the period and to report the unexpired cost (asset) at the end of the period.

At the time an asset is acquired, its useful life cannot be known with certainty. The asset may be useful for a longer or shorter time than expected, depending on such factors as actual use, deterioration due to the elements or obsolescence. Thus, you should recognize that **depreciation is an estimate** rather than a factual measurement of the cost that has expired. A common procedure in computing depreciation expense is to divide the cost of the asset by its useful life. For example, if cost is $10,000 and useful life is expected to be 10 years, annual depreciation is $1,000.[1]

[1]Additional consideration is given to computing depreciation expense in Chapter 11.

For Premier Staffing, depreciation on the office equipment is estimated to be $480 a year, or $40 per month. Accordingly, depreciation for October is recognized by the following adjusting entry.

A	=	L	+	SE
−40				−40

Oct. 31	Depreciation Expense	40	
	Accumulated Depreciation—Office Equipment		40
	(To record monthly depreciation)		

After the adjusting entry is posted, the accounts look like Illustration 4-7.

Illustration 4-7

Accounts after adjustment for depreciation

Office Equipment

10/1	5,000		

Accumulated Depreciation—Office Equipment

		10/31 **Adj.**	**40**

Depreciation Expense

10/31 **Adj.**	**40**		

The balance in the accumulated depreciation account will increase $40 each month. After journalizing and posting the adjusting entry at November 30, the balance will be $80; at December 31, $120; and so on.

HELPFUL HINT

All contra accounts have increases, decreases, and normal balances opposite to the account to which they relate.

Statement Presentation. Accumulated Depreciation—Office Equipment is a contra asset account. A **contra asset account** is one that is offset against an asset account on the balance sheet. This accumulated depreciation account appears just after Office Equipment on the balance sheet. Its normal balance is a credit. An alternative would be to credit (decrease) Office Equipment directly for the depreciation each month. But use of the contra account provides disclosure of **both the original cost** of the equipment **and the total cost that has expired to date**. In the balance sheet, Accumulated Depreciation—Office Equipment is deducted from the related asset account as follows.

Illustration 4-8

Balance sheet presentation of accumulated depreciation

Office equipment	$5,000	
Less: Accumulated depreciation—office equipment	40	**$4,960**

ALTERNATIVE TERMINOLOGY

Book value is sometimes referred to as *carrying value* or *unexpired cost*.

The difference between the cost of any depreciable asset and its related accumulated depreciation is referred to as the **book value** of that asset. In Illustration 4-8, the book value of the equipment at the balance sheet date is $4,960. You should realize that the book value is generally different from the market value (the price at which the asset could be sold in the marketplace). The reason the two are different is that depreciation is a means of cost allocation, not a matter of valuation.

Depreciation expense also identifies that portion of the asset's cost that has expired in October. As in the case of other prepaid adjustments, the omission of this adjusting entry would cause total assets, total stockholders' equity, and net income to be overstated and depreciation expense to be understated.

If the company owns additional equipment, such as delivery or store equipment, or if it has buildings, a separate depreciation expense is recorded on each of those items. Related accumulated depreciation accounts also are established, such as: Accumulated Depreciation—Delivery Equipment; Accumulated Depreciation—Store Equipment; and Accumulated Depreciation—Buildings.

Unearned Revenues

Unearned Revenues

Oct. 2

Cash is received in advance; liability is recorded

Oct. 31

Service is provided; revenue is recorded

As stated on page 116, cash received and recorded as liabilities before revenue is earned is called **unearned revenues**. Such items as rent, magazine subscriptions, and customer deposits for future service may result in unearned revenues. Airlines such as **United**, **American**, and **Delta** treat receipts from the sale of tickets as unearned revenue until the flight service is provided. Similarly, college tuition received prior to the start of a semester is considered unearned revenue. Unearned revenues are the opposite of prepaid expenses. Indeed, unearned revenue on the books of one company is likely to be a prepayment on the books of the company that has made the advance payment. For example, if identical accounting periods are assumed, a landlord will have unearned rent revenue when a tenant has prepaid rent.

When the payment is received for services to be provided in a future accounting period, an unearned revenue account (a liability) should be credited (increased) to recognize the obligation that exists. Later, unearned revenues are earned by providing service to a customer. It may not be practical to make daily journal entries as the revenue is earned. In such cases, recognition of earned revenue is delayed until the end of the period. Then an adjusting entry is made to record the revenue that has been earned and to show the liability that remains. In the typical case, liabilities are overstated and revenues are understated prior to adjustment. Thus, **the adjusting entry for unearned revenues results in a debit (decrease) to a liability account and a credit (increase) to a revenue account.**

ALTERNATIVE TERMINOLOGY
Unearned revenue is sometimes referred to as *deferred revenue.*

Premier Staffing Agency Inc. received $1,200 on October 2 from R. Knox for staffing services expected for a New Year's Eve party to be completed by December 31. The payment was credited to Unearned Revenue; this account shows a balance of $1,200 in the October 31 trial balance. Analysis reveals that $400 of those fees was earned in October. The following adjusting entry is made.

Oct. 31	Unearned Revenue	400	
	Service Revenue		400
	(To record revenue for services provided)		

A	=	L	+	SE
		−400		+400

After the adjusting entry is posted, the accounts look like Illustration 4-9:

Unearned Revenue

10/31 **Adj.**	**400**	10/2	1,200
		10/31 Bal.	800

Service Revenue

		10/31 Bal.	10,000
		31 **Adj.**	**400**

Illustration 4-9
Revenue accounts after prepayments adjustment

The liability Unearned Revenue now shows a balance of $800. This amount represents the remaining prepaid staffing services to be performed in the future. At the same time, Service Revenue shows total revenue of $10,400 earned in October. **If this adjustment is not made, revenues and net income would be understated by $400 in the income statement. Also, liabilities would be overstated and stockholders' equity would be understated by $400 on the October 31 balance sheet.**

ACCOUNTING IN ACTION e-Business Insight

Many early dot-com investors focused almost entirely on revenue growth instead of net income. Many early dot-com companies earned most of their revenue from selling advertising space on their Web sites. To boost reported revenue, some companies began swapping Web site ad space. Company A would put an ad for its Web site on company B's Web site, and company B would put an ad for its Web site on company A's Web site. No money ever changed hands, but each company recorded revenue (for the value of the space that it gave up on its site) and expense (for the value of its ad that it placed on the other company's site). This transaction resulted in no change to net income or cash flow, but it did boost *reported* revenue. This practice was quickly put to an end because accountants felt that it did not meet the criteria of the revenue recognition principle.

BEFORE YOU GO ON...

REVIEW IT

1. What are the four types of adjusting entries?
2. What is the effect on assets, stockholders' equity, expenses, and net income if a prepaid expense adjusting entry is not made?
3. What is the effect on liabilities, stockholders' equity, revenues, and net income if an unearned revenue adjusting entry is not made?
4. Using **Hilton's** financial statements, what was the amount of depreciation and amortization expense for 2001 and for 2000? The answer to this question is provided on page 141.

Hilton™

DO IT

The ledger of Hammond, Inc. on March 31, 2004, includes the following selected accounts before adjusting entries.

	Debit	Credit
Prepaid Insurance	3,600	
Office Supplies	2,800	
Office Equipment	25,000	
Accumulated Depreciation—Office Equipment		5,000
Unearned Revenue		9,200

An analysis of the accounts shows the following.

1. Insurance expires at the rate of $100 per month.
2. Supplies on hand total $800.
3. The office equipment depreciates $200 a month.
4. One-half of the unearned revenue was earned in March.

Prepare the adjusting entries for the month of March.

ACTION PLAN

- Make adjusting entries at the end of the period for revenues earned and expenses incurred in the period.
- Don't forget to make adjusting entries for prepayments. Failure to adjust for prepayments leads to overstatement of the asset or liability and related understatement of the expense or revenue.

SOLUTION

1. Insurance Expense	100	
Prepaid Insurance		100
(To record insurance expired)		

2. Office Supplies Expense	2,000	
Office Supplies		2,000
(To record supplies used)		
3. Depreciation Expense	200	
Accumulated Depreciation—Office Equipment		200
(To record monthly depreciation)		
4. Unearned Revenue	4,600	
Service Revenue		4,600
(To record revenue for services provided)		

Related exercise material: 4-3, 4-6, 4-7, and 4-8.

THE NAVIGATOR

ADJUSTING ENTRIES FOR ACCRUALS

STUDY OBJECTIVE 6

Prepare adjusting entries for accruals.

The second category of adjusting entries is **accruals**. Adjusting entries for accruals are required to record revenues earned and expenses incurred in the current accounting period that have not been recognized through daily entries.

An accrual adjustment is needed when various accounts are understated: the revenue account and the related asset account, and/or the expense account and the related liability account. Thus, the adjusting entry for accruals will **increase both a balance sheet and an income statement account**. Adjusting entries for accruals are graphically depicted in Illustration 4-10.

Illustration 4-10

Adjusting entries for accruals

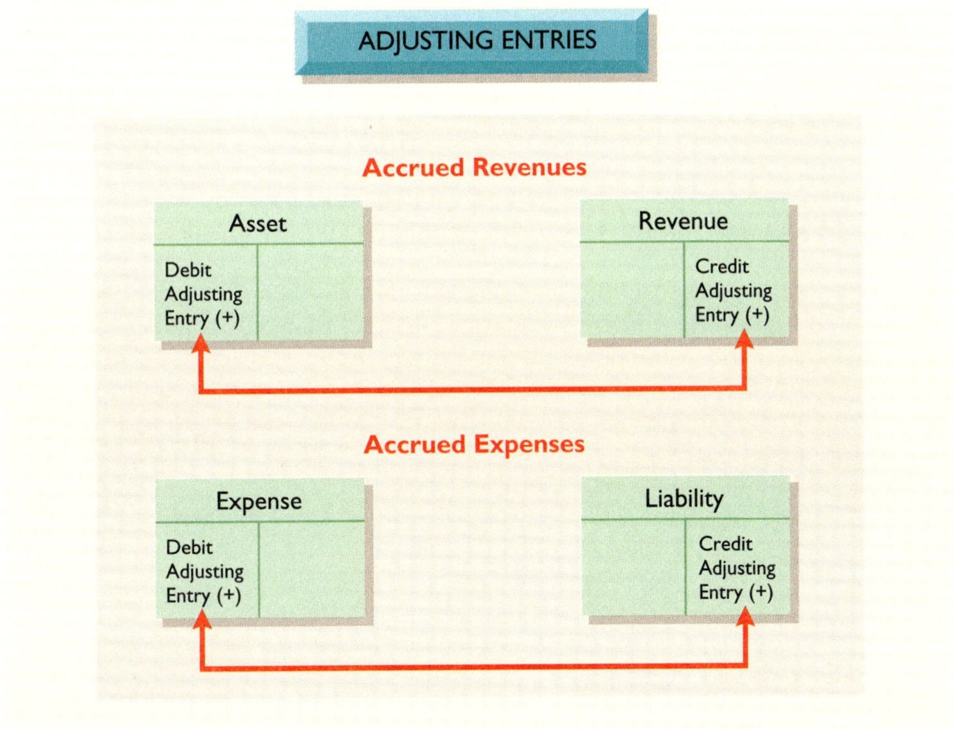

Accrued Revenues
Oct. 31
My fee is $200
Revenue and receivable are recorded for unbilled services
$
Nov. 10
Cash is received; receivable is reduced

Accrued Revenues

As explained on page 116, revenues earned but not yet received in cash or recorded at the statement date are **accrued revenues**. Accrued revenues may accumulate (accrue) with the passing of time, as in the case of interest revenue and rent revenue. Or they may result from services that have been performed but neither billed nor collected, as in the case of commissions and fees. The former are unrecorded because the earning of interest and rent does not involve daily transactions. The latter may be unrecorded because only a portion of the total service has been provided.

An adjusting entry is required for two purposes: (1) to show the receivable that exists at the balance sheet date, and (2) to record the revenue that has been earned during the period. Prior to adjustment both assets and revenues are understated. Thus, **an adjusting entry for accrued revenues results in a debit (increase) to an asset account and a credit (increase) to a revenue account.**

In October Premier Staffing Agency Inc. earned $200 for services that were not billed to clients before October 31. Because these services have not been billed, they have not been recorded. The following adjusting entry is made.

A	=	L	+	SE
+200				+200

Oct. 31	Accounts Receivable	200	
	Service Revenue		200
	(To record revenue for services provided)		

After the adjusting entry is posted, the accounts look like Illustration 4-11.

Illustration 4-11

Receivable and revenue accounts after accrual adjustment

Accounts Receivable				Service Revenue		
10/31 Adj.	200				10/31	10,000
					31	400
					31 Adj.	200
					10/31 Bal.	10,600

ALTERNATIVE TERMINOLOGY
Accrued revenues are also called *accrued receivables.*

The asset Accounts Receivable shows that $200 is owed by clients at the balance sheet date. The balance of $10,600 in Service Revenue represents the total revenue earned during the month ($10,000 + $400 + $200). **If the adjusting entry is not made, the following will all be understated: assets and stockholders' equity on the balance sheet, and revenues and net income on the income statement.**

In the next accounting period, the clients will be billed. The entry to record the billing should recognize that a portion has already been recorded in the previous month's adjusting entry. To illustrate, assume that bills totaling $3,000 are mailed to clients on November 10. Of this amount, $200 represents revenue earned in October and recorded as Service Revenue in the October 31 adjusting entry. The remaining $2,800 represents revenue earned in November. Thus, the following entry is made.

A	=	L	+	SE
+2,800				+2,800

Nov. 10	Accounts Receivable	2,800	
	Service Revenue		2,800
	(To record revenue for services provided)		

This entry records service revenue between November 1 and November 10. The subsequent collection of revenue from clients (including the $200 earned in October) will be recorded with a debit (increase) to Cash and a credit (decrease) to Accounts Receivable.

Accrued Expenses

ALTERNATIVE TERMINOLOGY
Accrued expenses are also called *accrued liabilities.*

As indicated on page 116, expenses incurred but not yet paid or recorded at the statement date are called **accrued expenses**. Interest, rent, taxes, and salaries can be accrued expenses. Accrued expenses result from the same causes as accrued revenues. In fact, an accrued expense on the books of one company is an accrued revenue to another company. For example, the $200 accrual of fees by Premier is an accrued expense to the client that received the service.

Adjustments for accrued expenses are needed for two purposes: (1) to record the obligations that exist at the balance sheet date, and (2) to recognize the expenses that apply to the current accounting period. Prior to adjustment, both liabilities and expenses are understated. Thus, **the adjusting entry for accrued expenses results in a debit (increase) to an expense account and a credit (increase) to a liability account**.

ACCRUED INTEREST. Premier Staffing Agency Inc. signed a $5,000, 3-month note payable on October 1. The note requires interest at an annual rate of 12 percent. The amount of the interest accumulation is determined by three factors: (1) the face value of the note, (2) the interest rate, which is always expressed as an annual rate, and (3) the length of time the note is outstanding. In this instance, the total interest due on the $5,000 note at its due date 3 months hence is $150 ($5,000 × 12% × 3/12), or $50 for one month. The formula for computing interest and its application to Premier Staffing Agency Inc. for the month of October[2] are shown in Illustration 4-12. Note that the time period is expressed as a fraction of a year.

HELPFUL HINT
Interest is a cost of borrowing money that accumulates with the passage of time.

Illustration 4-12
Formula for computing interest

Face Value of Note	×	Annual Interest Rate	×	Time in Terms of One Year	=	Interest
$5,000	×	12%	×	1/12	=	$50

The accrued expense adjusting entry at October 31 is:

Oct. 31	Interest Expense	50	
	Interest Payable		50
	(To record interest on notes payable)		

A	=	L	+	SE
		+50		−50

After this adjusting entry is posted, the accounts look like Illustration 4-13.

Illustration 4-13
Interest accounts after adjustment

Interest Expense		Interest Payable	
10/31 **Adj.** **50**			10/31 **Adj.** **50**

Interest Expense shows the interest charges for the month. The amount of interest owed at the statement date is shown in Interest Payable. It will not be paid until the note comes due at the end of 3 months. The Interest Payable account is used instead of crediting (increasing) Notes Payable. The reason for using the two accounts is to disclose the two types of obligations (interest and principal) in the accounts and statements. **If this adjusting entry is not made, liabilities and interest expense will be understated, and net income and stockholders' equity will be overstated.**

ACCRUED SALARIES. Some types of expenses are paid for after the services have been performed. Examples are employee salaries and commissions. At

[2] The computation of interest will be considered in more depth in later chapters.

Premier Staffing Inc., salaries were last paid on October 26; the next payday is November 9. As shown in the calendar in Illustration 4-14, three working days remain in October (October 29–31).

Illustration 4-14

Calendar showing Premier's pay periods

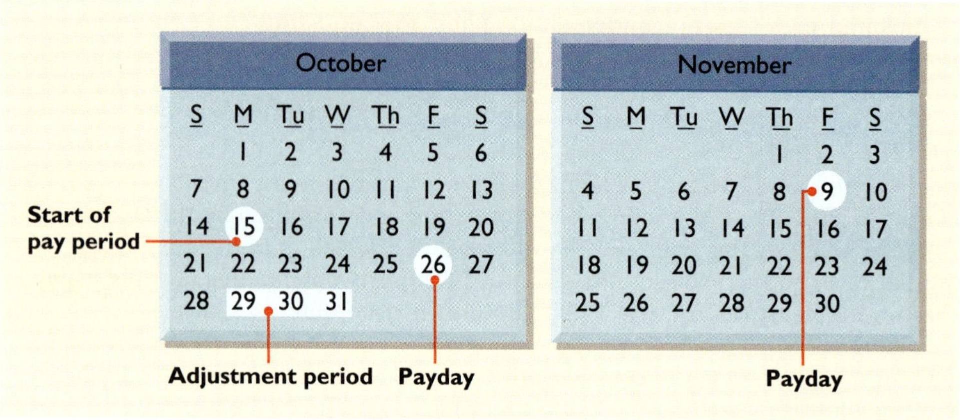

At October 31, the salaries for the last three days of the month represent an accrued expense and a related liability. The employees receive total salaries of $2,000 for a five-day workweek, or $400 per day. Thus, accrued salaries at October 31 are $1,200 ($400 × 3). The adjusting entry is:

A	=	L	+	SE
		+1,200		−1,200

Oct. 31	Salaries Expense	1,200	
	Salaries Payable		1,200
	(To record accrued salaries)		

After this adjusting entry is posted, the accounts look like Illustration 4-15.

Illustration 4-15

Salary accounts after adjustment

Salaries Expense

10/26	4,000		
31 **Adj.**	**1,200**		
10/31 Bal.	5,200		

Salaries Payable

		10/31 **Adj.**	**1,200**

After this adjustment, the balance in Salaries Expense of $5,200 (13 days × $400) is the actual salary expense for October. (The employees started work on October 15.) The balance in Salaries Payable of $1,200 is the amount of the liability for salaries owed as of October 31. **If the $1,200 adjustment for salaries is not recorded, Premier's expenses will be understated $1,200, and its liabilities will be understated $1,200.**

At Premier Staffing, salaries are payable every two weeks. The next payday is November 9, when total salaries of $4,000 will again be paid. The payment will consist of $1,200 of salaries payable at October 31 plus $2,800 of salaries expense for November (seven working days as shown in the November calendar × $400). Therefore, the following entry is made on November 9.

A	=	L	+	SE
−4,000		−1,200		−2,800

Nov. 9	Salaries Payable	1,200	
	Salaries Expense	2,800	
	Cash		4,000
	(To record November 9 payroll)		

This entry does two things: (1) It eliminates the liability for Salaries Payable that was recorded in the October 31 adjusting entry. (2) It records the proper amount of Salaries Expense for the period between November 1 and November 9.

TECHNOLOGY IN ACTION

In many computer systems, the adjusting process is handled like any other transaction, with the accountant inputting the adjustment at the time required. The main difference between adjusting entries and regular transactions is that with adjusting entries, one part of the computer system may perform the required calculation for such items as depreciation or interest and then "feed" these figures to the journalizing process.

Such systems are also able to display information before and after changes were made. Management may be interested in such information to highlight the impact that adjustments have on the various accounts and financial statements.

BEFORE YOU GO ON...

REVIEW IT

1. If an accrued revenue adjusting entry is not made, what is the effect on assets, stockholders' equity, revenues, and net income?
2. If an accrued expense adjusting entry is not made, what is the effect on liabilities, stockholders' equity, and interest expense?

DO IT

Hector and Jeremy are the new owners of Micro Property Management System Services Inc. At the end of August 2004, their first month of ownership, Hector and Jeremy are trying to prepare monthly financial statements. They have the following information for the month.

1. At August 31, Micro Property owed employees $800 in salaries that will be paid on September 1.
2. On August 1, Micro Property borrowed $30,000 from a local bank on a 15-year mortgage. The annual interest rate is 10%.
3. Service revenue unrecorded in August totaled $1,100.

Prepare the adjusting entries needed at August 31, 2004.

ACTION PLAN

- Make adjusting entries at the end of the period for revenues earned and expenses incurred in the period.
- Don't forget to make adjusting entries for accruals. Adjusting entries for accruals will increase both a balance sheet and an income statement account.

SOLUTION

1. Salaries Expense	800	
Salaries Payable		800
(To record accrued salaries)		
2. Interest Expense	250	
Interest Payable		250
(To record interest)		
($30,000 × 10% × 1/12 = $250)		
3. Accounts Receivable	1,100	
Service Revenue		1,100
(To record revenue for services provided)		

Related exercise material: 4-4, 4-6, 4-7, and 4-8.

THE NAVIGATOR

SUMMARY OF BASIC RELATIONSHIPS

The four basic types of adjusting entries are summarized in Illustration 4-16. Take some time to study and analyze the adjusting entries shown in the summary. Be sure to note that **each adjusting entry affects one balance sheet account and one income statement account**.

Illustration 4-16

Summary of adjusting entries

Type of Adjustment	Reason for Adjustment	Accounts before Adjustment	Adjusting Entry
1. Prepaid expenses	Prepaid expenses originally recorded in asset accounts have been used.	Assets overstated Expenses understated	Dr. Expenses Cr. Assets
2. Unearned revenues	Unearned revenues initially recorded in liability accounts have been earned.	Liabilities overstated Revenues understated	Dr. Liabilities Cr. Revenues
3. Accrued revenues	Revenues have been earned but not yet received in cash or recorded.	Assets understated Revenues understated	Dr. Assets Cr. Revenues
4. Accrued expenses	Expenses have been incurred but not yet paid in cash or recorded.	Expenses understated Liabilities understated	Dr. Expenses Cr. Liabilities

The journalizing and posting of adjusting entries for Premier Staffing Agency Inc. on October 31 are shown in Illustrations 4-17 and 4-18. All adjustments are identified in the ledger by the reference J2 because they have been journalized on page 2 of the general journal. A center caption entitled "Adjusting Entries" may be inserted between the last transaction entry and the first adjusting entry to identify these entries. When reviewing the general ledger in Illustration 4-18, note that the adjustments are highlighted in color.

Illustration 4-17

General journal showing adjusting entries

GENERAL JOURNAL — J2

Date	Account Titles and Explanation	Ref.	Debit	Credit
2004	Adjusting Entries			
Oct. 31	Supplies Expense	611	1,500	
	Supplies	129		1,500
	(To record supplies used)			
31	Insurance Expense	722	50	
	Prepaid Insurance	130		50
	(To record insurance expired)			
31	Depreciation Expense	711	40	
	Accumulated Depreciation—Office Equipment	158		40
	(To record monthly depreciation)			
31	Unearned Revenue	209	400	
	Service Revenue	400		400
	(To record revenue for services provided)			
31	Accounts Receivable	112	200	
	Service Revenue	400		200
	(To record revenue for services provided)			
31	Interest Expense	905	50	
	Interest Payable	230		50
	(To record interest on notes payable)			
31	Salaries Expense	726	1,200	
	Salaries Payable	212		1,200
	(To record accrued salaries)			

HELPFUL HINT

(1) Adjusting entries should not involve debits or credits to cash.
(2) Evaluate whether the adjustment makes sense. For example, an adjustment to recognize supplies used should increase supplies expense.
(3) Double-check all computations.

Illustration 4-18

General ledger after adjustment

GENERAL LEDGER

Cash No. 101

Date	Explanation	Ref.	Debit	Credit	Balance
2004					
Oct. 1		J1	10,000		10,000
2		J1	1,200		11,200
3		J1		900	10,300
4		J1		600	9,700
20		J1		500	9,200
26		J1		4,000	5,200
31		J1	10,000		15,200

Accounts Receivable No. 112

Date	Explanation	Ref.	Debit	Credit	Balance
2004					
Oct. 31	Adj. entry	J2	200		200

Supplies No. 129

Date	Explanation	Ref.	Debit	Credit	Balance
2004					
Oct. 5		J1	2,500		2,500
31	Adj. entry	J2		1,500	1,000

Prepaid Insurance No. 130

Date	Explanation	Ref.	Debit	Credit	Balance
2004					
Oct. 4		J1	600		600
31	Adj. entry	J2		50	550

Office Equipment No. 157

Date	Explanation	Ref.	Debit	Credit	Balance
2004					
Oct. 1		J1	5,000		5,000

Accumulated Depreciation—Office Equipment No. 158

Date	Explanation	Ref.	Debit	Credit	Balance
2004					
Oct. 31	Adj. entry	J2		40	40

Notes Payable No. 200

Date	Explanation	Ref.	Debit	Credit	Balance
2004					
Oct. 1		J1		5,000	5,000

Accounts Payable No. 201

Date	Explanation	Ref.	Debit	Credit	Balance
2004					
Oct. 5		J1		2,500	2,500

Unearned Revenue No. 209

Date	Explanation	Ref.	Debit	Credit	Balance
2004					
Oct. 2		J1		1,200	
31	Adj. entry	J2	400		800

Salaries Payable No. 212

Date	Explanation	Ref.	Debit	Credit	Balance
2004					
Oct. 31	Adj. entry	J2		1,200	1,200

Interest Payable No. 230

Date	Explanation	Ref.	Debit	Credit	Balance
2004					
Oct. 31	Adj. entry	J2		50	50

Common Stock No. 311

Date	Explanation	Ref.	Debit	Credit	Balance
2004					
Oct. 1		J1		10,000	10,000

Retained Earnings No. 320

Date	Explanation	Ref.	Debit	Credit	Balance
2004					

Dividends No. 332

Date	Explanation	Ref.	Debit	Credit	Balance
2004					
Oct. 20		J1	500		500

Service Revenue No. 400

Date	Explanation	Ref.	Debit	Credit	Balance
2004					
Oct. 31		J1		10,000	10,000
31	Adj. entry	J2		400	10,400
31	Adj. entry	J2		200	10,600

Supplies Expense No. 611

Date	Explanation	Ref.	Debit	Credit	Balance
2004					
Oct. 31	Adj. entry	J2	1,500		1,500

Depreciation Expense No. 711

Date	Explanation	Ref.	Debit	Credit	Balance
2004					
Oct. 31	Adj. entry	J2	40		40

Insurance Expense No. 722

Date	Explanation	Ref.	Debit	Credit	Balance
2004					
Oct. 31	Adj. entry	J2	50		50

Salaries Expense No. 726

Date	Explanation	Ref.	Debit	Credit	Balance
2004					
Oct. 26		J1	4,000		4,000
31	Adj. entry	J2	1,200		5,200

Rent Expense No. 729

Date	Explanation	Ref.	Debit	Credit	Balance
2004					
Oct. 3		J1	900		900

Interest Expense No. 905

Date	Explanation	Ref.	Debit	Credit	Balance
2004					
Oct. 31	Adj. entry	J2	50		50

STUDY OBJECTIVE 7

Describe the nature and purpose of an adjusted trial balance.

THE ADJUSTED TRIAL BALANCE AND FINANCIAL STATEMENTS

After all adjusting entries have been journalized and posted, another trial balance is prepared from the ledger accounts. This is called an **adjusted trial balance**. Its purpose is to **prove the equality** of the total debit balances and the total credit balances in the ledger after all adjustments have been made. The accounts in the adjusted trial balance contain all data that are needed for the preparation of financial statements.

PREPARING THE ADJUSTED TRIAL BALANCE

The adjusted trial balance for Premier Staffing Agency Inc. is shown in Illustration 4-19. It has been prepared from the ledger accounts in Illustration 4-18. The amounts affected by the adjusting entries are highlighted in color. Compare these amounts to those in the unadjusted trial balance in Illustration 4-3 on page 116.

Illustration 4-19

Adjusted trial balance

PREMIER STAFFING AGENCY INC.
Adjusted Trial Balance
October 31, 2004

	Dr.	Cr.
Cash	$15,200	
Accounts Receivable	**200**	
Supplies	**1,000**	
Prepaid Insurance	**550**	
Office Equipment	5,000	
Accumulated Depreciation—Office Equipment		$ **40**
Notes Payable		5,000
Accounts Payable		2,500
Unearned Revenue		**800**
Salaries Payable		**1,200**
Interest Payable		**50**
Common Stock		10,000
Retained Earnings		–0–
Dividends	500	
Service Revenue		**10,600**
Salaries Expense	**5,200**	
Supplies Expense	**1,500**	
Rent Expense	900	
Insurance Expense	**50**	
Interest Expense	**50**	
Depreciation Expense	**40**	
	$30,190	$30,190

PREPARING FINANCIAL STATEMENTS

Financial statements can be prepared directly from the adjusted trial balance. Illustrations 4-20 and 4-21 show the interrelationships of data in the adjusted trial balance and the financial statements.

As shown in Illustration 4-20, the income statement is first prepared from the revenue and expense accounts. The retained earnings statement is derived from the retained earnings and dividends accounts and the net income (or net loss) shown in the income statement. As shown in Illustration 4-21, the balance sheet is then prepared from the asset and liability accounts, the common stock account, and the ending retained earnings balance as reported in the retained earnings statement.

Illustration 4-20

Preparation of the income statement and retained earnings statement from the adjusted trial balance

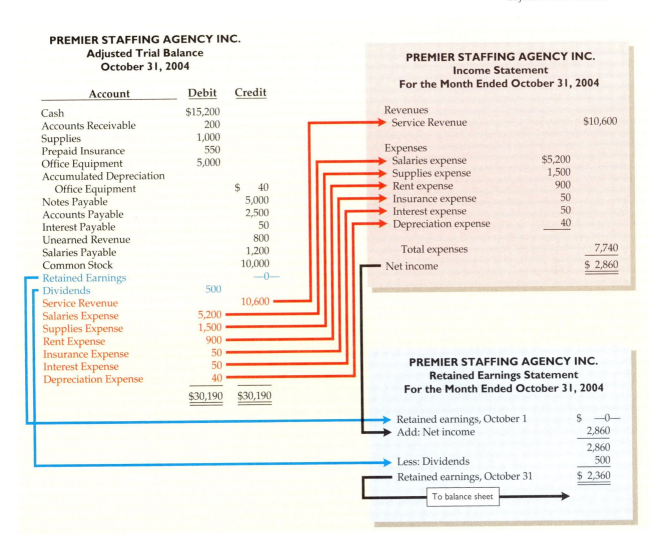

PREMIER STAFFING AGENCY INC.
Adjusted Trial Balance
October 31, 2004

Account	Debit	Credit
Cash	$15,200	
Accounts Receivable	200	
Supplies	1,000	
Prepaid Insurance	550	
Office Equipment	5,000	
Accumulated Depreciation—Office Equipment		$ 40
Notes Payable		5,000
Accounts Payable		2,500
Interest Payable		50
Unearned Revenue		800
Salaries Payable		1,200
Common Stock		10,000
Retained Earnings		—0—
Dividends	500	
Service Revenue		10,600
Salaries Expense	5,200	
Supplies Expense	1,500	
Rent Expense	900	
Insurance Expense	50	
Interest Expense	50	
Depreciation Expense	40	
	$30,190	$30,190

PREMIER STAFFING AGENCY INC.
Income Statement
For the Month Ended October 31, 2004

Revenues		
Service Revenue		$10,600
Expenses		
Salaries expense	$5,200	
Supplies expense	1,500	
Rent expense	900	
Insurance expense	50	
Interest expense	50	
Depreciation expense	40	
Total expenses		7,740
Net income		$ 2,860

PREMIER STAFFING AGENCY INC.
Retained Earnings Statement
For the Month Ended October 31, 2004

Retained earnings, October 1	$ —0—
Add: Net income	2,860
	2,860
Less: Dividends	500
Retained earnings, October 31	$ 2,360

To balance sheet

Illustration 4-21

Preparation of the balance sheet from the adjusted trial balance

PREMIER STAFFING AGENCY INC.
Adjusted Trial Balance
October 31, 2004

Account	Debit	Credit
Cash	$15,200	
Accounts Receivable	200	
Supplies	1,000	
Prepaid Insurance	550	
Office Equipment	5,000	
Accumulated Depreciation—Office Equipment		$ 40
Notes Payable		5,000
Accounts Payable		2,500
Interest Payable		50
Unearned Revenue		800
Salaries Payable		1,200
Common Stock		10,000
Retained Earnings		-0-
Dividends	500	
Service Revenue		10,600
Salaries Expense	5,200	
Supplies Expense	1,500	
Rent Expense	900	
Insurance Expense	50	
Interest Expense	50	
Depreciation Expense	40	
	$30,190	$30,190

PREMIER STAFFING AGENCY INC.
Balance Sheet
October 31, 2004

Assets		
Cash		$15,200
Accounts receivable		200
Supplies		1,000
Prepaid insurance		550
Office equipment	$5,000	
Less: Accumulated depreciation	40	4,960
Total assets		$21,910
Liabilities and Stockholder's Equity		
Liabilities		
Notes payable		$ 5,000
Accounts payable		2,500
Interest payable		50
Unearned revenue		800
Salaries payable		1,200
Total liabilities		9,550
Stockholders' equity		
Common Stock		10,000
Retained earnings		2,360
Total liabilities and stockholder's equity		$21,910

Balance at Oct. 31 from Retained Earnings Statement in Illustration 4-20

BEFORE YOU GO ON...

REVIEW IT

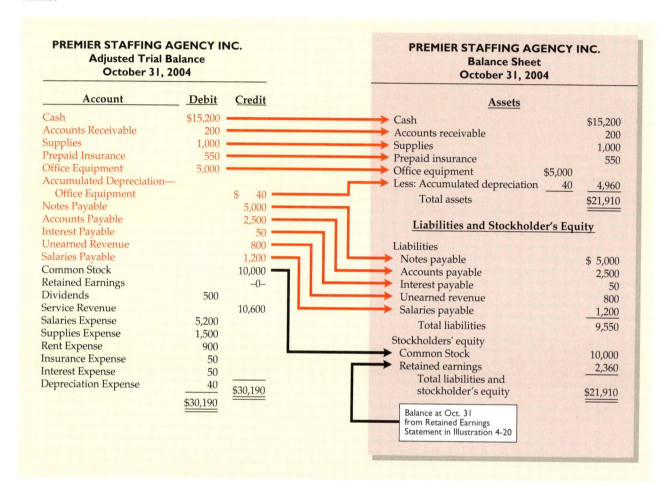

1. What is the purpose of an adjusted trial balance?
2. How is an adjusted trial balance prepared?

ALTERNATIVE TREATMENT OF PREPAID EXPENSES AND UNEARNED REVENUES

STUDY OBJECTIVE 8

Prepare adjusting entries for the alternative treatment of prepayments.

In our discussion of adjusting entries for prepaid expenses and unearned revenues, we illustrated transactions for which the initial entries were made to balance sheet accounts. In the case of prepaid expenses, the prepayment was debited to an asset account. In the case of unearned revenue, the cash received was credited to a liability account. Some businesses use an alternative treatment: (1) At the time an expense is prepaid, it is debited to an expense account. (2) At the time of a receipt for future services, it is credited to a revenue account. The circumstances that justify such entries and the different adjusting entries that may be required are described below. The alternative treatment of prepaid expenses and unearned revenues has the same effect on the financial statements as the procedures described in the chapter.

PREPAID EXPENSES

Prepaid expenses become expired costs either through the passage of time (e.g., insurance) or through consumption (e.g., supplies). If, at the time of purchase, the company expects to consume the supplies before the next financial statement date, **it may be more convenient initially to debit (increase) an expense account rather than an asset account**.

Assume that Premier Staffing Agency Inc. expects that all of the supplies purchased on October 5 will be used before the end of the month. A debit of $2,500 to Supplies Expense (rather than to the asset account Supplies) on October 5 will eliminate the need for an adjusting entry on October 31, if all the supplies are used. At October 31, the Supplies Expense account will show a balance of $2,500, which is the cost of supplies used between October 5 and October 31.

But what if the company does not use all the supplies, and an inventory of $1,000 of supplies remains on October 31? Obviously, an adjusting entry is needed. Prior to adjustment, the expense account Supplies Expense is overstated $1,000, and the asset account Supplies is understated $1,000. Thus the following adjusting entry is made.

Oct. 31	Supplies	1,000	
	Supplies Expense		1,000
	(To record supplies inventory)		

A	=	L	+	SE
+1,000				+1,000

After posting the adjusting entry, the accounts show:

Illustration 4-22

Prepaid expenses accounts after adjustment

Supplies					**Supplies Expense**			
10/31 **Adj.**	**1,000**				10/5	2,500	10/31 **Adj.**	**1,000**
					10/31 **Bal.**	**1,500**		

After adjustment, the asset account Supplies shows a balance of $1,000, which is equal to the cost of supplies on hand at October 31. In addition, Supplies Expense shows a balance of $1,500, which is equal to the cost of supplies used between October 5 and October 31. If the adjusting entry is not made, expenses will be overstated and net income will be understated by $1,000 in the October income statement. Also, both assets and stockholders' equity will be understated by $1,000 on the October 31 balance sheet.

A comparison of the entries and accounts for advertising supplies is shown in Illustration 4-23.

Illustration 4-23

Adjustment approaches—a comparison

Prepayment Initially Debited to Asset Account				**Prepayment Initially Debited to Expense Account (alternative)**			
Oct. 5	Supplies	2,500		Oct. 5	Supplies Expense	2,500	
	Accounts Payable		2,500		Accounts Payable		2,500
Oct. 31	Supplies Expense	1,500		Oct. 31	Supplies	1,000	
	Advertising Supplies		1,500		Advertising Supplies Expense		1,000

After posting the entries, the accounts look like Illustration 4-24.

Illustration 4-24

Comparison of accounts

Supplies

10/5	2,500	10/31 **Adj.**	**1,500**
10/31 **Bal.**	**1,000**		

Supplies Expense

10/31 **Adj.**	**1,500**		

(alternative)
Supplies

10/31 **Adj.**	**1,000**		

Supplies Expense

10/5	2,500	10/31 **Adj.**	**1,000**
10/31 **Bal.**	**1,500**		

Note that the account balances under each alternative are the same at October 31: Supplies $1,000, and Supplies Expense $1,500.

UNEARNED REVENUES

Unearned revenues become earned either through the passage of time (e.g., unearned rent) or through providing the service (e.g., unearned fees). Similar to the case for prepaid expenses, a revenue account may be credited (increased) when cash is received for future services.

To illustrate, assume that Premier Staffing received $1,200 for future services on October 2. The services were expected to be performed before October 31.[3] In such a case, Service Revenue is credited. If revenue is in fact earned before October 31, no adjustment is needed.

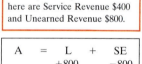

HELPFUL HINT
The required adjusted balances here are Service Revenue $400 and Unearned Revenue $800.

However, if at the statement date $800 of the services have not been performed, an adjusting entry is required. The revenue account Service Revenue is overstated $800, and the liability account Unearned Revenue is understated $800. Thus, the following adjusting entry is made.

A	=	L	+	SE
		+800		−800

Oct. 31	Service Revenue	800	
	Unearned Revenue		800
	(To record unearned revenue)		

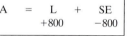

After posting the adjusting entry, the accounts look like Illustration 4-25.

Illustration 4-25

Unearned revenue accounts after adjustment

Unearned Revenue

		10/31 **Adj.**	**800**

Service Revenue

10/31 **Adj.**	**800**	10/2	1,200
		10/31 **Bal.**	**400**

The liability account Unearned Revenue shows a balance of $800. This is equal to the services that will be provided in the future. In addition, the balance in Service Revenue equals the services provided in October. If the adjusting entry is not made, both revenues and net income will be overstated by $800 in the October income statement. Also, liabilities will be understated by $800, and stockholders' equity will be overstated by $800 on the October 31 balance sheet.

[3]This example focuses only on the alternative treatment of unearned revenues. In the interest of simplicity, the entries to Service Revenue pertaining to the immediate earning of revenue ($10,000) and the adjusting entry for accrued revenue ($200) have been ignored.

A comparison of the entries and accounts for service revenue earned and unearned is shown in Illustration 4-26.

Illustration 4-26

Adjustment approaches—a comparison

Unearned Revenue Initially Credited to Liability Account				Unearned Revenue Initially Credited to Revenue Account (alternative)			
Oct. 2	Cash	1,200		Oct. 2	Cash	1,200	
	Unearned Revenue		1,200		Service Revenue		1,200
Oct. 31	Unearned Revenue	400		Oct. 31	Service Revenue	800	
	Service Revenue		400		Unearned Revenue		800

After posting the entries, the accounts look like Illustration 4-27.

Illustration 4-27

Comparison of accounts

Unearned Revenue

Debit		Credit	
10/31 **Adj.**	**400**	10/2	1,200
		10/31 **Bal.**	**800**

Service Revenue

Debit		Credit	
		10/31 **Adj.**	**400**

(alternative) Unearned Revenue

Debit		Credit	
		10/31 **Adj.**	**800**

Service Revenue

Debit		Credit	
10/31 **Adj.**	**800**	10/2	1,200
		10/31 **Bal.**	**400**

Note that the balances in the accounts are the same under the two alternatives: Unearned Revenue $800, and Service Revenue $400.

SUMMARY OF ADDITIONAL ADJUSTMENT RELATIONSHIPS

The use of alternative adjusting entries requires additions to the summary of basic relationships presented earlier in Illustration 4-16. The additions are shown in color in Illustration 4-28.

Alternative adjusting entries **do not apply** to accrued revenues and accrued expenses because **no entries occur before these types of adjusting entries are made.** Therefore, the entries in Illustration 4-16 for these two types of adjustments remain unchanged.

Illustration 4-28

Summary of basic relationships for prepayments

Type of Adjustment	Reason for Adjustment	Account Balances before Adjustment	Adjusting Entry
1. Prepaid expenses	(a) Prepaid expenses initially recorded in asset accounts have been used.	Assets overstated Expenses understated	Dr. Expenses Cr. Assets
	(b) Prepaid expenses initially recorded in expense accounts have not been used.	**Assets understated Expenses overstated**	**Dr. Assets Cr. Expenses**
2. Unearned revenues	(a) Unearned revenues initially recorded in liability accounts have been earned.	Liabilities overstated Revenues understated	Dr. Liabilities Cr. Revenues
	(b) Unearned revenues initially recorded in revenue accounts have not been earned.	**Liabilities understated Revenues overstated**	**Dr. Revenues Cr. Liabilities**

A LOOK BACK AT OUR FEATURE STORY

Refer back to the Feature Story about **Lake Swan Resort**, **Juneau Country Club**, **Cuisine-on-the-Go**, and **Hospitality Purveyors** at the beginning of the chapter, and answer the following questions.

1. What are the purposes of adjusting entries?
2. What do these four companies have in common relative to accrual accounting?
3. What other types of adjusting entries do you believe these companies might make?

SOLUTION

1. Adjusting entries are necessary to make the financial statements complete and accurate. Adjusting entries are made to record revenues in the period in which they are earned and to recognize expenses in the period in which they are incurred. Therefore, adjustments ensure that the revenue recognition and matching principles are followed.
2. Each of the companies misstated net income by either overstating revenues (sales) or understating expenses. They failed to properly time the reporting of revenues or expenses.
3. (a) Accrued expenses: rent, salaries, utilities, interest, taxes.
   (b) Accrued revenues: interest earned, rent, commissions, fees.
   (c) Prepaid expenses: insurance, rent, supplies, advertising.
   (d) Unearned revenues: rent, subscriptions, customer deposits, and prepayments.

THE NAVIGATOR

DEMONSTRATION PROBLEM

Terry Thomas opens the Green Thumb Lawn Care Company to provide lawn-care services to hotels, restaurants, and theme parks on April 1. At April 30, the trial balance shows the following balances for selected accounts.

Prepaid Insurance	$ 3,600
Equipment	28,000
Notes Payable	20,000
Unearned Revenue	4,200
Service Revenue	1,800

Analysis reveals the following additional data.

1. Prepaid insurance is the cost of a 2-year insurance policy, effective April 1.
2. Depreciation on the equipment is $500 per month.
3. The note payable is dated April 1. It is a 6-month, 12 percent note.
4. Seven customers paid for the company's 6 months' lawn service package of $600 beginning in April. These customers were serviced in April.
5. Lawn services provided other customers but not billed at April 30 totaled $1,500.

Instructions

Prepare the adjusting entries for the month of April. Show computations.

ACTION PLAN

- Note that adjustments are being made for one month.
- Make computations carefully.
- Select account titles carefully.
- Make sure debits are made first and credits are indented.
- Check that debits equal credits for each entry.

SOLUTION TO DEMONSTRATION PROBLEM

GENERAL JOURNAL **J1**

Date	Account Titles and Explanation	Ref.	Debit	Credit
	Adjusting Entries			
Apr. 30	Insurance Expense		150	
	Prepaid Insurance			150
	(To record insurance expired: $3,600 ÷ 24 = $150 per month)			

30	Depreciation Expense	500	
	Accumulated Depreciation—Equipment		500
	(To record monthly depreciation)		
30	Interest Expense	200	
	Interest Payable		200
	(To record interest on notes payable: $20,000 × 12% × 1/12 = $200)		
30	Unearned Revenue	700	
	Service Revenue		700
	(To record service revenue: $600 ÷ 6 = $100; $100 per month × 7 = $700)		
30	Accounts Receivable	1,500	
	Service Revenue		1,500
	(To record revenue for services provided)		

SUMMARY OF STUDY OBJECTIVES

1. *Explain the time period assumption.* The time period assumption assumes that the economic life of a business can be divided into artificial time periods.

2. *Explain the accrual basis of accounting.* Accrual-basis accounting means that events that change a company's financial statements are recorded in the periods in which the events occur, rather than in the periods in which the company receives or pays cash.

3. *Explain why adjusting entries are needed.* Adjusting entries are made at the end of an accounting period. They ensure that revenues are recorded in the period in which they are earned and that expenses are recognized in the period in which they are incurred.

4. *Identify the major types of adjusting entries.* The major types of adjusting entries are prepaid expenses, unearned revenues, accrued revenues, and accrued expenses.

5. *Prepare adjusting entries for prepayments.* Prepayments are either prepaid expenses or unearned revenues. Adjusting entries for prepayments are required at the statement date to record the portion of the prepayment that represents the expense incurred or the revenue earned in the current accounting period.

6. *Prepare adjusting entries for accruals.* Accruals are either accrued revenues or accrued expenses. Adjusting entries for accruals are required to record revenues earned and expenses incurred in the current accounting period that have not been recognized through daily entries.

7. *Describe the nature and purpose of an adjusted trial balance.* An adjusted trial balance shows the balances of all accounts, including those that have been adjusted, at the end of an accounting period. Its purpose is to show the effects of all financial events that have occurred during the accounting period.

8. *Prepare adjusting entries for the alternative treatment of prepayments.* Prepayments may be initially debited to an expense account. Unearned revenues may be credited to a revenue account. At the end of the period, these accounts may be overstated. The adjusting entries for prepaid expenses are a debit to an asset account and a credit to an expense account. Adjusting entries for unearned revenues are a debit to a revenue account and a credit to a liability account.

GLOSSARY

Accrual-basis accounting Accounting basis in which transactions that change a company's financial statements are recorded in the periods in which the events occur (p. 113).

Accrued expenses Expenses incurred but not yet paid in cash or recorded (p. 116).

Accrued revenues Revenues earned but not yet received in cash or recorded (p. 116).

Adjusted trial balance A list of accounts and their balances after all adjustments have been made (p. 130).

Adjusting entries Entries made at the end of an accounting period to ensure that the revenue recognition and matching principles are followed (p. 115).

Book value The difference between the cost of a depreciable asset and its related accumulated depreciation (p. 120).

Calendar year An accounting period that extends from January 1 to December 31 (p. 113).

Cash-basis accounting Accounting basis in which revenue is recorded when cash is received and an expense is recorded when cash is paid (p. 113).

Contra asset account An account that is offset against an asset account on the balance sheet (p. 120).

Depreciation The allocation of the cost of an asset to expense over its useful life in a rational and systematic manner (p. 119).

Fiscal year An accounting period that is one year in length (p. 113).

Interim periods Monthly or quarterly accounting time periods (p. 113).

Matching principle The principle that efforts (expenses) be matched with accomplishments (revenues) (p. 114).

Prepaid expenses Expenses paid in cash and recorded as assets before they are used or consumed (p. 116).

Revenue recognition principle The principle that revenue be recognized in the accounting period in which it is earned (p. 114).

Time period assumption An assumption that the economic life of a business can be divided into artificial time periods (p. 113).

Unearned revenues Cash received and recorded as liabilities before revenue is earned (p. 116).

Useful life The length of service of a productive facility (p. 119).

EXERCISES

Indicate why adjusting entries are needed.
(SO 3)

4-1 The ledger of Heavenly Cruiselines includes the following accounts. Explain why each account may require adjustment.

(a) Prepaid Insurance
(b) Depreciation Expense
(c) Unearned Revenue
(d) Interest Payable

Identify the major types of adjusting entries.
(SO 4)

4-2 Riko Cigar Company accumulates the following adjustment data at December 31. Indicate **(a)** the type of adjustment (prepaid expense, accrued revenues and so on), and **(b)** the accounts before adjustment (overstated or understated).

1. Supplies of $100 are on hand.
2. Services provided but unbilled total $900.
3. Interest of $200 has accumulated on a note payable.
4. Rent collected in advance totaling $800 has been earned.

Prepare adjusting entry for supplies.
(SO 5)

4-3 Sain Design Company specializes in menu design for foodservices. Its trial balance at December 31 shows Supplies $8,700 and Supplies Expense $0. On December 31, there are $1,700 of supplies on hand. Prepare the adjusting entry at December 31, and using T accounts, enter the balances in the accounts, post the adjusting entry, and indicate the adjusted balance in each account.

Prepare adjusting entries for accruals.
(SO 6)

4-4 The bookkeeper for Rosenberg Consulting Company asks you to prepare the following accrued adjusting entries at December 31.

1. Interest on notes payable of $300 is accrued.
2. Services provided but unbilled total $1,250.
3. Salaries earned by employees of $900 have not been recorded.

Use the following account titles: Service Revenue, Accounts Receivable, Interest Expense, Interest Payable, Salaries Expense, and Salaries Payable.

Analyze accounts in an adjusted trial balance.
(SO 7)

4-5 The trial balance of Hoi Catering Company includes the following balance sheet accounts. Identify the accounts that require adjustment. For each account that requires adjustment, indicate **(a)** the type of adjusting entry (prepaid expenses, unearned revenues, accrued revenues, and accrued expenses) and **(b)** the related account in the adjusting entry.

Accounts Receivable	Interest Payable
Prepaid Insurance	Unearned Service Revenue
Accumulated Depreciation—Equipment	

Identify types of adjustments and account relationships.
(SO 4, 5, 6)

4-6 Jawson Catering accumulates the following adjustment data at December 31.

1. Services provided but unbilled total $750.
2. Store supplies of $300 have been used.
3. Utility expenses of $225 are unpaid.
4. Unearned revenue of $260 has been earned.
5. Salaries of $900 are unpaid.
6. Prepaid insurance totaling $350 has expired.

Instructions

For each of the above items, indicate the following.

(a) The type of adjustment (prepaid expense, unearned revenue, accrued revenue, or accrued expense).
(b) The accounts before adjustment (overstatement or understatement).

Prepare adjusting entries from selected account data.
(SO 5, 6, 7)

4-7 The ledger of Easy Party Supplies Rental Agency on March 31 of the current year includes the following selected accounts before adjusting entries have been prepared.

	Debit	Credit
Prepaid Insurance	$ 3,600	
Supplies	2,800	
Equipment	25,000	
Accumulated Depreciation—Equipment		$ 8,400
Notes Payable		20,000
Unearned Rent Revenue		9,900
Rent Revenue		60,000
Interest Expense	–0–	
Wage Expense	14,000	

An analysis of the accounts shows the following.

1. The equipment depreciates $250 per month.
2. One-third of the unearned rent was earned during the quarter.
3. Interest of $500 is accrued on the notes payable.
4. Supplies on hand total $650.
5. Insurance expires at the rate of $300 per month.

Instructions

Prepare the adjusting entries at March 31, assuming that adjusting entries are made quarterly. Additional accounts are: Depreciation Expense, Insurance Expense, Interest Payable, and Supplies Expense.

Prepare adjusting entries. (SO 5, 6, 7)

4-8 Karen Tong, D.D.S., opened a flower shop on January 1, 2004. During the first month of operations the following transactions occurred.

1. Performed services for hotel clients. At January 31, $875 of such services was earned but not yet billed to the hotel companies.
2. Utility expenses incurred but not paid prior to January 31 totaled $520.
3. Purchased furniture on January 1 for $80,000, paying $20,000 in cash and signing a $60,000, 3-year note payable. The furniture depreciates $400 per month. Interest is $500 per month.
4. Purchased a one-year insurance policy on January 1 for $12,000.
5. Purchased $1,600 of supplies. On January 31, determined that $700 of supplies were on hand.

Instructions

Prepare the adjusting entries on January 31. Account titles are: Accumulated Depreciation—Furniture, Depreciation Expense, Service Revenue, Accounts Receivable, Insurance Expense, Interest Expense, Interest Payable, Prepaid Insurance, Supplies, Supplies Expense, Utilities Expense, and Utilities Payable.

Prepare adjusting entries, post to ledger accounts, and prepare adjusted trial balance. (SO 5, 6, 7)

4-9 Samwise Gamgee started his own hospitality consulting firm, Gamgee Company, on June 1, 2004. Gamgee Company performs feasibility studies to determine if restaurants should be opened at certain locations. The trial balance at June 30 is as follows.

GAMGEE COMPANY
Trial Balance
June 30, 2004

Account Number		Debit	Credit
100	Cash	$ 7,750	
110	Accounts Receivable	6,000	
120	Prepaid Insurance	2,400	
130	Supplies	2,000	
135	Office Equipment	15,000	
200	Accounts Payable		$ 4,500
230	Unearned Service Revenue		4,000
311	Common Stock		21,750
400	Service Revenue		7,900
510	Salaries Expense	4,000	
520	Rent Expense	1,000	
		$38,150	$38,150

In addition to those accounts listed on the trial balance, the chart of accounts for Gamgee Company also contains the following accounts and account numbers: No. 136 Accumulated Depreciation—Office Equipment, No. 210 Utilities Payable, No. 220 Salaries Payable, No. 530 Depreciation Expense, No. 540 Insurance Expense, No. 550 Utilities Expense, and No. 560 Supplies Expense.

Other data:

1. Supplies on hand at June 30 are $1,300.
2. A utility bill for $150 has not been recorded and will not be paid until next month.
3. The insurance policy is for a year.
4. $2,500 of unearned service revenue has been earned at the end of the month.
5. Salaries of $1,500 are accrued at June 30.
6. The office equipment has a 5-year life with no salvage value. It is being depreciated at $250 per month for 60 months.
7. Invoices representing $3,000 of services performed during the month have not been recorded as of June 30.

Instructions

(a) Prepare the adjusting entries for the month of June. Use J3 as the page number for your journal.

(b) Post the adjusting entries to the ledger accounts. Enter the totals from the trial balance as beginning account balances and place a check mark in the posting reference column.

(c) Prepare an adjusted trial balance at June 30, 2004.

Prepare adjusting entries, post to ledger accounts, and prepare an adjusted trial balance. (SO 5, 6, 7)

4-10 Julie Brown started her own consulting firm, Wedding Consulting, on May 1, 2004. The trial balance at May 31 is as follows.

WEDDING CONSULTING
Trial Balance
May 31, 2004

Account Number		Debit	Credit
101	Cash	$ 6,500	
110	Accounts Receivable	4,000	
120	Prepaid Insurance	3,600	
130	Supplies	1,500	
135	Office Furniture	12,000	
200	Accounts Payable		$ 3,500
230	Unearned Service Revenue		3,000
311	Common Stock		19,100
400	Service Revenue		6,000
510	Salaries Expense	3,000	
520	Rent Expense	1,000	
		$31,600	$31,600

In addition to those accounts listed on the trial balance, the chart of accounts for Wedding Consulting also contains the following accounts and account numbers: No. 136 Accumulated Depreciation—Office Furniture, No. 210 Travel Payable, No. 220 Salaries Payable, No. 530 Depreciation Expense, No. 540 Insurance Expense, No. 550 Travel Expense, and No. 560 Supplies Expense.

Other data:

1. $500 of supplies have been used during the month.
2. Travel expense incurred but not paid on May 31, 2003, $200.
3. The insurance policy is for 2 years.
4. $1,000 of the balance in the unearned service revenue account remains unearned at the end of the month.
5. May 31 is a Wednesday, and employees are paid on Fridays. Wedding Consulting has two employees, who are paid $500 each for a 5-day workweek.
6. The office furniture has a 5-year life with no salvage value. It is being depreciated at $200 per month for 60 months.
7. Invoices representing $2,000 of services performed during the month have not been recorded as of May 31.

Instructions

(a) Prepare the adjusting entries for the month of May. Use J4 as the page number for your journal.

(b) Post the adjusting entries to the ledger accounts. Enter the totals from the trial balance as beginning account balances and place a check mark in the posting reference column.

(c) Prepare an adjusted trial balance at May 31, 2004.

FINANCIAL REPORTING PROBLEM: Hilton Hotels Corporation

4-11 The financial statements of **Hilton** are presented in the Appendix at the end of this textbook.

Instructions

(a) Using the consolidated financial statements and related information, identify items that may result in adjusting entries for prepayments.

(b) Using the consolidated financial statements and related information, identify items that may result in adjusting entries for accruals.

(c) Using the Income Statement, what has been the trend since 1999 for depreciation and amortization expense?

EXPLORING THE WEB

4-12 A wealth of accounting-related information is available via the Internet. For example, the Rutgers Accounting Web offers access to a great variety of sources.

Address: **www.accounting.rutgers.edu/raw**

Steps: Click on **Accounting Resources**, or click on **RAW's Features**. (*Note:* Once on this page, you may have to click on the **text only** box to access the available information.)

Instructions

(a) List the categories of information available through the **Accounting Resources** page.

(b) Select any one of these categories and briefly describe the types of information available.

ETHICS CASE

4-13 Die Hard Company is a pest control company providing services to hotels and clubs. Its sales declined greatly this year due to the passage of legislation outlawing the sale of several of Die Hard's chemical pesticides. In the coming year, Die Hard will have environmentally safe and competitive chemicals to replace these discontinued products. Sales in the next year are expected to greatly exceed any prior year's. The decline in sales and profits appears to be a one-year aberration. But even so, the company president fears a large dip in the current year's profits. He believes that such a dip could cause a significant drop in the market price of Die Hard's stock and make the company a takeover target.

To avoid this possibility, the company president calls in Becky Freeman, controller, to discuss this period's year-end adjusting entries. He urges her to accrue every possible revenue and to defer as many expenses as possible. He says to Becky, "We need the revenues this year, and next year can easily absorb expenses deferred from this year. We can't let our stock price be hammered down!" Becky didn't get around to recording the adjusting entries until January 17, but she dated the entries December 31 as if they were recorded then. Becky also made every effort to comply with the president's request.

Instructions

(a) Who are the stakeholders in this situation?

(b) What are the ethical considerations of (1) the president's request and (2) Becky's dating the adjusting entries December 31?

(c) Can Becky accrue revenues and defer expenses and still be ethical?

Answer to Hilton Review It Question 4, p. 122

2001 depreciation and amortization expense is $391 million; 2000 depreciation and amortization expense is $382 million.

Remember to go back to the Navigator box on the chapter-opening page and check off your completed work.

THE NAVIGATOR ✓

- Understand *Concepts for Review* ❑
- Read *Feature Story* ❑
- Scan *Study Objectives* ❑
- Read *Preview* ❑
- Read text and answer *Before You Go On*
  p. 150 ❑ *p.* 160 ❑ *p.* 166 ❑
- Work *Demonstration Problem* ❑
- Review *Summary of Study Objectives* ❑
- Complete *Assignments* ❑

CONCEPTS FOR REVIEW

Before studying this chapter, you should know or, if necessary, review:

a. How to apply the revenue recognition and matching principles. (Ch. 4, p. 114)

b. How to make adjusting entries. (Ch. 4, pp. 115–126)

c. How to prepare an adjusted trial balance. (Ch. 4, p. 130)

d. How to prepare a balance sheet, income statement, and retained earnings statement. (Ch. 4, pp. 131–132)

THE NAVIGATOR ✓

FEATURE STORY

Everyone Likes to Win

When Ted Castle was a hockey coach at the University of Vermont, his players were self-motivated by their desire to win. Hockey was a game you either won or lost. But at **Rhino Foods, Inc.**, a specialty-bakery-foods company he founded in Burlington, Vermont, he discovered that manufacturing-line workers were not so self-motivated. Ted thought, what if he turned the food-making business into a game, with rules, strategies, and trophies?

Ted knew that in a game knowing the score is all-important. He felt that only if the employees know the score—know exactly how the business is doing daily, weekly, monthly—could he turn food-making into a game. But Rhino is a closely held, family-owned business, and its financial statements and profits were confidential. Should Ted open Rhino's books to the employees?

A consultant he was working with put Ted's concerns in perspective. The consultant said, "Imagine you're playing touch football. You play for an hour or two, and the whole time I'm sitting there with a book, keeping score. All of a sudden I blow the whistle, and I say, 'OK, that's it. Everybody go home.' I close my book and walk away. How would you feel?" Ted opened his books and revealed the financial statements to his employees.

The next step was to teach employees the rules and strategies of how to win at making food. The first lesson: "Your opponent at Rhino is expenses. You must cut and control expenses." Ted and his staff distilled those lessons into daily scorecards (production reports and income statements) that keep Rhino's employees up to date on the game. At noon each day, Ted posts the previous day's results at the entrance to the production room. Everyone checks whether they made or lost money on what they produced the day before. And it's not just an academic exercise; there's a bonus check for each employee at the end of every four-week "game" that meets profitability guidelines. Everyone can be a winner!

Rhino has flourished since the first game, three years ago. Employment has nearly tripled to 58, while both revenues and profits have grown by about 600 percent.

THE NAVIGATOR

STUDY OBJECTIVES

After studying this chapter, you should be able to

1. Prepare a work sheet.
2. Explain the process of closing the books.
3. Describe the content and purpose of a post-closing trial balance.
4. State the required steps in the accounting cycle.
5. Explain the approaches to preparing correcting entries.
6. Identify the sections of a classified balance sheet.

THE NAVIGATOR

PREVIEW OF CHAPTER 5

As was true at **Rhino Foods, Inc.** financial statements can help employees understand what is happening in the business. In Chapter 4, we prepared financial statements directly from the adjusted trial balance. However, with so many details involved in the end-of-period accounting procedures, it is easy to make errors. Locating and correcting errors can cost much time and effort. One way to minimize errors in the records and to simplify the end-of-period procedures is to use a work sheet.

In this chapter we will explain the role of the work sheet in accounting as well as the remaining steps in the accounting cycle, most especially, the closing process, again using Premier Staffing Agency as an example. Then we will consider (1) correcting entries and (2) classified balance sheets. The content and organization of Chapter 5 are as follows.

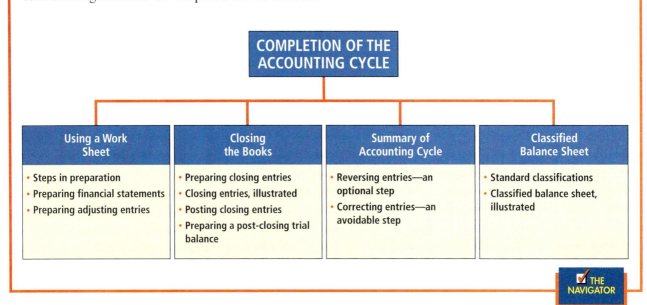

COMPLETION OF THE ACCOUNTING CYCLE

Using a Work Sheet
- Steps in preparation
- Preparing financial statements
- Preparing adjusting entries

Closing the Books
- Preparing closing entries
- Closing entries, illustrated
- Posting closing entries
- Preparing a post-closing trial balance

Summary of Accounting Cycle
- Reversing entries—an optional step
- Correcting entries—an avoidable step

Classified Balance Sheet
- Standard classifications
- Classified balance sheet, illustrated

THE NAVIGATOR

USING A WORK SHEET

STUDY OBJECTIVE 1

Prepare a work sheet.

A **work sheet** is a multiple-column form that may be used in the adjustment process and in preparing financial statements. As its name suggests, the work sheet is a working tool. **A work sheet is not a permanent accounting record**; it is neither a journal nor a part of the general ledger. The work sheet is merely a device used to make it easier to prepare adjusting entries and the financial statements. In small companies with relatively few accounts and adjustments, a work sheet may not be needed. In large companies with numerous accounts and many adjustments, it is almost indispensable.

The basic form of a work sheet and the procedure (five steps) for preparing it are shown in Illustration 5-1. Each step must be performed in the prescribed sequence.

The use of a work sheet is optional. When one is used, financial statements are prepared from the work sheet. The adjustments are entered in the work sheet columns and are then journalized and posted after the financial statements have been prepared. Thus, management and other interested parties can receive the financial statements at an earlier date when a work sheet is used.

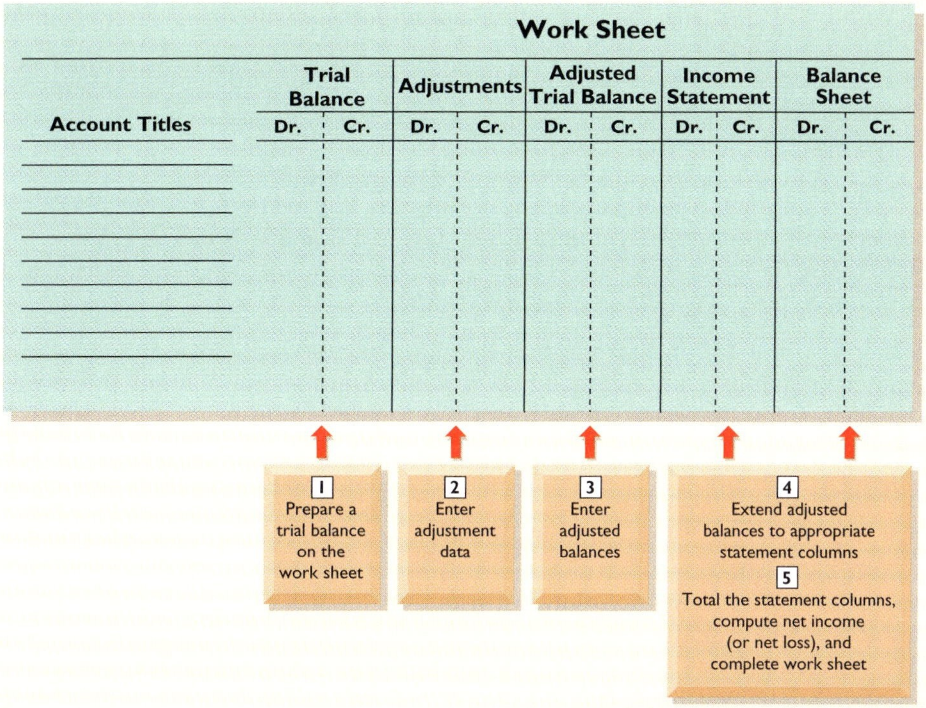
Work Sheet
Account Titles
Trial Balance
Adjustments
Adjusted Trial Balance
Income Statement
Balance Sheet
Dr.
Cr.
1 Prepare a trial balance on the work sheet
2 Enter adjustment data
3 Enter adjusted balances
4 Extend adjusted balances to appropriate statement columns
5 Total the statement columns, compute net income (or net loss), and complete work sheet

Illustration 5-1

Form and procedure for a work sheet

STEPS IN PREPARING A WORK SHEET

We will use the October 31 trial balance and adjustment data of Premier Staffing in Chapter 4 to illustrate the preparation of a work sheet. Each step of the process is described below and demonstrated in Illustrations 5-2 and 5-3A, B, C, and D following page 147.

Step 1. Prepare a Trial Balance on the Work Sheet

All ledger accounts with balances are entered in the account title space. Debit and credit amounts from the ledger are entered in the trial balance columns. The work sheet trial balance for Premier Staffing Agency is shown in Illustration 5-2.

Step 2. Enter the Adjustments in the Adjustments Columns

Turn over the first transparency, Illustration 5-3A. When a work sheet is used, all adjustments are entered in the adjustments columns. In entering the adjustments, applicable trial balance accounts should be used. If additional accounts are needed, they are inserted on the lines immediately below the trial balance totals. Each adjustment is indexed and keyed; this practice facilitates the journalizing of the adjusting entry in the general journal. **The adjustments are not journalized until after the work sheet is completed and the financial statements have been prepared.**

The adjustments for Premier Staffing Agency are the same as the adjustments illustrated on page 128. They are keyed in the adjustments columns of the work sheet as follows.

(a) An additional account Supplies Expense is debited $1,500 for the cost of supplies used, and Supplies is credited $1,500.
(b) An additional account Insurance Expense is debited $50 for the insurance that has expired, and Prepaid Insurance is credited $50.

(c) Two additional depreciation accounts are needed. Depreciation Expense is debited $40 for the month's depreciation, and Accumulated Depreciation—Office Equipment is credited $40.
(d) Unearned Revenue is debited $400 for services provided, and Service Revenue is credited $400.
(e) An additional account Accounts Receivable is debited $200 for services provided but not billed, and Service Revenue is credited $200.
(f) Two additional accounts relating to interest are needed. Interest Expense is debited $50 for accrued interest, and Interest Payable is credited $50.
(g) Salaries Expense is debited $1,200 for accrued salaries, and an additional account Salaries Payable is credited $1,200.

Note in the illustration that after all the adjustments have been entered, the adjustments columns are totaled and the equality of the column totals is proved.

Step 3. Enter Adjusted Balances in the Adjusted Trial Balance Columns

Turn over the second transparency, Illustration 5-3B. The adjusted balance of an account is obtained by combining the amounts entered in the first four columns of the work sheet for each account. For example, the Prepaid Insurance account in the trial balance columns has a $600 debit balance and a $50 credit in the adjustments columns. The result is a $550 debit balance recorded in the adjusted trial balance columns. **For each account on the work sheet, the amount in the adjusted trial balance columns is the account balance that will appear in the ledger after the adjusting entries have been journalized and posted.** The balances in these columns are the same as those in the adjusted trial balance in Illustration 4-19 (page 130).

After all account balances have been entered in the adjusted trial balance columns, the columns are totaled and their equality is proved. The agreement of the column totals facilitates the completion of the work sheet. If these columns are not in agreement, the financial statement columns will not balance and the financial statements will be incorrect.

Step 4. Extend Adjusted Trial Balance Amounts to Appropriate Financial Statement Columns

HELPFUL HINT
Every adjusted trial balance amount must be extended to one of the four statement columns. Debit amounts go to debit columns and credit amounts go to credit columns.

Turn over the third transparency, Illustration 5-3C. The fourth step is to extend adjusted trial balance amounts to the income statement and balance sheet columns of the work sheet. Balance sheet accounts are entered in the appropriate balance sheet debit and credit columns. For instance, Cash is entered in the balance sheet debit column, and Notes Payable is entered in the credit column. Accumulated Depreciation is extended to the balance sheet credit column. The reason is that accumulated depreciation is a contra-asset account with a credit balance.

Because the work sheet does not have columns for the retained earnings statement, the balances in Common Stock and Retained Earnings, if any, are extended to the balance sheet credit column. In addition, the balance in Dividends is extended to the balance sheet debit column because it is a stockholders' equity account with a debit balance.

The expense and revenue accounts such as Salaries Expense and Service Revenue are entered in the appropriate income statement columns.

All of these extensions are shown in Illustration 5-3C.

Step 5. Total the Statement Columns, Compute the Net Income (or Net Loss), and Complete the Work Sheet

Turn over the fourth transparency, Illustration 5-3D. Each of the financial statement columns must be totaled. The net income or loss for the period is then found by computing the difference between the totals of the two income statement columns. If total credits exceed total debits, net income has resulted. In such a case, as shown in Illustration 5-3D, the words "Net Income" are inserted in the account titles space. The amount then is entered in the income statement debit column and the balance sheet credit column. **The debit amount balances the income statement columns, and the credit amount balances the balance sheet columns.** In addition, the credit in the balance sheet column indicates the increase in stockholders' equity resulting from net income.

If, instead, total debits in the income statement columns exceed total credits, a net loss has occurred. The amount of the net loss is entered in the income statement credit column and the balance sheet debit column.

After the net income or net loss has been entered, new column totals are determined. The totals shown in the debit and credit income statement columns will match. The totals shown in the debit and credit balance sheet columns will also match. If either the income statement columns or the balance sheet columns are not equal after the net income or net loss has been entered, an error has been made in the work sheet. The completed work sheet for Premier Staffing Agency Inc. is shown in Illustration 5-3D.

HELPFUL HINT
All pairs of columns must balance for a work sheet to be complete.

TECHNOLOGY IN ACTION

The work sheet can be computerized using an electronic spreadsheet program. The Excel supplement for this textbook is one of the most popular versions of such spreadsheet packages. With a program like Excel, you can produce any type of work sheet (accounting or otherwise) that you could produce with paper and pencil on a columnar pad. The tremendous advantage of an electronic work sheet over the paper-and-pencil version is the ability to change selected data easily. When data are changed, the computer updates the balance of your computations instantly. More specific applications of electronic spreadsheets will be noted as we proceed.

PREPARING FINANCIAL STATEMENTS FROM A WORK SHEET

After a work sheet has been completed, all the data that are required for the preparation of financial statements are at hand. The income statement is prepared from the income statement columns. The balance sheet and retained earnings statement are prepared from the balance sheet columns. The financial statements prepared from the work sheet for Premier Staffing Agency Inc. are shown in Illustration 5-4. At this point, adjusting entries have not been journalized and posted. Therefore, the ledger does not support all financial statement amounts.

The amount shown for common stock on the work sheet does not change from the beginning to the end of the period unless additional stock is issued by the company during the period. Because there was no balance in Premier's retained earnings, the account is not listed on the work sheet. Only after dividends and net income (or loss) are posted to retained earnings does this account have a balance at the end of the first year of the business.

Using a work sheet, financial statements can be prepared before adjusting entries are journalized and posted. **However, the completed work sheet is not a substitute for formal financial statements.** Data in the financial statement columns of the work sheet are not properly arranged for statement purposes. Also, as noted above, the financial statement presentation for some accounts differs from their statement columns on the work sheet. **A work sheet is essentially a working tool of the accountant; it is not distributed to management and other parties.**

(**Note:** Text continues on page 149, following acetate overlays.)

Illustration 5-2

Preparing a trial balance

PREMIER STAFFING AGENCY INC.
Work Sheet
For the Month Ended October 31, 2004

	Trial Balance		Adjustments		Adjusted Trial Balance		Income Statement		Balance Sheet	
Account Titles	Dr.	Cr.	Dr.	Cr.	Dr.	Cr.	Dr.	Cr.	Dr.	Cr.
Cash	15,200									
Supplies	2,500									
Prepaid Insurance	600									
Office Equipment	5,000									
Notes Payable		5,000								
Accounts Payable		2,500								
Unearned Revenue		1,200								
Common Stock		10,000								
Dividends	500									
Service Revenue		10,000								
Salaries Expense	4,000									
Rent Expense	900									
Totals	28,700	28,700								

Include all accounts from ledger with balances.

Trial balance amounts are taken directly from ledger accounts.

Illustration 5-4

Financial statements from a work sheet

PREMIER STAFFING AGENCY INC.
Income Statement
For the Month Ended October 31, 2004

Revenues		
Service revenue		$10,600
Expenses		
Salaries expense	$5,200	
Supplies expense	1,500	
Rent expense	900	
Insurance expense	50	
Interest expense	50	
Depreciation expense	40	
Total expenses		7,740
Net income		$ 2,860

PREMIER STAFFING AGENCY INC.
Retained Earnings Statement
For the Month Ended October 31, 2004

Retained earnings, October 1	$ –0–
Add: Net income	2,860
	2,860
Less: Dividends	500
Retained earnings, October 31	$2,360

PREMIER STAFFING AGENCY INC.
Balance Sheet
October 31, 2004

Assets

Cash		$15,200
Accounts receivable		200
Supplies		1,000
Prepaid insurance		550
Office equipment	$5,000	
Less: Accumulated depreciation	40	4,960
Total assets		$21,910

Liabilities and Stockholders' Equity

Liabilities	
Notes payable	$ 5,000
Accounts payable	2,500
Interest payable	50
Unearned revenue	800
Salaries payable	1,200
Total liabilities	9,550
Stockholders' equity	
Common stock	10,000
Retained earnings	2,360
Total liabilities and stockholders' equity	$21,910

PREPARING ADJUSTING ENTRIES FROM A WORK SHEET

A work sheet is not a journal, and it cannot be used as a basis for posting to ledger accounts. To adjust the accounts, it is necessary to journalize the adjustments and post them to the ledger. **The adjusting entries are prepared from the adjustments columns of the work sheet.** The reference letters in the adjustments columns and the explanations of the adjustments at the bottom of the work sheet help identify the adjusting entries. However, writing the explanation to the adjustments at the bottom of the work sheet is not required. As indicated previously, the journalizing and posting of adjusting entries follows the preparation of financial statements when a work sheet is used. The adjusting entries on October 31 for Premier Staffing Agency Inc. are the same as those shown in Illustration 4-17 (page 128).

BEFORE YOU GO ON...

REVIEW IT

1. What are the five steps in preparing a work sheet?
2. How is net income or net loss shown in a work sheet?
3. How does a work sheet relate to preparing financial statements and adjusting entries?

DO IT

Susan Elbe is preparing a work sheet for her travel agency. Explain to Susan how the following adjusted trial balance accounts should be extended to the financial statement columns of the work sheet: Cash; Accumulated Depreciation; Accounts Payable; Dividends; Service Revenue; and Salaries Expense.

ACTION PLAN

- Extend asset balances to the balance sheet debit column. Extend liability balances to the balance sheet credit column. Extend accumulated depreciation to the balance sheet credit column.
- Extend the Dividends account to the balance sheet debit column.
- Extend expenses to the income statement debit column.
- Extend revenue accounts to the income statement credit column.

SOLUTION

Income statement debit column—Salaries Expense
Income statement credit column—Service Revenue
Balance sheet debit column—Cash; Dividends
Balance sheet credit column—Accumulated Depreciation; Accounts Payable

As indicated in the Technology in Action box on page 147, the work sheet is an ideal application for electronic spreadsheet software like Microsoft Excel and LOTUS 1–2–3.

Related exercise material: 5-1, 5-2, and 5-8.

THE NAVIGATOR

CLOSING THE BOOKS

STUDY OBJECTIVE 2

Explain the process of closing the books.

At the end of the accounting period, the accounts are made ready for the next period. This is called **closing the books**. In closing the books, it is necessary to distinguish between temporary and permanent accounts. **Temporary** or **nominal accounts** relate only to a given accounting period. They include all income statement accounts and dividends. All temporary accounts are closed. In contrast, **permanent** or **real accounts** relate to one or more future accounting periods. They consist of all balance sheet accounts, including common stock and retained earnings. Permanent accounts are not closed. Instead, their balances are carried forward into the next accounting period. Illustration 5-5 identifies the accounts in each category.

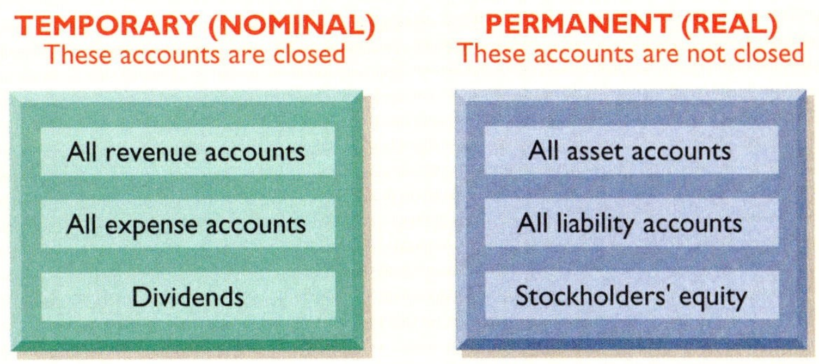

Illustration 5-5

Temporary versus permanent accounts

HELPFUL HINT
A contra-asset account, such as accumulated depreciation, is a real account also.

PREPARING CLOSING ENTRIES

At the end of the accounting period, the temporary account balances are transferred to the permanent stockholders' equity account, Retained Earnings, through the preparation of closing entries. **Closing entries** formally recognize in the ledger the transfer of net income (or net loss) and Dividends to Retained Earnings as shown in the retained earnings statement. **These entries also produce a zero balance in each temporary account. These accounts are then ready to be used to accumulate data in the next accounting period separate from the data of prior periods.** Permanent accounts are not closed.

Journalizing and posting closing entries is a required step in the accounting cycle. (See Illustration 5-12 on page 158.) This step is performed after financial statements have been prepared. In contrast to the steps in the cycle that you have already studied, closing entries are generally journalized and posted **only at the end of a company's annual accounting period**. This practice facilitates the preparation of annual financial statements because all temporary accounts will contain data for the entire year.

In preparing closing entries, each income statement account could be closed directly to Retained Earnings. However, to do so would result in excessive detail in the Retained Earnings account. Instead, the revenue and expense accounts are closed to another temporary account, **Income Summary**; only the net income or net loss is transferred from this account to Retained Earnings.

Closing entries are journalized in the general journal. A center caption entitled Closing Entries, inserted in the journal between the last adjusting entry and the first closing entry, identifies these entries. Then the closing entries are posted to the ledger accounts.

HELPFUL HINT
When the work sheet is used, revenue and expense account data are found in the income statement columns, and Dividends is in the balance sheet debit column.

Closing entries may be prepared directly from the adjusted balances in the ledger, from the income statement and balance sheet columns of the work sheet, or from the income and retained earnings statements. Separate closing entries could be prepared for each nominal account, but the following four entries accomplish the desired result more efficiently:

1. Debit each revenue account for its balance, and credit Income Summary for total revenues.
2. Debit Income Summary for total expenses, and credit each expense account for its balance.
3. Debit Income Summary and credit Retained Earnings for the amount of net income.
4. Debit Retained Earnings for the balance in the Dividends account, and credit Dividends for the same amount.

The four entries are referenced in the diagram of the closing process shown in Illustration 5-6 and in the journal entries in Illustration 5-7. The posting of closing entries is shown in Illustration 5-8.

Illustration 5-6

Diagram of closing process—corporation

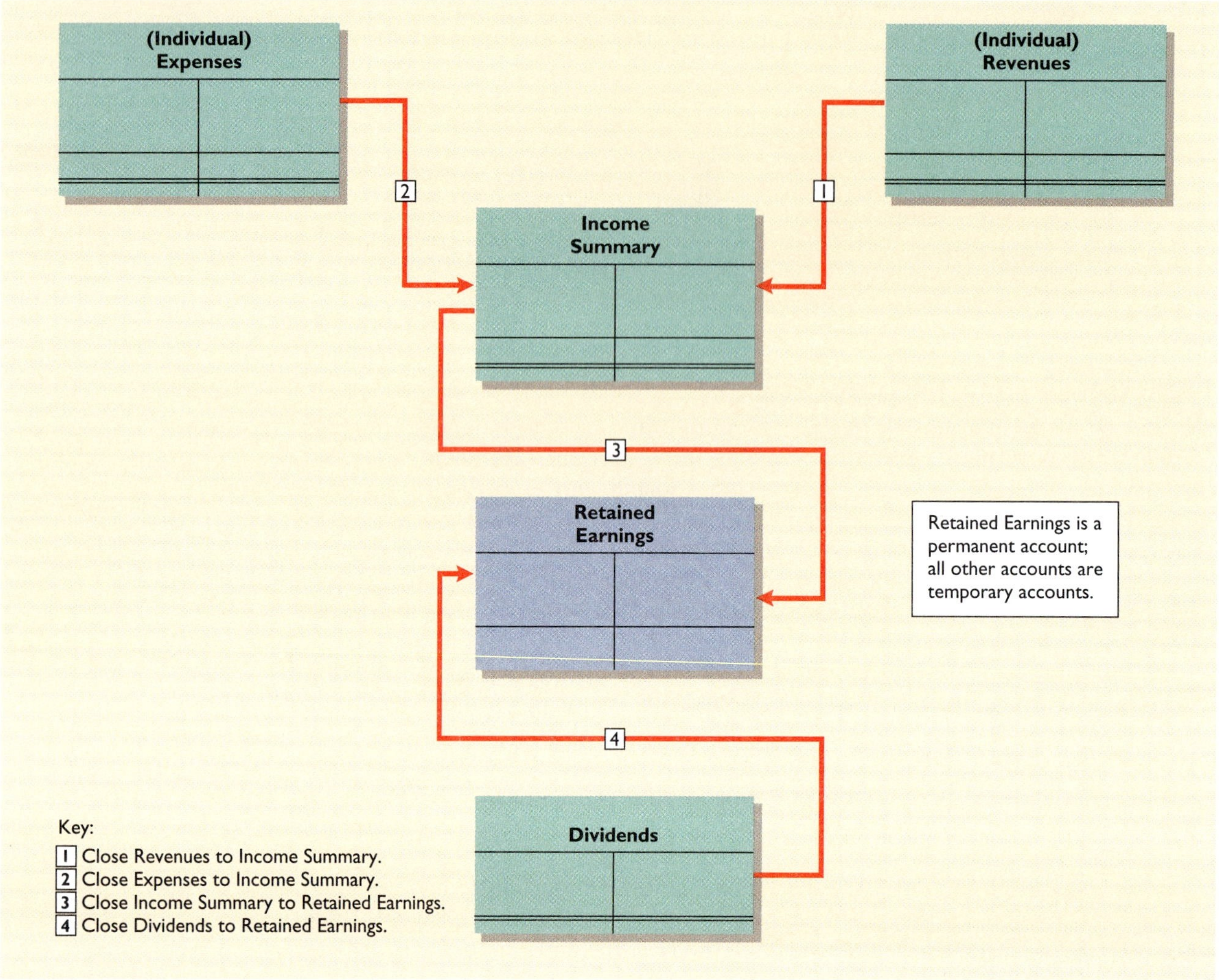

(Individual) Expenses
(Individual) Revenues
Income Summary
Retained Earnings
Dividends
Retained Earnings is a permanent account; all other accounts are temporary accounts.
Key:
1 Close Revenues to Income Summary.
2 Close Expenses to Income Summary.
3 Close Income Summary to Retained Earnings.
4 Close Dividends to Retained Earnings.

HELPFUL HINT

Dividends is closed directly to Retained Earnings and *not* to Income Summary because Dividends is not an expense.

If a net loss has occurred, entry (3) credits Income Summary and debits Retained Earnings.

ACCOUNTING IN ACTION *Business Insight*

Until Sam Walton had opened twenty Wal-Mart stores, he used what he called the "ESP method" of closing the books. ESP was a pretty basic method: If the books didn't balance, Walton calculated the amount by which they were off and entered that amount under the heading ESP—which stood for "Error Some Place." As Walton noted, "It really sped things along when it came time to close those books."

SOURCE: Sam Walton, *Made in America* (New York: Doubleday, 1992), p. 53.

CLOSING ENTRIES, ILLUSTRATED

In practice, closing entries are generally prepared only at the end of a company's annual accounting period. However, to illustrate the journalizing and posting of closing entries, we will assume that Premier Staffing Agency Inc. closes its books monthly. The closing entries at October 31 are shown in Illustration 5-7.

Illustration 5-7

Closing entries journalized

GENERAL JOURNAL J3

Date	Account Titles and Explanation	Ref.	Debit	Credit
	Closing Entries			
	(1)			
Oct. 31	Service Revenue	400	10,600	
	Income Summary	350		10,600
	(To close revenue account)			
	(2)			
31	Income Summary	350	7,740	
	Supplies Expense	611		1,500
	Depreciation Expense	711		40
	Insurance Expense	722		50
	Salaries Expense	726		5,200
	Rent Expense	729		900
	Interest Expense	905		50
	(To close expense accounts)			
	(3)			
31	Income Summary	350	2,860	
	Retained Earnings	320		2,860
	(To close net income to retained earnings)			
	(4)			
31	Retained Earnings	320	500	
	Dividends	332		500
	(To close dividends to retained earnings)			

HELPFUL HINT
Income Summary is a very descriptive title: total revenues are closed to Income Summary, total expenses are closed to Income Summary, and the balance in the Income Summary is a net income or net loss.

Note that the amounts for Income Summary in entries (1) and (2) are the totals of the income statement credit and debit columns, respectively, in the work sheet.

A couple of cautions in preparing closing entries: (1) Avoid unintentionally doubling the revenue and expense balances rather than zeroing them. (2) Do not close Dividends through the Income Summary account. **Dividends are not expenses, and they are not a factor in determining net income.**

POSTING OF CLOSING ENTRIES

The posting of the closing entries and the ruling of the accounts are shown in Illustration 5-8. Note that all temporary accounts have zero balances after posting the closing entries. In addition, you should realize that the balance in Retained Earnings represents the accumulated undistributed earnings of the corporation at the end of the accounting period. This balance is shown on the balance sheet and is the ending amount reported on the retained earnings statement, as shown in Illustration 5-4. **The Income Summary account is used only in closing.** No entries are journalized and posted to this account during the year.

As part of the closing process, the **temporary accounts**—revenues, expenses, and Dividends—in T-account form are totaled, balanced, and double-ruled, as shown in Illustration 5-8. The **permanent accounts**—assets, liabilities, and stockholders' equity (Common Stock and Retained Earnings)—are not closed. A single rule is drawn beneath the current-period entries, and the account balance carried forward to the next period is entered below the single rule. (For example, see Retained Earnings.)

HELPFUL HINT
The balance in Income Summary before it is closed must equal the net income or net loss for the period.

Illustration 5-8

Posting of closing entries

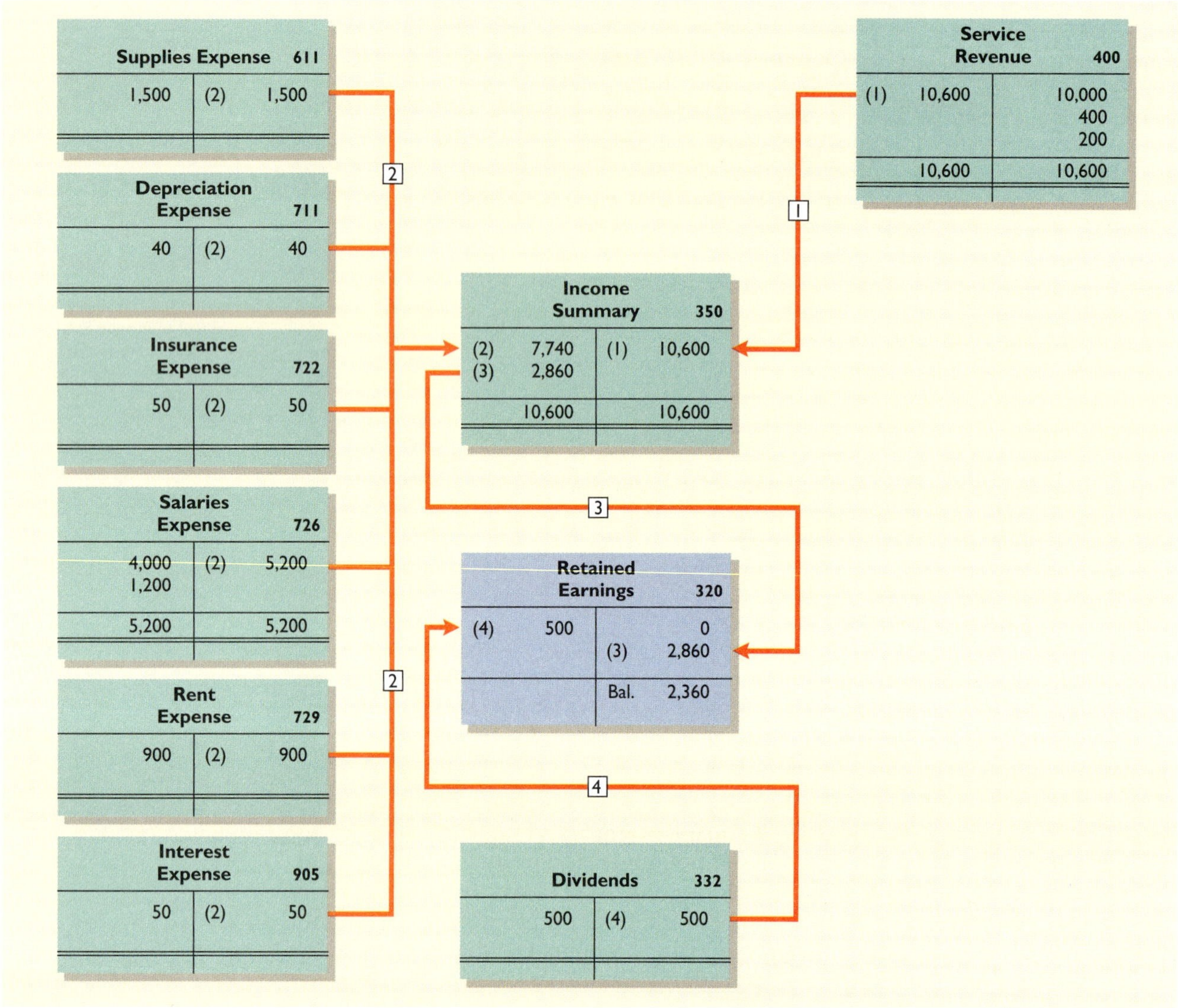

ACCOUNTING IN ACTION *Business Insight*

The **River Oaks Country Club** is an exclusive private club in the Houston metropolitan area. It has more than 1,500 members, and monthly billing can be a big project without the use of computers. Mel Samuelson, chief financial officer of the club, comments that he could not imagine how cumbersome the system would be if month-end closing and billing had to be done manually. "It only takes us one day to do our month-end closing with computers," said Samuelson. "If every transaction for all 1,530 members has to be done by hand, it may take at least a week just for the closing." Mr. Samuelson also adds that with the use of computers, all postings are updated on a daily basis, making information accessible and real-time.

As Mr. Samuelson suggests, computers do provide more accurate and updated information. More important, this also means the associates in the accounting office can now use the time saved to do other, more meaningful, analysis of data, thereby providing better information to management and better service to its members.

PREPARING A POST-CLOSING TRIAL BALANCE

STUDY OBJECTIVE 3

Describe the content and purpose of a post-closing trial balance.

After all closing entries have been journalized and posted, another trial balance, called a **post-closing trial balance**, is prepared from the ledger. The post-closing trial balance lists permanent accounts and their balances after closing entries have been journalized and posted. **The purpose of this trial balance is to prove the equality of the permanent account balances that are carried forward into the next accounting period.** Since all temporary accounts will have zero balances, the post-closing trial balance will contain only permanent—that is, *balance sheet*—accounts.

The procedure for preparing a post-closing trial balance again consists entirely of listing the accounts and their balances. The post-closing trial balance for Premier Staffing Agency Inc. is shown in Illustration 5-9. These balances are the same as those reported in the company's balance sheet in Illustration 5-4.

Illustration 5-9

Post-closing trial balance

PREMIER STAFFING AGENCY INC.
Post-Closing Trial Balance
October 31, 2004

	Debit	Credit
Cash	$15,200	
Accounts Receivable	200	
Supplies	1,000	
Prepaid Insurance	550	
Office Equipment	5,000	
Accumulated Depreciation—Office Equipment		$ 40
Notes Payable		5,000
Accounts Payable		2,500
Unearned Revenue		800
Salaries Payable		1,200
Interest Payable		50
Common Stock		10,000
Retained Earnings		2,360
	$21,950	$21,950

HELPFUL HINT

Will total debits in a post-closing trial balance equal total assets on the balance sheet? Answer: No. Accumulated depreciation is deducted from assets on the balance sheet but added to the credit balance total in a post-closing trial balance.

The post-closing trial balance is prepared from the permanent accounts in the ledger. The permanent accounts of Premier Staffing are shown in the general ledger in Illustration 5-10 on page 156. Remember that the balance of each permanent account is computed after every posting. Therefore, no additional work on these accounts is needed as part of the closing process.

A post-closing trial balance provides evidence that the journalizing and posting of closing entries have been properly completed. It also shows that the accounting equation is in balance at the end of the accounting period. However, like the trial balance, it does not prove that all transactions have been recorded or that the ledger is correct. For example, the post-closing trial balance will balance if a transaction is not journalized and posted or if a transaction is journalized and posted twice.

The remaining accounts in the general ledger are temporary accounts (shown in Illustration 5-11 on page 157). After the closing entries are correctly posted, each temporary account has a zero balance. These accounts are double-ruled to finalize the closing process.

(Permanent Accounts Only)

General Ledger

Cash — **No. 101**

Date	Explanation	Ref.	Debit	Credit	Balance
2004					
Oct. 1		J1	10,000		10,000
2		J1	1,200		11,200
3		J1		900	10,300
4		J1		600	9,700
20		J1		500	9,200
26		J1		4,000	5,200
31		J1	10,000		15,200

Accounts Receivable — **No. 112**

Date	Explanation	Ref.	Debit	Credit	Balance
2004					
Oct. 31	Adj. entry	J2	200		200

Supplies — **No. 129**

Date	Explanation	Ref.	Debit	Credit	Balance
2004					
Oct. 5		J1	2,500		2,500
31	Adj. entry	J2		1,500	1,000

Prepaid Insurance — **No. 130**

Date	Explanation	Ref.	Debit	Credit	Balance
2004					
Oct. 4		J1	600		600
31	Adj. entry	J2		50	550

Office Equipment — **No. 157**

Date	Explanation	Ref.	Debit	Credit	Balance
2004					
Oct. 1		J1	5,000		5,000

Accumulated Depreciation—Office Equipment — **No. 158**

Date	Explanation	Ref.	Debit	Credit	Balance
2004					
Oct. 31	Adj. entry	J2		40	40

Notes Payable — **No. 200**

Date	Explanation	Ref.	Debit	Credit	Balance
2004					
Oct. 1		J1		5,000	5,000

Accounts Payable — **No. 201**

Date	Explanation	Ref.	Debit	Credit	Balance
2004					
Oct. 5		J1		2,500	2,500

Unearned Revenue — **No. 209**

Date	Explanation	Ref.	Debit	Credit	Balance
2004					
Oct. 2		J1		1,200	1,200
31	Adj. entry	J2	400		800

Salaries Payable — **No. 212**

Date	Explanation	Ref.	Debit	Credit	Balance
2004					
Oct. 31	Adj. entry	J2		1,200	1,200

Interest Payable — **No. 230**

Date	Explanation	Ref.	Debit	Credit	Balance
2004					
Oct. 31	Adj. entry	J2		50	50

Common Stock — **No. 311**

Date	Explanation	Ref.	Debit	Credit	Balance
2004					
Oct. 1		J1		10,000	10,000

Retained Earnings — **No. 320**

Date	Explanation	Ref.	Debit	Credit	Balance
2004					
Oct. 1					–0–
31	Closing entry	J3		2,860	2,860
31	Closing entry	J3	500		2,360

Note: The permanent accounts for Premier Staffing Agency Inc. are shown here; the temporary accounts are shown in Illustration 5-11. Both permanent and temporary accounts are part of the general ledger; they are segregated here to aid in learning.

Illustration 5-10

General ledger, permanent accounts

SUMMARY OF THE ACCOUNTING CYCLE

STUDY OBJECTIVE 4

State the required steps in the accounting cycle.

The required steps in the accounting cycle are shown in Illustration 5-12 on page 158. From the graphic you can see that the cycle begins with the analysis of business transactions and ends with the preparation of a post-closing trial balance. The steps in the cycle are performed in sequence and are repeated in each accounting period.

(Temporary Accounts Only)

GENERAL LEDGER

Dividends No. 332

Date	Explanation	Ref.	Debit	Credit	Balance
2004					
Oct. 31		J1	500		500
31	Closing entry	J3		500	–0–

Income Summary No. 350

Date	Explanation	Ref.	Debit	Credit	Balance
2004					
Oct. 31	Closing entry	J3		10,600	10,600
31	Closing entry	J3	7,740		2,860
31	Closing entry	J3	2,860		–0–

Service Revenue No. 400

Date	Explanation	Ref.	Debit	Credit	Balance
2004					
Oct. 31		J1		10,000	10,000
31	Adj. entry	J2		400	10,400
31	Adj. entry	J2		200	10,600
31	Closing entry	J3	10,600		–0–

Supplies Expense No. 611

Date	Explanation	Ref.	Debit	Credit	Balance
2004					
Oct. 31	Adj. entry	J2	1,500		1,500
31	Closing entry	J3		1,500	–0–

Depreciation Expense No. 711

Date	Explanation	Ref.	Debit	Credit	Balance
2004					
Oct. 31	Adj. entry	J2	40		40
31	Closing entry	J3		40	–0–

Insurance Expense No. 722

Date	Explanation	Ref.	Debit	Credit	Balance
2004					
Oct. 31	Adj. entry	J2	50		50
31	Closing entry	J3		50	–0–

Salaries Expense No. 726

Date	Explanation	Ref.	Debit	Credit	Balance
2004					
Oct. 26		J1	4,000		4,000
31	Adj. entry	J2	1,200		5,200
31	Closing entry	J3		5,200	–0–

Rent Expense No. 729

Date	Explanation	Ref.	Debit	Credit	Balance
2004					
Oct. 3		J1	900		900
31	Closing entry	J3		900	–0–

Interest Expense No. 905

Date	Explanation	Ref.	Debit	Credit	Balance
2004					
Oct. 31	Adj. entry	J2	50		50
31	Closing entry	J3		50	–0–

Note: The temporary accounts for Premier Staffing Agency Inc. are shown here; the permanent accounts are shown in Illustration 5-10. Both permanent and temporary accounts are part of the general ledger; they are segregated here to aid in learning.

Illustration 5-11

General ledger, temporary accounts

Steps 1–3 may occur daily during the accounting period, as explained in Chapter 3. Steps 4–7 are performed on a periodic basis, such as monthly, quarterly, or annually. Steps 8 and 9, closing entries, and a post-closing trial balance, are usually prepared only at the end of a company's *annual* accounting period. As you have seen, a work sheet may also be used in preparing adjusting entries and financial statements.

Illustration 5-12

Steps in the accounting cycle

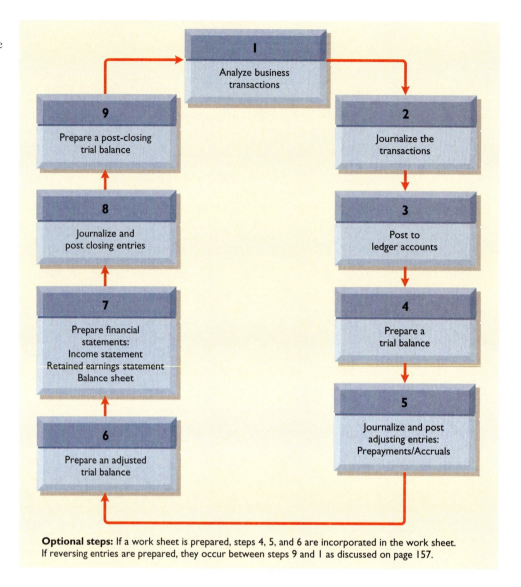

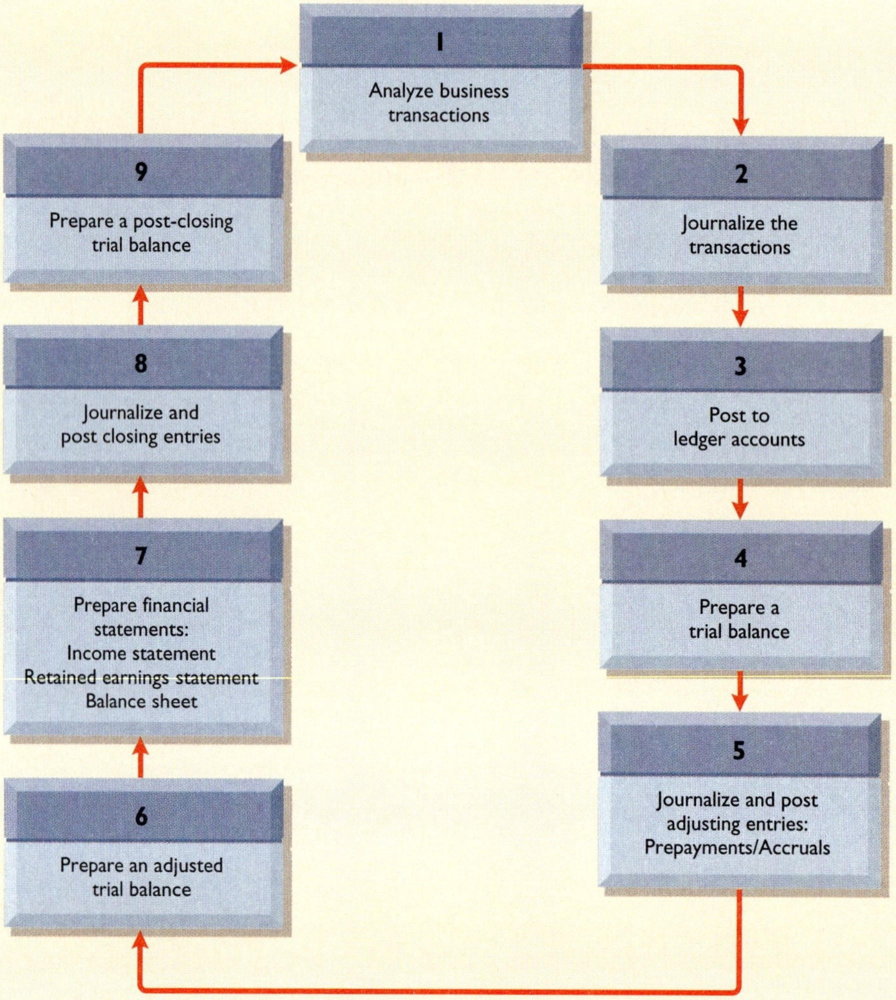
1
Analyze business transactions
2
Journalize the transactions
3
Post to ledger accounts
4
Prepare a trial balance
5
Journalize and post adjusting entries: Prepayments/Accruals
6
Prepare an adjusted trial balance
7
Prepare financial statements: Income statement Retained earnings statement Balance sheet
8
Journalize and post closing entries
9
Prepare a post-closing trial balance

Optional steps: If a work sheet is prepared, steps 4, 5, and 6 are incorporated in the work sheet. If reversing entries are prepared, they occur between steps 9 and 1 as discussed on page 157.

CORRECTING ENTRIES—AN AVOIDABLE STEP

STUDY OBJECTIVE 5

Explain the approaches to preparing correcting entries.

Unfortunately, errors may occur in the recording process. Errors should be corrected **as soon as they are discovered** by journalizing and posting **correcting entries**. If the accounting records are free of errors, no correcting entries are necessary.

You should recognize three differences between correcting entries and adjusting entries:

1. Adjusting entries are an integral part of the accounting cycle. Correcting entries, on the other hand, are unnecessary if the records are free of errors.
2. Adjustments are journalized and posted only at the end of an accounting period. In contrast, correcting entries are made whenever an error is discovered.
3. Adjusting entries always affect at least one balance sheet account and one income statement account. In contrast, correcting entries may involve any combination of accounts in need of correction. **Correcting entries must be posted before closing entries.**

To determine the correcting entry, it is useful to compare the incorrect entry with the correct entry. Doing so helps identify the accounts and amounts that should—and should not—be corrected. After comparison, a correcting entry is made to correct the accounts. This approach is illustrated in the following two cases.

ETHICS NOTE

Citigroup once reported a correcting entry reducing reported revenue by $23 million, while firing 11 employees. Company officials did not specify why the employees had apparently intentionally inflated the revenue figures, although it was noted that their bonuses were tied to their unit's performance.

CASE 1 On May 10, a $50 cash collection on account from a customer is journalized and posted as a debit to Cash $50 and a credit to Service Revenue $50. The error is discovered on May 20, when the customer pays the remaining balance in full.

Illustration 5-13
Comparison of entries

Incorrect Entry (May 10)			Correct Entry (May 10)		
Cash	50		Cash	50	
Service Revenue		50	Accounts Receivable		50

A comparison of the incorrect entry with the correct entry reveals that the debit to Cash $50 is correct. However, the $50 credit to Service Revenue should have been credited to Accounts Receivable. As a result, both Service Revenue and Accounts Receivable are overstated in the ledger. The following correcting entry is required.

Illustration 5-14
Correcting entry

Correcting Entry

May 20	Service Revenue	50	
	Accounts Receivable		50
	(To correct entry of May 10)		

A	=	L	+	SE
−50				−50

CASE 2 On May 18, office equipment costing $450 is purchased on account. The transaction is journalized and posted as a debit to Delivery Equipment $45 and a credit to Accounts Payable $45. The error is discovered on June 3, when the monthly statement for May is received from the creditor.

Illustration 5-15
Comparison of entries

Incorrect Entry (May 18)			Correct Entry (May 18)		
Delivery Equipment	45		Office Equipment	450	
Accounts Payable		45	Accounts Payable		450

A comparison of the two entries shows that three accounts are incorrect. Delivery Equipment is overstated $45; Office Equipment is understated $450; and Accounts Payable is understated $405. The correcting entry is shown in Illustration 5-16:

Illustration 5-16
Correcting entry

Correcting Entry

June 3	Office Equipment	450	
	Delivery Equipment		45
	Accounts Payable		405
	(To correct entry of May 18)		

A	=	L	+	SE
+450				
−45		+405		

Instead of preparing a correcting entry, **it is possible to reverse the incorrect entry and then prepare the correct entry**. This approach will result in more entries and postings than a correcting entry, but it will accomplish the desired result.

ACCOUNTING IN ACTION *Business Insight*

In the hospitality industry, much work is done behind the scenes so that guests can enjoy their experience, whether they are on a cruise, staying in a hotel for business, at a resort for their vacation, playing tennis at their country club, or dining out with good friends. All the products that make the ultimate service a reality have to be transported and shipped by various carriers. The produce may be grown in California and freighted to Texas; the grill in the kitchen may be manufactured in Ohio and shipped to Florida. Consider the following events with two freight companies.

Yale Express, a short-haul trucking firm, turned over much of its cargo to local truckers for delivery completion. Yale collected the entire delivery charge and, when billed by the local trucker, sent payment for the final phase to the local trucker. Yale used a cutoff period of 20 days into the next accounting period in making its adjusting entries for accrued liabilities. That is, it waited 20 days to receive the local truckers' bills to determine the amount of the unpaid but incurred delivery charges as of the balance sheet date.

In contrast, **Republic Carloading**, a nationwide, long-distance freight forwarder, frequently did not receive transportation bills from truckers to whom it passed on cargo until months after the year-end. In making its year-end adjusting entries, Republic waited for months in order to include all of these outstanding transportation bills.

When Yale Express merged with Republic Carloading, Yale's vice president employed the 20-day cutoff procedure for both firms. As a result, millions of dollars of Republic's accrued transportation bills went unrecorded. When the erroneous procedure was detected and correcting entries were made, these and other errors changed a reported profit of $1.14 million into a loss of $1.88 million!

BEFORE YOU GO ON...

REVIEW IT

1. How do permanent accounts differ from temporary accounts?
2. What four different types of entries are required in closing the books?
3. What is the content and purpose of a post-closing trial balance?
4. What are the required and optional steps in the accounting cycle?

DO IT

The work sheet for Hancock Health and Exercise Club shows the following in the financial statement columns: Common Stock $98,000, Dividends $15,000, Retained Earnings $42,000, and Net Income $18,000. Prepare the closing entries at December 31 that affect stockholders' equity.

ACTION PLAN

- Remember to make closing entries in the correct sequence.
- Make the first two entries to close revenues and expenses.
- Make the third entry to close net income to retained earnings.
- Make the final entry to close dividends to retained earnings.

SOLUTION

Dec. 31	Income Summary	18,000	
	Retained Earnings		18,000
	(To close net income to retained earnings)		
31	Retained Earnings	15,000	
	Dividends		15,000
	(To close dividends to retained earnings)		

Related exercise material: 5-3, 5-5, and 5-9.

THE NAVIGATOR

CLASSIFIED BALANCE SHEET

The financial statements illustrated up to this point were purposely kept simple. We classified items as assets, liabilities, and stockholders' equity in the balance sheet, and as revenues and expenses in the income statement. **Financial statements, however, become more useful to management, creditors, and potential investors when the elements are classified into significant subgroups.** In the remainder of this chapter we will introduce you to the primary balance sheet classifications. The classified income statement will be presented in Chapter 6. The classified financial statements are what Ted Castle, owner of **Rhino Foods, Inc.** gave to his employees to understand what was happening in the business.

STUDY OBJECTIVE 6

Identify the sections of a classified balance sheet.

STANDARD CLASSIFICATIONS

A **classified balance sheet** usually contains these standard classifications:

Assets	Liabilities and Stockholders' Equity
Current assets	Current liabilities
Long-term investments	Long-term liabilities
Property, plant, and equipment	Stockholders' equity
Intangible assets	

Illustration 5-17

Standard balance sheet classifications

These sections help the financial statement user determine such matters as (1) the availability of assets to meet debts as they come due and (2) the claims of short- and long-term creditors on total assets. A classified balance sheet also makes it easier to compare companies in the same industry, such as **Four Seasons**, **Forte Hotels**, and **John Q. Hammons Hotels** in the hotel industry. Each of the sections is explained below.

A complete set of specimen financial statements for **Hilton Hotels Corporation** is shown in the Appendix at the back of the book.

Current Assets

Current assets are cash and other resources that are reasonably expected to be realized in cash or sold or consumed in the business within one year of the balance sheet date or the company's operating cycle, whichever is longer. For example, accounts receivable are current assets because they will be realized in cash through collection within one year. A prepayment such as supplies is a current asset because of its expected use or consumption in the business within one year.

The **operating cycle** of a company is the average time that is required to go from cash to cash in producing revenues. The term *cycle* suggests a circular flow, which in this case, starts and ends with cash. For example, in municipal transit companies, the operating cycle would tend to be short because services are provided entirely on a cash basis. On the other hand, the operating cycle in manufacturing companies is longer: they purchase goods and materials, manufacture and sell products, bill customers, and collect cash. This is a cash-to-cash cycle that may extend for several months. Most companies have operating cycles of less than one year. More will be said about operating cycles in later chapters.

INTERNATIONAL NOTE

Other countries use a different format for the balance sheet. In Great Britain, for example, property, plant, and equipment are reported first on the balance sheet; assets and liabilities are netted and grouped into net current and net total assets.

In a service enterprise, it is customary to recognize four types of current assets: (1) cash, (2) short-term investments such as U.S. government bonds,

(3) receivables (notes receivable, accounts receivable, and interest receivable), and (4) prepaid expenses (insurance and supplies). **These items are listed in the order of liquidity.** That is, they are listed in the order in which they are expected to be converted into cash. This arrangement is illustrated in Illustration 5-18 in the presentation of **UAL, Inc. (United Airlines)**.

Illustration 5-18

Current assets section

UAL, INC. (UNITED AIRLINES)
Balance Sheet (partial)
(in millions)

Current assets	
Cash	$ 310
Short-term investments	379
Receivables	1,284
Aircraft fuel, spare parts, and supplies	340
Prepaid expenses	368
Other current assets	254
Total current assets	$2,935

A company's current assets are important in assessing the company's short-term debt-paying ability, as explained later in the chapter.

Long-Term Investments

HELPFUL HINT
Long-term investments are investments *made by* the business—not investments by the stockholders *in* the business. Investments by the stockholders in the business are reported as part of stockholders' equity (see pp. 164–165).

Like current assets, **long-term investments** are resources that can be realized in cash. However, the conversion into cash is not expected within one year or the operating cycle, whichever is longer. In addition, long-term investments are not intended for use or consumption within the business. This category, often just called *investments*, normally includes stocks and bonds of other corporations. **Deluxe Corporation** reported the balance sheet shown in Illustration 5-19.

Illustration 5-19

Long-term investments section

DELUXE CORPORATION
Balance Sheet (partial)

Long-term investments		
Investment in stock of Data Card Corporation	$20,468,000	
Other long-term investments	16,961,000	$37,429,000

Property, Plant, and Equipment

ALTERNATIVE TERMINOLOGY
Property, plant, and equipment are sometimes referred to as *plant assets* or *fixed assets*.

Property, plant, and equipment are tangible resources of a relatively permanent nature that are used in the business and not intended for sale. This category includes land, buildings, machinery and equipment, delivery equipment, and furniture and fixtures. Assets subject to depreciation should be reported at cost less accumulated depreciation. Illustration 5-20 shows this practice for **Delta Air Lines**.

DELTA AIR LINES, INC. Balance Sheet (partial) (in millions)			
Property, plant, and equipment			
Flight equipment	$9,619		
Less: Accumulated depreciation	3,510	$6,109	
Ground property and equipment	3,032		
Less: Accumulated depreciation	1,758	1,274	$7,383

Illustration 5-20

Property, plant, and equipment section

Intangible Assets

Intangible assets are noncurrent resources that do not have physical substance. Intangible assets include patents, copyrights, and trademarks or trade names that give the holder **exclusive right** of use for a specified period of time. Their value to a company is generally derived from the rights or privileges granted by governmental authority (such as the U.S. Patent Office and the Copyright Office). Intangibles are recorded at cost, and this cost is expensed (amortized) over the useful life of the intangible. Intangibles with indefinite lives are not amortized.

In its balance sheet, **Brunswick Corporation** reported the following.

BRUNSWICK CORPORATION Balance Sheet (partial)	
Intangible assets	
Patents, trademarks, and other intangibles	$10,460,000

Illustration 5-21

Intangible assets section

Current Liabilities

Listed first in the liabilities and stockholders' equity section of the balance sheet are current liabilities. **Current liabilities** are obligations that are reasonably expected to be paid from existing current assets or through the creation of other current liabilities. As in the case of current assets, the time period for payment is one year or the operating cycle, whichever is longer. Current liabilities include (1) debts related to the operating cycle, such as accounts payable and wages and salaries payable, and (2) other short-term debts, such as bank loans payable, interest payable, taxes payable, and current maturities of long-term obligations (payments to be made within the next year on long-term obligations).

The arrangement of items within the current liabilities section has evolved through custom rather than from a prescribed rule. Notes payable is usually listed first, followed by accounts payable. Other items are then listed in any order. The current liabilities section adapted from the balance sheet of **UAL, Inc. (United Airlines)** is shown in Illustration 5-22.

Illustration 5-22
Current liabilities section

UAL, INC. (UNITED AIRLINES) Balance Sheet (partial) (in thousands)	
Current liabilities	
Notes payable	$ 297,518
Accounts payable	382,967
Current maturities of long-term obligations	81,525
Unearned ticket revenue	432,979
Salaries and wages payable	435,622
Taxes payable	80,390
Other current liabilities	240,652
Total current liabilities	$1,951,653

Users of financial statements look closely at the relationship between current assets and current liabilities. This relationship is important in evaluating a company's **liquidity**—its ability to pay obligations that are expected to become due within the next year or operating cycle. When current assets exceed current liabilities at the balance sheet date, the likelihood for paying the liabilities is favorable. When the reverse is true, short-term creditors may not be paid, and the company may ultimately be forced into bankruptcy.

Long-Term Liabilities

ALTERNATIVE TERMINOLOGY
Long-term liabilities are also called *long-term debt* or *noncurrent liabilities.*

Obligations expected to be paid after one year or an operating cycle, whichever is longer, are classified as **long-term liabilities**. Liabilities in this category include bonds payable, mortgages payable, long-term notes payable, lease liabilities, and obligations under employee pension plans. Many companies report long-term debt maturing after one year as a single amount in the balance sheet. They then show the details of the debt in the notes that accompany the financial statements. Others list the various sources of long-term liabilities. In its balance sheet, **Consolidated Freightways, Inc.** reported the following.

Illustration 5-23
Long-term liabilities section

CONSOLIDATED FREIGHTWAYS, INC. Balance Sheet (partial) (in thousands)	
Long-term liabilities	
Bank notes payable	$10,000
Mortgage payable	2,900
Bonds payable	53,422
Other long-term debt	9,597
Total long-term liabilities	$75,919

Stockholders' (Owners') Equity

The content of the owners' equity section varies with the form of business organization. In a proprietorship, there is one capital account. In a partnership, there is a capital account for each partner. For a corporation, owners' (stockholders') equity is divided into two accounts—Common Stock and Retained Earnings. As previously indicated, investments of capital in the business by the stockholders are recorded in the Common Stock account. Income retained for use in the business is recorded in the Retained Earnings account. These two accounts are combined and reported as **stockholders' equity** on the balance sheet.

In its balance sheet, **Round Top Tours** recently reported its stockholders' equity section as follows.

Illustration 5-24

Stockholders' equity section

ROUND TOP TOURS	
Stockholders' equity	
Common stock, 1,000,000 shares	$1,781,000
Retained earnings	540,000
Total stockholders' equity	$2,321,000

CLASSIFIED BALANCE SHEET, ILLUSTRATED

An unclassified, report form balance sheet of Premier Staffing Agency Inc. was presented in Illustration 4-21 on page 132. Using the same adjusted trial balance accounts at October 31, 2004, we can prepare the classified balance sheet shown in Illustration 5-25. For illustrative purposes, assume that $1,000 of the notes payable is due currently and $4,000 is long term.

The balance sheet is most often presented in **report form**, with assets listed above liabilities and stockholders' equity. The balance sheet may also be presented in **account form**: the assets section is placed on the left and the liabilities and stockholders' equity sections on the right, as shown in Illustration 5-25.

Illustration 5-25

Classified balance sheet in account form

PREMIER STAFFING AGENCY INC.
Balance Sheet
October 31, 2004

Assets			Liabilities and Stockholders' Equity		
Current assets			Current liabilities		
Cash		$15,200	Notes payable		$ 1,000
Accounts receivable		200	Accounts payable		2,500
Supplies		1,000	Unearned revenue		800
Prepaid insurance		550	Salaries payable		1,200
Total current assets		16,950	Interest payable		50
Property, plant, and equipment			Total current liabilities		5,550
Office equipment	$5,000		Long-term liabilites		
Less: Accumulated depreciation	40	4,960	Notes payable		4,000
Total assets		$21,910	Total liabilities		9,550
			Stockholders' equity		
			Common stock	$10,000	
			Retained earnings	2,360	
			Total stockholders' equity		12,360
			Total liabilities and stockholders' equity		$21,910

Another, more complete example of a classified balance sheet is presented in report form in Illustration 5-26.

Illustration 5-26

Classified balance sheet in report form

FRANKLIN CORPORATION **Balance Sheet** **October 31, 2004**			
Assets			
Current assets			
Cash		$ 6,600	
Short-term investments		2,000	
Accounts receivable		7,000	
Inventories		4,000	
Supplies		2,100	
Prepaid insurance		400	
Total current assets			$22,100
Long-term investments			
Investment in stock of Walters Corp.			7,200
Property, plant, and equipment			
Land		10,000	
Office equipment	$24,000		
Less: Accumulated depreciation	5,000	19,000	29,000
Intangible assets			
Patents			3,100
Total assets			$61,400
Liabilities and Stockholders' Equity			
Current liabilities			
Notes payable		$11,000	
Accounts payable		2,100	
Unearned revenue		900	
Salaries payable		1,600	
Interest payable		450	
Total current liabilities			$16,050
Long-term liabilities			
Notes payable		1,300	
Mortgage payable		10,000	
Total long-term liabilities			11,300
Total liabilities			27,350
Stockholders' equity			
Common stock		20,000	
Retained earnings		14,050	
Total stockholders' equity			34,050
Total liabilities and stockholders' equity			$61,400

BEFORE YOU GO ON...

REVIEW IT

1. What are the major sections in a classified balance sheet?
2. Using the **Hilton** annual report, determine its current liabilities at December 31, 2001, and December 31, 2000. Were current liabilities higher or lower than current assets in these two years? The answer to this question is provided on page 173.
3. What is the difference between the report form and the account form of the classified balance sheet?

A LOOK BACK AT OUR FEATURE STORY

Refer back to the Feature Story about **Rhino Foods, Inc.** at the beginning of the chapter, and answer the following questions.

1. What is the lesson of the Rhino Foods story and Ted Castle's innovations?
2. How did Rhino's employees' knowledge of financial statements, especially production reports and the income statement, contribute to their effectiveness as employees?

SOLUTION

1. If you give employees equity in the company and provide them with the training and the information to understand the financial consequences of their decisions and actions, they will act more responsibly and make a greater contribution to the sales and income of the company. In other words, they begin to think like owners.
2. By understanding the income statement, they now recognize the impact of revenues and expenses in arriving at net income—as well as how productivity and expenses affect their bonuses.

THE NAVIGATOR

DEMONSTRATION PROBLEM

At the end of its first month of operations, Watson Island Tour Service, Inc. has the following unadjusted trial balance.

WATSON ISLAND TOUR SERVICE, INC.
August 31, 2004
Trial Balance

	Debit	Credit
Cash	$ 5,400	
Accounts Receivable	8,800	
Prepaid Insurance	2,400	
Supplies	1,300	
Equipment	60,000	
Notes Payable		$40,000
Accounts Payable		2,400
Common Stock		30,000
Dividends	1,000	
Service Revenue		10,900
Salaries Expense	3,200	
Utilities Expense	800	
Advertising Expense	400	
	$83,300	$83,300

Other data consist of the following:

1. Insurance expires at the rate of $200 per month.
2. There are $1,000 of supplies on hand at August 31.
3. Monthly depreciation on the equipment is $900.
4. Interest of $500 on the notes payable has accrued during August.

Instructions

(a) Prepare a work sheet.

(b) Prepare a classified balance sheet assuming $35,000 of the notes payable are long term.

(c) Journalize the closing entries.

ACTION PLAN

- In completing the work sheet, be sure to (a) key the adjustments, (b) start at the top of the adjusted trial balance columns and extend adjusted balances to the correct statement columns, and (c) enter net income (or net loss) in the proper columns.
- In preparing a classified balance sheet, know the contents of each of the sections.
- In journalizing closing entries, remember that there are only four entries and that dividends are closed to retained earnings.

SOLUTION TO DEMONSTRATION PROBLEM

(a)

WATSON ISLAND TOUR SERVICE, INC.
Work Sheet
For the Month Ended August 31, 2004

Account Titles	Trial Balance Dr.	Trial Balance Cr.	Adjustments Dr.	Adjustments Cr.	Adjusted Trial Balance Dr.	Adjusted Trial Balance Cr.	Income Statement Dr.	Income Statement Cr.	Balance Sheet Dr.	Balance Sheet Cr.
Cash	5,400				5,400				5,400	
Accounts Receivable	8,800				8,800				8,800	
Prepaid Insurance	2,400			(a) 200	2,200				2,200	
Supplies	1,300			(b) 300	1,000				1,000	
Equipment	60,000				60,000				60,000	
Notes Payable		40,000				40,000				40,000
Accounts Payable		2,400				2,400				2,400
Common Stock		30,000				30,000				30,000
Dividends	1,000				1,000				1,000	
Service Revenue		10,900				10,900		10,900		
Salaries Expense	3,200				3,200		3,200			
Utilities Expense	800				800		800			
Advertising Expense	400				400		400			
Totals	83,300	83,300								
Insurance Expense			(a) 200		200		200			
Supplies Expense			(b) 300		300		300			
Depreciation Expense			(c) 900		900		900			
Accumulated Depreciation—Equipment				(c) 900		900				900
Interest Expense			(d) 500		500		500			
Interest Payable				(d) 500		500				500
Totals			1,900	1,900	84,700	84,700	6,300	10,900	78,400	73,800
Net Income							4,600			4,600
Totals							10,900	10,900	78,400	78,400

Explanation: (a) Insurance expired, (b) Supplies used, (c) Depreciation expensed, (d) Interest accrued.

(b)

WATSON ISLAND TOUR SERVICE, INC.
Balance Sheet
August 31, 2004

Assets

Current assets		
Cash		$ 5,400
Accounts receivable		8,800
Prepaid insurance		2,200
Supplies		1,000
Total current assets		17,400
Property, plant, and equipment		
Equipment	$60,000	
Less: Accumulated depreciation—equipment	900	59,100
Total assets		$76,500

Liabilities and Stockholders' Equity

Current liabilities	
Notes payable	$ 5,000
Accounts payable	2,400
Interest payable	500
Total current liabilities	7,900
Long-term liabilities	
Notes payable	35,000
Total liabilities	42,900
Stockholders' equity	
Common stock	30,000
Retained earnings	3,600*
Total liabilities and stockholders' equity	$76,500

*Net income of $4,600 less dividends of $1,000.

(c)

Aug. 31	Service Revenue	10,900	
	Income Summary		10,900
	(To close revenue account)		
31	Income Summary	6,300	
	Salaries Expense		3,200
	Depreciation Expense		900
	Utilities Expense		800
	Interest Expense		500
	Advertising Expense		400
	Supplies Expense		300
	Insurance Expense		200
	(To close expense accounts)		
31	Income Summary	4,600	
	Retained Earnings		4,600
	(To close net income to retained earnings)		
31	Retained Earnings	1,000	
	Dividends		1,000
	(To close dividends to retained earnings)		

THE NAVIGATOR

SUMMARY OF STUDY OBJECTIVES

1. *Prepare a work sheet.* The steps in preparing a work sheet are: (a) prepare a trial balance on the work sheet, (b) enter the adjustments in the adjustment columns, (c) enter adjusted balances in the adjusted trial balance columns, (d) extend adjusted trial balance amounts to appropriate financial statement columns, and (e) total the statement columns, compute net income (or net loss), and complete the work sheet.

2. *Explain the process of closing the books.* Closing the books occurs at the end of an accounting period. The process is to journalize and post closing entries and then rule and balance all accounts. In closing the books, separate entries are made to close revenues and expenses to Income Summary, Income Summary to Retained Earnings, and Dividends to Retained Earnings. Only temporary accounts are closed.

3. *Describe the content and purpose of a post-closing trial balance.* A post-closing trial balance contains the balances in permanent accounts that are carried forward to the next accounting period. The purpose of this trial balance is to prove the equality of these balances.

4. *State the required steps in the accounting cycle.* The required steps in the accounting cycle are: (a) analyze business transactions, (b) journalize the transactions, (c) post to ledger accounts, (d) prepare a trial balance, (e) journalize and post adjusting entries, (f) prepare an adjusted trial balance, (g) prepare financial statements, (h) journalize and post closing entries, and (i) prepare a post-closing trial balance.

5. *Explain the approaches to preparing correcting entries.* One approach for determining the correcting entry is to compare the incorrect entry with the correct entry. After comparison, a correcting entry is made to correct the accounts. An alternative to a correcting entry is to reverse the incorrect entry and then prepare the correct entry.

6. *Identify the sections of a classified balance sheet.* In a classified balance sheet, assets are classified as current assets; long-term investments; property, plant, and equipment; or intangibles. Liabilities are classified as either current or long-term. There is also an owners' equity section, which varies with the form of business organization. The classified balance sheet can be presented in either report form or account form.

THE NAVIGATOR

GLOSSARY

Classified balance sheet A balance sheet that contains a number of standard classifications or sections (p. 161).

Closing entries Entries made at the end of an accounting period to transfer the balances of temporary accounts to a permanent stockholders' equity account, Retained Earnings (p. 151).

Correcting entries Entries to correct errors made in recording transactions (p. 158).

Current assets Cash and other resources that are reasonably expected to be realized in cash or sold or consumed in the business within one year or the operating cycle, whichever is longer (p. 161).

Current liabilities Obligations reasonably expected to be paid from existing current assets or through the creation of other current liabilities within the next year or operating cycle, whichever is longer (p. 162).

Income Summary A temporary account used in closing revenue and expense accounts (p. 151).

Intangible assets Noncurrent resources that do not have physical substance (p. 163).

Liquidity The ability of a company to pay obligations that are expected to become due within the next year or operating cycle (p. 164).

Long-term investments Resources not expected to be realized in cash within the next year or operating cycle (p. 162).

Long-term liabilities (Long-term debt) Obligations expected to be paid after one year (p. 164).

Operating cycle The average time required to go from cash to cash in producing revenues (p. 161).

Permanent (real) accounts Balance sheet accounts whose balances are carried forward to the next accounting period (p. 150).

Post-closing trial balance A list of permanent accounts and their balances after closing entries have been journalized and posted (p. 155).

Property, plant, and equipment Assets of a relatively permanent nature that are being used in the business and not intended for resale (p. 162).

Stockholders' equity The ownership claim of shareholders on total assets (p. 165).

Temporary (nominal) accounts Revenue, expense, and Dividends accounts whose balances are transferred to Retained Earnings at the end of an accounting period (p. 150).

Work sheet A multiple-column form that may be used in the adjustment process and in preparing financial statements (p. 144).

EXERCISES

List the steps in preparing a work sheet.
(SO 1)

5-1 The steps in using a work sheet are presented in random order below. List the steps in the proper order by placing numbers 1–5 in the blank spaces.

(a) _____ Prepare a trial balance on the work sheet.
(b) _____ Enter adjusted balances.
(c) _____ Extend adjusted balances to appropriate statement columns.
(d) _____ Total the statement columns, compute net income (loss), and complete the work sheet.
(e) _____ Enter adjustment data.

Prepare partial work sheet.
(SO 1)

5-2 The ledger of Giovanni Party Decorations Company includes the following unadjusted balances: Prepaid Insurance $4,000, Service Revenue $58,000, and Salaries Expense $25,000. Adjusting entries are required for **(a)** expired insurance $1,200; **(b)** services provided $900, but unbilled and uncollected; and **(c)** accrued salaries payable $800. Enter the unadjusted balances and adjustments into a work sheet and complete the work sheet for all accounts. (*Note:* You will need to add the following accounts: Accounts Receivable, Salaries Payable, and Insurance Expense.)

Journalize and post closing entries using the three-column form of account.
(SO 2)

5-3 The income statement for Edgebrook Golf Club for the month ending July 31 shows Green Fee Revenue $14,000, Salaries Expense $8,200, Maintenance Expense $2,500, and Net Income $3,300. Prepare the entries to close the revenue and expense accounts. Post the entries to the revenue and expense accounts, and complete the closing process for these accounts using the three-column form of account.

5-4 Using the data in 5-3, identify the accounts that would be included in a post-closing trial balance.

Identify post-closing trial balance accounts.
(SO 3)

5-5 The steps in the accounting cycle are listed in random order below. List the steps in proper sequence, assuming no work sheet is prepared, by placing numbers 1–9 in the blank spaces.

List the required steps in the accounting cycle in sequence.
(SO 4)

(a) _____ Prepare a trial balance.
(b) _____ Journalize the transactions.
(c) _____ Journalize and post closing entries.
(d) _____ Prepare financial statements.
(e) _____ Journalize and post adjusting entries.
(f) _____ Post to ledger accounts.
(g) _____ Prepare a post-closing trial balance.
(h) _____ Prepare an adjusted trial balance.
(i) _____ Analyze business transactions.

5-6 At Piccola Pasta Sauce, the following errors were discovered after the transactions had been journalized and posted. Prepare the correcting entries.

Prepare correcting entries.
(SO 5)

1. A collection on account from a customer for $780 was recorded as a debit to Cash $780 and a credit to Service Revenue $780.
2. The purchase of store supplies on account for $1,730 was recorded as a debit to Store Supplies $1,370 and a credit to Accounts Payable $1,370.

5-7 The balance sheet debit column of the work sheet for Salsa Picante includes the following accounts: Accounts Receivable $12,500; Prepaid Insurance $3,600; Cash $18,400; Supplies $5,200, and Short-term Investments $8,200. Prepare the current assets section of the balance sheet, listing the accounts in proper sequence.

Prepare the current assets section of a balance sheet.
(SO 6)

5-8 The adjusted trial balance columns of the work sheet for Jose Tortilla Company are as follows:

Complete work sheet.
(SO 1)

JOSE TORTILLA COMPANY
Work Sheet (partial)
For the Month Ended April 30, 2004

Account Titles	Adjusted Trial Balance Dr.	Adjusted Trial Balance Cr.	Income Statement Dr.	Income Statement Cr.	Balance Sheet Dr.	Balance Sheet Cr.
Cash	15,052					
Accounts Receivable	7,840					
Prepaid Rent	2,280					
Equipment	23,050					
Accumulated Depreciation		4,921				
Notes Payable		5,700				
Accounts Payable		5,972				
Common Stock		30,000				
Retained Earnings		3,960				
Dividends	3,650					
Service Revenue		12,590				
Salaries Expense	9,840					
Rent Expense	760					
Depreciation Expense	671					
Interest Expense	57					
Interest Payable		57				
Totals	63,200	63,200				

Instructions
Complete the work sheet.

5-9 The adjusted trial balance of Mozart D.J., Inc. at the end of its fiscal year is as follows.

Journalize and post closing entries and prepare a post-closing trial balance.
(SO 2, 3, 6)

MOZART D.J., INC.
Adjusted Trial Balance
July 31, 2004

No.	Account Titles	Debits	Credits
101	Cash	$ 14,940	
112	Accounts Receivable	8,780	
157	Equipment	15,900	
167	Accumulated Depreciation		$ 5,400
201	Accounts Payable		4,220
208	Unearned Rent Revenue		1,800
311	Common Stock		20,000
320	Retained Earnings		25,200
332	Dividends	14,000	
404	Commission Revenue		65,100
429	Rent Revenue		6,500
711	Depreciation Expense	4,000	
720	Salaries Expense	55,700	
732	Utilities Expense	14,900	
		$128,220	$128,220

Instructions

(a) Prepare the closing entries using page J15.

(b) Post to Retained Earnings and No. 350 Income Summary accounts. (Use the three-column form.)

(c) Prepare a post-closing trial balance at July 31.

(d) Prepare an income statement and a retained earnings statement for the year ended July 31, 2004. There were no issuances of stock during the year.

(e) Prepare a classified balance sheet at July 31.

Prepare work sheet, financial statements, and adjusting and closing entries.
(SO 1, 2, 3, 6)

5-10 Susanne Perfect began operations as a mystery shopper on January 1, 2004. The trial balance columns of the work sheet for Susanne Perfect, Inc. at March 31 are as follows.

SUSANNE PERFECT, INC.
Work Sheet
For the Quarter Ended March 31, 2004

	Trial Balance	
Account Titles	**Dr.**	**Cr.**
Cash	11,400	
Accounts Receivable	5,620	
Supplies	1,050	
Prepaid Insurance	2,400	
Equipment	30,000	
Notes Payable		10,000
Accounts Payable		12,350
Common Stock		20,000
Dividends	600	
Service Revenue		13,620
Salaries Expense	2,200	
Travel Expense	1,300	
Rent Expense	1,200	
Miscellaneous Expense	200	
	55,970	55,970

Other data:

1. Supplies on hand total $750.
2. Depreciation is $500 per quarter.
3. Interest accrued on 6-month note payable, issued January 1, $300.

4. Insurance expires at the rate of $150 per month.
5. Services provided but unbilled at March 31 total $750.

Instructions

(a) Enter the trial balance on a work sheet and complete the work sheet.
(b) Prepare an income statement and a retained earnings statement for the quarter and a classified balance sheet at March 31.
(c) Journalize the adjusting entries from the adjustments columns of the work sheet.
(d) Journalize the closing entries from the financial statement columns of the work sheet.

FINANCIAL REPORTING PROBLEM: Hilton Hotels Corporation

5-11 The financial statements of **Hilton** are presented in the Appendix at the end of this textbook.

Instructions

Answer the following questions using the Consolidated Balance Sheet and the Notes to Consolidated Financial Statements section.

(a) What were Hilton's total current assets at December 31, 2001, and December 31, 2000?
(b) Are assets that Hilton's included under current assets listed in proper order? Explain.
(c) How are Hilton's assets classified?
(d) What are "cash equivalents"?
(e) What were Hilton's total current liabilities at December 31, 2001, and December 31, 2000?

EXPLORING THE WEB

5-12 Numerous companies have established home pages on the Internet, e.g., **Hyatt Corporation (www.hyatt.com/corporate)** and **Four Seasons Hotels and Resorts (www.fourseasons.com)**. You may have noticed company Internet addresses in television commercials or magazine advertisements.

Instructions

Examine the home pages of any two companies and answer the following questions.

(a) What type of information is available?
(b) Is any accounting-related information presented?
(c) Would you describe the home page as informative, promotional, or both? Why?

ETHICS CASE

5-13 As the controller of TellTale Ice Cream Company, you discover a misstatement that significantly overstated net income in the prior year's financial statements. The misleading financial statements appear in the company's annual report which was issued to banks and other creditors less than a month ago. After much thought about the consequences of telling the president, Eddie Lieman, about this misstatement, you gather your courage to inform him. Eddie says, "Hey! What they don't know won't hurt them. But, just so we set the record straight, we'll adjust this year's financial statements for last year's misstatement. We can absorb that misstatement better in this year than in last year anyway! Just don't make such a mistake again."

Instructions

(a) Who are the stakeholders in this situation?
(b) What are the ethical issues in this situation?
(c) What would you do as the controller in this situation?

Answers to Hilton Review It Question 2, p. 166

Current liabilities in 2001 were $996 million. Current liabilities in 2000 were $840 million. In both 2001 and 2000, current liabilities were considerably less than current assets.

Remember to go back to the Navigator box on the chapter-opening page and check off your completed work.

6

SUBSIDIARY LEDGERS AND SPECIAL JOURNALS

THE NAVIGATOR

- Understand *Concepts for Review* ❑
- Read *Feature Story* ❑
- Scan *Study Objectives* ❑
- Read *Preview* ❑
- Read text and answer *Before You Go On* *p.* 178 ❑ *p.* 191 ❑
- Work *Demonstration Problem* ❑
- Review *Summary of Study Objectives* ❑
- Complete *Assignments* ❑

CONCEPTS FOR REVIEW

Before studying this chapter, you should know or, if necessary, review:

a. What a double-entry system is (Ch. 3, p. 77)

b. How to post a transaction (Ch. 3, pp. 87–88)

c. The steps in the accounting cycle (Ch. 5, pp. 156–158)

THE NAVIGATOR

FEATURE STORY

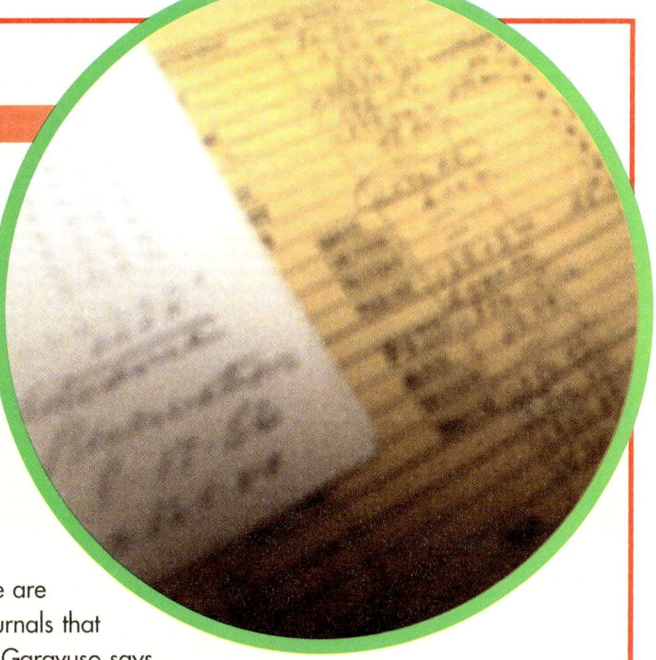

Different Roads for Different Folks

Most people begin working in the hospitality industry in one functional area and progress up the career ladder to become general managers, and then reach the district, regional, and finally corporate level, if they so choose.

Brian P. Garavuso is one of the rare breeds in the hospitality business. He has worked in the accounting and financial aspects of the industry and then became intrigued with the ever-changing technology. Rather than being a controller, then a general manager, and finally corporate, or going strictly the financial route and becoming a chief financial officer, he is currently the chief technology officer of **Interstate Hotels and Resorts.**

Garavuso states some specific types of journals that are unique to the hospitality industry. "The city ledger is basically an accounts receivable journal, and the guest ledger represents the amount of money owed to the hotel for those guests that are staying in the hotel," says Garavuso. "Another important and unique journal in our industry is the advance deposit ledger. This gives a detailed listing of amounts received from future guests to secure their reservations. This is a liability and cannot be taken as revenue until the guest arrives."

Of course, there are also the special journals that all businesses use. Garavuso says the cash receipts journal is quite useful when reconciling deposits to the bank statements. This journal helps the business identify deposits in transit, and is also useful for reconciling accounts receivable accounts. The cash payments or disbursements journal, by contrast, is very important for managing cash flow. This journal also assists managers and owners in analyzing income statements when researching actual versus budget variances. For expense management, the purchases journal is the key. In some systems, the purchases journal is also the accounts payable expense journal, which represents invoices entered in the system.

As you can see from the previous chapters, Mr. Garavuso has made a smart career choice—accounting and technology really go hand in hand. Recalling his accounting days, he is one who will always insist on the use of subsidiary ledgers and special journals. With computers, and even in a manual system, all subsidiary ledgers and special journals allow businesses to keep transactions grouped by type, eliminate all of the posting detail from the general ledger, and free up time for true management.

THE NAVIGATOR

STUDY OBJECTIVES

After studying this chapter, you should be able to

1. Describe the nature and purpose of a subsidiary ledger.
2. Explain how special journals are used in journalizing.
3. Indicate how a multicolumn journal is posted.

THE NAVIGATOR

PREVIEW OF CHAPTER 6

In the last five chapters, you have seen how you can complete an entire accounting cycle so that transactions can be accounted for in any given business. However, that is only the first step. All the examples and practice exercises you have completed thus far are exactly what they are—examples and practices. Think of all the individual transactions that happen at all the **Disney** businesses on any given day, from guests staying at their hotels, to guests eating at their restaurants, to guests paying at the entrance of a theme park, to guests buying souvenirs at a Disney store at a local mall. Then you also have Disney buying food from a purveyor, paying its employees, paying bills to a linen cleaning company, to paying its electricity bill, to many others. If Disney has one general ledger and one general journal to account for all its transactions, it will be very difficult for Disney to do any analysis or look up any specific information.

The ease of obtaining information and analyses—and other reasons such as facilitating the recording process and better organization of data—are why special ledgers and journals are useful in the accounting process.

The content and organization of Chapter 6 are as follows.

SUBSIDIARY LEDGERS AND SPECIAL JOURNALS

Expanding the Ledger	Expanding the Journal	Effect of Special Journals on General Journal
• Nature and purpose of subsidiary ledgers • Advantages of subsidiary ledgers	• Sales journal • Cash receipts journal • Purchases journal • Cash payments journal	• Journalizing • Posting

THE NAVIGATOR

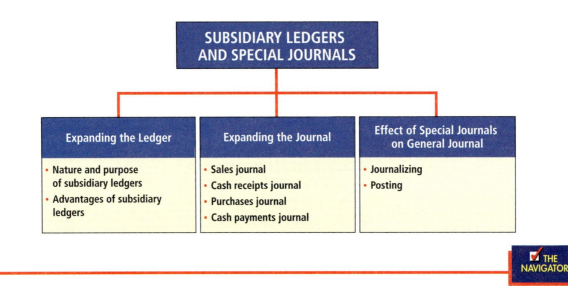

EXPANDING THE LEDGER—SUBSIDIARY LEDGERS

STUDY OBJECTIVE 1

Describe the nature and purpose of a subsidiary ledger.

NATURE AND PURPOSE OF SUBSIDIARY LEDGERS

Imagine a business that has several thousand charge (credit) customers and shows the transactions with these customers in only one general ledger account—Accounts Receivable. It would be virtually impossible to determine the balance owed by an individual customer at any specific time. Similarly, the amount payable to one creditor would be difficult to locate quickly from a single Accounts Payable account in the general ledger.

Instead, companies use subsidiary ledgers to keep track of individual balances. A **subsidiary ledger** is a group of accounts with a common characteristic (for example, all accounts receivable). The subsidiary ledger frees the general ledger from the details of individual balances. A subsidiary ledger is an addition to, and an expansion of, the general ledger.

There are two common subsidiary ledgers:

1. The **accounts receivable** (or **customers'**) **subsidiary ledger**, which collects transaction data of individual customers.
2. The **accounts payable** (or **creditors'**) **subsidiary ledger**, which collects transaction data of individual creditors.

In each of these subsidiary ledgers, individual accounts are usually arranged in alphabetical order.

The detailed data from a subsidiary ledger are summarized in a general ledger account. For example, the detailed data from the accounts receivable subsidiary ledger are summarized in Accounts Receivable in the general ledger. The general ledger account that summarizes subsidiary ledger data is called a **control account**. An overview of the relationship of subsidiary ledgers to the general ledger is shown in Illustration 6-1. The general ledger control accounts and subsidiary ledger accounts are shown in green. Note that cash and stockholders' equity in this illustration are not control accounts because there are no subsidiary ledger accounts related to these accounts.

Illustration 6-1

Relationship of general ledger and subsidiary ledgers

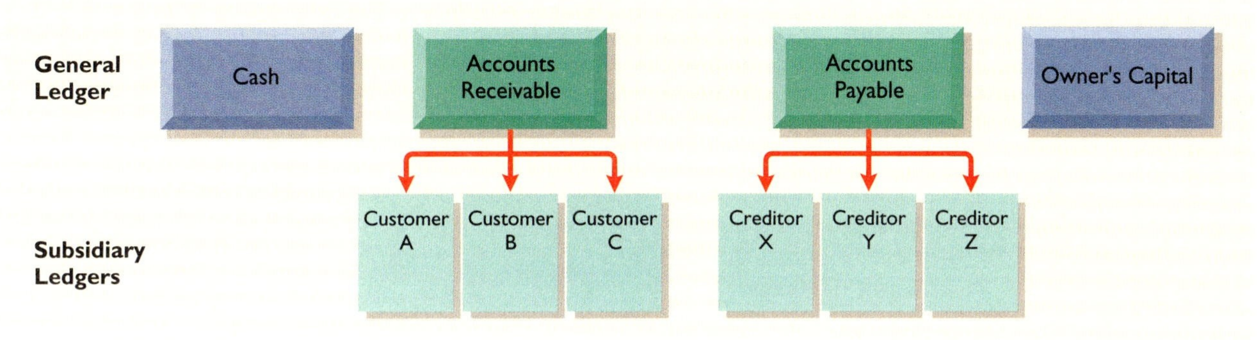

Each general ledger control account balance must equal the composite balance of the individual accounts in the related subsidiary ledger at the end of an accounting period. For example, the balance in Accounts Payable in Illustration 6-1 must equal the total of the subsidiary balances of Creditors X + Y + Z.

EXAMPLE

An example of a control account and subsidiary ledger for Larson Enterprises, a firm that sells souvenirs and children's giveaways for restaurants, is provided in Illustration 6-2. (The explanation column in these accounts is not shown in this and subsequent illustrations due to space considerations.)

Illustration 6-2

Relationship between general and subsidiary ledgers

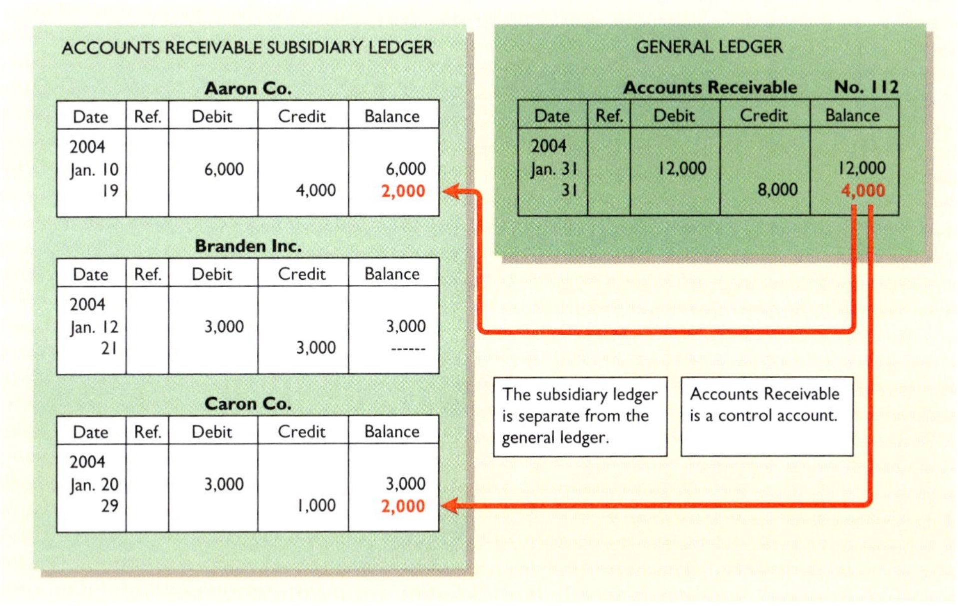

ACCOUNTS RECEIVABLE SUBSIDIARY LEDGER

Aaron Co.

Date	Ref.	Debit	Credit	Balance
2004				
Jan. 10		6,000		6,000
19			4,000	2,000

Branden Inc.

Date	Ref.	Debit	Credit	Balance
2004				
Jan. 12		3,000		3,000
21			3,000	------

Caron Co.

Date	Ref.	Debit	Credit	Balance
2004				
Jan. 20		3,000		3,000
29			1,000	2,000

GENERAL LEDGER

Accounts Receivable No. 112

Date	Ref.	Debit	Credit	Balance
2004				
Jan. 31		12,000		12,000
31			8,000	4,000

The subsidiary ledger is separate from the general ledger.

Accounts Receivable is a control account.

The example is based on the transactions listed in Illustration 6-3.

Illustration 6-3

Sales and collection transactions

Credit Sales			Collections on Account		
Jan. 10	Aaron Co.	$ 6,000	Jan. 19	Aaron Co.	$ 4,000
12	Branden Inc.	3,000	21	Branden Inc.	3,000
20	Caron Co.	3,000	29	Caron Co.	1,000
		$12,000			$ 8,000

The total debits ($12,000) and credits ($8,000) in Accounts Receivable in the general ledger are reconcilable to the detailed debits and credits in the subsidiary accounts. Also, the balance of $4,000 in the control account agrees with the total of the balances in the individual accounts (Aaron Co. $2,000 + Branden Inc. $0 + Caron Co. $2,000) in the subsidiary ledger.

As shown, postings are made monthly to the control accounts in the general ledger. This practice allows monthly financial statements to be prepared. Postings to the individual accounts in the subsidiary ledger are made daily. Daily posting ensures that account information is current. This enables the company to monitor credit limits, bill customers, and answer inquiries from customers about their account balances.

ADVANTAGES OF SUBSIDIARY LEDGERS

Subsidiary ledgers have at least four advantages:

1. **They show transactions affecting one customer or one creditor in a single account**, thus providing up-to-date information on specific account balances.
2. **They free the general ledger of excessive details.** As a result, a trial balance of the general ledger does not contain vast numbers of individual account balances.
3. **They help locate errors in individual accounts** by reducing the number of accounts in one ledger and by using control accounts.
4. **They make possible a division of labor** in posting. One employee can post to the general ledger while someone else posts to the subsidiary ledgers.

TECHNOLOGY IN ACTION

Rather than relying on customer or creditor names in a subsidiary ledger, a computerized system expands the account number of the control account in a prespecified manner. For example, if Accounts Receivable was numbered 10010, the first account in the accounts receivable subsidiary ledger might be numbered 10010-0001. Most systems allow inquiries about specific accounts in the subsidiary ledger (by account number) or about the control account. With the latter, the system would automatically total all the subsidiary accounts whenever an inquiry to the control account was made.

BEFORE YOU GO ON...

REVIEW IT

1. What is a subsidiary ledger, and what purpose does it serve?

2. What are two common subsidiary ledgers? What is the relationship between subsidiary ledgers and a general ledger?
3. What are the advantages of using maintaining subsidiary ledgers?

DO IT

Presented below is information related to Sims Frozen Slushies for its first month of operations. Determine the balances that appear in the accounts payable subsidiary ledger. What Accounts Payable balance appears in the general ledger at the end of January?

Credit Purchases			**Cash Paid**		
Jan. 5	Devon Co.	$11,000	Jan. 9	Devon Co.	$7,000
11	Shelby Co.	7,000	14	Shelby Co.	2,000
22	Taylor Co.	14,000	27	Taylor Co.	9,000

ACTION PLAN

- Subtract cash paid from credit purchases to determine the balances in the accounts payable subsidiary ledger.
- Sum the individual balances to determine the Accounts Payable balance.

SOLUTION

Subsidiary ledger balances: Devon Co. $4,000 ($11,000 – $7,000); Shelby Co. $5,000 ($7,000 – $2,000); Taylor Co. $5,000 ($14,000 – $9,000). General ledger Accounts Payable balance: $14,000 ($4,000 + $5,000 + $5,000).

Related exercise material: 6-1, 6-5, 6-6, and 6-7.

EXPANDING THE JOURNAL—SPECIAL JOURNALS

STUDY OBJECTIVE 2

Explain how special journals are used in journalizing.

So far you have learned to journalize transactions in a two-column general journal and post each entry to the general ledger. This procedure is satisfactory in only the very smallest companies. To expedite journalizing and posting, most companies use special journals *in addition to the general journal.*

A **special journal** is used to record similar types of transactions. Examples would be all sales of merchandise on account, or all cash receipts. What special journals a company uses depends largely on the types of transactions that occur frequently. Most merchandising enterprises use the journals shown in Illustration 6-4 to record transactions daily.

Illustration 6-4

Use of special journals and the general journal

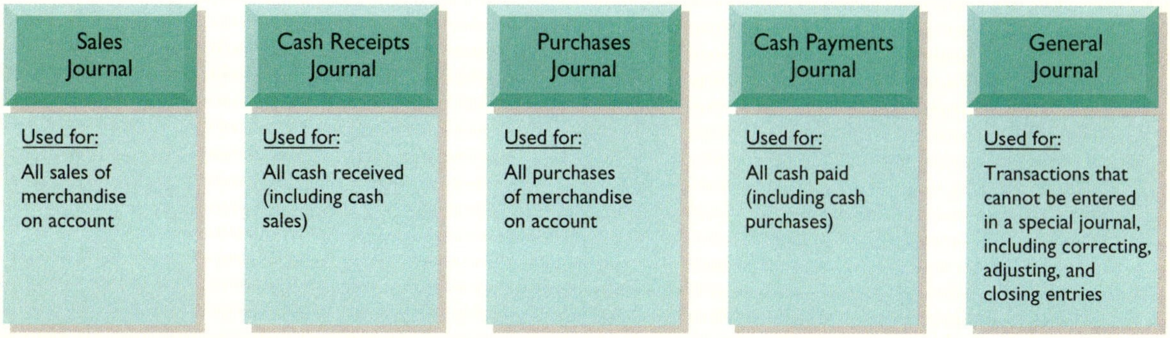

If a transaction cannot be recorded in a special journal, it is recorded in the general journal. For example, if you had special journals only for the four types of transactions listed above, purchase returns and allowances would be recorded in the general journal. So would sales returns and allowances. Similarly, **correcting, adjusting, and closing entries are recorded in the general journal**. Other types of special journals may sometimes be used in some situations. For example, when sales returns and allowances are frequent, special journals may be used to record these transactions.

The use of special journals *permits greater division of labor* because several people can record entries in different journals at the same time. For example, one employee may journalize all cash receipts, and another may journalize all credit sales. Also, the use of special journals *reduces the time needed to complete the posting process*. With special journals, some accounts may be posted monthly, instead of daily, as will be illustrated later in the chapter.

SALES JOURNAL

The **sales journal** is used to record sales of merchandise on account. Cash sales of merchandise are entered in the cash receipts journal. Credit sales of assets other than merchandise are entered in the general journal.

Journalizing Credit Sales

HELPFUL HINT
Postings are also made daily to individual ledger accounts in the inventory subsidiary ledger to maintain a perpetual inventory.

Karns Food Wholesale uses a **perpetual inventory** system. Under this system, each entry in the sales journal results in one entry *at selling price*—a debit to Accounts Receivable (a control account) and a credit of equal amount to Sales—and another entry at cost. The entry *at cost* is a debit to Cost of Goods Sold and a credit of equal amount to Merchandise Inventory (a control account). A sales journal with two amount columns can show on only one line a sales transaction at both selling price and cost. The two-column sales journal of Karns Food Wholesale is shown in Illustration 6-5, using assumed credit sales transactions (for sales invoices 101–107). The reference (Ref.) column is not used in journalizing. It is used in posting the sales journal, as explained in the next section. Also, note that, unlike the general journal, an explanation is not required for each entry in a special journal. Finally, note that each invoice is prenumbered to ensure that all invoices are journalized.

Illustration 6-5

Journalizing the sales journal—perpetual inventory system

Karns Food Wholesale
SALES JOURNAL **S1**

Date	Account Debited	Invoice No.	Ref.	Accts. Receivable Dr. Sales Cr.	Cost of Goods Sold Dr. Merchandise Inventory Cr.
2004					
May 3	Abbot Sisters	101		10,600	6,360
7	Babson Co.	102		11,350	7,370
14	Carson Bros.	103		7,800	5,070
19	Deli Co.	104		9,300	6,510
21	Abbot Sisters	105		15,400	10,780
24	Deli Co.	106		21,210	15,900
27	Babson Co.	107		14,570	10,200
				90,230	62,190

Posting the Sales Journal

Postings from the sales journal are made *daily* to the individual accounts receivable in the subsidiary ledger. Posting to the general ledger is made *monthly*. Illustration 6-6 (on page 181) shows both the daily and monthly postings.

Illustration 6-6

Posting the sales journal

Karns Food Wholesale
SALES JOURNAL
S1

Date	Account Debited	Invoice No.	Ref.	Accts. Receivable Dr. Sales Cr.	Cost of Goods Sold Dr. Merchandise Inventory Cr.
2004					
May 3	Abbot Sisters	101	√	10,600	6,360
7	Babson Co.	102	√	11,350	7,370
14	Carson Bros.	103	√	7,800	5,070
19	Deli Co.	104	√	9,300	6,510
21	Abbot Sisters	105	√	15,400	10,780
24	Deli Co.	106	√	21,210	15,900
27	Babson Co.	107	√	14,570	10,200
				90,230	62,190
				(112) / (401)	(505) / (120)

Totals are posted at the end of the accounting period to the general ledger.

Individual amounts are posted daily to the subsidiary ledger.

ACCOUNTS RECEIVABLE SUBSIDIARY LEDGER

Abbot Sisters

Date	Ref.	Debit	Credit	Balance
2004				
May 3	S1	10,600		10,600
21	S1	15,400		26,000

Babson Co.

Date	Ref.	Debit	Credit	Balance
2004				
May 7	S1	11,350		11,350
27	S1	14,570		25,920

Carson Bros.

Date	Ref.	Debit	Credit	Balance
2004				
May 14	S1	7,800		7,800

Deli Co.

Date	Ref.	Debit	Credit	Balance
2004				
May 19	S1	9,300		9,300
24	S1	21,210		30,510

GENERAL LEDGER

Accounts Receivable **No. 112**

Date	Ref.	Debit	Credit	Balance
2004				
May 31	S1	90,230		90,230

Merchandise Inventory **No. 120**

Date	Ref.	Debit	Credit	Balance
2004				
May 31	S1		62,190	62,190[1]

Sales **No. 401**

Date	Ref.	Debit	Credit	Balance
2004				
May 31	S1		90,230	90,230

Cost of Goods Sold **No. 505**

Date	Ref.	Debit	Credit	Balance
2004				
May 31	S1	62,190		62,190

The subsidiary ledger is separate from the general ledger.

Accounts Receivable is a control account.

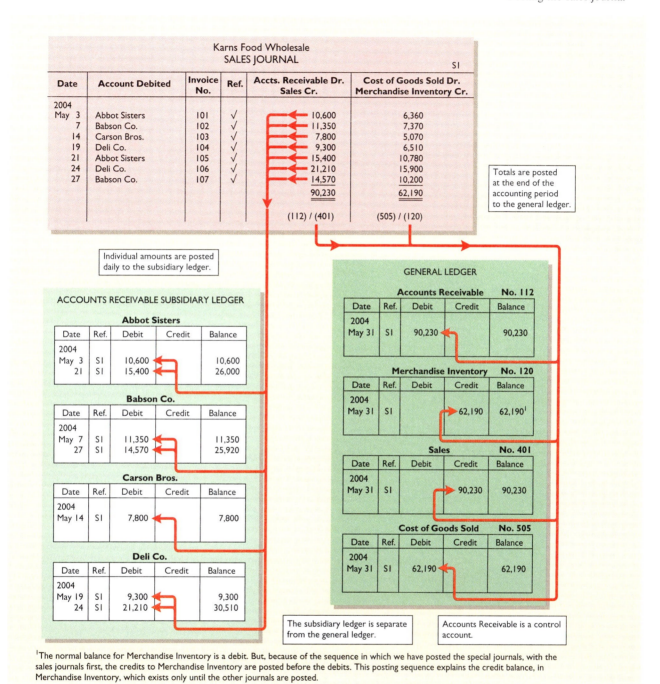

[1]The normal balance for Merchandise Inventory is a debit. But, because of the sequence in which we have posted the special journals, with the sales journals first, the credits to Merchandise Inventory are posted before the debits. This posting sequence explains the credit balance, in Merchandise Inventory, which exists only until the other journals are posted.

A check mark (✓) is inserted in the reference posting column to indicate that the daily posting to the customer's account has been made. A check mark (✓) is used in this illustration because the subsidiary ledger accounts are not numbered. At the end of the month, the column totals of the sales journal are posted to the general ledger. Here, the column totals are a debit of $90,230 to Accounts Receivable (account No. 112), a credit of $90,230 to Sales (account No. 401), a debit of $62,190 to Cost of Goods Sold (account No. 505), and a credit of $62,190 to Merchandise Inventory (account No. 120). Insertion of the account numbers below the column total indicates that the postings have been made. In both the general ledger and subsidiary ledger accounts, the reference **S1** indicates that the posting came from page 1 of the sales journal.

Proving the Ledgers

The next step is to "prove" the ledgers. To do so, we must determine two things: (1) The total of the general ledger debit balances must equal the total of the general ledger credit balances. (2) The sum of the subsidiary ledger balances must equal the balance in the control account. The proof of the postings from the sales journal to the general and subsidiary ledger is shown in Illustration 6-7.

Illustration 6-7

Proving the equality of the postings from the sales journal

Postings to General Ledger

General Ledger	
Credits	
Merchandise Inventory	$62,190
Sales	90,230
	$152,420
Debits	
Accounts Receivable	$90,230
Cost of Goods Sold	62,190
	$152,420

Debit Postings to the Accounts Receivable Subsidiary Ledger

Subsidiary Ledger	
Abbot Sisters	$26,000
Babson Co.	25,920
Carson Bros.	7,800
Deli Co.	30,510
	$90,230

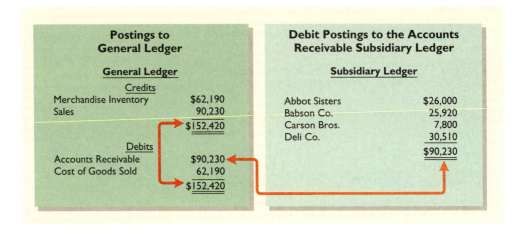

Advantages of the Sales Journal

The use of a special journal to record sales on account has a number of advantages. First, the one-line entry for each sales transaction saves time. In the sales journal, it is not necessary to write out the four account titles for each transaction. Second, only totals, rather than individual entries, are posted to the general ledger. This saves posting time and reduces the possibilities of errors in posting. Finally, **a division of labor results**, because one individual can take responsibility for the sales journal.

CASH RECEIPTS JOURNAL

All receipts of cash are recorded in the **cash receipts journal**. The most common types of cash receipts are cash sales of merchandise and collections of accounts receivable. Many other possibilities exist, such as receipt of money from bank loans and cash proceeds from disposal of equipment. A one- or two-column cash receipts journal would not have space enough for all possible cash receipt transactions. Therefore, a multiple-column cash receipts journal is used.

Generally, a cash receipts journal includes the following columns: debit columns for cash and sales discounts; and credit columns for accounts receivable, sales, and "other" accounts. The Other Accounts category is used when the cash receipt does not involve a cash sale or a collection of accounts receivable. Under a perpetual inventory system, each sales entry is accompanied by another entry that debits Cost of Goods Sold and credits Merchandise Inventory for the cost of the merchandise sold. This entry may be recorded separately. A six-column cash receipts journal is shown in Illustration 6-8 (on page 183).

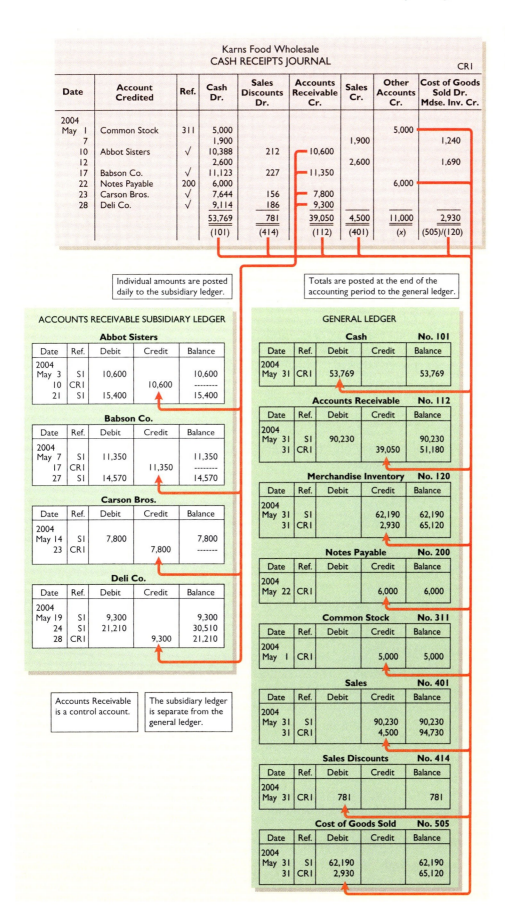

Illustration 6-8

Journalizing and posting the cash receipts journal

Karns Food Wholesale
CASH RECEIPTS JOURNAL

CR1

Date	Account Credited	Ref.	Cash Dr.	Sales Discounts Dr.	Accounts Receivable Cr.	Sales Cr.	Other Accounts Cr.	Cost of Goods Sold Dr. Mdse. Inv. Cr.
2004								
May 1	Common Stock	311	5,000				5,000	
7			1,900			1,900		1,240
10	Abbot Sisters	√	10,388	212	10,600			
12			2,600			2,600		1,690
17	Babson Co.	√	11,123	227	11,350			
22	Notes Payable	200	6,000				6,000	
23	Carson Bros.	√	7,644	156	7,800			
28	Deli Co.	√	9,114	186	9,300			
			53,769	781	39,050	4,500	11,000	2,930
			(101)	(414)	(112)	(401)	(x)	(505)/(120)

Individual amounts are posted daily to the subsidiary ledger.

Totals are posted at the end of the accounting period to the general ledger.

ACCOUNTS RECEIVABLE SUBSIDIARY LEDGER

Abbot Sisters

Date	Ref.	Debit	Credit	Balance
2004				
May 3	S1	10,600		10,600
10	CR1		10,600	--------
21	S1	15,400		15,400

Babson Co.

Date	Ref.	Debit	Credit	Balance
2004				
May 7	S1	11,350		11,350
17	CR1		11,350	--------
27	S1	14,570		14,570

Carson Bros.

Date	Ref.	Debit	Credit	Balance
2004				
May 14	S1	7,800		7,800
23	CR1		7,800	-------

Deli Co.

Date	Ref.	Debit	Credit	Balance
2004				
May 19	S1	9,300		9,300
24	S1	21,210		30,510
28	CR1		9,300	21,210

Accounts Receivable is a control account.

The subsidiary ledger is separate from the general ledger.

GENERAL LEDGER

Cash **No. 101**

Date	Ref.	Debit	Credit	Balance
2004				
May 31	CR1	53,769		53,769

Accounts Receivable **No. 112**

Date	Ref.	Debit	Credit	Balance
2004				
May 31	S1	90,230		90,230
31	CR1		39,050	51,180

Merchandise Inventory **No. 120**

Date	Ref.	Debit	Credit	Balance
2004				
May 31	S1		62,190	62,190
31	CR1		2,930	65,120

Notes Payable **No. 200**

Date	Ref.	Debit	Credit	Balance
2004				
May 22	CR1		6,000	6,000

Common Stock **No. 311**

Date	Ref.	Debit	Credit	Balance
2004				
May 1	CR1		5,000	5,000

Sales **No. 401**

Date	Ref.	Debit	Credit	Balance
2004				
May 31	S1		90,230	90,230
31	CR1		4,500	94,730

Sales Discounts **No. 414**

Date	Ref.	Debit	Credit	Balance
2004				
May 31	CR1	781		781

Cost of Goods Sold **No. 505**

Date	Ref.	Debit	Credit	Balance
2004				
May 31	S1	62,190		62,190
31	CR1	2,930		65,120

Additional credit columns may be used if they significantly reduce postings to a specific account. For example, a loan company, such as **Household International**, receives thousands of cash collections from customers. A significant saving in posting would result from using separate credit columns for Loans Receivable and Interest Revenue, rather than using the Other Accounts credit column. In contrast, a retailer that has only one interest collection a month would not find it useful to have a separate column for Interest Revenue.

Journalizing Cash Receipts Transactions

To illustrate the journalizing of cash receipts transactions, we will continue with the May transactions of Karns Food Wholesale. Collections from customers relate to the entries recorded in the sales journal in Illustration 6-5. The entries in the cash receipts journal are based on the following cash receipts.

May	1	Stockholders invest $5,000 in the business.
	7	Cash sales of merchandise total $1,900 (cost, $1,240).
	10	A check for $10,388 is received from Abbot Sisters in payment of invoice No. 101 for $10,600 less a 2 percent discount.
	12	Cash sales of merchandise total $2,600 (cost, $1,690).
	17	A check for $11,123 is received from Babson Co. in payment of invoice No. 102 for $11,350 less a 2 percent discount.
	22	Cash is received by signing a note for $6,000.
	23	A check for $7,644 is received from Carson Bros. in full for invoice No. 103 for $7,800 less a 2 percent discount.
	28	A check for $9,114 is received from Deli Co. in full for invoice No. 104 for $9,300 less a 2 percent discount.

Further information about the columns in the cash receipts journal (see Illustration 6-8) is listed below.

DEBIT COLUMNS

1. **Cash.** The amount of cash actually received in each transaction is entered in this column. The column total indicates the total cash receipts for the month.
2. **Sales Discounts.** Karns includes a Sales Discounts column in its cash receipts journal. By doing so, it is not necessary to enter sales discount items in the general journal. As a result, the collection of an account receivable within the discount period is expressed on one line in the appropriate columns of the cash receipts journal.

CREDIT COLUMNS

3. **Accounts Receivable.** The Accounts Receivable column is used to record cash collections on account. The amount entered here is the amount to be credited to the individual customer's account.
4. **Sales.** The Sales column records all cash sales of merchandise. Cash sales of other assets (plant assets, for example) are not reported in this column.
5. **Other Accounts.** The Other Accounts column is used whenever the credit is other than to Accounts Receivable or Sales. For example, in the first entry, $5,000 is entered as a credit to Common Stock. This column is often referred to as the **sundry accounts column.**

> **HELPFUL HINT**
> When is an account title entered in the "Account Credited" column of the cash receipts journal?
> Answer: A *subsidiary ledger* title is entered there whenever the entry involves a collection of accounts receivable. A *general ledger* account title is entered there whenever the entry involves an account that is not the subject of a special column (and an amount must be entered in the Other Accounts column). No account title is entered there if neither of the foregoing applies.

DEBIT AND CREDIT COLUMN

6. **Cost of Goods Sold and Merchandise Inventory.** This column records debits to Cost of Goods Sold and credits to Merchandise Inventory.

In a multicolumn journal, generally only one line is needed for each entry. Debit and credit amounts for each line must be equal. When the collection from Abbot Sisters on May 10 is journalized, for example, three amounts are indicated. Note also that the Account Credited column is used to identify both general ledger and subsidiary ledger account titles. General ledger accounts are illustrated in the May 1 and May 22 entries. A subsidiary account is illustrated in the May 10 entry for the collection from Abbot Sisters.

When the journalizing of a multicolumn journal has been completed, the amount columns are totaled, and the totals are compared to prove the equality of debits and credits. The proof of the equality of Karns's cash receipts journal is shown in Illustration 6-9. Totaling the columns of a journal and proving the equality of the totals is called **footing** and **cross-footing** a journal.

Illustration 6-9

Proving the equality of the cash receipts journal

Debits	
Cash	$53,769
Sales Discounts	781
Cost of Goods Sold	2,930
	$57,480

Credits	
Accounts Receivable	$39,050
Sales	4,500
Other Accounts	11,000
Merchandise Inventory	2,930
	$57,480

Posting the Cash Receipts Journal

STUDY OBJECTIVE 3

Indicate how a multicolumn journal is posted.

Posting a multicolumn journal involves the following steps.

1. *All column totals except for the Other Accounts total are posted once at the end of the month to the account title(s) specified in the column heading (such as Cash or Accounts Receivable).* Account numbers are entered below the column totals to show that they have been posted. Cash is posted to account No. 101, accounts receivable to account No. 112, merchandise inventory to account No. 120, sales to account No. 401, sales discounts to account No. 414, and cost of goods sold to account No. 505.
2. *The individual amounts making up the Other Accounts total are posted separately to the general ledger accounts specified in the Account Credited column.* See, for example, the credit posting to Common Stock. The total amount of this column is not posted. The symbol (X) is inserted below the total to this column to indicate that the amount has not been posted.
3. *The individual amounts in a column, posted in total to a control account (Accounts Receivable, in this case), are posted daily to the subsidiary ledger account specified in the Account Credited column.* See, for example, the credit posting of $10,600 to Abbot Sisters.

The symbol **CR** is used in both the subsidiary and general ledgers to identify postings from the cash receipts journal.

Proving the Ledgers

After posting of the cash receipts journal is completed, it is necessary to prove the ledgers. As shown in Illustration 6-10, the general ledger totals are in agreement. Also, the sum of the subsidary ledger balances equals the control account balance.

Illustration 6-10

Proving the ledgers after posting the sales and the cash receipts journals

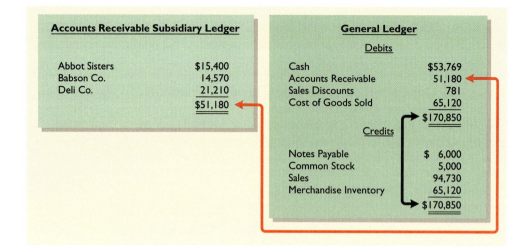

Accounts Receivable Subsidiary Ledger

Abbot Sisters	$15,400
Babson Co.	14,570
Deli Co.	21,210
	$51,180

General Ledger

Debits	
Cash	$53,769
Accounts Receivable	51,180
Sales Discounts	781
Cost of Goods Sold	65,120
	$170,850
Credits	
Notes Payable	$ 6,000
Common Stock	5,000
Sales	94,730
Merchandise Inventory	65,120
	$170,850

Illustration 6-11

Journalizing and posting the purchases journal

HELPFUL HINT

A single-column purchases journal needs only to be footed to prove the equality of debits and credits.

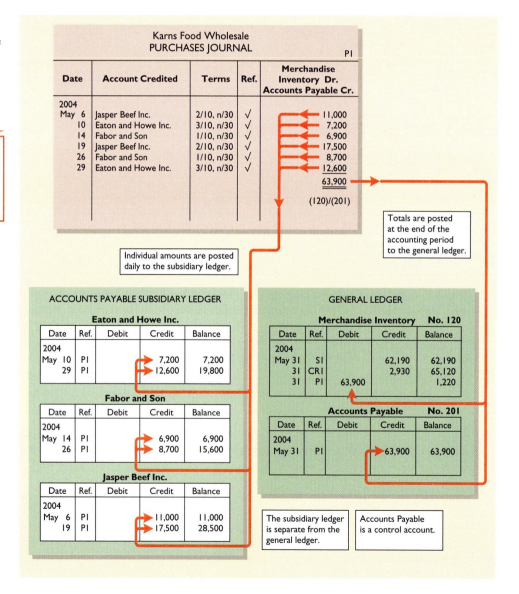

Karns Food Wholesale
PURCHASES JOURNAL

P1

Date	Account Credited	Terms	Ref.	Merchandise Inventory Dr. Accounts Payable Cr.
2004				
May 6	Jasper Beef Inc.	2/10, n/30	√	11,000
10	Eaton and Howe Inc.	3/10, n/30	√	7,200
14	Fabor and Son	1/10, n/30	√	6,900
19	Jasper Beef Inc.	2/10, n/30	√	17,500
26	Fabor and Son	1/10, n/30	√	8,700
29	Eaton and Howe Inc.	3/10, n/30	√	12,600
				63,900
				(120)/(201)

Individual amounts are posted daily to the subsidiary ledger.

Totals are posted at the end of the accounting period to the general ledger.

ACCOUNTS PAYABLE SUBSIDIARY LEDGER

Eaton and Howe Inc.

Date	Ref.	Debit	Credit	Balance
2004				
May 10	P1		7,200	7,200
29	P1		12,600	19,800

Fabor and Son

Date	Ref.	Debit	Credit	Balance
2004				
May 14	P1		6,900	6,900
26	P1		8,700	15,600

Jasper Beef Inc.

Date	Ref.	Debit	Credit	Balance
2004				
May 6	P1		11,000	11,000
19	P1		17,500	28,500

GENERAL LEDGER

Merchandise Inventory No. 120

Date	Ref.	Debit	Credit	Balance
2004				
May 31	S1		62,190	62,190
31	CR1		2,930	65,120
31	P1	63,900		1,220

Accounts Payable No. 201

Date	Ref.	Debit	Credit	Balance
2004				
May 31	P1		63,900	63,900

The subsidiary ledger is separate from the general ledger.

Accounts Payable is a control account.

PURCHASES JOURNAL

All purchases of merchandise on account are recorded in the **purchases journal**. Each entry in this journal results in a debit to Merchandise Inventory and a credit to Accounts Payable. When a one-column purchases journal is used (as in Illustration 6-11), other types of purchases on account and cash purchases cannot be journalized in it. For example, credit purchases of equipment or supplies must be recorded in the general journal. Likewise, all cash purchases are entered in the cash payments journal. As illustrated later, where credit purchases for items other than merchandise are numerous, the purchases journal is often expanded to a multicolumn format. The purchases journal for Karns Food Wholesale is shown in Illustration 6-11 (on page 186).

Journalizing Credit Purchases of Merchandise

Entries in the purchases journal are made from purchase invoices. The journalizing procedure is similar to that for a sales journal. In contrast to the sales journal, the purchases journal may not have an invoice number column, because invoices received from different suppliers will not be in numerical sequence. To assure that all purchase invoices are recorded, some companies consecutively number each invoice upon receipt and then use an internal document number column in the purchases journal.

The entries for Karns Food Wholesale are based on the assumed credit purchases shown in Illustration 6-12.

Illustration 6-12

Credit purchases transactions

Date	Supplier	Amount
5/6	Jasper Beef Inc.	$11,000
5/10	Eaton and Howe Poultry Inc.	7,200
5/14	Fabor and Son Seafood	6,900
5/19	Jasper Beef Inc.	17,500
5/26	Fabor and Son Seafood	8,700
5/29	Eaton and Howe Poultry Inc.	12,600

Posting the Purchases Journal

The procedures for posting the purchases journal are similar to those for the sales journal. In this case, postings are made daily to the **accounts payable ledger** and monthly to Merchandise Inventory and Accounts Payable in the **general ledger**. In both ledgers, P1 is used in the reference column to show that the postings are from page 1 of the purchases journal.

Proof of the equality of the postings from the purchases journal to both ledgers is shown by the following.

HELPFUL HINT

Postings to subsidiary ledger accounts are done daily because it is often necessary to know a current balance for the subsidiary accounts.

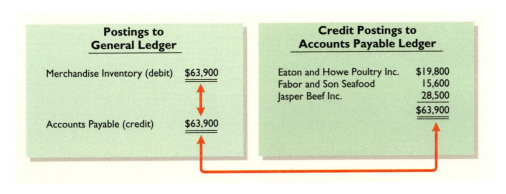

Illustration 6-13

Proving the equality of the purchases journal

Postings to General Ledger	
Merchandise Inventory (debit)	$63,900
Accounts Payable (credit)	$63,900

Credit Postings to Accounts Payable Ledger	
Eaton and Howe Poultry Inc.	$19,800
Fabor and Son Seafood	15,600
Jasper Beef Inc.	28,500
	$63,900

HELPFUL HINT
A multicolumn purchases journal must be footed and cross-footed to prove the equality of debits and credits.

Expanding the Purchases Journal

Some companies expand the purchases journal to include all types of purchases on account. Instead of one column for merchandise inventory and accounts payable, they use a multiple-column format. The multicolumn format usually includes a credit column for accounts payable and debit columns for purchases of merchandise, of office supplies, of store supplies, and other accounts. Illustration 6-14 is an example of a multicolumn purchases journal for Hanover Table Linen Co. The posting procedures are similar to those illustrated earlier for posting the cash receipts journal.

Illustration 6-14
Multicolumn purchases journal

Hanover Table Linen Co.
PURCHASES JOURNAL **P1**

Date	Account Credited	Ref.	Accounts Payable Cr.	Merchandise Inventory Dr.	Office Supplies Dr.	Store Supplies Dr.	Other Accounts Dr. Account	Ref.	Amount
2004									
June 1	Signe Audio	✓	2,000		2,000				
3	Wright Co.	✓	1,500	1,500					
5	Orange Tree Co.	✓	2,600				Equipment	157	2,600
30	Sue's Business Forms	✓	800			800			
			56,600	43,000	7,500	1,200			4,900

CASH PAYMENTS JOURNAL

ALTERNATIVE TERMINOLOGY
The cash payments journal is sometimes called the *cash disbursements journal.*

All disbursements of cash are entered in a **cash payments journal**. Entries are made from prenumbered checks. Because cash payments are made for various purposes, the cash payments journal has multiple columns. A four-column journal is shown in Illustration 6-15 (on page 189).

Journalizing Cash Payments Transactions

The procedures for journalizing transactions in this journal are similar to those described earlier for the cash receipts journal. Each transaction is entered on one line, and for each line there must be equal debit and credit amounts. The entries in the cash payments journal in Illustration 6-15 are based on the following transactions for Karns Food Wholesale.

May 1 Check No. 101 for $1,200 issued for the annual premium on a fire insurance policy.
3 Check No. 102 for $100 issued in payment of freight when terms were FOB shipping point.
8 Check No. 103 for $4,400 issued for the purchase of merchandise.
10 Check No. 104 for $10,780 sent to Jasper Beef Inc. in payment of May 6 invoice for $11,000 less a 2 percent discount.
19 Check No. 105 for $6,984 mailed to Eaton and Howe Poultry in payment of May 10 invoice for $7,200 less a 3 percent discount.
23 Check No. 106 for $6,831 sent to Fabor and Son Seafood in payment of May 14 invoice for $6,900 less a 1 percent discount.
28 Check No. 107 for $17,150 sent to Jasper Beef Inc. in payment of May 19 invoice for $17,500 less a 2 percent discount.
30 Check No. 108 for $500 issued to stockholders as a cash dividend.

Note that whenever an amount is entered in the Other Accounts column, a specific general ledger account must be identified in the Account Debited column.

Illustration 6-15

Journalizing and posting the cash payments journal

Karns Food Wholesale
CASH PAYMENTS JOURNAL

CP1

Date	Ck. No.	Account Debited	Ref.	Other Accounts Dr.	Accounts Payable Dr.	Merchandise Inventory Cr.	Cash Cr.
2004							
May 1	101	Prepaid Insurance	130	1,200			1,200
3	102	Mdse. Inventory	120	100			100
8	103	Mdse. Inventory	120	4,400			4,400
10	104	Jasper Beef Inc.	√		11,000	220	10,780
19	105	Eaton & Howe Poultry	√		7,200	216	6,984
23	106	Fabor and Son Seafood	√		6,900	69	6,831
28	107	Jasper Beef Inc.	√		17,500	350	17,150
30	108	Dividends	332	500			500
				6,200	42,600	855	47,945
				(x)	(201)	(120)	(101)

Individual amounts are posted daily to the subsidiary ledger.

Totals are posted at the end of the accounting period to the general ledger.

ACCOUNTS PAYABLE SUBSIDIARY LEDGER

Eaton and Howe Poultry

Date	Ref.	Debit	Credit	Balance
2004				
May 10	P1		7,200	7,200
19	CP1	7,200		-------
29	P1		12,600	12,600

Fabor and Son Seafood

Date	Ref.	Debit	Credit	Balance
2004				
May 14	P1		6,900	6,900
23	CP1	6,900		-------
26	P1		8,700	8,700

Jasper Beef Inc.

Date	Ref.	Debit	Credit	Balance
2004				
May 6	P1		11,000	11,000
10	CP1	11,000		--------
19	P1		17,500	17,500
28	CP1	17,500		--------

Accounts Payable is a control account.

The subsidiary ledger is separate from the general ledger.

GENERAL LEDGER

Cash **No. 101**

Date	Ref.	Debit	Credit	Balance
2004				
May 31	CR1	53,769		53,769
31	CP1		47,945	5,824

Merchandise Inventory **No. 120**

Date	Ref.	Debit	Credit	Balance
2004				
May 3	CP1	100		100
8	CP1	4,400		4,500
31	S1		62,190	57,690
31	CR1		2,930	60,620
31	P1	63,900		3,280
31	CP1		855	2,425

Prepaid Insurance **No. 130**

Date	Ref.	Debit	Credit	Balance
2004				
May 1	CP1	1,200		1,200

Accounts Payable **No. 201**

Date	Ref.	Debit	Credit	Balance
2004				
May 31	P1		63,900	63,900
31	CP1	42,600		21,300

Dividends **No. 332**

Date	Ref.	Debit	Credit	Balance
2004				
May 30	CP1	500		500

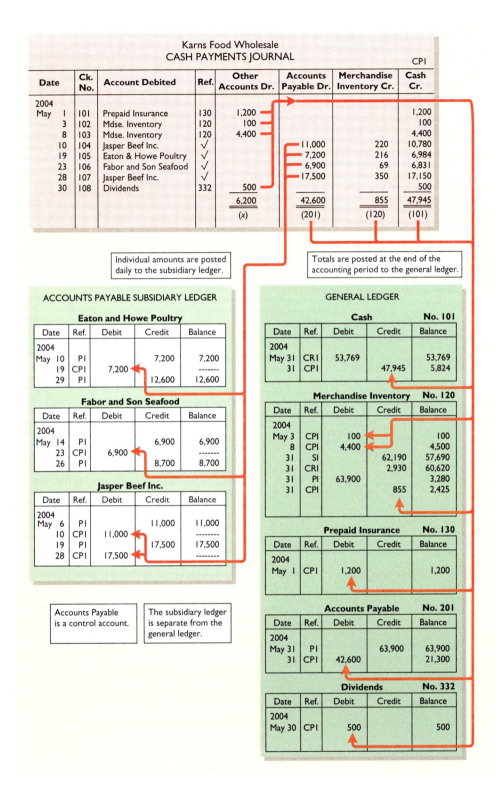

The entries for checks No. 101, 102, and 103 illustrate this situation. Similarly, a subsidiary account must be identified in the Account Debited column whenever an amount is entered in the Accounts Payable column. See, for example, the entry for check No. 104.

After the cash payments journal has been journalized, the columns are totaled. The totals are then balanced to prove the equality of debits and credits.

Posting the Cash Payments Journal

The procedures for posting the cash payments journal are similar to those for the cash receipts journal. The amounts recorded in the Accounts Payable column are posted individually to the subsidiary ledger and in total to the control account. Merchandise Inventory and Cash are posted only in total at the end of the month. Transactions in the Other Accounts column are posted individually to the appropriate account(s) affected. No totals are posted for this column.

The posting of the cash payments journal is shown in Illustration 6-15. Note that the symbol *CP* is used as the posting reference. After postings are completed, the equality of the debit and credit balances in the general ledger should be determined. In addition, the control account balances should agree with the subsidiary ledger total balance. The agreement of these balances is shown in Illustration 6-16.

Illustration 6-16

Proving the ledgers after postings from the sales, cash receipts, purchases, and cash payments journals

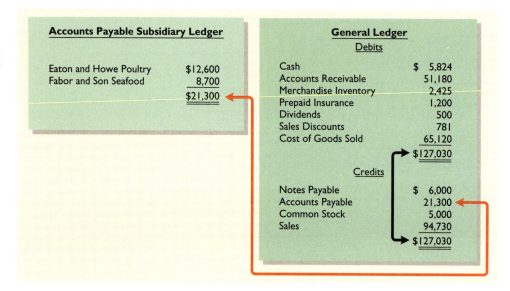

Accounts Payable Subsidiary Ledger

Eaton and Howe Poultry	$12,600
Fabor and Son Seafood	8,700
	$21,300

General Ledger

Debits	
Cash	$ 5,824
Accounts Receivable	51,180
Merchandise Inventory	2,425
Prepaid Insurance	1,200
Dividends	500
Sales Discounts	781
Cost of Goods Sold	65,120
	$127,030

Credits	
Notes Payable	$ 6,000
Accounts Payable	21,300
Common Stock	5,000
Sales	94,730
	$127,030

EFFECTS OF SPECIAL JOURNALS ON GENERAL JOURNAL

Special journals for sales, purchases, and cash substantially reduce the number of entries that are made in the general journal. **Only transactions that cannot be entered in a special journal are recorded in the general journal.** For example, the general journal may be used to record such transactions as granting of credit to a customer for a sales return or allowance, granting of credit from a supplier for purchases returned, acceptance of a note receivable from a customer, and purchase of equipment by issuing a note payable. Also, correcting, adjusting, and closing entries are made in the general journal.

The general journal has columns for date, account title and explanation, reference, and debit and credit amounts. When control and subsidiary accounts are not involved, the procedures for journalizing and posting of transactions are the same as those described in earlier chapters. When control and subsidiary accounts are involved, two changes from the earlier procedures are required:

1. In *journalizing*, both the control and the subsidiary accounts must be identified.
2. In *posting*, there must be a dual posting: once to the control account and once to the subsidiary account.

To illustrate, assume that on May 31, Karns Food Wholesale returns $500 of merchandise for credit to Fabor and Son. The entry in the general journal and the posting of the entry are shown in Illustration 6-17. Note that if cash is received instead of credit granted on this return, then the transaction is recorded in the cash receipts journal.

Illustration 6-17

Journalizing and posting the general journal

Karns Food Wholesale
GENERAL JOURNAL G1

Date	Account Title and Explanation	Ref.	Debit	Credit
2004				
May 31	Accounts Payable–Fabor and Son	201/√	500	
	Merchandise Inventory	120		500
	(Received credit for returned goods)			

ACCOUNTS PAYABLE SUBSIDIARY LEDGER

Fabor and Son Seafood

Date	Ref.	Debit	Credit	Balance
2004				
May 14	P1		6,900	6,900
23	CP1	6,900		....
26	P1		8,700	8,700
31	**G1**	500		**8,200**

GENERAL LEDGER

Merchandise Inventory **No. 120**

Date	Ref.	Debit	Credit	Balance
2004				
May 31	**G1**		500	**500**

Accounts Payable **No. 201**

Date	Ref.	Debit	Credit	Balance
2004				
May 31	P1		63,900	63,900
31	CP1	42,600		21,300
31	**G1**	500		**20,800**

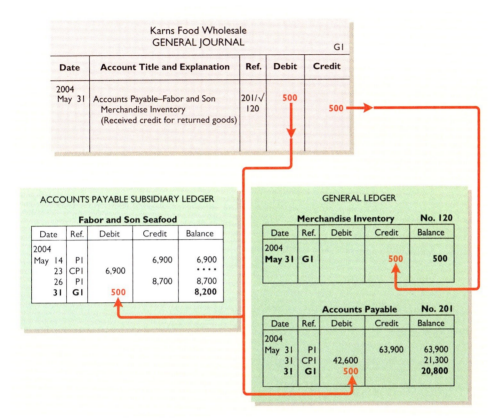

Observe in the journal that two accounts are indicated for the debit, and two postings ("201/✓") are indicated in the reference column. One amount is posted to the control account and the other to the creditor's account in the subsidiary ledger.

BEFORE YOU GO ON...

▶ *REVIEW IT*

1. What types of special journals are frequently used to record transactions? Why are special journals used?
2. Explain how transactions recorded in the sales journal and the cash receipts journal are posted.
3. Indicate the types of transactions that are recorded in the general journal when special journals are used.

▶ *DO IT*

Vilas Company has the following selected transactions: (1) purchase of equipment for cash, (2) cash sales, (3) sales returns and allowances, (4) payment of cash dividends, and (5) sales of merchandise on account. Identify the journals in which each transaction should be entered.

ACTION PLAN

- Know the content of each special journal.
- Understand the effect of special journals on the general journal.

SOLUTION: (1) Purchase of equipment for cash—cash payments journal. (2) Cash sale—cash receipts journal. (3) Sales return and allowance—general journal. (4) Payment of cash dividends—cash payments journal. (5) Sale of merchandise on account—sales journal.

Related exercise material: 6-2, 6-3, 6-4, 6-5, and 6-6.

DEMONSTRATION PROBLEM

Dion Restaurant Equipment Company uses a six-column cash receipts journal with the following columns: Cash (Dr.), Sales Discounts (Dr.), Accounts Receivable (Cr.), Sales (Cr.), Other Accounts (Cr.), and Cost of Goods Sold (Dr.) and Merchandise Inventory (Cr.). Cash receipts transactions for the month of July 2002 are as follows.

July 3 Cash sales total $5,800 (cost, $3,480).
5 A check for $6,370 is received from Jeltz Deli in payment of an invoice dated June 26 for $6,500, terms 2/10, n/30.
9 An additional investment of $5,000 in cash is made in the business by stockholders.
10 Cash sales total $12,519 (cost, $7,511).
12 A check for $7,275 is received from R. Eliot Seafood House in payment of a $7,500 invoice dated July 3, terms 3/10, n/30.
15 A customer advance of $700 cash is received for future sales.
20 Cash sales total $15,472 (cost, $9,283).
22 A check for $5,880 is received from Beck Hamburger in payment of $6,000 invoice dated July 13, terms 2/10, n/30.
29 Cash sales total $17,660 (cost, $10,596).
31 Cash of $200 is received on interest earned for July.

Instructions

(a) Journalize the transactions in the cash receipts journal.
(b) Contrast the posting of the Accounts Receivable and Other Accounts columns.

ACTION PLAN

- Record all cash receipts in the cash receipts journal.
- The "account credited" indicates items posted individually to the subsidiary ledger or general ledger.
- Record cash sales in the cash receipts journal—not in the sales journal.
- The total debits must equal the total credits.

SOLUTION TO DEMONSTRATION PROBLEM

(a)

Dion Restaurant Equipment Company
CASH RECEIPTS JOURNAL **CR1**

Date	Account Credited	Ref.	Cash Dr.	Sales Discounts Dr.	Accounts Receivable Cr.	Sales Cr.	Other Accounts Cr.	Cost of Goods Sold Dr. Mdse. Inv. Cr.
2004								
7/3			5,800			5,800		3,480
5	Jeltz Deli		6,370	130	6,500			
9	Common Stock		5,000				5,000	
10			12,519			12,519		7,511
12	R. Eliot Seafood House		7,275	225	7,500			
15	Unearned Revenues		700				700	
20			15,472			15,472		9,283
22	Beck Hamburger		5,880	120	6,000			
29			17,660			17,660		10,596
31	Interest Revenue		200				200	
			76,876	475	20,000	51,451	5,900	30,870

(b) The Accounts Receivable column is posted as a credit to Accounts Receivable. The individual amounts are credited to the customers' accounts identified in the Account Credited column, which are maintained in the accounts receivable subsidiary ledger.

The amounts in the Other Accounts column are only posted individually. They are credited to the account titles identified in the Account Credited column.

SUMMARY OF STUDY OBJECTIVES

1. *Describe the nature and purpose of a subsidiary ledger.* A subsidiary ledger is a group of accounts with a common characteristic. It facilitates the recording process by freeing the general ledger from details of individual balances.

2. *Explain how special journals are used in journalizing.* A special journal is used to group similar types of transactions. In a special journal, generally only one line is used to record a complete transaction.

3. *Indicate how a multicolumn journal is posted.* In posting a multicolumn journal:

(a) All column totals except for the Other Accounts column are posted once at the end of the month to the account title specified in the column heading.

(b) The total of the Other Accounts column is not posted. Instead, the individual amounts comprising the total are posted separately to the general ledger accounts specified in the Account Credited column.

(c) The individual amounts in a column posted in total to a control account are posted daily to the subsidiary ledger accounts specified in the Account Credited column.

GLOSSARY

Accounts payable (creditors') subsidiary ledger A subsidiary ledger that contains accounts of individual creditors (p. 176).

Accounts receivable (customers') subsidiary ledger A subsidiary ledger that contains individual customer accounts (p. 176).

Cash payments journal A special journal used to record all cash paid (p. 188).

Cash receipts journal A special journal used to record all cash received (p. 182).

Control account An account in the general ledger that summarizes a subsidiary ledger (p. 177).

Cross-footing The proving of the equality of the totals in a journal (p. 185).

Footing The totaling of a column of a journal (p. 185).

Purchases journal A special journal used to record all purchases of merchandise on account (p. 187).

Sales journal A special journal used to record all sales of merchandise on account (p. 180).

Special journal A journal that is used to record similar types of transactions, such as all credit sales (p. 179).

Subsidiary ledger A group of accounts with a common characteristic (p. 176).

EXERCISES

6-1 Presented below is information related to Bradley Bed & Breakfast for its first month of operations. Identify the balances that appear in the accounts receivable subsidiary ledger and the accounts receivable balance that appears in the general ledger at the end of January.

Identify subsidiary ledger balances.
(SO 1)

Credit Sales			Cash Collections		
Jan. 7	Avon Co.	$8,000	Jan. 17	Avon Co.	$7,000
15	Barto Co.	6,000	24	Barto Co.	5,000
23	Cecil Co.	9,000	29	Cecil Co.	9,000

6-2 Indicate whether each of the following debits and credits is included in the cash receipts journal. (Use "Yes" or "No" to answer this question.)

Identify entries to cash receipts journal.
(SO 2)

1. Debit to Sales
2. Credit to Merchandise Inventory
3. Credit to Accounts Receivable
4. Debit to Accounts Payable

6-3 Steering Rental Car uses a multicolumn cash receipts journal. Indicate which column(s) is/are posted only in total, only daily, or both in total and daily.

Indicate postings to cash receipts journal.
(SO 3)

1. Accounts Receivable
2. Sales Discounts
3. Cash
4. Other Accounts

6-4 Cohen Noodles Manufacturing uses special journals and a general journal. Identify the journal in which each of the following transactions is recorded.

Identify transactions for special journals.
(SO 2)

(a) Purchased equipment on account.
(b) Purchased merchandise on account.
(c) Paid utility expense in cash.
(d) Sold merchandise on account.

6-5 On September 1 the balance of the Accounts Receivable control account in the general ledger of Odesto Restaurant Equipment Company was $11,960. The customers' subsidiary ledger

Post various journals to control and subsidiary accounts.
(SO 1, 2)

contained account balances as follows: Edmonds $2,440, Park $2,640, Roemer $2,060, Schulz $4,820. At the end of September the various journals contained the following information.

Sales journal: Sales to Schulz Burger $800; to Edmonds Taco $1,350; to Henry Fried Chicken $1,030; to Roemer Pasta $1,100.

Cash receipts journal: Cash received from Roemer Pasta $1,310; from Schulz Burger $2,300; from Henry Fried Chicken $410; from Park Ice Cream & Yogurt $1,800; from Edmonds Taco $1,240.

General journal: An allowance is granted to Schulz Burger $220.

Instructions

(a) Set up control and subsidiary accounts and enter the beginning balances. Do not construct the journals.

(b) Post the various journals. Post the items as individual items or as totals, whichever would be the appropriate procedure. (No sales discounts given.)

(c) Prepare a list of customers and prove the agreement of the controlling account with the subsidiary ledger at September 30, 2004.

Record transactions in sales and purchases journals.
(SO 1, 2)

6-6 Hurley Hotel Bedding Company uses special journals and a general journal. The following transactions occurred during September 2004.

Sept.	2	Sold merchandise on account to Rusch Motel, invoice no. 101, $480, terms n/30. The cost of the merchandise sold was $300.
	10	Purchased merchandise on account from Dayne Hotel $600, terms 2/10, n/30.
	12	Purchased office equipment on account from Piazza Resorts $6,500.
	21	Sold merchandise on account to Perez Motel, invoice no. 102 for $800, terms 2/10, n/30. The cost of the merchandise sold was $480.
	25	Purchased merchandise on account from Sage Linen $900, terms n/30.
	27	Sold merchandise to Deitrich Hotel for $700 cash. The cost of the merchandise sold was $420.

Instructions

(a) Draw a sales journal (see Illustration 6-6) and a single-column purchase journal (see Illustration 6-11). (Use page 1 for each journal.)

(b) Record the transaction(s) for September that should be journalized in the sales journal and the purchases journal.

Explain posting to control account and subsidiary ledger.
(SO 1, 3)

6-7 The general ledger of Williams Greek Gyros contained the following Accounts Payable control account (in T-account form). Also shown is the related subsidiary ledger.

GENERAL LEDGER

Accounts Payable

Feb.	15 General journal	1,400	Feb.	1	Balance	26,025
	28 ?	?		5	General journal	265
				11	General journal	550
				28	Purchases	13,900
			Feb.	28	Balance	9,840

ACCOUNTS PAYABLE LEDGER

Sealy Bakery

	Feb. 28 Bal. 4,600

Gates Meats

	Feb. 28 Bal. 2,000

Wolcott Condiments, Inc.

	Feb. 28 Bal. ?

Instructions

(a) Indicate the missing posting reference and amount in the control account, and the missing ending balance in the subsidiary ledger.

(b) Indicate the amounts in the control account that were dual-posted (i.e., posted to the control account and the subsidiary accounts).

Journalize transactions in cash receipts journal; post to control account and subsidiary ledger.
(SO 1, 2, 3)

6-8 Lemon Ice Company produces a unique 4-oz cup of frozen ice treats to many growing stores. Its chart of accounts includes the following selected accounts.

101 Cash	401 Sales
112 Accounts Receivable	414 Sales Discounts
120 Merchandise Inventory	505 Cost of Goods Sold
311 Common Stock	

On April 1 the accounts receivable ledger of Lemon Ice Company showed the following balances: Horner Foods $1,550, Harris Grocery $1,200, Northeast $2,900, and Smith Foods $1,700. The April transactions involving the receipt of cash were as follows.

Apr.	1	Stockholders invested additional cash in the business, $6,000, for common stock.
	4	Received check for payment of account from Smith Foods less 2 percent cash discount.
	5	Received check for $620 in payment of invoice no. 307 from Northeast.
	8	Made cash sales of merchandise totaling $7,245. The cost of the merchandise sold was $4,347.
	10	Received check for $800 in payment of invoice no. 309 from Horner Foods.
	11	Received cash refund from a supplier for damaged merchandise $550.
	23	Received check for $1,500 in payment of invoice no. 310 from Northeast.
	29	Received check for payment of account from Harris Grocery.

Instructions

(a) Journalize the transactions above in a six-column cash receipts journal with columns for Cash Dr., Sales Discounts Dr., Accounts Receivable Cr., Sales Cr., Other Accounts Cr., and Cost of Goods Sold Dr./Merchandise Inventory Cr. Foot and cross-foot the journal.

(b) Insert the beginning balances in the Accounts Receivable control and subsidiary accounts, and post the April transactions to these accounts.

(c) Prove the agreement of the control account and subsidiary account balances.

Journalize transactions in cash payments journal; post to control account and subsidiary ledgers.
(SO 1, 2, 3)

6-9 Simpson's caters food to area corporate offices for their partices. Its chart of accounts includes the following selected accounts.

101 Cash	201 Accounts Payable
120 Merchandise Inventory	332 Dividends
130 Prepaid Insurance	505 Cost of Goods Sold
157 Equipment	

On October 1 the accounts payable ledger of Simpson Company showed the following balances: Hester Foods $1,700, Milo Sausages $2,500, Ontario Fruits $1,400, and Pagan Produce $3,700. The October transactions involving the payment of cash were as follows.

Oct.	1	Purchased merchandise, check no. 63, $700.
	3	Purchased equipment, check no. 64, $800.
	5	Paid Hester Foods balance due of $1,700, less 2 percent discount, check no. 65, $1,666.
	10	Purchased merchandise, check no. 66, $2,250.
	15	Paid Ontario Fruits balance due of $1,400, check no. 67.
	16	A cash dividend is paid in the amount of $400, check no. 68.
	19	Paid Milo Sausages in full for invoice no. 610, $1,400 less 2 percent cash discount, check no. 69, $1,372.
	29	Paid Pagan Produce in full for invoice no. 264, $2,600, check no. 70.

Instructions

(a) Journalize the transactions above in a four-column cash payments journal with columns for Other Accounts Dr., Accounts Payable Dr., Merchandise Inventory Cr., and Cash Cr. Foot and cross-foot the journal.

(b) Insert the beginning balances in the Accounts Payable control and subsidiary accounts, and post the October transactions to these accounts.
(c) Prove the agreement of the control account and the subsidiary account balances.

Journalize transactions in multi-column purchases journal; post to the general and subsidiary ledgers.
(SO 1, 2, 3)

6-10 The chart of accounts of Hernandez Executive Catering includes the following selected accounts.

112 Accounts Receivable	401 Sales
120 Merchandise Inventory	412 Sales Returns and Allowances
126 Supplies	505 Cost of Goods Sold
157 Equipment	610 Advertising Expense
201 Accounts Payable	

In July the following selected transactions were completed. All purchases and sales were on account. The cost of all merchandise sold was 70 percent of the sales price.

July	1	Purchased merchandise from Denton Meats, $7,000.
	2	Received freight bill from Johnson Shipping on Denton purchase, $400.
	3	Made sales to Lyons Company, $1,300, and to Franklin Bros., $1,900.
	5	Purchased merchandise from Grant Foods, $3,200.
	8	Received credit on merchandise returned to Grant Foods, $300.
	13	Purchased store supplies from Brent Meats, $720.
	15	Purchased merchandise from Denton Meats $3,600 and from Ruiz Coffee, $2,900.
	16	Made sales to Martin Company $3,450 and to Franklin Bros., $1,570.
	18	Received bill for advertising from Marlin Advertisements, $600.
	21	Made sales to Lyons Company $310 and to Randee Company, $2,300.
	22	Granted allowance to Lyons Company for merchandise damaged in shipment, $40.
	24	Purchased merchandise from Grant Foods, $3,000.
	26	Purchased equipment from Brent Meats, $600.
	28	Received freight bill from Johnson Shipping on Grant purchase of July 24, $380.
	30	Made sales to Martin Company, $4,900.

Instructions

(a) Journalize the transactions above in a purchases journal, a sales journal, and a general journal. The purchases journal should have the following column headings: Date, Account Credited (Debited), Ref., Other Accounts Dr., and Merchandise Inventory Dr., Accounts Payable Cr.
(b) Post to both the general and subsidiary ledger accounts. (Assume that all accounts have zero beginning balances.)
(c) Prove the agreement of the control and subsidiary accounts.

EXPLORING THE WEB

6-11 **Great Plains' Accounting** is one of the leading accounting software packages. Information related to this package is found at its Web site.

Address: **www.greatplains.com/accounting/productinfo.asp**

Steps

1. Go to the site shown above.
2. Choose **General Ledger**. Answer question (a) below.
3. Choose **Accounts Payable**. Answer question (b) below.

Instructions

(a) What are three key features of the general ledger module highlighted by the company?
(b) What are three key features of the payables management module highlighted by the company?

GROUP DECISION CASE

6-12 Ehlert & Ramos is a wholesaler of small restaurant appliances and parts. Ehlert & Ramos is operated by two owners, Bill Ehlert and Denise Ramos. In addition, the company has one employee, a repair specialist, who is on a fixed salary. Revenues are earned through the sale of appliances to retailers (approximately 75% of total revenues), appliance parts to do-it-yourselfers (10%), and the repair of appliances brought to the store (15%). Appliance sales are made on both a credit and cash basis. Customers are billed on prenumbered sales invoices. Credit terms are always net/30 days. All parts sales and repair work are cash only.

Merchandise is purchased on account from the manufacturers of both the appliances and the parts. Practically all suppliers offer cash discounts for prompt payments, and it is company policy to take all discounts. Most cash payments are made by check. Checks are most frequently issued to suppliers, to trucking companies for freight on merchandise purchases, and to newspapers, radio, and TV stations for advertising. All advertising bills are paid as received. Bill and Denise each make a monthly drawing in cash for personal living expenses. The salaried repairman is paid twice monthly. Ehlert & Ramos currently has a manual accounting system.

Instructions

With the class divided into groups, answer the following.

(a) Identify the special journals that Ehlert & Ramos should have in its manual system. List the column headings appropriate for each of the special journals.

(b) What control and subsidiary accounts should be included in Ehlert & Ramos's manual system? Why?

ETHICS CASE

6-13 Tyler Resorts operates three properties, each with its own personnel, including a marketing/sales force. The corporate headquarters and central accounting office are in Tyler, and the properties are in Freeport, Rockport, and Bayport, all within 50 miles of Tyler. Corporate management treats each resort as an independent profit center and encourages competition among them. They each have similar but different product lines. As a competitive incentive, bonuses are awarded each year to the employees of the fastest growing and most profitable division.

Don Henke is the manager of Tyler's centralized computer accounting operation that keyboards the sales transactions and maintains the accounts receivable for all three divisions. Don came up in the accounting ranks from the Bayport resort where his wife, several relatives, and many friends still work.

As sales documents are keyboarded into the computer, the originating property is identified by code. Most sales documents (95%) are coded, but some (5%) are not coded or are coded incorrectly. As the manager, Don has instructed the keyboard operators to assign the Bayport code to all uncoded and incorrectly coded sales documents. This is done he says, "in order to expedite processing and to keep the computer files current since they are updated daily." All receivables and cash collections for all three properties are handled by Tyler as one subsidiary accounts receivable ledger.

Instructions

(a) Who are the stakeholders in this situation?

(b) What are the ethical issues in this case?

(c) How might the system be improved to prevent this situation?

Remember to go back to the Navigator box on the chapter-opening page and check off your completed work.

THE NAVIGATOR ✓

- Understand *Concepts for Review* ❑
- Read *Feature Story* ❑
- Scan *Study Objectives* ❑
- Read *Preview* ❑
- Read text and answer *Before You Go On*
  p. 208 ❑ *p.* 210 ❑ *p.* 215 ❑
- Work *Demonstration Problem* ❑
- Review *Summary of Study Objectives* ❑
- Complete *Assignments* ❑

CONCEPTS FOR REVIEW

Before studying this chapter, you should know or, if necessary, review:

a. How to close revenue, expense, and dividend accounts. (Ch. 5, pp. 152–156)

b. The steps in the accounting cycle. (Ch. 5, pp. 156–158)

THE NAVIGATOR

FEATURE STORY

Pricing for Profitable Margins

For most of the last decade, **Wendy's** has set the rules of the 99-cent menu items. Other quick-service restaurants may have a 2-for-$2 special during the year 2002 to have the play on numbers, but not have set a 99-cent menu board. This has changed in the last several years as the market has become more and more saturated. **Burger King** began a 99-cent Great Tastes Menu in 1998, and by 2002 a flood of television spots were promoting it. Even regional chains such as **Checkers Drive-In Restaurants** are offering 99-cent menu items. In June 2002, **McDonald's** announced its 10-item dollar menu, which is instituted in about a third of their 13,000 stores in the United States.

How can a burger be sold for 99 cents and make a profit? How much does it cost to make a hamburger? Will 99-cent items be available forever? These are questions quick-service restaurants have analyzed in great detail before launching any campaign.

The fact is that every item has a cost. Quick-service restaurants buy the meat, buns, french fries, oil, cheese, pickles, tomatoes, lettuce, ketchup, and all other ingredients from somebody. These somebodies range from a local produce house to a giant food wholesaler and distributor like **SYSCO**. Quick-service restaurants are not like the staffing companies. While staffing companies provide services, the quick-service restaurants buy merchandise, and with the service provided make the merchandise into finished products, selling them to customers. Therefore, it is important for these restaurants to know what they are buying and how much they are paying for it, so they can price their finish products correctly and make a profit.

Do 99-cent items make a good profit for these quick-service restaurants? Some do, some do not. For example, it does not cost much to produce a 99-cent soft drink, combining syrup and carbon dioxide. When the cost is less, the gross profit margin is higher. It does, however, cost more to produce the 99-cent hamburger. In this case, the gross profit margin is much lower. In certain cases, it may even be at a loss. It is the hope of the quick-service restaurants that they can use these "loss leaders" to attract you to the restaurant, and then upscale you on certain items in order to average out the cost structure. Of course, it is also the hope of these restaurants that they will impress you not just with the food but also with their friendly service, bringing you back in the future.

THE NAVIGATOR

STUDY OBJECTIVES

After studying this chapter, you should be able to

1. Identify the differences between a service enterprise and a merchandiser.
2. Explain the entries for purchases under a perpetual inventory system.
3. Explain the entries for sales revenues under a perpetual inventory system.
4. Explain the steps in the accounting cycle for a merchandiser.
5. Prepare a work sheet for a merchandiser.

THE NAVIGATOR

PREVIEW OF CHAPTER 7

As indicated in the Feature Story, hospitality companies generate revenues by selling food and other items to customers rather than simply performing services. Merchandisers that purchase and sell directly to consumers—such as **Wendy's**, **Burger King**, and **McDonald's**—are called retailers. In contrast, merchandisers that sell to retailers are known as wholesalers. For example, retailer **Landry's** might buy canned goods from wholesaler **SYSCO**.

The steps in the accounting cycle for a merchandiser are the same as the steps for a service enterprise. But merchandisers use additional accounts and entries that are required in recording merchandising transactions.

The content and organization of Chapter 7 are as follows.

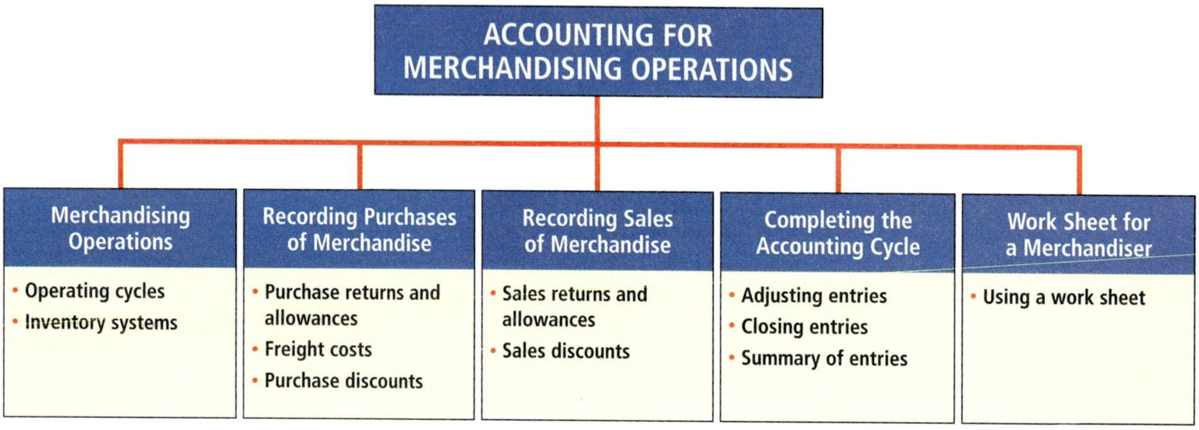

THE NAVIGATOR

MERCHANDISING OPERATIONS

STUDY OBJECTIVE 1

Identify the differences between a service enterprise and a merchandiser.

Measuring net income for a merchandiser is conceptually the same as for a service enterprise. That is, net income (or loss) results from the matching of expenses with revenues. For a merchandiser, the primary source of revenues is the sale of merchandise. This revenue source is often referred to as **sales revenue** or **sales**. Unlike expenses for a service company, expenses for a merchandiser are divided into two categories: (1) the cost of goods sold and (2) operating expenses.

The **cost of goods sold** is the total cost of merchandise sold during the period. This expense is directly related to the revenue recognized from the sale of the goods. Sales revenue less cost of goods sold is called **gross profit** on sales. For example, when a calculator costing $15 is sold for $25, the gross profit is $10. Merchandisers report gross profit on sales in the income statement.

After gross profit is calculated, operating expenses are deducted to determine net income (or net loss). **Operating expenses** are expenses incurred in the process of earning sales revenue. Examples of operating expenses are sales salaries, advertising expense, and insurance expense. The operating expenses of a merchandiser include many of the expenses found in a service company.

The income measurement process for a merchandiser is diagrammed in Illustration 7-1. The items in the three blue boxes are peculiar to a merchandiser. They are not used by a service company.

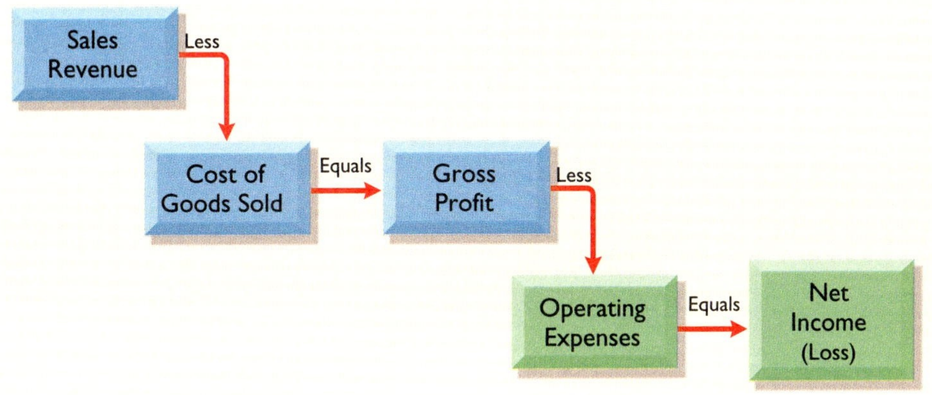

Illustration 7-1

Income measurement process for a merchandiser

In hospitality, the cost of goods sold concept is further divided into cost of food sold and cost of beverage sold. All food items, including all meat products, produce, coffee, baked goods, tea, candy and cigarettes, and soft drinks and other nonalcoholic beverages are considered food. Only alcoholic beverages, namely liquor, beer, and wine, are included as beverages. These two items have to be separated and accounted for differently because they have unique cost structure and tax implications.

Food cost percentage can be anywhere from 20 percent to more than 50 percent, depending on the type of establishment. Quick-service restaurants and cafeterias normally have lower food costs while country clubs have higher food costs. This is the case because members pay their monthly dues to the club. Thus, to encourage members to dine at the club, the menu prices are often lower than a freestanding restaurant or one that is in a hotel. Therefore, with the same quality of food served, the percentage is higher. As for beverages, each state alcoholic beverage commission needs to keep track of alcohol sales and consumption. Therefore, alcoholic beverages must be accounted for separately.

As for the accounting procedure, the calculation is the same as cost of goods sold. Sales less cost is gross profit on sales. For example, if a prime rib dinner is sold for $19.95 and the plate cost is $8.00, then food sales is $19.95, cost of food sold is $8.00, and gross profit on food is $11.95. Similarly, if a bottle of wine that costs $7.25 is sold for $25.00, then beverage sales is $25.00, cost of beverage sold is $7.25, and gross profit on beverages is $17.75.

OPERATING CYCLES

The operating cycle of a merchandiser differs from that of a service company, as shown in Illustration 7-2. The operating cycle of a merchandiser ordinarily is longer than that of a service company. The purchase of merchandise inventory and its eventual sale lengthen the cycle. Note that the added asset account for a merchandising company is an **inventory** account. It is usually titled Merchandise Inventory. Merchandise inventory is reported as a current asset on the balance sheet.

Illustration 7-2

Operating cycles for a service company and a merchandiser

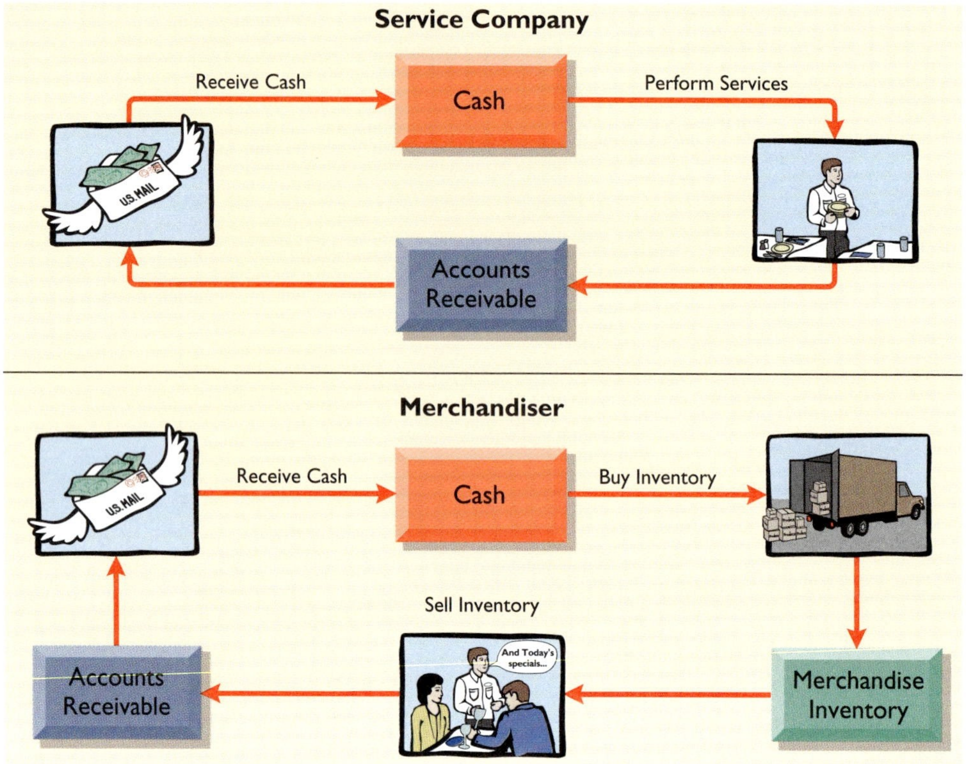

INVENTORY SYSTEMS

A merchandiser keeps track of its inventory to determine what is available for sale and what has been sold. One of two systems is used to account for inventory: a perpetual inventory system or a periodic inventory system.

Perpetual System

In a **perpetual inventory system**, detailed records of the cost of each inventory purchase and sale are maintained. This system continuously—perpetually—shows the inventory that should be on hand for every item. For example, a wine cellar has separate inventory records for each variety of Chardonnay, Merlot, Beaujolais, or Cabernet. With the use of bar codes and optical scanners, a grocery store can keep a daily running record of every box of cereal and every jar of jelly that it buys and sells. Under a perpetual inventory system, the cost of goods sold is determined *each time a sale occurs.*

HELPFUL HINT

For control purposes a physical inventory count is taken under the perpetual system, even though it is not needed to determine cost of goods sold.

TECHNOLOGY IN ACTION

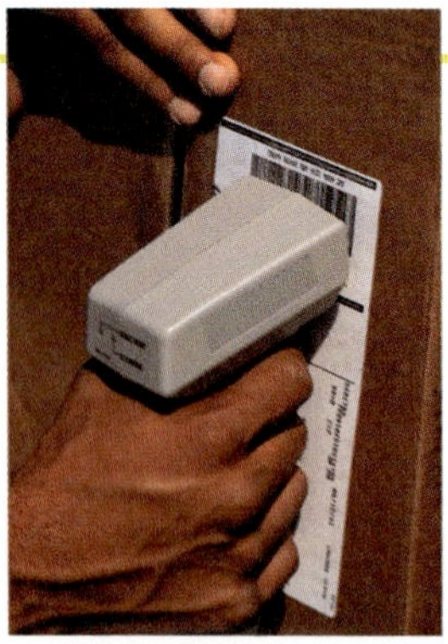

What's in a bar code? First, the bar code usually doesn't contain descriptive data (just as your Social Security number or car's license plate number doesn't have anything about your name or where you live). For example, the bar codes found on food items at grocery stores don't contain the price or description of the food item. Instead, the bar code has a 12-digit "product number" in it. When read by a bar code reader and transmitted to the computer, the computer finds the disk file item record(s) associated with that item number. In the disk file is the price, vendor name, quantity on hand, description, and so on. The computer does a "price lookup" by reading the bar code, and then it creates a register of the items and adds the price to the subtotal of the groceries sold. It also subtracts the quantity from the "on-hand" total.

SOURCE: Excerpted from *A Bar Code Primer*, © 1997 Worth Data.

Periodic System

In a **periodic inventory system**, detailed inventory records of the goods on hand are not kept throughout the period. The cost of goods sold is determined *only at the end of the accounting period*—that is, periodically. At that time, a physical inventory count is taken to determine the cost of goods on hand (Merchandise Inventory). To determine the cost of goods sold under a periodic inventory system, the following steps are necessary: (1) Determine the cost of goods on hand at the beginning of the accounting period. (2) Add to it the cost of goods purchased. (3) Subtract the cost of goods on hand at the end of the accounting period.

Illustration 7-3 graphically compares the sequence of activities and the timing of the cost of goods sold computation under the two inventory systems.

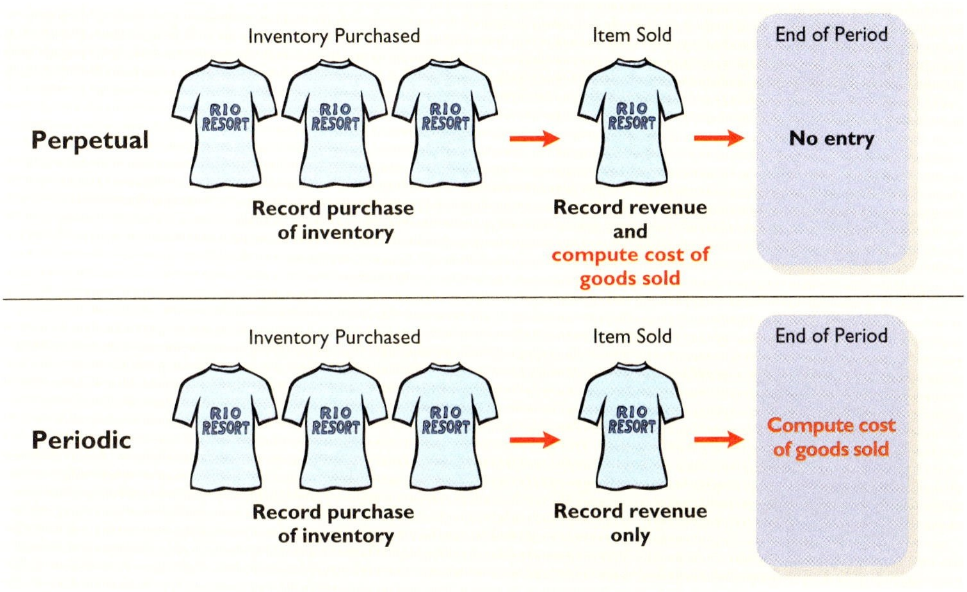

Illustration 7-3

Comparing periodic and perpetual inventory systems

Additional Considerations

Perpetual systems have traditionally been used by companies that sell merchandise with high unit values. Examples are automobiles, furniture, and major home appliances. The widespread use of computers and electronic scanners now enables many more companies to install perpetual inventory systems. The perpetual inventory system is so named because the accounting records continuously—perpetually—show the quantity and cost of the inventory that should be on hand at any time.

A perpetual inventory system provides better control over inventories than a periodic system. The inventory records show the quantities that should be on hand. So, the goods can be counted at any time to see whether the amount of goods actually on hand agrees with the inventory records. Any shortages uncovered can be investigated immediately. A perpetual inventory system does require additional clerical work and additional cost to maintain the subsidiary records. But a computerized system can minimize this cost.

RECORDING PURCHASES OF MERCHANDISE

STUDY OBJECTIVE 2

Explain the entries for purchases under a perpetual inventory system.

Purchases of inventory may be made for cash or on account (credit). Purchases are normally recorded when the goods are received from the seller. Every purchase should be supported by business documents that provide written evidence of the transaction. Each cash purchase should be supported by a canceled check or a cash register receipt indicating the items purchased and amounts paid. Cash purchases are recorded by an increase in Merchandise Inventory and a decrease in Cash.

Each credit purchase should be supported by a **purchase invoice**. This document indicates the total purchase price and other relevant information. But the purchaser does not prepare a separate purchase invoice. Instead, the copy of the sales invoice sent by the seller is used by the buyer as a purchase invoice. Illustration 7-4, for example, describes a transaction between Beyer Theme Park and Sellers T-Shirts. Beyer purchases logo T-shirts and other merchandise from Sellers to be sold in its retail outlets all throughout the theme park. The sales invoice prepared by Sellers T-Shirts (the seller) is used as a purchase invoice by Beyer (the buyer).

Illustration 7-4

Sales invoice used as purchase invoice by Beyer Theme Park

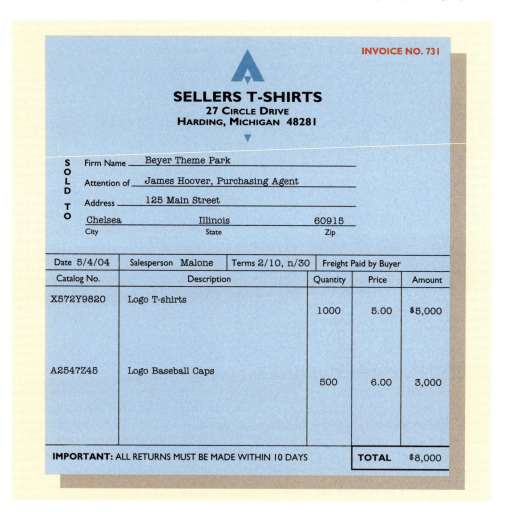

INVOICE NO. 731

SELLERS T-SHIRTS
27 CIRCLE DRIVE
HARDING, MICHIGAN 48281

SOLD TO
Firm Name: Beyer Theme Park
Attention of: James Hoover, Purchasing Agent
Address: 125 Main Street
City: Chelsea State: Illinois Zip: 60915

Date 5/4/04	Salesperson Malone	Terms 2/10, n/30	Freight Paid by Buyer	
Catalog No.	**Description**	**Quantity**	**Price**	**Amount**
X572Y9820	Logo T-shirts	1000	5.00	$5,000
A2547Z45	Logo Baseball Caps	500	6.00	3,000
IMPORTANT: ALL RETURNS MUST BE MADE WITHIN 10 DAYS			TOTAL	$8,000

HELPFUL HINT

To better understand the contents of this invoice, identify these items:

1. Seller
2. Invoice date
3. Purchaser
4. Salesperson
5. Credit terms
6. Freight terms
7. Goods sold: catalog number, description, quantity, price per unit
8. Total invoice amount

The associated entry for Beyer Theme Park for the invoice from Sellers T-Shirts looks like this:

A	=	L	+ SE
+8,000		+8,000	

May 4	Merchandise Inventory	8,000	
	Accounts Payable		8,000
	(To record goods purchased on account from Sellers T-Shirts)		

Under the perpetual inventory system, purchases of merchandise for sale are recorded in the Merchandise Inventory account. Thus, a retailer of general merchandise such as **Wal-Mart** would debit Merchandise Inventory for clothing, sporting goods, and anything else purchased for resale to customers.

Not all purchases are debited to Merchandise Inventory, however. Purchases of assets acquired for use and not for resale (such as supplies, equipment, and similar items) are recorded as increases to specific asset accounts rather than to Merchandise Inventory. Beyer would increase Supplies to record the purchase of materials used to make shelf signs or for cash register receipt paper.

PURCHASE RETURNS AND ALLOWANCES

A purchaser may be dissatisfied with the merchandise received. The goods may be damaged or defective, of inferior quality, or perhaps they do not meet the purchaser's specifications. In such cases, the purchaser may return the goods to the seller. The purchaser is granted credit if the sale was made on credit, or a cash refund if the purchase was for cash. This transaction is known as a **purchase return**. Or the purchaser may choose to keep the merchandise if the seller is willing to grant an allowance (deduction) from the purchase price. This transaction is known as a **purchase allowance**.

The purchaser initiates the request for a reduction of the balance due through the issuance of a **debit memorandum**. A debit memorandum is a document issued by a purchaser to inform a supplier that a debit has been made to the supplier's account on the purchaser's books. The original copy of the memorandum is sent to the supplier, and one copy is retained by the purchaser. The information contained in a debit memorandum is shown in Illustration 7-5; it relates to the sales invoice shown in Illustration 7-4.

Illustration 7-5

Debit memorandum

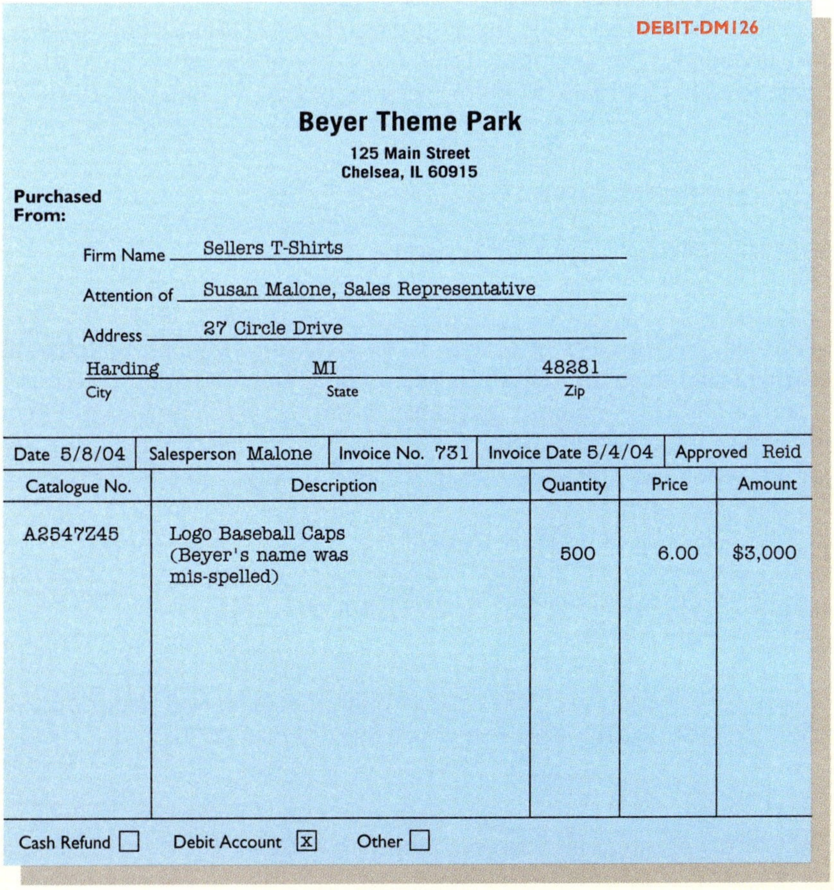
DEBIT-DM126

Beyer Theme Park
125 Main Street
Chelsea, IL 60915

Purchased From:

Firm Name Sellers T-Shirts

Attention of Susan Malone, Sales Representative

Address 27 Circle Drive

Harding (City) MI (State) 48281 (Zip)

Date 5/8/04	Salesperson Malone	Invoice No. 731	Invoice Date 5/4/04	Approved Reid

Catalogue No.	Description	Quantity	Price	Amount
A2547Z45	Logo Baseball Caps (Beyer's name was mis-spelled)	500	6.00	$3,000

Cash Refund ☐ Debit Account ☒ Other ☐

HELPFUL HINT

Note that the debit memorandum is prenumbered to help ensure that all memoranda are accounted for.

As shown in the debit memorandum, Beyer returned goods costing $3,000 to Sellers on May 8. The entry by Beyer Theme Park for the returned merchandise looks like this:

A	=	L	+	SE
−3,000		−3,000		

May 8	Accounts Payable	3,000	
	Merchandise Inventory		3,000
	(To record return of defective logo caps received from Sellers T-Shirts, DM No. 126)		

Beyer Theme Park increased Merchandise Inventory when the goods were received. So, Beyer decreases Merchandise Inventory when it returns the goods or when it is granted an allowance.

FREIGHT COSTS

The sales agreement should indicate whether the seller or the buyer is to pay the cost of transporting the goods to the buyer's place of business. When a common carrier such as a railroad, trucking company, or airline is used, the transportation company prepares a freight bill (often called a bill of lading) in accordance with the sales agreement. Freight terms are expressed as either **FOB shipping point** or **FOB destination**. The letters FOB mean *free on board*. Thus, *FOB shipping point* means that goods are placed free on board the carrier by the seller, and the buyer pays the freight costs. Conversely, *FOB destination* means that the goods are placed free on board to the buyer's place of business, and the seller pays the freight. For example, the sales invoice in Illustration 7-4 on page 204 indicates that the buyer (Beyer Theme Park) pays the freight charges.

HELPFUL HINT
Freight terms may be stated by location. A Chicago seller may use "FOB Chicago" for FOB shipping point and the buyer's city for FOB destination.

When the purchaser directly incurs the freight costs, the account Merchandise Inventory is debited. For example, if upon delivery of the goods on May 6, Beyer pays Acme Freight Company $150 for freight charges, the entry on Beyer's books looks like this:

A	=	L	+	SE
+150				
−150				

May 6	Merchandise Inventory	150	
	Cash		150
	(To record payment of freight on goods purchased)		

In contrast, **freight costs incurred by the seller on outgoing merchandise are an operating expense to the seller**. These costs increase an expense account titled Freight-out or Delivery Expense. If the freight terms on the invoice in Illustration 7-4 had required that Sellers T-Shirts pay the $150 freight charges, the entry by Sellers would look like this:

A	=	L	+	SE
−150				−150

May 4	Freight-out (or Delivery Expense)	150	
	Cash		150
	(To record payment of freight on goods sold)		

When the freight charges are paid by the seller, the seller will usually establish a higher invoice price for the goods to cover the expense of shipping.

PURCHASE DISCOUNTS

The credit terms of a purchase on account may permit the buyer to claim a cash discount for prompt payment. The buyer calls this cash discount a **purchase discount**. This incentive offers advantages to both parties: The purchaser saves money, and the seller is able to shorten the operating cycle by converting the accounts receivable into cash earlier.

The **credit terms** specify the amount of the cash discount and time period during which it is offered. They also indicate the length of time in which the purchaser is expected to pay the full invoice price. In the sales invoice in Illustration 7-4, credit terms are 2/10, n/30. This is read "two-ten, net thirty." It means that a 2 percent cash discount may be taken on the invoice price, less ("net of") any returns or allowances, if payment is made within 10 days of the invoice date (the *discount period*). If payment is not made in that time, the invoice price, less any returns or allowances, is due 30 days from the invoice date. Or, the discount period may extend to a specified number of days after the month in which the sale occurs. For example, 1/10 EOM (end of month) means that a 1 percent discount is available if the invoice is paid within the first 10 days of the next month.

HELPFUL HINT

The term *net* in "net 30" means the remaining amount due after subtracting any sales returns and allowances and partial payments.

The seller may elect not to offer a cash discount for prompt payment. In that case, credit terms will specify only the maximum time period for paying the balance due. For example, the time period may be stated as n/30, n/60, or n/10 EOM. These mean, respectively, that the net amount must be paid in 30 days, 60 days, or within the first 10 days of the next month.

Purchase Discount

"Get that check in the mail this week so we can save 2%."
Invoice
$XXX
2/10 n30

Merchandise Inventory	
	XXX

When an invoice is paid within the discount period, the amount of the discount decreases Merchandise Inventory. Inventory is recorded at its cost and, by paying within the discount period, the merchandiser has reduced its cost. To illustrate, assume Beyer Theme Park pays the balance due of $5,000 (gross invoice price of $8,000 less purchase returns and allowances of $3,000) on May 14, the last day of the discount period. The cash discount is $100 ($5,000 × 2%), and the amount of cash paid by Beyer is $4,900 ($5,000 − $100). The entry to record the May 14 payment by Beyer looks like this:

May 14	Accounts Payable	5,000	
	Cash		4,900
	Merchandise Inventory		100
	(To record payment within discount period)		

A	=	L	+ SE
−4,900		−5,000	
−100			

ACCOUNTING IN ACTION *Business Insight*

In the 1990s, **Sears** wielded its retail clout by telling its suppliers that, rather than pay its obligations in the standard 30-day period, it would now pay in 60 days. This practice is often adopted by firms that are experiencing a shortage of cash. A Sears spokesperson insisted, however, that Sears did not have cash problems. Rather, it was simply utilizing "vendor-financed inventory methods to improve its return on investment." Supplier trade groups were outspoken critics of Sears's policy. They suggested that consumers would be the ultimate victims, because the financing costs would eventually be passed on to them.

In the hospitality industry, hotels, restaurants, and larger corporations may or may not have the clout that is described in the Sears example. However, they can change the pricing structure if they negotiate properly and have good credit. For instance, produce houses will normally grant big hotel chains or a school district purchases on credit to be paid net in 30 days, with no discounts. However, if these hospitality companies are willing to pay the produce houses on a weekly basis, they may get a 2 percent purchase discount. As you will see in this chapter, taking a 2 percent discount is effectively taking a 36.5 percent return on the money.

Small "mom and pop" restaurants and start-up businesses may not have the credit history needed and are often faced with paying terms such as *cash on delivery* (COD) until they have proven themselves.

If Beyer failed to take the discount and instead made full payment on June 3, Beyer's entry would be:

A	=	L	+ SE
−5,000		−5,000	

June 3	Accounts Payable	5,000	
	Cash		5,000
	(To record payment with no discount taken)		

HELPFUL HINT
So as not to miss purchase discounts, unpaid invoices should be filed by due dates. This procedure helps the purchaser remember the discount date, prevents early payment of bills, and maximizes the time that cash can be used for other purposes.

A merchandiser usually should take all available discounts. Passing up the discount may be viewed as *paying interest* for use of the money. For example, if Beyer passed up the discount, it would be like paying an interest rate of 2 percent for the use of $5,000 for 20 days. This is the equivalent of an annual interest rate of approximately 36.5 percent (2% × 365/20). Obviously, it would be better for Beyer to borrow at prevailing bank interest rates of 8 percent to 12 percent than to lose the discount.

BEFORE YOU GO ON...

REVIEW IT

1. How does the measurement of net income in a merchandising company differ from that in a service enterprise?
2. In what ways is a perpetual inventory system different from a periodic system?
3. Under the perpetual inventory system, what entries are made to record purchases, purchase returns and allowances, purchase discounts, and freight costs?

THE NAVIGATOR

RECORDING SALES OF MERCHANDISE

STUDY OBJECTIVE 3
Explain the entries for sales revenues under a perpetual inventory system.

Sales revenues, like service revenues, are recorded when earned. This is done in accord with the revenue recognition principle. Typically, sales revenues are earned when the goods are transferred from the seller to the buyer. At this point the sales transaction is completed, and the sales price has been established.

Sales may be made on credit or for cash. Every sales transaction should be supported by a business document that provides written evidence of the sale. **Cash register tapes** provide evidence of cash sales. A **sales invoice**, like the one that was shown in Illustration 7-4 (page 204), provides support for a credit sale. The original copy of the invoice goes to the customer. A copy is kept by the seller for use in recording the sale. The invoice shows the date of sale, customer name, total sales price, and other relevant information.

Two entries are made for each sale. The first entry records the sale: Cash (or Accounts Receivable, if a credit sale) is increased by a debit, and Sales is increased by a credit at the selling (invoice) price of the goods. The second entry records the cost of the merchandise sold: Cost of Goods Sold is increased by a debit, and Merchandise Inventory is decreased by a credit for the cost of those goods. As a result, the Merchandise Inventory account will show at all times the amount of inventory that should be on hand.

To illustrate a credit sales transaction, Sellers sale of $8,000 on May 4 to Beyer (see Illustration 7-4, page 204) is recorded as follows. (Assume the merchandise cost Sellers $1,600.)

May 4	Accounts Receivable	8,000	
	Sales		8,000
	(To record credit sale to Beyer Theme Park per invoice #731)		
4	Cost of Goods Sold	1,600	
	Merchandise Inventory		1,600
	(To record cost of merchandise sold on invoice #731 to Beyer Theme Park)		

A	=	L	+	SE
+8,000				+8,000

A	=	L	+	SE
−1,600				−1,600

For internal decision-making purposes, merchandisers may use more than one sales account. For example, Sellers T-Shirts may keep separate sales accounts for its key chains, sweatshirts, and pens. By using separate sales accounts for major product lines, company management can monitor sales trends more closely and respond more strategically to changes in sales patterns. For example, if key chain sales are increasing while sweatshirt sales are decreasing, the company could reevaluate its advertising and pricing policies on each of these items.

HELPFUL HINT
The Sales account is credited only for sales of goods held for resale. Sales of assets not held for resale (such as equipment or land) are credited directly to the asset account.

However, on its income statement presented to outside investors, a merchandiser would normally provide only a single sales figure—the sum of all of its individual sales accounts. This is done for two reasons. First, providing detail on individual sales accounts would add length to the income statement. Second, companies do not want their competitors to know the details of their operating results.

SALES RETURNS AND ALLOWANCES

We now look at the "flip side" of purchase returns and allowances, which are **sales returns and allowances** recorded on the books of the seller.

To grant the customer a sales return or allowance, the seller normally prepares a **credit memorandum**. This document informs a customer that a credit has been made to the customer's account receivable for a sales return or allowance. The information contained in a credit memorandum is similar to the information found in the debit memorandum in Illustration 7-5 (page 205). The original copy of the credit memorandum is sent to the customer, and a copy is kept by the seller as evidence of the transaction.

HELPFUL HINT
If the customer is sent cash, then credit Cash rather than Accounts Receivable.

Sellers T-Shirts' entries to record credit for returned goods involve two entries: (1) The first is an increase in Sales Returns and Allowances and a decrease in Accounts Receivable at the $3,000 selling price. (2) The second is an increase in Merchandise Inventory (assume a $900 cost) and a decrease in Cost of Goods Sold. The entries are as follows.

May 8	Sales Returns and Allowances	3,000	
	Accounts Receivable		3,000
	(To record credit granted to Beyer Theme Park for returned goods)		
8	Merchandise Inventory	900	
	Cost of Goods Sold		900
	(To record cost of goods returned)		

A	=	L	+	SE
−3,000				−3,000

A	=	L	+	SE
+900				+900

HELPFUL HINT
Remember that the increases, decreases, and normal balances of contra accounts are the opposite of the accounts to which they correspond.

If goods are returned because they are damaged or defective, then the entry to Merchandise Inventory and Cost of Goods Sold should be for the estimated value of the returned goods, rather than their cost. For example, if the goods returned to Sellers were defective and had a scrap value of $50, Merchandise Inventory would be debited for $50, and Cost of Goods Sold would be credited for $50.

Sales Returns and Allowances is a **contra revenue account** to Sales. The normal balance of Sales Returns and Allowances is a debit. A contra account is used, instead of debiting Sales, to disclose in the accounts the amount of sales returns and allowances. This information is important to management. Excessive returns and allowances suggest inferior merchandise, inefficiencies in filling orders, errors in billing customers, and mistakes in delivery or shipment of goods. Also, a debit recorded directly to Sales could distort comparisons between total sales in different accounting periods.

SALES DISCOUNTS

Sales Discount

"That's right, pay within 10 days and you'll get a 2% discount."

Sales Discounts	
XXX	

As mentioned in our discussion of purchase transactions, the seller may offer the customer a cash discount for the prompt payment of the balance due. From the seller's point of view, this is called a **sales discount**. Like a purchase discount, a sales discount is based on the invoice price less returns and allowances, if any. The Sales Discounts account is debited for discounts that are taken. The entry by Sellers T-Shirts to record the cash receipt on May 15 from Beyer Theme Park within the discount period looks like this:

May 15	Cash	4,900	
	Sales Discounts	100	
	Accounts Receivable		5,000
	(To record collection within 2/10, n/30 discount period from Beyer Theme Park)		

A	=	L	+	SE
+4,900				−100
−5,000				

Like Sales Returns and Allowances, Sales Discounts is a contra revenue account to Sales. Its normal balance is a debit. This account is used, instead of debiting Sales, to disclose cash discounts taken by customers. If the discount is not taken, Sellers T-Shirts debits Cash for $5,000 and credits Accounts Receivable for the same amount at the date of collection.

BEFORE YOU GO ON...

REVIEW IT

1. Under a perpetual inventory system, what are the two entries that must be recorded at the time of each sale?
2. Why is it important to use the Sales Returns and Allowances account, rather than simply reducing the Sales account, when goods are returned?

DO IT

On September 5, De La Hoya Hotels buys merchandise on account from Junot Diaz Company. The selling price of the goods is $1,500, and the cost to Diaz Company was $800. On September 8, defective goods with a selling price of $200 and a scrap value of $80 are returned. Record the transaction on the books of both companies.

ACTION PLAN

- Purchaser: Record purchases of inventory at its cost and directly reduce the Merchandise Inventory account for returned goods.

- Seller: Record both the sale and the cost of goods sold at the time of the sale. Record returns in a contra account, Sales Returns and Allowances.

SOLUTION

De La Hoya Hotels

Sept. 5	Merchandise Inventory	1,500	
	Accounts Payable		1,500
	(To record goods purchased on account)		
8	Accounts Payable	200	
	Merchandise Inventory		200
	(To record return of defective goods)		

Junot Diaz Company

Sept. 5	Accounts Receivable	1,500	
	Sales		1,500
	(To record credit sale)		
5	Cost of Goods Sold	800	
	Merchandise Inventory		800
	(To record cost of goods sold on account)		
8	Sales Returns and Allowances	200	
	Accounts Receivable		200
	(To record credit granted for receipt of returned goods)		
8	Merchandise Inventory	80	
	Cost of Goods Sold		80
	(To record scrap value of goods returned)		

Related exercise material: 7-1, 7-2, 7-3, 7-7, and 7-8.

THE NAVIGATOR

COMPLETING THE ACCOUNTING CYCLE

Up to this point, we have illustrated the basic entries in recording transactions relating to purchases and sales in a perpetual inventory system. Now we consider the remaining steps in the accounting cycle for a merchandiser. Each of the required steps described in Chapter 5 for a service company applies to a merchandising company. Use of a work sheet by a merchandiser (an optional step) is shown in the next section.

STUDY OBJECTIVE 4

Explain the steps in the accounting cycle for a merchandiser.

ADJUSTING ENTRIES

A merchandiser generally has the same types of adjusting entries as a service company. But a merchandiser using a perpetual system will require one additional adjustment to make the records agree with the actual inventory on hand. Here's why: At the end of each period, a merchandiser using a perpetual system will take a physical count of its goods on hand for control purposes. A company's unadjusted

HELPFUL HINT

The steps required to determine the actual inventory on hand are discussed in Chapter 10.

balance in Merchandise Inventory will usually not agree with the actual amount of inventory on hand at year-end. The perpetual inventory records may be incorrect due to a variety of causes such as recording errors, theft, or waste. As a result, the perpetual records need adjustment to ensure that the recorded inventory amount agrees with the actual inventory on hand. **This involves adjusting Merchandise Inventory and Cost of Goods Sold.**

For example, suppose that the records of Sellers T-Shirts report an unadjusted balance in Merchandise Inventory of $40,500. Through a physical count, the company determines that its actual merchandise inventory on hand at year-end is $40,000. The adjusting entry would be to debit Cost of Goods Sold for $500 and to credit Merchandise Inventory for $500.

CLOSING ENTRIES

For a merchandiser, like a service enterprise, all accounts that affect the determination of net income are closed to Income Summary. In journalizing, all temporary accounts with debit balances are credited, and all temporary accounts with credit balances are debited, as shown below for Sellers T-Shirts. Cost of goods sold is a new account that must be closed to Income Summary.

HELPFUL HINT
The easiest way to prepare the first two closing entries is to identify the temporary accounts by their balances and then prepare one entry for the credits and one for the debits.

Dec. 31	Sales	480,000	
	Income Summary		480,000
	(To close income statement accounts with credit balances)		
31	Income Summary	450,000	
	Sales Returns and Allowances		12,000
	Sales Discounts		8,000
	Cost of Goods Sold		316,000
	Store Salaries Expense		45,000
	Salaries Expense		19,000
	Freight-out		7,000
	Advertising Expense		16,000
	Utilities Expense		17,000
	Depreciation Expense		8,000
	Insurance Expense		2,000
	(To close income statement accounts with debit balances)		
31	Income Summary	30,000	
	Retained Earnings		30,000
	(To close net income to retained earnings)		
31	Retained Earnings	15,000	
	Dividends		15,000
	(To close dividends to retained earnings)		

After the closing entries are posted, all temporary accounts have zero balances. In addition, Retained Earnings has a credit balance of $48,000: beginning balance + net income − dividends ($33,000 + $30,000 − $15,000).

SUMMARY OF MERCHANDISING ENTRIES

The entries for the merchandising accounts using a perpetual inventory system are summarized in Illustration 7-6.

Illustration 7-6

Daily recurring and adjusting and closing entries

	Transactions	Daily Recurring Entries	Dr.	Cr.
Sales Transactions	Sell merchandise to customers.	Cash or Accounts Receivable	XX	
		Sales		XX
		Cost of Goods Sold	XX	
		Merchandise Inventory		XX
	Grant sales returns or allowances to customers.	Sales Returns and Allowances	XX	
		Cash or Accounts Receivable		XX
		Merchandise Inventory	XX	
		Cost of Goods Sold		XX
	Pay freight costs on sales; FOB destination.	Freight-out	XX	
		Cash		XX
	Receive payment from customers within discount period.	Cash	XX	
		Sales Discounts	XX	
		Accounts Receivable		XX
Purchase Transactions	Purchase merchandise for resale.	Merchandise Inventory	XX	
		Cash or Accounts Payable		XX
	Pay freight costs on merchandise purchased; FOB shipping point.	Merchandise Inventory	XX	
		Cash		XX
	Receive purchase returns or allowances from suppliers.	Cash or Accounts Payable	XX	
		Merchandise Inventory		XX
	Pay suppliers within discount period.	Accounts Payable	XX	
		Merchandise Inventory		XX
		Cash		XX
	Events	**Adjusting and Closing Entries**		
	Adjust because book amount is higher than the inventory amount determined to be on hand.	Cost of Goods Sold	XX	
		Merchandise Inventory		XX
	Close temporary accounts with credit balances.	Sales	XX	
		Income Summary		XX
	Close temporary accounts with debit balances.	Income Summary	XX	
		Sales Returns and Allowances		XX
		Sales Discounts		XX
		Cost of Goods Sold		XX
		Freight-out		XX
		Expenses		XX

WORK SHEET FOR A MERCHANDISER

USING A WORK SHEET

STUDY OBJECTIVE 5

Prepare a work sheet for a merchandiser.

As indicated in Chapter 5, a work sheet enables financial statements to be prepared before the adjusting entries are journalized and posted. The steps in preparing a work sheet for a merchandiser are the same as they are for a service enterprise (see page 145). The work sheet for Sellers T-Shirts is shown in Illustration 7-7. The unique accounts for a merchandiser using a perpetual inventory system are shown in capital letters in red.

Illustration 7-7

Work sheet for merchandiser

SELLERS T-SHIRTS
Work Sheet
For the Year Ended December 31, 2004

	Trial Balance		Adjustments		Adjusted Trial Balance		Income Statement		Balance Sheet	
	Dr.	Cr.	Dr.	Cr.	Dr.	Cr.	Dr.	Cr.	Dr.	Cr.
Cash	9,500				9,500				9,500	
Accounts Receivable	16,100				16,100				16,100	
MERCHANDISE INVENTORY	**40,500**			(a) 500	**40,000**				**40,000**	
Prepaid Insurance	3,800			(b) 2,000	1,800				1,800	
Equipment	80,000				80,000				80,000	
Accumulated Depreciation		16,000		(c) 8,000		24,000				24,000
Accounts Payable		20,400				20,400				20,400
Common Stock		50,000				50,000				50,000
Retained Earnings		33,000				33,000				33,000
Dividends	15,000				15,000				15,000	
SALES		**480,000**				**480,000**		**480,000**		
SALES RETURNS AND ALLOWANCES	**12,000**				**12,000**		**12,000**			
SALES DISCOUNTS	**8,000**				**8,000**		**8,000**			
COST OF GOODS SOLD	**315,500**		(a) 500		**316,000**		**316,000**			
Freight-out	7,000				7,000		7,000			
Advertising Expense	16,000				16,000		16,000			
Salaries Expense	19,000				19,000		19,000			
Store Salaries Expense	40,000		(d) 5,000		45,000		45,000			
Utilities Expense	17,000				17,000		17,000			
Totals	599,400	599,400								
Insurance Expense			(b) 2,000		2,000		2,000			
Depreciation Expense			(c) 8,000		8,000		8,000			
Salaries Payable				(d) 5,000		5,000				5,000
Totals			15,500	15,500	612,400	612,400	450,000	480,000	162,400	132,400
Net Income							30,000			30,000
Totals							480,000	480,000	162,400	162,400

Key: (a) Adjustment to inventory on hand, (b) Insurance expired, (c) Depreciation expense, (d) Salaries accrued.

Trial Balance Columns

Data for the trial balance are obtained from the ledger balances of Sellers T-Shirts at December 31. The amount shown for Merchandise Inventory, $40,500, is the year-end inventory amount from the perpetual inventory system.

Adjustments Columns

A merchandiser generally has the same types of adjustments as a service company. As you see in the work sheet, adjustments (b), (c), and (d) are for insurance, depreciation, and salaries. These adjustments were also required for

Premier Staffing Agency, as illustrated in previous chapters. Adjustment (a) was required to adjust the perpetual inventory carrying amount to the actual count.

After all adjustments data are entered on the work sheet, the equality of the adjustments column totals is established. The balances in all accounts are then extended to the adjusted trial balance columns.

Adjusted Trial Balance

The adjusted trial balance shows the balance of all accounts after adjustment at the end of the accounting period.

Income Statement Columns

The accounts and balances that affect the income statement are transferred from the adjusted trial balance columns to the income statement columns. For Sellers T-Shirts, Sales of $480,000 is shown in the credit column. The contra revenue accounts Sales Returns and Allowances $12,000 and Sales Discounts $8,000 are shown in the debit column.

Finally, all the credits in the income statement column should be totaled and compared to the total of the debits in the income statement column. If the credits exceed the debits, the company has net income. In Sellers T-Shirts' case, there was net income of $30,000. If the debits exceed the credits, the company would report a net loss.

Balance Sheet Columns

The major difference between the balance sheets of a service company and a merchandiser is inventory. For Sellers T-Shirts, the ending inventory amount of $40,000 is shown in the balance sheet debit column. The information to prepare the retained earnings statement is also found in these columns. That is, the retained earnings account beginning balance is $33,000. The dividends are $15,000. Net income results when the total of the debit column exceeds the total of the credit column in the balance sheet columns. A net loss results when the total of the credits exceeds the total of the debit balances.

BEFORE YOU GO ON...

REVIEW IT

1. Why is an adjustment to the Merchandise Inventory account usually needed?
2. What merchandising account(s) will appear in the post-closing trial balance?

DO IT

The trial balance of Revere Finest Foods at December 31 shows Merchandise Inventory $25,000, Sales $162,400, Sales Returns and Allowances $4,800, Sales Discounts $3,600, Cost of Goods Sold $110,000, Rental Revenue $6,000, Freight-out $1,800, Rent Expense $8,800, and Salaries and Wages Expense $22,000. Prepare the closing entries for the above accounts.

ACTION PLAN

- Close all temporary accounts with credit balances to Income Summary by debiting these accounts.
- Close all temporary accounts with debit balances to Income Summary by crediting these accounts.

SOLUTION: The two closing entries are:

Dec. 31	Sales	162,400	
	Rental Revenue	6,000	
	Income Summary		168,400
	(To close accounts with credit balances)		
Dec. 31	Income Summary	151,000	
	Cost of Goods Sold		110,000
	Sales Returns and Allowances		4,800
	Sales Discounts		3,600
	Freight-out		1,800
	Rent Expense		8,800
	Salaries and Wages Expense		22,000
	(To close accounts with debit balances)		

Related exercise material: 7-5 and 7-9.

THE NAVIGATOR

A LOOK BACK AT OUR FEATURE STORY

Refer back to the Feature Story about **Wendy's**, **Burger King**, and **McDonald's** on their 99-cent menu items, and answer the following questions:

1. What types of inventory do quick-service restaurants carry?
2. How does the operating cycle from quick-service restaurants differ from other retailer such as a department store or a car manufacturing plant?
3. How do quick-service restaurants carry these 99-cent items and still maintain a profit?

SOLUTION

1. Quick-service restaurants mainly carry food inventory in terms of bread items, meat, frozen items, produce, cheese and dairy, condiments, coffee, and other beverages. They also carry dry goods such as all the packaging and single-service utensils, and cleaning supplies from towels to chemicals.
2. Inventory in department stores and car manufacturing plants are much less perishable than the inventory in quick-service restaurants. In a car manufacturing plant, the inventory is further divided into raw materials (the steel), work in process (parts of a car), and finished products (actual car). In a department store, summer clothing may be put on sale in early autumn to make space for the display of new winter clothing. It may take a while to make a car and sell it, and this is also the same for clothing or other items found in a department store. However, it should take just a few minutes from the time a customer orders a burger until the customer can eat it. Therefore, the operating cycle in quick-service restaurants has a much shorter time span than a department store or car manufacturing plant.
3. Many of the 99-cent items have different cost structures. Some might cost only a few cents to produce, while others might actually be sold at a price less than the cost. However, using the law of averages and aggressive and effective marketing techniques, quick-service restaurants are trying to attract customers and then sell them not only the food, but the entire dining experience, from fast and prompt service, to service with a smile, to filling correct orders. The hoped-for result is that the restaurants can gain new or repeat customers for the future who will not only purchase the 99-cent items but try other regular-priced items, as well.

THE NAVIGATOR

DEMONSTRATION PROBLEM

Gregory Scott, a former professional golf star, operates Greg's Pro Shop at Bay Golf Course. At the beginning of the current season on April 1, the ledger of Greg's Pro Shop showed Cash $2,500, Merchandise Inventory $3,500, and Common Stock $6,000. The following transactions were completed during April.

Apr. 5 Purchased golf bags, clubs, and balls on account from Hardy Co., $1,600, FOB shipping point, terms 2/10, n/60.
7 Paid freight on Hardy purchase, $80.
9 Received credit from Hardy Co. for merchandise returned, $100.
10 Sold merchandise on account to members, $1,100, terms n/30. The merchandise sold had a cost of $730.
12 Purchased golf shoes, sweaters, and other accessories on account from Titleist Sportswear, $660, terms 1/10, n/30.
14 Paid Hardy Co. in full, less discount.
17 Received credit from Titleist Sportswear for merchandise returned, $60.
20 Made sales on account to members, $700, terms n/30. The cost of the merchandise sold was $490, less discount.
21 Paid Titleist Sportswear in full.
27 Granted an allowance to members for clothing that did not fit properly, $30.
30 Received payments on account from members, $1,200.

The chart of accounts for the pro shop includes the following: No. 101 Cash, No. 112 Accounts Receivable, No. 120 Merchandise Inventory, No. 201 Accounts Payable, No. 311 Common Stock, No. 401 Sales, No. 412 Sales Returns and Allowances, No. 505 Cost of Goods Sold.

Instructions

(a) Journalize the April transactions using a perpetual inventory system.

(b) Enter the beginning balances in the ledger accounts and post the April transactions. (Use J1 for the journal reference.)

(c) Prepare a trial balance on April 30, 2004.

SOLUTION TO DEMONSTRATION PROBLEM

(a) **GENERAL JOURNAL** **J1**

Date	Account Titles and Explanation	Ref.	Debit	Credit
Apr. 5	Merchandise Inventory	120	1,600	
	Accounts Payable	201		1,600
7	Merchandise Inventory	120	80	
	Cash	101		80
9	Accounts Payable	201	100	
	Merchandise Inventory	120		100
10	Accounts Receivable	112	1,100	
	Sales	401		1,100
	Cost of Goods Sold	505	730	
	Merchandise Inventory	120		730
12	Merchandise Inventory	120	660	
	Accounts Payable	201		660
14	Accounts Payable ($1,600 − $100)	201	1,500	
	Merchandise Inventory ($1,500 × 2%)	120		30
	Cash	101		1,470
17	Accounts Payable	201	60	
	Merchandise Inventory	120		60
20	Accounts Receivable	112	700	
	Sales	401		700
	Cost of Goods Sold	505	490	
	Merchandise Inventory	120		490
21	Accounts Payable ($660 − $60)	201	600	
	Merchandise Inventory ($600 × 1%)	120		6
	Cash	101		594

J1

Date	Account Titles and Explanation	Ref.	Debit	Credit
Apr. 27	Sales Returns and Allowances	412	30	
	Accounts Receivable	112		30
30	Cash	101	1,200	
	Accounts Receivable	112		1,200

(b)

GENERAL LEDGER

Cash — **No. 101**

Date	Explanation	Ref.	Debit	Credit	Balance
Apr. 1	Balance	✓			2,500
7		J1		80	2,420
14		J1		1,470	950
21		J1		594	356
30		J1	1,200		1,556

Accounts Receivable — **No. 112**

Date	Explanation	Ref.	Debit	Credit	Balance
Apr. 10		J1	1,100		1,100
20		J1	700		1,800
27		J1		30	1,770
30		J1		1,200	570

Merchandise Inventory — **No. 120**

Date	Explanation	Ref.	Debit	Credit	Balance
Apr. 1	Balance	✓			3,500
5		J1	1,600		5,100
7		J1	80		5,180
9		J1		100	5,080
10		J1		730	4,350
12		J1	660		5,010
14		J1		30	4,980
17		J1		60	4,920
20		J1		490	4,430
21		J1		6	4,424

Accounts Payable — **No. 201**

Date	Explanation	Ref.	Debit	Credit	Balance
Apr. 5		J1		1,600	1,600
9		J1	100		1,500
12		J1		660	2,160
14		J1	1,500		660
17		J1	60		600
21		J1	600		0

Common Stock — **No. 311**

Date	Explanation	Ref.	Debit	Credit	Balance
Apr. 1	Balance	✓			6,600

Sales — **No. 401**

Date	Explanation	Ref.	Debit	Credit	Balance
Apr. 10		J1		1,100	1,100
Apr. 20		J1		700	1,800

Sales Returns and Allowances — **No. 412**

Date	Explanation	Ref.	Debit	Credit	Balance
Apr. 27		J1	30		30

Cost of Goods Sold — **No. 505**

Date	Explanation	Ref.	Debit	Credit	Balance
Apr. 10		J1	730		730
Apr. 20		J1	490		1,220

(c)

GREG'S PRO SHOP
Trial Balance
April 30, 2004

	Debit	Credit
Cash	$1,556	
Accounts Receivable	570	
Merchandise Inventory	4,424	
Common Stock		$6,000
Sales		1,800
Sales Returns and Allowances	30	
Cost of Goods Sold	1,220	
	$7,800	$7,800

THE NAVIGATOR

SUMMARY OF STUDY OBJECTIVES

1. ***Identify the differences between a service enterprise and a merchandiser.*** Because of inventory, a merchandiser has sales revenue, cost of goods sold, and gross profit. To account for inventory, a merchandiser must choose between a perpetual inventory system and a periodic inventory system.

2. ***Explain the entries for purchases under a perpetual inventory system.*** The Merchandise Inventory account is debited for all purchases of merchandise, freight-in, and other costs, and it is credited for purchase discounts and purchase returns and allowances.

3. ***Explain the entries for sales revenues under a perpetual inventory system.*** When inventory is sold, Accounts Receivable (or Cash) is debited, and Sales is credited for the *selling price* of the merchandise. At the same time, Cost of Goods Sold is debited, and Merchandise Inventory is credited for the **cost** of the inventory items sold.

4. ***Explain the steps in the accounting cycle for a merchandiser.*** Each of the required steps in the accounting cycle for a service enterprise applies to a merchandiser. A work sheet is again an optional step. Under a perpetual inventory system, the Merchandise Inventory account must be adjusted to agree with the physical count.

5. ***Prepare a work sheet for a merchandiser.*** The steps in preparing a work sheet for a merchandiser are the same as they are for a service company. The unique accounts for a merchandiser are Merchandise Inventory, Sales, Sales Returns and Allowances, Sales Discounts, and Cost of Goods Sold.

THE NAVIGATOR

GLOSSARY

Contra revenue account An account that is offset against a revenue account on the income statement (p. 210).

Cost of goods sold The total cost of merchandise sold during the period (p. 200).

Credit memorandum A document issued by a seller to inform a customer that a credit has been made to the customer's account receivable for a sales return or allowance (p. 208).

credit terms Conditions specified on a sales invoice as to when and in what amount a cash discount will be offered (p. 207).

Debit memorandum A document issued by a buyer to inform a seller that a debit has been made to the seller's account because of unsatisfactory merchandise (p. 205).

FOB destination Freight terms indicating that the goods will be placed free on board at the buyer's place of business, and the seller pays the freight costs (p. 206).

FOB shipping point Freight terms indicating that goods are placed free on board the carrier by the seller, and the buyer pays the freight costs (p. 206).

Gross profit The excess of net sales over the cost of goods sold (p. 200).

Operating expenses Expenses incurred in the process of earning sales revenues that are deducted from gross profit in the income statement (p. 200).

Periodic inventory system An inventory system in which detailed records are not maintained throughout the accounting period and the cost of goods sold is determined only at the end of an accounting period (p. 203).

Perpetual inventory system An inventory system in which the cost of each inventory item is maintained throughout the accounting period and detailed records continuously show the inventory that should be on hand (p. 202).

Purchase allowance A transaction in which the seller deducts from the purchase price to compensate the buyer for less-than-satisfactory merchandise (p. 205).

Purchase discount A cash discount claimed by a buyer for prompt payment of a balance due (p. 206).

Purchase invoice A document that supports each credit purchase (p. 204).

Purchase return A transaction in which a dissatisfied purchaser returns the goods for credit or cash (p. 205).

Sales discount A reduction given by a seller for prompt payment of a credit sale (p. 210).

Sales invoice A document that supports each credit sale (p. 208).

Sales revenue (sales) Primary source of revenue in a merchandising company (p. 208).

EXERCISES

Compute missing amounts in determining net income.
(SO 1)

7-1 Presented below are the components in Sang Nam Asian Garden's income statement. Determine the missing amounts.

	Sales	Cost of Goods Sold	Gross Profit	Operating Expenses	Net Income
(a)	$75,000	?	$31,500	?	$10,800
(b)	$108,000	$70,000	?	?	$29,500
(c)	?	$71,900	$99,600	$39,500	?

Journalize perpetual inventory entries.
(SO 2, 3)

7-2 Keo Salad Buffet buys merchandise on account from Cesar Company. The selling price of the goods is $800, and the cost of the goods is $560. Both companies use perpetual inventory systems. Journalize the transaction on the books of both companies.

Journalize sales transactions.
(SO 3)

7-3 Prepare the journal entries to record the following transactions on Rowen Oven & Range books using a perpetual inventory system.

(a) On March 2, Rowen sold $800,000 of merchandise to Mosquera Eateries, terms 2/10, n/30. The cost of the merchandise sold was $580,000.
(b) On March 6, Mosquera returned $120,000 of the merchandise purchased on March 2 because it was defective. The cost of the returned merchandise was $90,000.
(c) On March 12, Rowen received the balance due from Mosquera.

Prepare adjusting entry for merchandise inventory.
(SO 4)

7-4 At year-end the perpetual inventory records of Kren Foods showed merchandise inventory of $98,000. The company determined, however, that its actual inventory on hand was $97,100. Record the necessary adjusting entry.

Prepare closing entries for merchandise accounts.
(SO 4)

7-5 Prasad Pasta Manufacturing has the following merchandise account balances: Sales $180,000, Sales Discounts $2,000, Cost of Goods Sold $105,000, and Merchandise Inventory $40,000. Prepare the entries to record the closing of these items to Income Summary.

Identify work sheet columns for selected accounts.
(SO 5)

7-6 Presented below is the format of the work sheet presented in the chapter.

Trial Balance		Adjustments		Adjusted Trial Balance		Income Statement		Balance Sheet	
Dr.	Cr.	Dr.	Cr.	Dr.	Cr.	Dr.	Cr.	Dr.	Cr.

Indicate where the following items will appear on the work sheet: **(a)** Cash, **(b)** Merchandise Inventory, **(c)** Sales, **(d)** Cost of Goods Sold.

Example:
Cash: Trial balance debit column; Adjusted trial balance debit column; and Balance sheet debit column.

Journalize purchases transactions.
(SO 2)

7-7 Information related to Munoz Pizza is presented below.

1. On April 5, purchased merchandise from Freeman Tomato Sauce for $17,000 terms 2/10, net/30, FOB shipping point.
2. On April 6 paid freight costs of $900 on merchandise purchased from Freeman.
3. On April 7, purchased equipment on account for $26,000.
4. On April 8, returned damaged merchandise to Freeman and was granted a $3,000 allowance.
5. On April 15 paid the amount due to Freeman in full.

Instructions

(a) Prepare the journal entries to record these transactions on the books of Munoz Pizza under a perpetual inventory system.
(b) Assume that Munoz Pizza paid the balance due to Freeman Company on May 4 instead of April 15. Prepare the journal entry to record this payment.

Journalize perpetual inventory entries.
(SO 2, 3)

7-8 On September 1, Roth Seafood had an inventory of 30 golf shirts that bear the restaurant's logo at a cost of $20 each. The company uses a perpetual inventory system. During September, the following transactions occurred.

Sept.	6	Purchased 80 shirts at $19 each from Lanza Fashion for cash.
	9	Paid freight of $80 on shirts purchased from Lanza Fashion.
	10	Returned 2 shirts to Lanza for $40 credit (including freight) because they did not meet specifications.
	12	Sold 26 shirts costing $20 (including freight) for $31 each to ABC Company for their office party, terms n/30.
	14	Granted credit of $31 to ABC for the return of one shirt that was not ordered.
	20	Sold 30 shirts costing $20 for $31 each to Mallik Company, terms n/30.

Instructions
Journalize the September transactions.

7-9 Presented is information related to Croce Yogurt for the month of January 2004.

Prepare adjusting and closing entries.
(SO 4)

Ending inventory per perpetual records	$ 21,600	Salary expense	$ 61,000
Ending inventory actually on hand	21,200	Sales discounts	8,000
Cost of goods sold	208,000	Sales returns and allowances	13,000
Freight-out	7,000	Sales	350,000
Insurance expense	12,000		
Rent expense	20,000		

Instructions

(a) Prepare the necessary adjusting entry for inventory.
(b) Prepare the necessary closing entries.

7-10 Presented below are selected accounts for Garland Decorating as reported in the work sheet at the end of May 2004.

Complete work sheet.
(SO 5)

Accounts	Adjusted Trial Balance		Income Statement		Balance Sheet	
	Dr.	Cr.	Dr.	Cr.	Dr.	Cr.
Cash	9,000					
Merchandise Inventory	80,000					
Sales		450,000				
Sales Returns and Allowances	10,000					
Sales Discounts	7,000					
Cost of Goods Sold	250,000					

Instructions

Complete the work sheet by extending amounts reported in the adjusted trial balance to the appropriate columns in the work sheet. Do not total individual columns.

7-11 Mike Young, a former professional tennis star, operates Mike's Tennis Shop at the Jackson Lake Resort. At the beginning of the current season, the ledger of Mike's Tennis Shop showed Cash $2,500, Merchandise Inventory $1,700, and Common Stock $4,200. The following transactions were completed during April.

Journalize, post, and prepare a trial balance.
(SO 2, 3, 4)

Apr. 4 Purchased racquets and balls from Sampras Co., $640, FOB shipping point, terms 3/10, n/30.
6 Paid freight on purchase from Sampras Co., $40.
8 Sold merchandise to members $1,150, terms n/30. The merchandise sold had a cost of $750.
10 Received credit of $40 from Sampras Co. for a damaged racquet that was returned.
11 Purchased tennis shoes from Alan Sports for cash, $300.
13 Paid Sampras Co. in full.
14 Purchased tennis shirts and shorts from Tiger's Sportswear, $700, FOB shipping point, terms 2/10, n/60.
15 Received cash refund of $50 from Alan Sports for damaged merchandise that was returned.
17 Paid freight on Tiger's Sportswear purchase, $30.
18 Sold merchandise to members $800, terms n/30. The cost of the merchandise sold was $530.
20 Received $500 in cash from members in settlement of their accounts.
21 Paid Tiger's Sportswear in full.
27 Granted an allowance of $30 to members for tennis clothing that did not fit properly.
30 Received cash payments on account from members, $675.

The chart of accounts for the tennis shop includes the following: No. 101 Cash, No. 112 Accounts Receivable, No. 120 Merchandise Inventory, No. 201 Accounts Payable, No. 311 Common Stock, No. 401 Sales, No. 412 Sales Returns and Allowances, No. 505 Cost of Goods Sold.

Instructions

(a) Journalize the April transactions using a perpetual inventory system.

(b) Enter the beginning balances in the ledger accounts and post the April transactions. (Use J1 for the journal reference.)

(c) Prepare a trial balance on April 30, 2004.

EXPLORING THE WEB

7-12 No financial decision maker should ever rely solely on the financial information reported in the annual report to make decisions. It is important to keep abreast of financial news. This activity demonstrates how to search for financial news on the Web.

Address: **biz.yahoo.com/i**

Steps

1. Type in either Hilton Hotels or Disney.
2. Choose **News**.
3. Select an article that sounds interesting to you.

Instructions

(a) What was the source of the article? (For example, Reuters, Businesswire, PR Newswire.)

(b) Pretend that you are a personal financial planner and that one of your clients owns stock in the company. Write a brief memo to your client, summarizing the article and explaining the implications of the article for their investment.

ETHICS CASE

7-13 Rita Pelzer was just hired as the assistant treasurer of Yorkshire Store. The company is a specialty chain store with nine retail stores concentrated in one metropolitan area. Among other things, the payment of all invoices is centralized in one of the departments Rita will manage. Her primary responsibility is to maintain the company's high credit rating by paying all bills when due and to take advantage of all cash discounts.

Jamie Caterino, the former assistant treasurer who has been promoted to treasurer, is training Rita in her new duties. He instructs Rita that she is to continue the practice of preparing all checks "net of discount" and dating the checks the last day of the discount period. "But," Jamie continues, "we always hold the checks at least 4 days beyond the discount period before mailing them. That way we get another 4 days of interest on our money. Most of our creditors need our business and don't complain. And, if they scream about our missing the discount period, we blame it on the mail room or the post office. We've only lost one discount out of every hundred we take that way. I think everybody does it. By the way, welcome to our team!"

Instructions

(a) What are the ethical considerations in this case?

(b) Who are the stakeholders that are harmed or benefited in this situation?

(c) Should Rita continue the practice started by Jamie? Does she have any choice?

Remember to go back to the Navigator box on the chapter-opening page and check off your completed work.

8

FINANCIAL STATEMENTS

THE NAVIGATOR ✓

- Understand *Concepts for Review* ❑
- Read *Feature Story* ❑
- Scan *Study Objectives* ❑
- Read *Preview* ❑
- Read text and answer *Before You Go On* *p.* 239 ❑ *p.* 249 ❑ *p.* 262 ❑
- Work *Demonstration Problem* ❑
- Review *Summary of Study Objectives* ❑
- Complete *Assignments* ❑

CONCEPTS FOR REVIEW

Before studying this chapter, you should know or, if necessary, review:

a. The difference between the accrual basis and the cash basis of accounting. (Ch. 4, pp. 113–114)

b. The major items included in a corporation's balance sheet. (Ch. 5, pp. 161–166)

THE NAVIGATOR

FEATURE STORY

Cash Is King

Cash flow is important, and "Cash is king" is a phase used in almost all industries. For the most part, cash is the only difference between successful operations and closure. We all know that the income statement is important because it tells us how much money the operation has made. But, due to the accrual basis of accounting, we record sales when the transaction occurs, not when the cash is received. Thus, while an income statement may show a profit, if the sales made are still in the form of accounts receivables, there is no cash on hand to pay bills.

We also know that the balance sheet is important because it gives us, in a snapshot, the financial picture of our business. As with the income statement, it is done on an accrual basis. The balance sheet might show $200,000 in the cash account, but if there is also $400,000 in accounts payable, this is not a comfortable picture.

Therefore, you will want to use a statement of cash flows to give you an exact idea of where the money comes from, how it is spent, and, most important, how much cash you really have on hand for the business. But while the statement of cash flows is fundamental, it is also the most complex of the three statements. In November 1987, the Financial Accounting Standards Board (FASB) issued a new requirement—known as FASB 95—that all annual financial statements for fiscal years ending after July 15, 1988, must include the statement of cash flows as one of its components. This requirement has been viewed as one of the more important changes made in the accounting profession in recent years. As a result, the statement of cash flows and the topic of cash flow itself has become very important.

The cash-flow crunch experienced by the hospitality industry in recent years due to overbuilding and a weak economy has hospitality managers placing extra importance on cash flow. Cash is not only a prerequisite for a successful hospitality business, but also a continued essential element for business survival. A few years ago, print advertising spoke to the importance of profits. Today, profits are still important, but eye-catching phrases that contain the word *cash* are more prominent in stating the health of a business.

THE NAVIGATOR

Source: A. L. DeFranco & R. S. Schmidgall, "Cash Flow Practices and Procedures in the Club Industry," *Bottomline*, 11 (8) (1996/1997), 16–20.

STUDY OBJECTIVES

After studying this chapter, you should be able to

1. Distinguish between multiple-step and single-step income statements.
2. Explain the computation and importance of gross profit.
3. Distinguish between departmental and consolidated income statements.
4. Indicate the primary purpose of the statement of cash flows.
5. Distinguish among operating, investing, and financing activities.
6. Prepare a statement of cash flows using the indirect method.
7. Prepare a statement of cash flows using the direct method.

THE NAVIGATOR

PREVIEW OF CHAPTER 8

As you know by now, the three financial statements, income statement, balance sheet, and statement of cash flow, are all very important to each and every hospitality manager. Why would one want to use a multiple-step income statement when a single-step one is available? How many departmental statements are there in a hotel or a theme park? Can we just use departmental statements or the consolidated one but not both? How can a hotel company spend $400 million buying another property when it has just reported a loss of $10 million? Where does the money come from? Answers to these and similar questions can be found in this chapter, which presents the three financial statements.

The content and organization of Chapter 8 are as follows.

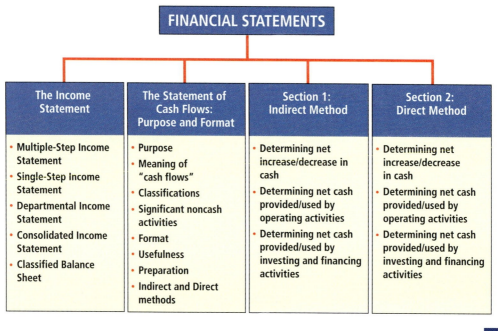

FINANCIAL STATEMENTS

The Income Statement	The Statement of Cash Flows: Purpose and Format	Section 1: Indirect Method	Section 2: Direct Method
• Multiple-Step Income Statement • Single-Step Income Statement • Departmental Income Statement • Consolidated Income Statement • Classified Balance Sheet	• Purpose • Meaning of "cash flows" • Classifications • Significant noncash activities • Format • Usefulness • Preparation • Indirect and Direct methods	• Determining net increase/decrease in cash • Determining net cash provided/used by operating activities • Determining net cash provided/used by investing and financing activities	• Determining net increase/decrease in cash • Determining net cash provided/used by operating activities • Determining net cash provided/used by investing and financing activities

THE NAVIGATOR

THE INCOME STATEMENT

STUDY OBJECTIVE 1

Distinguish between a multiple-step and a single-step income statement.

Two forms of the income statement are widely used by merchandisers. Also, merchandisers use the classified balance sheet, introduced in Chapter 5. The use of these financial statements by merchandisers is explained below.

MULTIPLE-STEP INCOME STATEMENT

The **multiple-step income statement** is so named because it shows the steps in determining net income (or net loss). It shows two main steps: (1) Cost of goods sold is subtracted from net sales, to determine gross profit. (2) Operating expenses are deducted from gross profit, to determine net income. These steps relate to the company's principal operating activities. A multiple-step statement also distinguishes between *operating* and *nonoperating activities*. This distinction provides users with more information about a company's income performance. The statement also highlights intermediate components of income and shows subgroupings of expenses.

Income Statement Presentation of Sales

The multiple-step income statement begins by presenting sales revenue. As contra revenue accounts, sales returns and allowances, and sales discounts are deducted from sales to arrive at **net sales**. The sales revenues section for Sellers T-Shirts, using assumed data, is as follows.

Illustration 8-1

Computation of net sales

SELLERS T-SHIRTS Income Statement (partial)		
Sales revenues		
Sales		$480,000
Less: Sales returns and allowances	$12,000	
Sales discounts	8,000	20,000
Net sales		**$460,000**

This presentation discloses the key aspects of the company's principal revenue-producing activities.

Gross Profit

STUDY OBJECTIVE 2

Explain the computation and importance of gross profit.

From the previous chapter, you learned that cost of goods sold is deducted from sales revenue to determine **gross profit**. Net sales revenue are used for this computation. On the basis of the sales data presented in Illustration 8-1 (net sales of $460,000) and the cost of goods sold under the perpetual inventory system (assume $316,000), the gross profit for Sellers T-Shirts is $144,000, computed as follows:

Illustration 8-2

Computation of gross profit

Net sales	$460,000
Cost of goods sold	316,000
Gross profit	**$144,000**

A company's gross profit may also be expressed as a percentage. This is done by dividing the amount of gross profit by net sales. For Sellers T-Shirts the **gross profit rate** is 31.3 percent, computed as shown in Illustration 8-3.

Illustration 8-3

Gross profit rate formula and computation

Gross Profit	÷	Net Sales	=	Gross Profit Rate
$144,000	÷	$460,000	=	31.3%

The gross profit rate is generally considered to be more useful than the gross profit amount. The rate expresses a more meaningful (qualitative) relationship between net sales and gross profit. For example, a gross profit of $1,000,000 may be impressive. But, if it is the result of a gross profit rate of only 7 percent, it is not so impressive. The gross profit rate tells how many cents of each sales dollar go to gross profit.

Gross profit represents the **merchandising profit** of a company. It is not a measure of the overall profitability, because operating expenses have not been deducted. But the amount and trend of gross profit is closely watched by management and other interested parties. They compare current gross profit with amounts reported in past periods. They also compare the company's gross profit rate with rates of competitors and with industry averages. Such comparisons provide information about the effectiveness of a company's purchasing function and the soundness of its pricing policies.

Operating Expenses and Net Income

Operating expenses are the third component in measuring net income for a merchandiser. As indicated earlier, these expenses are similar in merchandising and service enterprises. At Sellers T-Shirts, operating expenses were $114,000. The firm's net income is determined by subtracting operating expenses from gross profit. Thus, net income is $30,000, as shown in Illustration 8-4.

Illustration 8-4

Operating expenses in computing net income

Gross profit	$144,000
Operating expenses	**114,000**
Net income	$ 30,000

The net income amount is the "bottom line" of a company's income statement.

Nonoperating Activities

Nonoperating activities consist of (1) revenues and expenses from auxiliary operations and (2) gains and losses that are unrelated to the company's operations. The results of nonoperating activities are shown in two sections: **Other revenues and gains** and **Other expenses and losses**. For a merchandiser, these sections will typically include the items shown in Illustration 8-5.

Illustration 8-5

Items reported in nonoperating sections

Nonoperating Activities

Other revenues and gains	Other expenses and losses
Interest revenue from notes receivable and marketable securities	Interest expense on notes and loans payable
Dividend revenue from investments in capital stock	Casualty losses from recurring causes such as vandalism and accidents
Rent revenue from subleasing a portion of the store	Loss from the sale or abandonment of property, plant, and equipment
Gain from the sale of property, plant, and equipment	Loss from strikes by employees and suppliers

The nonoperating activities are reported in the income statement immediately after the company's primary operating activities. These sections are shown in Illustration 8-6, using assumed data for Sellers T-Shirts.

Illustration 8-6

Multiple-step income statement—nonoperating sections and subgroupings of operating expenses

SELLERS T-SHIRTS
Income Statement
For the Year Ended December 31, 2004

Calculation of gross profit	**Sales revenues**		
	Sales		$480,000
	Less: Sales returns and allowances	$12,000	
	Sales discounts	8,000	20,000
	Net sales		460,000
	Cost of goods sold		316,000
	Gross profit		144,000
Calculation of income from operations	**Operating expenses**		
	Selling expenses		
	Store salaries expense	45,000	
	Advertising expense	16,000	
	Depreciation expense—store equipment	8,000	
	Freight-out	7,000	
	Total selling expenses	76,000	
	Administrative expenses		
	Salaries expense	19,000	
	Utilities expense	17,000	
	Insurance expense	2,000	
	Total administrative expenses	38,000	
	Total operating expenses		114,000
	Income from operations		30,000
Results of nonoperating activities	**Other revenues and gains**		
	Interest revenue	3,000	
	Gain on sale of equipment	600	
		3,600	
	Other expenses and losses		
	Interest expense	1,800	
	Casualty loss from vandalism	200	
		2,000	
			1,600
	Net income		$ 31,600

When the two nonoperating sections are included, the label **Income from operations** (or Operating income) precedes them. It clearly identifies the results of the company's normal operations. Income from operations is determined by subtracting cost of goods sold and operating expenses from net sales.

In the nonoperating activities sections, items are generally reported at the net amount. Thus, if a company received a $2,500 insurance settlement on vandalism losses of $2,700, the loss is reported at $200. Note, too, that the results of the two nonoperating sections are netted. The difference is added to or subtracted from income from operations to determine net income. It is not uncommon for companies to combine these two nonoperating sections into a single "Other revenues and expenses" section.

HELPFUL HINT
Operating income relates to the sale of primary goods in the ordinary course of business.

Subgrouping of Operating Expenses

In larger companies, operating expenses are often subdivided into selling expenses and administrative expenses, as illustrated in Illustration 8-6. **Selling expenses** are those associated with making sales. They include expenses for sales promotion as well as expenses of completing the sale, such as delivery and shipping. **Administrative expenses** (sometimes called general expenses) relate to general operating activities such as personnel management, accounting, and security.

When subgroupings are made, some expenses may have to be prorated (e.g., 70% to selling and 30% to administrative expenses). For example, if a store building is used for both selling and general functions, building expenses such as depreciation, utilities, and property taxes will need to be allocated.

Any reasonable classification of expenses that serves to inform those who use the statement is satisfactory. The tendency in statements prepared for management's internal use is to present in considerable detail expense data grouped along lines of responsibility.

ETHICS NOTE

At the end of a celebratory lunch the employees of a sales department each gave the manager $10, and he paid the bill with his charge card. During the next week you notice that the manager reported the full amount of the lunch bill on his expense report (and requested reimbursement). When this question was posed to the CEO of Intel, he suggested that an appropriate action would be to report the problem anonymously to the internal audit staff for investigation. What would you do? Does it make a difference if the company is large or small?

SINGLE-STEP INCOME STATEMENT

Another income statement format is the **single-step income statement**. The statement is so named because only one step, subtracting total expenses from total revenues, is required in determining net income (or net loss).

In a single-step statement, all data are classified under two categories: (1) revenues and (2) expenses. The Revenues category includes both operating revenues and other revenues and gains. The Expenses category includes cost of goods sold, operating expenses, and other expenses and losses. A condensed single-step statement for Sellers T-Shirts is shown in Illustration 8-7.

Illustration 8-7

Single-step income statement

SELLERS T-SHIRTS
Income Statement
For the Year Ended December 31, 2004

Revenues		
Net sales		$460,000
Interest revenue		3,000
Gain on sale of equipment		600
Total revenues		463,600
Expenses		
Cost of goods sold	$316,000	
Selling expenses	76,000	
Administrative expenses	38,000	
Interest expense	1,800	
Casualty loss from vandalism	200	
Total expenses		432,000
Net income		$ 31,600

There are two primary reasons for using the single-step format: (1) A company does not realize any type of profit or income until total revenues exceed total expenses, so it makes sense to divide the statement into these two categories. (2) The format is simpler and easier to read than the multiple-step format. But for homework problems, the single-step format should be used only when it is specifically requested.

DEPARTMENTAL INCOME STATEMENT

Imagine working in a theme park with different types of rides. While little kids might want to go on the bumper cars and trains, teenagers might prefer the roller coasters, others might want to take the monorail to view the entire park. Of course, these are not the only services a theme park offers. As guests, you will also visit the souvenir stores, have a snack at one of the food stands, or sit down for dinner at one of the theme restaurants.

STUDY OBJECTIVE 3

Distinguish between departmental and consolidated income statements.

In a hotel, a similar picture of a variety of options is depicted. Although the guests all stay in the guest rooms, some might want to have their meals in the hotel restaurant or order room service, while others might have their meals away from the hotel facilities. There are also services such as those at a business center, fax, and Internet access that will be used by some but not all.

So, how can a hotel or a theme park decide which service is making the property the most money? Are all these services, or departments, needed? Are there departments that are money losers but are necessary for the operation of the entire property?

This is the reason why *departmental income statements* are needed. In Chapter 2, you learned the various departments of a hotel and how they all work together to provide a total experience for the guests. Each of these departments has its own departmental income statement. Although each department provides a different service, each departmental income statement has the same format. For revenue-generating departments such as rooms and food and beverage, you will have revenues and expenses, very similar to the multiple-step and the single-step income statements discussed earlier. The statements for departments such as engineering, accounting, and security show only expenses as they do not generate any revenues. For a theme park, the departments will be rides instead of rooms or arcade games instead of a business center. Illustration 8-8 presents an example of a department income statement.

Illustration 8-8

Departmental Income Statement

DEPARTMENTAL INCOME STATEMENT
ROOMS DEPARTMENT
For the Month Ending April 30, 2004

Revenues	
Gross sales	$650,000
Less: Allowances	10,500
Net Sales	639,500
Expenses	
Salaries and wages	95,240
Benefits	28,500
Linen	12,340
Guests supplies	4,800
Guests transportation	1,060
Long distance calls	367
Total Expenses	(142,307)
Departmental Income	$497,193

CONSOLIDATED INCOME STATEMENT

Once all departmental income statements are put together, added, and summarized, the company now has a **consolidated income statement**. Its format is similar to the single-step and multiple-step income statements, but rather being headed as Rooms Department, it is named for the business, (i.e., Belleview Hotel). A sample consolidated income statement is presented in Illustration 8-9.

Illustration 8-9

Consolidated Income Statement

CONSOLIDATED INCOME STATEMENT SAVOY RESORT For the Month Ending June 30, 2004	
Revenues	
Rooms	$ 854,300
Food and beverage	1,788,560
Telecommunications	38,992
Garage and valet	85,000
Salon and spa	50,000
Total Departmental Income	$2,816,852
Expenses	
Rooms	$ 196,489
Food and beverage	1,466,619
Telecommunications	15,597
Garage and valet	22,100
Salon and spa	16,500
Administrative and general	208,447
Human resources	126,758
Information systems	92,956
Security	30,985
Marketing	64,788
Property operations and maintenance	67,604
Utilities	112,674
Occupation costs	45,000
Interest expense	3,680
Depreciation and amortization	42,253
Total Expenses	($2,512,451)
Gross Income	304,401
Less: Income tax	(103,496)
Net Income	$ 200,905

HELPFUL HINT

Merchandise inventory is a current asset because it is expected to be sold within one year or the operating cycle, whichever is longer.

CLASSIFIED BALANCE SHEET

In the balance sheet, merchandise inventory is reported as a current asset immediately below accounts receivable. Recall from Chapter 5 that items are listed under current assets in their order of liquidity. Merchandise inventory is less liquid than accounts receivable because the goods must first be sold and then collection must be made from the customer. Illustration 8-10 presents the assets section of a classified balance sheet for Sellers T-Shirts and also that of Fame Restaurant. Sellers, as was used in our illustrations, sells merchandise to hospitality companies. In the case of a restaurant, it also sells gifts and sundries to its customers. Therefore, you may also see "gift shop and sundries," which represents the merchandise.

SELLERS T-SHIRTS Balance Sheet (partial) December 31, 2004		
Assets		
Current assets		
Cash		$ 9,500
Accounts receivable		16,100
Merchandise inventory		**40,000**
Prepaid insurance		1,800
Total current assets		67,400
Property, plant, and equipment		
Store equipment	$80,000	
Less: Accumulated depreciation—store equipment	24,000	56,000
Total assets		$123,400

Illustration 8-10

Assets section of a classified balance sheet (partial)

HELPFUL HINT
The $40,000 is the cost of the inventory on hand, not its expected selling price.

FAME RESTAURANT Balance Sheet (partial) December 31, 2004		
Current Assets		
Cash—Petty		$ 500
Cash—Bank		200,000
Accounts Receivables	$25,000	
Less: Allowance of Doubtful Accounts	1,000	
Net Accounts Receivables		24,000
Inventories—Food		40,000
Inventories—Beverage		15,800
Gift Shop and Sundries		2,590
Supplies		4,587
Prepaid Expenses		34,877
Total Current Assets		$322,354

THE STATEMENT OF CASH FLOWS: PURPOSE AND FORMAT

STUDY OBJECTIVE 4

Indicate the primary purpose of the statement of cash flows.

The three basic financial statements we've studied so far present only fragmentary information about a company's cash flows (cash receipts and cash payments). For example, **comparative balance sheets** show the increase in property, plant, and equipment during the year. But they do not show how the additions were financed or paid for. The **income statement** shows net income. But it does not indicate the amount of cash generated by operating activities Similarly, the **retained earnings statement** shows cash dividends declared but not the cash dividends paid during the year. None of these statements presents a detailed summary of the net change in cash as a result of operating, investing, and financing activities during the period.

PURPOSE OF THE STATEMENT OF CASH FLOWS

The primary purpose of the statement of cash flows is to provide information about an entity's cash receipts and cash payments during a period. A secondary objective is to provide information about its operating, investing, and financing activities.[1] The **statement of cash flows** reports the cash receipts, cash payments, and net change in cash resulting from operating, investing, and financing activities during a period. It does so in a format that reconciles the beginning and ending cash balances.

Reporting the causes of changes in cash helps investors, creditors, and other interested parties understand what is happening to a company's most liquid resource—its cash. A statement of cash flows helps us understand what is happening. It provides answers to the following simple, but important, questions about an enterprise:

1. Where did the cash come from during the period?
2. What was the cash used for during the period?
3. What was the change in the cash balance during the period?

MEANING OF CASH FLOWS

The statement of cash flows is generally prepared using **cash and cash equivalents** as its basis. *Cash equivalents* are short-term, highly liquid investments that have two characteristics:

1. They are readily convertible to known amounts of cash.
2. They are so near their maturity that their market value is relatively insensitive to changes in interest rates.

Generally, only investments with original maturities of three months or less qualify under this definition. Examples of cash equivalents are Treasury bills, commercial paper (short-term corporate notes), and money market funds. All typically are purchased with cash that is in excess of immediate needs.

Note that since cash and cash equivalents are viewed as the same, transfers between cash and cash equivalents are not treated as cash receipts and cash payments. That is, such transfers are not reported in the statement of cash flows. The term *cash* when used in this chapter includes cash and cash equivalents.

CLASSIFICATION OF CASH FLOWS

STUDY OBJECTIVE 5

Distinguish among operating, investing, and financing activities.

The statement of cash flows classifies cash receipts and cash payments as operating, investing, and financing activities, as follows:

1. **Operating activities** include the cash effects of transactions that create revenues and expenses. They thus enter into the determination of net income.
2. **Investing activities** include (a) acquiring and disposing of investments and productive long-lived assets, and (b) lending money and collecting the loans.
3. **Financing activities** include (a) obtaining cash from issuing debt and repaying the amounts borrowed, and (b) obtaining cash from stockholders and providing them with a return on their investment.

The category of operating activities is the most important because it shows the cash provided by company operations. This source of cash is generally considered to be the best measure of a company's ability to generate sufficient cash to continue as a going concern.

Illustration 8-11 below lists typical cash receipts and cash payments within each of the three classifications. *Study the list carefully.* It will prove very useful in solving homework exercises and problems.

---

[1] "Statement of Cash Flows," *Statement of Financial Accounting Standards No. 95* (Stamford, Conn.: FASB, 1987).

Illustration 8-11

Typical receipts and payments classified by business activity and shown in the statement of cash flows

Operating activities

Investing activities

Financing activities

Types of Cash Inflows and Outflows

Operating activities
- Cash inflows:
  - From sale of goods or services.
  - From returns on loans (interest received) and on equity securities (dividends received)
- Cash outflows:
  - To suppliers for inventory.
  - To employees for services.
  - To government for taxes.
  - To lenders for interest.
  - To others for expenses.

Investing activities
- Cash inflows:
  - From sale of property, plant, and equipment.
  - From sale of debt or equity securities of other entities.
  - From collection of principal on loans to other entities.
- Cash outflows:
  - To purchase property, plant, and equipment.
  - To purchase debt or equity securities of other entities.
  - To make loans to other entities.

Financing activities
- Cash inflows:
  - From sale of equity securities (company's own stock).
  - From issuance of debt (bonds and notes).
- Cash outflows:
  - To stockholders as dividends.
  - To redeem long-term debt or reacquire capital stock.

HELPFUL HINT

Operating activities generally relate to changes in current assets and current liabilities. Investing activities generally relate to changes in noncurrent assets. Financing activities relate to changes in long-term liabilities and stockholders' equity accounts.

As you can see, some cash flows related to investing or financing activities are classified as operating activities. For example, receipts of investment revenue (interest and dividends) are classified as operating activities. So are payments of interest to lenders. Why are these considered operating activities? **Because these items are reported in the income statement, where results of operations are shown.**

Note the following general guidelines: (1) Operating activities involve income determination (income statement) items. (2) Investing activities involve cash flows resulting from changes in investments and long-term asset items. (3) Financing activities involve cash flows resulting from changes in long-term liability and stockholders' equity items.

SIGNIFICANT NONCASH ACTIVITIES

Not all of a company's significant activities involve cash. Examples of significant noncash activities include the following:

- Issuance of common stock to purchase assets
- Conversion of bonds into common stock
- Issuance of debt to purchase assets
- Exchanges of plant assets

Significant financing and investing activities that do not affect cash are not reported in the body of the statement of cash flows. However, these activities are reported in either a *separate schedule* at the bottom of the statement of cash flows or in a *separate note or supplementary schedule* to the financial statements.

HELPFUL HINT

Do not include noncash investing and financing activities in the body of the statement of cash flows. Report this information in a separate schedule.

The reporting of these noncash activities in a separate schedule satisfies the **full disclosure principle**. In solving homework assignments you should present significant noncash investing and financing activities in a separate schedule at the bottom of the statement of cash flows. (See lower section of Illustration 8-12 for an example.)

ACCOUNTING IN ACTION *Business Insight*

Net income is not the same as net cash provided by operating activities. The differences are illustrated by the following results from recent annual reports for the same fiscal year (all data are in millions of dollars).

Company	Net Income (Loss)	Net Cash from Operations
Morton's Restaurant Group Inc. Fiscal year 2001	$ 989,000	$ 4,160,000
Darden Restaurants, Inc. Fiscal year 2002	$237,788,000	$508,142,000
Brinker International Inc. Fiscal year 2002	$152,713,000	$390,033,000
Starwood Hotels & Resorts Worldwide, Inc. Fiscal year 2001	$145,000,000	$761,000,000
Hilton Hotels Corp. Fiscal year 2001	$166,000,000	$585,000,000
Marriott International Inc. Fiscal year 2001	$236,000,000	$400,000,000
Choice Hotels International Inc. Fiscal year 2001	$ 14,327,000	$101,712,000

SOURCE: FISonline database.

Note the disparity among the companies that engaged in both the foodservice and hotel industries.

FORMAT OF THE STATEMENT OF CASH FLOWS

The general format of the statement of cash flows is the three activities discussed previously—operating, investing, and financing—plus the significant noncash investing and financing activities. A widely used form of the statement of cash flows is shown in Illustration 8-12.

Illustration 8-12

Format of statement of cash flows

COMPANY NAME
Statement of Cash Flows
Period Covered

Cash flows from operating activities		
(List of individual items)	XX	
Net cash provided (used) by operating activities		XXX
Cash flows from investing activities		
(List of individual inflows and outflows)	XX	
Net cash provided (used) by investing activities		XXX
Cash flows from financing activities		
(List of individual inflows and outflows)	XX	
Net cash provided (used) by financing activities		XXX
Net increase (decrease) in cash		XXX
Cash at beginning of period		XXX
Cash at end of period		XXX
Noncash investing and financing activities		
(List of individual noncash transactions)		XXX

As illustrated, the cash flows from operating activities section always appears first. It is followed by the investing activities and the financing activities sections.

Note also that **the individual inflows and outflows from investing and financing activities are reported separately**. Thus, cash outflow for the purchase of property, plant, and equipment is reported separately from the cash inflow from the sale of property, plant, and equipment. Similarly, the cash inflow from the issuance of debt securities is reported separately from the cash outflow for the retirement of debt. If a company did not report the inflows and outflows separately, it would obscure the investing and financing activities of the enterprise. This would make it more difficult to assess future cash flows.

The reported operating, investing, and financing activities result in either net cash *provided or used* by each activity. The amounts of net cash provided or used by each activity then are totaled. The result is the net increase (decrease) in cash for the period. This amount is then added to or subtracted from the beginning-of-period cash balance. This gives the end-of-period cash balance. Finally, any significant noncash investing and financing activities are reported in a separate schedule, usually at the bottom of the statement.

USEFULNESS OF THE STATEMENT OF CASH FLOWS

The information in a statement of cash flows should help investors, creditors, and others assess the following aspects of the firm's financial position.

1. **The entity's ability to generate future cash flows.** By examining relationships between items in the statement of cash flows, investors and others can make predictions of the amounts, timing, and uncertainty of future cash flows better than they can from accrual basis data.
2. **The entity's ability to pay dividends and meet obligations.** If a company does not have adequate cash, employees cannot be paid, debts settled, or dividends paid. Employees, creditors, and stockholders should be particularly interested in this statement, because it alone shows the flows of cash in a business.
3. **The reasons for the difference between net income and net cash provided (used) by operating activities.** Net income provides information on the success or failure of a business enterprise. However, some are critical of accrual basis net income because it requires many estimates. As a result, the reliability of the number is often challenged. Such is not the case with cash. Many readers of the statement of cash flows want to know the reasons for the difference between net income and net cash provided by operating activities. Then they can assess for themselves the reliability of the income number.
4. **The cash investing and financing transactions during the period.** By examining a company's investing and financing transactions, a financial statement reader can better understand why assets and liabilities changed during the period.

   In summary, the information in the statement of cash flows is useful in answering the following questions:

- How did cash increase when there was a net loss for the period?
- How were the proceeds of the bond issue used?
- How was the expansion in the plant and equipment financed?
- Why were dividends not increased?
- How was the retirement of debt accomplished?
- How much money was borrowed during the year?
- Is cash flow greater or less than net income?

ETHICS NOTE

Many investors believe that "Cash is cash and everything else is accounting." That is, they feel that cash flow is less susceptible to management manipulation than traditional accounting measures such as net income. Though we would discourage reliance on cash flows to the exclusion of accrual accounting, comparing cash from operations to net income can reveal important information about the "quality" of reported net income. Such a comparison can reveal the extent to which net income provides a good measure of actual performance.

HELPFUL HINT

Income from operations and cash flow from operating activities are different. Income from operations is based on accrual accounting: cash flow from operating activities is prepared on a cash basis.

PREPARING THE STATEMENT OF CASH FLOWS

The statement of cash flows is prepared differently from the three other basic financial statements. First, it is not prepared from an adjusted trial balance. The statement requires detailed information concerning the changes in account balances that occurred between two periods of time. An adjusted trial balance will not provide the necessary data. Second, the statement of cash flows deals with cash receipts and payments. As a result, **the accrual concept is not used in the preparation of a statement of cash flows**.

The information to prepare this statement usually comes from three sources:

1. **Comparative balance sheets.** Information in the comparative balance sheets indicates the amount of the changes in assets, liabilities, and stockholders' equities from the beginning to the end of the period.
2. **Current income statement.** Information in this statement helps determine the amount of cash provided or used by operations during the period.
3. **Additional information.** Such information includes transaction data that are needed to determine how cash was provided or used during the period.

Preparing the statement of cash flows from these data sources involves three major steps, explained in Illustration 8-13.

Illustration 8-13

Three major steps in preparing the statement of cash flows

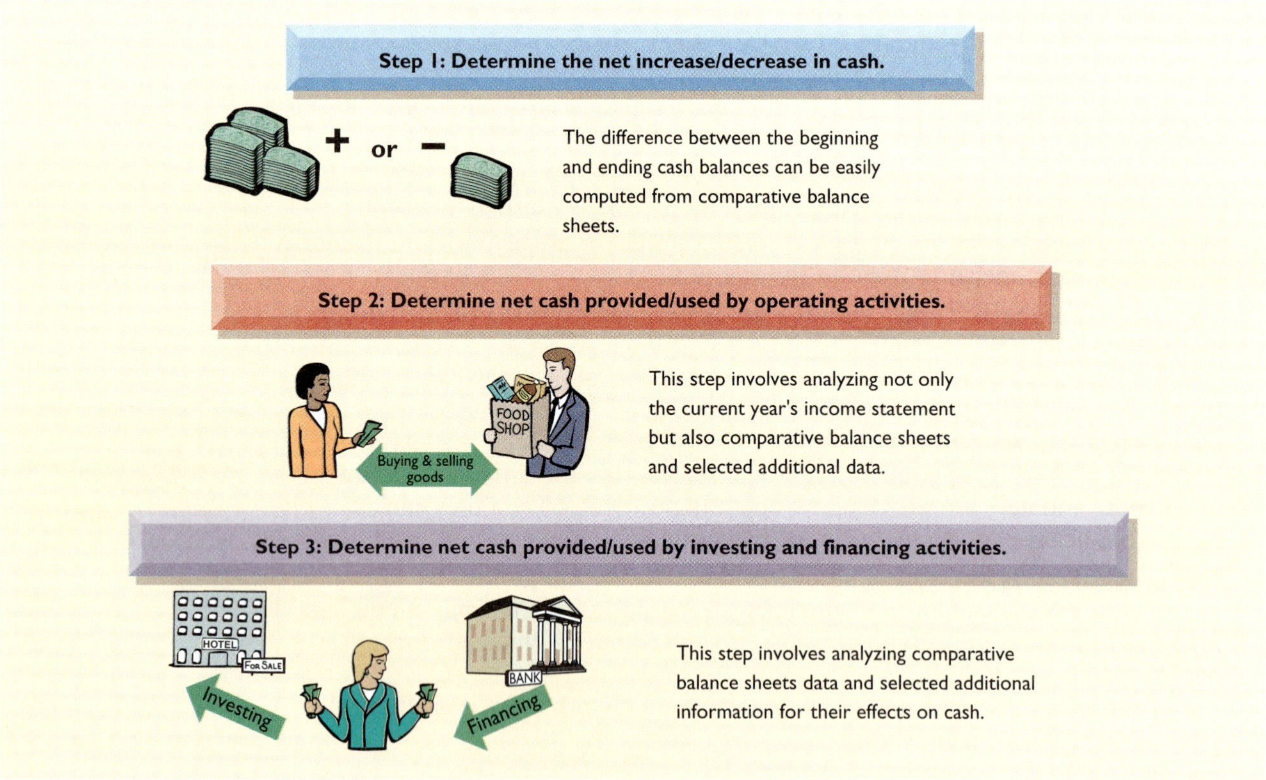

Step 1: Determine the net increase/decrease in cash.
+ or −
The difference between the beginning and ending cash balances can be easily computed from comparative balance sheets.
Step 2: Determine net cash provided/used by operating activities.
FOOD SHOP
Buying & selling goods
This step involves analyzing not only the current year's income statement but also comparative balance sheets and selected additional data.
Step 3: Determine net cash provided/used by investing and financing activities.
HOTEL
FOR SALE
BANK
Investing
Financing
This step involves analyzing comparative balance sheets data and selected additional information for their effects on cash.

INDIRECT AND DIRECT METHODS

In order to perform step 2, the operating activities section must be converted from an accrual basis to a cash basis. This conversion may be done by either of two methods: (1) the indirect method or (2) the direct method. Both methods arrive at the same total amount for "Net cash provided by operating activities." They differ in disclosing the items that comprise the total amount.

The indirect method is used extensively in practice. Companies (98.8%) favor the indirect method for two reasons: (1) It is easier to prepare, and (2) it focuses on the differences between net income and net cash flow from operating activities.

A minority of companies favor the direct method. This method shows operating cash receipts and payments, and so it is more consistent with the objective of a statement of cash flows. The FASB has expressed a preference for the direct method, but allows the use of either method. When the direct method is used, the net cash flow from operating activities as computed using the indirect method must also be reported in a separate schedule.

BEFORE YOU GO ON...

REVIEW IT

1. What is the primary purpose of a statement of cash flows?
2. What are the major classifications of cash flows on the statement of cash flows?
3. Why is the statement of cash flows useful? What key information does it convey?
4. What are the three major steps in preparing a statement of cash flows?

DO IT

During its first week of existence, Plano Submarine Sandwiches had the following transactions.

1. Issued 100,000 shares of $5 par value common stock for $800,000 cash.
2. Borrowed $200,000 from State Bank, signing a 5-year note bearing 8 percent interest.
3. Purchased two delivery trucks for $170,000 cash.
4. Paid employees $12,000 for salaries and wages.
5. Collected $20,000 cash for services provided.

Classify each of these transactions by type of cash flow activity.

ACTION PLAN

- Identify the three types of activities used to report all cash inflows and outflows.
- Report as operating activities the cash effects of transactions that create revenues and expenses and enter into the determination of net income.
- Report as investing activities transactions that (a) acquire and dispose of investments and productive long-lived assets, and (b) lend money and collect loans.
- Report as financing activities transactions that (a) obtain cash from issuing debt and repay the amounts borrowed, and (b) obtain cash from stockholders and pay them dividends.

SOLUTION

1. Financing activity
2. Financing activity
3. Investing activity
4. Operating activity
5. Operating activity

Related exercise material: 8-3, 8-8, and 8-10.

THE NAVIGATOR

INTERNATIONAL NOTE

International accounting requirements are quite similar in most respects with regard to the cash flow statement. Some interesting exceptions: In Japan, operating and investing activities are combined. In Australia, the direct method is mandatory. In Spain, the indirect method is mandatory. Also, in a number of European and Scandinavian countries a cash flow statement is not required at all, although in practice most publicly traded firms provide one.

On the following pages, in two separate sections, we describe the two cash flow methods. Section 1 illustrates the indirect method. Section 2 illustrates the direct method. These sections are independent of each other. *Only one or the other needs to be covered in order to understand and prepare the statement of cash flows.*

SECTION 1: INDIRECT METHOD FOR STATEMENT OF CASH FLOWS

STUDY OBJECTIVE 6

Prepare a statement of cash flows using the indirect method.

To explain and illustrate the indirect method, we will use the transactions of the Airport Shuttle Services Company for two years, 2004 and 2005, to prepare annual statements of cash flows. We will show basic transactions in the first year, with additional transactions added in the second year.

FIRST YEAR OF OPERATIONS—2004

Airport Shuttle Services Company started on January 1, 2004. At that time it issued 50,000 shares of $1.00 par value common stock for $50,000 cash. The company rented its office space and furniture and performed consulting services throughout the first year. The comparative balance sheets at the beginning and end of 2004, showing changes in each account, appear in Illustration 8-14. The income statement and additional information for Airport Shuttle Services Company are shown in Illustration 8-15.

Illustration 8-14

Comparative balance sheets, 2004, with increases and decreases

AIRPORT SHUTTLE SERVICES COMPANY
Comparative Balance Sheets

Assets	**Dec. 31, 2004**	**Jan. 1, 2004**	**Change Increase/Decrease**
Cash	$34,000	$–0–	$34,000 Increase
Accounts receivable	30,000	–0–	30,000 Increase
Equipment	10,000	–0–	10,000 Increase
Total	$74,000	$–0–	
Liabilities and Stockholders' Equity			
Accounts payable	$ 4,000	$–0–	$ 4,000 Increase
Common stock	50,000	–0–	50,000 Increase
Retained earnings	20,000	–0–	20,000 Increase
Total	$74,000	$–0–	

HELPFUL HINT
Although each of the balance sheet items increased, their individual effects are not the same. Some of these increases are cash inflows, and some are cash outflows.

Illustration 8-15

Income statement and additional information, 2004

AIRPORT SHUTTLE SERVICES COMPANY
Income Statement
For the Year Ended December 31, 2004

Revenues	$85,000
Operating expenses	40,000
Income before income taxes	45,000
Income tax expense	10,000
Net income	$35,000

Additional information:
1. A dividend of $15,000 was declared and paid during the year.
2. The equipment was purchased at the end of 2004. No depreciation was taken in 2004.

Step 1: Determine the Net Increase/Decrease in Cash

To prepare a statement of cash flows, the first step is to **determine the net increase or decrease in cash**. This is a simple computation. For example, Airport Shuttle Services Company had no cash on hand at the beginning of 2004. It had $34,000 on hand at the end of 2004. Thus, the change in cash for 2004 was an increase of $34,000.

HELPFUL HINT

You may wish to insert immediately into the statement of cash flows the beginning and ending cash balances and the increase/decrease in cash necessitated by these balances. The net increase/decrease is the target amount. The net cash flows from the three classes of activity must equal the target amount.

Step 2: Determine Net Cash Provided/Used by Operating Activities

To determine net cash provided by operating activities under the indirect method, **net income is adjusted for items that did not affect cash**. A useful starting point is to understand *why* net income must be converted. Under generally accepted accounting principles, most companies use the accrual basis of accounting. As you have learned, this basis requires that revenue be recorded when earned and that expenses be recorded when incurred. Earned revenues may include credit sales that have not been collected in cash. Expenses incurred may not have been paid in cash. Thus, under the accrual basis of accounting, net income is not the same as net cash provided by operating activities. Therefore, under the indirect method, net income must be adjusted to convert certain items to the cash basis.

The **indirect method** (or reconciliation method) starts with net income and converts it to net cash provided by operating activities. In other words, **the indirect method adjusts net income for items that affected reported net income but did not affect cash**. Illustration 8-16 shows this adjustment. That is, noncash charges in the income statement are added back to net income. Likewise, noncash credits are deducted. The result is net cash provided by operating activities.

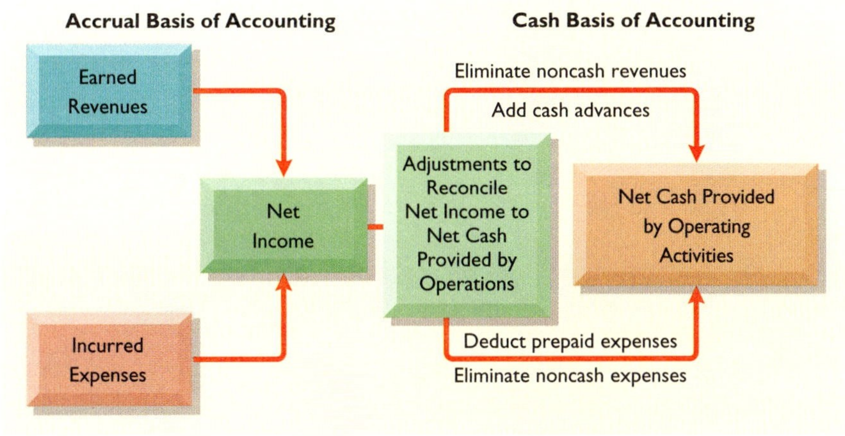

Illustration 8-16

Net income versus net cash provided by operating activities

A useful starting point in identifying the adjustments to net income is the current asset and current liability accounts other than cash. Those accounts—receivables, payables, prepayments, and inventories—should be analyzed for their effects on cash.

INCREASE IN ACCOUNTS RECEIVABLE. When accounts receivable increase during the year, revenues on an accrual basis are higher than revenues on a cash basis. In other words, operations of the period led to revenues, *but not all of these revenues resulted in an increase in cash*. Some of the revenues resulted in an increase in accounts receivable.

Illustration 8-17 shows that Airport Shuttle Services Company had $85,000 in revenues, but it collected only $55,000 in cash. To convert net income to net cash provided by operating activities, the increase of $30,000 in accounts receivable must be deducted from net income.

Illustration 8-17

Analysis of accounts receivable

Accounts Receivable				
1/1/04	Balance	–0–	Receipts from customers	55,000
	Revenues	**85,000**		
12/31/04	Balance	30,000		

INCREASE IN ACCOUNTS PAYABLE. In the first year, operating expenses incurred on account were credited to Accounts Payable. When accounts payable increase during the year, operating expenses on an accrual basis are higher than they are on a cash basis. For Airport Shuttle Services, operating expenses reported in the income statement were $40,000. But, since Accounts Payable increased $4,000, only $36,000 ($40,000 − $4,000) of the expenses were paid in cash. To adjust net income to net cash provided by operating activities, the increase of $4,000 in accounts payable must be added to net income. A T-account analysis indicates that payments to creditors are less than operating expenses.

Illustration 8-18

Analysis of accounts payable

Accounts Payable				
Payments to creditors	**36,000**	1/1/04	Balance	–0–
			Operating expenses	**40,000**
		12/31/04	Balance	4,000

For Airport Shuttle Services, the changes in accounts receivable and accounts payable were the only changes in current asset and current liability accounts. This means that any other revenues or expenses reported in the income statement were received or paid in cash. Thus, the income tax expense of $10,000 was paid in cash, and no adjustment of net income is necessary.

The operating activities section of the statement of cash flows for Airport Shuttle Services Company is shown in Illustration 8-19.

Illustration 8-19

Presentation of net cash provided by operating activities, 2004—indirect method

AIRPORT SHUTTLE SERVICES COMPANY
Statement of Cash Flows—Indirect Method (partial)
For the Year Ended December 31, 2004

Cash flows from operating activities		
Net income		$35,000
Adjustments to reconcile net income to net cash provided by operating activities:		
Increase in accounts receivable	$(30,000)	
Increase in accounts payable	4,000	(26,000)
Net cash provided by operating activities		**$ 9,000**

Step 3: Determine Net Cash Provided/Used by Investing and Financing Activities

The third and final step in preparing the statement of cash flows begins with a study of the balance sheet. We look at it to determine changes in noncurrent accounts. The change in each noncurrent account is then analyzed to determine the effect, if any, the change had on cash.

In Airport Shuttle Services Company, the three noncurrent accounts are Equipment, Common Stock, and Retained Earnings. All three have increased during the year. What caused these increases? No transaction data are given in the balance sheet for the increases in Equipment of $10,000 and Common Stock of $50,000. In solving your homework, you should assume that any unexplained differences in noncurrent accounts involve *cash*. Thus, the increase in Equipment is assumed to be a purchase of equipment for $10,000 cash. This purchase of equipment is reported as a cash outflow in the investing activities section of the statement of cash flows. The increase in Common Stock is assumed to result from the issuance of common stock for $50,000 cash. The issuance of common stock is reported as an inflow of cash in the financing activities section.

What caused the net increase of $20,000 in the Retained Earnings account? First, net income increased retained earnings by $35,000. Second, the additional information provided below the income statement in Illustration 8-15 indicates that a cash dividend of $15,000 was declared and paid.

This analysis can also be made directly from the Retained Earnings account in the ledger of Airport Shuttle Services Company, as shown in Illustration 8-20.

Illustration 8-20

Analysis of retained earnings

Retained Earnings

12/31/04	**Cash dividend**	**15,000**	1/1/04	Balance	–0–
			12/31/04	**Net income**	**35,000**
			12/31/04	Balance	20,000

The $20,000 increase in Retained Earnings in 2004 is a *net* change. When a net change in a noncurrent balance sheet account has occurred during the year, it generally is necessary to report the individual items that cause the net change. Therefore, the $35,000 increase due to net income is reported in the operating activities section. The cash dividend paid is reported in the financing activities section.

Statement of Cash Flows—2004

We now can prepare the statement of cash flows. The statement starts with the operating activities, followed by the investing activities, and then the financing activities. The 2004 statement of cash flows for Airport Shuttle Services is shown in Illustration 8-21.

Airport Shuttle Services' statement of cash flows for 2004 shows the following: Operating activities *provided* $9,000 cash. Investing activities *used* $10,000 cash. Financing activities *provided* $35,000 cash. The increase in cash of $34,000 reported in the statement of cash flows agrees with the increase of $34,000 shown as the change in the cash account in the comparative balance sheets.

Illustration 8-21

Statement of cash flows, 2004—indirect method

AIRPORT SHUTTLE SERVICES COMPANY
Statement of Cash Flows—Indirect Method
For the Year Ended December 31, 2004

Cash flows from operating activities		
Net income		$35,000
Adjustments to reconcile net income to net cash provided by operating activities:		
Increase in accounts receivable	$(30,000)	
Increase in accounts payable	4,000	(26,000)
Net cash provided by operating activities		9,000
Cash flows from investing activities		
Purchase of equipment	(10,000)	
Net cash used by investing activities		(10,000)
Cash flows from financing activities		
Issuance of common stock	50,000	
Payment of cash dividends	(15,000)	
Net cash provided by financing activities		35,000
Net increase in cash		34,000
Cash at beginning of period		-0-
Cash at end of period		$34,000

SECOND YEAR OF OPERATIONS—2005

Illustrations 8-22 and 8-23 present information related to the second year of operations for Airport Shuttle Services Company.

Illustration 8-22

Comparative balance sheets, 2005, with increases and decreases

AIRPORT SHUTTLE SERVICES COMPANY
Comparative Balance Sheets
December 31

Assets	2005	2004	Change Increase/Decrease
Cash	$ 56,000	$34,000	$ 22,000 Increase
Accounts receivable	20,000	30,000	10,000 Decrease
Prepaid expenses	4,000	-0-	4,000 Increase
Land	130,000	-0-	130,000 Increase
Building	160,000	-0-	160,000 Increase
Accumulated depreciation—building	(11,000)	-0-	11,000 Increase
Equipment	27,000	10,000	17,000 Increase
Accumulated depreciation—equipment	(3,000)	-0-	3,000 Increase
Total	$383,000	$74,000	
Liabilities and Stockholders' Equity			
Accounts payable	$ 59,000	$ 4,000	$ 55,000 Increase
Bonds payable	130,000	-0-	130,000 Increase
Common stock	50,000	50,000	-0-
Retained earnings	144,000	20,000	124,000 Increase
Total	$383,000	$74,000	

Illustration 8-23

Income statement and additional information, 2003

AIRPORT SHUTTLE SERVICES COMPANY
Income Statement
For the Year Ended December 31, 2005

Revenues		$507,000
Operating expenses (excluding depreciation)	$261,000	
Depreciation expense	15,000	
Loss on sale of equipment	3,000	279,000
Income from operations		228,000
Income tax expense		89,000
Net income		$139,000

Additional information:

1. In 2005, the company declared and paid a $15,000 cash dividend.
2. The company obtained land through the issuance of $130,000 of long-term bonds.
3. A building costing $160,000 was purchased for cash. Equipment costing $25,000 was also purchased for cash.
4. During 2005, the company sold equipment with a book value of $7,000 (cost $8,000, less accumulated depreciation $1,000) for $4,000 cash.

Step 1: Determine the Net Increase/Decrease in Cash

To prepare a statement of cash flows from this information, the first step is to determine the net increase or decrease in cash. As indicated from the information presented, cash increased $22,000 ($56,000 − $34,000).

Step 2: Determine Net Cash Provided/Used by Operating Activities

As in step 2 in 2004, net income on an accrual basis must be adjusted to arrive at net cash provided/used by operating activities. Explanations for the adjustments to net income for Airport Shuttle Services in 2005 follow.

HELPFUL HINT

Decrease in accounts receivable indicates that cash collections were greater than sales.
Increase in accounts receivable indicates that sales were greater than cash collections.
Increase in prepaid expenses indicates that the amount paid for the prepayments exceeded the amount that was recorded as an expense.
Decrease in prepaid expenses indicates that the amount recorded as an expense exceeded the amount of cash paid for the prepayments.
Increase in accounts payable indicates that expenses incurred exceed the cash paid for expenses that period.

DECREASE IN ACCOUNTS RECEIVABLE. Accounts receivable decreases during the period because cash receipts are higher than revenues reported on the accrual basis. To adjust net income to net cash provided by operating activities, the decrease of $10,000 in accounts receivable must be added to net income.

INCREASE IN PREPAID EXPENSES. Prepaid expenses increase during a period because cash paid for expenses is higher than expenses reported on the accrual basis. Cash payments have been made in the current period, but expenses (as charges to the income statement) have been deferred to future periods. To adjust net income to net cash provided by operating activities, the $4,000 increase in prepaid expenses must be deducted from net income. An increase in prepaid expenses results in a decrease in cash during the period.

INCREASE IN ACCOUNTS PAYABLE. Like the increase in 2004, the 2005 increase of $55,000 in accounts payable must be added to net income to convert to net cash provided by operating activities.

DEPRECIATION EXPENSE. During 2005, the company reported depreciation expense of $15,000. Of this amount, $11,000 related to the building and $4,000 to the equipment. These two amounts were determined by analyzing the accumulated depreciation accounts in the balance sheets.

- **Increase in Accumulated Depreciation—Building.** The Accumulated Depreciation—Building account increased $11,000. This change represents the depreciation expense on the building for the year. **Depreciation expense is a noncash charge. So it is added back to net income** in order to arrive at net cash provided by operating activities.
- **Increase in Accumulated Depreciation—Equipment.** The Accumulated Depreciation—Equipment account increased $3,000. But this change does not represent depreciation expense for the year. The additional information at the bottom of the income statement indicates why not: This account was decreased (debited $1,000) as a result of the sale of some equipment. Thus depreciation expense for 2005 was $4,000 ($3,000 + $1,000). That amount is added to net income to determine net cash provided by operating activities. The T-account in Illustration 8-24 provides information about the changes that occurred in this account in 2005.

Illustration 8-24

Analysis of accumulated depreciation—equipment

Accumulated Depreciation—Equipment

Accumulated depreciation on equipment sold	1,000	1/1/05	Balance	–0–
			Depreciation expense	**4,000**
		12/31/05	Balance	3,000

Depreciation expense on the building ($11,000) plus depreciation expense on the equipment ($4,000) equals the depreciation expense of $15,000 reported in the income statement.

Other charges to expense that do not require the use of cash, such as the amortization of intangible assets and depletion expense, are treated in the same way as depreciation. Depreciation and similar noncash charges are frequently listed in the statement of cash flows as the first adjustments to net income.

LOSS ON SALE OF EQUIPMENT. In the income statement, Airport Shuttle Services Company reported a $3,000 loss on the sale of equipment (book value $7,000, less cash proceeds $4,000). The loss reduced net income but *did not reduce cash.* So the loss is *added to net income* in determining net cash provided by operating activities.[2]

As a result of the previous adjustments, net cash provided by operating activities is $218,000, as computed in Illustration 8-25.

[2]If a gain on sale occurs, a different situation results. To allow a gain to flow through to net cash provided by operating activities would be double-counting the gain—once in net income and again in the investing activities section as part of the cash proceeds from sale. As a result, a gain is deducted from net income in reporting net cash provided by operating activities.

Illustration 8-25

Presentation of net cash provided by operating activities, 2005—indirect method

AIRPORT SHUTTLE SERVICES COMPANY
Statement of Cash Flows—Indirect Method (partial)
For the Year Ended December 31, 2005

Cash flows from operating activities		
Net income		$139,000
Adjustments to reconcile net income to net cash provided by operating activities:		
Depreciation expense	$15,000	
Loss on sale of equipment	3,000	
Decrease in accounts receivable	10,000	
Increase in prepaid expenses	(4,000)	
Increase in accounts payable	55,000	79,000
Net cash provided by operating activities		**$218,000**

Step 3: Determine Net Cash Provided/Used by Investing and Financing Activities

The next step involves analyzing the remaining changes in balance sheet accounts to determine net cash provided (used) by investing and financing activities.

INCREASE IN LAND. As indicated from the change in the Land account and the additional information, land of $130,000 was purchased through the issuance of long-term bonds. The issuance of bonds payable for land has no effect on cash. But it is a significant noncash investing and financing activity that merits disclosure in a separate schedule.

INCREASE IN BUILDING. As the additional data indicate, an office building was acquired for $160,000 cash. This is a cash outflow reported in the investing section.

INCREASE IN EQUIPMENT. The Equipment account increased $17,000. The additional information explains that this was a net increase that resulted from two transactions: (1) a purchase of equipment of $25,000 and (2) the sale for $4,000 of equipment costing $8,000. These transactions are classified as investing activities. Each transaction should be reported separately. Thus the purchase of equipment should be reported as an outflow of cash for $25,000. The sale should be reported as an inflow of cash for $4,000. The T-account below shows the reasons for the change in this account during the year.

Illustration 8-26

Analysis of equipment

Equipment

1/1/05	Balance	10,000	Cost of equipment sold	8,000
	Purchase of equipment	**25,000**		
12/31/05	Balance	27,000		

The following entry shows the details of the equipment sale transaction.

Cash	4,000	
Accumulated Depreciation	1,000	
Loss on Sale of Equipment	3,000	
Equipment		8,000

A	=	L	+	SE
+4,000				−3,000
+1,000				
−8,000				

HELPFUL HINT
When stocks or bonds are issued for cash, the actual proceeds will appear in the statement of cash flows as a financing inflow (rather than the par value of the stocks or face value of bonds).

INCREASE IN BONDS PAYABLE. The Bonds Payable account increased \$130,000. As indicated in the additional information, land was acquired from the issuance of these bonds. This noncash transaction is reported in a separate schedule at the bottom of the statement.

HELPFUL HINT
It is the **payment** of dividends, not the declaration, that appears in the cash flow statement.

INCREASE IN RETAINED EARNINGS. Retained earnings increased \$124,000 during the year. This increase can be explained by two factors: (1) Net income of \$139,000 increased retained earnings. (2) Dividends of \$15,000 decreased retained earnings. Net income is adjusted to net cash provided by operating activities in the operating activities section. **Payment of the dividends is a cash outflow that is reported as a financing activity**.

Statement of Cash Flows—2005

Combining the previous items, we obtain a statement of cash flows for 2005 for Airport Shuttle Services Company as presented in Illustration 8-27.

Illustration 8-27

Statement of cash flows, 2005—indirect method

AIRPORT SHUTTLE SERVICES COMPANY
Statement of Cash Flows—Indirect Method
For the Year Ended December 31, 2005

Cash flows from operating activities		
Net income		\$139,000
Adjustments to reconcile net income to net cash provided by operating activities:		
Depreciation expense	\$ 15,000	
Loss on sale of equipment	3,000	
Decrease in accounts receivable	10,000	
Increase in prepaid expenses	(4,000)	
Increase in accounts payable	55,000	79,000
Net cash provided by operating activities		218,000
Cash flows from investing activities		
Purchase of building	(160,000)	
Purchase of equipment	(25,000)	
Sale of equipment	4,000	
Net cash used by investing activities		(181,000)
Cash flows from financing activities		
Payment of cash dividends	(15,000)	
Net cash used by financing activities		(15,000)
Net increase in cash		22,000
Cash at beginning of period		34,000
Cash at end of period		\$ 56,000
Noncash investing and financing activities		
Issuance of bonds payable to purchase land		\$130,000

HELPFUL HINT
Note that in the investing and financing activities sections, positive numbers indicate cash inflows (receipts), and negative numbers indicate cash outflows (payments).

Summary of Conversion to Net Cash Provided by Operating Activities—Indirect Method

As shown in the previous illustrations, the statement of cash flows prepared by the indirect method starts with net income. It then adds (or deducts) items not affecting cash, to arrive at net cash provided by operating activities. The additions and deductions consist of (1) changes in specific current assets and current liabilities and (2) noncash charges reported in the income statement. A summary of the adjustments for current assets and current liabilities is provided in Illustration 8-28.

	Adjustments to Convert Net Income to Net Cash Provided by Operating Activities	
Current Assets and Current Liabilities	**Add to Net Income a(n):**	**Deduct from Net Income a(n):**
Accounts receivable	Decrease	Increase
Inventory	Decrease	Increase
Prepaid expenses	Decrease	Increase
Accounts payable	Increase	Decrease
Accrued expenses payable	Increase	Decrease

Illustration 8-28

Adjustments for current assets and current liabilities

HELPFUL HINT

1. An increase in a current asset is deducted from net income.
2. A decrease in a current asset is added to net income.
3. An increase in a current liability is added to net income.
4. A decrease in a current liability is deducted from net income.

Adjustments for the noncash charges reported in the income statement are made as shown in Illustration 8-29.

Noncash Charges	Adjustments to Convert Net Income to Net Cash Provided by Operating Activities
Depreciation expense	Add
Patent amortization expense	Add
Depletion expense	Add
Loss on sale of asset	Add

Illustration 8-29

Adjustments for noncash charges

BEFORE YOU GO ON...

REVIEW IT

1. What is the format of the operating activities section of the statement of cash flows using the indirect method?
2. Where is depreciation expense shown on a statement of cash flows using the indirect method?
3. Where are significant noncash investing and financing activities shown in a statement of cash flows? Give some examples.

DO IT

Presented below is information related to Reynolds Gourmet Foods Company. Use it to prepare a statement of cash flows using the indirect method.

REYNOLDS GOURMET FOODS COMPANY
Comparative Balance Sheets
December 31

Assets	**2005**	**2004**	**Change Increase/Decrease**
Cash	$ 54,000	$ 37,000	$ 17,000 Increase
Accounts receivable	68,000	26,000	42,000 Increase
Inventories	54,000	–0–	54,000 Increase
Prepaid expenses	4,000	6,000	2,000 Decrease
Land	45,000	70,000	25,000 Decrease
Buildings	200,000	200,000	–0–
Accumulated depreciation—buildings	(21,000)	(11,000)	10,000 Increase
Equipment	193,000	68,000	125,000 Increase
Accumulated depreciation—equipment	(28,000)	(10,000)	18,000 Increase
Totals	$569,000	$386,000	
Liabilities and Stockholders' Equity			
Accounts payable	$ 23,000	$ 40,000	$ 17,000 Decrease
Accrued expenses payable	10,000	–0–	10,000 Increase
Bonds payable	110,000	150,000	40,000 Decrease
Common stock ($1 par)	220,000	60,000	160,000 Increase
Retained earnings	206,000	136,000	70,000 Increase
Totals	$569,000	$386,000	

REYNOLDS GOURMET FOODS COMPANY
Income Statement
For the Year Ended December 31, 2005

Revenues		$890,000
Cost of goods sold	$465,000	
Operating expenses	221,000	
Interest expense	12,000	
Loss on sale of equipment	2,000	700,000
Income from operations		190,000
Income tax expense		65,000
Net income		$125,000

Additional information:

1. Operating expenses include depreciation expense of $33,000 and charges from prepaid expenses of $2,000.
2. Land was sold at its book value for cash.
3. Cash dividends of $55,000 were declared and paid in 2005.
4. Interest expense of $12,000 was paid in cash.
5. Equipment with a cost of $166,000 was purchased for cash. Equipment with a cost of $41,000 and a book value of $36,000 was sold for $34,000 cash.
6. Bonds of $10,000 were redeemed at their book value for cash. Bonds of $30,000 were converted into common stock.
7. Common stock ($1 par) of $130,000 was issued for cash.
8. Accounts payable pertain to merchandise suppliers.

ACTION PLAN

- Determine the net increase/decrease in cash.
- Determine net cash provided/used by operating activities by adjusting net income for items that did not affect cash.
- Determine net cash provided/used by investing activities.
- Determine net cash provided/used by financing activities.

SOLUTION

REYNOLDS GOURMENT FOODS COMPANY Statement of Cash Flows—Indirect Method For the Year Ended December 31, 2005		
Cash flows from operating activities		
Net income		$125,000
Adjustments to reconcile net income to net cash provided by operating activities:		
Depreciation expense	$ 33,000	
Increase in accounts receivable	(42,000)	
Increase in inventories	(54,000)	
Decrease in prepaid expenses	2,000	
Decrease in accounts payable	(17,000)	
Increase in accrued expenses payable	10,000	
Loss on sale of equipment	2,000	(66,000)
Net cash provided by operating activities		59,000
Cash flows from investing activities		
Sale of land	25,000	
Sale of equipment	34,000	
Purchase of equipment	(166,000)	
Net cash used by investing activities		(107,000)
Cash flows from financing activities		
Redemption of bonds	(10,000)	
Sale of common stock	130,000	
Payment of dividends	(55,000)	
Net cash provided by financing activities		65,000
Net increase in cash		17,000
Cash at beginning of period		37,000
Cash at end of period		$ 54,000
Noncash investing and financing activities		
Conversion of bonds into common stock		$ 30,000

HELPFUL HINT

1. Determine net cash provided/used by operating activities, recognizing that operating activities generally relate to changes in current assets and current liabilities.
2. Determine net cash provided/used by investing activities, recognizing that investing activities generally relate to changes in noncurrent assets.
3. Determine net cash provided/used by financing activities, recognizing that financing activities generally relate to changes in long-term liabilities and stockholders' equity accounts.

Related exercise material: 8-2 and 8-9.

THE NAVIGATOR

SECTION 2: DIRECT METHOD FOR STATEMENT OF CASH FLOWS

STUDY OBJECTIVE 7

Prepare a statement of cash flows using the direct method.

To explain and illustrate the direct method, we will use the transactions of Juarez Motel for two years, 2004 and 2005, to prepare annual statements of cash flows. We will show basic transactions in the first year, with additional transactions added in the second year.

FIRST YEAR OF OPERATIONS—2004

Juarez Motel began business on January 1, 2004. At that time it issued 300,000 shares of $1 par value common stock for $300,000 cash. The company rented office and sales space along with equipment. The comparative balance sheets at the beginning and end of 2004, showing changes in each account, appear in Illustration 8-30. The income statement and additional information for Juarez Motel are shown in Illustration 8-31.

Illustration 8-30

Comparative balance sheet, 2002, with increases and decreases

JUAREZ MOTEL
Comparative Balance Sheet

Assets	Dec. 31, 2004	Jan. 1, 2004	Change Increase/Decrease
Cash	$159,000	$-0-	$159,000 Increase
Accounts receivable	15,000	-0-	15,000 Increase
Inventory	160,000	-0-	160,000 Increase
Prepaid expenses	8,000	-0-	8,000 Increase
Land	80,000	-0-	80,000 Increase
Total	$422,000	$-0-	
Liabilities and Stockholders' Equity			
Accounts payable	$ 60,000	$-0-	$ 60,000 Increase
Accrued expenses payable	20,000	-0-	20,000 Increase
Common stock	300,000	-0-	300,000 Increase
Retained earnings	42,000	-0-	42,000 Increase
Total	$422,000	$-0-	

Illustration 8-31

Income statement and additional information, 2004

JUAREZ MOTEL
Income Statement
For the Year Ended December 31, 2004

Revenues	$780,000
Cost of goods sold	450,000
Gross profit	330,000
Operating expenses	170,000
Income before income taxes	160,000
Income tax expense	48,000
Net income	$112,000

Additional information:
1. Dividends of $70,000 were declared and paid in cash.
2. The accounts payable increase resulted from the purchase of merchandise.

The three steps cited on page 238 for preparing the statement of cash flows are used in the direct method.

Step 1: Determine the Net Increase/Decrease in Cash

The comparative balance sheets for Juarez Motel show a zero cash balance at January 1, 2004, and a cash balance of $159,000 at December 31, 2004. Thus, the change in cash for 2004 was a net increase of $159,000.

Step 2: Determine Net Cash Provided/Used by Operating Activities

Under the **direct method**, net cash provided by operating activities is computed by *adjusting each item in the income statement* from the accrual basis to the cash basis. To simplify and condense the operating activities section, **only major classes of operating cash receipts and cash payments are reported**. For these major classes, the difference between cash receipts and cash payments is the net cash provided by operating activities. These relationships are as shown in Illustration 8-32.

Illustration 8-32

Major classes of cash receipts and payments

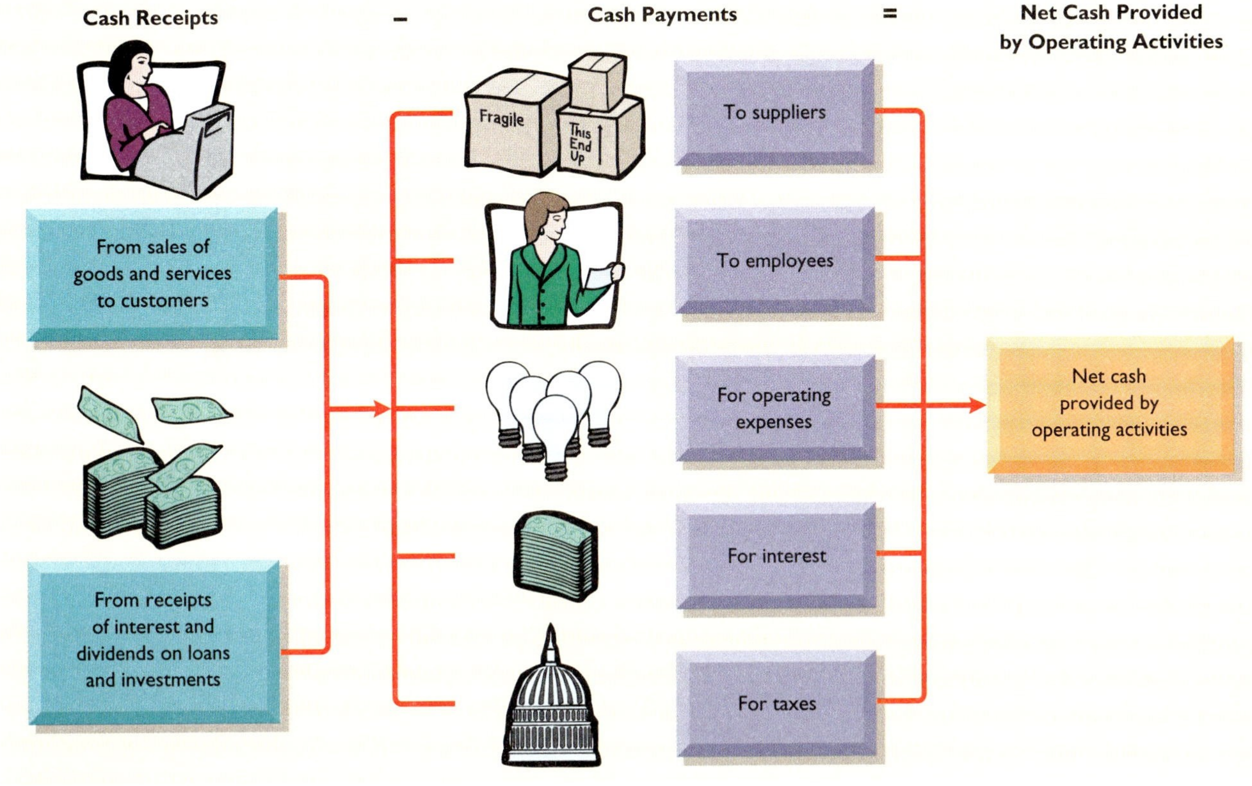

An efficient way to apply the direct method is to analyze the items reported in the income statement in the order in which they are listed. Cash receipts and cash payments related to these revenues and expenses are then determined. The direct method adjustments for Juarez Motel in 2004 to determine net cash provided by operating activities are presented on the following pages.

CASH RECEIPTS FROM CUSTOMERS. The income statement for Juarez Motel reported revenues from customers of $780,000. How much of that was cash receipts? To answer that, it is necessary to consider the change in accounts receivable during the year. When accounts receivable increase during the year, revenues on an accrual basis are higher than cash receipts from customers. Operations led to revenues, but not all of these revenues resulted in cash receipts. To determine the amount of cash receipts, the increase in accounts receivable is deducted from sales revenues. On the other hand, there may be a decrease in accounts receivable. That would occur if cash receipts from customers exceeded sales revenues. In that case, the decrease in accounts receivable is added to sales revenues.

For Juarez Motel, accounts receivable increased $15,000. Thus, cash receipts from customers were $765,000, computed as follows.

Illustration 8-33

Computation of cash receipts from customers

Revenues from sales	$780,000
Deduct: Increase in accounts receivable	15,000
Cash receipts from customers	**$765,000**

Cash receipts from customers may also be determined from an analysis of the Accounts Receivable account, as shown in Illustration 8-34.

Illustration 8-34

Analysis of accounts receivable

Accounts Receivable

1/1/04	Balance	–0–	**Receipts from customers**	**765,000**
	Revenues from sales	780,000		
12/31/04	Balance	15,000		

HELPFUL HINT

The T-account shows that revenue less increase in receivables equals cash receipts.

The relationships among cash receipts from customers, revenues from sales, and changes in accounts receivable are shown in Illustration 8-35.

Illustration 8-35

Formula to compute cash receipts from customers—direct method

Cash receipts from customers = Revenues from sales { + Decrease in accounts receivable or − Increase in accounts receivable }

CASH PAYMENTS TO SUPPLIERS. Juarez Motel reported cost of goods sold of $450,000 on its income statement. How much of that was cash payments to suppliers? To answer that, it is first necessary to find purchases for the year. To find purchases, cost of goods sold is adjusted for the change in inventory. When inventory increases during the year, purchases for the year have exceeded cost of goods sold. As a result, to determine the amount of purchases, the increase in inventory is added to cost of goods sold.

In 2004, Juarez's inventory increased $160,000. Purchases are computed as shown in Illustration 8-36.

Illustration 8-36

Computation of purchases

Cost of goods sold	$450,000
Add: Increase in inventory	160,000
Purchases	**$610,000**

After purchases are computed, cash payments to suppliers can be determined. This is done by adjusting purchases for the change in accounts payable. When accounts payable increase during the year, purchases on an accrual basis are higher than they are on a cash basis. As a result, to determine cash payments to suppliers, an increase in accounts payable is deducted from purchases. On the other hand, there may be a decrease in accounts payable. That would occur if cash payments to suppliers exceed purchases. In that case, the decrease in accounts payable is added to purchases.

For Juarez Motel, cash payments to suppliers were $550,000, shown in Illustration 8-37.

Illustration 8-37

Computation of cash payments to suppliers

Purchases	$610,000
Deduct: Increase in accounts payable	60,000
Cash payments to suppliers	**$550,000**

Cash payments to suppliers may also be determined from an analysis of the Accounts Payable account as shown in Illustration 8-38.

Illustration 8-38

Analysis of accounts payable

Accounts Payable

Payments to suppliers	**550,000**	1/1/04	Balance	–0–
			Purchases	610,000
		12/31/04	Balance	60,000

HELPFUL HINT

The T-account shows that purchases less increase in accounts payable equals payments to suppliers.

The relationships among cash payments to suppliers, cost of goods sold, changes in inventory, and changes in accounts payable are shown in the following formula.

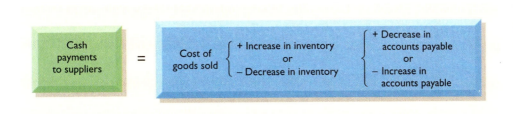

Illustration 8-39

Formula to compute cash payments to suppliers—direct method

Cash payments to suppliers = Cost of goods sold { + Increase in inventory or – Decrease in inventory } { + Decrease in accounts payable or – Increase in accounts payable }

CASH PAYMENTS FOR OPERATING EXPENSES. Operating expenses of $170,000 were reported on Juarez's income statement. How much of that amount was cash paid for operating expenses? To answer that, we need to adjust this amount for any changes in prepaid expenses and accrued expenses payable. For example, when prepaid expenses increased $8,000 during the year, cash paid for operating expenses was $8,000 higher than operating expenses reported on the income statement. To convert operating expenses to cash payments for operating expenses, the increase must be added to operating expenses. On the other hand, if prepaid expenses decrease during the year, the decrease must be deducted from operating expenses.

Operating expenses must also be adjusted for changes in accrued expenses payable. When accrued expenses payable increase during the year, operating expenses on an accrual basis are higher than they are on a cash basis. As a result, to determine cash payments for operating expenses, an increase in accrued expenses payable is deducted from operating expenses. On the other hand, a decrease in accrued expenses payable is added to operating expenses because cash payments exceed operating expenses.

Juarez Motel's cash payments for operating expenses were $158,000, computed as shown in Illustration 8-40.

HELPFUL HINT

Decrease in accounts receivable indicates that cash collections were greater than sales.
Increase in accounts receivable indicates that sales were greater than cash collections.
Increase in prepaid expenses indicates that the amount paid for the prepayments exceeded the amount that was recorded as an expense.
Decrease in prepaid expenses indicates that the amount recorded as an expense exceeded the amount of cash paid for the prepayments.
Increase in accrued expenses payable indicates that expenses incurred exceed the cash paid for expenses that period.

Illustration 8-40

Computation of cash payments for operating expenses

Operating expenses	$170,000
Add: Increase in prepaid expenses	8,000
Deduct: Increase in accrued expenses payable	(20,000)
Cash payments for operating expenses	**$158,000**

The relationships among cash payments for operating expenses, changes in prepaid expenses, and changes in accrued expenses payable are shown in Illustration 8-41.

Illustration 8-41

Formula to compute cash payments for operating expenses—direct method

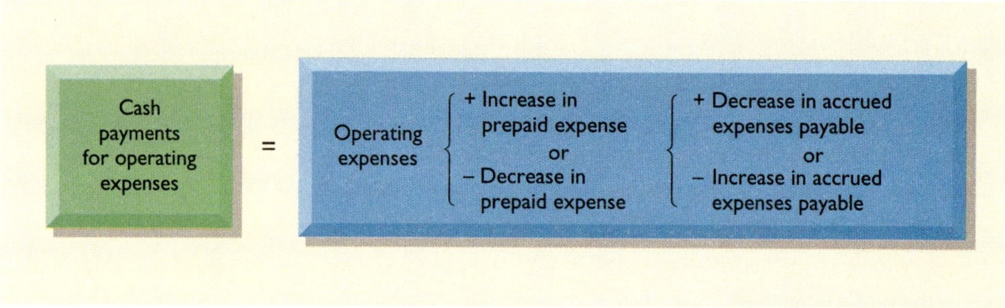

CASH PAYMENTS FOR INCOME TAXES. The income statement for Juarez Motel shows income tax expense of $48,000. This amount equals the cash paid. The comparative balance sheets indicated no income taxes payable at either the beginning or end of the year.

All of the revenues and expenses in the 2004 income statement have now been adjusted to a cash basis. The operating activities section of the statement of cash flows is shown in Illustration 8-42.

Illustration 8-42

Operating activities section—direct method

JUAREZ MOTEL
Statement of Cash Flows—Direct Method (partial)
For the Year Ended December 31, 2004

Cash flows from operating activities		
Cash receipts from customers		$765,000
Cash payments:		
To suppliers	$550,000	
For operating expenses	158,000	
For income taxes	48,000	756,000
Net cash provided by operating activities		**$ 9,000**

Step 3: Determine Net Cash Provided/Used by Investing and Financing Activities

HELPFUL HINT
This is the same procedure used under the indirect method. The investing and financing activities are measured and reported the same under both methods.

Preparing the investing and financing activities sections of the statement of cash flows begins by determining the changes in noncurrent accounts reported in the comparative balance sheets. The change in each account is then analyzed to determine the effect, if any, the change had on cash.

INCREASE IN LAND. No additional information is given for the increase in land. In such case, you should assume that the increase affected cash. In solving homework problems, you should assume that any unexplained differences in noncurrent accounts involve cash. The purchase of land is an investing activity. Thus, an outflow of cash of $80,000 for the purchase of land should be reported in the investing activities section.

INCREASE IN COMMON STOCK. As indicated earlier, 300,000 shares of $1 par value stock were sold for $300,000 cash. The issuance of common stock is a financing activity. Thus, a cash inflow of $300,000 from the issuance of common stock is reported in the financing activities section.

INCREASE IN RETAINED EARNINGS. What caused the net increase of $42,000 in the Retained Earnings account? First, net income increased retained earnings by $112,000. Second, the additional information section indicates that a cash dividend of $70,000 was declared and paid. The adjustment of revenues and expenses to arrive at net cash provided by operations was done in step 2 above. The cash dividend paid is reported as an outflow of cash in the financing activities section.

This analysis can also be made directly from the Retained Earnings account in the ledger of Juarez Motel as shown in Illustration 8-43.

HELPFUL HINT
It is the *payment* of dividends, not the declaration, that appears on the cash flow statement.

Illustration 8-43
Analysis of retained earnings

Retained Earnings

12/31/04	**Cash dividend**	**70,000**	1/1/04	Balance	–0–
			12/31/04	**Net income**	**112,000**
			12/31/04	Balance	42,000

The $42,000 increase in Retained Earnings in 2004 is a net change. When a net change in a noncurrent balance sheet account has occurred during the year, it generally is necessary to report the individual items that cause the net change.

Statement of Cash Flows—2004

We can now prepare the statement of cash flows. The operating activities section is reported first, followed by the investing and financing activities sections. The statement of cash flows for Juarez Motel for 2004 is shown in Illustration 8-44.

Illustration 8-44
Statement of cash flows, 2004—direct method

JUAREZ MOTEL
Statement of Cash Flows—Direct Method
For the Year Ended December 31, 2004

Cash flows from operating activities		
Cash receipts from customers		$765,000
Cash payments:		
To suppliers	$550,000	
For operating expenses	158,000	
For income taxes	48,000	756,000
Net cash provided by operating activities		9,000
Cash flows from investing activities		
Purchase of land	(80,000)	
Net cash used by investing activities		(80,000)
Cash flows from financing activities		
Issuance of common stock	300,000	
Payment of cash dividend	(70,000)	
Net cash provided by financing activities		230,000
Net increase in cash		159,000
Cash at beginning of period		–0–
Cash at end of period		$159,000

HELPFUL HINT
Note that in the investing and financing activities sections, positive numbers indicate cash inflows (receipts), and negative numbers indicate cash outflows (payments).

The statement of cash flows shows the following: Operating activities *provided* $9,000 of the net increase in cash. Investing activities *used* $80,000 of cash. Financing activities *provided* $230,000 of cash. The $159,000 net increase in cash for the year agrees with the increase in cash of $159,000 reported in the comparative balance sheets.

SECOND YEAR OF OPERATIONS—2005

Illustrations 8-45 and 8-46 present information related to the second year of operations for Juarez Motel.

Illustration 8-45

Comparative balance sheets, 2005, with increases and decreases

JUAREZ MOTEL
Comparative Balance Sheets
December 31

Assets	**2005**	**2004**	**Change Increase/Decrease**
Cash	$191,000	$159,000	$ 32,000 Increase
Accounts receivable	12,000	15,000	3,000 Decrease
Inventory	130,000	160,000	30,000 Decrease
Prepaid expenses	6,000	8,000	2,000 Decrease
Land	180,000	80,000	100,000 Increase
Equipment	160,000	–0–	160,000 Increase
Accumulated depreciation—equipment	(16,000)	–0–	16,000 Increase
Total	$663,000	$422,000	
Liabilities and Stockholders' Equity			
Accounts payable	$ 52,000	$ 60,000	$ 8,000 Decrease
Accrued expenses payable	15,000	20,000	5,000 Decrease
Income taxes payable	12,000	–0–	12,000 Increase
Bonds payable	90,000	–0–	90,000 Increase
Common stock	400,000	300,000	100,000 Increase
Retained earnings	94,000	42,000	52,000 Increase
Total	$663,000	$422,000	

Illustration 8-46

Income statement and additional information, 2005

JUAREZ MOTEL
Income Statement
For the Year Ended December 31, 2005

Revenues		$975,000
Cost of goods sold	$660,000	
Operating expenses (excluding depreciation)	176,000	
Depreciation expense	18,000	
Loss on sale of store equipment	1,000	855,000
Income before income taxes		120,000
Income tax expense		36,000
Net income		$ 84,000

Additional information:

1. In 2005, the company declared and paid a $32,000 cash dividend.
2. Bonds were issued at face value for $90,000 in cash.
3. Equipment costing $180,000 was purchased for cash.
4. Equipment costing $20,000 was sold for $17,000 cash when the book value of the equipment was $18,000.
5. Common stock of $100,000 was issued to acquire land.

Step 1: Determine the Net Increase/Decrease in Cash

The comparative balance sheets show a beginning cash balance of $159,000 and an ending cash balance of $191,000. Thus, there was a net increase in cash in 2005 of $32,000.

Step 2: Determine Net Cash Provided/Used by Operating Activities

CASH RECEIPTS FROM CUSTOMERS. Revenues from sales were $975,000. Since accounts receivable decreased $3,000, cash receipts from customers were greater than sales revenues. Cash receipts from customers were $978,000, computed as shown in Illustration 8-47.

Revenues from sales	$975,000
Add: Decrease in accounts receivable	3,000
Cash receipts from customers	**$978,000**

Illustration 8-47

Computation of cash receipts from customers

CASH PAYMENTS TO SUPPLIERS. The conversion of cost of goods sold to purchases and purchases to cash payments to suppliers is similar to the computations made in 2004. For 2005, purchases are computed using cost of goods sold of $660,000 from the income statement and the decrease in inventory of $30,000 from the comparative balance sheets. Purchases are then adjusted by the decrease in accounts payable of $8,000. Cash payments to suppliers were $638,000, computed as shown in Illustration 8-48.

Cost of goods sold	$660,000
Deduct: Decrease in inventory	30,000
Purchases	630,000
Add: Decrease in accounts payable	8,000
Cash payments to suppliers	**$638,000**

Illustration 8-48

Computation of cash payments to suppliers

CASH PAYMENTS FOR OPERATING EXPENSES. Operating expenses (exclusive of depreciation expense) for 2005 were reported at $176,000. This amount is then adjusted for changes in prepaid expenses and accrued expenses payable to determine cash payments for operating expenses.

As shown in the comparative balance sheets, prepaid expenses decreased $2,000 during the year. This means that $2,000 was allocated to operating expenses (thereby increasing operating expenses), but cash payments did not increase by that $2,000. To determine cash payments for operating expenses, the decrease in prepaid expenses is deducted from operating expenses.

Accrued operating expenses decreased $5,000 during the period. As a result, cash payments were higher by $5,000 than the amount reported for operating expenses. The decrease in accrued expenses payable is added to operating expenses. Cash payments for operating expenses were $179,000, computed in Illustration 8-49.

Illustration 8-49

Computation of cash payments for operating expenses

Operating expenses, exclusive of depreciation	$176,000
Deduct: Decrease in prepaid expenses	(2,000)
Add: Decrease in accrued expenses payable	5,000
Cash payments for operating expenses	**$179,000**

DEPRECIATION EXPENSE AND LOSS ON SALE OF EQUIPMENT. Operating expenses are shown exclusive of depreciation. Depreciation expense in 2005 was $18,000. Depreciation expense is not shown on a statement of cash flows because it is a noncash charge. If the amount for operating expenses includes depreciation expense, operating expenses must be reduced by the amount of depreciation to determine cash payments for operating expenses.

The loss on sale of equipment of $1,000 is also a noncash charge. The loss on sale of equipment reduces net income, but it does not reduce cash. Thus, the loss on sale of equipment is not reported on a statement of cash flows.

Other charges to expense that do not require the use of cash, such as the amortization of intangible assets and depletion expense, are treated in the same manner as depreciation.

CASH PAYMENTS FOR INCOME TAXES. Income tax expense reported on the income statement was $36,000. Income taxes payable, however, increased $12,000. This increase means that $12,000 of the income taxes have not been paid. As a result, income taxes paid were less than income taxes reported in the income statement. Cash payments for income taxes were, therefore, $24,000 as shown in Illustration 8-50.

Illustration 8-50

Computation of cash payments for income taxes

Income tax expense	$36,000
Deduct: Increase in income taxes payable	12,000
Cash payments for income taxes	**$24,000**

The relationships among cash payments for income taxes, income tax expense, and changes in income taxes payable are shown in Illustration 8-51.

Illustration 8-51

Formula to compute cash payments for income taxes—direct method

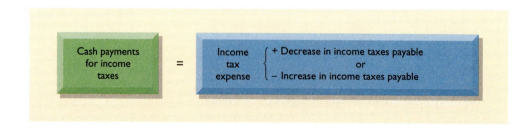

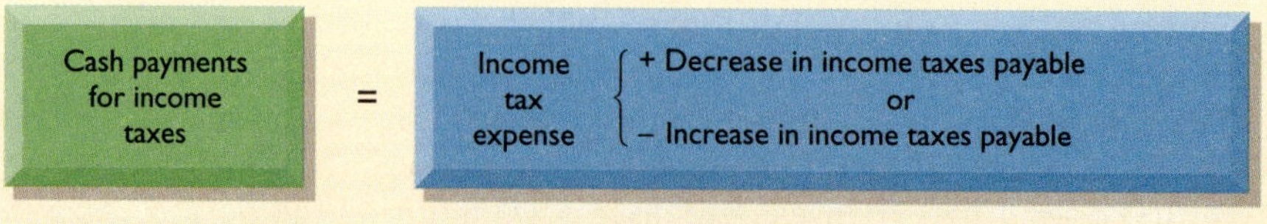

Step 3: Determine Net Cash Provided/Used by Investing and Financing Activities

INCREASE IN LAND. Land increased $100,000. The additional information section indicates that common stock was issued to purchase the land. The issuance of common stock for land has no effect on cash. **But it is a significant noncash investing and financing transaction**. This transaction requires disclosure in a separate schedule at the bottom of the statement of cash flows.

INCREASE IN EQUIPMENT. The comparative balance sheets show that equipment increased $160,000 in 2005. The additional information in Illustration 8-46 indicates that the increase resulted from two investing transactions: (1) Equipment costing $180,000 was purchased for cash. And (2) equipment costing $20,000 was sold for $17,000 cash when its book value was $18,000. The relevant data for the statement of cash flows is the cash paid for the purchase and the cash proceeds from the sale. For Juarez Motel, the investing activities section will show the following: The $180,000 purchase of equipment as an outflow of cash, and the $17,000 sale of equipment also as an inflow of cash. **The two amounts should not be netted. Both individual outflows and inflows of cash should be shown.**

The analysis of the changes in equipment should include the related Accumulated Depreciation account. These two accounts for Juarez Motel are shown in Illustration 8-52.

Illustration 8-52

Analysis of equipment and related accumulated depreciation

Equipment

1/1/05	Balance	–0–		Cost of equipment sold	20,000
	Cash purchase	**180,000**			
12/31/05	Balance	160,000			

Accumulated Depreciation—Equipment

	Sale of equipment	2,000	1/1/05	Balance	–0–
				Depreciation expense	18,000
			12/31/05	Balance	16,000

INCREASE IN BONDS PAYABLE. Bonds Payable increased $90,000. The additional information in Illustration 8-46 indicated that bonds with a face value of $90,000 were issued for $90,000 cash. The issuance of bonds is a financing activity. For Juarez Motel, there is an inflow of cash of $90,000 from the issuance of bonds.

INCREASE IN COMMON STOCK. The Common Stock account increased $100,000. The additional information indicated that land was acquired from the issuance of common stock. **This transaction is a significant noncash investing and financing transaction** that should be reported separately at the bottom of the statement.

INCREASE IN RETAINED EARNINGS. The $52,000 net increase in Retained Earnings resulted from net income of $84,000 and the declaration and payment of a cash dividend of $32,000. **Net income is not reported in the statement of cash flows under the direct method.** Cash dividends paid of $32,000 are reported in the financing activities section as an outflow of cash.

Statement of Cash Flows—2005

The statement of cash flows for Juarez Motel is shown in Illustration 8-53.

Illustration 8-53

Statement of cash flows, 2005—direct method

JUAREZ MOTEL
Statement of Cash Flows—Direct Method
For the Year Ended December 31, 2005

Cash flows from operating activities		
Cash receipts from customers		$978,000
Cash payments:		
To suppliers	$638,000	
For operating expenses	179,000	
For income taxes	24,000	841,000
Net cash provided by operating activities		137,000
Cash flows from investing activities		
Purchase of equipment	(180,000)	
Sale of equipment	17,000	
Net cash used by investing activities		(163,000)
Cash flows from financing activities		
Issuance of bonds payable	90,000	
Payment of cash dividends	(32,000)	
Net cash provided by financing activities		58,000
Net increase in cash		32,000
Cash at beginning of period		159,000
Cash at end of period		$191,000
Noncash investing and financing activities		
Issuance of common stock to purchase land		$100,000

BEFORE YOU GO ON...

REVIEW IT

1. What is the format of the operating activities section of the statement of cash flows using the direct method?
2. Where is depreciation expense shown on a statement of cash flows using the direct method?
3. Where are significant noncash investing and financing activities shown on a statement of cash flows? Give some examples.

DO IT

Presented below is information related to Reynolds Gourmet Foods Company. Use it to prepare a statement of cash flows using the direct method.

REYNOLDS GOURMET FOODS COMPANY
Comparative Balance Sheets
December 31

Assets	**2005**	**2004**	**Change Increase/Decrease**
Cash	$ 54,000	$ 37,000	$ 17,000 Increase
Accounts receivable	68,000	26,000	42,000 Increase
Inventories	54,000	–0–	54,000 Increase
Prepaid expenses	4,000	6,000	2,000 Decrease
Land	45,000	70,000	25,000 Decrease
Buildings	200,000	200,000	–0–
Accumulated depreciation—buildings	(21,000)	(11,000)	10,000 Increase
Equipment	193,000	68,000	125,000 Increase
Accumulated depreciation—equipment	(28,000)	(10,000)	18,000 Increase
Totals	$569,000	$386,000	
Liabilities and Stockholders' Equity			
Accounts payable	$ 23,000	$ 40,000	$ 17,000 Decrease
Accrued expenses payable	10,000	–0–	10,000 Increase
Bonds payable	110,000	150,000	40,000 Decrease
Common stock ($1 par)	220,000	60,000	160,000 Increase
Retained earnings	206,000	136,000	70,000 Increase
Totals	$569,000	$386,000	

REYNOLDS GOURMET FOODS COMPANY
Income Statement
For the Year Ended December 31, 2005

Revenues		$890,000
Cost of goods sold	$465,000	
Operating expenses	221,000	
Interest expense	12,000	
Loss on sale of equipment	2,000	700,000
Income from operations		190,000
Income tax expense		65,000
Net income		$125,000

Additional information:

1. Operating expenses include depreciation expense of $33,000 and charges from prepaid expenses of $2,000.
2. Land was sold at its book value for cash.
3. Cash dividends of $55,000 were declared and paid in 2005.
4. Interest expense of $12,000 was paid in cash.
5. Equipment with a cost of $166,000 was purchased for cash. Equipment with a cost of $41,000 and a book value of $36,000 was sold for $34,000 cash.
6. Bonds of $10,000 were redeemed at their book value for cash. Bonds of $30,000 were converted into common stock.
7. Common stock ($1 par) of $130,000 was issued for cash.
8. Accounts payable pertain to merchandise suppliers.

ACTION PLAN

- Determine the net increase/decrease in cash.
- Determine net cash provided/used by operating activities by adjusting each item in the income statement from the accrual basis to the cash basis.
- Determine net cash provided/used by investing activities.
- Determine net cash provided/used by financing activities.

SOLUTION

REYNOLDS GOURMET FOODS COMPANY
Statement of Cash Flows—Direct Method
For the Year Ended December 31, 2005

Cash flows from operating activities		
Cash receipts from customers		$848,000[a]
Cash payments:		
To suppliers	$536,000[b]	
For operating expenses	176,000[c]	
For interest expense	12,000	
For income taxes	65,000	789,000
Net cash provided by operating activities		59,000
Cash flows from investing activities		
Sale of land	25,000	
Sale of equipment	34,000	
Purchase of equipment	(166,000)	
Net cash used by investing activities		(107,000)
Cash flows from financing activities		
Redemption of bonds	(10,000)	
Sale of common stock	130,000	
Payment of dividends	(55,000)	
Net cash provided by financing activities		65,000
Net increase in cash		17,000
Cash at beginning of period		37,000
Cash at end of period		$ 54,000
Noncash investing and financing activities		
Conversion of bonds into common stock		$ 30,000

Computations:

[a]$848,000 = $890,000 − $42,000
[b]$536,000 = $465,000 + $54,000 + $17,000
[c]$176,000 = $221,000 − $33,000 − $2,000 − $10,000

Technically, an additional schedule reconciling net income to net cash provided by operating activities should be presented as part of the statement of cash flows when using the direct method.

HELPFUL HINT

1. Determine net cash provided/used by operating activities, recognizing that each item in the income statement must be adjusted to the cash basis.
2. Determine net cash provided/used by investing activities, recognizing that investing activities generally relate to changes in noncurrent assets.
3. Determine net cash provided/used by financing activities, recognizing that financing activities generally relate to changes in long-term liabilities and stockholders' equity accounts.

Related exercise material: 8-4 and 8-11.

THE NAVIGATOR

DEMONSTRATION PROBLEM 1

The income statement for the year ended December 31, 2004, for Tuscany Bay Resort contains the following condensed information.

TUSCANY BAY RESORT
Income Statement

Revenues		$6,583,000
Operating expenses (excluding depreciation)	$4,920,000	
Depreciation expense	880,000	5,800,000
Income before income taxes		783,000
Income tax expense		353,000
Net income		$ 430,000

Included in operating expenses is a $24,000 loss resulting from the sale of guest room furniture for $270,000 cash. Guest room furniture was purchased at a cost of $750,000.

The following balances are reported on Tuscany Bay's comparative balance sheets at December 31.

TUSCANY BAY RESORT
Comparative Balance Sheets (partial)

	2004	2003
Cash	$672,000	$130,000
Accounts receivable	775,000	610,000
Inventories	834,000	867,000
Accounts payable	521,000	501,000

Income tax expense of $353,000 represents the amount paid in 2004. Dividends declared and paid in 2004 totaled $200,000.

Instructions

(a) Prepare the statement of cash flows using the indirect method.

OR

(b) Prepare the statement of cash flows using the direct method.

SOLUTION TO DEMONSTRATION PROBLEM

(a)

TUSCANY BAY RESORT
Statement of Cash Flows—Indirect Method
For the Year Ended December 31, 2004

Cash flows from operating activities		
Net income		$ 430,000
Adjustments to reconcile net income to net cash provided by operating activities:		
Depreciation expense	$ 880,000	
Loss on sale of guest room furniture	24,000	
Increase in accounts receivable	(165,000)	
Decrease in inventories	33,000	
Increase in accounts payable	20,000	792,000
Net cash provided by operating activities		1,222,000
Cash flows from investing activities		
Sale of guest room furniture	270,000	
Purchase of guest room furniture	(750,000)	
Net cash used by investing activities		(480,000)
Cash flows from financing activities		
Payment of cash dividends		(200,000)
Net increase in cash		542,000
Cash at beginning of period		130,000
Cash at end of period		$ 672,000

ACTION PLAN

- Apply the same data to the preparation of a statement of cash flows under both the indirect and direct methods.
- Note the similarities of the two methods: Both methods report the same information in the investing and financing sections.
- Note the differences between the two methods: The cash flows from operating activities sections report different information (but the amount of net cash provided by operating activities is the same for both methods).

(b)

TUSCANY BAY RESORT
Statement of Cash Flows—Direct Method
For the Year Ended December 31, 2004

Cash flows from operating activities		
Cash receipts from customers		$6,418,000*
Cash payments:		
For operating expenses	$4,843,000**	
For income taxes	353,000	5,196,000
Net cash provided by operating activities		1,222,000
Cash flows from investing activities		
Sale of guest room furniture	270,000	
Purchase of guest room furniture	(750,000)	
Net cash used by investing activities		(480,000)
Cash flows from financing activities		
Payment of cash dividends		(200,000)
Net increase in cash		542,000
Cash at beginning of period		130,000
Cash at end of period		$ 672,000

Direct Method Computations:

* Computation of cash receipts from customers:	
Revenues per the income statement	$6,583,000
Less increase in accounts receivable	165,000
Cash receipts from customers	$6,418,000
** Computation of cash payments for operating expenses:	
Operating expenses per the income statement	$4,920,000
Deduct loss from sale of guest room furniture	(24,000)
Deduct decrease in inventories	(33,000)
Deduct increase in accounts payable	(20,000)
Cash payments for operating expenses	$4,843,000

THE NAVIGATOR

DEMONSTRATION PROBLEM 2

The adjusted trial balance columns of the work sheet for the year ended December 31, 2004, for Tournament Souvenir and Pro Shop are as follows.

Debit		Credit	
Cash	14,500	Accumulated Depreciation	18,000
Accounts Receivable	11,100	Notes Payable	25,000
Merchandise Inventory	29,000	Accounts Payable	10,600
Prepaid Insurance	2,500	Common Stock	50,000
Store Equipment	95,000	Retained Earnings	31,000
Dividends	12,000	Sales	536,800
Sales Returns and Allowances	6,700	Interest Revenue	2,500
Sales Discounts	5,000		673,900
Cost of Goods Sold	363,400		
Freight-out	7,600		
Advertising Expense	12,000		
Store Salaries Expense	56,000		
Utilities Expense	18,000		
Rent Expense	24,000		
Depreciation Expense	9,000		
Insurance Expense	4,500		
Interest Expense	3,600		
	673,900		

Instructions

Prepare an income statement assuming Tournament Souvenir and Pro Shop does not use subgroupings for operating expenses.

SOLUTION TO DEMONSTRATION PROBLEM

TOURNAMENT SOUVENIR AND PRO SHOP
Income Statement
For the Year Ended December 31, 2004

Sales revenues		
Sales		$536,800
Less: Sales returns and allowances	$6,700	
Sales discounts	5,000	11,700
Net sales		525,100
Cost of goods sold		363,400
Gross profit		161,700
Operating expenses		
Store salaries expense	56,000	
Rent expense	24,000	
Utilities expense	18,000	
Advertising expense	12,000	
Depreciation expense	9,000	
Freight-out	7,600	
Insurance expense	4,500	
Total operating expenses		131,100
Income from operations		30,600
Other revenues and gains		
Interest revenue	2,500	
Other expenses and losses		
Interest expense	3,600	1,100
Net income		$ 29,500

ACTION PLAN

- Remember that the key components of the income statement are net sales, cost of goods sold, gross profit, total operating expenses, and net income (loss). Report these components in the right-hand column of the income statement.
- Put nonoperating items after income from operations.

THE NAVIGATOR

SUMMARY OF STUDY OBJECTIVES

1. *Distinguish between multiple-step and single-step income statements.* A multiple-step income statement shows numerous steps in determining net income, including nonoperating activities sections. In a single-step income statement, all data are classified under two categories (revenues or expenses) and net income is determined in one step.

2. *Explain the computation and importance of gross profits.* Gross profit is computed by subtracting cost of goods sold from net sales. Gross profit represents the merchandising profit of a company. The amount and trend of gross profit are closely watched by management and other interested parties.

3. *Distinguish between departmental and consolidated income statements.* A consolidated income statement is a summary statement of all the departmental income statements of a property.

4. *Indicate the primary purpose of the statement of cash flows.* The primary purpose of the statement of cash flows is to provide information about the cash receipts and cash payments during a period. A secondary objective is to provide information about the operating, investing, and financing activities during the period.

5. *Distinguish among operating, investing, and financing activities.* Operating activities include the cash effects of transactions that enter into the determination of net income. Investing activities involve cash flows resulting from changes in investments and long-term asset items. Financing activities involve cash flows resulting from changes in long-term liability and stockholders' equity items.

6. *Prepare a statement of cash flows using the indirect method.* The preparation of a statement of cash flows involves three major steps: (1) Determine the net increase or decrease in cash. (2) Determine net cash provided (used) by operating activities. (3) Determine net cash flows provided (used) by investing and financing activities. Under the indirect method, accrual basis net income is adjusted to net cash provided by operating activities.

7. *Prepare a statement of cash flows using the direct method.* The preparation of the statement of cash flows involves three major steps: (1) Determine the net increase or decrease in cash. (2) Determine net cash provided (used) by operating activities. (3) Determine net cash flows provided (used) by investing and financing activities. To determine net cash provided by operating activities, the direct method reports cash receipts less cash payments.

THE NAVIGATOR

GLOSSARY

Administrative expenses Expenses relating to general operating activities such as personnel management, accounting, and store security (p. 230).

Consolidated income statement A combined income statement of all departmental income statements of an entity (p. 231)

Direct method A method of determining the net cash provided by operating activities by adjusting each item in the income statement from the accrual basis to the cash basis (p. 252).

Financing activities Cash flow activities that include (a) obtaining cash from issuing debt and repaying the amounts borrowed and (b) obtaining cash from stockholders and providing them with a return on their investment (p. 234).

Income from operations Income from a company's principal operating activity; determined by subtracting cost of goods sold and operating expenses from net sales (p. 228).

Indirect method A method of preparing a statement of cash flows in which net income is adjusted for items that did not affect cash, to determine net cash provided by operating activities (p. 241).

Investing activities Cash flow activities that include (a) acquiring and disposing of investments and productive long-lived assets and (b) lending money and collecting on those loans (p. 234).

Multiple-step income statement An income statement that shows numerous steps in determining net income (or net loss) (p. 226).

Net sales Sales less sales returns and allowances and sales discounts (p. 227).

Operating activities Cash flow activities that include the cash effects of transactions that create revenues and expenses and thus enter into the determination of net income (p. 234).

Other expenses and losses A nonoperating activities section of the income statement that shows expenses from auxiliary operations and losses unrelated to the company's operations (p. 228).

Other revenues and gains A nonoperating activities section of the income statement that shows revenues from auxiliary operations and gains unrelated to the company's operations (p. 228).

Selling expenses Expenses associated with making sales (p. 229).

Single-step income statement An income statement that shows only one step in determining net income (or net loss) (p. 230).

Statement of cash flows A financial statement that provides information about the cash receipts and cash payments of an entity during a period, classified as operating, investing, and financing activities, in a format that reconciles the beginning and ending cash balances (p. 234).

EXERCISES

Contrast presentation in multiple-step and single-step income statements. (SO 1)

8-1 Explain where each of the following items would appear on (1) a multiple-step income statement, and on (2) a single-step income statement: **(a)** gain on sale of equipment, **(b)** casualty loss from vandalism, and **(c)** cost of goods sold.

Compute cash provided by operating activities—indirect method. (SO 6)

8-2 Titanic Candy reported net income of $2.5 million in 2004. Depreciation for the year was $260,000, accounts receivable decreased $350,000, and accounts payable decreased $310,000. Compute net cash provided by operating activities using the indirect approach.

Classify items by activities. (SO 5)

8-3 Classify the following items as an operating, investing, or financing activity. Assume all items involve cash unless there is information to the contrary.

(a) Purchase of equipment.
(b) Sale of building.
(c) Redemption of bonds.
(d) Depreciation.
(e) Payment of dividends.
(f) Issuance of capital stock.

Compute receipts from customers using direct method. (SO 7)

8-4 Kate's Uniforms Co. has accounts receivable of $14,000 at January 1, 2004, and $24,000 at December 31, 2004. Sales revenues for 2004 were $470,000. What is the amount of cash receipts from customers in 2004?

Determine cash received in sale of equipment. (SO 6, 7)

8-5 The T-accounts for Equipment and the related Accumulated Depreciation for Stone Kitchen Equipment Company at the end of 2004 are as follows.

Equipment

Beg. bal.	80,000	Disposals	22,000
Acquisitions	41,600		
End. bal.	99,600		

Accumulated Depreciation

Disposals	5,500	Beg. bal.	44,500
		Depr.	12,000
		End. bal.	51,000

Stone Kitchen Equipment Company's income statement reported a loss on the sale of equipment of $4,900. What amount was reported on the statement of cash flows as "cash flow from sale of equipment"?

8-6 The following T-account is a summary of the cash account of Amy's Candied Apples.

Identify financing activity transactions.
(SO 5)

Cash (Summary Form)

Balance, 1/1/04	8,000		
Receipts from customers	364,000	Payments for goods	200,000
Dividends on stock investments	6,000	Payments for operating expenses	140,000
Proceeds from sale of equipment	36,000	Interest paid	10,000
Proceeds from issuance of bonds payable	200,000	Taxes paid	8,000
		Dividends paid	45,000
Balance, 12/31/04	211,000		

8-7 Presented below is financial information for two different companies.

Compute missing amounts.
(SO 1)

	Amoruso Company	Tamburri Company
Sales	$90,000	(d)
Sales returns	(a)	$ 5,000
Net sales	83,000	95,000
Cost of goods sold	56,000	(e)
Gross profit	(b)	38,000
Operating expenses	15,000	(f)
Net income	(c)	15,000

Instructions

Determine the missing amounts.

8-8 Britney Hotels Corporation had the following transactions during 2004.

Classify transactions by type of activity.
(SO 5)

1. Issued $50,000 par value common stock for cash.
2. Collected $16,000 of accounts receivable.
3. Declared and paid a cash dividend of $25,000.
4. Sold a long-term investment with a cost of $15,000 for $15,000 cash.
5. Issued $200,000 par value common stock upon conversion of bonds having a face value of $200,000.
6. Paid $18,000 on accounts payable.
7. Purchased a machine for $30,000, giving a long-term note in exchange.

Instructions

Analyze the transactions above and indicate whether each transaction resulted in a cash flow from **(a)** operating activities, **(b)** investing activities, **(c)** financing activities, or **(d)** noncash investing and financing activities.

8-9 The current sections of Depeche Ice balance sheets at December 31, 2003 and 2004, are presented below.

Prepare the operating activities section—indirect method.
(SO 6)

DEPECHE ICE
Comparative Balance Sheets (partial)
December 31

	2004	2003
Current assets		
Cash	$105,000	$ 99,000
Accounts receivable	110,000	89,000
Inventory	171,000	186,000
Prepaid expenses	27,000	32,000
Total current assets	$413,000	$406,000
Current liabilities		
Accrued expenses payable	$ 15,000	$ 5,000
Accounts payable	$ 85,000	$ 92,000
Total current liabilities	$100,000	$ 97,000

Depeche Ice's net income for 2004 was $163,000. Depreciation expense was $30,000.

Instructions

Prepare the net cash provided by operating activities section of Depeche Ice's statement of cash flows for the year ended December 31, 2004, using the indirect method.

Classify transactions by type of activity. (SO 5)

8-10 An analysis of comparative balance sheets, the current year's income statement, and the general ledger accounts of Winfrey Movies uncovered the following items. Assume all items involve cash unless there is information to the contrary.

1. Issuance of capital stock.
2. Amortization of patent.
3. Issuance of bonds for land.
4. Payment of interest on notes payable.
5. Conversion of bonds into common stock.
6. Sale of land at a loss.
7. Receipt of dividends on investment in stock.
8. Purchase of land.
9. Payment of dividends.
10. Sale of building at book value.
11. Exchange of land for patent.
12. Depreciation.
13. Redemption of bonds.
14. Receipt of interest on notes receivable.

Instructions

Indicate how the above items should be classified in the statement of cash flows using the following four major classifications: operating activity (indirect method), investing activity, financing activity, and significant noncash investing and financing activity.

Compute cash flow from operating activities—direct method. (SO 5, 7)

8-11 The 2004 accounting records of Ryder Beer Co. reveal the following transactions and events.

Payment of interest	$ 6,000	Collection of accounts receivable	$180,000
Cash sales	38,000	Payment of salaries and wages	65,000
Receipt of dividend revenue	14,000	Depreciation expense	18,000
Payment of income taxes	15,000	Proceeds from sale of aircraft	812,000
Net income	38,000	Purchase of equipment for cash	22,000
Payment of accounts payable		Loss on sale of aircraft	3,000
for merchandise	90,000	Payment of dividends	14,000
Payment for land	74,000	Payment of operating expenses	20,000

Instructions

Prepare the cash flows from operating activities section using the direct method. (Not all of the above items will be used.)

Prepare the operating activities section—indirect method. (SO 3)

8-12 The income statement of Rebecca Sherrick Company is shown below.

REBECCA SHERRICK COMPANY
Income Statement
For the Year Ended December 31, 2004

Sales		$7,100,000
Cost of goods sold		
Beginning inventory	$1,700,000	
Purchases	5,430,000	
Goods available for sale	7,130,000	
Ending inventory	1,920,000	
Cost of goods sold		5,210,000
Gross profit		1,890,000
Operating expenses		
Selling expenses	380,000	
Administrative expense	525,000	
Depreciation expense	75,000	
Amortization expense	30,000	1,010,000
Net income		$ 880,000

Additional information:

1. Accounts receivable increased $490,000 during the year.
2. Prepaid expenses increased $170,000 during the year.

3. Accounts payable to merchandise suppliers increased $40,000 during the year.
4. Accrued expenses payable decreased $180,000 during the year.

Instructions
Prepare the operating activities section of the statement of cash flows for the year ended December 31, 2004, for Rebecca Sherrick Company using the indirect method.

EXPLORING THE WEB

8-13 ***Purpose:*** Learn about the SEC.

Address: **www.sec.gov/index.html**

Steps
1. From the SEC homepage, choose **About the SEC**.

Instructions
Answer the following questions.

(a) How many enforcement actions does the SEC take each year against securities law violators? What are typical infractions?
(b) After the Depression, Congress passed the Securities Acts of 1933 and 1934 to improve investor confidence in the markets. What two commonsense notions are these laws based on?
(c) Who was the president of the United States at the time of the creation of the SEC? Who was the first SEC chairperson?

ETHICS CASE

8-14 Puebla Corporation is a medium-sized hotel corporation. It has ten stockholders, who have been paid a total of $1 million in cash dividends for eight consecutive years. The policy of the board of directors requires that in order for this dividend to be declared, net cash provided by operating activities as reported in Puebla's current year's statement of cash flows must be in excess of $1 million. President and CEO Phil Monat's job is secure so long as he produces annual operating cash flows to support the usual dividend.

At the end of the current year, controller Rick Rodgers presents President Monat with some disappointing news: The net cash provided by operating activities is calculated, by the indirect method, to be only $970,000. The president says to Rick, "We must get that amount above $1 million. Isn't there some way to increase operating cash flow by another $30,000?" Rick answers, "These figures were prepared by my assistant. I'll go back to my office and see what I can do." The president replies, "I know you won't let me down, Rick."

Upon close scrutiny of the statement of cash flows, Rick concludes that he can get the operating cash flows above $1 million by reclassifying a $60,000, two-year note payable listed in the financing activities section as "Proceeds from bank loan—$60,000." He will report the note instead as "Increase in payables—$60,000" and treat it as an adjustment of net income in the operating activities section. He returns to the president saying, "You can tell the Board to declare their usual dividend. Our net cash flow provided by operating activities is $1,030,000." "Good man, Rick! I knew I could count on you," exults the president.

Instructions
(a) Who are the stakeholders in this situation?
(b) Was there anything unethical about the president's actions? Was there anything unethical about the controller's actions?
(c) Are the board members or anyone else likely to discover the misclassification?

Remember to go back to the Navigator box on the chapter-opening page and check off your completed work.

PAYROLL

THE NAVIGATOR ✓

- Understand *Concepts for Review* ❑
- Read *Feature Story* ❑
- Scan *Study Objectives* ❑
- Read *Preview* ❑
- Read text and answer *Before You Go On* *p.* 288 ❑ *p.* 290 ❑
- Work *Demonstration Problem* ❑
- Review *Summary of Study Objectives* ❑
- Complete *Assignments* ❑

CONCEPTS FOR REVIEW

Before studying this chapter, you should know or, if necessary, review:

a. The assumptions and principles of accounting. (Ch. 2, pp. 40–45)

b. The difference between the accrual basis and the cash basis of accounting (Ch. 4, pp. 113–114)

c. The accounting and financial management departments in hospitality organizations (Ch. 2, pp. 57–63)

THE NAVIGATOR

FEATURE STORY

Payroll: The Important Cost in the Service Industry

Payroll and related fringe benefits often make up a large percentage of the cost in any hospitality business. Why? The answer is quite simple: The hospitality industry is all about service. Yes, the products are always important. However, a good meal can be ruined by a bad waiter, and a rude front-desk agent can make your $400-a-night room at a spa resort a nightmarish rather than a relaxing experience.

Service is the key to the hospitality industry. Service and product go hand in hand. Employee compensation is often the most significant expense a company incurs. **Darden Restaurants, Inc.**, reported an approximate number of 133,220 full-time associates, and its fiscal year ending May 27, 2001, indicated restaurant labor cost of more than $1.26 billion. This is 31.4 percent of sales. In other words, for every dollar of sales Darden brings in through its restaurants, more than 31 cents goes toward paying its labor to service the guests. Considering that the entire restaurant industry has more than $400 billion in sales, more than 850,000 locations, and employs more than 11.6 million people, labor cost is an important line item on any income statement.

It is also important to understand that labor cost is not limited to salary and wages. Labor cost includes benefits such as vacation, holiday pay, health insurance, dental insurance, life insurance, disability insurance, and so on. Therefore, you can see why proper accounting and control of payroll are stressed in this chapter.

Companies are also required by law to maintain payroll records for each employee, file and pay payroll taxes, and comply with numerous state and federal tax laws related to employee compensation. Accounting for payroll has become much more complex due to these regulations.

Source: National Restaurant Association 2002 Restaurant Industry Pocket Fact Book.

THE NAVIGATOR

STUDY OBJECTIVES

After studying this chapter, you should be able to

1. Discuss the objectives of internal control for payroll.
2. Compute and record the payroll for a pay period.
3. Compute and record tips under the 8 percent tip regulation.
4. Describe and record employer payroll taxes.

THE NAVIGATOR

PREVIEW OF CHAPTER 9

What you see from the feature story is the magnitude of the cost of labor in the restaurant business. Imagine adding the lodging business, the casino business, the club business, the tourism business, and other hospitality enterprises, and you get the picture. In this chapter, we will discuss the reasons for payroll and its internal control mechanisms, determination of payroll with all the rules and regulations, recording and payment of payroll of regular and tipped employees, and the recording and filing of payroll taxes.

The content and organization of Chapter 9 are as follows:

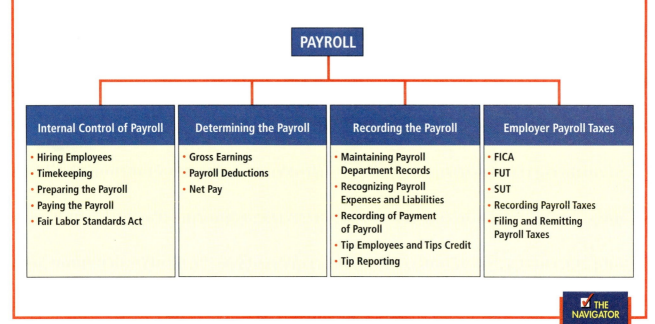

PAYROLL

Internal Control of Payroll	Determining the Payroll	Recording the Payroll	Employer Payroll Taxes
• Hiring Employees • Timekeeping • Preparing the Payroll • Paying the Payroll • Fair Labor Standards Act	• Gross Earnings • Payroll Deductions • Net Pay	• Maintaining Payroll Department Records • Recognizing Payroll Expenses and Liabilities • Recording of Payment of Payroll • Tip Employees and Tips Credit • Tip Reporting	• FICA • FUT • SUT • Recording Payroll Taxes • Filing and Remitting Payroll Taxes

THE NAVIGATOR

PAYROLL DEFINED

The term *payroll* pertains to both salaries and wages. Managerial, administrative, and sales personnel are generally paid **salaries**. Salaries are often expressed in terms of a specified amount per month or per year rather than an hourly rate. For example, the faculty and administrative personnel at the college or university you are attending are paid salaries. In contrast, wait staff, line cooks, room attendants, and bell staff are normally paid **wages**. Wages are based on a rate per hour or on a piecework basis (such as per room cleaned). Frequently, the terms *salaries* and *wages* are used interchangeably.

Payroll does not apply to payments made for services of professionals such as certified public accountants, attorneys, and architects. Such professionals are independent contractors rather than salaried employees. Payments to them are called **fees**, rather than salaries or wages. This distinction is important because government regulations relating to the payment and reporting of payroll taxes apply only to employees.

INTERNAL CONTROL OF PAYROLL

STUDY OBJECTIVE 1

Discuss the objectives of internal control for payroll.

Internal control will be discussed in depth in Chapter 10. As applied to payrolls, the objectives of internal control are (1) to safeguard company assets against unauthorized payments of payrolls, and (2) to ensure the accuracy and reliability of the accounting records pertaining to payrolls.

Irregularities often result if internal control is lax. Overstating hours, using unauthorized pay rates, adding fictitious employees to the payroll, continuing terminated employees on the payroll, and distributing duplicate payroll checks are all methods of stealing from a company. Moreover, inaccurate records will result in incorrect paychecks, financial statements, and payroll tax returns.

TECHNOLOGY IN ACTION

No, it is not Halloween, but don't get spooked by a ghost employee! In the old days, when businesses were small and payroll was given in cash or paychecks were given to employees in person, this was not a problem. With technology and direct deposits, ghost employees seem to surface. Who are ghost employees? These are people who do not exist in your casino, cruise ships, theme parks, and hotels. They are fictitious employees that are created or are terminated or deceased employees not removed from payroll records by the perpetrator. This dishonest person continues to collect and cash paychecks for people who do not exist. What can be done? Detecting fraud takes a team. Always check bank account numbers, Social Security or identification numbers, addresses, deductions, work location and department, and the like. It may not be a bad idea to also look at sick leave and vacation. Even ghosts need a break. If someone on your payroll is not taking the normal level of sick leave and vacations, you either have a very dedicated employee or a dead one. Either way, it is good for you to find out so you can reward the former or delete the latter.

Payroll activities involve four functions: hiring employees, timekeeping, preparing the payroll, and paying the payroll. For effective internal control, these four functions should be assigned to different departments or individuals. To illustrate these functions, we will examine the case of Academy Waterparks and one of its employees, Mark Jordan.

HIRING EMPLOYEES

The human resources (personnel) department is responsible for posting job openings, screening and interviewing applicants, and hiring employees. From a control standpoint, this department provides significant documentation and authorization. When an employee is hired, the human resources department prepares an authorization form. The one used by Academy Waterparks for Mark Jordan is shown in Illustration 9-1.

Hiring Employees

Human Resources department documents and authorizes employment.

The authorization form is sent to the payroll department, where it is used to place the new employee on the payroll. A chief concern of the human resources department is ensuring the accuracy of this form. The reason is quite simple: one of the most common types of payroll frauds is adding fictitious employees to the payroll.

The human resources department is also responsible for authorizing changes in employment status. Specifically, they must authorize (1) changes in pay rates and (2) terminations of employment. Every authorization should be in writing, and a copy of the change in status should be sent to the payroll department. Notice in Illustration 9-1 on page 276 that Jordan received a pay increase of $2 per hour.

TIMEKEEPING

Another area in which internal control is important is timekeeping. Hourly employees are usually required to record time worked by punching a time clock. Times of arrival and departure are automatically recorded by the employee by in-

Illustration 9-1

Authorization form prepared by the human resources department

ACADEMY WATERPARKS

Employee Name: Jordan, (LAST) Mark (FIRST) (MI) Starting Date: 9/01/01

Classification: Skilled-Level 10 Social Security No.: 329-36-9547

Department: Guest Relations Division: Entertainment

NEW HIRE	Classification: Guest Service Agent Salary Grade: Level 10 Trans. from Temp. ☐ Rate $ 10.00 per hour Bonus N/A Non-exempt ☒ Exempt ☐
RATE CHANGE	New Rate $ 12.00 Effective Date 9/1/03 Present Rate $ 10.00 Merit ☒ Promotion ☐ Decrease ☐ Other ____ Previous Increase Date None Amount $ ____ per ____ Type ____
SEPARATION	Resignation ☐ Discharge ☐ Retirement ☐ Reason ____ Leave of absence ☐ From ____ to ____ Type ____ Last Day Worked ____
APPROVALS	BEW — BRANCH OR DEPT. MANAGER — 9/1/03 DATE EMW — DIVISION V.P. — 9-1-03 DATE James E. Speer — PERSONNEL DEPARTMENT

Timekeeping

Supervisors monitor hours worked through time cards and time reports.

serting a time card into the clock. Mark Jordan's time card is shown in Illustration 9-2 on page 277.

In large companies, time clock procedures are often monitored by a supervisor or security guard to make sure an employee punches only one card. At the end of the pay period, each employee's supervisor approves the hours shown by signing the time card. When overtime hours are involved, approval by a supervisor is usually mandatory. This guards against unauthorized overtime. The approved time cards are then sent to the payroll department. For salaried employees, a manually prepared weekly or monthly time report kept by a supervisor may be used to record time worked.

Preparing the Payroll

Two (or more) employees verify payroll amounts; supervisor approves.

PREPARING THE PAYROLL

The payroll is prepared in the payroll department on the basis of two inputs: (1) human resources department authorizations and (2) approved time cards. Numerous calculations are involved in determining gross wages and payroll deductions. Therefore, a second payroll department employee, working independently, verifies all calculated amounts, and a payroll department supervisor then approves the payroll. The payroll department is also responsible for preparing (but not signing) payroll checks, maintaining payroll records, and preparing payroll tax returns.

Paying the Payroll

Treasurer signs and distributes checks.

PAYING THE PAYROLL

The payroll is paid by the treasurer's department. **Payment by check minimizes the risk of loss from theft, and the endorsed check provides proof of payment.** For good internal control, payroll checks should be prenumbered, and all checks should be accounted for. All checks must be signed by the treasurer (or a des-

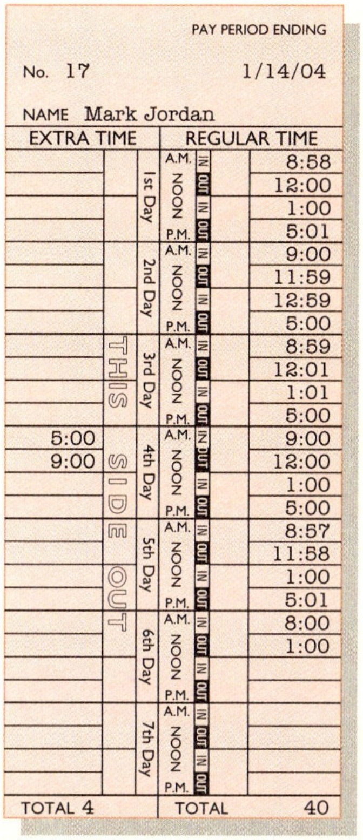
PAY PERIOD ENDING
No. 17 1/14/04
NAME Mark Jordan

EXTRA TIME			REGULAR TIME
		1st Day	8:58
			12:00
			1:00
			5:01
		2nd Day	9:00
			11:59
			12:59
			5:00
		3rd Day	8:59
			12:01
			1:01
			5:00
5:00		4th Day	9:00
9:00			12:00
			1:00
			5:00
		5th Day	8:57
			11:58
			1:00
			5:01
		6th Day	8:00
			1:00
		7th Day	
TOTAL 4			TOTAL 40

THIS SIDE OUT

Illustration 9-2

Time card

ignated agent). Distribution of the payroll checks to employees should be controlled by the treasurer's department. Checks may be distributed by the treasurer or paymaster.

Occasionally the payroll is paid in currency. In such cases it is customary to have a second person count the cash in each pay envelope. The paymaster should obtain a signed receipt from the employee upon payment. If alleged discrepancies arise, adequate safeguards have been established to protect each party involved.

FAIR LABOR STANDARDS ACT

The **Fair Labor Standards Act** was instituted in 1938 and was amended with additional provisions in 1977. It is commonly known as *the Act* or **FLSA**, and it provides minimum standards for both wages and overtime entitlement. It also spells out administrative procedures by which covered work time must be compensated. Included in the Act are other provisions such as equal pay and child labor. Although you might think that an act or any law applies to everyone, the FSLA exempts specified employees or groups of employees from certain of its provisions. According to the Act, employees can be covered by the law under the *enterprise coverage* or *individual coverage*. Therefore, in the hospitality industry, if an enterprise has two or fewer employees and less than $500,000 a year in business, those two employees will not be covered. As you can see, the Act does apply to most hospitality businesses.

The FLSA Act began applying to employees of the U.S. federal government in 1974. The U.S. Office of Personnel Management works with federal agencies to apply the Act to employees of the U.S. federal government.

As mentioned, one item the FLSA regulates is overtime. For the hospitality industry, this means all employees covered by the Act will get one and a half times their regular pay for all hours worked over 40 hours per week. The FLSA, however, does not require extra pay for Saturdays and Sundays, and makes no special provisions for vacation pay, sick pay, holiday pay, or severances. Of course certain union contracts or states have established more advantageous overtime provisions than those stipulated by the FSLA, and these are the ones that will be in effect. This also holds true for conflicting state and federal regulations. In addition, the FLSA has certain rules such as requiring employers to maintain records of worked time of hourly employees. The form of recordkeeping used is up to the employer. In today's technologically advanced world, some businesses have replaced signing in and out on time cards with a fingerprint as a record of clocking in and out.

DETERMINING THE PAYROLL

STUDY OBJECTIVE 2

Compute and record the payroll for a pay period.

Determining the payroll involves computing three amounts: (1) gross earnings, (2) payroll deductions, and (3) net pay.

GROSS EARNINGS

Gross earnings is the total compensation earned by an employee. It consists of wages or salaries, plus any bonuses and commissions.

Total *wages* for an employee are determined by multiplying the hours worked by the hourly rate of pay. In addition to the hourly pay rate, most companies are required by law to pay hourly workers a minimum of one and a half times the regular hourly rate for overtime work in excess of 8 hours per day or 40 hours per week. In addition, many employers pay overtime rates for work done at night, on weekends, and on holidays.

HELPFUL HINT
The law that governs pay rates is the Federal Fair Labor Standards Act. It applies to all companies involved in interstate commerce.

Mark Jordan's time card shows that he worked 44 hours for the weekly pay period ending January 14. The computation of his gross earnings (total wages) is shown in Illustration 9-3.

Illustration 9-3

Computation of total wages

Type of Pay	Hours	×	Rate	=	Gross Earnings
Regular	40	×	$12.00	=	$480.00
Overtime	4	×	18.00	=	72.00
Total wages					**$552.00**

This computation assumes that Jordan receives one and a half times his regular hourly rate ($12.00 × 1.5) for his overtime hours. Union contracts often require that overtime rates be as much as twice the regular rates.

The *salary* for an employee is generally based on a monthly or yearly rate. These rates are then prorated to the payroll periods used by the company. Most executive and administrative positions are salaried. Federal law does not require overtime pay for employees in such positions.

ETHICS NOTE
Bonuses often reward outstanding individual performance; but successful corporations also need considerable teamwork. A challenge is to motivate individuals while preventing an unethical employee from taking another's idea for his or her own advantage.

Many companies have **bonus** agreements for management personnel and other employees. Bonus arrangements may be based on such factors as increased sales or net income. Bonuses may be paid in cash and/or by granting executives and employees the opportunity to acquire shares of company stock at favorable prices (called *stock option plans*).

PAYROLL DEDUCTIONS

As anyone who has received a paycheck knows, gross earnings are usually very different from the amount actually received. The difference is due to **payroll deductions**. Such deductions do not result in payroll tax expense to the employer. The employer is merely a collection agent, and it subsequently transfers the amounts deducted to the government and designated recipients. Payroll deductions may be mandatory or voluntary. Mandatory deductions are required by law and consist of FICA taxes and income taxes. Voluntary deductions are at the option of the employee. Illustration 9-4 summarizes the types of payroll deductions.

Illustration 9-4

Payroll deductions

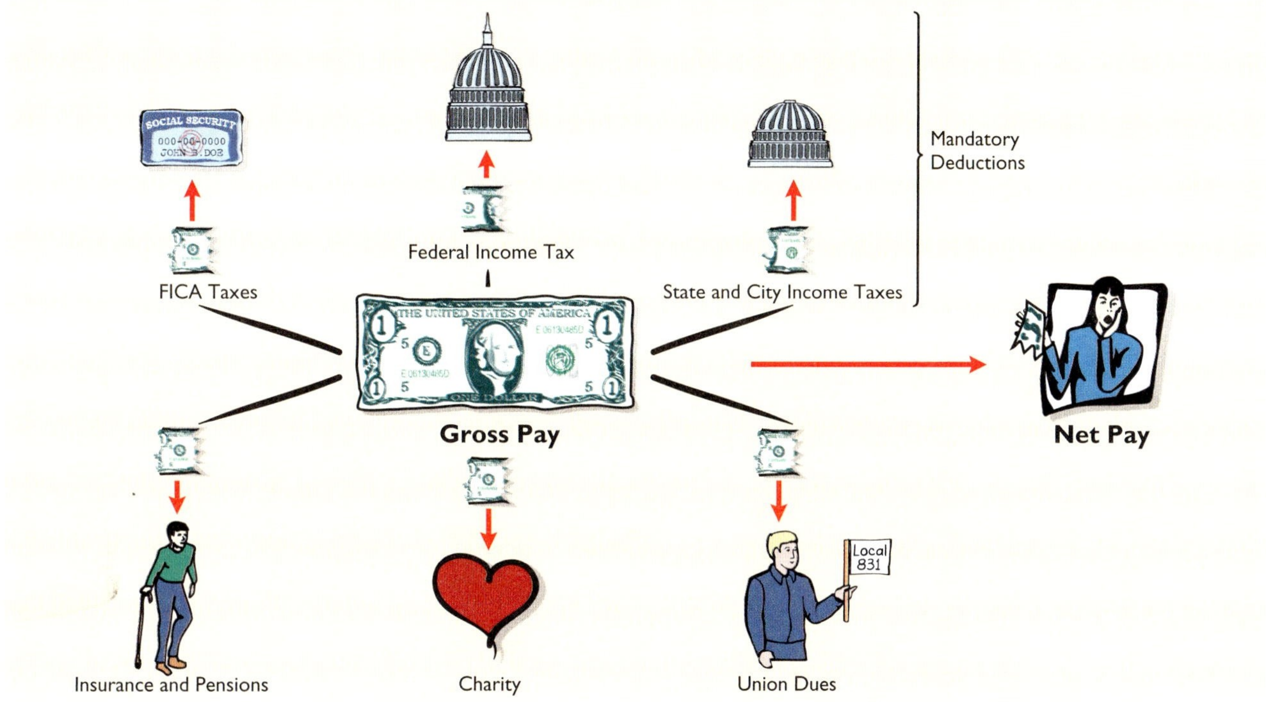

FICA Taxes

In 1937 Congress enacted the Federal Insurance Contribution Act (FICA). **FICA taxes are designed to provide workers with supplemental retirement, employment disability, and medical benefits.** In 1965, benefits were expanded to include Medicare for individuals over 65 years of age. The benefits are financed by a tax levied on employees' earnings. FICA taxes are commonly referred to as *Social Security taxes*.

The tax rate and the tax base for FICA taxes are set by Congress. When FICA taxes were first imposed, the rate was 1 percent on the first $3,000 of gross earnings, or a maximum of $30 per year. The rate and base have changed dramatically since that time! In 2002, the rate was 7.65 percent (6.2% Social Security plus 1.45% Medicare) on the first $84,900 of gross earnings for each employee.[1] For purpose

[1]The Medicare provision also includes a tax of 1.45 percent on gross earnings in excess of $84,900. In the interest of simplification, we ignore this 1.45 percent charge in our end-of-chapter assignment material. We assume zero FICA withholdings on gross earnings above $65,000.

of illustration in this chapter, we will assume a rate of 8 percent on the first $65,000 of gross earnings, or a maximum of $5,200. Using the 8 percent rate, the FICA withholding for Jordan for the weekly pay period ending January 14 is $44.16 (wages of $552 × 8%).

Income Taxes

Under the U.S. pay-as-you-go system of federal income taxes, employers are required to withhold income taxes from employees each pay period. The amount to be withheld is determined by three variables: (1) the employee's gross earnings; (2) the number of allowances claimed by the employee; and (3) the length of the pay period. The number of allowances claimed typically includes the employee, his or her spouse, and other dependents. To indicate to the Internal Revenue Service the number of allowances claimed, the employee must complete an **Employee's Withholding Allowance Certificate (Form W-4)**. As shown in Illustration 9-5, Mark Jordan claims two allowances on his W-4.

Illustration 9-5

W-4 form

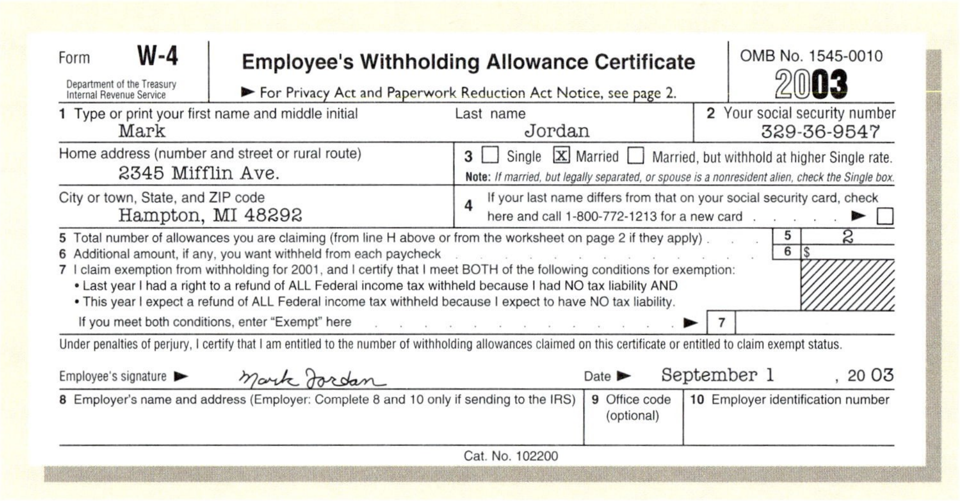
Form **W-4** Employee's Withholding Allowance Certificate OMB No. 1545-0010 **2003**
Department of the Treasury Internal Revenue Service ► For Privacy Act and Paperwork Reduction Act Notice, see page 2.
1 Type or print your first name and middle initial: Mark Last name: Jordan 2 Your social security number: 329-36-9547
Home address (number and street or rural route): 2345 Mifflin Ave.
3 ☐ Single ☒ Married ☐ Married, but withhold at higher Single rate.
Note: If married, but legally separated, or spouse is a nonresident alien, check the Single box.
City or town, State, and ZIP code: Hampton, MI 48292
4 If your last name differs from that on your social security card, check here and call 1-800-772-1213 for a new card ► ☐
5 Total number of allowances you are claiming (from line H above or from the worksheet on page 2 if they apply) 5 2
6 Additional amount, if any, you want withheld from each paycheck 6 $
7 I claim exemption from withholding for 2001, and I certify that I meet BOTH of the following conditions for exemption:
• Last year I had a right to a refund of ALL Federal income tax withheld because I had NO tax liability AND
• This year I expect a refund of ALL Federal income tax withheld because I expect to have NO tax liability.
If you meet both conditions, enter "Exempt" here ► 7
Under penalties of perjury, I certify that I am entitled to the number of withholding allowances claimed on this certificate or entitled to claim exempt status.
Employee's signature ► Mark Jordan Date ► September 1, 20 03
8 Employer's name and address (Employer: Complete 8 and 10 only if sending to the IRS) 9 Office code (optional) 10 Employer identification number
Cat. No. 102200

Withholding tables furnished by the Internal Revenue Service indicate the amount of income tax to be withheld. Withholding amounts are based on gross wages and the number of allowances claimed. Separate tables are provided for weekly, biweekly, semimonthly, and monthly pay periods. The withholding tax table for Mark Jordan (assuming he earns $552 per week) is shown in Illustration 9-6. For a weekly salary of $552 with two allowances, the income tax to be withheld is $49.

Most states (and some cities) also require *employers* to withhold income taxes from employees' earnings. As a rule, the amounts withheld are a percentage (specified in the state revenue code) of the amount withheld for the federal income tax. Or they may be a specified percentage of the employee's earnings. For the sake of simplicity, we have assumed that Jordan's wages are subject to state income taxes of 2 percent, or $11.04 (2% × $552) per week.

There is no limit on the amount of gross earnings subject to income tax withholdings. In fact, the higher the earnings, the higher the amount of taxes withheld.

Other Deductions

Employees may voluntarily authorize withholdings for charitable, retirement, and other purposes. All voluntary deductions from gross earnings should be author-

Illustration 9-6

Withholding tax table

MARRIED Persons — **WEEKLY** Payroll Period
(For Wages Paid in 2004)

If the wages are –		And the number of withholding allowances claimed is –										
At least	But less than	0	1	2	3	4	5	6	7	8	9	10
		The amount of income tax to be withheld is –										
490	**500**	56	48	40	32	24	17	9	1	0	0	0
500	**510**	57	49	42	34	26	18	10	3	0	0	0
510	**520**	59	51	43	35	27	20	12	4	0	0	0
520	**530**	60	52	45	37	29	21	13	6	0	0	0
530	**540**	62	54	46	38	30	23	15	7	0	0	0
540	**550**	63	55	48	40	32	24	16	9	1	0	0
550	**560**	65	57	**49**	41	33	26	18	10	2	0	0
560	**570**	66	58	51	43	35	27	19	12	4	0	0
570	**580**	68	60	52	44	36	29	21	13	5	0	0
580	**590**	69	61	54	46	38	30	22	15	7	0	0
590	**600**	71	63	55	47	39	32	24	16	8	1	0
600	**610**	72	64	57	49	41	33	25	18	10	2	0
610	**620**	74	66	58	50	42	35	27	19	11	4	0
620	**630**	75	67	60	52	44	36	28	21	13	5	0
630	**640**	77	69	61	53	45	38	30	22	14	7	0
640	**650**	78	70	63	55	47	39	31	24	16	8	0
650	**660**	80	72	64	56	48	41	33	25	17	10	2
660	**670**	81	73	66	58	50	42	34	27	19	11	3
670	**680**	83	75	67	59	51	44	36	28	20	13	5
680	**690**	84	76	69	61	53	45	37	30	22	14	6

ized in writing by the employee. The authorization(s) may be made individually or as part of a group plan. Deductions for charitable organizations, such as the United Fund, or for financial arrangements, such as U.S. savings bonds and repayment of loans from company credit unions, are made individually. Deductions for union dues, health and life insurance, and pension plans are often made on a group basis. We will assume that Jordan has weekly voluntary deductions of $10 for the United Fund and $5 for union dues.

NET PAY

Net pay is determined by subtracting payroll deductions from gross earnings. For Mark Jordan, net pay for the pay period is $432.80, computed in Illustration 9-7.

ALTERNATIVE TERMINOLOGY
Net pay is also called *take-home pay.*

Illustration 9-7

Computation of net pay

Gross earnings		$552.00
Payroll deductions:		
FICA taxes	$44.16	
Federal income taxes	49.00	
State income taxes	11.04	
United Fund	10.00	
Union dues	5.00	119.20
Net pay		**$432.80**

Assuming that Mark Jordan's wages for each week during the year are $552, total wages for the year are $28,704 (52 × $552). Thus, all of Jordan's wages are subject to FICA tax during the year. Let's assume that Jordan's department head earns $1,350 per week, or $70,200 for the year. Since only the first $65,000 is subject to

FICA taxes, the maximum FICA withholdings on the department head's earnings would be $5,200 ($65,000 × 8%).

RECORDING THE PAYROLL

Recording the payroll involves maintaining payroll department records, recognizing payroll expenses and liabilities, and recording payment of the payroll.

MAINTAINING PAYROLL DEPARTMENT RECORDS

To comply with state and federal laws, an employer must keep a cumulative record of each employee's gross earnings, deductions, and net pay during the year. The record that provides this information is the **employee earnings record**. Mark Jordan's employee earnings record is shown in Illustration 9-8.

Illustration 9-8

Employee earnings record

ACADEMY WATERPARKS
Employee Earnings Record
For the Year 2004

Name	Mark Jordan	**Address**	2345 Mifflin Ave.
Social Security Number	329-36-9547		Hampton, Michigan 48292
Date of Birth	December 24, 1962	**Telephone**	555-238-9051
Date Employed	September 1, 2001	**Date Employment Ended**	
Sex	Male	**Exemptions**	2
Single		**Married**	x

2004 Period Ending	Total Hours	Gross Earnings: Regular	Overtime	Total	Cumulative	Deductions: FICA	Fed. Inc. Tax	State Inc. Tax	United Fund	Union Dues	Total	Payment: Net Amount	Check No.
1/7	42	480.00	36.00	516.00	516.00	41.28	43.00	10.32	10.00	5.00	109.60	406.40	974
1/14	44	480.00	72.00	552.00	1,068.00	44.16	49.00	11.04	10.00	5.00	119.20	432.80	1028
1/21	43	480.00	54.00	534.00	1,602.00	42.72	46.00	10.68	10.00	5.00	114.40	419.60	1077
1/28	42	480.00	36.00	516.00	2,118.00	41.28	43.00	10.32	10.00	5.00	109.60	406.40	1133
Jan. Total		1,920.00	198.00	2,118.00		169.44	181.00	42.36	40.00	20.00	452.80	1,665.20	

A separate earnings record is kept for each employee. It is updated after each pay period. The cumulative payroll data on the earnings record are used by the employer to: (1) determine when an employee has earned the maximum earnings subject to FICA taxes, (2) file state and federal payroll tax returns (as explained later in the chapter), and (3) provide each employee with a statement of gross earnings and tax withholdings for the year. Illustration 9-12 on page 287 shows this statement.

In addition to employee earnings records, many companies find it useful to prepare a **payroll register**. This record accumulates the gross earnings, deductions, and net pay by employee for each pay period. It provides the documentation for preparing a paycheck for each employee. Academy's payroll register is presented in Illustration 9-9. It shows the data for Mark Jordan in the wages section. In this example, Academy Waterparks' total weekly payroll is $17,210, as shown in the gross earnings column.

Illustration 9-9

Payroll register

ACADEMY WATERPARKS
Payroll Register
For the Week Ending January 14, 2004

		Earnings			Deductions						Paid		Accounts Debited	
Employee	**Total Hours**	**Regular**	**Over-time**	**Gross**	**FICA**	**Federal Income Tax**	**State Income Tax**	**United Fund**	**Union Dues**	**Total**	**Net Pay**	**Check No.**	**Office Salaries Expense**	**Wages Expense**
Office Salaries														
Arnold, Patricia	40	580.00		580.00	46.40	61.00	11.60	15.00		134.00	446.00	998	580.00	
Canton, Matthew	40	590.00		590.00	47.20	63.00	11.80	20.00		142.00	448.00	999	590.00	
Mueller, William	40	530.00		530.00	42.40	54.00	10.60	11.00		118.00	412.0	1000	530.00	
Subtotal		5,200.00		5,200.00	416.00	1,090.00	104.00	120.00		1,730.00	3,470.00		5,200.00	
Wages														
Bennett, Robin	42	480.00	36.00	516.00	41.28	43.00	10.32	18.00	5.00	117.60	398.40	1025		516.00
Jordan, Mark	**44**	**480.00**	**72.00**	**552.00**	**44.16**	**49.00**	**11.04**	**10.00**	**5.00**	**119.20**	**432.80**	**1028**		**552.00**
Milroy, Lee	43	480.00	54.00	534.00	42.72	46.00	10.68	10.00	5.00	114.40	419.60	1029		534.00
Subtotal		11,000.00	1,010.00	12,010.00	960.80	2,400.00	240.20	301.50	115.00	4,017.50	7,992.50			12,010.00
Total		16,200.00	1,010.00	17,210.00	1,376.80	3,490.00	344.20	421.50	115.00	5,747.50	11,462.50		5,200.00	12,010.00

Note that this record is a listing of each employee's payroll data for the pay period. In some companies, a payroll register is a journal or book of original entry. Postings are made from it directly to ledger accounts. In other companies, the payroll register is a memorandum record that provides the data for a general journal entry and subsequent posting to the ledger accounts. At Academy Waterparks, the latter procedure is followed.

RECOGNIZING PAYROLL EXPENSES AND LIABILITIES

From the payroll register in Illustration 9-9, a journal entry is made to record the payroll. For the week ending January 14 the entry is:

Jan. 14	Office Salaries Expense	5,200.00	
	Wages Expense	12,010.00	
	FICA Taxes Payable		1,376.80
	Federal Income Taxes Payable		3,490.00
	State Income Taxes Payable		344.20
	United Fund Payable		421.50
	Union Dues Payable		115.00
	Salaries and Wages Payable		11,462.50
	(To record payroll for the week ending January 14)		

A	=	L	+	SE
		+1,376.80		−5,200.00
		+3,490.00		−12,010.00
		+344.20		
		+421.50		
		+115.00		
		+11,462.50		

Specific liability accounts are credited for the mandatory and voluntary deductions made during the pay period. In the example, debits to Office Salaries and Wages Expense are used for gross earnings because office workers are on a salary and other employees are paid on an hourly rate. In other companies, there may be debits to other accounts such as Store Salaries or Sales Salaries. The amount credited to Salaries and Wages Payable is the sum of the individual checks the employees will receive.

RECORDING PAYMENT OF THE PAYROLL

Payment by check is made either from the employer's regular bank account or a payroll bank account. Each paycheck is usually accompanied by a detachable **statement of earnings** document. This shows the employee's gross earnings, payroll deductions, and net pay for the period and for the year to date. The Academy Waterparks uses its regular bank account for payroll checks. The paycheck and statement of earnings for Mark Jordan are shown in Illustration 9-10.

Illustration 9-10

Paycheck and statement of earnings

AW

ACADEMY WATERPARKS
19 Center St.
Hampton, MI 48291

No. 1028

January 14, 2004 62-1113/610

Pay to the order of Mark Jordan $ 432.80

Four Hundred Thirty-two and 80/100 Dollars

City Bank & Trust
P.O. Box 3000
Hampton, MI 48291

For Payroll Randall E. Barnes

0032447" 7 6 0

DETACH AND RETAIN THIS PORTION FOR YOUR RECORDS

NAME				SOC. SEC. NO.		EMPL. NUMBER	NO. EXEMP	PAY PERIOD ENDING
Mark Jordan				329-36-9547			2	1/14/04
REG. HRS.	O.T. HRS.	OTH. HRS. (1)	OTH. HRS. (2)	REG. EARNINGS	O.T. EARNINGS	OTH. EARNINGS (1)	OTH. EARNINGS (2)	GROSS
40	4			480.00	72.00			$552.00
FED. W/H TAX	FICA	STATE TAX	LOCAL TAX	OTHER DEDUCTIONS (1)	(2)	(3)	(4)	NET PAY
49.00	44.16	11.04		10.00	5.00			$432.80

YEAR TO DATE								
FED. W/H TAX	FICA	STATE TAX	LOCAL TAX	OTHER DEDUCTIONS (1)	(2)	(3)	(4)	NET PAY
92.00	85.44	21.36		20.00	10.00			$839.20

HELPFUL HINT

Do any of the income tax liabilities result in payroll tax expense for the employer? Answer: No. The employer is acting only as a collection agent for the government.

Following payment of the payroll, the check numbers are entered in the payroll register. The entry to record payment of the payroll for Academy Waterparks is as follows.

A	=	L	+	SE
		−11,462.50		

−11,462.50

Jan. 14	Salaries and Wages Payable	11,462.50	
	Cash		11,462.50
	(To record payment of payroll)		

When currency is used in payment, one check is prepared for the payroll's total amount of net pay. This check is then cashed, and the coins and currency are inserted in individual pay envelopes for disbursement to individual employees.

TECHNOLOGY IN ACTION

In addition to supplying the entry to record the payroll, the output for a computerized payroll system would include (1) payroll checks, (2) a payroll check register sorted by check and department, and (3) updated employee earnings records. Those employee records become the source for monthly, quarterly, and annual reporting of wages to taxing agencies.

TIPPED EMPLOYEES

Although other industries pay straight wages to their employees, the hospitality industry has regular wage employees and tipped employees. It is said that TIPS is the acronym for "To insure prompt service." As a tipped employee, you earn your wage from two sources: a specified rate from your employer and tips from guests. All income earned by an employee, whether it is a wage from the employer or tips from guests, is taxable. Employers also need to record tip amounts carefully as such amounts affect the amount of tax the business will pay on behalf of the employee.

What is considered a tip? In a restaurant, any amount left by a guest for the wait staff or any service charge on a bill distributed to the waitstaff is defined as a tip. As for wages, as mentioned earlier, the FLSA specifies the amount of minimum wage. The Act also allows an employer to take a $3.02 tip credit on tipped employees. In other words, if the minimum wage set by the Act is $5.15 an hour, an employer need only pay a tipped employee $2.13 an hour as long as the actual tips earned by the employee are not less than the FLSA maximum allowable tip credit. For example, if a tipped employee earns only $2.00 in tips rather than the allowable credit of $3.02, the employer has to pay the employee $3.15 for the hour. Thus, with the tip of $2.00 and the employer's wage of $3.15, the employee will still make the minimum wage of $5.15 an hour.

As mentioned, the FLSA is strictly federal. Many states have variations of this $3.02 credit. The Department of Labor Web site does offer a minimum wage and tip credit table that spells out the details of each state (www.dol.gov). Since this information changes according to the state and federal legislatures, please refer to the latest information on the Internet as guidelines.

TIP REPORTING

Obviously, not all food and beverage operations are the same. You would likely tip in a full-service restaurant but would not leave a tip if you are picking up fast food at a drive-through window. To address these differences, the 1982 **Tax Equity and Fiscal Responsibility Act (TEFRA)** instituted regulations guiding food and beverage operations on tip reporting requirements. This 8 percent regulation means that if a tipped employee has gross sales of $100, then it is expected that he or she will at least earn 8 percent of that, or $8.00, in tips; and thus will have to report at least $8.00 as part of his or her wages.

This 8 percent rule applies to all foodservices except cafeteria and fast-food operations. It also has other provisions to make sure that certain items not usually tipped by guests do not count as gross sales, including takeout orders, complimentary snacks at the bar area, state and local taxes, and a few others. The complimentary items, however, do apply to casinos, because it is customary that guests in casinos will tip for such service. This rule is established so that the true wage earned by a tipped employee can be calculated and the appropriate taxes are assessed to both the employee and the employer. Although it is customary for guests to tip about 15 percent of the bill, some will pay more, while others will pay less. As the TEFRA rule says, tipped employees need to report only 8 percent of the tips.

In 2002, the U.S. Supreme Court passed a ruling that holds businesses responsible for the shortfall of tip collection. The case resulted when an audit revealed employees at a Californian restaurant did not report at least 8 percent of the tips by customers left on credit cards receipts, let alone the 8 percent collected in the form of cash. If a food and beverage operation reports under the 8 percent regulation, it must file an 8027, the Employer's Annual Information Return of Tip Income and Allocated Tips. If you are an owner or manager of a food and beverage establishment, consult the IRS. An agent will be pleased to visit your operation, at no cost to you, and educate your employees on the requirements and forms they need to file.

What happens if employees did not report at least 8 percent of the legitimate gross receipts during a particular period? Do you as an employer need to do anything? Absolutely! It is the employer's responsibility to determine the amount of the shortfall that no reported and allocate such amount to the directly tipped employees. The two methods to determine this are the gross receipts method and the hours worked method.

The **gross receipts method** adds all gross receipts of each employee and multiplies the total by 8 percent. This is the amount the employer should report. The difference between this amount and the amount reported by the employee is the shortfall. Each employee's gross receipts are then divided into the total gross re-

Illustration 9-11

The Gross Receipts Method

Step 1. Determining the amount of shortfall to be allocated

Employees	Gross Receipts	Tips Reported	
A	$ 31,500	$ 2,125	
B	33,450	2,000	
C	30,050	2,260	
D	24,500	1,400	
E	30,500	2,105	
	$150,000	$ 9,890	
Indirectly Tipped Employees		$ 750	
Total actual tips reported		$10,640	
Total tips according to 8% rule ($150,000 × 8%)			$12,000.00
Total actual tips reported			$ 10,640
Shortfall to be allocated			$ 1,360.00
Total tips according to 8% rule			$12,000.00
Tips reported by indirectly tipped employees			$ 750.00
Tips should have been reported by tipped employees			$11,250.00

Step 2. Determining individual shortfall amounts

Employee	Tips that Should Have Been Reported		Gross Receipts Ratios		Employee's Share of the 8%		Actual Reported		Shortfall portion
A	$11,250.00	×	31,500/150,000	=	$ 2,362.50	−	$2,125	=	$ 237.50
B	$11,250.00	×	33,450/150,000	=	$ 2,508.75	−	$2,000	=	$ 508.75
C	$11,250.00	×	30,050/150,000	=	$ 2,253.75	−	$2,260	=	$ —
D	$11,250.00	×	24,500/150,000	=	$ 1,837.50	−	$1,400	=	$ 437.50
E	$11,250.00	×	30,500/150,000	=	$ 2,287.50	−	$2,105	=	$ 182.50
			Total		$11,250.00		$9,890		$1,366.25 Total shortfall

Step 3. Allocation of shortfall

Employee	Shortfall Ratio		Shortfall to be Allocated		Tip Allocation
A	237.5/1,366.25	×	1,360	=	$ 236.41
B	508.75/1,366.25	×	1,360	=	$ 506.42
C	0	×	1,360	=	$ —
D	437.5/1,366.25	×	1,360	=	$ 435.50
E	182.5/1,366.25	×	1,360	=	$ 181.67
					$1,360.00

ceipts to obtain a weighted ratio. The ratio is multiplied by the employee's 8 percent amount to determine the part of the 8 percent amount that should be reported by each employee. This is then compared to the amounts actually reported by each employee. For those employees who report at least their fair share of 8 percent, there is no allocation. For those who report less than their fair share of 8 percent, an allocation will be made to their paycheck and taxes will be assessed accordingly.

The **hours worked method** is essentially the same in terms of mathematic procedures. The difference is the use of total hours worked rather than the gross receipts as the benchmark for calculation. Illustrations 9-11 and 9-12 are examples of the gross receipts method and the hours worked method, respectively.

Illustration 9-12

The Hours Worked Method

Step 1. Determining the amount of shortfall to be allocated

Employees	Hours Worked	Tips Reported	
A	40	$ 2,125	
B	45	2,000	
C	40	2,260	
D	30	1,400	
E	30	2,105	
	185	$ 9,890	
Indirectly Tipped Employees		750	
Total actual tips reported		$10,640	
Total tips according to 8% rule ($150,000 × 8%)			$12,000.00
Total actual tips reported			$ 10,640
Shortfall to be allocated			$ 1,360.00
Total tips according to 8% rule			$12,000.00
Tips reported by indirectly tipped employees			$ 750.00
Tips should have been reported by tipped employees			$11,250.00

Step 2. Determining individual shortfall amounts

Employee	Tips that Should Have Been Reported	Gross Receipts Ratios		Employee's Share of the 8%		Actual Reported		Shortfall portion
A	$11,250.00 ×	40/185	=	$ 2,432.43	−	$2,125	=	$ 307.43
B	$11,250.00 ×	45/185	=	$ 2,736.49	−	$2,000	=	$ 736.49
C	$11,250.00 ×	40/185	=	$ 2,432.43	−	$2,260	=	$ —
D	$11,250.00 ×	30/185	=	$ 1,824.32	−	$1,400	=	$ 424.32
E	$11,250.00 ×	30/185	=	$ 1,824.32	−	$2,105	=	$ —
		Total		$11,250.00		$9,890		$1,468.24 Total shortfall

Step 3. Allocation of shortfall

Employee	Shortfall Ratio	Shortfall to be Allocated		Tip Allocation
A	307.42/1,468.24 ×	1,360	=	$ 284.77
B	763.49/1,468.24 ×	1,360	=	$ 682.19
C	0 ×	1,360	=	$ —
D	424.32/1,468.24 ×	1,360	=	$ 393.04
E	0 ×	1,360	=	$ —
				$1,360.00

BEFORE YOU GO ON...

REVIEW IT

1. Identify two internal control procedures that apply to each payroll function.
2. What are the primary sources of gross earnings?
3. What payroll deductions are (a) mandatory and (b) voluntary?
4. What account titles are used in recording a payroll, assuming only mandatory payroll deductions are involved?

DO IT

Your cousin Stan is establishing a small catering business and will have a number of employees working for him. He is aware that documentation procedures are an important part of internal control. But he is confused about the difference between an employee earnings record and a payroll register. He asks you to explain the principal differences, because he wants to be sure that he sets up the proper payroll procedures.

ACTION PLAN

- Determine the earnings and deductions data that must be recorded and reported for each employee.
- Design a record that will accumulate earnings and deductions data and will serve as a basis for journal entries to be prepared and posted to the general ledger accounts.
- Explain the difference between the employee earnings record and the payroll register.

SOLUTION: An employee earnings record is kept for *each* employee. It shows gross earnings, payroll deductions, and net pay for each pay period. It provides cumulative payroll data for that employee. In contrast, a payroll register is a listing of *all* employees' gross earnings, payroll deductions, and net pay for each pay period. It is the documentation for preparing paychecks and for recording the payroll. Of course, Stan will need to keep both documents.

Related exercise material: 9-1 and 9-5.

EMPLOYER PAYROLL TAXES

STUDY OBJECTIVE 3

Describe and record employer payroll taxes.

Payroll tax expense for businesses results from three taxes *levied on employers* by governmental agencies. These taxes are: (1) FICA, (2) federal unemployment tax, and (3) state unemployment tax. These taxes plus such items as paid vacations and pensions are collectively referred to as **fringe benefits**. As indicated earlier, the cost of fringe benefits in many companies is substantial.

FICA TAXES

We have seen that each employee must pay FICA taxes. An employer must match each employee's FICA contribution. The matching contribution results in **payroll tax expense** to the employer. The employer's tax is subject to the same rate and maximum earnings applicable to the employee. The account, FICA Taxes Payable, is used for both the employee's and the employer's FICA contributions. For the January 14 payroll, Academy Waterparks' FICA tax contribution is \$1,376.80 (\$17,210.00 × 8%).

FEDERAL UNEMPLOYMENT TAXES

The Federal Unemployment Tax Act (FUTA) is another feature of the federal Social Security program. **Federal unemployment taxes** provide benefits for a limited period of time to employees who lose their jobs through no fault of their own. Under provisions of the Act, the employer is required to pay a tax of 6.2 percent on the first $9,000 of gross wages paid to each employee during a calendar year. The law allows the employer a maximum credit of 5.4 percent on the federal rate for contributions to state unemployment taxes. Because of this provision, state unemployment tax laws generally provide for a 5.4 percent rate. The effective federal unemployment tax rate thus becomes 0.8 percent (6.2% − 5.4%). **This tax is borne entirely by the employer.** There is no deduction or withholding from employees.

The account Federal Unemployment Taxes Payable is used to recognize this liability. The federal unemployment tax for Academy Waterparks for the January 14 payroll is $137.68 ($17,210.00 × 0.8%).

HELPFUL HINT
FICA taxes are paid by both the employer and employee. Federal unemployment taxes and (in most states) the state unemployment taxes are borne entirely by the employer.

STATE UNEMPLOYMENT TAXES

All states have unemployment compensation programs under state unemployment tax acts (SUTA). Like federal unemployment taxes, **state unemployment taxes** provide benefits to employees who lose their jobs. These taxes are levied on employers.[2] The basic rate is usually 5.4 percent on the first $9,000 of wages paid to an employee during the year. The basic rate is adjusted according to the employer's experience rating: Companies with a history of unstable employment may pay more than the basic rate. Companies with a history of stable employment may pay less than 5.4 percent. Regardless of the rate paid, the credit on the federal unemployment tax is still 5.4 percent.

The account State Unemployment Taxes Payable is used for this liability. The state unemployment tax for Academy Waterparks for the January 14 payroll is $929.34 ($17,210.00 × 5.4%).

Illustration 9-13 on page 290 summarizes the types of employer payroll taxes.

RECORDING EMPLOYER PAYROLL TAXES

Employer payroll taxes are usually recorded at the same time the payroll is journalized. The entire amount of gross pay ($17,210.00) shown in the payroll register in Illustration 9-9 is subject to each of the three taxes mentioned above. Accordingly, the entry to record the payroll tax expense associated with the January 14 payroll is:

Jan. 14	Payroll Tax Expense	2,443.82	
	FICA Taxes Payable		1,376.80
	Federal Unemployment Taxes Payable		137.68
	State Unemployment Taxes Payable		929.34
	(To record employer's payroll taxes on January 14 payroll)		

A	=	L	+	SE
		+1,376.80		−2,443.82
		+137.68		
		+929.34		

Separate liability accounts are used instead of a single credit to Payroll Taxes Payable. Why? Because these liabilities are payable to different taxing authorities at different dates. The liability accounts are classified in the balance sheet as cur-

[2]In a few states, the employee is also required to make a contribution. In this textbook, including the homework, we will assume that the tax is only on the employer.

rent liabilities since they will be paid within the next year. Payroll Tax Expense is classified on the income statement as an operating expense.

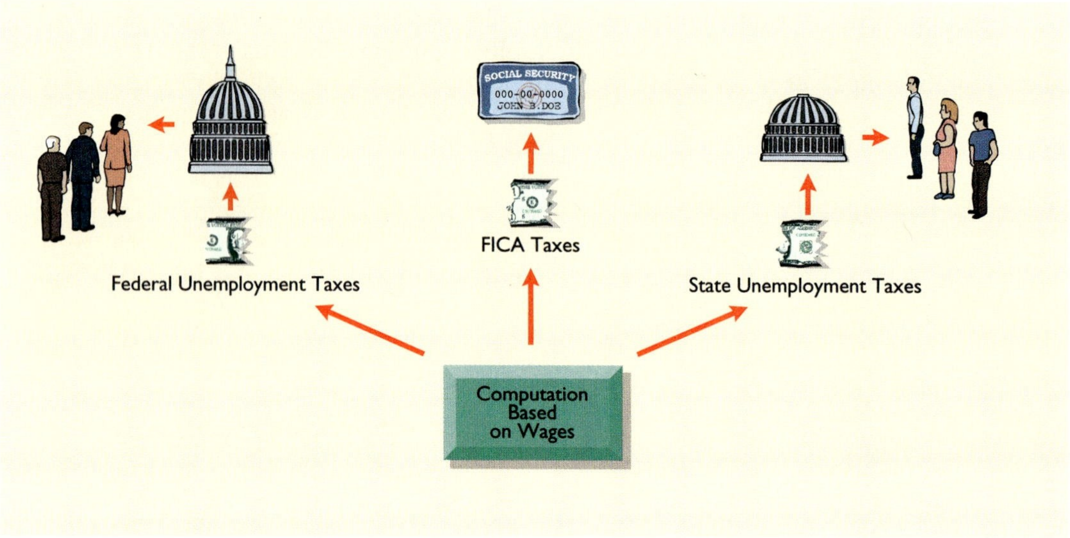

Illustration 9-13

Employer payroll taxes

FILING AND REMITTING PAYROLL TAXES

Preparation of payroll tax returns is the responsibility of the payroll department. Payment of the taxes is made by the treasurer's department. Much of the information for the returns is obtained from employee earnings records.

For purposes of reporting and remitting to the IRS, FICA taxes and federal income taxes that were withheld are combined. **The taxes must be reported quarterly, no later than one month following the close of each quarter.** The remitting requirements depend on the amount of taxes withheld and the length of the pay period. Remittances are made through deposits in either a Federal Reserve bank or an authorized commercial bank.

Federal unemployment taxes are generally filed and remitted *annually* on or before January 31 of the subsequent year. Earlier payments are required when the tax exceeds a specified amount. State unemployment taxes usually *must be filed and paid by the end of the month following each quarter.* When payroll taxes are paid, payroll liability accounts are debited, and Cash is credited.

The employer is also required to provide each employee with a **Wage and Tax Statement (Form W-2)** by January 31 following the end of a calendar year. This statement shows gross earnings, FICA taxes withheld, and income taxes withheld for the year. The required W-2 form for Mark Jordan, using assumed annual data, is shown in Illustration 9-14 on page 291.

The employer must send a copy of each employee's Wage and Tax Statement (Form W-2) to the Social Security Administration. This agency subsequently furnishes the Internal Revenue Service with the income data required.

BEFORE YOU GO ON...

REVIEW IT

1. What payroll taxes are levied on employers?
2. What accounts are involved in accruing employer payroll taxes?

Illustration 9-14

W-2 form

a Control number	OMB No. 1545-0008	
b Employer's identification number 36-2167852	1 Wages, tips, other compensation $26,300.00	2 Federal income tax withheld $2,248.00
c Employer's name, address and ZIP code Academy Waterparks 19 Center St. Hampton, MI 48291	3 Social security wages $26,300.00	4 Social security tax withheld $2,104.00
	5 Medicare wages and tips	6 Medicare tax withheld
	7 Social security tips	8 Allocated tips
d Employee's social security number 329-36-9547	9 Advance EIC payment	10 Dependent care benefits
e Employee's first name and initial Last name Mark Jordan 2345 Mifflin Ave. Hampton, MI 48292	11 Nonqualified plans	12a Code
	13 Statutory employee ☐ Retirement plan ☐ Third-party sick pay ☐	12b Code
	14 Other	12c Code
f Employee's address, and ZIP code		12d Code

15 State Employer's state ID number	16 State wages, tips, etc.	17 State income tax	18 Local wages, tips, etc.	19 Local income tax	20 Locality name
		$526.00			Michigan

Form **W-2** **Wage and Tax Statement** 2004 Department of the Treasury—Internal Revenue Service

▶ *DO IT*

In January, the payroll supervisor determines that gross earnings in Halo Company are \$70,000. All earnings are subject to 8 percent FICA taxes, 5.4 percent state unemployment taxes, and 0.8 percent federal unemployment taxes. You are asked to record the employer's payroll taxes.

ACTION PLAN

- Compute the employer's payroll taxes on the period's gross earnings.
- Identify the expense account(s) to be debited.
- Identify the liability account(s) to be credited.

SOLUTION: The entry to record the employer's payroll taxes is:

Payroll Tax Expense	9,940	
FICA Taxes Payable (\$70,000 × 8%)		5,600
Federal Unemployment Taxes Payable (\$70,000 × 0.8%)		560
State Unemployment Taxes Payable (\$70,000 × 5.4%)		3,780
(To record employer's payroll taxes on January payroll)		

Related exercise material: 9-2, 9-3, 9-4, and 9-5.

DEMONSTRATION PROBLEM

Indiana Jones Company had the following payroll transactions.

Feb. 28 The payroll for the month consists of Sales Salaries \$32,000 and Office Salaries \$18,000. All wages are subject to 8 percent FICA taxes. A total of \$8,900 federal income taxes are withheld. The salaries are paid on March 1.

28 Employer payroll taxes include 8 percent FICA taxes, a 5.4 percent state unemployment tax, and a 0.8 percent federal unemployment tax.

Instructions

(a) Journalize the February payroll transaction.

(b) Journalize the payroll adjusting entry at February 28.

ACTION PLAN

- Base employees' payroll taxes on gross earnings.
- Base employer's payroll taxes on gross earnings.

SOLUTION TO DEMONSTRATION PROBLEM

(a) Feb. 28	Sales Salaries Expense	32,000	
	Office Salaries Expense	18,000	
	FICA Taxes Payable (8% × $50,000)		4,000
	Federal Income Taxes Payable		8,900
	Salaries Payable		37,100
	(To record February salaries)		
(b) Feb. 28	Payroll Tax Expense	7,100	
	FICA Taxes Payable		4,000
	Federal Unemployment Taxes Payable (0.8% × $50,000)		400
	State Unemployment Taxes Payable (5.4% × $50,000)		2,700
	(To record employer's payroll taxes on February payroll)		

SUMMARY OF STUDY OBJECTIVES

1. *Discuss the objectives of internal control for payroll.* The objectives of internal control for payroll are (1) to safeguard company assets against unauthorized payments of payrolls, and (2) to ensure the accuracy of the accounting records pertaining to payrolls.

2. *Compute and record the payroll for a pay period.* The computation of the payroll involves gross earnings, payroll deductions, and net pay. In recording the payroll, Salaries (or Wages) Expense is debited for gross earnings, individual tax and other liability accounts are credited for payroll deductions, and Salaries (Wages) Payable is credited for net pay. When the payroll is paid, Salaries and Wages Payable is debited, and Cash is credited.

3. *Compute and record tips under the 8 percent tip regulation.* The computation and recording of the 8 percent tip regulation is based on 8 percent of the gross receipts. The Tax Equity and Fiscal Responsibility Act (TEFRA) details the calculation of gross receipts and what types of establishments are included in this reporting. If all the employees' tips reporting do not meet at least 8 percent of the gross receipts of the business, the employer needs to perform an allocation by either the gross receipts method or hours worked method to allocate such shortfall to the appropriate employee.

4. *Describe and record employer payroll taxes.* Employer payroll taxes consist of FICA, federal unemployment taxes, and state unemployment taxes. The taxes are usually accrued at the time the payroll is recorded by debiting Payroll Tax Expense and crediting separate liability accounts for each type of tax.

THE NAVIGATOR

GLOSSARY

Bonus Compensation to management personnel and other employees, based on factors such as increased sales or the amount of net income (p. 278).

Employee earnings record A cumulative record of each employee's gross earnings, deductions, and net pay during the year (p. 282).

Employee's Withholding Allowance Certificate (Form W-4) An Internal Revenue Service form on which the employee indicates the number of allowances claimed for withholding federal income taxes (p. 280).

The Fair Labor Standards Act (FLSA) 1938 law, amended with additional provisions in 1977, commonly known as *the Act* or FLSA. It provides minimum standards for both wages and overtime entitlement, equal pay, child labor, and spells out administrative procedures by which covered work time must be compensated (p. 277).

Federal unemployment taxes Taxes imposed on the employer that provide benefits for a limited time period to employees who lose their jobs through no fault of their own (p. 289).

FICA taxes Taxes designed to provide workers with supplemental retirement, employment disability, and medical benefits (p. 288).

Fringe benefits Any form of employee compensation except salary and wages. This may include insurance, retirement, bonus plans, or leaves (p. 288).

Gross earnings Total compensation earned by an employee (p. 278).

Gross receipts method A method of tip reporting which all gross receipts of employees are totaled and then multiplied by 8 percent to determine the amount of tips an employee should report (p. 286).

Hours worked method A method of tip reporting where the total hours worked by all employees is used as the benchmark for tip calculation (p. 287).

Net pay Gross earnings less payroll deductions (p. 281).

Payroll deductions Deductions from gross earnings to determine the amount of a paycheck (p. 281).

Payroll register A payroll record that accumulates the gross earnings, deductions, and net pay by employee for each pay period (p. 282).

Salaries Specified amount per month or per year paid to executive and administrative personnel (p. 274).

Statement of earnings A document attached to a paycheck that indicates the employee's gross earnings, payroll deductions, and net pay (p. 284).

State unemployment taxes Taxes imposed on the employer that provide benefits to employees who lose their jobs (p. 289).

The Tax Equity and Fiscal Responsibility Act (TEFRA) 1982 law that institutes regulations guiding food and beverage operations on tip reporting (p. 285).

Wage and Tax Statement (Form W-2) A form showing gross earnings, FICA taxes withheld, and income taxes withheld which is prepared annually by an employer for each employee (p. 290).

Wages Amounts paid to employees based on a rate per hour or on a piecework basis (p. 274).

EXERCISES

9-1 Gutierrez Yacht Club has the following payroll procedures.

Identify payroll functions. (SO 1)

(a) Supervisor approves overtime work.
(b) The human resources department prepares hiring authorization forms for new hires.
(c) A second payroll department employee verifies payroll calculations.
(d) The treasurer's department pays employees.

Identify the payroll function to which each procedure pertains.

9-2 Becky Sherrick's regular hourly wage rate is $14, and she receives an hourly rate of $21 for work in excess of 40 hours. During a January pay period, Becky works 45 hours. Becky's federal income tax withholding is $95, and she has no voluntary deductions. Compute Becky Sherrick's gross earnings and net pay for the pay period.

Compute gross earnings and net pay. (SO 2)

9-3 In January, gross earnings in Bri Ski Resort totaled $70,000. All earnings are subject to 8 percent FICA taxes, 5.4 percent state unemployment taxes, and 0.8 percent federal unemployment taxes. Prepare the entry to record January payroll tax expense.

Record employer payroll taxes. (SO 4)

9-4 Employee earnings records for Borelias Restaurant reveal the following gross earnings for four employees through the pay period of December 15.

Compute maximum FICA deductions. (SO 2)

C. Mull	$62,500	D. Chambers	$64,300
L. Church	$64,600	T. Olejnik	$65,000

For the pay period ending December 31, each employee's gross earnings is $2,000. The FICA tax rate is 8 percent on gross earnings of $65,000.

Instructions

Compute the FICA withholdings that should be made for each employee for the December 31 pay period. (Show computations.)

9-5 Martinez Theater has the following data for the weekly payroll ending January 31.

Prepare payroll register and record payroll and payroll tax expense. (SO 2, 4)

	Hours								
Employee	**M**	**T**	**W**	**T**	**F**	**S**	**Hourly Rate**	**Federal Income Tax Withholding**	**Health Insurance**
M. Miller	8	8	9	8	10	3	$10	$34	$10
E. Neupert	8	8	8	8	8	2	12	37	15
K. Mann	9	10	8	8	9	0	13	58	15

Employees are paid $1^1/_2$ times the regular hourly rate for all hours worked in excess of 40 hours per week. FICA taxes are 8 percent on the first $65,000 of gross earnings. Martinez is subject to 5.4 percent state unemployment taxes and 0.8 percent federal unemployment taxes on the first $7,000 of gross earnings.

Instructions

(a) Prepare the payroll register for the weekly payroll.
(b) Prepare the journal entries to record the payroll and Martinez's payroll tax expense.

Identify internal control weaknesses and make recommendations for improvement.
(SO 1)

9-6 Selected payroll procedures of Palm Travel are described below.

1. Department managers interview applicants and on the basis of the interview either hire or reject the applicants. When an applicant is hired, the applicant fills out a W-4 form (Employer's Withholding Exemption Certificate). One copy of the form is sent to the human resources department, and one copy is sent to the payroll department as notice that the individual has been hired. On the copy of the W-4 sent to payroll, the managers manually indicate the hourly pay rate for the new hire.
2. The payroll checks are manually signed by the chief accountant and given to the department managers for distribution to employees in their department. The managers are responsible for seeing that any absent employees receive their checks.
3. There are two clerks in the payroll department. The payroll is divided alphabetically; one clerk has employees A to L and the other has employees M to Z. Each clerk computes the gross earnings, deductions, and net pay for employees in the section and posts the data to the employee earning records.

Instructions

(a) Indicate the weaknesses in internal control.
(b) For each weakness, describe the control procedures that will provide effective internal control. Use the following format for your answer:

(a) Weaknesses	(b) Recommended Procedures

Prepare payroll register and payroll entries.
(SO 2, 3)

9-7 Happy Vacations has four employees who are paid on an hourly basis plus time-and-a half for all hours worked in excess of 40 a week. Payroll data for the week ended March 15, 2004, are presented below.

Employee	Hours Worked	Hourly Rate	Federal Income Tax Withholdings	United Fund
Joe McKane	40	$14.00	$?	$5.00
Mary Miller	42	13.00	?	5.00
Andy Manion	44	13.00	60	8.00
Kim Cheng	46	13.00	51	5.00

McKane and Miller are married. They claim 0 and 4 withholding allowances, respectively. The following tax rates are applicable: FICA 8 percent, state income taxes 3 percent, state unemployment taxes 5.4 percent, and federal unemployment 0.8 percent. The first three employees are sales clerks for booking travel arrangements for clients (wages expense). The fourth employee performs administrative duties (office wages expense).

Instructions

(a) Prepare a payroll register for the weekly payroll. (Use the wage-bracket withholding table in the text for federal income tax withholdings.)
(b) Journalize the payroll on March 15, 2004, and the accrual of employer payroll taxes.
(c) Journalize the payment of the payroll on March 16, 2004.
(d) Journalize the deposit in a Federal Reserve bank on March 31, 2004, of the FICA and federal income taxes payable to the government.

Journalize payroll transactions and adjusting entries.
(SO 2, 4)

9-8 The following payroll liability accounts are included in the ledger of Pho Nam Noodle House on January 1, 2004.

FICA Taxes Payable	$ 760.00
Federal Income Taxes Payable	1,004.60
State Income Taxes Payable	108.95
Federal Unemployment Taxes Payable	288.95
State Unemployment Taxes Payable	1,954.40
Union Dues Payable	870.00
U.S. Savings Bonds Payable	360.00

In January, the following transactions occurred.

Jan.	10	Sent check for $870.00 to union treasurer for union dues.
	12	Deposited check for $1,764.60 in Federal Reserve bank for FICA taxes and federal income taxes withheld.
	15	Purchased U.S. Savings Bonds for employees by writing check for $360.00.
	17	Paid state income taxes withheld from employees.
	20	Paid federal and state unemployment taxes.
	31	Completed monthly payroll register, which shows office salaries $14,600, store wages $28,400, FICA taxes withheld $3,440, federal income taxes payable $1,684, state income taxes payable $360, union dues payable $400, United Fund contributions payable $1,888, and net pay $35,228.
	31	Prepared payroll checks for the net pay and distributed checks to employees.

At January 31, the company also makes the following accrued adjustments pertaining to employee compensation.

1. Employer payroll taxes: FICA taxes 8 percent, federal unemployment taxes 0.8 percent, and state unemployment taxes 5.4 percent.
2. Vacation pay: 6 percent of gross earnings.

Instructions

(a) Journalize the January transactions.

(b) Journalize the adjustments pertaining to employee compensation at January 31.

9-9 The payroll procedures used by three different companies are described below.

Identify internal control weaknesses and make recommendations for improvement.
(SO 1)

1. In Ecom Motel each employee is required to mark on a clock card the hours worked. At the end of each pay period, the employee must have this clock card approved by the department manager. The approved card is then given to the payroll department by the employee. Subsequently, the accounting department pays the employee by check.
2. In Yerkes Casino clock cards and time clocks are used. At the end of each pay period, the department manager initials the cards, indicates the rates of pay, and sends them to payroll. A payroll register is prepared from the cards by the payroll department. Cash equal to the total net pay in each department is given to the department manager, who pays the employees in cash.
3. In Min Wu Fortune Cookies employees are required to record hours worked by "punching" clock cards in a time clock. At the end of each pay period, the clock cards are collected by the department manager. The manager prepares a payroll register in duplicate and forwards the original to payroll. In payroll, the summaries are checked for mathematical accuracy, and a payroll supervisor pays each employee by check.

Instructions

(a) Indicate the weakness(es) in internal control in each company.

(b) For each weakness, describe the control procedure(s) that will provide effective internal control. Use the following format for your answer:

(a) Weaknesses	(b) Recommended Procedures

9-10 Mama's Barbeque employs six waitstaff. The details of their gross receipts, hours worked, and tips reported are offered below. The restaurant also had two buspersons with whom the waitstaff will share their tips. The owner, Mrs. Brown, knows the employees did not report the required 8 percent of gross receipts. Using both the gross receipts and hours worked method, please help her identify what amount of tip should be allocated to each employee, if any.

Compute and record tips under the 8 percent tip regulation.
(SO 3)

Employee	Gross Receipts	Hours Worked	Tips Reported
1	$40,000	30	$3,000
2	48,550	40	3,500
3	39,000	25	2,500
4	42,860	35	3,500
5	50,110	40	4,300
6	20,000	20	1,050

EXPLORING THE WEB

9-11 The Internal Revenue Service provides considerable information over the Internet. The following demonstrates how useful one of its sites is in answering payroll tax questions faced by employers.

Address: **www.irs.ustreas.gov/prod/forms_pubs/index.html**

Steps

1. Go to the site shown above.
2. Choose **Publications Online**.
3. Choose **Circular E, Employer's Tax Guide**.

Instructions
Answer each of the following questions.

(a) How does the government define *employees*?
(b) What are the special rules for Social Security and Medicare regarding children who are employed by their parents?

GROUP DECISION CASE

9-12 Kishwaukee Catering Company provides catering services for banquets, events, and other catering functions within a university community. The work is fairly steady throughout the year, but peaks significantly in December and May as a result of holiday parties and graduation events.

Two years ago, the company attempted to meet the peak demand by hiring part-time help. However, this led to numerous errors and considerable customer dissatisfaction. A year ago, the company hired four experienced employees on a permanent basis instead of using part-time help. This proved to be much better in terms of productivity and customer satisfaction. But, it has caused an increase in annual payroll costs and a significant decline in annual net income.

Recently, Valarie Flynn, a sales representative of Harrington Services Inc., has made a proposal to the company. Under her plan, Harrington Services will provide up to four experienced workers at a daily rate of $110 per person for an eight-hour workday. Harrington workers are not available on an hourly basis. Kishwaukee Catering would have to pay only the daily rate for the workers used.

The owner of Kishwaukee, Martha Bell, asks you, as the company's accountant, to prepare a report on the expenses that are pertinent to the decision. If the Harrington plan is adopted, Martha will terminate the employment of two permanent employees and will keep two permanent employees. At the moment, each employee earns an annual income of $30,000. Kishwaukee pays 8 percent FICA taxes, 0.8 percent federal unemployment taxes, and 5.4 percent state unemployment taxes. The unemployment taxes apply to only the first $7,000 of gross earnings. In addition, Kishwaukee Catering pays $40 per month for each employee for medical and dental insurance.

Martha indicates that if the Harrington Services plan is accepted, Kishwaukee's needs for Harrington's workers will be as follows.

Months	Number	Working Days per Month
January–March	2	20
April–May	3	25
June–October	2	18
November–December	3	23

Instructions
With the class divided into groups, answer the following.

(a) Prepare a report showing the comparative payroll expense of continuing to employ permanent workers compared to adopting the Harrington Services Inc. plan.
(b) What other factors should Martha consider before finalizing her decision?

ETHICS CASE

9-13 Harry Smith owns and manages Harry's Restaurant, a 24-hour restaurant near the city's medical complex. Harry employs 9 full-time employees and 16 part-time employees. He pays all of the full-time employees by check, the amounts of which are determined by Harry's public accountant, Pam Web. Harry pays all of his part-time employees in cash. He computes their wages and withdraws the cash directly from his cash register.

Pam has repeatedly urged Harry to pay all employees by check. But as Harry has told his competitor and friend, Steve Hill, who owns the Greasy Diner, "First of all, my part-time employees prefer the cash over a check, and second, I don't withhold or pay any taxes or workmen's compensation insurance on those wages because they go totally unrecorded and unnoticed."

Instructions

(a) Who are the stakeholders in this situation?
(b) What are the legal and ethical considerations regarding Harry's handling of his payroll?
(c) Pam Web is aware of Harry's payment of the part-time payroll in cash. What are her ethical responsibilities in this case?
(d) What internal control principle is violated in this payroll process?

Remember to go back to the Navigator box on the chapter-opening page and check off your completed work.

INVENTORIES, COST CALCULATIONS, AND INTERNAL CONTROLS

10

THE NAVIGATOR ✓

- Understand *Concepts for Review* ❑
- Read *Feature Story* ❑
- Scan *Study Objectives* ❑
- Read *Preview* ❑
- Read text and answer *Before You Go On*
  p. 304 ❑ *p.* 310 ❑ *p.* 319 ❑ *p.* 322 ❑
  p. 328 ❑ *p.* 333 ❑ *p.* 341 ❑
- Work *Demonstration Problem* ❑
- Review *Summary of Study Objectives* ❑
- Complete *Assignments* ❑

CONCEPTS FOR REVIEW

Before studying this chapter, you should know or, if necessary, review:

a. The cost principle (Ch. 1, p. 9) and matching principle of accounting. (Ch. 4, p. 114)

b. How to record purchases, sales, and cost of goods sold under a perpetual inventory system. (Ch. 7, pp. 200–210)

c. How to prepare multiple-step income statements. (Ch. 7, pp. 226–229)

d. How to prepare a classified balance sheet. (Ch. 5, pp. 161–169)

e. The role ethics plays in proper financial reporting. (Ch. 1, p. 8)

✓ THE NAVIGATOR

FEATURE STORY

Minding the Money in Moose Jaw

If you're ever looking for a cappuccino in Moose Jaw, Saskatchewan, stop by **Stephanie's Gourmet Coffee and More**, located on Main Street. Staff there serve, on average, 646 cups of coffee a day—including both regular and specialty coffees—not to mention soups, Italian sandwiches, and a wide assortment of gourmet cheesecakes.

"We've got high school students who come here, and students from the community college," says owner/manager Stephanie Mintenko, who has run the place since opening it in 1995. "We have customers who are retired, and others who are working people and have only 30 minutes for lunch. We have to be pretty quick."

That means that the cashiers have to be efficient. Like most businesses where purchases are low-cost and high-volume, cash control has to be simple.

"We have an electronic cash register, but it's not the fancy new kind where you just punch in the item," explains Ms. Mintenko. "You have to punch in the prices." The machine does keep track of sales in several categories, however. Cashiers punch a button to indicate whether each item is a beverage, a meal, or a charge for the cafe's Internet connections. All transactions are recorded on an internal tape in the machine; the customer receives a receipt only upon request.

There is only one cash register. "Up to three of us might operate it on any given shift, including myself," says Ms. Mintenko.

She and her staff do two "cashouts" each day—one with the shift change at 5:00, and one when the shop closes at 10:00. The cash in the register drawer is counted. That amount, minus the cash change carried forward (the float), should match the shift total on the register tape. If there's a discrepancy, they do another count. Then, if necessary, "we go through the whole tape to find the mistake," she explains. "It usually turns out to be someone who punched in $18 instead of $1.80, or something like that."

Ms. Mintenko sends all the cash tapes and float totals to a bookkeeper, who double-checks everything and provides regular reports. "We try to keep the accounting simple, so we can concentrate on making great coffee and food."

THE NAVIGATOR

STUDY OBJECTIVES

After studying this chapter, you should be able to

1. Describe the steps in determining inventory quantities.
2. Prepare the entries for purchases and sales of inventory under a periodic inventory system.
3. Determine cost of goods sold under a periodic inventory system.
4. Identify the unique features of the income statement for a merchandiser using a periodic inventory system.
5. Explain the basis of accounting for inventories, and describe the inventory cost flow methods.
6. Explain the financial statement and tax effects of each of the inventory cost flow methods.

Continued

PREVIEW OF CHAPTER 10

As the story about recording cash sales at **Stephanie's Gourmet Coffee and More** indicates, control of cash is important. Equally important is the control of inventories. Controls are needed to safeguard all types of assets. For example, Stephanie's undoubtedly has controls to prevent the theft of its food and supplies inventories, and controls to prevent the theft of silverware and dishes from its kitchen.

In this chapter, we will first explain the methods used in determining the cost of inventory on hand at the balance sheet date. Then, we will discuss the differences in perpetual and periodic inventory systems, and the effects of inventory errors on a company's financial statements. We will also explain the essential features of an internal control system and describe how those controls apply to cash. The applications include some controls with which you may already be familiar. Toward the end of the chapter, we describe the use of a bank and explain how cash is reported on the balance sheet.

The content and organization of Chapter 10 are as follows.

INVENTORIES, COST CALCULATIONS, AND INTERNAL CONTROLS

- **Inventory Basics**
  - Classifications
  - Determining inventory quantities
  - Inventory accounting systems
- **Periodic Inventory**
  - Recording transactions
  - Cost of goods sold
  - Cost of goods purchased
  - Income statement presentation
- **Inventory Costing**
  - Actual inventory costs
  - Assumed inventory costs
  - Financial statement effects
  - Consistent use
- **Inventory Errors**
  - Income statement effects
  - Balance sheet effects
- **Statement Presentation**
  - Presentation
  - Analysis
- **Internal Control**
  - Principles
  - Limitations
- **Cash Controls**
  - Control over cash receipts
  - Control over cash disbursements
- **Use of a Bank**
  - Making deposits
  - Writing checks
  - Bank statements
  - Reconciling the bank account

STUDY OBJECTIVES (CONTINUED)

7. Indicate the effects of inventory errors on financial statements.
8. Compute and interpret inventory turnover.
9. Define internal control.
10. Identify the principles of internal control.
11. Explain the applications of internal control principles to cash receipts.
12. Explain the applications of internal control principles to cash disbursements.
13. Indicate the control features of a bank account.
14. Prepare a bank reconciliation.

INVENTORY BASICS

In our economy, inventories are an important barometer of business activity. The U.S. Commerce Department publishes monthly inventory data for retailers, wholesalers, and manufacturers. The amount of inventories and the time required to sell the goods on hand are two closely watched indicators. During downturns in the economy, there is an initial buildup of inventories, as it takes longer to sell existing quantities. Inventories generally decrease with an upturn in business activity. A delicate balance must be maintained between too little inventory and too much. A company with too little inventory to meet demand will have dissatisfied customers and sales personnel. One with too much inventory will be burdened with unnecessary carrying costs.

Inventories affect both the balance sheet and the income statement. In the **balance sheet** of merchandising companies, inventory is frequently the most significant current asset. Of course, its amount and relative importance can vary, even for companies in the same industry. For example, **Marriott** reported inventory of $96 million, representing 4.51 percent of total current assets. For the same period, **Starwood Hotels and Resorts Worldwide, Inc.**, reported $219 million of inventory, representing 24.4 percent of total current assets. In the **income statement**, inventory is vital in determining the results of operations for a particular period. Also, gross profit (net sales less cost of goods sold) is closely watched by management, owners, and other interested parties (as explained in Chapter 8).

CLASSIFYING INVENTORY

How a company classifies its inventory depends on whether the firm is a merchandiser or a manufacturer. A *merchandiser's* inventory consists of many different items. For example, in a grocery store, canned goods, dairy products, meats, and produce are just a few of the inventory items on hand. These items have two common characteristics: (1) They are owned by the company, and (2) they are in a form ready for sale in the ordinary course of business. Only one inventory classification, **merchandise inventory**, is needed to describe the many different items that make up the total inventory.

A *manufacturer's* inventories are also owned by the company, but some goods may not yet be ready for sale. As a result, inventory is usually classified into three categories: finished goods, work in process, and raw materials. For example, **General Motors** classifies vehicles completed and ready for sale as **finished goods**. The vehicles in various stages of production are classified as **work in process**. The steel, glass, upholstery, and other components that are on hand waiting to be used in production are **raw materials**.

HELPFUL HINT
Regardless of the classification, all inventories are reported under current assets on the balance sheet.

DETERMINING INVENTORY QUANTITIES

STUDY OBJECTIVE 1
Describe the steps in determining inventory quantities.

Many businesses take a physical inventory count on the last day of the year. Businesses using the periodic inventory system must make such a count to determine the inventory on hand at the balance sheet date and to compute cost of goods sold. Even businesses using a perpetual inventory system must take a physical inventory at some time during the year.

Determining inventory quantities consists of two steps: (1) taking a physical inventory of goods on hand, and (2) determining the ownership of goods.

Taking a Physical Inventory

Taking a physical inventory involves actually counting, weighing, or measuring each kind of inventory on hand. In many companies, taking an inventory is a formidable task. An inventory count is generally more accurate when goods are not being sold or received during the counting. So, companies often "take inventory" when the business is closed or when business is slow. This, however, is difficult in the hospitality business as most are open 365 days a year.

To minimize errors in taking the inventory, a company should adhere to **internal control principles** and practices that safeguard inventory:

1. The counting should be done by employees who do not have custodial responsibility for the inventory.
2. Each counter should establish the authenticity of each inventory item. For example, does each box contain four sheetcakes? Is each bottle of liquor a full or a partial?
3. There should be a second count by another employee.
4. Prenumbered inventory tags should be used. All inventory tags should be accounted for.
5. At the end of the count, a designated supervisor should check that all inventory items are tagged and that no items have more than one tag.

After the physical inventory is taken, the quantity of each kind of inventory is listed on **inventory summary sheets**. To ensure accuracy, the listing should be verified by a second employee. Later, unit costs will be applied to the quantities in order to determine a total cost of the inventory—which is the topic of later sections.[1]

ACCOUNTING IN ACTION *Business Insight*

Failure to observe the foregoing internal control procedures contributed to the Great Salad Oil Swindle. In this case, management intentionally overstated its salad oil inventory, which was stored in large holding tanks. Three procedures contributed to overstating the oil inventory: (1) Water added to the bottom of the holding tanks caused the oil to float to the top. Inventory-taking crews who viewed the holding tanks from the top observed only salad oil. In fact, as much as 37 out of 40 feet of many of the holding tanks contained water. (2) The company's inventory records listed more holding tanks than it actually had. The company repainted numbers on the tanks after inventory crews examined them, so the crews counted the same tanks twice. (3) Underground pipes pumped oil from one holding tank to another during the inventory taking. Therefore, the same salad oil was counted more than once. Although the salad oil swindle was unusual, it demonstrates the complexities involved in assuring that inventory is properly counted.

Determining Ownership of Goods

Before we can begin to calculate the cost of inventory, we need to consider the ownership of goods. Specifically, we need to be sure that we have not included in the inventory any goods that do not belong to the company.

GOODS IN TRANSIT. Goods are considered *in transit* when they are in the hands of a public carrier (such as a railroad, trucking, or airline company) at the statement date. Goods in transit should be included in the inventory of the party

[1] To estimate the cost of inventory when a physical inventory cannot be taken (the inventory is destroyed) or when it is inconvenient (during interim periods), estimating methods are applied.

that has legal title to the goods. Legal title is determined by the terms of sale, as shown in Illustration 10-1 and described below.

1. **FOB (free on board) shipping point:** Ownership of the goods passes to the buyer when the public carrier accepts the goods from the seller.
2. **FOB destination:** Legal title to the goods remains with the seller until the goods reach the buyer.

Illustration 10-1

Terms of sale

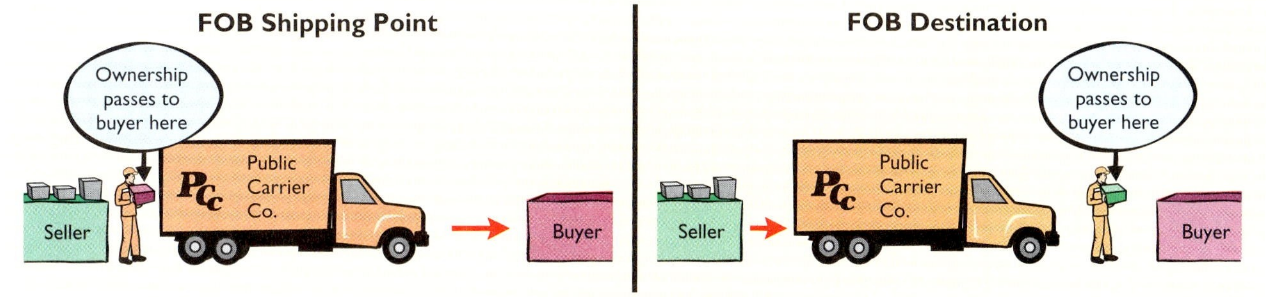

Inventory quantities may be seriously miscounted if goods in transit at the statement date are ignored. Assume that Hargrove Meat Company has 20,000 units of inventory on hand on December 31. It also has the following goods in transit: (1) **sales** of 1,500 units shipped December 31 FOB destination, and (2) **purchases** of 2,500 units shipped FOB shipping point by the seller on December 31. Hargrove has legal title to both the units sold and the units purchased. If units in transit are ignored, inventory quantities would be understated by 4,000 units (1,500 + 2,500).

TECHNOLOGY IN ACTION

Many companies have invested large amounts of time and money in automated inventory systems. One of the most sophisticated is **Federal Express's** Digitally Assisted Dispatch System (DADS). It uses handheld "Super-Trackers" to transmit data about the packages and documents to the firm's computer system. Based on bar codes, the system allows the firm to know where any package is at any time to prevent losses and to fulfill the firm's delivery commitments. More recently, FedEx's software enables customers to track shipments on their own PCs.

INVENTORY ACCOUNTING SYSTEMS

One of two basic systems of accounting for inventories may be used: (1) the perpetual inventory system, or (2) the periodic inventory system. Chapter 6 discussed and illustrated the perpetual inventory system. This chapter discusses and illustrates the **periodic inventory system** and compares the periodic inventory system with the perpetual inventory system. The chapter then continues coverage of the perpetual inventory system.

Some businesses find it either unnecessary or uneconomical to invest in a computerized perpetual inventory system. As illustrated in Chapter 6, a perpetual inventory system keeps track of inventory in number of units *and* in dollar costs per unit. Many small merchandising business managers still feel that a perpetual inventory system costs more than it is worth. These managers can control merchandise and manage day-to-day operations either without detailed inventory records or with a perpetual **units only** inventory system.

BEFORE YOU GO ON...

REVIEW IT

1. What steps are involved in determining inventory quantities?
2. How is ownership determined for goods in transit at the balance sheet date?

DO IT

Hasbeen Company completed its inventory count. It arrived at a total inventory value of $200,000. You have been informed of the information listed below. Discuss how this information affects the reported cost of inventory.

1. Purchased goods of $10,000 which were in transit (terms: FOB shipping point) were not included in the count.
2. Sold inventory with a cost of $12,000 which was in transit (terms: FOB shipping point) was not included in the count.

ACTION PLAN

- Apply the rules of ownership to goods held on consignment.
- Apply the rules of ownership to goods in transit FOB shipping point.

SOLUTION

The goods of $10,000 purchased FOB shipping point should be added to the inventory count. Sold goods of $12,000 which were in transit FOB shipping point should not be included in the ending inventory. Thus, inventory should be carried at $195,000.

Related exercise material: 10-1.

THE NAVIGATOR

PERIODIC INVENTORY SYSTEM

STUDY OBJECTIVE 2

Prepare the entries for purchases and sales of inventory under a periodic inventory system.

In a periodic inventory system, revenues from the sale of merchandise are recorded when sales are made, in the same way as in a perpetual system. But, no attempt is made on the date of sale to record the cost of the merchandise sold. Instead, a physical inventory count is taken at the end of the period. This count determines (1) the cost of the merchandise on hand and (2) the cost of the goods sold during the period. There is another key difference: Under a periodic system, purchases of merchandise are recorded in a Purchases account rather than a Merchandise Inventory account. Also, under a periodic system, it is customary to record the following in separate accounts: purchase returns and allowances, purchase discounts, and freight-in on purchases. That way, accumulated amounts for each are known.

RECORDING TRANSACTIONS

To illustrate the recording of merchandise transactions under a periodic inventory system, we will use the purchase/sale transactions between Sellers T-Shirts and Beyer Theme Park discussed in Chapter 7.

HELPFUL HINT

Be careful not to fall into the trap of debiting purchases of equipment or supplies to Purchases.

RECORDING PURCHASES OF MERCHANDISE

On the basis of the sales invoice (Illustration 7-4 shown on page 204) and receipt of the merchandise ordered from Sellers T-Shirts, Beyer Theme Park records the $8,000 purchase as follows.

May 4	Purchases	8,000		
	Accounts Payable		8,000	
	(To record goods purchased on account, terms 2/10, n/30)			

A	=	L	+	SE
		+8,000		−8,000

Purchases is a temporary account whose normal balance is a debit.

Purchase Returns and Allowances

Some of the merchandise received from Sellers T-Shirts is defective. Beyer Theme Park returns $3,000 worth of the goods and prepares the following entry to recognize the purchase return.

May 8	Accounts Payable	3,000	
	Purchase Returns and Allowances		3,000
	(To record return of defective goods purchased from Sellers T-Shirts)		

A	=	L	+	SE
		−3,000		+3,000

Purchase Returns and Allowances is a temporary account whose normal balance is a credit.

Freight Costs

When the purchaser directly incurs the freight costs, the account Freight-in is debited. For example, upon delivery of the goods on May 6, Beyer pays Acme Freight Company $150 for freight charges on its purchase from Sellers. The entry on Beyer's books looks like this:

May 6	Freight-in	150	
	Cash		150
	(To record payment of freight, terms FOB shipping point)		

A	=	L	+	SE
−150				−150

Like Purchases, Freight-in is a temporary account whose normal balance is a debit. **Freight-in is part of cost of goods purchased**. In accordance with the cost principle, cost of goods purchased should include any freight charges necessary to bring the goods to the purchaser. Freight costs are not subject to a purchase discount. Purchase discounts apply only on the invoice cost of the merchandise.

ALTERNATIVE TERMINOLOGY
Freight-in is frequently called *transportation-in*.

Purchase Discounts

On May 14 Beyer Theme Park pays the balance due on account to Sellers. Beyer takes the 2 percent cash discount allowed by Sellers for payment within 10 days. The payment and discount are recorded by Beyer as follows.

May 14	Accounts Payable	5,000	
	Purchase Discounts		100
	Cash		4,900
	(To record payment to Sellers T-Shirts within the discount period)		

A	=	L	+	SE
−4,900		−5,000		+100

Purchase Discounts is a temporary account whose normal balance is a credit.

RECORDING SALES OF MERCHANDISE

The sale of $8,000 of merchandise to Beyer on May 4 (sales invoice No. 731, Illustration 7-4 on page 204) is recorded by Sellers T-Shirts as follows.

A	=	L	+	SE
+8,000				+8,000

Date	Account	Debit	Credit
May 4	Accounts Receivable	8,000	
	Sales		8,000
	(To record credit sales per invoice #731 to Beyer Theme Park)		

Sales Returns and Allowances

Based on the receipt of returned goods from Beyer on May 8, Sellers records the $3,000 sales return as follows.

A	=	L	+	SE
−3,000				−3,000

Date	Account	Debit	Credit
May 8	Sales Returns and Allowances	3,000	
	Accounts Receivable		3,000
	(To record return of goods from Beyer Theme Park)		

Sales Discounts

On May 15, Sellers receives payment of $5,000 on account from Beyer. Sellers honors the 2 percent cash discount and records the payment of Beyer's account receivable in full as follows.

A	=	L	+	SE
+5,000				−100
−5,000				

Date	Account	Debit	Credit
May 15	Cash	5,000	
	Sales Discounts	100	
	Accounts Receivable		5,000
	(To record collection from Beyer Theme Park within 2/10, n/30 discount period)		

COST OF GOODS SOLD

STUDY OBJECTIVE 3

Determine cost of goods sold under a periodic inventory system.

As the entries above indicate, under a periodic inventory system a running account of the changes in inventory is not recorded as either purchases or sales transactions occur. Neither the daily amount of merchandise on hand is known, nor is the cost of goods sold. **To determine the cost of goods sold under a periodic inventory system, three steps are required:** (1) Record purchases of merchandise (as shown above). (2) Determine the cost of goods purchased. (3) Determine the cost of goods on hand at the beginning and end of the accounting period. The cost of goods on hand must be determined by a physical inventory count and application of the cost to the items counted in the inventory. In this section, we look in more detail at this process.

DETERMINING COST OF GOODS PURCHASED

Earlier in this chapter we used four accounts to record the purchase of inventory under a periodic inventory system. These accounts are illustrated in Illustration 10-2.

Illustration 10-2

Normal balances: cost of goods purchased accounts

Account	Normal Balance
Purchases	Debit
Purchase Returns and Allowances	Credit
Purchase Discounts	Credit
Freight-in	Debit

All of these accounts are **temporary accounts**. They are used to determine the cost of goods sold, which is an expense disclosed on the income statement. Therefore, the balances in these accounts must be reduced to zero at the end of each accounting period. Information about cost of goods sold can then be accumulated for the next accounting period.

The procedure for determining the cost of goods purchased is as follows.

1. The accounts with credit balances (Purchase Returns and Allowances, Purchase Discounts) are subtracted from Purchases. The result is **net purchases**.
2. Freight-in is then added to net purchases. The result is **cost of goods purchased**.

To illustrate, assume that Sellers T-Shirts shows the following balances for the accounts above: Purchases \$325,000; Purchase Returns and Allowances \$10,400; Purchase Discounts \$6,800; and Freight-in \$12,200. Net purchases is \$307,800, and cost of goods purchased is \$320,000, as computed in Illustration 10-3.

Purchases		\$325,000
(1) Less: Purchase returns and allowances	\$10,400	
Purchase discounts	6,800	17,200
Net purchases		**307,800**
(2) Add: Freight-in		12,200
Cost of goods purchased		**\$320,000**

Illustration 10-3

Computation of net purchases and cost of goods purchased

Determining Cost of Goods on Hand

To determine the cost of inventory on hand, Sellers T-Shirts must take a **physical inventory**. Taking a physical inventory involves three steps:

1. Counting the units on hand for each item of inventory.
2. Applying unit costs to the total units on hand for each item.
3. Totaling the costs for each item of inventory, to determine the total cost of goods on hand.

A physical inventory should be taken at or near the balance sheet date. In the hospitality industry, due to the perishable nature of our inventory, taking inventory on a weekly or monthly basis is quite common and often necessary.

The account Merchandise Inventory is used to record the cost of inventory on hand at the balance sheet date. This amount becomes the beginning inventory for the next accounting period. For Sellers T-Shirts, the balance in Merchandise Inventory at December 31, 2003, is \$36,000. This amount is also the January 1, 2004, balance in Merchandise Inventory. During the year, *no entries are made to Merchandise Inventory*. At the end of the year, entries are made to eliminate the beginning inventory and to record the ending inventory. We will assume that Sellers' ending inventory on December 31, 2004, is \$40,000.

Computing Cost of Goods Sold

We have now reached the point where we can compute cost of goods sold. Doing so involves two steps:

1. Add the cost of goods purchased to the cost of goods on hand at the beginning of the period (beginning inventory). The result is the **cost of goods available for sale**.
2. Subtract the cost of goods on hand at the end of the period (ending inventory) from the cost of goods available for sale. The result is the **cost of goods sold**.

ALTERNATIVE TERMINOLOGY

Some use the term *cost of sales* instead of *cost of goods sold*.

For Sellers T-Shirts the cost of goods available for sale is $356,000, and the cost of goods sold is $316,000, as shown in Illustration 10-4.

Illustration 10-4

Computation of cost of goods available for sale and cost of goods sold

Beginning inventory	$ 36,000
(1) Add: Cost of goods purchased	320,000
Cost of goods available for sale	**356,000**
(2) Less: Ending inventory	40,000
Cost of goods sold	**$316,000**

Gross profit, operating expenses, and net income are computed and reported in a periodic inventory system in the same manner as under a perpetual inventory system, as shown in Illustration 10-5.

Illustration 10-5

Income statement for a merchandiser using a periodic inventory system

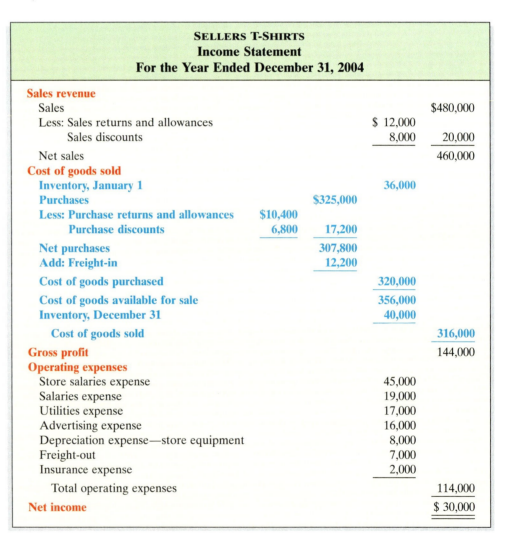

SELLERS T-SHIRTS
Income Statement
For the Year Ended December 31, 2004

Sales revenue				
Sales				$480,000
Less: Sales returns and allowances			$ 12,000	
Sales discounts			8,000	20,000
Net sales				460,000
Cost of goods sold				
Inventory, January 1			**36,000**	
Purchases		**$325,000**		
Less: Purchase returns and allowances	**$10,400**			
Purchase discounts	**6,800**	**17,200**		
Net purchases		**307,800**		
Add: Freight-in		**12,200**		
Cost of goods purchased			**320,000**	
Cost of goods available for sale			**356,000**	
Inventory, December 31			**40,000**	
Cost of goods sold				**316,000**
Gross profit				144,000
Operating expenses				
Store salaries expense			45,000	
Salaries expense			19,000	
Utilities expense			17,000	
Advertising expense			16,000	
Depreciation expense—store equipment			8,000	
Freight-out			7,000	
Insurance expense			2,000	
Total operating expenses				114,000
Net income				$ 30,000

HELPFUL HINT
The far right column identifies the major subdivisions of the income statement. The next column identifies the primary items comprising cost of goods sold of $316,000 and operating expenses of $114,000; in addition, contra revenue items of $20,000 are reported. The third column explains cost of goods purchased of $320,000. The fourth column reports contra purchase items of $17,200.

HELPFUL HINT

Beginning inventory
\+
Cost of goods purchased
=
Ending inventory + Cost of goods sold

TRANSFERS IN AND OUT

As suggested by the Helpful Hint sidebar, you can simply add beginning inventory to cost of goods purchased, then deduct from this total the ending inventory amount to get to cost of goods sold. The same formula can be slightly modified for food or for beverage in the hospitality industry. In such cases, changing the word *goods* to *food* or to *beverage* will provide you with the result. Yet, due to the complexity of the hospitality industry (e.g., a hospitality operation can be departmentalized, and it is customary that a meal be provided to its employees during a shift), the formula to compute the true and accurate cost of food sold needs to be modified a bit more.

A hotel may be divided into banquet and room service operations, or banquet, restaurant, lounge, and room service operations, or any different venues of food and beverage operations. As such, although each operation may order its food supplies from the central storage area, there are times that things may run out and an employee may need to "borrow" items from another outlet so as to be able to fill the order of the guests. Take, for example, an example where a bartender at a lounge forgets to order lemons for the evening shift. The storeroom is now closed and he cannot make another requisition. He therefore asks the restaurant chef to give him ten lemons to carry him over to finish his shift. This transfer of food is known as a *transfer out* from the restaurant and a *transfer in* for the lounge. Although these two operations are in the same hotel, it is important to do a separate cost calculation for each food and beverage outlet so that managers can better assess the efficiency and profitability of each operation. It should also be expected that if everything is performed correctly, such transfers in and out should be minimal or zero.

In this case, a more complete formula for the calculation of cost of food sold would be as shown below.

Beginning inventory	$ 4,000
(1) Add: Cost of food purchased	12,500
(2) Add: Transfers in	50
Cost of food available for sale	16,550
(3) Less: Transfer out	73
(4) Less: Ending inventory	3,540
Cost of food consumed	$12,937

Notice that the ending number is only known as cost of food *consumed* and not cost of food *sold*. As mentioned, it is customary in the hospitality business, especially any establishment that serves food, that the employees are provided a meal during their shift. Of course, there is a cost of food involved. However, the cost of employee meals is part of employee benefits and should not be added to the cost of the food sold to the guests. Thus, an extra step needs to be added:

Cost of food consumed	$12,937
(5) Less: Employee meals	854
Cost of food sold	$12,083

This final amount, $12,083 can now be used by management to calculate food cost percentages and other meaningful tracking and assessment data.

FOOD COST CALCULATIONS

Besides figuring out cost of inventories, it is also useful in the hospitality industry to be able to calculate and track food cost, beverage cost, and labor cost. These costs are often known as the prime costs of a food and beverage operation. The calculation for food cost is very similar to that of regular inventory cost.

However, in a hospitality business, if you are a manager of a restaurant and somebody asks you about the food cost of your operation, you will not quote them a dollar amount. Rather, you will give them a percentage, such as 30 or 35 percent. Why? Percentages are better for comparison and tracking purposes. The more food you are able to sell, the higher will be the sales dollar amount, and so is the cost. Thus, the cost varies with sales, and therefore food cost is called a *variable cost*.

So, how is food cost percentage calculated? Simply, it is the cost of food sold divided by total sales. For example, if your food cost is $4,146.50 and the total sales amount generated by that cost is $11,847, then the food cost percentage would be

35 percent. Most fast-food restaurants are able to maintain a food cost percentage in the 15 percent to 25 percent range, depending on the menu items; most free-standing restaurants or those in hotels will run 30 percent to 40 percent. The food cost percentage is highest in clubs, as high as 50 percent. This is because club members pay a membership fee every month already. Some clubs even require members to pay a food and beverage minimum. Thus, menu prices at clubs are normally lower to offset the other revenues collected from members. With lower sales figures but the same cost to produce food items, the food cost percentage is higher.

BEVERAGE COST CALCULATIONS

The calculation of beverage cost and beverage cost percentage is exactly the same as that of food cost. First, you need to compute the inventory amounts, calculate the cost of beverage sold, and then divide the cost by the total sales dollars to obtain the percentage. However, what should be included in beverage cost? Should all soft drinks and coffee be included since they are beverages? What about liquor, beer, and wine?

There are good reasons why food and beverage are separated. Beverage costs only include alcoholic beverages, such as liquor, beer, and wine since taxes need to be paid by the establishments to the government. In Texas, for instance, the tax is 14 percent. Iced tea, soft drinks, milk, and coffee, although they are beverages, are considered food items and they are not taxable. The markup and pricing of beverages are always higher than food. Beverage cost percentages run in the 15 percent to 25 percent range. They might be higher if a restaurant is running a special at a lower price or trying to sell inventory.

INCOME STATEMENT PRESENTATION

STUDY OBJECTIVE 4

Identify the unique features of the income statement for a merchandiser using a periodic inventory system.

The income statement for merchandisers under a periodic inventory system contains three features not found in the income statement of a service enterprise. These features are: (1) a sales revenue section, (2) a cost of goods sold section, and (3) gross profit. These same three features appear for a merchandiser under a perpetual inventory system. But under a periodic inventory system, the cost of goods sold section generally will contain more detail. Using assumed data for specific operating expenses, the income statement for Sellers T-Shirts using a periodic inventory system is shown in Illustration 10-5. Whether the periodic or the perpetual inventory system is used, merchandise inventory is reported at the same amount in the current assets section.

ALTERNATIVE TERMINOLOGY

Gross profit is sometimes referred to as *merchandising profit* or *gross margin*.

BEFORE YOU GO ON...

REVIEW IT

1. Name two basic systems of accounting for inventory.
2. Identify the three steps in determining cost of goods sold.
3. What accounts are used in determining the cost of goods purchased?
4. What is included in cost of goods available for sale?

DO IT

Aerosmith Company's accounting records show the following at year-end: Purchase discounts, \$3,400; Freight-in, \$6,100; Sales, \$240,000; Purchases, \$162,500; Beginning inventory, \$18,000; Ending inventory, \$20,000; Sales discounts, \$10,000; Purchase returns, \$5,200; and Operating expenses, \$57,000. Compute the following amounts for Aerosmith Company: net sales, cost of goods purchased, cost of goods sold, gross profit, and net income.

ACTION PLAN

- Understand the relationships of the cost components in measuring net income for a merchandising company.
- Compute net sales.

- Compute cost of goods purchased.
- Compute cost of goods sold.
- Compute gross profit.
- Compute net income.

SOLUTION
Net sales: \$240,000 − \$10,000 = \$230,000.
Cost of goods purchased: \$162,500 − \$5,200 − \$3,400 + \$6,100 = \$160,000.
Cost of goods sold: \$18,000 + \$160,000 − \$20,000 = \$158,000.
Gross profit: \$230,000 − \$158,000 = \$72,000.
Net income: \$72,000 − \$57,000 = \$15,000.

THE NAVIGATOR

INVENTORY COSTING UNDER A PERIODIC INVENTORY SYSTEM

STUDY OBJECTIVE 5

Explain the basis of accounting for inventories, and describe the inventory cost flow methods.

All expenditures needed to acquire goods and to make them ready for sale are included as inventoriable costs. **Inventoriable costs** may be regarded as a pool of costs that consists of two elements: (1) the cost of the beginning inventory and (2) the cost of goods purchased during the year. The sum of these two equals the cost of goods available for sale.

Conceptually, the costs of the purchasing, receiving, and warehousing departments (whose efforts make the goods available for sale) should also be included in inventoriable costs. But, there are practical difficulties in allocating these costs to inventory. So these costs are generally accounted for as **operating expenses** in the period in which they are incurred.

Inventoriable costs are allocated either to ending inventory or to cost of goods sold. Under a periodic inventory system, the allocation is made at the end of the accounting period. First, the costs for the ending inventory are determined. Next, the cost of the ending inventory is subtracted from the cost of goods available for sale, to determine the cost of goods sold.

HELPFUL HINT
Under a perpetual inventory system, described in Chapter 7, the allocation of costs is recognized continuously as purchases and sales are made.

To illustrate, assume that General Suppliers has a cost of goods available for sale of \$120,000. This amount is based on a beginning inventory of \$20,000 and cost of goods purchased of \$100,000. The physical inventory indicates that 5,000 units are on hand. The costs applicable to the units are \$3.00 per unit. The allocation of the pool of costs is shown in Illustration 10-6. As shown, the \$120,000 of goods available for sale are allocated \$15,000 to ending inventory (5,000 × \$3.00) and \$105,000 to cost of goods sold.

Illustration 10-6
Allocation (matching) of pool of costs

Pool of Costs
Cost of Goods Available for Sale

Beginning inventory	\$ 20,000
Cost of goods purchased	100,000
Cost of goods available for sale	**\$120,000**

Step 1 — Ending Inventory

Units	Unit Cost	Total Cost
5,000	\$3.00	**\$15,000**

Step 2 — Cost of Goods Sold

Cost of goods available for sale	\$120,000
Less: Ending inventory	15,000
Cost of goods sold	**\$105,000**

USING ACTUAL PHYSICAL FLOW COSTING—SPECIFIC IDENTIFICATION

Costing of the inventory is complicated because specific items of inventory on hand may have been purchased at different prices. For example, a company may experience several increases in the cost of identical goods within a given year. Or, unit costs may decline. Under such circumstances, how should different unit costs be allocated between the ending inventory and cost of goods sold?

One answer is to use the **specific identification method** of the units purchased. This method tracks the *actual physical flow* of the goods. **Each item of inventory is marked, tagged, or coded with its "specific" unit cost.** At the end of the year the specific costs of items still in inventory make up the total cost of the ending inventory. This method is most accurate because it looks at the exact cost of every single item. At any point in time, as long as you count the inventory and add up all the tags, you will get the exact cost of inventory. However, for the hospitality industry, this method is not the most practical. Imagine tagging every can of tomato juice at a restaurant. Imagine putting a price on each bar of soap a hotel puts in guest rooms. Imagine having to put a tag on each bottle of beer at a piano lounge in a casino. These items are often indistinguishable from one another. In such cases (as the next section will show), we must make assumptions about which units were sold.

Illustration 10-7

Specific identification method

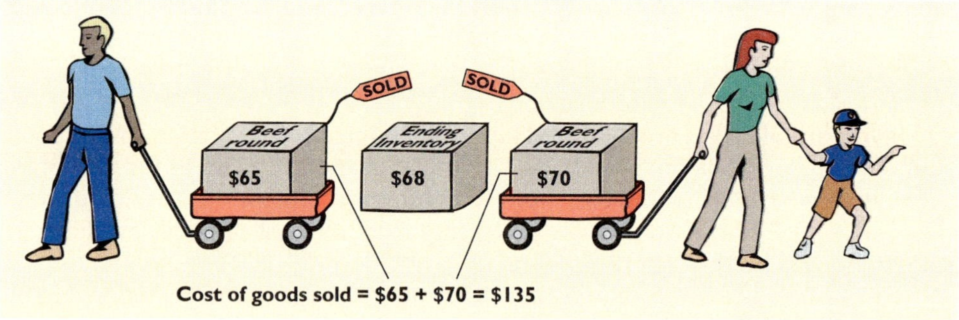

HELPFUL HINT
A major disadvantage of the specific identification method is that management may be able to manipulate net income through specific identification of items sold.

The general rule is this: When feasible, specific identification is the ideal method of allocating cost of goods available for sale. It reports ending inventory at actual cost and matches the actual cost of goods sold against sales revenue.

USING ASSUMED COST FLOW METHODS — FIFO, LIFO, AND AVERAGE COST

Because specific identification is often impractical, other cost flow methods are allowed. These assume flows of costs that may be unrelated to the physical flow of goods. For this reason we call them **assumed cost flow methods** or **cost flow assumptions**:

INTERNATIONAL NOTE
A survey of accounting standards in 21 major industrial countries found that all three methods were permissible. In Ireland and the U.K., LIFO is permitted only in extreme circumstances.

1. First-in, first-out (FIFO)
2. Last-in, first-out (LIFO)
3. Average cost

To illustrate these three inventory cost flow methods, we will assume that Bow Foods uses a *periodic inventory system*. The information shown in Illustration 10-8 relates to one of its products, cheddar cheese.

Illustration 10-8

Inventoriable units and costs for Bow Foods

BOW FOODS
Cheddar Cheese Blocks

Date	Explanation	Units	Unit Cost	Total Cost
1/1	Beginning inventory	100	$10	$ 1,000
4/15	Purchase	200	11	2,200
8/24	Purchase	300	12	3,600
11/27	Purchase	400	13	5,200
	Total	1,000		$12,000

During the year, 550 units were sold, and 450 units are on hand at 12/31.

There is no accounting requirement that the cost flow assumption be consistent with the physical movement of the goods. Management selects the appropriate cost flow method. Even in the same industry, different companies may reach different conclusions as to the most appropriate method.

First-in, First-out (FIFO)

The **first-in, first-out (FIFO) method** assumes that the *earliest goods* purchased are the first to be sold. FIFO often parallels the actual physical flow of merchandise because it generally is good business practice to sell the earliest units first. Under the FIFO method, the *costs* of the earliest goods purchased are the first to be recognized as cost of goods sold. (Note that this does not necessarily mean that the earliest units *are* sold first, but that the costs of the earliest units are recognized first. In a bin of sunglasses at a theme park souvenir shop, for example, no one really knows, nor would it matter, which sunglasses are sold first.) The allocation of the cost of goods available for sale at Bow Foods under FIFO is shown in Illustrations 10-9 and 10-10.

Note that the ending inventory is based on the latest units purchased. That is, **under FIFO, the cost of the ending inventory is found by taking the unit cost of the most recent purchase and working backward until all units of inventory are costed.**

Illustration 10-9

Allocation of costs—FIFO method

Pool of Costs
Cost of Goods Available for Sale

Date	Explanation	Units	Unit Cost	Total Cost
1/1	Beginning inventory	100	$10	$ 1,000
4/15	Purchase	200	11	2,200
8/24	Purchase	300	12	3,600
11/27	Purchase	400	13	5,200
	Total	1,000		$12,000

Step 1
Ending Inventory

Date	Units	Unit Cost	Total Cost
11/27	400	$13	$5,200
8/24	50	12	600
Total	450		$5,800

Step 2
Cost of Goods Sold

Cost of goods available for sale	$12,000
Less: Ending inventory	5,800
Cost of goods sold	$ 6,200

HELPFUL HINT
Note the sequencing of the allocation: (1) Compute ending inventory. (2) Determine cost of goods sold.

Illustration 10-10

FIFO—First costs in are first costs out in computing cost of goods sold

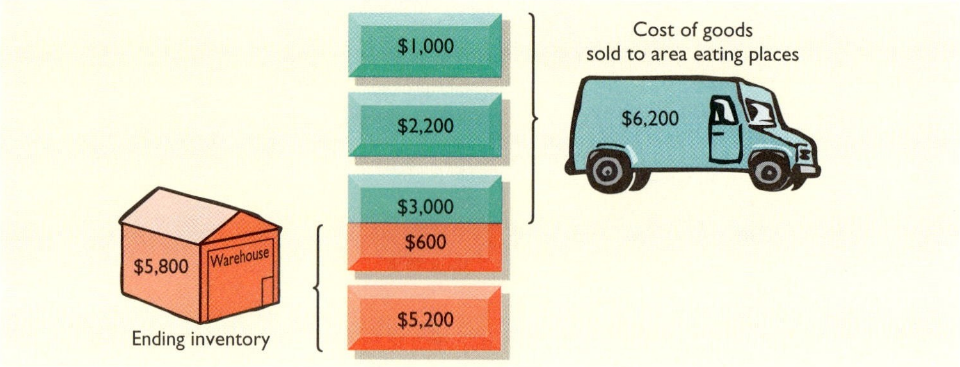

We can verify the accuracy of the cost of goods sold by recognizing that the *first units acquired are the first units sold*. The computations for the 550 units sold are shown in Illustration 10-11.

Illustration 10-11

Proof of cost of goods sold

Date	Units		Unit Cost		Total Cost
1/1	100	×	$10	=	$1,000
4/15	200	×	11	=	2,200
8/24	250	×	12	=	3,000
Total	550				**$6,200**

Last-in, First-out (LIFO)

The **last-in, first-out (LIFO) method** assumes that the *latest goods* purchased are the first to be sold. LIFO seldom coincides with the actual physical flow of inventory. Only for goods in piles, such as hay, coal, or produce at the grocery store would LIFO match the physical flow of inventory. Under the LIFO method, the *costs* of the latest goods purchased are the first to be assigned to cost of goods sold. The allocation of the cost of goods available for sale at Bow Foods under LIFO is shown in Illustration 10-12.

Illustration 10-12

Allocation of costs—LIFO method

Pool of Costs

Cost of Goods Available for Sale

Date	Explanation	Units	Unit Cost	Total Cost
1/1	Beginning inventory	100	$10	$ 1,000
4/15	Purchase	200	11	2,200
8/24	Purchase	300	12	3,600
11/27	Purchase	400	13	5,200
	Total	1,000		**$12,000**

Step 1

Ending Inventory

Date	Units	Unit Cost	Total Cost
1/1	100	$10	$1,000
4/15	200	11	2,200
8/24	150	12	1,800
Total	450		**$5,000**

Step 2

Cost of Goods Sold

Cost of goods available for sale	$12,000
Less: Ending inventory	5,000
Cost of goods sold	**$ 7,000**

HELPFUL HINT

The costs allocated to ending inventory ($5,000) plus the costs allocated to CGS ($7,000) must equal CGAS ($12,000).

Illustration 10-13 graphically displays the LIFO cost flow.

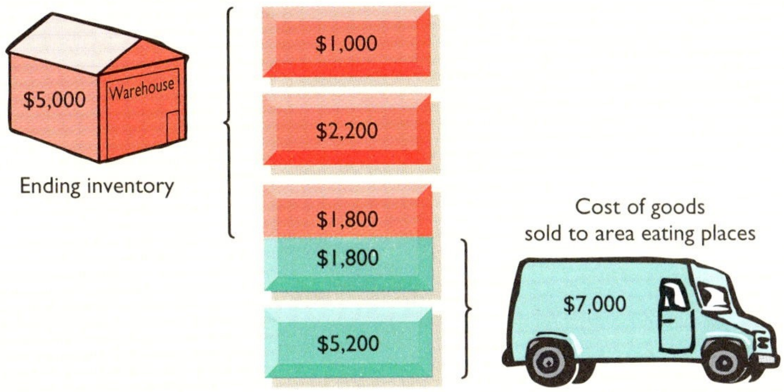

Illustration 10-13

LIFO—Last costs in are first costs out in computing cost of goods sold

Under the LIFO method, **the cost of the ending inventory is found by taking the unit cost of the oldest goods and working forward until all units of inventory are costed**. As a result, the first costs assigned to ending inventory are the costs of the beginning inventory. Proof of the costs allocated to cost of goods sold is shown in Illustration 10-14.

Illustration 10-14

Proof of cost of goods sold

Date	Units		Unit Cost		Total Cost
11/27	400	×	$13	=	$5,200
8/24	150	×	12	=	1,800
Total	550				$7,000

Under a periodic inventory system, **all goods purchased during the period are assumed to be available for the first sale, regardless of the date of purchase**.

Average Cost

The **average cost method** assumes that the goods available for sale have the same (average) cost per unit. Generally such goods are identical. Under this method, the cost of goods available for sale is allocated on the basis of the **weighted-average unit cost**. Illustration 10-15 shows the formula and a sample computation of the weighted-average unit cost.

Illustration 10-15

Formula for weighted-average unit cost

Cost of Goods Available for Sale	÷	Total Units Available for Sale	=	Weighted-Average Unit Cost
$12,000	÷	1,000	=	$12.00

The weighted-average unit cost is then applied to the units on hand. This computation determines the cost of the ending inventory. The allocation of the cost of goods available for sale at Bow Foods using average cost is shown in Illustrations 10-16 and 10-17.

Illustration 10-16

Allocation of costs—average cost method

Pool of Costs

Cost of Goods Available for Sale

Date	Explanation	Units	Unit Cost	Total Cost
1/1	Beginning inventory	100	$10	$ 1,000
4/15	Purchase	200	11	2,200
8/24	Purchase	300	12	3,600
11/27	Purchase	400	13	5,200
	Total	1,000		**$12,000**

Step 1

Ending Inventory

$12,000	÷	1,000	=	$12.00
		Unit		**Total**
Units		**Cost**		**Cost**
450	×	$12.00	=	**$5,400**

Step 2

Cost of Goods Sold

Cost of goods available for sale	$12,000
Less: Ending inventory	5,400
Cost of goods sold	**$ 6,600**

Illustration 10-17

Average cost—the average cost of the goods available for sale during the period is the cost used to compute cost of goods sold

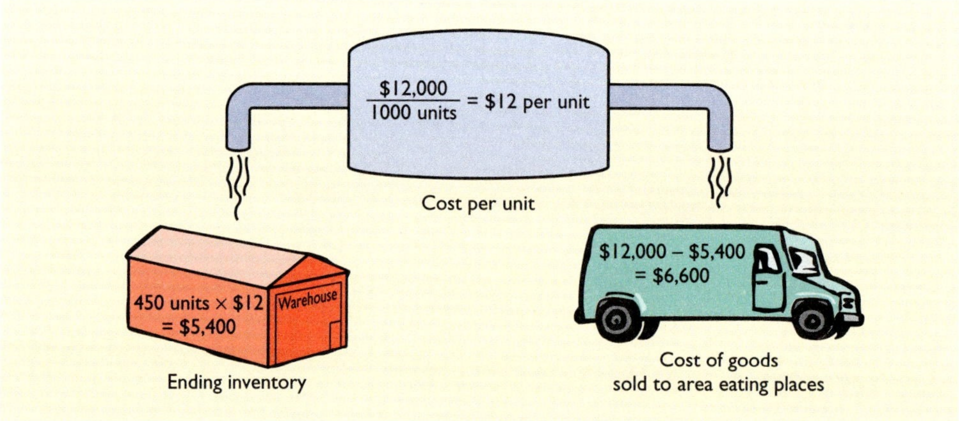

To verify the cost of goods sold data in Illustration 10-16, multiply the units sold by the weighted-average unit cost (550 × $12 = $6,600). Note that this method does not use the average of the unit costs. That average is $11.50 ($10 + $11 + $12 + $13 = $46; $46 ÷ 4). Instead, the average cost method uses the average *weighted* by the quantities purchased at each unit cost.

FINANCIAL STATEMENT EFFECTS OF COST FLOW METHODS

Each of the three cost flow methods is acceptable. For example, **Wendy's International** currently uses the FIFO method. **Campbell Soup Company** uses LIFO, while **Isle of Capri Casinos** uses the average cost method. A company may also use more than one cost flow method at the same time. **Del Monte Corporation** uses LIFO for domestic inventories and FIFO for foreign inventories. Companies adopt different inventory cost flow methods for various reasons. Usually, one of the following factors is involved:

1. Income statement effects
2. Balance sheet effects
3. Tax effects

Income Statement Effects

STUDY OBJECTIVE 6

Explain the financial statement and tax effects of each of the inventory cost flow methods.

To understand why companies might choose a particular cost flow method, let's compare their effects on the financial statements of Bow Foods. The condensed income statements in Illustration 10-18 assume that Bow Foods sold its 550 units for $11,500, and its operating expenses were $2,000. Its income tax rate is 30 percent.

Illustration 10-18

Comparative effects of cost flow methods

BOW FOODS
Condensed Income Statements

	FIFO	LIFO	Average Cost
Sales	$11,500	$11,500	$11,500
Beginning inventory	1,000	1,000	1,000
Purchases	11,000	11,000	11,000
Cost of goods available for sale	12,000	12,000	12,000
Ending inventory	5,800	5,000	5,400
Cost of goods sold	6,200	7,000	6,600
Gross profit	5,300	4,500	4,900
Operating expenses	2,000	2,000	2,000
Income before income taxes[2]	3,300	2,500	2,900
Income tax expense (30%)	990	750	870
Net income	$ 2,310	$ 1,750	$ 2,030

The cost of goods available for sale ($12,000) is the same under each of the three inventory cost flow methods. But the ending inventory is different in each method, and this difference affects cost of goods sold. Each dollar of difference in ending inventory therefore results in a corresponding dollar difference in income before income taxes. For Bow Foods, there is an $800 difference between FIFO and LIFO.

In a period of rising prices, FIFO produces a higher net income. This happens because the expenses matched against revenues are the lower unit costs of the first units purchased. In a period of rising prices (as is the case here), FIFO reports the highest net income ($2,310) and LIFO the lowest ($1,750); average cost falls in the middle ($2,030). To management, higher net income is an advantage: It causes external users to view the company more favorably. Also, if management bonuses are based on net income, FIFO will provide the basis for higher bonuses.

HELPFUL HINT
If prices are falling, the results from the use of FIFO and LIFO are reversed: FIFO will report the lowest net income and LIFO the highest.

Some argue that the use of LIFO in a period of rising prices enables the company to avoid reporting **paper** or **phantom profit** as economic gain. To illustrate, assume that Kralik Resorts buys golf shirts to be sold to its guests at $20 per unit on January 10. It buys 200 more on December 31 at $24 each. During the year, it sells 200 units at $30 each. The results under FIFO and LIFO are shown in Illustration 10-19.

Illustration 10-19

Income statement effects compared

	FIFO	LIFO
Sales (200 × $30)	$6,000	$6,000
Cost of goods sold	4,000 (200 × $20)	4,800 (200 × $24)
Gross profit	$2,000	$1,200

[2]It is assumed that Bow Foods is a corporation, and corporations are required to pay income taxes.

Under LIFO, the company has recovered the current replacement cost ($4,800) of the units sold. The gross profit in economic terms under LIFO is real. Under FIFO, the company has recovered only the January 10 cost ($4,000). To replace the units sold, it must reinvest $800 (200 × $4) of the gross profit. Thus, $800 of the gross profit under FIFO is phantom, or illusory. As a result, reported net income under FIFO is also overstated in real terms.

Balance Sheet Effects

A major advantage of FIFO is that in a period of rising prices, the costs allocated to ending inventory will be close to their current cost. For Bow Foods, for example, 400 of the 450 units in the ending inventory are costed at the November 27 unit cost of $13.

A major shortcoming of LIFO is that in a period of rising prices, the costs allocated to ending inventory may be understated in terms of current cost. This is true for Bow Foods: The cost of the ending inventory includes the $10 unit cost of the beginning inventory. The understatement becomes even greater if the inventory includes goods purchased in one or more prior accounting periods.

Tax Effects

We have seen that both inventory on the balance sheet and net income on the income statement are higher when FIFO is used in a period of rising prices. Why, then, would a company use LIFO? The reason is that LIFO results in the lowest income taxes during times of rising prices. The lower net income reported by LIFO translates to a lower tax liability. For example, at Bow Foods, income taxes are $750 under LIFO, compared to $990 under FIFO. The tax saving of $240 makes more cash available for use in the business.

USING INVENTORY COST FLOW METHODS CONSISTENTLY

Whatever cost flow method a company chooses, it should be used consistently from one period to another. Consistent application makes financial statements more comparable over successive time periods. In contrast, using FIFO in one year and LIFO in the next would make it difficult to compare the net incomes of the two years.

Although consistent application is preferred, a company *may* change its method of inventory costing. Such a change and its effects on net income should be disclosed in the financial statements. A typical disclosure is shown in Illustration 10-20, using information from recent financial statements of **Quaker Oats Company**.

Illustration 10-20

Disclosure of change in cost flow method

QUAKER

QUAKER OATS COMPANY
Notes to the Financial Statements

Note 1 Effective July 1, the Company adopted the LIFO cost flow assumption for valuing the majority of U.S. Grocery Products inventories. The Company believes that the use of the LIFO method better matches current costs with current revenues. The effect of this change on the current year was to decrease net income by $16.0 million.

BEFORE YOU GO ON...

REVIEW IT

1. How do the cost and matching principles apply to inventoriable costs?
2. How are the three assumed cost flow methods applied in allocating inventoriable costs?
3. What factors should be considered by management in selecting an inventory cost flow method?
4. Which inventory cost flow method produces (a) the highest net income in a period of rising prices, and (b) the lowest income taxes?

DO IT

The accounting records of Shumway Eggrolls show the following data.

Beginning inventory	4,000 units at $3
Purchases	6,000 units at $4
Sales	5,000 units at $12

Determine the cost of goods sold during the period under a periodic inventory system using (a) the FIFO method, (b) the LIFO method, and (c) the average cost method.

ACTION PLAN

- Understand the periodic inventory system.
- Compute the cost of goods sold under the periodic inventory system using the FIFO cost flow method.
- Compute the cost of goods sold under the periodic inventory system using the LIFO cost flow method.
- Compute the cost of goods sold under the periodic inventory system using the average cost method.

SOLUTION

(a) FIFO: (4,000 @ $3) + (1,000 @ $4) = $12,000 + $4,000 = $16,000.
(b) LIFO: 5,000 @ $4 = $20,000.
(c) Average cost: [(4,000 @ $3) + (6,000 @ $4)] ÷ 10,000 = ($12,000 + $24,000) ÷ 10,000 = $3.60 per unit; 5,000 @ $3.60 = $18,000.

Related exercise material: 10-2.

THE NAVIGATOR

INVENTORY ERRORS

STUDY OBJECTIVE 7

Indicate the effects of inventory errors on the financial statements.

Unfortunately, errors occasionally occur in taking or costing inventory. Some errors are caused by counting or pricing the inventory incorrectly. Others occur because of improper recognition of the transfer of legal title to goods in transit. When errors occur, they affect both the income statement and the balance sheet.

INCOME STATEMENT EFFECTS

Remember that both the beginning and ending inventories are used to determine cost of goods sold in a periodic system. The ending inventory of one period automatically becomes the beginning inventory of the next period. Inventory errors thus affect the determination of cost of goods sold and net income.

The effects on cost of goods sold can be determined by using the formula in Illustration 10-21. First enter the incorrect data in the formula. Then substitute the correct data, and find the difference between the two CGS amounts.

If beginning inventory is understated, cost of goods sold will be understated. If ending inventory is understated, cost of goods sold will be overstated. The effects of inventory errors on the current year's income statement are shown in Illustration 10-22.

Illustration 10-21

Formula for cost of goods sold

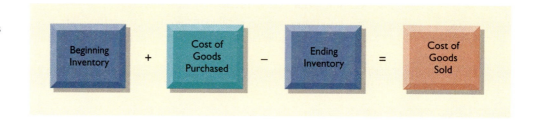

Beginning Inventory + Cost of Goods Purchased − Ending Inventory = Cost of Goods Sold

Illustration 10-22

Effects of inventory errors on current year's income statement

Inventory Error	Cost of Goods Sold	Net Income
Beginning inventory understated	Understated	Overstated
Beginning inventory overstated	Overstated	Understated
Ending inventory understated	Overstated	Understated
Ending inventory overstated	Understated	Overstated

ETHICS NOTE

Inventory fraud includes pricing inventory at amounts in excess of their actual value, or claiming to have inventory when no inventory exists. Inventory fraud is usually done to overstate ending inventory, which understates cost of goods sold and creates higher income.

An error in ending inventory in the current period will have a *reverse effect on net income of the next period.* This is shown in Illustration 10-23 below. Note that understating ending inventory in 2004 understates beginning inventory in 2005 and overstates net income in 2005.

Over the two years, total net income is correct. The errors offset one another. Notice that for 2004 and 2005 total income using incorrect data is $35,000 ($22,000 + $13,000). This is the same as the total income of $35,000 ($25,000 + $10,000) using correct data. Also note in this example that an error in the beginning inventory does not result in a corresponding error in the ending inventory. The correctness of the ending inventory depends entirely on the accuracy of taking and costing the inventory at the balance sheet date.

Illustration 10-23

Effects of inventory errors on two years' income statements

Condensed Income Statement

	2004				2005			
	Incorrect		Correct		Incorrect		Correct	
Sales		$80,000		$80,000		$90,000		$90,000
Beginning inventory	$20,000		$20,000		$12,000		$15,000	
Cost of goods purchased	40,000		40,000		68,000		68,000	
Cost of goods available for sale	60,000		60,000		80,000		83,000	
Ending inventory	12,000		15,000		23,000		23,000	
Cost of goods sold		48,000		45,000		57,000		60,000
Gross profit		32,000		35,000		33,000		30,000
Operating expenses		10,000		10,000		20,000		20,000
Net income		$22,000		$25,000		$13,000		$10,000

($3,000) Net income understated

$3,000 Net income overstated

Total income for 2 years correct

BALANCE SHEET EFFECTS

The effect of ending-inventory errors on the balance sheet can be determined by the basic accounting equation: Assets = Liabilities + Stockholders' Equity. Errors in the ending inventory have the following effects on these components.

Ending Inventory Error	Assets	Liabilities	Stockholders' Equity
Overstated	Overstated	None	Overstated
Understated	Understated	None	Understated

Illustration 10-24
Ending inventory error—balance sheet effects

The effect of an error in ending inventory on the next period was shown in Illustration 10-23. If the error is not corrected, total net income for the two periods would be correct. Thus, total stockholders' equity reported on the balance sheet at the end of the next period will also be correct.

STATEMENT PRESENTATION AND ANALYSIS

PRESENTATION

As indicated in Chapter 6, inventory is classified as a current asset after receivables in the balance sheet. In a multiple-step income statement, cost of goods sold is subtracted from sales. There also should be disclosure of (1) the major inventory classifications, (2) the basis of accounting (cost, or lower of cost or market), and (3) the costing method (FIFO, LIFO, or average).

Disney, for example, in its September 30, 2000, consolidated balance sheet, reported inventory of $702 million under current assets. The accompanying notes to the financial statements, as shown in Illustration 10-25, disclosed the following information.

THE WALT DISNEY COMPANY AND SUBSIDIARIES
Notes to the Financial Statements

Note 1. Description of the Business and Summary of Significant Accounting Policies
Inventories
Carrying amounts of merchandise, materials and supplies inventories are generally determined on a moving average cost basis and area stated at the lower of cost or market.

Illustration 10-25
Inventory disclosures by **The Walt Disney Company**. Information from Disney Worldwide Industries.

ANALYSIS

The amount of inventory carried by a company has significant economic consequences. And inventory management is a double-edged sword that requires constant attention. On the one hand, management wants to have a great variety and quantity on hand so that customers have a wide selection and items are always in stock. But such a policy may incur high carrying costs (e.g., investment, storage, insurance, obsolescence, and damage). On the other hand, low inventory levels lead to stockouts and lost sales.

Common ratios used to manage and evaluate inventory levels are inventory turnover and a related measure, average days to sell the inventory.

STUDY OBJECTIVE 8
Compute and interpret inventory turnover.

Inventory turnover measures the number of times on average the inventory is sold during the period. Its purpose is to measure the liquidity of the inventory. The inventory turnover is computed by dividing cost of goods sold by the average inventory during the period. Unless seasonal factors are significant, average inventory can be computed from the beginning and ending inventory balances. For example, **Darden Restaurants** reported in its 2002 Annual Report a beginning inventory of $148,429,000 and an ending inventory of $172,413,000, and cost of goods sold for the year ended May 26, 2002, of $1,384,481,000. The inventory turnover formula and computation for Darden are shown in Illustration 10-26.

Illustration 10-26

Inventory turnover formula and computation for **Darden Restaurants**

Cost of Goods Sold	÷	Average Inventory	=	Inventory Turnover
$1,384,481,000	÷	$\frac{\$148{,}429{,}000 + \$172{,}413{,}000}{2}$	=	8.63 times

A variant of the inventory turnover ratio is the **average days to sell inventory**. For example, the inventory turnover for Darden of 8.63 times divided into 365 is approximately 42 days. This is the approximate age of the inventory.

There are typical levels of inventory in every industry. Companies that are able to keep their inventory at lower levels and higher turnovers and still satisfy customer needs are the most successful.

BEFORE YOU GO ON...

REVIEW IT

1. Why is it appropriate to report inventories at the lower of cost or market?
2. How do inventory errors affect financial statements?
3. What does inventory turnover reveal?

THE NAVIGATOR

INTERNAL CONTROL

STUDY OBJECTIVE 9

Define internal control.

Could there be dishonest employees where you work? Unfortunately, the answer sometimes is yes. For example, the press recently reported the following:

- A restaurateur in New York was arrested along with his bookkeeper and charged with stealing $185,000 by adding thousands of dollars in tips to credit card charges.
- A new manager, taking over a fast-food restaurant, took inventory of the food items in the freezer and found that the previous manager had filled four hamburger-patty boxes with rocks.
- A bar manager, after receiving complaints from guests about the diluted drinks, found that bottles of clear liquor were mostly water.
- A controller found "faked" invoices submitted for payment by a company that only exists at a post office box address.[3]

These situations emphasize the need for a good system of internal control.

Internal control consists of the plan of organization and all the related methods and measures adopted within a business to do the following:

[3]Sources: Milford Prewitt, "In the Soup: Ruggerio Charged in Tip Fraud," *Nation's Restaurant News, 32*(46) (1998), 1, 2.

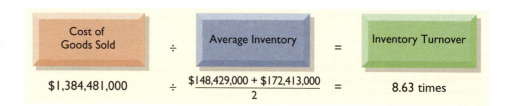

1. **Safeguard its assets** from employee theft, robbery, and unauthorized use.
2. **Enhance the accuracy and reliability of its accounting records.** This is done by reducing the risk of errors (unintentional mistakes) and irregularities (intentional mistakes and misrepresentations) in the accounting process.

The Foreign Corrupt Practices Act of 1977 requires all major U.S. corporations to maintain an adequate system of internal control. Companies that fail to comply are subject to fines, and company officers may be imprisoned. Also, the National Commission on Fraudulent Financial Reporting concluded that all companies whose stock is publicly traded should maintain internal controls that can provide reasonable assurance that fraudulent financial reporting will be prevented or subject to early detection.[4]

INTERNATIONAL NOTE

U.S. companies also adopt model business codes that guide their international operations to provide for a safe and healthy workplace, avoid child and forced labor, abstain from bribes, and follow sound environmental practices.

TECHNOLOGY IN ACTION

Good internal control must be designed into computerized systems. The starting point is usually flowcharts that graphically depict each component of a firm's operations. The assembled flow charts serve as the basis for writing detailed programs. An example of flowcharting is given in this chapter (see Illustration 10-32). When attempts to automate or improve accounting systems fail, it is often due to the absence of such well-documented procedures.

PRINCIPLES OF INTERNAL CONTROL

STUDY OBJECTIVE 10

Identify the principles of internal control.

To safeguard its assets and enhance the accuracy and reliability of its accounting records, a company follows specific control principles. Of course, internal control measures vary with the size and nature of the business and with management's control philosophy. The six principles listed in Illustration 10-27 apply to most enterprises. Each principle is explained in the following sections.

Illustration 10-27

Principles of internal control

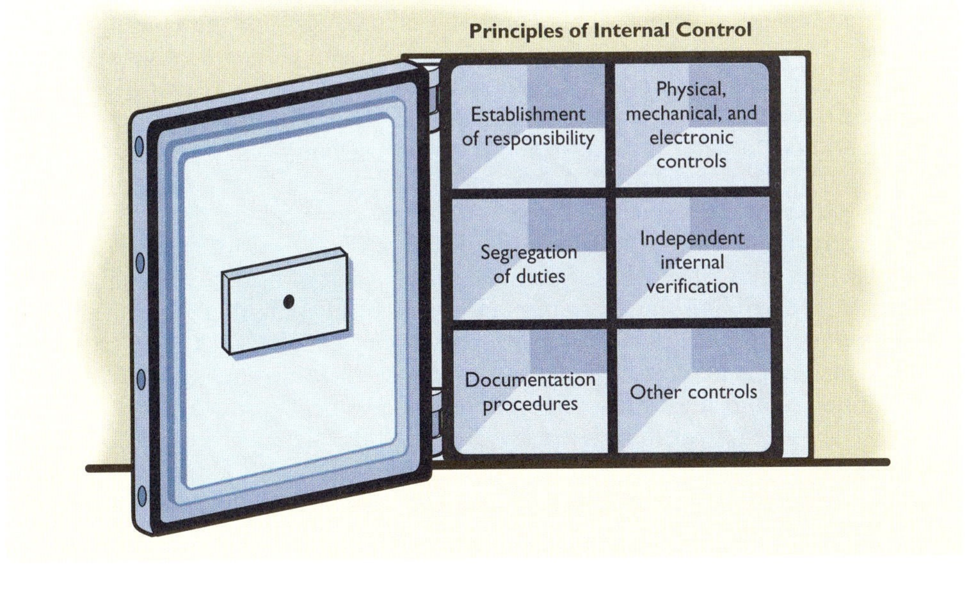

[4]Report of the National Commission on Fraudulent Financial Reporting, October 1987, p. 11.

It's your shift now. I'm turning in my cash drawer and heading home.

Transfer of cash drawers

Establishment of Responsibility

An essential characteristic of internal control is the assignment of responsibility to specific employees. **Control is most effective when only one person is responsible for a given task.** To illustrate, assume that the cash on hand at the end of the day in a breakfast restaurant is $10 short of the cash rung up on the cash register. If only one person has operated the register, responsibility for the shortage can be assessed quickly. If two or more individuals have worked the register, it may be impossible to determine who is responsible for the error unless each person is assigned a separate cash drawer and register key. The principle of establishing responsibility does not appear to be strictly applied by **Stephanie's** (in the Feature Story) since three people operate the cash register on any given shift. To identify any shortages quickly at Stephanie's, two cashouts are performed each day.

Establishing responsibility includes the authorization and approval of transactions. For example, the vice president of sales should have the authority to establish policies for making credit sales. The policies ordinarily will require written credit department approval of credit sales.

Segregation of Duties

Segregation of duties (also called *separation of functions* or *division of work*) is indispensable in a system of internal control. There are two common applications of this principle:

1. Related activities should be assigned to different individuals.
2. Establishing the accountability (keeping the records) for an asset should be separate from the physical custody of that asset.

The rationale for segregation of duties is this: **The work of one employee should, without a duplication of effort, provide a reliable basis for evaluating the work of another employee.**

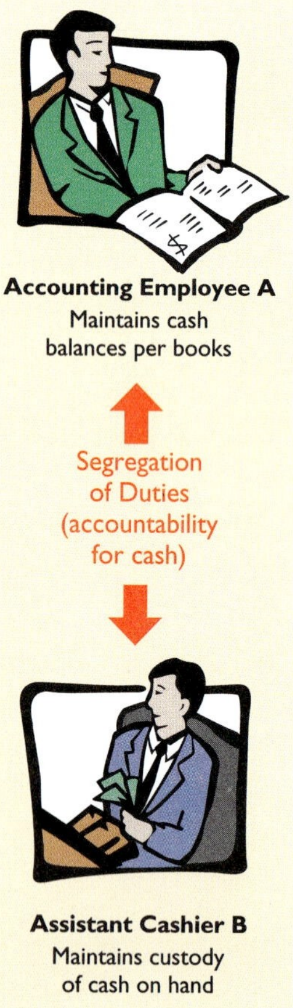

RELATED ACTIVITIES. Related activities that should be assigned to different individuals arise in both purchasing and selling. **When one individual is responsible for all of the related activities, the potential for errors and irregularities is increased.** Related purchasing activities include ordering merchandise, receiving the goods, and paying (or authorizing payment) for the merchandise. In purchasing, for example, orders could be placed with friends or with suppliers who give kickbacks. Or, only a cursory count and inspection could be made upon receiving the goods, which could lead to errors and poor-quality merchandise. Payment might be authorized without a careful review of the invoice. Even worse, fictitious invoices might be approved for payment. When the ordering, receiving, and paying are assigned to different individuals, the risk of such abuses is minimized.

Similarly, related sales activities should be assigned to different individuals. Related selling activities include making a sale, shipping (or delivering) the goods to the customer, billing the customer, and receiving payment. When one person handles related sales transactions, a salesperson could make sales at unauthorized prices to increase sales commissions; a shipping clerk could ship goods to himself; a billing clerk could understate the amount billed for sales made to friends and relatives. These abuses are reduced by dividing the sales tasks: the salespersons make the sale; the shipping department ships the goods on the basis of the sales order; and the billing department prepares the sales invoice after comparing the sales order with the report of goods shipped.

ACCOUNTABILITY FOR ASSETS. To provide a valid basis of accountability for an asset, the accountant should have neither physical custody of the asset nor access to it. Likewise, the custodian of the asset should not maintain or have access to the accounting records. **When one employee maintains the record of the asset that should be on hand, and a different employee has physical custody of the asset, the custodian of the asset is not likely to convert the asset to personal use.** The separation of accounting responsibility from the custody of assets is especially important for cash and inventories because these assets are vulnerable to unauthorized use or misappropriation.

TECHNOLOGY IN ACTION

Saving Cash through Controls

If control is so important in the hospitality business and if technology is supposed to make things better, is technology used in helping operators and businesses control their costs? Chevys, a restaurant chain that owns 131 Chevys Fresh Mex restaurant, 33 Rio Bravos, and 9 Fuzio Universal Pasta restaurants has the answer. They installed a system that has resulted in at least a 1 percent saving in food costs. With average sales at a Chevys Fresh Mex of over $2.5 million a year, 1 percent of sales translates to $25,000 and thus close to $3.3 million just for the Fresh Mex brand. The system allows management to do correct pricing with updated information from the vendor.

There are many technology systems available for restaurateurs, big or small, to take advantage of and to better operate their businesses. They can track menu additions, product mix, takeout orders, complimentary meals, voids, specialty requests, and perform many more functions, so that management and owners can stay competitive.

SOURCE: E. Rubenstein. "The menu is served," *Hospitality Technology, 19–21*, (April, 2003); and D. Kelley. "Analyze this," *Hospitality Technology, 32–32*, (April 2003).

Documentation Procedures

Documents provide evidence that transactions and events have occurred. At **Stephanie's Gourmet Coffee and More**, the cash register tape was the restaurant's documentation for the sale and the amount of cash received. Similarly, the shipping document indicates that the goods have been shipped, and the sales invoice indicates that the customer has been billed for the goods. By adding signatures (or initials) to the documents, the individual(s) responsible for the transaction or event can be identified. Documentation of transactions should be made when the transaction occurs. Documentation of events, such as those leading to adjusting entries, is generally developed when the adjustments are made.

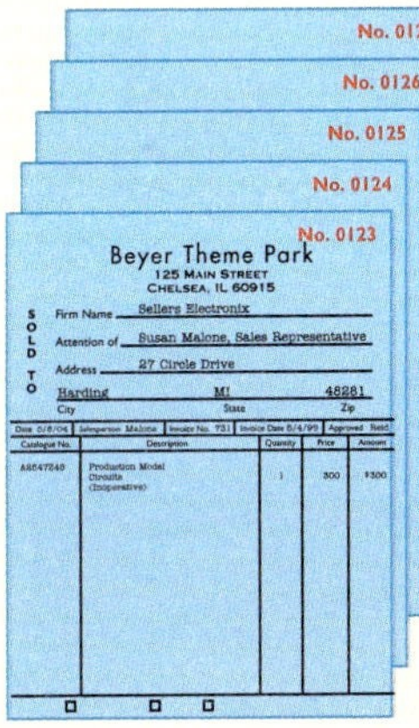

Prenumbered invoices

Two procedures should be established for documents.

1. **Whenever possible, documents should be prenumbered, and all documents should be accounted for**. Prenumbering helps to prevent a transaction from being recorded more than once. It also helps to prevent the transactions from not being recorded.
2. **Documents that are source documents for accounting entries should be promptly forwarded to the accounting department.** This control measure helps to ensure timely recording of the transaction and contributes directly to the accuracy and reliability of the accounting records.

HELPFUL HINT
An important corollary to prenumbering is that voided documents be kept until all documents are accounted for.

Physical, Mechanical, and Electronic Controls

Use of physical, mechanical, and electronic controls is essential. Physical controls relate primarily to the safeguarding of assets. Mechanical and electronic controls also safeguard assets; some enhance the accuracy and reliability of the accounting records. Examples of these controls are shown in Illustration 10-28.

Illustration 10-28

Physical, mechanical, and electronic controls

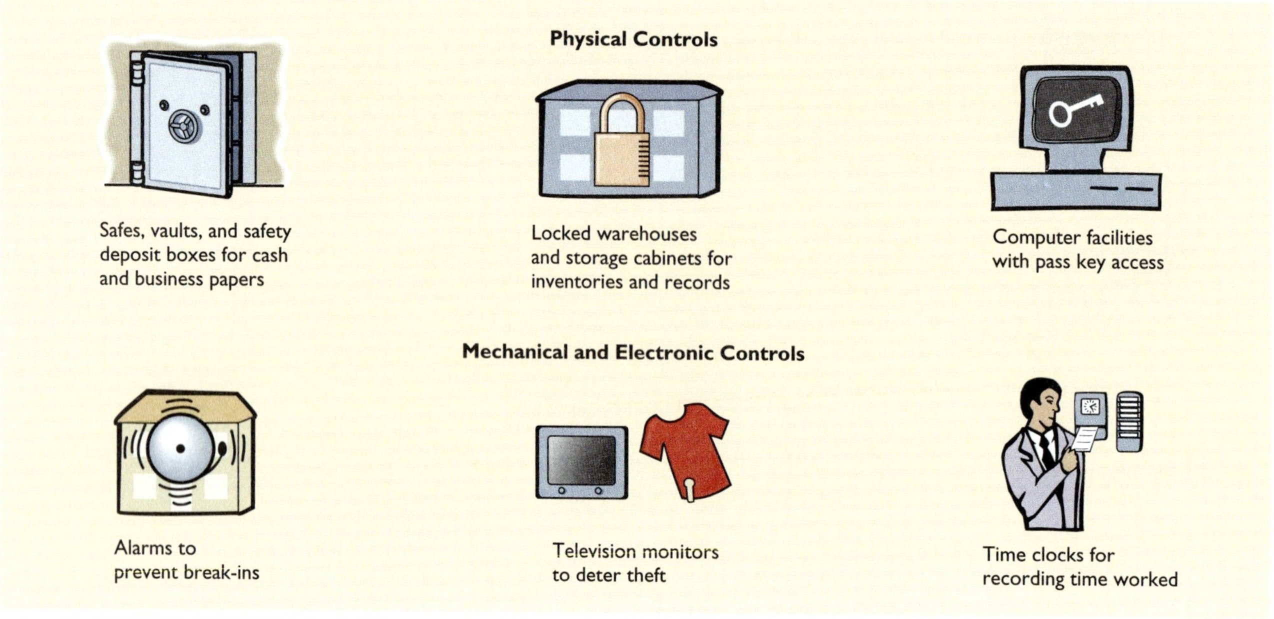

ACCOUNTING IN ACTION *Business Insight*

John Patterson, a young Ohio merchant, couldn't understand why his retail business didn't show a profit. There were lots of customers, but the money just seemed to disappear. Patterson suspected pilferage and sloppy bookkeeping by store clerks. Frustrated, he placed an order with a Dayton, Ohio, company for two rudimentary cash registers. A year later, Patterson's store was in the black.

"What is a good thing for this little store is a good thing for every retail store in the world," he observed. A few months later, in 1884, John Patterson and his brother, Frank, bought the tiny cash register maker for $6,500. The word around Dayton was that the Patterson boys got stung.

In the following 37 years, John Patterson built **National Cash Register Co.** into a corporate giant. Patterson died in 1922, the year in which NCR sold its two millionth cash register.

SOURCE: Wall Street Journal (January 28, 1989).

Independent Internal Verification

Most internal control systems provide for **independent internal verification**. This principle involves the review, comparison, and reconciliation of data prepared by other employees. To obtain maximum benefit from independent internal verification, three features must be present:

1. The verification should be made periodically or on a surprise basis.
2. The verification should be done by someone who is independent of the employee responsible for the information.
3. Discrepancies and exceptions should be reported to a management level that can take appropriate corrective action.

Independent internal verification is especially useful in comparing recorded accountability with existing assets. The reconciliation of the cash register tape with the cash in the register at **Stephanie's Gourmet Coffee and More** is an example of this internal control principle. Another common example is the reconciliation by an independent person of the cash balance per books with the cash balance per bank. The relationship between this principle and the segregation of duties principle is shown graphically in Illustration 10-29.

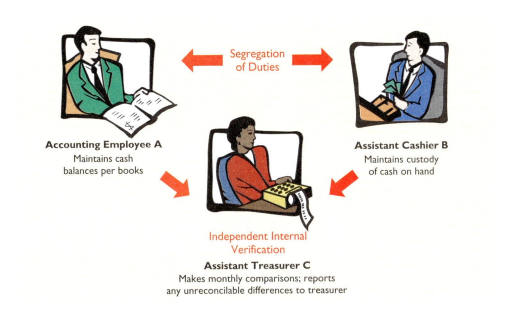

Illustration 10-29

Comparison of segregation of duties principle with independent internal verification principle

In large companies, independent internal verification is often assigned to internal auditors. **Internal auditors** are company employees who evaluate on a continuous basis the effectiveness of the company's system of internal control. They periodically review the activities of departments and individuals to determine whether prescribed internal controls are being followed. They also recommend improvements when needed. The importance of this function is illustrated by the number of internal auditors employed by companies.

Other Controls

Other control measures include the following:

1. **Bonding of employees who handle cash.** Bonding involves obtaining insurance protection against misappropriation of assets by dishonest employees. This measure contributes to the safeguarding of cash in two ways: First, the insurance company carefully screens all individuals before adding them to the policy and may reject risky applicants. Second, bonded employees know that the insurance company will vigorously prosecute all offenders.
2. **Rotating employees' duties and requiring employees to take vacations.** These measures are designed to deter employees from attempting any thefts because they will not be able to permanently conceal their improper actions. Many bank embezzlements, for example, have been discovered when the perpetrator was on vacation or assigned to a new position.

LIMITATIONS OF INTERNAL CONTROL

A company's system of internal control is generally designed to provide *reasonable* assurance that assets are properly safeguarded and that the accounting records

HELPFUL HINT
Controls may vary with the risk level of the activity. For example, management may consider cash to be high risk and maintaining inventories in the stock room as low risk. Thus management would have stricter controls for cash.

are reliable. **The concept of reasonable assurance rests on the premise that the costs of establishing control procedures should not exceed their expected benefit.** To illustrate, consider shoplifting losses in retail stores. Such losses could be eliminated by having a security guard stop and search customers as they leave the store. But, store managers have concluded that the negative effects of adopting such a procedure cannot be justified. Instead, stores have attempted to "control" shoplifting losses by less costly procedures such as: (1) posting signs saying, "We reserve the right to inspect all packages," and "All shoplifters will be prosecuted," (2) using hidden TV cameras and store detectives to monitor customer activity, and (3) using sensoring equipment at exits.

The **human element** is an important factor in every system of internal control. A good system can become ineffective as a result of employee fatigue, carelessness, or indifference. For example, a receiving clerk might not bother to count goods received or might just "fudge" the counts. Occasionally, two or more individuals may work together to get around prescribed controls. Such collusion can significantly impair the effectiveness of a system, eliminating the protection offered by segregation of duties. If a supervisor and a cashier collaborate to understate cash receipts, the system of internal control may be negated (at least in the short run). No system of internal control is perfect.

In addition, the size of the business may impose limitations on internal control. In a small company, for example, it may be difficult to segregate duties or to provide for independent internal verification.

BEFORE YOU GO ON...

REVIEW IT

1. What are the two primary objectives of internal control?
2. Identify and describe the principles of internal control.
3. What are the limitations of internal control?

DO IT

Li Song owns a small restaurant. Li wants to establish good internal control procedures but is confused about the difference between segregation of duties and independent internal verification. Explain the differences to Li.

ACTION PLAN

- Understand and explain the differences between (1) segregation of duties and (2) independent internal verification.

SOLUTION: Segregation of duties involves assigning responsibility so that the work of one employee evaluates the work of another employee. Segregation of duties occurs daily in executing and recording transactions. In contrast, independent internal verification involves reviewing, comparing, and reconciling data prepared by one or several employees. Independent internal verification occurs after the fact, as in the case of reconciling cash register totals at the end of the day with cash on hand.

Related exercise material: 10-5.

THE NAVIGATOR

INTERNATIONAL NOTE
Other countries also have control problems. For example, a judge in France has issued a 36-page "book" detailing many of the scams that are widespread, such as kickbacks in public-works contracts, the skimming of development aid money to Africa, and bribes on arms sales.

CASH CONTROLS

Just as cash is the beginning of a company's operating cycle, it is also usually the starting point for a company's system of internal control. Cash is the one asset that is readily convertible into any other type of asset. It is easily concealed and transported, and it is highly desired. Because of these characteristics, **cash is the asset**

most susceptible to improper diversion and use. Moreover, because of the large volume of cash transactions, numerous errors may occur in executing and recording them. To safeguard cash and to ensure the accuracy of the accounting records for cash, effective internal control over cash is imperative.

Cash consists of coins, currency (paper money), checks, money orders, and money on hand or on deposit in a bank or similar depository. The general rule is that if the bank will accept it for deposit, it is cash. Items such as postage stamps and postdated checks (checks payable in the future) are not cash. Stamps are a prepaid expense; the postdated checks are accounts receivable. In the following sections we explain the application of internal control principles to cash receipts and cash disbursements.

STUDY OBJECTIVE 11

Explain the applications of internal control principles to cash receipts.

INTERNAL CONTROL OVER CASH RECEIPTS

Cash receipts come from a variety of sources: cash sales; collections on account from customers; the receipt of interest, rent, and dividends; investments by owners; bank loans; and proceeds from the sale of noncurrent assets. Illustration 10-30 shows how the internal control principles explained earlier apply to cash receipts transactions.

Illustration 10-30

Application of internal control principles to cash receipts

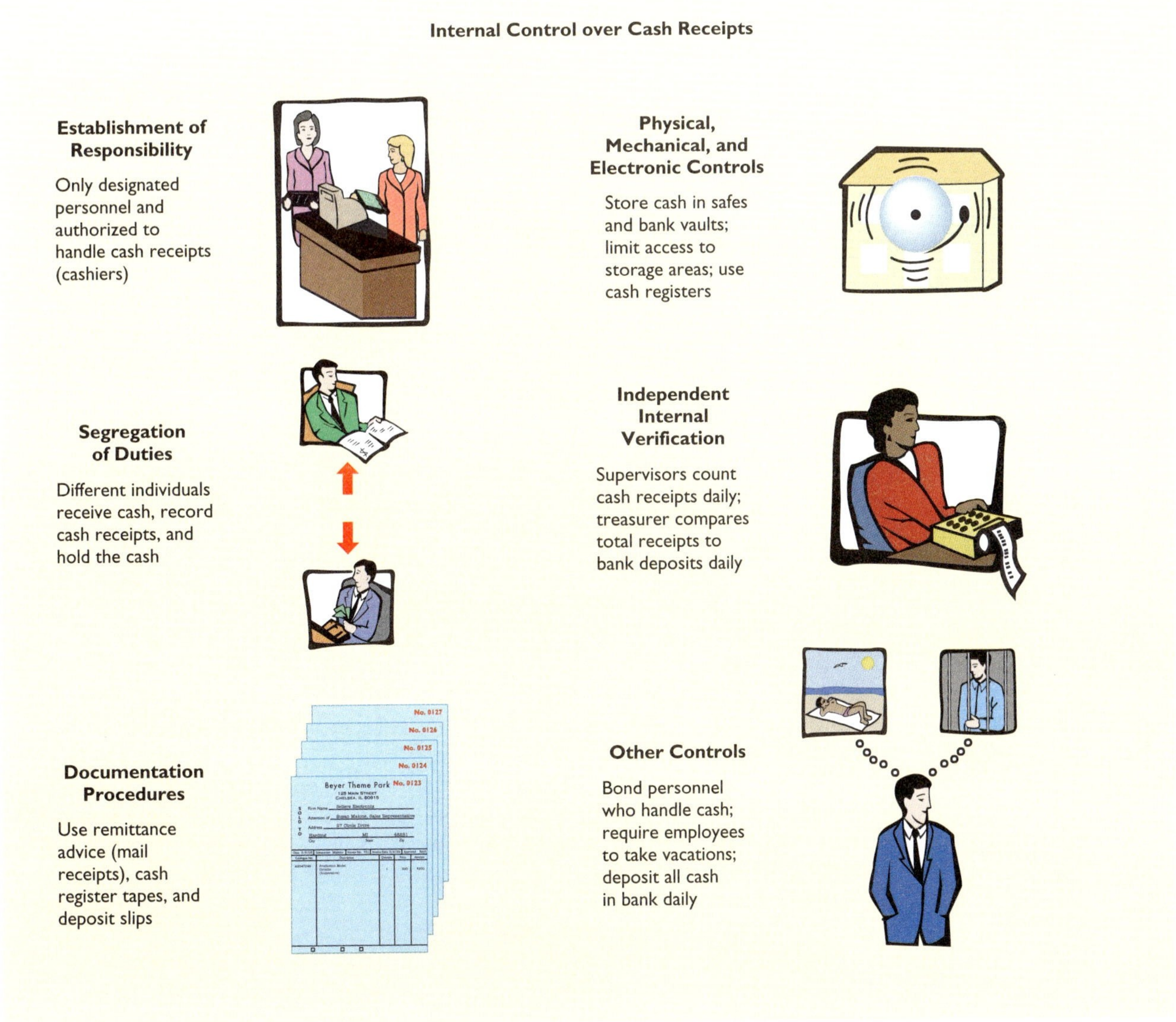
Internal Control over Cash Receipts
Establishment of Responsibility
Only designated personnel and authorized to handle cash receipts (cashiers)
Physical, Mechanical, and Electronic Controls
Store cash in safes and bank vaults; limit access to storage areas; use cash registers
Segregation of Duties
Different individuals receive cash, record cash receipts, and hold the cash
Independent Internal Verification
Supervisors count cash receipts daily; treasurer compares total receipts to bank deposits daily
Documentation Procedures
Use remittance advice (mail receipts), cash register tapes, and deposit slips
Other Controls
Bond personnel who handle cash; require employees to take vacations; deposit all cash in bank daily

As might be expected, companies vary considerably in how they apply these principles. To illustrate internal control over cash receipts, we will examine control measures for a retail store with both over-the-counter and mail receipts.

Over-the-Counter Receipts

Control of over-the-counter receipts in retail businesses is centered on cash registers that are visible to customers. In supermarkets and in variety stores, cash registers are placed in checkout lines near the exit. In hotels such as **Hilton** and **Marriott**, each department has its own cash register. A cash sale is "rung up" on a cash register *with the amount clearly visible to the customer*. This measure prevents the cashier from ringing up a lower amount and pocketing the difference. The customer receives an itemized cash register receipt slip and is expected to count the change received. A cash register tape is locked into the register until removed by a supervisor or manager. This tape accumulates the daily transactions and totals. When the tape is removed, the supervisor compares the total with the amount of cash in the register. The tape should show all registered receipts accounted for. The supervisor's findings are reported on a cash count sheet which is signed by both the cashier and supervisor. The cash count sheet used by Alrite Food is shown in Illustration 10-31.

Illustration 10-31

Cash count sheet

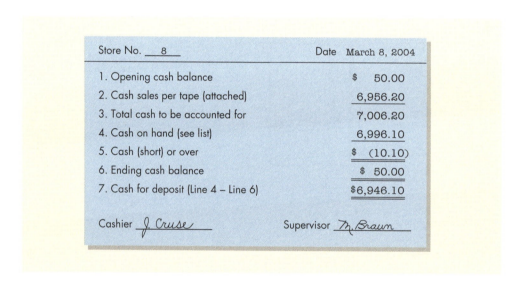

Store No. 8	Date March 8, 2004
1. Opening cash balance	$ 50.00
2. Cash sales per tape (attached)	6,956.20
3. Total cash to be accounted for	7,006.20
4. Cash on hand (see list)	6,996.10
5. Cash (short) or over	$ (10.10)
6. Ending cash balance	$ 50.00
7. Cash for deposit (Line 4 – Line 6)	$6,946.10
Cashier J. Cruse	Supervisor M. Braun

The count sheets, register tapes, and cash are then given to the head cashier. This individual prepares a daily cash summary showing the total cash received and the amount from each source, such as cash sales and collections on account. The head cashier sends one copy of the summary to the accounting department for entry into the cash receipts journal. The other copy goes to the treasurer's office for later comparison with the daily bank deposit.

Next, the head cashier prepares a deposit slip (see Illustration 10-34 on page 335) and makes the bank deposit. The total amount deposited should be equal to the total receipts on the daily cash summary. This will ensure that all receipts have been placed in the custody of the bank. In accepting the bank deposit, the bank stamps (authenticates) the duplicate deposit slip and sends it to the company treasurer, who makes the comparison with the daily cash summary.

These measures for cash sales are graphically presented in Illustration 10-32. The activities of the sales department are shown separately from those of the cashier's department to indicate the segregation of duties in handling cash.

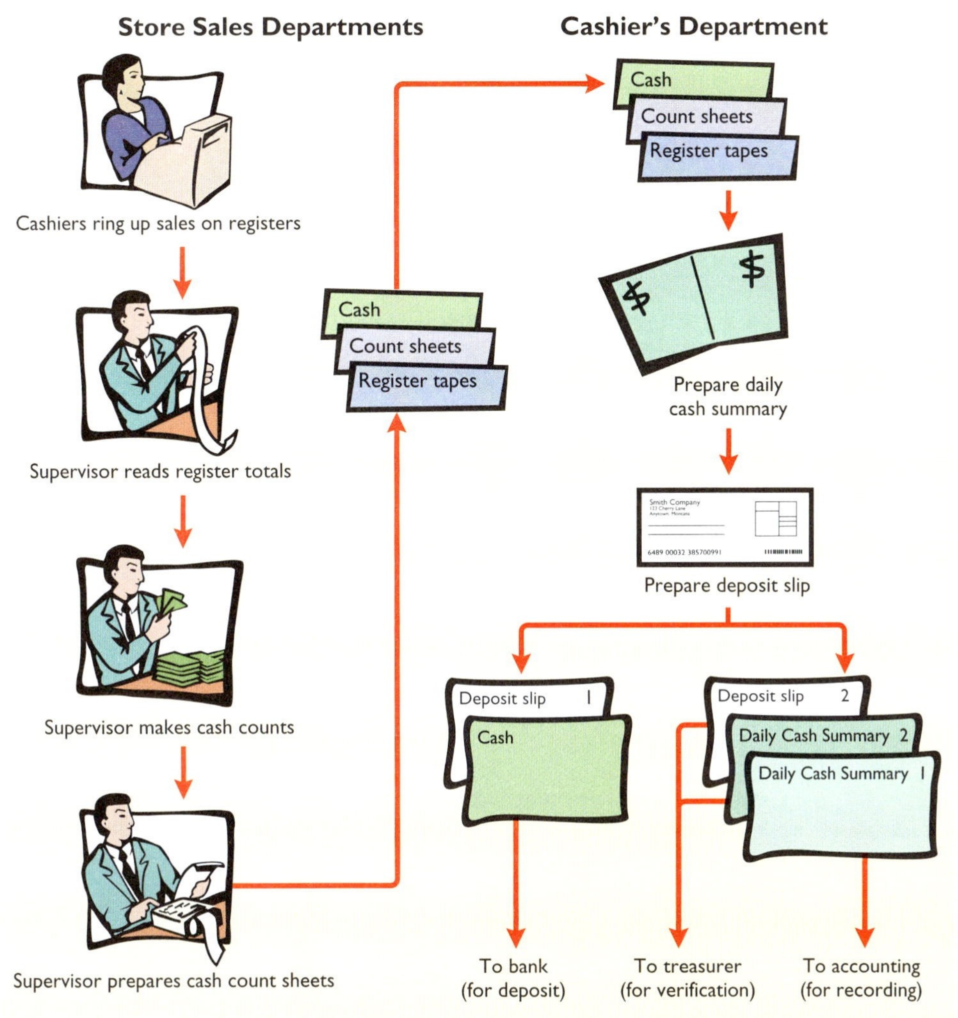

Illustration 10-32

Executing over-the-counter cash sales

HELPFUL HINT

Flowcharts such as this one enhance the understanding of the flow of documents, the processing steps, and the internal control procedures.

Mail Receipts

As an individual customer, you may be more familiar with over-the-counter receipts than with mail receipts. However, mail receipts resulting from billings and credit sales are by far the most common way cash is received by businesses. Think, for example, of the number of checks received through the mail daily by an international company such as **Disney**, **Marriott**, **Hilton**, or **Six Continents**.

All mail receipts should be opened in the presence of two mail clerks. These receipts are generally in the form of checks or money orders. They frequently are accompanied by a remittance advice stating the purpose of the check (sometimes attached to the check, but often a part of the bill that the customer tears off and returns). Each check should be promptly endorsed "For Deposit Only" by use of a company stamp. This **restrictive endorsement** reduces the likelihood that the check will be diverted to personal use. Banks will not give an individual any cash under this type of endorsement.

A list of the checks received each day should be prepared in duplicate. This list shows the name of the issuer of the check, the purpose of the payment, and the amount of the check. Each mail clerk should sign the list to establish responsibility for the data. The original copy of the list, along with the checks and remittance advices, are then sent to the cashier's department. There they are added to over-the-counter receipts (if any) in preparing the daily cash summary and in making the daily bank deposit. Also, a copy of the list is sent to the treasurer's office for comparison with the total mail receipts shown on the daily cash summary. This copy ensures that all mail receipts have been included.

INTERNAL CONTROL OVER CASH DISBURSEMENTS

STUDY OBJECTIVE 12

Explain the applications of internal control principles to cash disbursements.

Cash may be disbursed for a variety of reasons, such as to pay expenses and liabilities, or to purchase assets. **Generally, internal control over cash disbursements is more effective when payments are made by check, rather than by cash.** One exception is for incidental amounts that are paid out of *petty cash*. Payment by check generally occurs only after specified control procedures have been followed. In addition, the "paid" check provides proof of payment. Illustration 10-33 shows how principles of internal control apply to cash disbursements.

Illustration 10-33

Application of internal control principles to cash disbursements

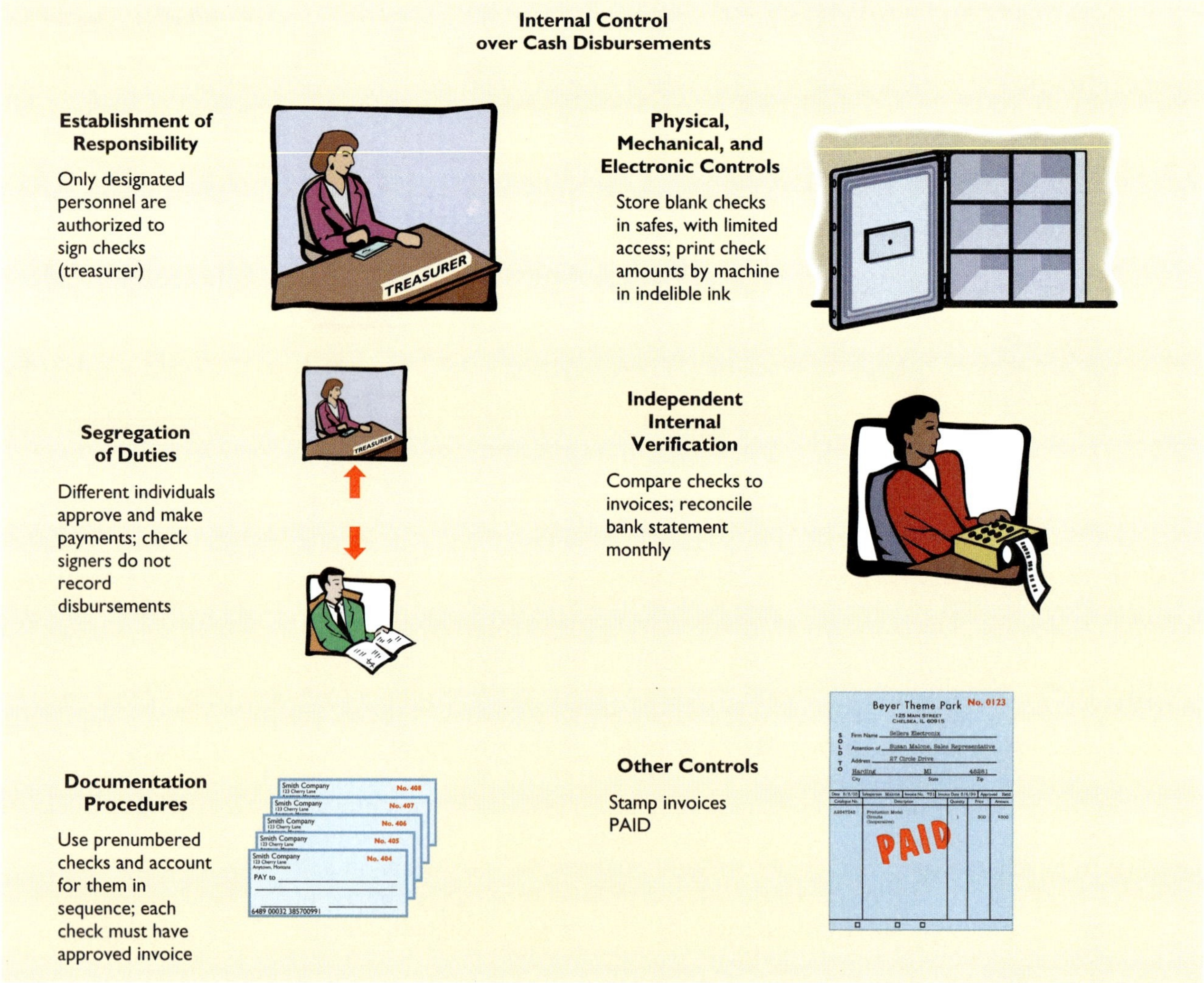

Voucher System

Most medium and large companies use vouchers as part of their internal control over cash disbursements. A **voucher system** is a network of approvals by authorized individuals acting independently to ensure that all disbursements by check are proper.

The system begins with the authorization to incur a cost or expense. It ends with the issuance of a check for the liability incurred. A **voucher** is an authorization form prepared for each expenditure. Vouchers are required for all types of cash disbursements except those from petty cash. The voucher generally is prepared in the accounts payable department.

The starting point in preparing a voucher is to fill in the appropriate information about the liability on the face of the voucher. The vendor's invoice provides most of the needed information. Then, the voucher must be recorded (in the journal called a **voucher register**) and filed according to the date on which it is to be paid. A check is sent on that date, the voucher is stamped "paid," and the paid voucher is sent to the accounting department for recording (in a journal called the **check register**). A voucher system involves two journal entries, similar to any accounts payable transaction, one to issue the voucher and a second to pay the voucher.

Electronic Funds Transfer (EFT) System

To account for and control cash is an expensive and time-consuming process. It was estimated recently that the cost to process a check through a bank system ranges from $0.55 to $1.00 and is increasing. It is not surprising that new approaches are being developed to transfer funds among parties without the use of paper (deposit tickets, checks, etc.). Such a procedure is called **electronic funds transfer (EFT)**. This disbursement system uses wire, telephone, telegraph, or computer to transfer cash from one location to another. Use of EFT is quite common. For example, the authors receive no formal payroll checks from their universities, which instead send magnetic tapes to the appropriate banks for deposit. Regular payments such as those for house, car, and utilities are frequently made by EFT.

TECHNOLOGY IN ACTION

The development of EFT will continue. Already it is estimated that more than 80 percent of the total volume of bank transactions in the United States is performed using EFT. The computer technology is available to create a "checkless" society. The only major barriers appear to be the individual's concern for privacy and protection and certain legislative constraints. Numerous safeguards have been built into EFT systems and are continuing to improve. However, the possibility of errors and fraud still exists because only a limited number of individuals are involved in the transfers, which may prevent appropriate segregation of duties.

BEFORE YOU GO ON...

REVIEW IT

1. How do the principles of internal control apply to cash receipts?
2. How do the principles of internal control apply to cash disbursements?

DO IT

L. R. Cortez is concerned about the control over cash receipts in his fast-food restaurant, Big Cheese. The restaurant has two cash registers. At no time do more than two employees take customer orders and ring up sales. Work shifts for employees range from four to eight hours. Cortez asks your help in installing a good system of internal control over cash receipts.

ACTION PLAN

- Differentiate among the internal control principles of (1) establishing responsibility, (2) using electronic controls, and (3) independent internal verification.
- Design an effective system of internal control over cash receipts.

SOLUTION: Cortez should assign a cash register to each employee at the start of each work shift, with register totals set at zero. Each employee should be instructed to use only the assigned register and to ring up all sales. At the end of each work shift, Cortez or a supervisor/manager should total the register and make a cash count to see whether all cash is accounted for.

Related exercise material: 10-6 and 10-7.

THE NAVIGATOR

USE OF A BANK

STUDY OBJECTIVE 13

Indicate the control features of a bank account.

The use of a bank contributes significantly to good internal control over cash. A company can safeguard its cash by using a bank as a depository and as a clearing house for checks received and checks written. Use of a bank minimizes the amount of currency that must be kept on hand. Also, the use of a bank facilitates the control of cash because it creates a double record of all bank transactions—one by the business and the other by the bank. The asset account Cash maintained by the depositor is the reciprocal of the bank's liability account for each depositor. It should be possible to *reconcile these accounts* (make them agree) at any time.

Opening a bank checking account is a relatively simple procedure. Typically, the bank makes a credit check on the new customer and the depositor is required to sign a **signature card**. The card contains the signatures of each person authorized to sign checks on the account. The signature card is used by bank employees to validate signatures on the checks.

Soon after an account is opened, the bank provides the depositor with serially numbered checks and deposit slips imprinted with the depositor's name and address. Each check and deposit slip is imprinted with both a bank and a depositor identification number. This number, printed in magnetic ink, permits computer processing of transactions.

Many companies have more than one bank account. For efficiency of operations and better control, national hospitality companies may have regional bank accounts. A company such as **Starwood** with more than 115,000 employees may have a payroll bank account, as well as one or more general bank accounts. Also, a company may maintain several bank accounts in order to have more than one source for short-term loans when needed.

MAKING BANK DEPOSITS

Bank deposits should be made by an authorized employee, such as the head cashier. Each deposit must be documented by a deposit slip (ticket), as shown in Illustration 10-34.

Deposit slips are prepared in duplicate. The original is retained by the bank; the duplicate, machine-stamped by the bank to establish its authenticity, is retained by the depositor.

WRITING CHECKS

A **check** is a written order signed by the depositor directing the bank to pay a specified sum of money to a designated recipient. There are three parties to a check: (1) the **maker** (or drawer) who issues the check; (2) the **bank** (or payer) on which the check is drawn; and (3) the **payee** to whom the check is payable. A

Illustration 10-34

Deposit slip

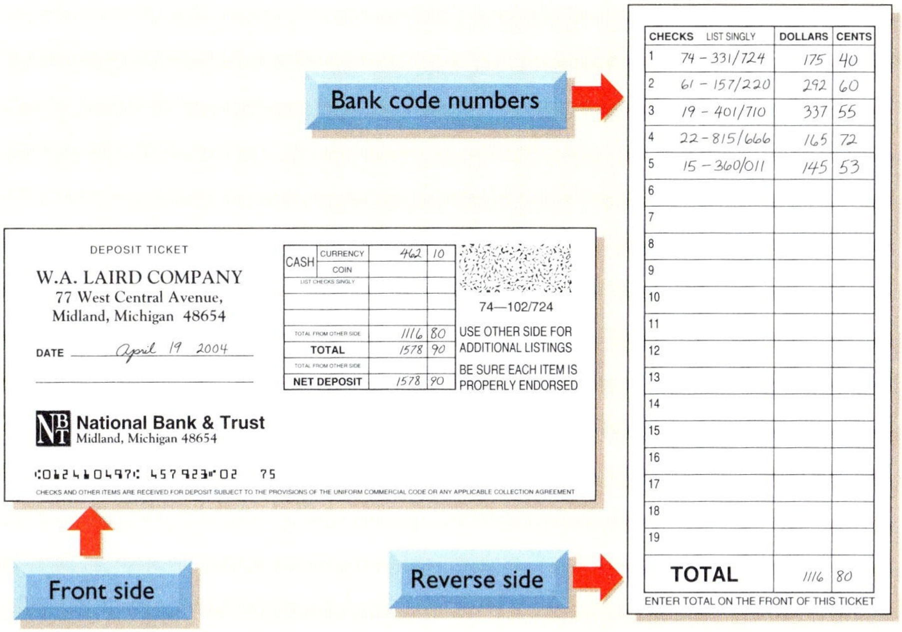

check is a **negotiable instrument** that can be transferred to another party by endorsement. Each check should be accompanied by an explanation of its purposes. In many businesses, this is done by a remittance advice attached to the check, as shown in Illustration 10-35.

Illustration 10-35

Check with remittance advice

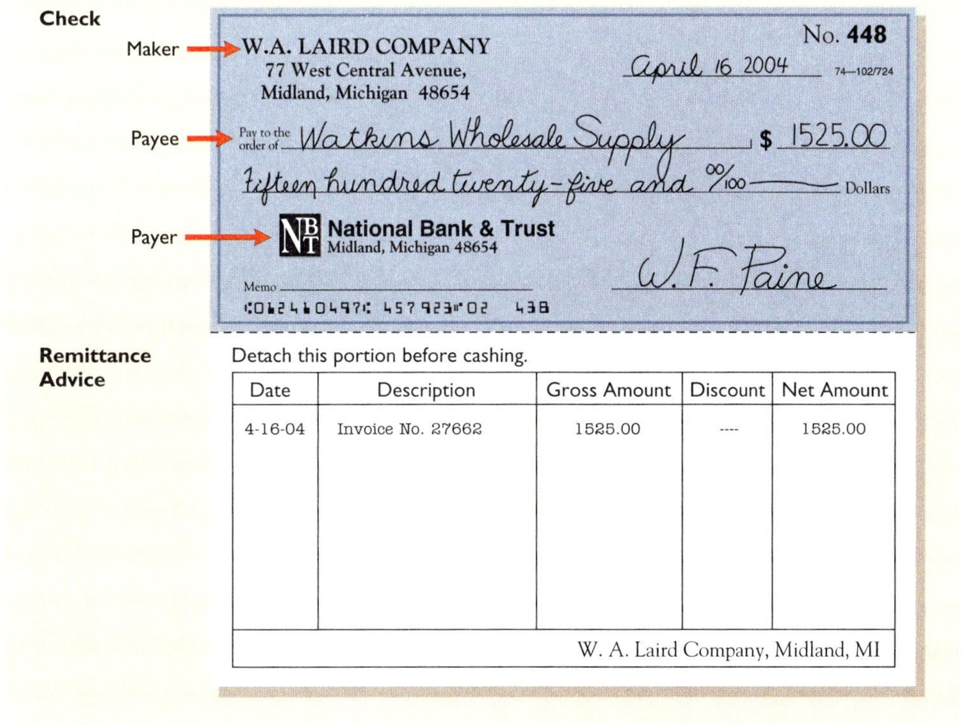

It is important to know the balance in the checking account at all times. To keep the balance current, each deposit and check should be entered on running balance memorandum forms provided by the bank or on the check stubs contained in the checkbook.

ACCOUNTING IN ACTION e Business Insight

Cash is virtually obsolete. We use debit cards and credit cards to pay for most of our purchases. But debit cards are usable only at specified locations, and credit cards are cumbersome for small transactions. They are no good for transferring cash between individuals or to small companies that don't want to pay credit card fees. Digital cash is the next online wave.

There are many digital-cash companies. One of the most flexible appears to be **PayPal.com.** PayPal has become popular with users of the auction site **eBay**, because it allows them to transfer funds to each other as easily as sending e-mail.

SOURCE: Mathew Ingram, "Will Digital Cash Work This Time?" *The Globe and Mail* (March 18, 2000), p. N4.

BANK STATEMENTS

HELPFUL HINT
Essentially, the bank statement is a copy of the bank's records sent to the customer for periodic review.

Each month, the depositor receives a bank statement from the bank. A **bank statement** shows the depositor's bank transactions and balances. A typical statement is presented in Illustration 10-36. It shows (1) checks paid and other debits that reduce the balance in the depositor's account, (2) deposits and other credits that

HELPFUL HINT
Every deposit received by the bank is *credited* to the customer's account. The reverse occurs when the bank "pays" a check issued by a company on its checking account balance: Payment reduces the bank's liability. Thus it is *debited* to the customer's account with the bank.

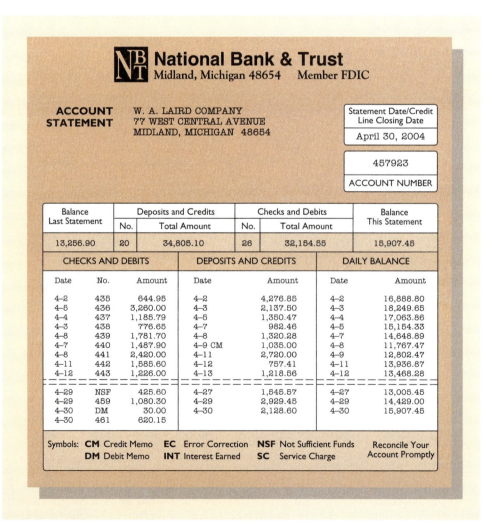

Illustration 10-36
Bank statement

National Bank & Trust
Midland, Michigan 48654 Member FDIC

ACCOUNT STATEMENT

W. A. LAIRD COMPANY
77 WEST CENTRAL AVENUE
MIDLAND, MICHIGAN 48654

Statement Date/Credit Line Closing Date: April 30, 2004

457923
ACCOUNT NUMBER

Balance Last Statement	Deposits and Credits		Checks and Debits		Balance This Statement
	No.	Total Amount	No.	Total Amount	
13,256.90	20	34,805.10	26	32,154.55	15,907.45

CHECKS AND DEBITS			DEPOSITS AND CREDITS		DAILY BALANCE	
Date	No.	Amount	Date	Amount	Date	Amount
4-2	435	644.95	4-2	4,276.85	4-2	16,888.80
4-5	436	3,260.00	4-3	2,137.50	4-3	18,249.65
4-4	437	1,185.79	4-5	1,350.47	4-4	17,063.86
4-3	438	776.65	4-7	982.46	4-5	15,154.33
4-8	439	1,781.70	4-8	1,320.28	4-7	14,648.89
4-7	440	1,487.90	4-9 CM	1,035.00	4-8	11,767.47
4-8	441	2,420.00	4-11	2,720.00	4-9	12,802.47
4-11	442	1,585.60	4-12	757.41	4-11	13,936.87
4-12	443	1,226.00	4-13	1,218.56	4-12	13,468.28
4-29	NSF	425.60	4-27	1,545.57	4-27	13,005.45
4-29	459	1,080.30	4-29	2,929.45	4-29	14,429.00
4-30	DM	30.00	4-30	2,128.60	4-30	15,907.45
4-30	461	620.15				

Symbols: **CM** Credit Memo **EC** Error Correction **NSF** Not Sufficient Funds **DM** Debit Memo **INT** Interest Earned **SC** Service Charge

Reconcile Your Account Promptly

increase the balance in the depositor's account, and (3) the account balance after each day's transactions.

All "paid" checks are listed in numerical sequence on the bank statement along with the date the check was paid and its amount. Upon paying a check, the bank stamps the check "paid"; a paid check is sometimes referred to as a **canceled** check. Most banks offer depositors the option of receiving "paid" checks with their bank statements. For those who decline, the bank keeps a record of each check on microfilm.

The bank also includes on the bank statement memoranda explaining other debits and credits made by the bank to the depositor's account.

Debit Memorandum

Banks charge a monthly fee for their services. Often the fee is charged only when the average monthly balance in a checking account falls below a specified amount. The fee, called a **bank service charge**, is identified on the bank statement by a code symbol such as SC. A debit memorandum explaining the charge is included with the bank statement and noted on the statement. Separate debit memoranda may also be issued for other bank services such as the cost of printing checks, issuing traveler's checks, and wiring funds to other locations. The symbol DM is often used for such charges.

A debit memorandum is also used by the bank when a deposited check from a customer "bounces" because of insufficient funds. In such a case, the check is marked NSF (not sufficient funds) by the customer's bank and is returned to the depositor's bank. The bank then debits the depositor's account, as shown by the symbol NSF on the bank statement in Illustration 10-36 (on page 336). The bank sends the **NSF check** and debit memorandum to the depositor as notification of the charge. The NSF check creates an account receivable for the depositor and reduces cash in the bank account.

Credit Memorandum

A depositor may ask the bank to collect its notes receivable. In such a case, the bank will credit the depositor's account for the cash proceeds of the note. This is illustrated on the W. A. Laird Company bank statement by the symbol CM. The bank will issue a credit memorandum, which is sent with the statement to explain the entry. Many banks also offer interest on checking accounts. The interest earned may be indicated on the bank statement by the symbol CM or INT.

RECONCILING THE BANK ACCOUNT

STUDY OBJECTIVE 14

Prepare a bank reconciliation.

The bank and the depositor maintain independent records of the depositor's checking account. If you've never had a checking account, you might assume that the respective balances will always agree. In fact, the two balances are seldom the same at any given time. It is therefore necessary to make the balance per books agree with the balance per bank—a process called *reconciling the bank account.* The lack of agreement between the two balances is due to:

1. **Time lags** that prevent one of the parties from recording the transaction in the same period.
2. **Errors** by either party in recording transactions.

Time lags occur frequently. For example, several days may elapse between the time a check is mailed to a payee and the date the check is paid by the bank.

ACCOUNTING IN ACTION *Ethics Insight*

During a class lecture, Mr. Alan E. Gallo, chief financial officer of The Houstonian Hotel, Club & Spa, shared some controls incidents with the students. He mentioned that a hotel received a complaint letter and a laundry bill from a guest. This guest claimed that food was spilled on his wife's dress, and he would like the hotel to pay for the laundry bill of an amount less than $10. To make the case more convincing, the guest also mentioned that he was a friend of another frequent guest of this establishment. When investigating the matter, the controller called the number on the laundry bill, trying to confirm the incident with the cleaner, and found that the cleaner did not exist. Most people will pay the small bill to take care of the complaint and move on to the next issue. The moral of the story: It is not the amount that matters, it is the principle. Follow set procedures and catch those crooks.

Similarly, when the depositor uses the bank's night depository to make its deposits, there will be a difference of at least one day between the time the receipts are recorded by the depositor and the time they are recorded by the bank. A time lag also occurs whenever the bank mails a debit or credit memorandum to the depositor.

Also, errors sometimes occur. The incidence of errors depends on the effectiveness of the internal controls of the depositor and the bank. Bank errors are infrequent. However, either party could inadvertently record a $450 check as $45 or $540. In addition, the bank might mistakenly charge a check drawn by C. D. Berg to the account of C. D. Burg.

Reconciliation Procedure

To obtain maximum benefit from a bank reconciliation, the reconciliation should be prepared by an employee who has no other responsibilities pertaining to cash. When the internal control principle of independent internal verification is not followed in preparing the reconciliation, cash embezzlements may go unnoticed. For example, a cashier who prepares the reconciliation can embezzle cash and conceal the embezzlement by misstating the reconciliation. Thus, the bank accounts would reconcile, and the embezzlement would not be detected.

In reconciling the bank account, it is customary to reconcile the balance per books and balance per bank to their adjusted (correct or true) cash balances. The reconciliation schedule is divided into two sections. The starting point in preparing the reconciliation is to enter the balance per bank statement and balance per books on the schedule. Adjustments are then made to each section, as shown in Illustration 10-37. Four steps should reveal all the reconciling items that cause the difference between the two balances:

1. **Deposits in transit.** Compare the individual deposits on the bank statement with deposits in transit from the preceding bank reconciliation and with the deposits per company records or duplicate deposit slips. Deposits recorded by the depositor that have not been recorded by the bank represent **deposits in transit**. They are added to the balance per bank.
2. **Outstanding checks.** Compare the paid checks shown on the bank statement or the paid checks returned with the bank statement with (a) checks outstanding from the preceding bank reconciliation, and (b) checks issued by the company as recorded in the cash payments journal. Issued checks recorded by the company that have not been paid by the bank represent **outstanding checks**. They are deducted from the balance per the bank.

HELPFUL HINT

Deposits in transit and outstanding checks are reconciling items because of time lags.

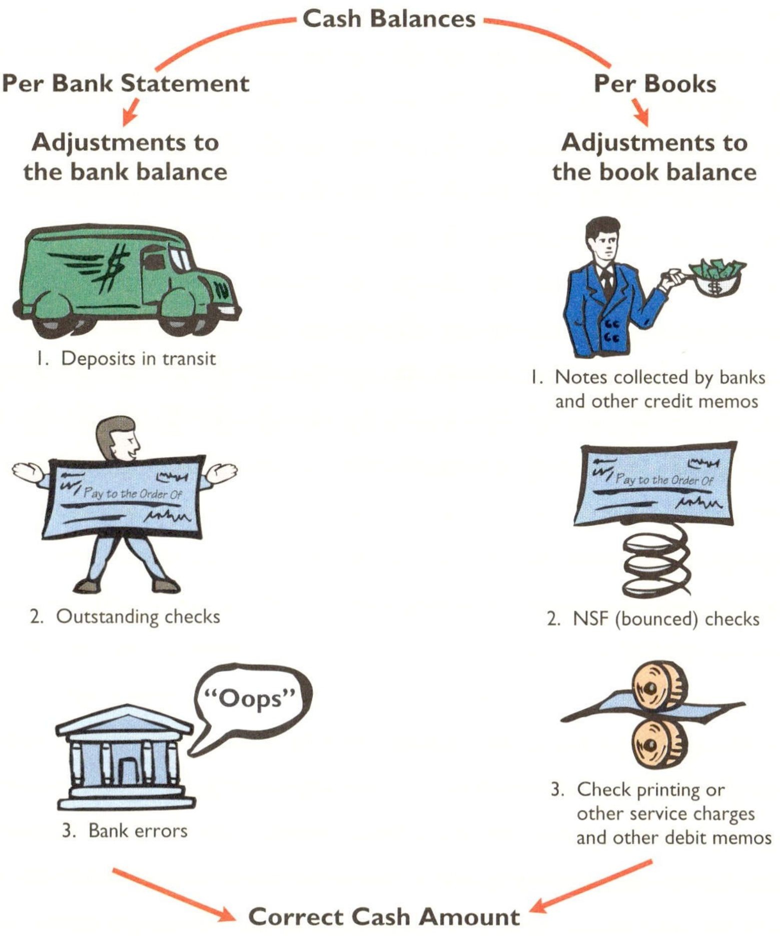

Illustration 10-37
Bank reconciliation procedures

3. **Errors.** Note any errors discovered in the foregoing steps. List them in the appropriate section of the reconciliation schedule. For example, if a paid check correctly written by the company for \$195 was mistakenly recorded by the company for \$159, the error of \$36 is deducted from the balance per books. All errors made by the depositor are reconciling items in determining the adjusted cash balance per books. In contrast, all errors made by the bank are reconciling items in determining the adjusted cash balance per the bank.
4. **Bank memoranda.** Trace bank memoranda to the depositor's records. Any unrecorded memoranda should be listed in the appropriate section of the reconciliation schedule. For example, a \$5 debit memorandum for bank service charges is deducted from the balance per books, and \$32 of interest earned is added to the balance per books.

Bank Reconciliation Illustrated

The bank statement for Laird Company was shown in Illustration 10-36. It shows a balance per bank of \$15,907.45 on April 30, 2004. On this date the balance of cash per books is \$11,589.45. From the foregoing steps, the following reconciling items are determined.

1. **Deposits in transit:** April 30 deposit (received by bank on May 1). \$2,201.40

HELPFUL HINT
Note in the bank statement that checks no. 459 and 461 have been paid but check no. 460 is not listed. Thus, this check is outstanding. If a complete bank statement were provided, checks no. 453 and 457 would also not be listed. The amounts for these three checks are obtained from the company's cash payments records.

2. **Outstanding checks:** No. 453, $3,000.00; no. 457, $1,401.30; no. 460, $1,502.70. — 5,904.00
3. **Errors:** Check no. 443 was correctly written by Laird for $1,226.00 and was correctly paid by the bank. However, it was recorded for $1,262.00 by Laird Company. — 36.00
4. **Bank memoranda:**
   a. Debit—NSF check from J. R. Baron for $425.60 — 425.60
   b. Debit—Printing company checks charge $30.00 — 30.00
   c. Credit—Collection of note receivable for $1,000 plus interest earned $50, less bank collection fee $15.00 — 1,035.00

The bank reconciliation is shown in Illustration 10-38.

Illustration 10-38
Bank reconciliation

ALTERNATIVE TERMINOLOGY
The terms *adjusted balance, true cash balance,* and *correct cash balance* may be used interchangeably.

W. A. LAIRD COMPANY
Bank Reconciliation
April 30, 2004

Cash balance per bank statement		$15,907.45
Add: Deposits in transit		2,201.40
		18,108.85
Less: Outstanding checks		
No. 453	$3,000.00	
No. 457	1,401.30	
No. 460	1,502.70	5,904.00
Adjusted cash balance per bank		**$12,204.85**
Cash balance per books		$11,589.45
Add: Collection of note receivable $1,000, plus interest earned $50, less collection fee $15	$1,035.00	
Error in recording check no. 443	36.00	1,071.00
		12,660.45
Less: NSF check	425.60	
Bank service charge	30.00	455.60
Adjusted cash balance per books		**$12,204.85**

Entries from Bank Reconciliation

HELPFUL HINT
The entries that follow are adjusting entries. In prior chapters, Cash was an account that did not require adjustment. That was a simplifying assumption for learning purposes, because a bank reconciliation had not been explained.

Each reconciling item in determining the **adjusted cash balance per books** should be recorded by the depositor. If these items are not journalized and posted, the Cash account will not show the correct balance. The entries for W. A. Laird Company on April 30 are as follows.

COLLECTION OF NOTE RECEIVABLE. This entry involves four accounts. Assuming that the interest of $50 has not been accrued and the collection fee is charged to Miscellaneous Expense, the entry looks like this:

A	=	L	+	SE
+1,035				−15
−1,000				+50

Apr. 30	Cash	1,035.00	
	Miscellaneous Expense	15.00	
	Notes Receivable		1,000.00
	Interest Revenue		50.00
	(To record collection of notes receivable by bank)		

BOOK ERROR. The cash disbursements journal shows that check no. 443 was a payment on account to Andrea Company, a supplier. Now there is a correcting entry:

Apr. 30	Cash	36.00	
	Accounts Payable—Andrea Company		36.00
	(To correct error in recording check no. 443)		

A	=	L	+	SE
+36		+36		

NSF CHECK. As indicated earlier, an NSF check becomes an account receivable to the depositor:

Apr. 30	Accounts Receivable—J. R. Baron	425.60	
	Cash		425.60
	(To record NSF check)		

A	=	L	+	SE
+425.60				
−425.60				

BANK SERVICE CHARGES. Check printing charges (DM) and other bank service charges (SC) are debited to Miscellaneous Expense. They are usually nominal in amount. The entry looks like this:

Apr. 30	Miscellaneous Expense	30.00	
	Cash		30.00
	(To record charge for printing company checks)		

A	=	L	+	SE
−30				−30

The foregoing four entries could also be combined into one compound entry.

After the entries are posted, the cash account will look like Illustration 10-39.

Cash

Apr. 30 Bal.	11,589.45	Apr. 30	425.60
30	1,035.00	30	30.00
30	36.00		
Apr. 30 Bal.	12,204.85		

Illustration 10-39

Adjusted balance in cash account

The adjusted cash balance in the ledger should agree with the adjusted cash balance per books in the bank reconciliation in Illustration 10-38.

What entries does the bank make? If any bank errors are discovered in preparing the reconciliation, the bank should be notified. It then can make the necessary corrections on its records. The bank does not make any entries for deposits in transit or outstanding checks. Only when these items reach the bank will the bank record these items.

BEFORE YOU GO ON...

REVIEW IT

1. Why is it necessary to reconcile a bank account?
2. What steps are involved in the reconciliation procedure?
3. What information is included in a bank reconciliation?

DO IT

Sally Kist owns Linen Kist Fabrics, which supplies fabrics for table linen in hotel and restaurants. Sally asks you to explain how the following reconciling items should be treated in reconciling the bank account: (1) a debit memorandum for an NSF check, (2) a credit memorandum for a note collected by the bank, (3) outstanding checks, and (4) a deposit in transit.

ACTION PLAN

- Understand the purpose of a bank reconciliation.
- Identify time lags and explain how they cause reconciling items.

SOLUTION: In reconciling the bank account, the reconciling items are treated as follows.
NSF check: Deducted from balance per books.
Collection of note: Added to balance per books.
Outstanding checks: Deducted from balance per bank.
Deposit in transit: Added to balance per bank.

Related exercise material: 10-8 and 10-9.

THE NAVIGATOR

A LOOK BACK AT OUR FEATURE STORY

Refer back to the Feature Story about **Stephanie's Gourmet Coffee and More** at the beginning of the chapter, and answer the following questions.

1. Does Stephanie Mintenko have a valid basis for establishing responsibility for overages or shortages? Why or why not?
2. What internal control principles are applicable to reconciling the cash register tape and the amount of cash in the cash drawer at the end of each shift?
3. What internal control principle is violated by not printing a receipt for each customer who purchases beverages, a meal, or uses the café's computers?
4. Do you think cashiers are, or should be, bonded (insured against misappropriation of assets)?
5. What adjusting entry would the bookkeeper likely make to record a cash shortage of $5?

SOLUTION

1. Establishing responsibility for overages or shortages occurs twice a day: at the end of the 5:00 P.M. shift, and at closing. This procedure provides a valid basis for evaluation only if one person worked an assigned register since the last reconciliation. Since up to three people work a single register during a shift, there is no valid basis for establishing who is responsible for any overage or shortage.
2. Internal control principles are: (a) Authorization—not applicable since cashiers are not assigned to a specific cash register for their shift. (b) Segregation of duties— cashiers (other than the owner/manager) are not involved in performing the reconciliation. (c) Documentation—the cash register tape provides the documentation for total receipts for the shift. (d) Safeguard assets—an electronic cash register is used with an internal tape whose access presumably is restricted. (e) Independent verification—a bookkeeper, in addition to Stephanie Mintenko, performs the reconciliation regularly.
3. The principle of documentation procedures is involved. If a customer making a purchase sees that a sale isn't rung up or if the customer doesn't request a receipt, there is a possibility that the transaction has not been recorded. But the internal control does not reside in the receipt itself. The control is forcing the cashier to ring up each sale so that a receipt is produced. Each receipt is recorded on an internal cash register tape. At the end of the day, the tape is used in determining overages or shortages.
4. It is doubtful that Stephanie's café would bond part-time employees. From the employer's standpoint, bonding is protection against major embezzlements by dishonest employees. The risk of this occurring in a small café, with the active participation of the owner/manager, is relatively low.
5. Cash Over and Short (miscellaneous expense account) and Cash:

Cash Over and Short (miscellaneous expense account)	5	
Cash		5

THE NAVIGATOR

DEMONSTRATION PROBLEM 1

Gerald D. Englehart Steakhouse has the following inventory, purchases, and sales data on its premium individually packaged beef for the month of March.

Inventory:	March 1	200 lbs @ $4.00	$ 800
Purchases:			
	March 10	500 lbs @ $4.50	2,250
	March 20	400 lbs @ $4.75	1,900
	March 30	300 lbs @ $5.00	1,500
Sales:			
	March 15	500 lbs	
	March 25	400 lbs	

The physical inventory count on March 31 shows 500 pounds on hand.

Instructions

Under a *periodic inventory system*, determine the cost of inventory on hand at March 31 and the cost of goods sold for March under the (a) first-in, first-out (FIFO) method, (b) last-in, first-out (LIFO) method, and (c) average cost method.

SOLUTION TO DEMONSTRATION PROBLEM 1

The cost of goods available for sale is $6,450, as follows.

Inventory:		200 lbs @ $4.00	$ 800
Purchases:			
	March 10	500 lbs @ $4.50	2,250
	March 20	400 lbs @ $4.75	1,900
	March 30	300 lbs @ $5.00	1,500
Total cost of goods available for sale			$6,450

Under a *periodic inventory system*, the cost of goods sold under each cost flow method is as follows.

FIFO Method

Ending inventory:

Date	Units	Unit Cost	Total Cost	
March 30	300	$5.00	$1,500	
March 20	200	4.75	950	$2,450

Cost of goods sold: $6,450 − $2,450 = $4,000

LIFO Method

Ending inventory:

Date	Units	Unit Cost	Total Cost	
March 1	200	$4.00	$ 800	
March 10	300	4.50	1,350	$2,150

Cost of goods sold: $6,450 − $2,150 = $4,300

Weighted-Average Cost Method

Weighted-average unit cost: $6,450 ÷ 1,400 = $4.607

Ending inventory: 500 × $4.607 = $2,303.50

Cost of goods sold: $6,450 − $2,303.50 = $4,146.50

ACTION PLAN

- Compute the cost of inventory under the periodic FIFO method by allocating to the units on hand the *latest costs*.
- Compute the cost of inventory under the periodic LIFO method by allocating to the units on hand the *earliest costs*.
- Compute the cost of inventory under the periodic average cost method by allocating to the units on hand a *weighted-average cost*.

THE NAVIGATOR

DEMONSTRATION PROBLEM 2

Trillo Beds and Mattresses sells beddings to resort and lodging operations. Its bank statement for May 2004 shows the following data.

Balance 5/1	$12,650	Balance 5/31	$14,280
Debit memorandum:		Credit memorandum:	
NSF check	$175	Collection of note receivable	$505

The cash balance per books at May 31 is $13,319. Your review of the data reveals the following.

1. The NSF check was from Hup Hotel Co., a customer.
2. The note collected by the bank was a $500, three-month, 12 percent note. The bank charged a $10 collection fee. No interest has been accrued.
3. Outstanding checks at May 31 total $2,410.
4. Deposits in transit at May 31 total $1,752.
5. A Trillo check for $352 dated May 10 cleared the bank on May 25. This check, which was a payment on account, was journalized for $325.

Instructions

(a) Prepare a bank reconciliation at May 31.

(b) Journalize the entries required by the reconciliation.

ACTION PLAN

- Follow the four steps in the reconciliation procedure. (p. 338).
- Work carefully to minimize mathematical errors in the reconciliation.
- Prepare adjusting entries from reconciling items per books.
- Make sure the cash ledger balance after posting the reconciling entries agrees with the adjusted cash balance per books.

THE NAVIGATOR

SOLUTION TO DEMONSTRATION PROBLEM 2

(a)

TRILLO BEDS AND MATTRESSES
Bank Reconciliation
May 31, 2004

Cash balance per bank statement		$14,280
Add: Deposits in transit		1,752
		16,032
Less: Outstanding checks		2,410
Adjusted cash balance per bank		$13,622
Cash balance per books		$13,319
Add: Collection of note receivable $500, plus $15 interest, less collection fee $10		505
		13,824
Less: NSF check	$175	
Error in recording check	27	202
Adjusted cash balance per books		$13,622

(b)

May 31	Cash	505	
	Miscellaneous Expense	10	
	Notes Receivable		500
	Interest Revenue		15
	(To record collection of note by bank)		
31	Accounts Receivable—Hup Hotel Co.	175	
	Cash		175
	(To record NSF check from Hup Hotel Co.)		
31	Accounts Payable	27	
	Cash		27
	(To correct error in recording check)		

SUMMARY OF STUDY OBJECTIVES

1. ***Describe the steps in determining inventory quantities.*** The steps in determining inventory quantities are (1) taking a physical inventory of goods on hand and (2) determining the ownership of goods in transit.

2. ***Prepare the entries for purchases and sales of inventory under a periodic inventory system.*** In recording purchases, entries are required for (a) cash and credit purchases, (b) purchase returns and allowances, (c) purchase discounts, and (d) freight costs. In recording sales, entries are required for (a) cash and credit sales, (b) sales returns and allowances, and (c) sales discounts.

3. ***Determine cost of goods sold under a periodic inventory system.*** The steps in determining cost of goods sold are (a) record the purchases of merchandise, (b) determine the cost of goods purchased, and (c) determine the cost of goods on hand at the beginning and end of the accounting period.

4. ***Identify the unique features of the income statement for a merchandiser using a periodic inventory system.*** The income statement for a merchandiser contains three sections: sales revenue, cost of goods sold, and operating expenses. The cost of goods sold section under a periodic inventory system generally reports beginning and ending inventory, cost of goods purchased, and cost of goods available for sale.

5. ***Explain the basis of accounting for inventories, and describe the inventory cost flow methods.*** The primary basis of accounting for inventories is cost. Cost includes all expenditures necessary to acquire goods and to make them ready for sale. Inventoriable costs include (1) the cost of beginning inventory and (2) the cost of goods purchased. The inventory cost flow methods are: specific identification, FIFO, LIFO, and average cost.

6. ***Explain the financial statement and tax effects of each of the inventory cost flow methods.*** The cost of goods available for sale may be allocated to cost of goods sold and ending inventory by specific identification or by a method based on an assumed cost flow. These methods have different effects on financial statements during periods of changing prices. When prices are rising, FIFO results in lower cost of goods sold and higher net income than the average cost and the LIFO methods. LIFO results in the lowest income taxes (because of lower net income). In the balance sheet, FIFO results in an ending inventory that is closest to current value. The inventory under LIFO is the farthest from current value.

7. ***Indicate the effects of inventory errors on the financial statements.*** In the income statement of the current year: (a) An error in beginning inventory will have a reverse effect on net income (overstatement of inventory results in understatement of net income); and (b) an error in ending inventory will have a similar effect on net income (overstatement of inventory results in overstatement of net income). If ending inventory errors are not corrected in the next period, their effect on net income for that period is reversed, and total net income for the two years will be correct. In the balance sheet, ending inventory errors will have the same effect on total assets and total stockholders' equity and no effect on liabilities.

8. ***Compute and interpret inventory turnover.*** Inventory turnover is calculated as cost of goods sold divided by average inventory. It can be converted to average days in inventory by dividing 365 days by the inventory turnover ratio. A higher turnover or lower average days in inventory suggests that management is trying to keep inventory levels low relative to sales.

9. ***Define internal control.*** Internal control is the plan of organization and related methods and procedures adopted within a business to safeguard its assets and to enhance the accuracy and reliability of its accounting records.

10. ***Identify the principles of internal control.*** The principles of internal control are: establishment of responsibility; segregation of duties; documentation procedures; physical, mechanical, and electronic controls; independent internal verification; and other controls.

11. ***Explain the applications of internal control principles to cash receipts.*** Internal controls over cash receipts include: (a) designating only personnel such as cashiers to handle cash; (b) assigning the duties of receiving cash, recording cash, and custody of cash to different individuals; (c) obtaining remittance advices for mail receipts, cash register tapes for over-the-counter receipts, and deposit slips for bank deposits; (d) using company safes and bank vaults to store cash with access limited to authorized personnel, and using cash registers in executing over-the-counter receipts; (e) making independent daily counts of register receipts and daily comparisons of total receipts with total deposits; and (f) bonding personnel that handle cash and requiring them to take vacations.

12. ***Explain the applications of internal control principles to cash disbursements.*** Internal controls over cash disbursements include: (a) having only specified individuals such as the treasurer authorized to sign checks; (b) assigning the duties of approving items for payment, paying the items, and recording the payment to different individuals; (c) using prenumbered checks and accounting for all checks, with each check supported by an approved invoice; (d) storing blank checks in a safe or vault with access restricted to authorized personnel, and using a checkwriter to imprint amounts on checks; (e) comparing each check with the approved invoice before issuing the check, and making monthly reconciliations of bank and book balances; and (f) after payment, stamping each approved invoice "paid."

13. ***Indicate the control features of a bank account.*** A bank account contributes to good internal control by providing physical controls for the storage of cash. It minimizes the amount of currency that must be kept on hand, and it creates a double record of a depositor's bank transactions.

14. ***Prepare a bank reconciliation.*** It is customary to reconcile the balance per books and balance per bank to their adjusted balances. The steps in determining the reconciling items are to ascertain deposits in transit, outstanding checks, errors by the depositor or the bank, and unrecorded bank memoranda.

THE NAVIGATOR

GLOSSARY

Average cost method Inventory costing method that assumes that the goods available for sale have the same (average) cost per unit; generally the goods are identical (p. 315).

Bank service charge A fee charged by a bank for the use of its services (p. 337).

Bank statement A statement received monthly from the bank that shows the depositor's bank transactions and balances (p. 336).

Cash Resources that consist of coins, currency, checks, money orders, and money on hand or on deposit in a bank or similar depository (p. 329).

Check A written order signed by the depositor directing the bank to pay a specified sum of money to a designated recipient (p. 334).

Cost of goods available for sale The sum of the beginning merchandise inventory plus the cost of goods purchased (p. 307).

Cost of goods purchased The sum of net purchases plus freight-in (p. 307).

Cost of goods sold The total cost of merchandise sold during the period, determined by subtracting ending inventory from the cost of goods available for sale (p. 307).

Deposits in transit Deposits recorded by the depositor that have not been recorded by the bank (p. 338).

Electronic funds transfer (EFT) A disbursement system that uses wire, telephone, telegraph, or computer to transfer cash from one location to another (p. 333).

First-in, first-out (FIFO) method Inventory costing method that assumes that the costs of the earliest goods acquired are the first to be recognized as cost of goods sold (p. 313).

Internal auditors Company employees who evaluate on a continuous basis the effectiveness of the company's system of internal control. (p. 327).

Internal control The plan of organization and all the related methods and measures adopted within a business to safeguard its assets and enhance the accuracy and reliability of its accounting records (p. 322).

Inventoriable costs All expenditures needed to acquire goods and to make them ready for sale. The pool of costs that consists of two elements: (1) the cost of the beginning inventory and (2) the cost of goods purchased during the period (p. 311).

Inventory turnover A measure of the number of times on average the inventory is sold during the period; computed by dividing cost of goods sold by the average inventory during the period (p. 321).

Last-in, first-out (LIFO) method Inventory costing method that assumes that the costs of the latest units purchased are the first to be allocated to cost of goods sold (p. 314).

Net purchases Purchases less purchase returns and allowances and purchase discounts (p. 307).

NSF check A check that is not paid by a bank because of insufficient funds in a customer's bank account (p. 337).

Outstanding checks Checks issued and recorded by a company that have not been paid by the bank (p. 338).

Periodic inventory system An inventory system in which inventoriable costs are allocated to ending inventory and cost of goods sold at the end of the period. Cost of goods sold is computed at the end of the period by subtracting the ending inventory (costs are assigned based on a physical count of items on hand) from the cost of goods available for sale (p. 304).

Segregation of duties A separation of functions or division of work so as to provide a reliable basis of evaluating the work of each employee (p. 324).

Specific identification method An actual, physical flow inventory costing method in which items still in inventory are specifically costed to arrive at the total cost of the ending inventory (p. 312).

Voucher An authorization form prepared for each payment by check in a voucher system (p. 333).

Voucher system A network of approvals by authorized individuals acting independently to ensure that all disbursements by check are proper (p. 332).

EXERCISES

Identify items to be included in taking a physical inventory.
(SO 1)

10-1 Fantasia Souvenir Company identifies the following items for possible inclusion in the taking of a physical inventory. Indicate whether each item should be included or excluded from the inventory taking.

(a) Goods in transit from a supplier shipped FOB destination.

(b) Goods sold but being held for customer pickup.

Compute ending inventory using FIFO, LIFO, and average costs.
(SO 5)

10-2 In its first month of operations, Manion Candies made three purchases of merchandise in the following sequence: (1) 300 units at $6, (2) 400 units at $7, and (3) 300 units at $8. Assuming there are 450 units on hand, compute the cost of the ending inventory under the **(a)** FIFO method, **(b)** LIFO method. Manion uses a periodic inventory system, **(c)** compute the cost of the ending inventory under the average cost method, assuming there are 450 units on hand.

10-3 At December 31, 2004, the following information was available for Sherrick Hotel: ending inventory \$80,000, beginning inventory \$60,000, cost of goods sold \$280,000, and sales revenue \$380,000. Calculate inventory turnover and days in inventory for B. Sherrick Company.

Compute inventory turnover and days in inventory.
(SO 9)

10-4 Rome Restaurants, Inc. reports net income of \$90,000 in 2004. However, ending inventory was understated \$5,000. What is the correct net income for 2004? What effect, if any, will this error have on total assets as reported in the balance sheet at December 31, 2004?

Determine correct income statement amounts.
(SO 8)

10-5 Jackie Bennett is the owner of Bennett's Pizza. Bennett's is operated strictly on a carry-out basis. Customers pick up their orders at a counter where a clerk exchanges the pizza for cash. While at the counter, the customer can see other employees making the pizzas and the large ovens in which the pizzas are baked.

Identify the principles of internal control.
(SO 10)

Instructions

Identify the six principles of internal control and give an example of each principle that you might observe when picking up your pizza. (*Note:* It may not be possible to observe all the principles.)

10-6 The following internal control procedures are used at Sheridan Bakery for over-the-counter cash receipts.

Identify internal control weaknesses over cash receipts and suggest improvements.
(SO 10, 11)

1. To minimize the risk of robbery, cash in excess of \$100 is stored in an unlocked attaché case in the stock room until it is deposited in the bank.
2. All over-the-counter receipts are registered by three clerks who use a cash register with a single cash drawer.
3. The company accountant makes the bank deposit and then records the day's receipts.
4. At the end of each day, the total receipts are counted by the cashier on duty and reconciled to the cash register total.
5. Cashiers are experienced; they are not bonded.

Instructions

(a) For each procedure, explain the weakness in internal control, and identify the internal control principle that is violated.

(b) For each weakness, suggest a change in procedure that will result in good internal control.

10-7 The following internal control procedures are used in Erin's Coffee House for cash disbursements.

Identify internal control weaknesses over cash disbursements and suggest improvements.
(SO 10, 12)

1. The company accountant prepares the bank reconciliation and reports any discrepancies to the owner.
2. The store manager personally approves all payments before signing and issuing checks.
3. Each week, Erin leaves 100 company checks in an unmarked envelope on a shelf behind the cash register.
4. After payment, bills are filed in a paid invoice folder.
5. The company checks are unnumbered.

Instructions

(a) For each procedure, explain the weakness in internal control, and identify the internal control principle that is violated.

(b) For each weakness, suggest a change in the procedure that will result in good internal control.

10-8 Cindy, a new owner of a Chinese restaurant, is unable to reconcile the bank balance at January 31. Cindy's reconciliation is as follows.

Prepare bank reconciliation and adjusting entries.
(SO 14)

Cash balance per bank	\$3,660.20
Add: NSF check	630.00
Less: Bank service charge	25.00
Adjusted balance per bank	\$4,265.20
Cash balance per books	\$3,875.20
Less: Deposits in transit	490.00
Add: Outstanding checks	930.00
Adjusted balance per books	\$4,315.20

Instructions

(a) Prepare a correct bank reconciliation.

(b) Journalize the entries required by the reconciliation.

Determine outstanding checks. (SO 14)

10-9 On April 30, the bank reconciliation of Hinckley Resorts shows three outstanding checks: no. 254, $650, no. 255, $720, and no. 257, $410. The May bank statement and the May cash payments journal show the following.

Bank Statement			Cash Payments Journal		
Checks Paid			Checks Issued		
Date	**Check No.**	**Amount**	**Date**	**Check No.**	**Amount**
5/4	254	650	5/2	258	159
5/2	257	410	5/5	259	275
5/17	258	159	5/10	260	925
5/12	259	275	5/15	261	500
5/20	261	500	5/22	262	750
5/29	263	480	5/24	263	480
5/30	262	750	5/29	264	560

Instructions

Using step 2 in the reconciliation procedure, list the outstanding checks at May 31.

Identify internal control principles over cash disbursements. (SO 10, 12)

10-10 Mexican Fare, a 50-year-old Mexican restaurant, recently changed its system of internal control over cash disbursements. The system includes the following features.

Instead of being unnumbered and manually prepared, all checks must now be prenumbered and written by using the new checkwriter purchased by the company. Before a check can be issued, each invoice must have the approval of Norma Hanson, the purchasing agent, and John Countryman, the controller department supervisor. Checks must be signed by either Linda Anderson, the treasurer, or Bob Skabo, the assistant controller. Before signing a check, the signer is expected to compare the amount of the check with the amount on the invoice.

After signing a check, the signer stamps the invoice PAID and inserts within the stamp, the date, check number, and amount of the check. The "paid" invoice is then sent to the accounting department for recording.

Blank checks are stored in a safe in the treasurer's office. The combination to the safe is known only by the treasurer and assistant treasurer. Each month, the bank statement is reconciled with the cash balance per books by the assistant chief accountant.

Instructions

Identify the internal control principles and their application to cash disbursements of Mexican Fare.

EXPLORING THE WEB

10-11 All organizations should have systems of internal control. Universities are no exception. This site discusses the basics of internal control in a university setting.

Address: **www.bc.edu/bc_org/fvp/ia/ic/intro.html**

Steps: Go the site shown above.

Instructions

The front page of this site provides links to pages that answer six critical questions. Use these links to answer the following questions.

(a) In a university setting who has responsibility for evaluating the adequacy of the system of internal control?

(b) What do reconciliations ensure in the university setting? Who should review the reconciliation?

(c) What are some examples of physical controls?

(d) What are two ways to accomplish inventory counts?

10-12 A company's annual report usually will identify the inventory method used. Knowing that, you can analyze the effects of the inventory method on the income statement and balance sheet.

Address: www.darden.com

Steps

1. From Darden Restaurants' homepage, choose **the Numbers**.
2. Choose **Financial Information**.
3. Choose **Annual Report & Financials**.
4. Choose **Annual Report 2002—HTML version**.
5. Click on **Financial Highlights** under the Table of Contents.

Instructions

Answer the following questions based on the 2002 Annual Report.

(a) At Darden's fiscal year-end, what was the net inventory on the balance sheet?
(b) How has this changed from the previous fiscal year-end?
(c) What inventory method does Darden use?

ETHICS CASE

10-13 J.K. Leask Wholesale Corp. uses the LIFO method of inventory costing. In the current year, profit at J.K. Leask is running unusually high. The corporate tax rate is also high this year, but it is scheduled to decline significantly next year. In an effort to lower the current year's net income and to take advantage of the changing income tax rate, the president of J.K. Leask Wholesale instructs the accountant to recommend to the purchasing department a large purchase of inventory for delivery three days before the end of the year. The price of the inventory to be purchased has doubled during the year, and the purchase will represent a major portion of the ending inventory value.

Instructions

(a) What is the effect of this transaction on this year's and next year's income statement and income tax expense? Why?
(b) If J.K. Leask Wholesale had been using the FIFO method of inventory costing, would the president give the same directive?
(c) Should the plant accountant order the inventory purchase to lower income? What are the ethical implications of this order?

Remember to go back to the Navigator box on the chapter-opening page and check off your completed work.

ACCOUNTING FOR RECEIVABLES AND PAYABLES

11

THE NAVIGATOR ✓

- Understand *Concepts for Review* ❑
- Read *Feature Story* ❑
- Scan *Study Objectives* ❑
- Read *Preview* ❑
- Read text and answer *Before You Go On* *p.* 361 ❑ *p.* 363 ❑ *p.* 370 ❑
- Work *Demonstration Problem* ❑
- Review *Summary of Study Objectives* ❑
- Complete *Assignments* ❑

CONCEPTS FOR REVIEW

Before studying this chapter, you should know or, if necessary, review:

a. How to record sales transactions. (Ch. 7, pp. 208–210)

b. Why adjusting entries are made. (Ch. 4, pp. 115–116)

c. How to compute interest. (Ch. 4, p. 125)

THE NAVIGATOR

FEATURE STORY

Show Me the Money

When businesses refer to accounts receivables, it is the money that is owed to them. Accounts payables, on the other hand, represent money that businesses owe to others. So, what about deposits on beer bottles paid by customers, refunds paid to customers when the bottles are returned, deposits paid by businesses when the beer sellers deliver the cases, and the refund checks beer sellers write to businesses when they pick up the bottles? They are all part of receivables and payables.

Ralph R. Miller, president of **Inntegrated Hospitality Management Ltd.** in Canada, started in the hospitality business as a chef, became a Chartered Account in Canada (equivalent to a Certified Public Accountant in the United States), worked for **Coopers and Lybrand**, an accounting firm, and started the hospitality arm for Coopers. In the early 1990s, he also managed a full-service hotel in Calgary.

This particular hotel is unique in that it has a license to operate a liquor store on premise. The liquor store alone generates $5 million in sales per year. The refrigerator for this liquor store could store 104 pallets of beer, each pallet holding 72 cases of 24 bottles per case. Customers who purchase beer pay a deposit on the bottles, and receive a refund later when they return the bottles to a liquor store. The store also takes in bottles from noncustomers and provides refunds. These refunds are recorded in the cash registers, and money therefore is taken out of the cash registers. At the end of the day, the amount of bottles refund is noted and the bottles are put in a bottle recycling bin. The beer seller picks up the bin content periodically and issues a check to the liquor store for the amount determined by the number of bottles recycled.

From the standpoint of accounting procedures, the amounts taken from the cash registers are recorded on a daily basis, offset by the amount received by the refund checks issued by the beer seller. All was well until six employees became a little too greedy. Each of them rung up fictitious refunds on the register without the bottles and kept the cash. All six of them did this daily, so the discrepancies between cash registers paid out and beer sellers' refund checks grew until the bottle refund checks from the supplier made little resemblance to the daily paid outs recorded by the liquor store cash register. Forensic accounting done on a six-month period revealed a total fraud of more than $57,000.

Miller gathered all the evidence and brought the issue to justice. All six employees had to pay restitution, with two employees serving jail time. He quoted an age-old adage, "You watch the pennies and the dollars will take care of themselves." Just think, even a $0.10-per-bottle refund can turn into a $57,000 fraud with jail time in six months!

THE NAVIGATOR

STUDY OBJECTIVES

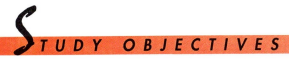

After studying this chapter, you should be able to

1. Identify the different types of receivables.
2. Explain how accounts receivable are recognized in the accounts.
3. Distinguish between the methods and bases used to value accounts receivable.
4. Describe the entries to record the disposition of accounts receivable.
5. Explain why credit policies are needed in the hospitality industry.

THE NAVIGATOR

Continued

PREVIEW OF CHAPTER 11

As indicated in the Feature Story, receivables are a significant asset on the books of many hospitality companies. As a consequence, companies must pay close attention to their receivables and carefully manage them. Although receivables are a significant asset, payables are a pertinent liability. These claims, debts, and obligations must be settled or paid at some time in the future by the transfer of assets or services. Failure in paying your bills on time, including sales taxes you collect on behalf of the government, can result in severe penalties. In this chapter, you will learn what journal entries hospitality companies make when products are sold, when cash is collected from those sales, when accounts that cannot be collected are written off, when debts are incurred, and when they are paid.

Thus, our discussion of receivables and current liabilities are as follows.

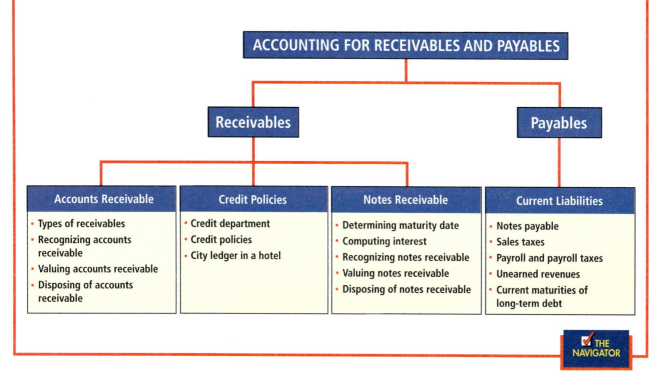

ACCOUNTING FOR RECEIVABLES AND PAYABLES

- **Receivables**
  - **Accounts Receivable**
    - Types of receivables
    - Recognizing accounts receivable
    - Valuing accounts receivable
    - Disposing of accounts receivable
  - **Credit Policies**
    - Credit department
    - Credit policies
    - City ledger in a hotel
  - **Notes Receivable**
    - Determining maturity date
    - Computing interest
    - Recognizing notes receivable
    - Valuing notes receivable
    - Disposing of notes receivable
- **Payables**
  - **Current Liabilities**
    - Notes payable
    - Sales taxes
    - Payroll and payroll taxes
    - Unearned revenues
    - Current maturities of long-term debt

THE NAVIGATOR

STUDY OBJECTIVES (CONTINUED)

6. Compute the maturity date of and interest on notes receivable.
7. Explain how notes receivable are recognized in the accounts.
8. Describe how notes receivable are valued.
9. Describe the entries to record the disposition of notes receivable.
10. Explain a current liability, and identify the major types of current liabilities.
11. Describe the accounting of notes payable.
12. Explain the accounting of other current liabilities.

ACCOUNTS RECEIVABLE

TYPES OF RECEIVABLES

STUDY OBJECTIVE 1

Identify the different types of receivables.

The term *receivables* refers to amounts due from individuals and other companies. They are claims that are expected to be collected in cash. Receivables are frequently classified as accounts, notes, and other:

- **Accounts receivable** are amounts owed by customers on account. They result from the sale of goods and services. These receivables generally are expected to be collected within 30 to 60 days. They are the most significant type of claim held by a company.
- **Notes receivable** are claims for which formal instruments of credit are issued as proof of the debt. A note receivable normally extends for time periods of 60 to 90 days or longer and requires the debtor to pay interest. Notes and accounts receivable that result from sales transactions are often called **trade receivables**.
- **Other receivables** include nontrade receivables. Examples are interest receivable, loans to company officers, advances to employees, and income taxes refundable. These are unusual. Therefore they are generally classified and reported as separate items in the balance sheet.

ETHICS NOTE

Receivables from employees and officers of a company are reported separately in the financial statements. The reason: Sometimes those assets are valued inappropriately or are not based on an "arm's length" transaction.

Three primary accounting issues are associated with accounts receivable:

1. **Recognizing** accounts receivable
2. **Valuing** accounts receivable
3. **Disposing of** accounts receivable

STUDY OBJECTIVE 2

Explain how accounts receivable are recognized in the accounts.

RECOGNIZING ACCOUNTS RECEIVABLE

Recognizing accounts receivable is relatively straightforward. In Chapter 7 we saw how accounts receivable are affected by the sale of merchandise. To illustrate, assume that Jordache Co. on July 1, 2004, sells merchandise on account to Polo Theme Park for $1,000 terms 2/10, n/30. On July 5, Polo returns merchandise worth $100 to Jordache Co. On July 11, Jordache receives payment from Polo for the balance due. The journal entries to record these transactions on the books of Jordache Co. are as follows.

July 1	Accounts Receivable—Polo Theme Park	1,000	
	Sales		1,000
	(To record sales on account)		
July 5	Sales Returns and Allowances	100	
	Accounts Receivable—Polo Theme Park		100
	(To record merchandise returned)		
July 11	Cash ($900 − $18)	882	
	Sales Discounts ($900 × .02)	18	
	Accounts Receivable—Polo Theme Park		900
	(To record collection of accounts receivable)		

A	=	L	+	SE
+1,000				+1,000

A	=	L	+	SE
−100				−100

A	=	L	+	SE
+882				−18
−900				

A discount is given in these situations either to encourage prompt payment or for competitive reasons.

Sometimes, a hospitality business may also need to pay interest. Take the example of Gary's Soup and Salad. Gary's buys produce from Fresh Produce for all its salad bar items. To illustrate, assume Gary's buy on credit. Fresh Produce will make the following entry at the date of sale.

Accounts Receivable	300	
Sales		300
(To record sale of merchandise)		

HELPFUL HINT

The preceding entries are the same as those described in Chapter 7. For simplicity, inventory and cost of goods sold are omitted from this set of journal entries and from end-of-chapter material.

A	=	L	+	SE
+300				+300

Fresh Produce will send Gary's a monthly statement of this transaction and any others that have occurred during the month. If Gary's does not pay in full within 30 days, Fresh Produce adds an interest (financing) charge to the balance due. Although the interest rates vary by region and over time, a common rate of interest is 18 percent per year (1.5% per month).

When financing charges are added, the seller recognizes interest revenue. Assuming that you owe $300 at the end of the month, and Fresh Produce charges 1.5 percent per month on the balance due, the adjusting entry to record interest revenue of $4.50 ($300 × 1.5%) is as follows:

A	=	L	+	SE
+4.50				+4.50

Accounts Receivable	4.50	
Interest Revenue		4.50
(To record interest on amount due)		

Interest revenue is often substantial for many retailers.

ACCOUNTING IN ACTION *Business Insight*

Interest rates on most credit cards are quite high, averaging 18.8 percent. As a result, consumers often look for companies that charge lower rates. Be careful—some companies offer lower interest rates but have eliminated the standard 25-day grace period before finance charges are incurred. Other companies encourage consumers to get more in debt by advertising that only a $1 minimum payment is due on a $1,000 account balance. The less you pay off, the more interest they earn! One bank markets a credit card that allows cardholders to skip a payment twice a year. However, the outstanding balance continues to incur interest. Other credit card companies calculate finance charges initially on two-month, rather than one-month, averages, a practice that often translates into higher interest charges. In short, read the fine print.

VALUING ACCOUNTS RECEIVABLE

STUDY OBJECTIVE 3

Distinguish between the methods and bases used to value accounts receivable.

Once receivables are recorded in the accounts, the next question is: How should receivables be reported in the financial statements? They are reported on the balance sheet as an asset. But determining the *amount* to report is sometimes difficult because some receivables will become uncollectible.

Each customer must satisfy the credit requirements of the seller before the credit sale is approved. Inevitably, though, some accounts receivable become uncollectible. For example, one of your customers may not be able to pay because of a decline in sales due to a downturn in the economy. Similarly, individuals may be laid off from their jobs or be faced with unexpected hospital bills. Credit losses are recorded as debits to **Bad Debts Expense** (or Uncollectible Accounts Expense). Such losses are considered a normal and necessary risk of doing business on a credit basis.

Two methods are used in accounting for uncollectible accounts: (1) the direct write-off method and (2) the allowance method. These methods are explained in the following sections.

Direct Write-off Method for Uncollectible Accounts

Under the **direct write-off method**, when a particular account is determined to be uncollectible, the loss is charged to Bad Debts Expense. Assume, for example, that Executive Conference Center writes off M. E. Doran's $200 balance as uncollectible on December 12. The entry looks like this:

Dec. 12	Bad Debts Expense	200	
	Accounts Receivable—M. E. Doran		200
	(To record write-off of M. E. Doran account)		

A	=	L	+	SE
−200				−200

When this method is used, bad debts expense will show only *actual losses* from uncollectibles. Accounts receivable will be reported at its gross amount.

Although this method is simple, its use can reduce the usefulness of both the income statement and balance sheet. Consider the following example. Assume that in 2004, Quick Buck Cruise Company decided it could increase its revenues by offering holiday cruises to college students without requiring any money down and with no credit-approval process. On campuses across the country it distributed 1,000,000 cruises with a selling price of $800 each. This increased Quick Buck's revenues and receivables by $800,000,000. The promotion was a huge success! The 2004 balance sheet and income statement looked great. Unfortunately, during 2005, nearly 40 percent of the college student customers defaulted on their loans. This made the 2005 income statement and balance sheet look terrible. Illustration 11-1 shows the effect of these events on the financial statements if the direct write-off method is used.

Illustration 11-1

Effects of direct write-off method

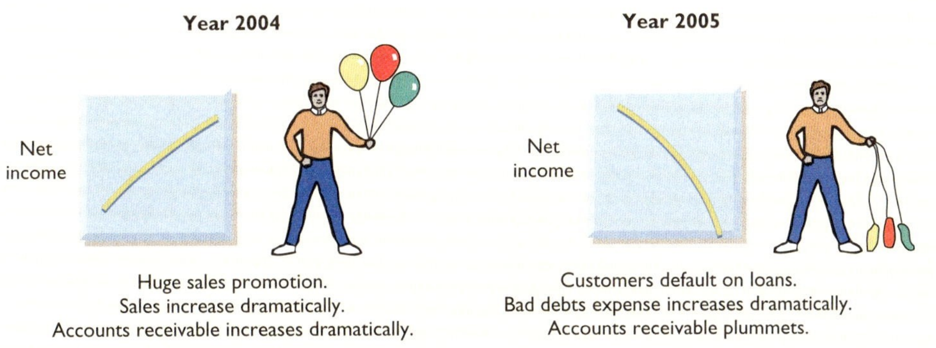

Year 2004
Net income
Huge sales promotion.
Sales increase dramatically.
Accounts receivable increases dramatically.
Year 2005
Net income
Customers default on loans.
Bad debts expense increases dramatically.
Accounts receivable plummets.

Under the direct write-off method, bad debts expense is often recorded in a period different from the period in which the revenue was recorded. No attempt is made to match bad debts expense to sales revenues in the income statement. Nor does the direct write-off method show accounts receivable in the balance sheet at the amount actually expected to be received. **Consequently, unless bad debts losses are insignificant, the direct write-off method is not acceptable for financial reporting purposes.**

Allowance Method for Uncollectible Accounts

The **allowance method** of accounting for bad debts involves estimating uncollectible accounts at the end of each period. This provides better matching on the income statement and ensures that receivables are stated at their cash (net) realizable value on the balance sheet. **Cash (net) realizable value** is the net amount expected to be received in cash. It excludes amounts that the company estimates it will not collect. Receivables are therefore reduced by estimated uncollectible receivables in the balance sheet through use of this method.

The allowance method is required for financial reporting purposes when bad debts are material in amount. It has three essential features:

HELPFUL HINT
In this context, *material* means significant or important to financial statement users.

1. Uncollectible accounts receivable are *estimated*. This estimate is treated as an expense and is matched against sales in the same accounting period in which the sales occurred.

2. Estimated uncollectibles are debited to Bad Debts Expense and are credited to Allowance for Doubtful Accounts (a contra asset account) through an adjusting entry at the end of each period.
3. When a specific account is written off, actual uncollectibles are debited to Allowance for Doubtful Accounts and credited to Accounts Receivable.

RECORDING ESTIMATED UNCOLLECTIBLES. To illustrate the allowance method, assume that Hampson Hotels has credit sales to various restaurants of $1,200,000 in 2004. Of this amount, $200,000 remains uncollected at December 31. The credit manager estimates that $12,000 of these sales will be uncollectible. The adjusting entry to record the estimated uncollectibles looks like this:

A	=	L	+	SE
−12,000				−12,000

Dec. 31	Bad Debts Expense	12,000	
	Allowance for Doubtful Accounts		12,000
	(To record estimate of uncollectible accounts)		

Bad Debts Expense is reported in the income statement as an operating expense (usually as a selling expense). Thus, the estimated uncollectibles are matched with sales in 2004. The expense is recorded in the same year the sales are made.

Allowance for Doubtful Accounts shows the estimated amount of claims on customers that are expected to become uncollectible in the future. This contra account is used instead of a direct credit to Accounts Receivable because we do not know which customers will not pay. The credit balance in the allowance account will absorb the specific write-offs when they occur. It is deducted from Accounts Receivable in the current assets section of the balance sheet as shown in Illustration 11-2.

Illustration 11-2

Presentation of allowance for doubtful accounts

HAMPSON HOTELS
Balance Sheet (partial)

Current assets		
Cash		$ 14,800
Accounts receivable	**$200,000**	
Less: Allowance for doubtful accounts	**12,000**	**188,000**
Merchandise inventory		310,000
Prepaid expense		25,000
Total current assets		$537,800

INTERNATIONAL NOTE

The Finance Ministry in Japan noted that financial institutions should make better disclosure of bad loans. This disclosure would help depositors pick healthy banks.

The amount of $188,000 in Illustration 11-2 represents the expected cash realizable value of the accounts receivable at the statement date. **Allowance for Doubtful Accounts is not closed at the end of the fiscal year.**

RECORDING THE WRITE-OFF OF AN UNCOLLECTIBLE ACCOUNT. Companies use various methods of collecting past-due accounts, such as letters, calls, and legal action. When all means of collecting a past-due account have been exhausted and collection appears impossible, the account should be written off. In the credit card industry, for example, it is standard practice to write off accounts that are 210 days past due. To prevent premature or unauthorized write-offs, each write-off should be formally approved in writing by management. To maintain good internal control, authorization to write off accounts should not be given to someone who also has daily responsibilities related to cash or receivables.

To illustrate a receivables write-off, assume that the vice president of finance of Hampson Hotel authorizes a write-off of the $500 balance owed by R. A. Cybercafe on March 1, 2005:

Mar. 1	Allowance for Doubtful Accounts	500	
	Accounts Receivable—R. A. Cybercafe		500
	(Write-off of R. A. Cybercafe account)		

A	=	L	+	SE
+500				
−500				

Bad Debts Expense is not increased when the write-off occurs. **Under the allowance method, every bad debt write-off is debited to the allowance account rather than to Bad Debts Expense.** A debit to Bad Debts Expense would be incorrect because the expense has already been recognized when the adjusting entry was made for estimated bad debts. Instead, the entry to record the write-off of an uncollectible account reduces both Accounts Receivable and the Allowance for Doubtful Accounts. After posting, the general ledger accounts will appear as in Illustration 11-3.

Illustration 11-3

General ledger balances after write-off

Accounts Receivable				Allowance for Doubtful Accounts			
Jan. 1 Bal.	200,000	Mar. 1	500	Mar. 1	500	Jan. 1 Bal.	12,000
Mar. 1 Bal.	199,500					Mar. 1 Bal.	11,500

A write-off affects only balance sheet accounts. The write-off of the account reduces both Accounts Receivable and Allowance for Doubtful Accounts. Cash realizable value in the balance sheet, therefore, remains the same, as shown in Illustration 11-4.

Illustration 11-4

Cash realizable value comparison

	Before Write-off	After Write-off
Accounts receivable	$200,000	$199,500
Allowance for doubtful accounts	12,000	11,500
Cash realizable value	**$188,000**	**$188,000**

RECOVERY OF AN UNCOLLECTIBLE ACCOUNT. Occasionally, a company collects from a customer after the account has been written off. Two entries are required to record the recovery of a bad debt: (1) The entry made in writing off the account is reversed to reinstate the customer's account. (2) The collection is journalized in the usual manner.

To illustrate, assume that on July 1, R. A. Ware pays the $500 amount that had been written off on March 1. These are the entries:

(1)

July 1	Accounts Receivable—R. A. Cybercafe	500	
	Allowance for Doubtful Accounts		500
	(To reverse write-off of R. A. Cybercafe account)		

A	=	L	+	SE
+500				
−500				

(2)

July 1	Cash	500	
	Accounts Receivable—R. A. Cybercafe		500
	(To record collection from R. A. Cybercafe)		

A	=	L	+	SE
+500				
−500				

Note that the recovery of a bad debt, like the write-off of a bad debt, affects only balance sheet accounts. The net effect of the two entries above is a debit to Cash and a credit to Allowance for Doubtful Accounts for $500. Accounts Receivable is debited and the Allowance for Doubtful Accounts is credited in entry (1) for two reasons: First, the company made an error in judgment when it wrote off the account receivable. Second, after R. A. Cybercafe did pay, Accounts Re-

HELPFUL HINT

Like the write-off, a recovery does not involve the income statement.

ceivable in the general ledger and R.A. Cybercafe's account in the subsidiary ledger should show the collection for possible future credit purposes.

BASES USED FOR ALLOWANCE METHOD. To simplify the preceding explanation, we assumed we knew the amount of the expected uncollectibles. In "real life," companies must estimate that amount if they use the allowance method. Two bases are used to determine this amount: (1) percentage of sales, and (2) percentage of receivables. Both bases are generally accepted. The choice is a management decision. It depends on the relative emphasis that management wishes to give to expenses and revenues on the one hand or to cash realizable value of the accounts receivable on the other. The choice is whether to emphasize income statement or balance sheet relationships. Illustration 11-5 compares the two bases.

Illustration 11-5

Comparison of bases for estimating uncollectibles

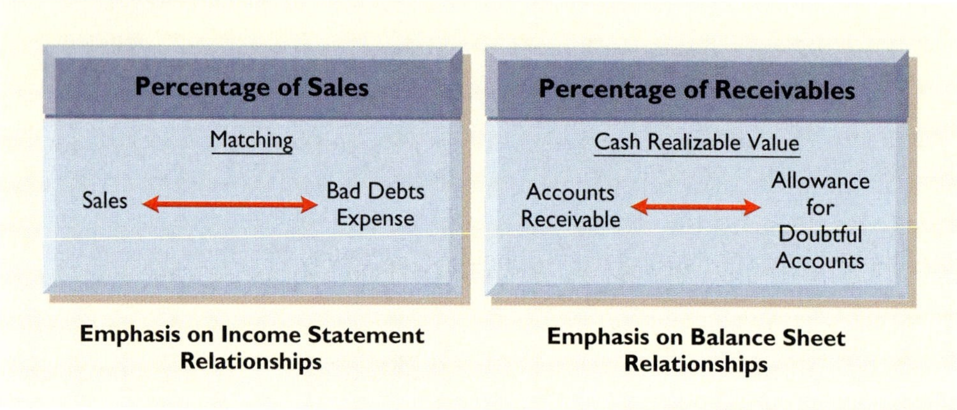

The **percentage of sales basis** results in a better matching of expenses with revenues—an income statement viewpoint. The **percentage of receivables basis** produces the better estimate of cash realizable value—a balance sheet viewpoint. Under both bases, it is necessary to determine the company's past experience with bad debt losses.

In the percentage of sales basis, management estimates what percentage of credit sales will be uncollectible. This percentage is based on past experience and anticipated credit policy.

The percentage is applied to either total credit sales or net credit sales of the current year. To illustrate, assume that the Gonzalez Hotel elects to use the percentage of sales basis. It concludes that 1 percent of net credit sales will become uncollectible. If net credit sales for 2004 are $800,000, the estimated bad debts expense is $8,000 (1% × $800,000). The adjusting entry is:

A	=	L	+	SE
−8,000				−8,000

Dec. 31	Bad Debts Expense	8,000	
	Allowance for Doubtful Accounts		8,000
	(To record estimated bad debts for year)		

After the adjusting entry is posted, assuming the allowance account already has a credit balance of $1,723, the accounts of Gonzalez Hotel will look like Illustration 11-6:

Illustration 11-6

Bad debts accounts after posting

Bad Debts Expense

Debit		Credit
Dec. 31 Adj.	**8,000**	

Allowance for Doubtful Accounts

Debit	Credit	
	Bal.	1,723
	Dec. 31 Adj.	**8,000**
	Bal.	9,723

This basis of estimating uncollectibles emphasizes the matching of expenses with revenues. As a result, Bad Debts Expense will show a direct percentage relationship to the sales base on which it is computed. **When the adjusting entry is made, the existing balance in Allowance for Doubtful Accounts is disregarded.** The adjusted balance in this account should be a reasonable approximation of the uncollectible receivables. If actual write-offs differ significantly from the amount estimated, the percentage for future years should be modified.

Under the *percentage of receivables basis*, management estimates what percentage of receivables will result in losses from uncollectible accounts. An **aging schedule** is prepared, in which customer balances are classified by the length of time they have been unpaid. Because of its emphasis on time, the analysis is often called **aging the accounts receivable**.

ACCOUNTING IN ACTION e Business Insight

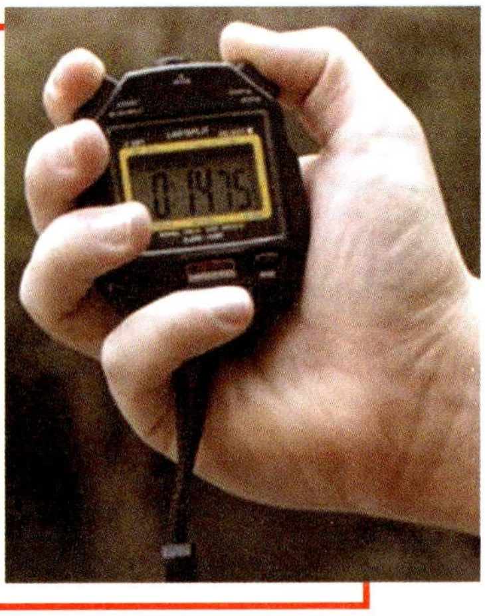

Accounts receivable in a country club is very important. It represents the majority of any additional income a club may earn besides the regular membership fees. Thus, on-time billing so that payments can be received will ensure a healthy cash flow for a club. Still today, many clubs need to mail the signed chits from their members with the month-end billing. The amount of paperwork involved can be tremendous. One country club adopted electronic document imaging whereby the chits are scanned into a PC and indexed so the image can be mailed to the members. With the advances in technology, such equipment has become very affordable. This process not only saves staff time in inefficient filing and copying procedures, but the accounting system can also be programmed so that it will compare its database to the imaging database to make certain proper billing is accomplished.

SOURCE: D. Pacheco, "Electronic document management," *Bottomline*, 15(8), 122–23, (2001).

After the accounts are aged, the expected bad debt losses are determined. This is done by applying percentages based on past experience to the totals in each category. The longer a receivable is past due, the less likely it is to be collected. So, the estimated percentage of uncollectible debts increases as the number of days past due increases. An aging schedule for Dart Day Spa is shown in Illustration 11-7. Note the increasing percentages from 2 to 40 percent.

Illustration 11-7
Aging schedule

			Number of Days Past Due			
Customer	**Total**	**Not Yet Due**	**1–30**	**31–60**	**61–90**	**Over 90**
T. E. Adert	$ 600		$ 300		$ 200	$ 100
R. C. Bortz	300	$ 300				
B. A. Carl	450		200	$ 250		
O. L. Diker	700	500			200	
T. O. Ebbet	600			300		300
Others	36,950	26,200	5,200	2,450	1,600	1,500
	$39,600	$27,000	$5,700	$3,000	$2,000	$1,900
Estimated Percentage Uncollectible		2%	4%	10%	20%	40%
Total Estimated Bad Debts	$ 2,228	$ 540	$ 228	$ 300	$ 400	$ 760

HELPFUL HINT
The higher percentages are used for the older categories because the longer an account is past due, the less likely it is to be collected.

Total estimated bad debts for Dart Day Spa ($2,228) represent the amount of existing customer claims expected to become uncollectible in the future. This amount represents the required balance in Allowance for Doubtful Accounts at the balance sheet date. **The amount of the bad debt adjusting entry is the difference between the required balance and the existing balance in the allowance account.** If the trial balance shows Allowance for Doubtful Accounts with a credit balance of $528, an adjusting entry for $1,700 ($2,228 − $528) is necessary, as shown below.

A	=	L	+	SE
−1,700				−1,700

Dec. 31	Bad Debts Expense	1,700	
	Allowance for Doubtful Accounts		1,700
	(To adjust allowance account to total estimated uncollectibles)		

After the adjusting entry is posted, the accounts of the Dart Day Spa will look like Illustration 11-8:

Illustration 11-8

Bad debts accounts after posting

Bad Debts Expense			Allowance for Doubtful Accounts	
Dec. 31 Adj.	1,700		Bal.	528
			Dec. 31 Adj.	1,700
			Bal.	2,228

Occasionally the allowance account will have a *debit balance* prior to adjustment. This occurs when write-offs during the year have exceeded previous provisions for bad debts. In such a case *the debit balance is added to the required balance* when the adjusting entry is made. Thus, if there had been a $500 debit balance in the allowance account before adjustment, the adjusting entry would have been for $2,728 ($2,228 + $500) to arrive at a credit balance of $2,228.

The percentage of receivables method will normally result in the better approximation of cash realizable value. But it will not result in the better matching of expenses with revenues if some customers' accounts are more than one year past due. In such a case, bad debts expense for the current period would include amounts related to the sales of a prior year.

ACCOUNTING IN ACTION *Business Insight*

Although many individuals pay for their hotel stay with a credit card, there are many others, especially business groups, that ask to be billed to a master account. These invoices are often thousands of dollars. An association holding an annual convention in a hotel might have 20 to 30 rooms blocked for its officers, meeting space rentals, breakfasts, luncheons, dinners, and breaks, all charged to a single master bill. It is, therefore, imperative that hotel controllers try to collect the funds as soon as possible. A number of hotel companies send bills to their customers via Federal Express or other courier services if such accounts are more than $25,000. Why? The customer will have to sign for the delivery of the bill. This eliminates the excuse some customers use, saying they never "received" the bill so they are not at fault for delinquent payment.

BEFORE YOU GO ON...

▶ *REVIEW IT*

1. What is the primary criticism of the direct write-off method?
2. Explain the difference between the percentage of sales and the percentage of receivables methods.

▶ *DO IT*

Brule Gourmet has been in business 5 years. The ledger at the end of the current year shows: Accounts Receivable $30,000, Sales $180,000, and Allowance for Doubtful Accounts with a **debit** balance of $2,000. Bad debts are estimated to be 10 percent of receivables. Prepare the entry to adjust the Allowance for Doubtful Accounts.

ACTION PLAN

- Report receivables at their cash (net) realizable value.
- Estimate the amount the company does not expect to collect.
- Consider the existing balance in the allowance account when using the percentage of receivables basis.

SOLUTION

The following entry should be made to bring the balance in the Allowance for Doubtful Accounts up to a balance of $3,000 (0.1 × $30,000):

Bad Debts Expense	5,000	
Allowance for Doubtful Accounts		5,000
(To record estimate of uncollectible accounts)		

Related exercise material: 11-3 and 11-11.

THE NAVIGATOR

DISPOSING OF ACCOUNTS RECEIVABLE

STUDY OBJECTIVE 4

Describe the entries to record the disposition of accounts receivable.

In the normal course of events, accounts receivable are collected in cash and removed from the books. However, as credit sales and receivables have grown in significance, their "normal course of events" has changed. Companies now frequently sell their receivables to another company for cash, thereby shortening the cash-to-cash operating cycle.

Receivables are sold for two major reasons:

1. **Receivables may be sold because they may be the only reasonable source of cash.** When money is tight, companies may not be able to borrow money in the usual credit markets. Or, if money is available, the cost of borrowing may be prohibitive.
2. **Billing and collection are often time consuming and costly.** It is often easier for a retailer to sell the receivable to another party with expertise in billing and collection matters. Credit card companies such as MasterCard, VISA, American Express, and Diners Club specialize in billing and collecting accounts receivable.

HELPFUL HINT

Two common expressions apply here:

1. Time is money. That is, waiting for the normal collection process costs money.
2. A bird in the hand is worth two in the bush. That is, getting cash now is better than getting it later.

Sale of Receivables

A common sale of receivables is a sale to a factor. A **factor** is a finance company or bank that buys receivables from businesses and then collects the payments directly from the customers. Factoring is a multibillion-dollar business.

Factoring arrangements vary widely. Typically the factor charges a commission to the company that is selling the receivables. This fee ranges from 1 to 3 percent of the amount of receivables purchased. To illustrate, assume that Hendredon Resort factors $600,000 of receivables to Federal Factors. Federal Factors assesses a service charge of 2 percent of the amount of receivables sold. The journal entry to record the sale by Hendredon Resort is as follows:

A	=	L	+	SE
+588,000				−12,000
−600,000				

Cash	588,000	
Service Charge Expense (2% × $600,000)	12,000	
Accounts Receivable		600,000
(To record the sale of accounts receivable)		

If the company often sells its receivables, the service charge expense (such as that incurred by Hendredon) is recorded as selling expense. If receivables are sold infrequently, this amount may be reported in the "other expenses and losses" section of the income statement.

Credit Card Sales

HELPFUL HINT
By accepting credit cards such as VISA, a retailer can increase its sales while reducing its bad debts expense.

One billion credit cards were estimated to be in use recently—more than three credit cards for every man, woman, and child in this country. Companies such as **VISA**, **MasterCard**, **Discover**, **American Express**, and **Diners Club** offer national credit cards. Three parties are involved when national credit cards are used in making retail sales: (1) the credit card issuer, who is independent of the retailer, (2) the retailer, and (3) the customer. A retailer's acceptance of a national credit card is another form of selling (factoring) the receivable.

The major advantages of these national credit cards to the retailer are shown in Illustration 11–9. In exchange for these advantages, the retailer pays the credit card issuer a fee of 2 to 6 percent of the invoice price for its services.

Illustration 11-9

Advantages of credit cards to the retailer

CASH SALES: VISA AND MASTERCARD. Sales resulting from the use of **VISA** and **MasterCard** are considered cash sales by the retailer. These cards are issued by banks. Upon receipt of credit card sales slips from a retailer, the bank immediately adds the amount to the seller's bank balance, deducting a fee of 2 to 4 percent of the credit card sales slips for this service. These credit card sales slips are recorded in the same manner as checks deposited from a cash sale.

To illustrate, Lee Lenertz purchases $1,000 of compact discs for her restaurant from Brieschke Music Co., using her VISA First Bank Card. The service fee that Castle Bank charges is 3 percent. The entry to record this transaction by Brieschke Music is as follows.

Cash	970	
Service Charge Expense	30	
Sales		1,000
(To record VISA credit card sales)		

A	=	L	+	SE
+970				−30
				+1,000

CREDIT SALES: AMERICAN EXPRESS AND DINERS CLUB. Sales using **American Express** and **Diners Club** cards are reported as credit sales, not cash sales. Conversion into cash does not occur until these companies remit the net amount to the seller. To illustrate, assume that Four Seasons restaurant accepts an American Express card for a $300 bill. The entry for the sale by Four Seasons, assuming a 5 percent service fee, looks like this:

Accounts Receivable—American Express	285	
Service Charge Expense	15	
Sales		300
(To record American Express credit card sales)		

A	=	L	+	SE
+285				−15
				+300

American Express will subsequently pay the restaurant $285. The restaurant will record this payment as follows.

Cash	285	
Accounts Receivable—American Express		285
(To record redemption of credit card billings)		

A	=	L	+	SE
+285				
−285				

Service Charge Expense is reported by the restaurant as a selling expense in the income statement.

BEFORE YOU GO ON...

REVIEW IT

1. Why do companies sell their receivables?
2. What is the journal entry when a company sells its receivables to a factor?
3. How are sales using a VISA or MasterCard reported? Is a sale using an American Express card recorded differently? Explain.

DO IT

Peter M. Dell Food Wholesalers Co. has been expanding faster than it can raise capital. According to its local banker, the company has reached its debt ceiling. Dell's customers are slow in paying (60–90 days), but its suppliers (creditors) are demanding 30-day payment. Dell has a cash-flow problem.

Dell needs $120,000 in cash to safely cover next Friday's employee payroll. Its balance of outstanding receivables totals $750,000. What might Dell do to alleviate this cash crunch? Record the entry that Dell would make when it raises the needed cash.

ACTION PLAN

- To speed up the collection of cash, sell receivables to a factor.
- Calculate service charge expense as a percentage of the factored receivables.

SOLUTION: Assuming that Dell Food Wholesalers factors $125,000 of its accounts receivable at a 1 percent service charge, the following entry would be made.

Cash	123,750	
Service Charge Expense	1,250	
Accounts Receivable		125,000
(To record sale of receivables to factor)		

Related exercise material: 11-6.

THE NAVIGATOR

CREDIT POLICIES

STUDY OBJECTIVE 5

Explain why credit policies are needed in the hospitality industry.

Credit policies are crucial in the hospitality industry, especially in the hotel industry where functions and parties are held. Good credit policies will ensure guest satisfaction, lessen misunderstanding, and ensure that the hospitality business will be able to collect its revenues in a timely manner.

THE CREDIT DEPARTMENT

The credit department of a hotel is normally part of the accounting department. Its function is to set policies and also work with the sales staff to check the credit of potential guests. For example, a student organization approaches a hotel for its year-end banquet. This hotel does not know the organization or any of its personnel. The credit department will ask the hotel sales representatives to have the student organization liaison complete a credit application form. The form asks for information such as bank accounts, businesses the student organization has dealt with before, address, phone number, and the like. The credit department will then do its due diligence to hopefully award credit to this organization while the sales personnel discusses the banquet and the needs of this new potential client. Once credit is approved, it is also customary for a hotel to ask for a deposit and have a contract signed. One might think that all these may be a bit too much work. However, consider a function that is $50 per person. If 100 people attend, it is $5,000. All you need is one bad incident and the hotel's profit for the event is gone.

THE CREDIT POLICY PRIOR, DURING, AND POST EVENT

Policies should always be followed; but in the hospitality business, when you are dealing with people, they may not be good event planners. This means that unexpected questions will arise. Imagine a wedding where the bride's parents have everything set with the hotel staff for a reception of 200 people. Despite the advice of the sales staff that the party might need more food since it is held during dinnertime, the family goes with its own estimate. The credit approval is only for a certain amount. The hotel approves the credit to a certain amount and requests and requires a deposit from the wedding party.

On the day of the wedding, 40 unexpected guests arrive. Within half an hour into the reception, the food is gone. The groom's family is telling the banquet captain to bring out more food. Some guests ask the waitstaff for additional canapés. Who actually has the authority to order more food on the spot? The bride wants to add more champagne for the guests. If champagne is $50 a bottle and the bride wants another 10 bottles, that is $500. Should the hotel staff take her order? What if later on the parents do not agree with this and do not want to pay? Should they write a check of $500 right there? Can they be billed later? When it comes to money, all these polices should be set ahead of time so that embarrassing moments like these will not occur.

CITY LEDGER OF A HOTEL

As mentioned in Chapter 2, a hotel keeps two ledgers: the guest ledger and the city ledger. The guest ledger is associated with guests staying at the hotel, while the city ledger contains all other billings. As you can well imagine, it is obviously easier to collect from people who are staying in your hotel because they are physically there. However, for city ledger accounts, collection can be challenging at times.

The city ledger can include individual billings, corporate accounts, group and travel agents, and banquet accounts. An individual might want to rent a function room for a meeting. Corporations might have training sessions for all their first-level managers. They might bring anywhere from 50 to 100 people to a hotel for a few days. The guest rooms, function rooms, and food and beverage bills can add up to thousands of dollars.

Besides training, corporations also hold incentive trips to reward their sales staff. These trips can be big affairs and are wonderful business for hotels. Associations hold annual membership conferences, trade shows, and conventions. Travel agencies book tour groups in hotels. Weddings, birthdays, and anniversaries are all common functions. Did we mention how much these functions can cost? A wealthy businessman once held a dinner for about 80 of his friends and spent more than $75,000, close to $1,000 per person. Of course, this wealthy person paid his bill.

What if, *just what if*, the hotel does not have a good credit policy, or no good accounting personnel to work its city ledger for collection? Well for one thing, the hotel would not be in business for long. Therefore, having a good credit department within the accounting office, good credit policies, and good management of the city ledger, are crucial to a successful operation.

In a restaurant, club, theme park, and other hospitality businesses, it is also important to have such practices. However, their businesses are less susceptible to losses in accounts receivables. Most customers pay by cash or credit cards in restaurants. Even if a restaurant caters functions, it will normally ask for a good amount of deposit up front. Clubs, due to their tax status, cannot take more than 15 percent of their business from nonmembers. In addition, such business normally is referred or sponsored by the members, so there is always a lead to collect if needed.

NOTES RECEIVABLE

Credit may also be granted in exchange for a promissory note. A **promissory note** is a written promise to pay a specified amount of money on demand or at a definite time. Promissory notes may be used (1) when individuals and companies lend or borrow money; (2) when the amount of the transaction and the credit period exceed normal limits; or (3) in settlement of accounts receivable.

In a promissory note, the party making the promise to pay is called the **maker**. The party to whom payment is to be made is called the **payee**. The payee may be specifically identified by name or may be designated simply as the bearer of the note. In the note shown in Illustration 11-10, Brent Company is the maker, Wilma Resort is the payee. To Wilma Resort, the promissory note is a note receivable; to Brent Company, it is a note payable.

Illustration 11-10

Promissory note

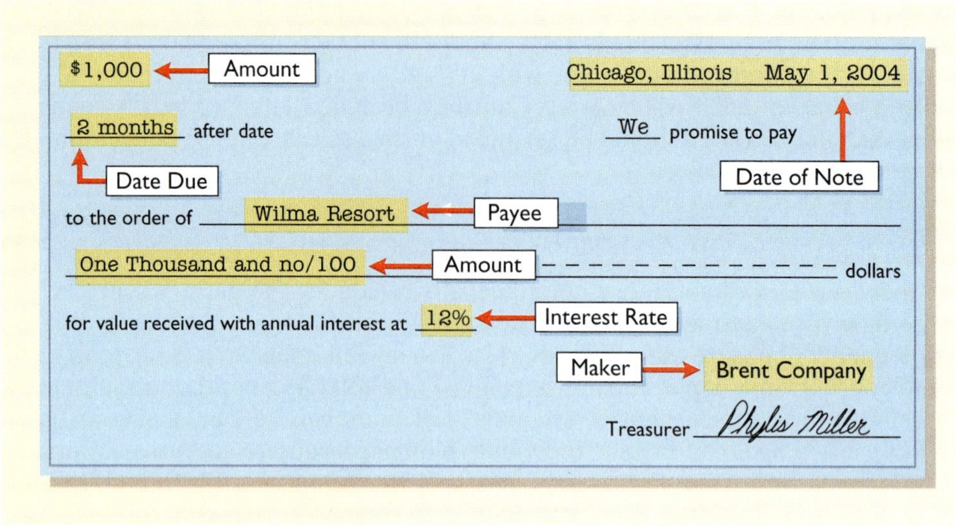

HELPFUL HINT

Who are the two key parties to a note, and what entry does each party make when the note is issued?

Answer:

1. The maker, Brent Company, credits Notes Payable.
2. The payee, Wilma Resort, debits Notes Receivable.

Notes receivable give the payee a stronger legal claim to assets than accounts receivable. Like accounts receivable, notes receivable can be readily sold to another party. Promissory notes are negotiable instruments (as are checks), which means that they can be transferred to another party by endorsement.

Notes receivable are frequently accepted from customers who need to extend the payment of an account receivable. They are often required from high-risk customers. In some industries (such as the pleasure boat industry), all credit sales are supported by notes. The majority of notes originate from loans. The basic issues in accounting for notes receivable are the same as those for accounts receivable:

1. **Recognizing** notes receivable
2. **Valuing** notes receivable
3. **Disposing of** notes receivable

On the following pages, we will look at these issues. Before we do, we need to consider two issues that did not apply to accounts receivable: maturity date and computing interest.

DETERMINING THE MATURITY DATE

STUDY OBJECTIVE 6

Compute the maturity date of and interest on notes receivable.

When the life of a note is expressed in terms of months, the due date when it matures is found by counting the months from the date of issue. For example, the maturity date of a three-month note dated May 1 is August 1. A note drawn on the last day of a month matures on the last day of a subsequent month. That is, a July 31 note due in two months matures on September 30. When the due date is stated in terms of days, you need to count the exact number of days to determine the maturity date. **In counting, the date the note is issued is omitted but the due date is included.** For example, the maturity date of a 60-day note dated July 17 is September 15, computed in Illustration 11-11.

Illustration 11-11

Computation of maturity date

Term of note		60 days
July (31 − 17)	14	
August	31	45
Maturity date: September		**15**

The due date (maturity date) of a promissory note may be stated in one of three ways, as shown in Illustration 11-12.

Illustration 11-12

Maturity date of different notes

COMPUTING INTEREST

As indicated in Chapter 4, Illustration 11-13 shows the basic formula for computing interest on an interest-bearing note:

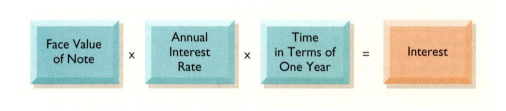

Illustration 11-13

Formula for computing interest

Face Value of Note × Annual Interest Rate × Time in Terms of One Year = Interest

The interest rate specified in a note is an *annual* rate of interest. The time factor in the formula above expresses the fraction of a year that the note is outstanding. When the maturity date is stated in days, the time factor is often the number of days divided by 360. When the due date is stated in months, the time factor is the number of months divided by 12. Computation of interest for various time periods is shown in Illustration 11-14.

HELPFUL HINT

The interest rate specified is the *annual* rate.

Illustration 11-14

Computation of interest

Terms of Note	Interest Computation
	Face × Rate × Time = Interest
\$ 730, 18%, 120 days	\$ 730 × 18% × 120/360 = \$ 43.80
\$1,000, 15%, 6 months	\$1,000 × 15% × 6/12 = \$ 75.00
\$2,000, 12%, 1 year	\$2,000 × 12% × 1/1 = \$240.00

There are many different ways to calculate interest. The computation above assumed 360 days for the length of the year. Many financial institutions use 365 days. It is more profitable to use 360 days; the holder of the note receives more interest than if 365 days are used. For homework problems, assume 360 days.

STUDY OBJECTIVE 7

Explain how notes receivable are recognized in the accounts.

RECOGNIZING NOTES RECEIVABLE

To illustrate the basic entry for notes receivable, we will use the $1,000, two-month, 12 percent promissory note on page 366. Assuming that the note was written to settle an open account, the entry for the receipt of the note by Wilma Resort is:

A	=	L	+	SE
+1,000				
−1,000				

May 1	Notes Receivable	1,000	
	Accounts Receivable—Brent Company		1,000
	(To record acceptance of Brent Company note)		

Observe that the note receivable is recorded at its **face value**, the value shown on the face of the note. No interest revenue is reported when the note is accepted because the revenue recognition principle does not recognize revenue until earned. Interest is earned (accrued) as time passes.

If a note is exchanged for cash, the entry is a debit to Notes Receivable and a credit to Cash in the amount of the loan.

STUDY OBJECTIVE 8

Describe how notes receivable are valued.

VALUING NOTES RECEIVABLE

Valuing short-term notes receivable is the same as valuing accounts receivable. Like accounts receivable, short-term notes receivable are reported at their **cash (net) realizable value**. The notes receivable allowance account is Allowance for Doubtful Accounts. The estimations involved in determining cash realizable value and in recording bad debts expense and related allowance are similar.

ACCOUNTING IN ACTION *International Insight*

Long-term receivables do pose additional estimation problems. For example, banks that loaned money to developing countries have often found it difficult to collect on those receivables. At one time, banks were owed $1.3 trillion by developing countries. (A trillion dollars is a lot of money—enough to give every man, woman, and child in the world $250 each.) Banks made these loans for various reasons: (1) to provide stability to these governments and increase trade, (2) in the belief that governments would never default on payment, and (3) with the desire to increase banks' income by lending. Determining the proper allowance is understandably difficult for these types of long-term receivables.

STUDY OBJECTIVE 9

Describe the entries to record the disposition of notes receivable.

DISPOSING OF NOTES RECEIVABLE

Notes may be held to their maturity date, at which time the face value plus accrued interest is due. Sometimes the maker of the note defaults and an adjustment to the accounts must be made. At other times the holder of the note speeds up the conversion to cash by selling the note. The entries for honoring and dishonoring notes are illustrated below.

Honor of Notes Receivable

A note is **honored** when it is paid in full at its maturity date. For an interest-bearing note, the amount due at maturity is the face value of the note plus interest for the length of time specified on the note.

To illustrate, assume that Betty Hospitality, Inc. lends Wayne Higley Inc. $10,000 on June 1, accepting a four-month, 9 percent interest note. Interest will be $300 ($10,000 × 9% × 4/12). The amount due, the maturity value, will be $10,300. To obtain payment, Betty Hospitality, Inc. (the payee) must present the note either to Wayne Higley Inc. (the maker) or to the maker's duly appointed agent, such as a bank. Assuming that Betty Hospitality, Inc. presents the note to Wayne Higley Inc. on the maturity date, the entry by Betty Hospitality, Inc. to record the collection is:

Oct. 1	Cash	10,300	
	Notes Receivable		10,000
	Interest Revenue		300
	(To record collection of Higley Inc. note)		

A	=	L	+	SE
+10,300				+300
−10,000				

If Betty Hospitality, Inc. prepares financial statements as of September 30, it would be necessary to accrue interest. In this case, the adjusting entry by Betty Hospitality, Inc. would be to record four months' interest ($300), as shown below.

Sept. 30	Interest Receivable	300	
	Interest Revenue		300
	(To accrue 4 months' interest)		

A	=	L	+	SE
+300				+300

When interest has been accrued, at maturity it is necessary to credit Interest Receivable. The entry by Betty Hospitality, Inc. to record the honoring of the Wayne Higley Inc. note on October 1 is:

Oct. 1	Cash	10,300	
	Notes Receivable		10,000
	Interest Receivable		300
	(To record collection of note at maturity)		

A	=	L	+	SE
+10,300				
−10,000				
−300				

In this case, Interest Receivable is credited because the receivable was established in the adjusting entry.

Dishonor of Notes Receivable

A **dishonored note** is a note that is not paid in full at maturity. A dishonored note receivable is no longer negotiable. However, the payee still has a claim against the maker of the note. Therefore the Notes Receivable account is usually transferred to an Account Receivable.

To illustrate, assume that Wayne Higley Inc. on October 1 indicates that it cannot pay at the present time. The entry to record the dishonor of the note depends on whether eventual collection is expected. If Betty Hospitality, Inc. expects eventual collection, the amount due (face value and interest) on the note is debited to Accounts Receivable. Betty Hospitality, Inc. would make the following entry at the time the note is dishonored (assuming no previous accrual of interest).

Oct. 1	Accounts Receivable—Wayne Higley Inc.	10,300	
	Notes Receivable		10,000
	Interest Revenue		300
	(To record the dishonor of Higley Inc. note)		

A	=	L	+	SE
+10,300				+300
−10,000				

If there is no hope of collection, the face value of the note would be written off by debiting the Allowance for Doubtful Accounts. No interest revenue would be recorded because collection will not occur.

Sale of Notes Receivable

The accounting for the sales of notes receivable is recorded similarly to the sale of accounts receivable. The accounting entries for the sale of notes receivable are left for a more advanced course.

BEFORE YOU GO ON...

REVIEW IT

1. What is the basic formula for computing interest?
2. At what value are notes receivable reported on the balance sheet?
3. Explain the difference between honoring and dishonoring a note receivable.

DO IT

Gambit Logo Shirts accepts from Leonard Golf Proshop a $3,400, 90-day, 12% note dated May 10 in settlement of Leonard's overdue account. What is the maturity date of the note? What is the entry made by Gambit at the maturity date, assuming Leonard pays the note and interest in full at that time?

ACTION PLAN

- Count the exact number of days to determine the maturity date. Omit the date the note is issued, but include the due date.
- Determine whether interest was accrued. The entry here assumes that no interest has been previously accrued on this note.

SOLUTION: The maturity date is August 8, computed as follows.

Term of note:		90 days
May (31 − 10)	21	
June	30	
July	31	82
Maturity date: August		8

The interest payable at maturity date is $102, computed as follows.

Face	× Rate	× Time	= Interest
$3,400	× 12%	× 90/360	= $102

The entry recorded by Gambit Logo Shirts at the maturity date is:

Cash	3,502	
Notes Receivable		3,400
Interest Revenue		102
(To record collection of Leonard note)		

Related exercise material: 11-4, 11-5, 11-12, and 11-13.

THE NAVIGATOR

ACCOUNTING IN ACTION *Business Insight*

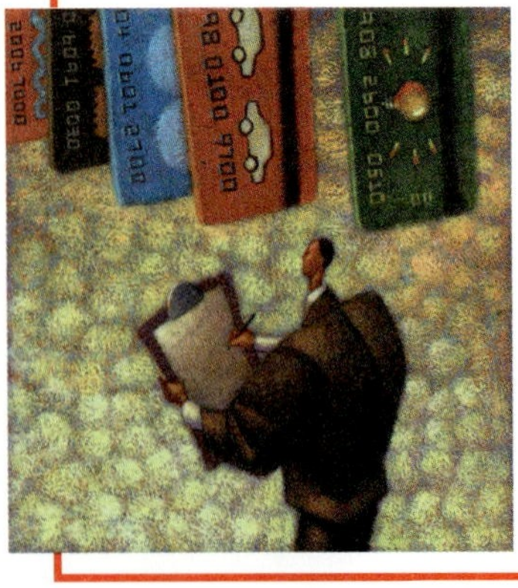

Give the man credit. Like most of us, John Galbreath receives piles of unsolicited, "preapproved" credit card applications in the mail. Galbreath doesn't just toss them out, though. He filled out a credit card application on which he stated he was 97 years old and had no income, no telephone, and no Social Security number. In a space inviting him to let the credit card company pay off his other credit card balances, Galbreath said he owed money to the Mafia.

Back came a credit card and a letter welcoming John to the fold with a $1,500 credit limit. Galbreath had requested the card under a false name, John C. Reath, an alias under which he had received two other credit cards—earning exemplary credit. John C. Reath might be a senior citizen with no means, but it seems he paid his bills on time.

SOURCE: "Forbes Informer," edited by Kate Bohner Lewis, *Forbes* (August 14, 1995), p. 19. Reprinted by permission of FORBES Magazine © Forbes Inc., 1995.

WHAT IS A CURRENT LIABILITY?

STUDY OBJECTIVE 10

Explain a current liability, and identify the major types of current liabilities.

As explained in Chapter 5, a **current liability** is a debt with two key features: (1) It can reasonably be expected to be paid from existing current assets or through the creation of other current liabilities. And (2) it will be paid within one year or the operating cycle, whichever is longer. Debts that do not meet *both criteria* are classified as long-term liabilities. Most companies pay current liabilities within one year out of current assets, rather than by creating other liabilities.

Companies must carefully monitor the relationship of current liabilities to current assets. This relationship is critical in evaluating a company's short-term debt-paying ability. A company that has more current liabilities than current assets is usually the subject of some concern because the company may not be able to meet its current obligations when they become due.

HELPFUL HINT

The current liabilities section of the balance sheet gives creditors a good idea of what obligations are coming due.

Current liabilities include notes payable, accounts payable, and unearned revenues. They also include accrued liabilities such as taxes, salaries and wages, and interest payable. The entries for accounts payable and adjusting entries for some current liabilities have been explained in previous chapters. Other types of current liabilities that are often encountered are discussed in the following sections.

NOTES PAYABLE

STUDY OBJECTIVE 11

Describe the accounting for notes payable.

Obligations in the form of written promissory notes are recorded as **notes payable**. Notes payable are often used instead of accounts payable. Doing so gives the lender formal proof of the obligation in case legal remedies are needed to collect the debt. Notes payable usually require the borrower to pay interest and frequently are issued to meet short-term financing needs.

Notes are issued for varying periods. **Those due for payment within one year of the balance sheet date are usually classified as current liabilities.** Most notes are interest bearing.

To illustrate the accounting for notes payable, assume that First National Bank agrees to lend $100,000 on March 1, 2004, if Williams Restaurant signs a $100,000, 12 percent, four-month note. With an interest-bearing promissory note, the amount of assets received upon issuance of the note generally equals the note's face value. Williams Restaurant therefore will receive $100,000 cash and will make the following journal entry:

Mar. 1	Cash	100,000	
	Notes Payable		100,000
	(To record issuance of 12%, 4-month note to First National Bank)		

A	=	L	+	SE
+100,000		+100,000		

Interest accrues over the life of the note and must be recorded periodically. If Williams Restaurant prepares financial statements semiannually, an adjusting entry is required at June 30 to recognize interest expense and interest payable of $4,000 ($100,000 × 12% × 4/12). The formula for computing interest and its application to Williams Restaurant's note are shown in Illustration 11-15.

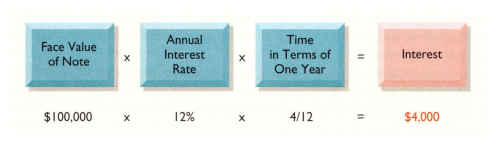

Illustration 11-15

Formula for computing interest

Face Value of Note	×	Annual Interest Rate	×	Time in Terms of One Year	=	Interest
$100,000	×	12%	×	4/12	=	$4,000

The adjusting entry looks like this:

A	=	L	+	SE
		+4,000		−4,000

Date	Account Titles and Explanation	Debit	Credit
June 30	Interest Expense	4,000	
	Interest Payable		4,000
	(To accrue interest for 4 months on First National Bank note)		

In the June 30 financial statements, the current liabilities section of the balance sheet will show notes payable $100,000 and interest payable $4,000. In addition, interest expense of $4,000 will be reported under "other expenses and losses" in the income statement. If Williams prepared financial statements monthly, the adjusting entry at the end of each month would have been $1,000 ($100,000 × 12% × 1/12).

At maturity (July 1, 2004), Williams must pay the face value of the note ($100,000) plus $4,000 interest ($100,000 × 12% × 4/12). The entry to record payment of the note and accrued interest is as follows.

A	=	L	+	SE
−104,000		−100,000		
		−4,000		

Date	Account Titles and Explanation	Debit	Credit
July 1	Notes Payable	100,000	
	Interest Payable	4,000	
	Cash		104,000
	(To record payment of First National Bank interest-bearing note and accrued interest at maturity)		

SALES TAXES PAYABLE

STUDY OBJECTIVE 12

Explain the accounting for other current liabilities.

As a consumer, you know that when you eat at a restaurant, the food is subject to sales taxes. The tax is expressed as a stated percentage of the sales price. The retailer collects the tax from the customer when the sale occurs. Periodically (usually monthly), the restaurant remits the collections to the state's department of revenue.

Under most state sales tax laws, the amount of the sale and the amount of the sales tax collected must be rung up separately on the cash register. The cash register readings are then used to credit Sales and Sales Taxes Payable. For example, if the March 25 cash register reading for Cooley Restaurant shows sales of $10,000 and sales taxes of $600 (sales tax rate of 6%), the entry looks like this:

A	=	L	+	SE
+10,600		+600		+10,000

Date	Account Titles and Explanation	Debit	Credit
Mar. 25	Cash	10,600	
	Sales		10,000
	Sales Taxes Payable		600
	(To record daily sales and sales taxes)		

When the taxes are remitted to the taxing agency, Sales Taxes Payable is debited and Cash is credited. The company does not report sales taxes as an expense. It simply forwards to the government the amount paid by the customers. Thus, Cooley serves only as a **collection agent** for the taxing authority.

When sales taxes are not rung up separately on the cash register, they must be extracted from the total receipts. To determine the amount of sales in such cases, divide total receipts by 100 percent plus the sales tax percentage. To illustrate, assume that in the above example Cooley rings up total receipts, which are $10,600. The receipts from the sales are equal to the sales price (100%) plus the tax percentage (6% of sales), or 1.06 times the sales total. We can compute the sales amount as follows.

$$\$10,600 \div 1.06 = \$10,000$$

Thus, Cooley Restaurant could find the sales tax amount it must remit to the state by subtracting sales from total receipts ($10,600 − $10,000).

HELPFUL HINT

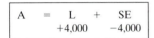

Alternatively, Cooley could find the tax by multiplying sales by the sales tax rate ($10,000 × 6%).

PAYROLL AND PAYROLL TAXES PAYABLE

Every employer incurs liabilities relating to employees' salaries and wages. One is the amount of wages and salaries owed to employees—**wages and salaries payable**. Another is the amount required by law to be withheld from employees' gross pay. Until these **withholding taxes** (federal and state income taxes, and Social Security taxes) are remitted to the governmental taxing authorities, they are credited to appropriate liability accounts. For example, if a corporation withholds taxes from its employees' wages and salaries, accrual and payment of a $100,000 payroll would be recorded as follows.

March 7	Salaries and Wages Expense	100,000	
	FICA Taxes Payable[1]		7,250
	Federal Income Taxes Payable		21,864
	State Income Taxes Payable		2,922
	Salaries and Wages Payable		67,964
	(To record payroll and withholding taxes for the week ending March 7)		

A	=	L	+	SE
		+7,250		−100,000
		+21,864		
		+2,922		
		+67,964		

March 11	Salaries and Wages Payable	67,964	
	Cash		67,964
	(To record payment of the March 7 payroll)		

A	=	L	+	SE
−67,964		−67,964		

Illustration 11-16 summarizes the types of payroll deductions.

Illustration 11-16

Payroll deductions

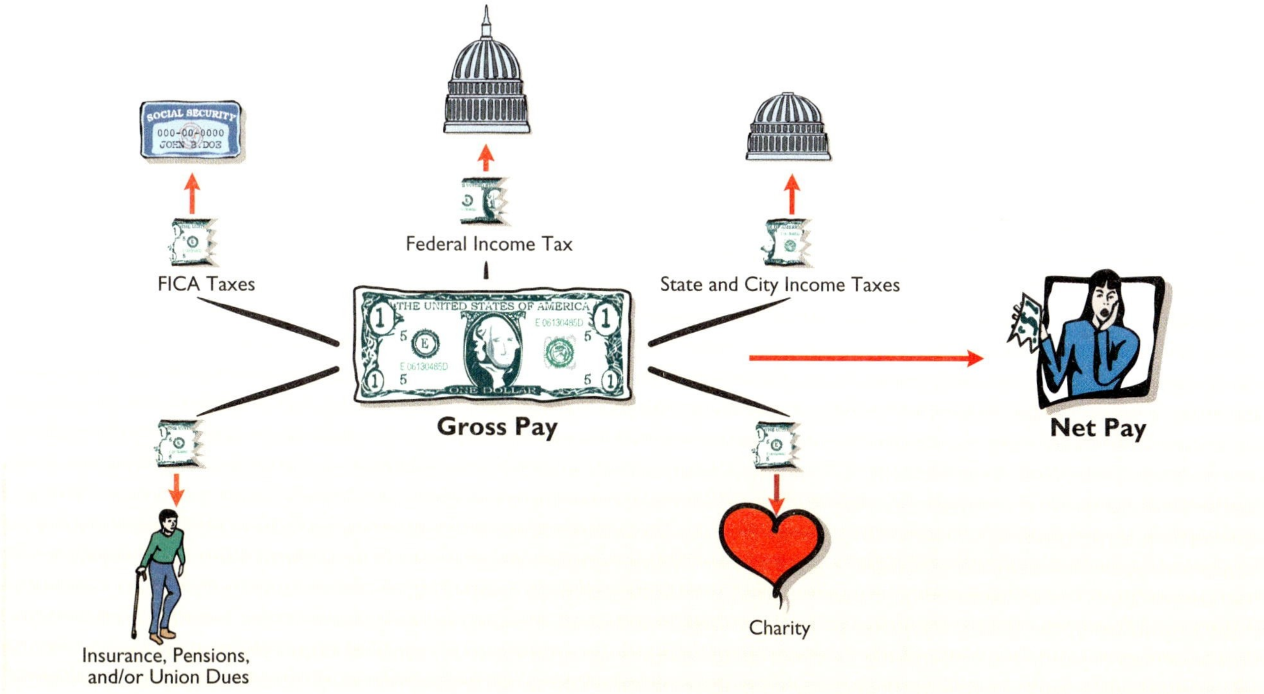

Also, with every payroll, the employer incurs liabilities to pay various **payroll taxes** levied upon the employer. These payroll taxes include the employer's share of Social Security taxes and the state and federal unemployment taxes.

[1]Social Security taxes are commonly referred to as FICA taxes. In 1937, Congress enacted the Federal Insurance Contribution Act (FICA). This act and other payroll issues are discussed in greater detail in Chapter 9.

Based on the $100,000 payroll in the previous example, the following entry would be made to record the employer's expense and liability for these payroll taxes:

A	=	L	+	SE
		+7,250		−13,450
		+800		
		+5,400		

March 7	Payroll Tax Expense	13,450	
	FICA Taxes Payable		7,250
	Federal Unemployment Taxes Payable		800
	State Unemployment Taxes Payable		5,400
	(To record employer's payroll taxes on March 7 payroll)		

Illustration 11-17

Employer payroll taxes

Illustration 11-17 shows the types of taxes levied on employers.

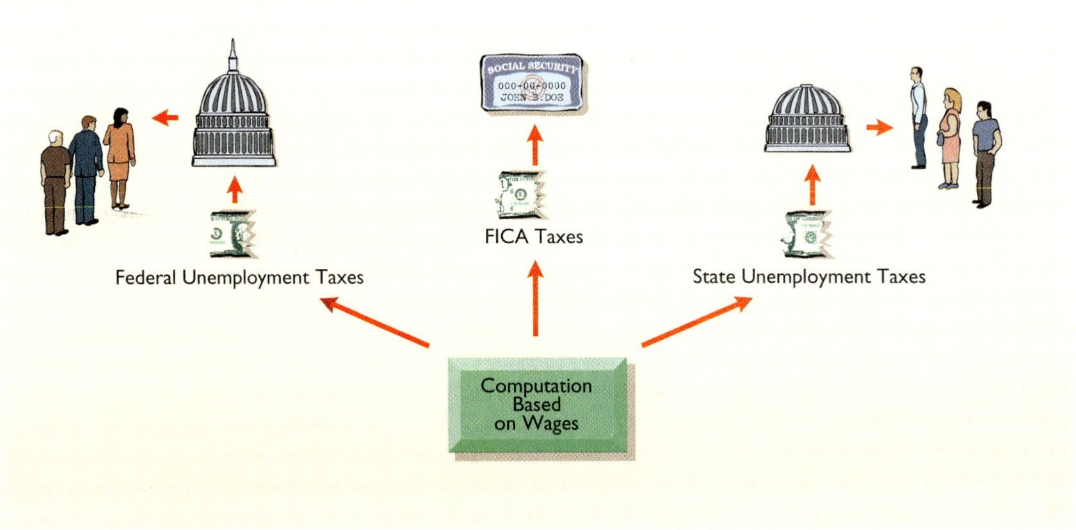

The payroll and payroll tax liability accounts are classified as current liabilities because they must be paid to employees or remitted to taxing authorities in the near term. Taxing authorities impose substantial fines and penalties on employers if the withholding and payroll taxes are not computed correctly and paid on time.

UNEARNED REVENUES

A hotel, such as **Hilton**, receives a customer's check when a banquet is ordered. An airline company, such as **American Airlines**, receives cash when it sells tickets for future flights. Through these transactions, both companies have incurred unearned revenues—revenues that are received before goods are delivered or services are rendered. How do companies account for unearned revenues?

1. When the advance payment is received, Cash is debited, and a current liability account identifying the source of the unearned revenue is credited.
2. When the revenue is earned, the Unearned Revenue account is debited, and an earned revenue account is credited.

To illustrate, assume that Superior Catering sells a party for 10,000 people at $50 each for a Thanksgiving event. The entry for the sale looks like this:

A	=	L	+	SE
+500,000		+500,000		

Aug. 6	Cash	500,000	
	Unearned Catering Revenue		500,000

As the function is completed, the following entry is made:

Sept. 7	Unearned Revenue	500,000	
	Sales Revenue		500,000
	(To record revenues earned)		

A	=	L	+	SE
		−500,000		+500,000

Any balance in an unearned revenue account is reported as a current liability in the balance sheet. As revenue is earned, a transfer from unearned revenue to earned revenue occurs. Unearned revenue is material for some companies: In the airline industry, for example, tickets sold for future flights represent almost 50 percent of total current liabilities. At **United Air Lines**, unearned ticket revenue is the largest current liability, recently amounting to more than $1 billion.

Illustration 11-18 shows specific unearned and earned revenue accounts used in selected types of businesses.

Illustration 11-18

Unearned and earned revenue accounts

Type of Business	Account Title	
	Unearned Revenue	**Earned Revenue**
Airline	Unearned Passenger Ticket Revenue	Passenger Revenue
Magazine publisher	Unearned Subscription Revenue	Subscription Revenue
Hotel	Unearned Rental Revenue	Rental Revenue
Insurance company	Unearned Premium Revenue	Premium Revenue

CURRENT MATURITIES OF LONG-TERM DEBT

Companies often have a portion of long-term debt that comes due in the current year. That amount would be considered a current liability. For example, assume that Wendy Construction issues a five-year interest-bearing $25,000 note on January 1, 2004. Each January 1, starting January 1, 2005, $5,000 of the note is due to be paid. When financial statements are prepared on December 31, 2004, $5,000 should be reported as a current liability. The remaining $20,000 on the note would be reported as a long-term liability. Current maturities of long-term debt are often termed **long-term debt due within one year**.

It is not necessary to prepare an adjusting entry to recognize the current maturity of long-term debt. The proper statement classification of each balance sheet account is recognized when the balance sheet is prepared.

DEMONSTRATION PROBLEM

The following selected transactions relate to Falcetto Souvenirs Company.

Mar.	1	Sold $20,000 of merchandise to Potter Hotels, terms 2/10, n/30.
	11	Received payment in full from Potter Hotels for balance due.
	12	Accepted Juno Resorts $20,000, 6-month, 12% note for balance due.
	15	Made American Express credit sales totaling $6,700. A 5% service fee is charged by American Express.
	30	Received payment in full from American Express Company.
Apr.	11	Sold accounts receivable of $8,000 to Harcot Factor. Harcot Factor assesses a service charge of 2% of the amount of receivables sold.
May	10	Wrote off as uncollectible $16,000 of accounts receivable. Falcetto uses the percentage of sales basis to estimate bad debts.
June	30	Credit sales for the first 6 months total $2,000,000. The bad debt percentage is 1% of credit sales. At June 30, the balance in the allowance account is $3,500.
July	16	One of the accounts receivable written off in May was from J. Simon, who pays the amount due, $4,000, in full.

Instructions

Prepare the journal entries for the transactions.

ACTION PLAN

- Generally, record accounts receivable at invoice price.
- Recognize that sales returns and allowances and cash discounts reduce the amount received on accounts receivable.
- Record a service charge expense on the seller's books when accounts receivable are sold.
- Prepare an adjusting entry for bad debts expense.
- Ignore any balance in the allowance account under the percentage of sales basis. Recognize the balance in the allowance account under the percentage of receivables basis.
- Record write-offs of accounts receivable only in balance sheet accounts.

THE NAVIGATOR

SOLUTION TO DEMONSTRATION PROBLEM

Mar. 1	Accounts Receivable–Potter	20,000	
	Sales		20,000
	(To record sales on account)		
11	Cash	19,600	
	Sales Discounts (2% × $20,000)	400	
	Accounts Receivable—Potter		20,000
	(To record collection of accounts receivable)		
12	Notes Receivable	20,000	
	Accounts Receivable—Juno		20,000
	(To record acceptance of Juno Company note)		
15	Accounts Receivable—American Express	6,365	
	Service Charge Expense (5% × $6,700)	335	
	Sales		6,700
	(To record credit card sales)		
Mar. 30	Cash	6,365	
	Accounts Receivable—American Express		6,365
	(To record redemption of credit card billings)		
Apr. 11	Cash	7,840	
	Service Charge Expense (2% × $8,000)	160	
	Accounts Receivable		8,000
	(To record sale of receivables to factor)		
May 10	Allowance for Doubtful Accounts	16,000	
	Accounts Receivable		16,000
	(To record write-off of accounts receivable)		
June 30	Bad Debts Expense ($2,000,000 × 1%)	20,000	
	Allowance for Doubtful Accounts		20,000
	(To record estimate of uncollectible accounts)		
July 16	Accounts Receivable—J. Simon	4,000	
	Allowance for Doubtful Accounts		4,000
	(To reverse write-off of accounts receivable)		
16	Cash	4,000	
	Accounts Receivable—J. Simon		4,000
	(To record collection of accounts receivable)		

SUMMARY OF STUDY OBJECTIVES

1. *Identify the different types of receivables.* Receivables are frequently classified as (1) accounts, (2) notes, and (3) other. Accounts receivable are amounts owed by customers on account. Notes receivable are claims for which formal instruments of credit are issued as proof of the debt. Other receivables include nontrade receivables such as interest receivable, loans to company officers, advances to employees, and income taxes refundable.

2. *Explain how accounts receivable are recognized in the accounts.* Accounts receivable are recorded at invoice price. They are reduced by Sales Returns and Allowances. Cash discounts reduce the amount received on accounts receivable. When interest is charged on a past due receivable, this interest is added to the accounts receivable balance and is recognized as interest revenue.

3. *Distinguish between the methods and bases used to value accounts receivable.* There are two methods of accounting for uncollectible accounts: (1) the allowance method and (2) the direct write-off method. Either the percentage of sales or the percentage of receivables basis may be used to estimate uncollectible accounts using the allowance method. The percentage of sales basis emphasizes the matching principle. The percentage of receivables basis emphasizes the cash realizable value of the accounts receivable. An aging schedule is often used with this basis.

4. ***Describe the entries to record the disposition of accounts receivable.*** When an account receivable is collected, Accounts Receivable is credited. When an account receivable is sold, a service charge expense is charged which reduces the amount collected.

5. ***Explain why credit policies are needed in the hospitality industry.*** Credit policies are needed in the hospitality industry, especially in the hotel industry where functions and parties are held. Good credit policies will ensure guest satisfaction, lessen misunderstanding, and ensure that the hospitality business will be able to collect its revenues in a timely manner.

6. ***Compute the maturity date of and interest on notes receivable.*** The maturity date of a note must be computed unless the due date is specified or the note is payable on demand. For a note stated in months, the maturity date is found by counting the months from the date of issue. For a note stated in days, the number of days is counted, omitting the issue date and counting the due date. The formula for computing interest is face value × interest rate × time.

7. ***Explain how notes receivable are recognized in the accounts.*** Notes receivable are recorded at face value. In some cases, it is necessary to accrue interest prior to maturity. In this case, Interest Receivable is debited and Interest Revenue is credited.

8. ***Describe how notes receivable are valued.*** Like accounts receivable, notes receivable are reported at their cash (net) realizable value. The notes receivable allowance account is the Allowance for Doubtful Accounts. The computation and estimations involved in valuing notes receivable at cash realizable value, and in recording the proper amount of bad debts expense and related allowance are similar to those for accounts receivable.

9. ***Describe the entries to record the disposition of notes receivable.*** Notes can be held to maturity. At that time the face value plus accrued interest is due, and the note is removed from the accounts. In many cases, the holder of the note speeds up the conversion by selling the receivable to another party. In some situations, the maker of the note dishonors the note (defaults), and the note is written off.

10. ***Explain a current liability, and identify the major types of current liabilities.*** A current liability is a debt that can be reasonably expected to be paid (1) from existing current assets or through the creation of other current liabilities, and (2) within one year or the operating cycle, whichever is longer. The major types of current liabilities are notes payable, accounts payable, sales taxes payable, unearned revenues, and accrued liabilities such as taxes, salaries and wages, and interest payable.

11. ***Describe the accounting of notes payable.*** When a promissory note is interest bearing, the amount of assets received upon the issuance of the note is generally equal to the face value of the note. Interest expense is accrued over the life of the note. At maturity, the amount paid is equal to the face value of the note plus accrued interest.

12. ***Explain the accounting for other current liabilities.*** Sales taxes payable are recorded at the time the related sales occur. The company serves as a collection agent for the taxing authority. Sales taxes are not an expense to the company. Until employee withholding taxes are remitted to governmental taxing authorities, they are credited to appropriate liability accounts. Unearned revenues are initially recorded in an unearned revenue account. As the revenue is earned, a transfer from unearned revenue to earned revenue occurs. The current maturities of long-term debt should be reported as a current liability in the balance sheet.

THE NAVIGATOR

GLOSSARY

Accounts receivable Amounts owed by customers on account as a result from the sale of goods and services (p. 353).

Aging of accounts receivable The analysis of customer balances by the length of time they have been unpaid (p. 359).

Allowance method A method of accounting for bad debts that involves estimating uncollectible accounts at the end of each period (p. 355).

Bad Debts Expense An expense account to record uncollectible receivables (p. 354).

Cash (net) realizable value The net amount expected to be received in cash (p. 355).

Direct write-off method A method of accounting for bad debts that involves expensing accounts at the time they are determined to be uncollectible (p. 354).

Dishonored note A note that is not paid in full at maturity (p. 369).

Factor A finance company or bank that buys receivables from businesses and then collects the payments directly from the customers (p. 361).

Maker The party in a promissory note who is making the promise to pay (p. 365).

Notes payable Obligations in the form of written promissory notes (p. 371).

Notes receivable Claims for which formal instruments of credit are issued as evidence of the debt (p. 354).

Other receivables Nontrade receivables such as interest receivable, loan to company officers, advances to employees, and income tax refundable (p. 353).

Payee The party to whom payment of a promissory note is to be made (p. 365).

Percentage of receivables basis Management establishes a percentage relationship between the amount of receivables and the expected losses from uncollectible accounts (p. 358).

Percentage of sales basis Management establishes a percentage relationship between the amount of credit sales and expected losses from uncollectible accounts (p. 358).

Promissory note A written promise to pay a specified amount of money on demand or at a definite time (p. 365).

Trade receivables Notes and accounts receivable that result from sales transactions (p. 353).

EXERCISES

Identify different types of receivables.
(SO 1)

11-1 Presented below are three receivables transactions. Indicate whether these receivables are reported as accounts receivable, notes receivable, or other receivables on a balance sheet.

(a) Sold merchandise on account for $70,000 to a customer.
(b) Received a promissory note of $57,000 for services performed.
(c) Advanced $10,000 to an employee.

Record basic accounts receivable transactions.
(SO 2)

11-2 Record the following transactions on the books of Essex Golf Supplies.

(a) On July 1, Essex sold merchandise on account to Harrard Golf Club for $16,000, terms 2/10, n/30.
(b) On July 8, Harrard returned merchandise worth $3,800 to Essex Co.
(c) On July 11, Harrard paid for the merchandise.

Prepare entries for write-off; determine cash realizable value.
(SO 3)

Prepare entries for collection of bad debts write-off.
(SO 3)

11-3 At the end of 2004, Searcy Hotel has accounts receivable of $700,000 and an allowance for doubtful accounts of $54,000. On January 24, 2005, the company learns that its receivable from Hunt Inc. is not collectible, and management authorizes a write-off of $7,000.

(a) Prepare the journal entry to record the write-off.
(b) What is the cash realizable value of the accounts receivable (1) before the write-off and (2) after the write-off?
(c) On March 4, 2005, Searcy Hotel receives payment of $7,000 in full from Hunt Inc. Prepare the journal entries to record this transaction.

Compute interest and determine maturity dates on notes.
(SO 6)

11-4 Compute interest and find the maturity date for the following notes.

Date of Note	Principal	Interest Rate (%)	Terms
(a) June 10	$100,000	9%	60 days
(b) July 14	$ 50,000	$7\frac{1}{2}$%	90 days
(c) April 27	$ 12,000	8%	75 days

Determine maturity dates and compute interest and rates on notes.
(SO 6)

11-5 Presented below are data on three promissory notes. Determine the missing amounts.

Date of Note	Terms	Maturity Date	Principal	Annual Interest Rate	Total Interest
(a) April 1	60 days	?	$900,000	9%	?
(b) July 2	30 days	?	90,000	?	$600
(c) March 7	6 months	?	120,000	12%	?

Prepare entries to dispose of accounts receivable.
(SO 4)

11-6 Presented below are two independent transactions.

(a) Raja Restaurant accepted a VISA card in payment of a $200 lunch bill. The bank charges a 3 percent fee. What entry should Raja make?
(b) Wendy Company sold its accounts receivable of $80,000. What entry should Wendy make, given a service charge of 3 percent on the amount of receivables sold?

Identify whether obligations are current liabilities.
(SO 10)

11-7 Ceneplex Theatre has the following obligations at December 31: (a) a note payable for $100,000 due in two years, (b) a ten-year mortgage payable of $200,000 payable in ten $20,000 annual payments, (c) interest payable of $15,000 on the mortgage, and (d) accounts payable of $60,000. For each obligation, indicate whether it should be classified as a current liability.

Prepare entries for an interest-bearing note payable.
(SO 11)

11-8 Banderas Spa borrows $60,000 on July 1 from the bank by signing a $60,000, 10 percent, one-year note payable. Prepare the journal entries to record (a) the proceeds of the note and (b) accrued interest at December 31, assuming adjusting entries are made only at the end of the year.

Compute and record sales taxes payable.
(SO 12)

11-9 Jurassic Theme Park does not segregate sales and sales taxes at the time of sale. The register total for March 16 is $9,975. All sales are subject to a 5 percent sales tax. Compute sales taxes payable and make the entry to record sales taxes payable and sales.

Compute gross earnings and net pay.
(SO 12)

11-10 Becky's Grill regular hourly wage rate is $14, and she receives an hourly rate of $21 for work in excess of 40 hours. During a January pay period, Becky works 45 hours. Becky's federal income tax withholding is $95, her FICA tax withheld is $53.20, and she has no voluntary deductions. Compute Becky Grill's gross earnings and net pay for the pay period.

11-11 Patillo Resort has accounts receivable of $97,500 at March 31. An analysis of the accounts shows the following.

Determine bad debts expense; prepare the adjusting entry for bad debts expense.
(SO 3)

Month of Sale	Balance, March 31
March	$65,000
February	17,600
January	8,500
Prior to January	6,400
	$97,500

Credit terms are 2/10, n/30. At March 31, Allowance for Doubtful Accounts has a credit balance of $1,600 prior to adjustment. The company uses the percentage of receivables basis for estimating uncollectible accounts. The company's estimate of bad debts is as follows:

Age of Accounts	Estimated Percentage Uncollectible
1–30 days	2.0%
31–60 days	5.0%
61–90 days	30.0%
Over 90 days	50.0%

Instructions

(a) Determine the total estimated uncollectibles.

(b) Prepare the adjusting entry at March 31 to record bad debts expense.

Journalize entries for notes receivable transactions.
(SO 6, 7)

11-12 Gore Food Supply Co. has the following transactions related to notes receivable during the last two months of the year.

Nov. 1 Loaned $18,000 cash to Sally Morgan Restaurant on a one-year, 10 percent note
Dec. 11 Sold goods to Adams BBQ receiving a $6,000, 90-day, 12 percent note
16 Received a $4,000, 180-day, 12% note on account from Prentice Bakery
31 Accrued interest revenue on all notes receivable

Instructions

Journalize the transactions for Gore Food Supply Co.

Journalize entries for notes receivable.
(SO 7, 8)

11-13 Record the following transactions for Icke Ice Co. in the general journal

2002

May 1 Received a $10,500, one-year, 10 percent note on account from Paul's Hamburger
Dec. 31 Accrued interest on the note
Dec. 31 Closed the interest revenue account

2003

May 1 Received principal plus interest on the note (No interest has been accrued in 2003.)

Journalize entries to record transactions related to bad debts.
(SO 2, 3)

11-14 Presented below is an aging schedule for Grifton Hotel.

			Number of Days Past Due			
Customer	**Total**	**Not Yet Due**	**1–30**	**31–60**	**61–90**	**Over 90**
Jones	$ 22,000		$10,000	$12,000		
Johnson	40,000	$ 40,000				
Klinger	57,000	16,000	6,000		$35,000	
Morgan	34,000					$34,000
Others	132,000	96,000	16,000	14,000		6,000
	$285,000	$152,000	$32,000	$26,000	$35,000	$40,000
Estimated Percentage Uncollectible		4%	7%	13%	25%	50%
Total Estimated Bad Debts	$ 40,450	$ 6,080	$ 2,240	$ 3,380	$ 8,750	$20,000

At December 31, 2004, the unadjusted balance in Allowance for Doubtful Accounts is a credit of $12,000.

Instructions

(a) Journalize and post the adjusting entry for bad debts at December 31, 2004.

(b) Journalize and post to the allowance account the following events and transactions in the year 2005.

  (1) On March 31, a $1,000 customer balance originating in 2004 is judged uncollectible.

  (2) On May 31, a check for $1,000 is received from the customer whose account was written off as uncollectible on March 31.

(c) Journalize the adjusting entry for bad debts on December 31, 2005, assuming that the unadjusted balance in Allowance for Doubtful Accounts is a debit of $800 and the aging schedule indicates that total estimated bad debts will be $30,300.

Journalize sales and related taxes.
(SO 12)

11-15 In providing accounting services to small businesses, you encounter the following situations pertaining to cash sales.

1. Cavanaugh Pizza rings up sales and sales taxes separately on its cash register. On April 10, the register totals are sales $25,000 and sales taxes $1,500.
2. Corelli Pasta does not segregate sales and sales taxes. Its register total for April 15 is $13,780, which includes a 6% sales tax.

Instructions

Prepare the entry to record the sales transactions and related taxes for each client.

EXPLORING THE WEB

11-16 ***Purpose:*** The Securities Exchange Act of 1934 requires any firm that is listed on one of the national exchanges to file annual reports (form 10-K), financial statements, and quarterly reports (form 10-Q) with the SEC. This exercise demonstrates how to search and access available SEC filings through the Internet.

Address: **http://biz.yahoo.com/i**

Steps

1. Type in a company's name, or use index to find a company name.
2. Choose **Profile**.
3. Choose **Raw SEC Filings**.

Instructions

Answer the following questions.

(a) Which SEC filings were available for the company you selected?

(b) In the company's quarterly report (SEC form 10-Q), what was one key point discussed in the "Management's Discussion and Analysis of Results of Operations and Financial Condition"?

(c) What was the net income for the period selected?

ETHICS CASE

11-17 The controller of Shirt Co. believes that the yearly allowance for doubtful accounts for Shirt Co. should be 2 percent of net credit sales. The president of Shirt Co., nervous that the stockholders might expect the company to sustain its 10 percent growth rate, suggests that the controller increase the allowance for doubtful accounts to 4 percent. The president thinks that the lower net income, which reflects a 6 percent growth rate, will be a more sustainable rate for Shirt Co.

Instructions

(a) Who are the stakeholders in this case?

(b) Does the president's request pose an ethical dilemma for the controller?

(c) Should the controller be concerned with Shirt Co.'s growth rate in estimating the allowance? Explain your answer.

Remember to go back to the Navigator box on the chapter-opening page and check off your completed work.

12 LONG-TERM AND INTANGIBLE ASSETS

THE NAVIGATOR ✓

- Understand *Concepts for Review* ❑
- Read *Feature Story* ❑
- Scan *Study Objectives* ❑
- Read *Preview* ❑
- Read text and answer *Before You Go On* *p.* 387 ❑ *p.* 396 ❑ *p.* 402 ❑
- Work *Demonstration Problems* ❑
- Review *Summary of Study Objectives* ❑
- Complete *Assignments* ❑

CONCEPTS FOR REVIEW

Before studying this chapter, you should know or, if necessary, review:

a. The time period assumption. (Ch. 4, p. 113)
b. The cost principle (Ch. 1, p. 9) and the matching principle. (Ch. 4, p. 114)
c. What is depreciation? (Ch. 4, p. 119)
d. How to make adjustments for depreciation. (Ch. 4, pp. 119–120)

THE NAVIGATOR

FEATURE STORY

Olympic Retrofit of the Homestead Resort in Midway, Utah—February 2002

In February 2002, Soldier Hollow hosted 40 percent of all the 2002 Olympic events and handled the majority of all spectators. Foreign Olympic teams began approaching **the Homestead Resort** more than two years before the games for alternate housing to the Olympic Village. Soldier Hollow is at 5,700 feet, whereas the Olympic Village, 50 miles away in Salt Lake City, is at 4,500 feet. The venue was at a record altitude for Cross Country, Biathlon, and Nordic Combined Olympic events. It was a competitive advantage to stay closer to the venue in order to acclimate and train at a higher altitude. It also significantly reduced transportation time. In addition, the resort's groomed golf course would provide a more convenient practice area.

The Controller of the Homestead Resort in Utah simply said, "It was a very profitable experience and we'd do it again. We also ended up with some significant long-term 'legacy' items and a tremendous sense of satisfaction and goodwill. Some funds were required for the preparation and the teardown phases for the 2002 Olympic guests. During the games, things went smoothly, and everyone who worked with us had a really good time."

So, what does a resort need to get ready for the athletes? More important, how were these transactions being paid for and recorded? First, major wiring was done for telecommunications. The Olympic sponsors, Nortel and Qwest, donated equipment, wiring, and labor. The Homestead Resort essentially became a telephone company "central office" with 12 pair or 24 strand fiber optic cable running to the all of the main buildings, including all banquet areas, for Internet access, additional phone lines as well as live and closed-circuit television broadcast. A year before the Olympics, the Homestead purchased a new phone switch: NEC 2400 on a three-year lease-purchase with a dollar buyout. The total cost was $108,000, and it will be depreciated as Computer Equipment.

To accommodate additional traffic and add additional security, the Salt Lake Olympic Committee (SLOC) donated $60,000 worth of grading and asphalt to create a new employee/service entrance to the property. The Homestead added $15,000 of wiring for lighting, poles, fixtures, and electrical connections. This was capitalized in Grounds to be written off over 12 years.

Of course, a great deal of funds was spent retrofitting the guest rooms. Each athlete required a separate bed. Thus, in each of the King/sofa bedrooms a single bed was added. The Queen rooms were already furnished with two beds. In the Condos, all the beds were removed and refurnished with two single beds in each bedroom. The Homestead purchased 120 single mattresses, boxes, and frames, as well as additional linens for these beds. The beds were purchased at a major discount from SLOC. After the games they were sold off for more than the original price to employees and a local university dormitory. Purchases were recorded in a prepaid account and sales were recorded against that account. Remaining profits were recorded in Other Income.

As the Olympics approached, demand for housing in the area overtook supply. Local residents rented out homes and apartments and took a vacation. The Homestead had an unfinished summer cabin that had been acquired during the construction of its golf course. It had been used as a makeshift stable operation. This cabin was completely remodeled and furnished to accommodate six guests. For this improvement, $60,000 was charged to Fixed Assets: $35,000 to Building & Improvements, and $25,000 to Furniture, Fixtures, and Equipment.

As you can see, this is a major project. But, it is also the Olympics!

THE NAVIGATOR

PREVIEW OF CHAPTER 12

The accounting for long-term assets has important implications for a company's reported results. In this chapter, we explain the application of the cost principle of accounting to property, plant, and equipment, such as the remodeling done at **the Homestead Resort**. We also describe the methods that may be used to allocate an asset's cost over its useful life. In addition, the accounting for expenditures incurred during the useful life of assets, such as the cost of replacing kitchen equipment and a catering delivery truck, is discussed.

The content and organization of Chapter 12 are as follows.

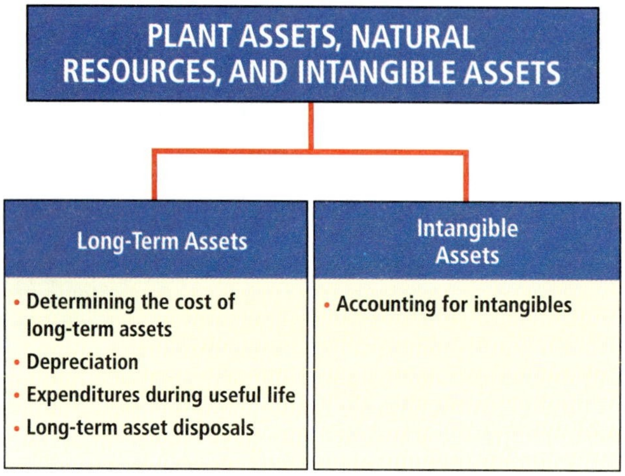

THE NAVIGATOR

STUDY OBJECTIVES

After studying this chapter, you should be able to

1. Describe the application of the cost principle to long-term assets.
2. Explain the concept of depreciation.
3. Compute periodic depreciation using different methods.
4. Describe the procedure for revising periodic depreciation.
5. Distinguish between revenue and capital expenditures, and explain the entries for these expenditures.
6. Explain how to account for the disposal of a long-term asset through retirement, sale, or exchange.
7. Contrast the accounting for intangible assets with the accounting for long-term assets.

THE NAVIGATOR

LONG-TERM ASSETS

Long-term assets are tangible resources that are used in the operations of a business and are not intended for sale to customers. They are also called **property, plant, and equipment; furniture, fixtures, and equipment;** or **fixed assets**. These assets are generally long-lived. They are expected to provide services to the company for a number of years. Except for land, long-term assets decline in service potential over their useful lives. Many companies have substantial investments in long-term assets. Illustration 12-1 shows the percentages of long-term assets in relation to total assets of companies in a number of industries.

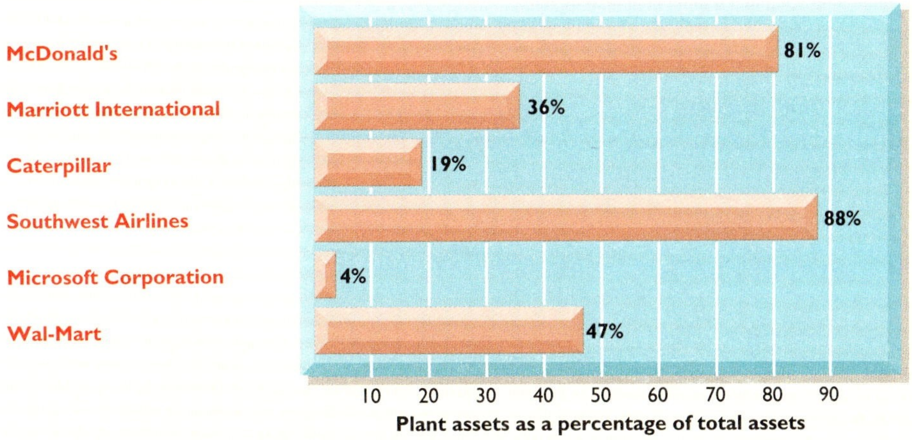

Illustration 12-1

Percentages of long-term assets in relation to total assets

Long-term assets are often subdivided into four classes:

1. **Land**, such as a building site.
2. **Land improvements**, such as driveways, parking lots, fences, and underground sprinkler systems.
3. **Buildings**, such as stores, offices, hotels, restaurants, retail shops, and warehouses.
4. **Equipment**, such as store checkout counters, cash registers, coolers, office furniture, and delivery equipment.

Like the purchase of a home by an individual, the acquisition of long-term assets is an important decision for a business. It is also important for a business to (1) keep assets in good operating condition, (2) replace worn-out or outdated assets, and (3) expand its productive resources as needed. The decline of rail travel in the United States can be traced in part to the failure of railroad companies to meet the first two conditions. The growth of U.S. air travel is due in part to airlines having generally met these conditions.

DETERMINING THE COST OF LONG-TERM ASSETS

STUDY OBJECTIVE 1

Describe the application of the cost principle to long-term assets.

Long-term assets are recorded *at cost* in accordance with the **cost principle** of accounting. Thus the delivery vehicles at a catering company are recorded at cost. **Cost consists of all expenditures necessary to acquire the asset and make it ready for its intended use.** For example, the cost of factory machinery includes the purchase price, freight costs paid by the purchaser, and installation costs. Once cost is established, it becomes the basis of accounting for the long-term asset over its useful life. Current market or replacement values are not used after acquisition.

The application of the cost principle to each of the major classes of long-term assets is explained in the following sections.

INTERNATIONAL NOTE

The United Kingdom (UK) is more flexible than the U.S. about asset valuation. Most companies in the UK make revaluations to fair value when they believe fair value is more relevant. Other countries that permit revaluations are Switzerland and the Netherlands.

LAND

The cost of land includes the cash purchase price plus other related costs. These costs might include closing costs such as title and attorney's fees, real estate broker's commissions, and accrued property taxes and other liens on the land assumed by the purchaser. For example, if the cash price is \$50,000 and the purchaser agrees to pay accrued taxes of \$5,000, the cost of the land is \$55,000.

All necessary costs incurred to make land *ready for its intended use* are debited to the Land account. For vacant land, these costs include expenditures for clearing, draining, filling, and grading. Sometimes the land has a building on it that must be removed before construction of a new building. In this case, all demolition and removal costs, less any proceeds from salvaged materials, are debited to the Land account. To illustrate, assume that Hayes Hotel Company acquires land for $100,000. An old warehouse on the property is razed at a net cost of $6,000 ($7,500 in costs less $1,500 proceeds from salvaged materials). Other expenditures are the attorney's fee, $1,000, and the real estate broker's commission, $8,000. The cost of the land is $115,000, computed in Illustration 12-2.

Illustration 12-2

Computation of cost of land

Land	
Cash price of property	$100,000
Net removal cost of warehouse	6,000
Attorney's fee	1,000
Real estate broker's commission	8,000
Cost of land	**$115,000**

In recording the acquisition, Land is debited for $115,000 and Cash is credited for $115,000.

LAND IMPROVEMENTS

The cost of land improvements includes all expenditures needed to make the improvements ready for their intended use. For example, the cost of a new hotel parking lot will include the amount paid for paving, fencing, and lighting. Thus, these costs are debited to Land Improvements. Because these improvements have limited useful lives and their maintenance and replacement are the responsibility of the company, *they are depreciated over their useful lives.*

BUILDINGS

All necessary costs related to the purchase or construction of a building are debited to the Buildings account. When a building is purchased, such costs include the purchase price, closing costs (attorney's fees, title insurance, etc.) and broker's commission. Costs to make the building ready for its intended use include expenditures for remodeling and replacing or repairing the roof, floors, electrical wiring, and plumbing.

When a new building is constructed, cost consists of the contract price plus payments for architects' fees, building permits, and excavation costs. Also, interest costs incurred to finance the project are included when a significant period of time is required to get the building ready for use. These interest costs are considered as necessary as materials and labor. The inclusion of interest costs is limited to the *construction period*, however. When construction has been completed, subsequent interest payments on funds borrowed to finance the construction are debited to Interest Expense.

EQUIPMENT

HELPFUL HINT

Two criteria apply in determining cost here: (1) the frequency of the cost—one-time or recurring, and (2) the benefit period—life of asset or one year.

The cost of equipment, such as vehicles, consists of the cash purchase price plus certain related costs. These costs include **sales taxes, freight charges, and insurance during transit paid by the purchaser**. They also include **expenditures required in assembling, installing, and testing the unit**. However, motor vehicle licenses and accident insurance on company trucks and cars are not included in the cost of equipment. They are treated as expenses as they are incurred. They represent annual recurring expenditures and do not benefit future periods.

To illustrate, assume Merten Hotels purchases kitchen equipment at a cash price of $50,000. Related expenditures consist of sales taxes $3,000, insurance during shipping $500, and installation and testing $1,000. The cost of the kitchen equipment is $54,500, computed in Illustration 12-3.

Illustration 12-3

Computation of cost of kitchen equipment

Kitchen Equipment	
Cash price	$50,000
Sales taxes	3,000
Insurance during shipping	500
Installation and testing	1,000
Cost of factory machinery	**$54,500**

A summary entry is made to record the purchase and related expenditures:

Kitchen Equipment	54,500	
Cash		54,500
(To record purchase of kitchen equipment)		

A	=	L	+	SE
+54,500				
−54,500				

For another example, assume that Lenard Catering purchases a delivery truck at a cash price of $22,000. Related expenditures consist of sales taxes $1,320, painting and lettering $500, motor vehicle license $80, and a three-year accident insurance policy $1,600. The cost of the delivery truck is $23,820, computed in Illustration 12-4.

Illustration 12-4

Computation of cost of delivery truck

Delivery Truck	
Cash price	$22,000
Sales taxes	1,320
Painting and lettering	500
Cost of delivery truck	**$23,820**

The motor vehicle license is expensed when incurred; the insurance policy is a prepaid asset. The summary entry to record the purchase of the truck and related expenditures looks like this:

Delivery Truck	23,820	
License Expense	80	
Prepaid Insurance	1,600	
Cash		25,500
(To record purchase of delivery truck and related expenditures)		

A	=	L	+	SE
+23,820				−80
+1,600				
−25,500				

BEFORE YOU GO ON...

REVIEW IT

1. What are long-term assets? What are the major classes of long-term assets? How is the cost principle applied to accounting for long-term assets?
2. What classifications and amounts does **Hilton** report on its balance sheet under the heading "Property and equipment, net"? The answer to this question is provided on p. 411.

Hilton

DO IT

Assume that a delivery truck is purchased for $15,000 cash, plus sales taxes of $900 and delivery costs to the dealer of $500. The restaurant also pays $200 for painting and lettering, $600 for an annual insurance policy, and $80 for a motor vehicle license. Explain how each of these costs would be accounted for.

ACTION PLAN

- Identify expenditures made in order to get delivery equipment ready for its intended use.
- Expense operating costs incurred during the useful life of the equipment.

SOLUTION: The first four payments ($15,000, $900, $500, and $200) are considered to be expenditures necessary to make the truck ready for its intended use. Thus, the cost of the truck is $16,600. The payments for insurance and the license are considered to be operating expenses incurred during the useful life of the asset.

Related exercise material: 12-1 and 12-5.

THE NAVIGATOR

DEPRECIATION

STUDY OBJECTIVE 2

Explain the concept of depreciation.

As explained in Chapter 3, **depreciation is the allocation of the cost of a plant asset to expense over its useful (service) life in a rational and systematic manner.** Cost allocation provides for the proper matching of expenses with revenues in accordance with the matching principle (see Illustration 12-5).

Illustration 12-5

Depreciation as an allocation concept

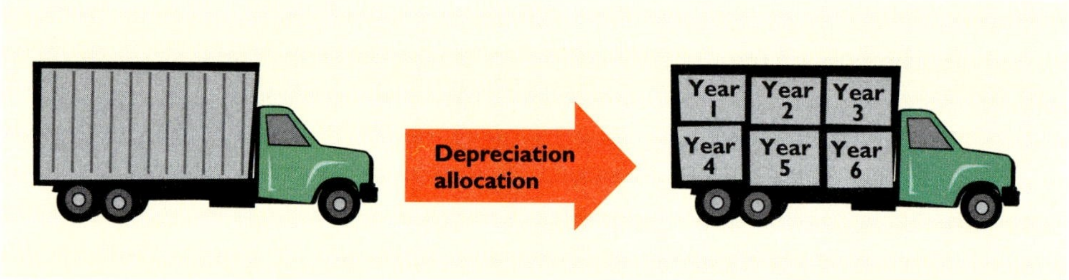

HELPFUL HINT
Remember that depreciation is the allocation of cost over the useful life of an asset. It is not a measure of value.

Depreciation is a process of cost allocation, not a process of asset valuation. The change in an asset's market value is not measured during ownership because plant assets are not held for resale. So, the **book value** (cost less accumulated depreciation) of a plant asset may be quite different from its market value.

Depreciation applies to three classes of plant assets: land improvements, buildings, and equipment. Each asset in these classes is considered to be a **depreciable asset**. Why? Because the usefulness to the company and revenue-producing ability of each asset will decline over the asset's useful life. Depreciation does not apply to land because its usefulness and revenue-producing ability generally remain intact over time. In fact, in many cases, the usefulness of land is greater over time because of the scarcity of good land sites. Thus, land is *not* a depreciable asset.

During a depreciable asset's useful life its revenue-producing ability will decline because of wear and tear. A delivery truck that has been driven 100,000 miles will be less useful to a company than one driven only 800 miles. Trucks and planes exposed to snow and salt will deteriorate faster than equipment that is not exposed to these elements.

Revenue-producing ability may also decline because of *obsolescence*. Obsolescence is the process of becoming out of date before the asset physically wears out. Major airlines were rerouted from Chicago's Midway Airport to Chicago-O'Hare International Airport because Midway's runways were too short for jumbo jets, for example.

It is important to understand that **recognizing depreciation on an asset does not result in an accumulation of cash for replacement of the asset.** The balance in Accumulated Depreciation represents the total cost that has been charged to expense. It is not a cash fund.

Factors in Computing Depreciation

Three factors affect the computation of depreciation:

1. **Cost.** Issues affecting the cost of a depreciable asset were explained earlier in this chapter. Recall that plant assets are recorded at cost, in accordance with the cost principle.
2. **Useful life.** **Useful life** is an estimate of the expected productive life, also called service life, of the asset. Useful life may be expressed in terms of time, units of activity (such as machine hours), or units of output. Useful life is an estimate. In making the estimate, management considers such factors as the intended use of the asset, its expected repair and maintenance, and its vulnerability to obsolescence. Past experience with similar assets is often helpful in deciding on expected useful life. We might reasonably expect the estimated useful life used by **Rent-A-Wreck** to differ from that used by **Avis**.
3. **Salvage value.** **Salvage value** is an estimate of the asset's value at the end of its useful life. This value may be based on the asset's worth as scrap or on its expected trade-in value. Like useful life, salvage value is an estimate. In making the estimate, management considers how it plans to dispose of the asset and its experience with similar assets.

ALTERNATIVE TERMINOLOGY
Another term sometimes used for salvage value is *residual value.*

Illustration 12-6 summarizes the three factors used in computing depreciation.

Illustration 12-6
Three factors in computing depreciation

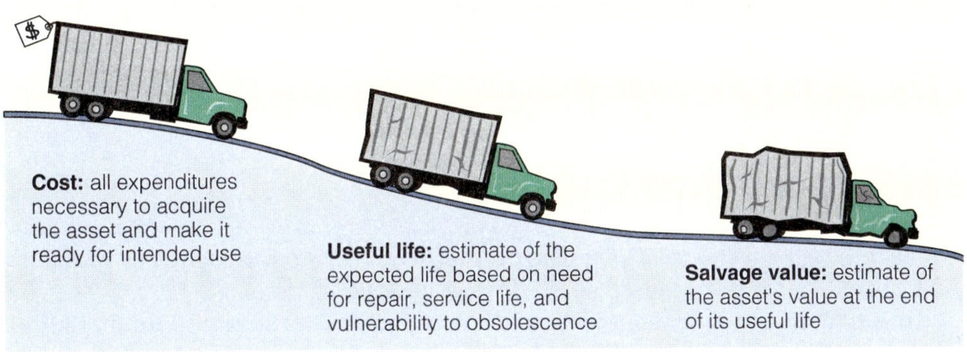

$
Cost: all expenditures necessary to acquire the asset and make it ready for intended use
Useful life: estimate of the expected life based on need for repair, service life, and vulnerability to obsolescence
Salvage value: estimate of the asset's value at the end of its useful life

HELPFUL HINT
Depreciation expense is reported on the income statement, and accumulated depreciation is reported as a deduction from plant assets on the balance sheet.

ACCOUNTING IN ACTION *Business Insight*

The Homestead Resort, highlighted in the feature story, also hosted athletes from around the world during the 2000 and 2001 Cross Country/Biathlon/Nordic Combined World Cup events held at Soldier Hollow. The demand for Internet access for the athletes, coaches, and officials was overwhelming. The resort accommodated that need with a request to **Gateway**, an official Olympic sponsor. They packed up the summer merchandise and fixtures in their Golf Shop and brought in comfortable chairs and sofas. Tables were placed around the room, and Gateway provided software and 14 brand-new flat-screen units that were linked to the Internet through the Olympic Village in Salt Lake for security purposes. The Salt Lake Olympic Committee (SLOC) brought in a live, commercial-free television feed from the various venues, and **IBM** installed other computers and printers with biographical and team information. This equipment provided instant times and results in several athlete lounge areas. The Homestead Resort provided wiring, hubs, a printer, and the use of their T-1 line that fed into the SLOC network. Local volunteers were organized to monitor the room from 7:00 A.M. to 10:00 P.M. The Internet Lounge was a very popular place, used by 200 to 300 athletes, coaches, and officials a day. As for the accounting procedures, the Homestead Resort capitalized the wiring and hubs as Computer Equipment, which is now used for banquets and other meetings.

Depreciation Methods

STUDY OBJECTIVE 3

Compute periodic depreciation using different methods.

Depreciation is generally computed using one of the following methods:

1. Straight-line
2. Units-of-activity
3. Declining-balance
4. Sum-of-years'-digits

Each method is acceptable under generally accepted accounting principles. Management selects the method(s) it believes to be appropriate. The objective is to select the method that best measures an asset's contribution to revenue over its useful life. Once a method is chosen, it should be applied consistently over the useful life of the asset. Consistency enhances the comparability of financial statements.

We will compare the three depreciation methods using the following data for a small delivery truck purchased by Barb's Florists on January 1, 2004. Barb's supplies many arrangement to hotels for weddings and special events.

Illustration 12-7

Delivery truck data

Cost	$13,000
Expected salvage value	$ 1,000
Estimated useful life in years	5
Estimated useful life in miles	100,000

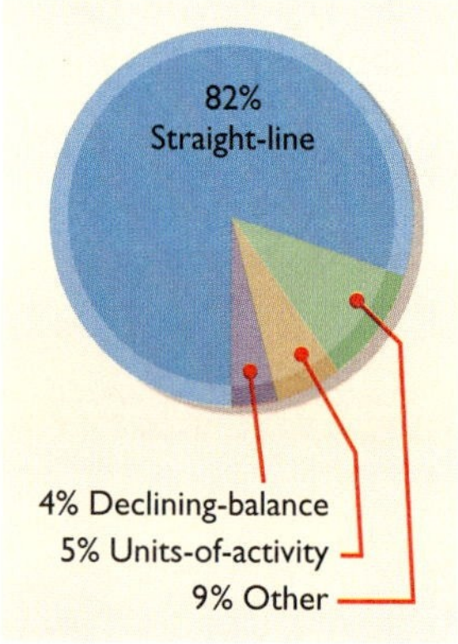

Illustration 12-8

Use of depreciation methods in 600 large U.S. companies

Depreciation affects the balance sheet through accumulated depreciation and the income statement through depreciation expense. Illustration 12-8 (in the margin) shows the use of the different depreciation methods in 600 of the largest companies in the United States.

Straight-Line

Under the **straight-line method**, depreciation is the same for each year of the asset's useful life. It is measured solely by the passage of time.

In order to compute depreciation expense under the straight-line method, it is necessary to determine depreciable cost. **Depreciable cost** is the cost of the asset less its salvage value. It represents the total amount subject to depreciation. Under the straight-line method, depreciable cost is divided by the asset's useful life to determine annual depreciation expense. The computation of depreciation expense in the first year for Barb's Florists is shown in Illustration 12-9.

Illustration 12-9

Formula for straight-line method

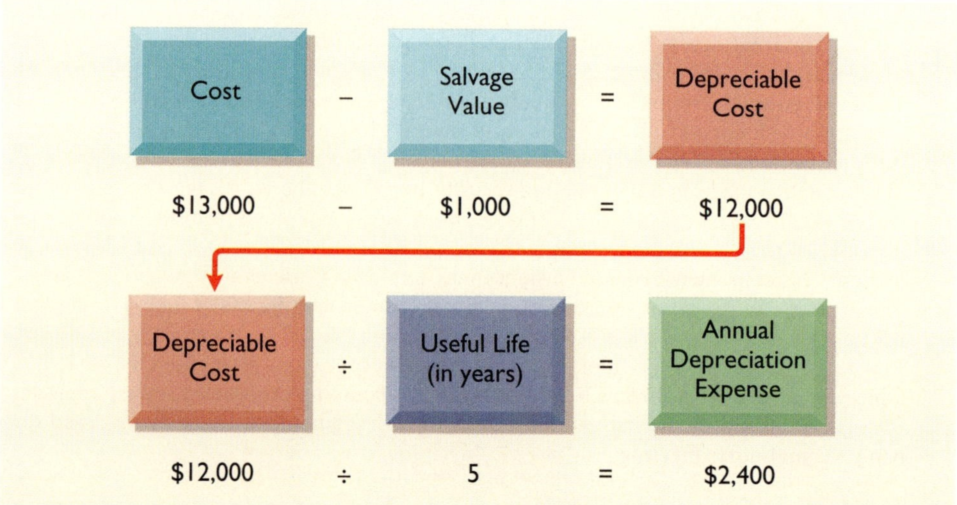

Alternatively, we also can compute an **annual rate of depreciation**. In this case, the rate is 20% (100% ÷ 5 years). When an annual straight-line rate is used, the percentage rate is applied to the depreciable cost of the asset. The use of an annual rate is shown in the **depreciation schedule** in Illustration 12-10.

Illustration 12-10

Straight-line depreciation schedule

BARB'S FLORISTS								
	Computation					End of Year	
Year	Depreciable Cost	×	Depreciation Rate	=	Annual Depreciation Expense	Accumulated Depreciation	Book Value
2004	$12,000		20%		**$2,400**	$ 2,400	$10,600*
2005	12,000		20		**2,400**	4,800	8,200
2006	12,000		20		**2,400**	7,200	5,800
2007	12,000		20		**2,400**	9,600	3,400
2008	12,000		20		**2,400**	12,000	**1,000**

*($13,000 − $2,400).

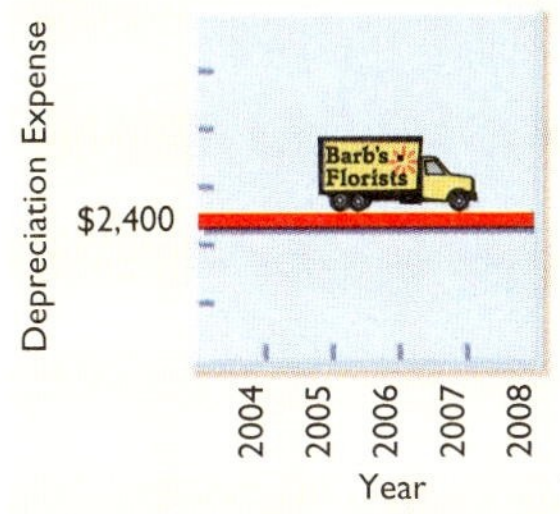

Note that the depreciation expense of $2,400 is the same each year. The book value at the end of the useful life is equal to the estimated $1,000 salvage value.

What happens when an asset is purchased *during* the year, rather than on January 1, as in our example? In that case, it is necessary to *prorate the annual depreciation* on a time basis. If Barb's Florists had purchased the delivery truck on April 1, 2004, the depreciation for 2004 would be $1,800 ($12,000 × 20% × 9/12 of a year).

The straight-line method predominates in practice. Such large companies as **Campbell Soup**, **Marriott Corporation**, and **General Mills** use the straight-line method. It is simple to apply, and it matches expenses with revenues when the use of the asset is reasonably uniform throughout the service life.

Units-of-Activity

Under the **units-of-activity method**, useful life is expressed in terms of the total units of production or use expected from the asset, rather than as a time period. The units-of-activity method is ideally suited to factory machinery. Production can be measured in units of output or in machine hours. This method can also be used for such assets as delivery equipment (miles driven) and airplanes (hours in use). The units-of-activity method is generally not suitable for buildings or furniture, because depreciation for these assets is more a function of time than of use.

ALTERNATIVE TERMINOLOGY
Another term often used is the *units-of-production method*.

To use this method, the total units of activity for the entire useful life are estimated, and these units are divided into depreciable cost. The resulting number represents the depreciation cost per unit. The depreciation cost per unit is then applied to the units of activity during the year to determine the annual depreciation expense.

To illustrate, assume that Barb's Florists' delivery truck is driven 15,000 miles in the first year. The computation of depreciation expense in the first year shown in Illustration 12-11:

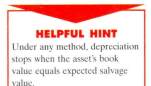

HELPFUL HINT
Under any method, depreciation stops when the asset's book value equals expected salvage value.

Illustration 12-11

Formula for units-of-activity method

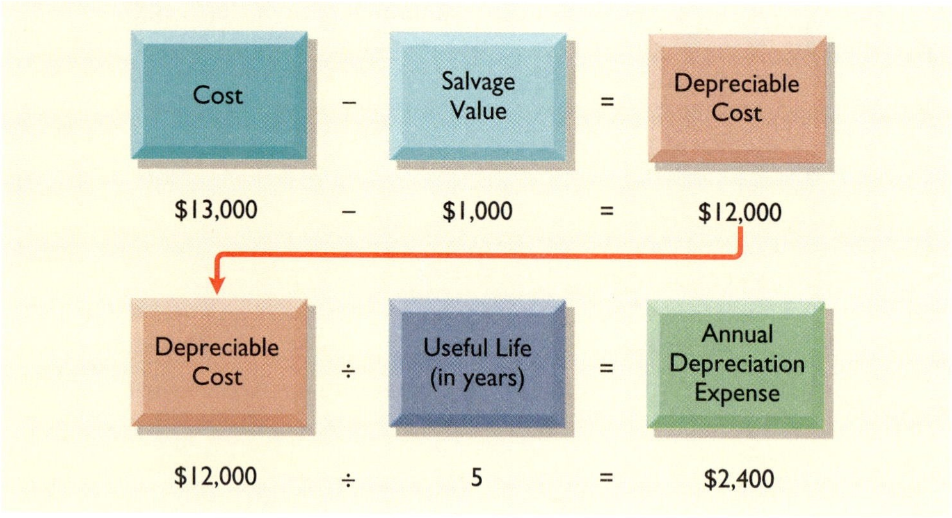

The units-of-activity depreciation schedule, using assumed mileage, is shown in Illustration 12-12:

Illustration 12-12

Units-of-activity depreciation schedule

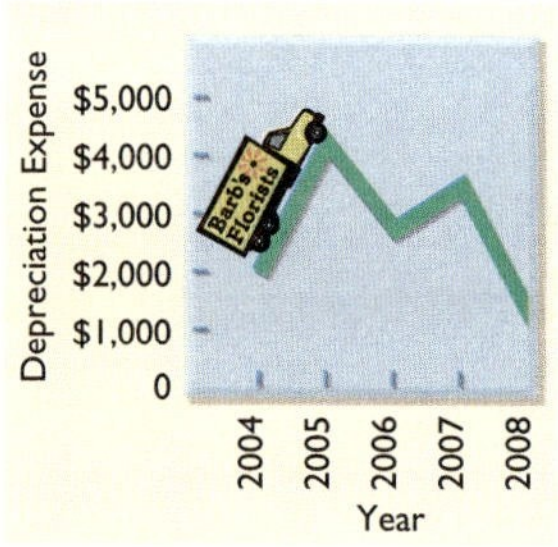

BARB'S FLORISTS

	Computation					End of Year	
Year	**Units of Activity**	×	**Depreciation Cost/Unit**	=	**Annual Depreciation Expense**	**Accumulated Depreciation**	**Book Value**
2004	15,000		$0.12		$1,800	$ 1,800	$11,200*
2005	30,000		0.12		3,600	5,400	7,600
2006	20,000		0.12		2,400	7,800	5,200
2007	25,000		0.12		3,000	10,800	2,200
2008	10,000		0.12		1,200	12,000	1,000

*($13,000 – $1,800)

This method is easy to apply when assets are purchased during the year. In such a case, the productivity of the asset for the partial year is used in computing the depreciation.

The units-of-activity method is not nearly as popular as the straight-line method (see Illustration 12-8), primarily because it is often difficult to make a reasonable estimate of total activity. It is also not widely used in hospitality businesses. However, this method is used by some very large companies, such as **ChevronTexaco Corp.** and **Boise Cascade Corporation** (a forestry company). When the productivity of an asset varies significantly from one period to another, the units-of-activity method results in the best matching of expenses with revenues.

Declining-Balance

The **declining-balance method** produces a decreasing annual depreciation expense over the asset's useful life. The method is so named because the periodic depreciation is based on a *declining book value* (cost less accumulated depreciation) of the asset. Annual depreciation expense is computed by multiplying the book value at the beginning of the year by the declining-balance depreciation rate. **The depreciation rate remains constant from year to year, but the book value to which the rate is applied declines each year.**

HELPFUL HINT

Book value is variable and the depreciation rate is constant for this method.

Book value at the beginning of the first year is the cost of the asset. This is so because the balance in accumulated depreciation at the beginning of the asset's useful life is zero. In subsequent years, book value is the difference between cost and accumulated depreciation to date. Unlike the other depreciation methods, the declining-balance method does not use depreciable cost. That is, **salvage value is ignored in determining the amount to which the declining-balance rate is applied**. Salvage value, however, does limit the total depreciation that can be taken. Depreciation stops when the asset's book value equals expected salvage value.

A common declining-balance rate is double the straight-line rate. As a result, the method is often referred to as the **double-declining-balance method**. If Barb's Florists uses the double-declining-balance method, the depreciation rate is 40 percent (2 × the straight-line rate of 20%). The computation of depreciation for the first year on the delivery truck is shown in Illustration 12-13:

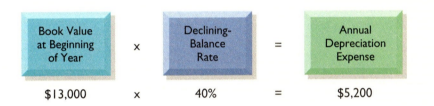

Illustration 12-13

Formula for declining-balance method

Book Value at Beginning of Year	×	Declining-Balance Rate	=	Annual Depreciation Expense
$13,000	×	40%	=	$5,200

Illustration 12-14 shows the depreciation schedule under this method.

Illustration 12-14

Double-declining-balance depreciation schedule

BARB'S FLORISTS

	Computation					End of Year	
Year	Book Value Beginning of Year	×	Depreciation Rate	=	Annual Depreciation Expense	Accumulated Depreciation	Book Value
2004	$13,000		40%		**$5,200**	$ 5,200	$7,800
2005	7,800		40		**3,120**	8,320	4,680
2006	4,680		40		**1,872**	10,192	2,808
2007	2,808		40		**1,123**	11,315	1,685
2008	1,685		40		685*	12,000	**1,000**

*Computation of $674 ($1,685 × 40%) is adjusted to $685 in order for book value to equal salvage value.

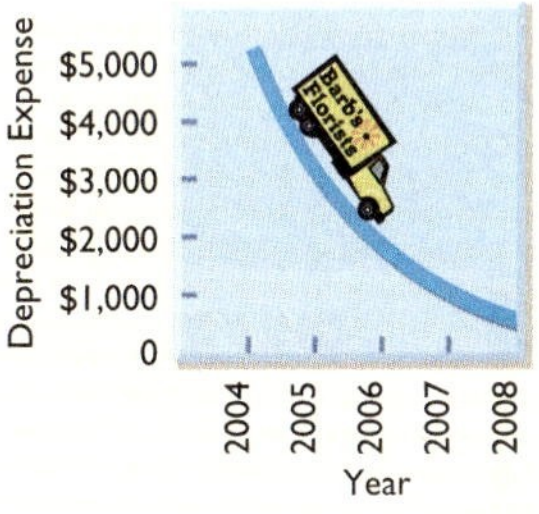

You can see that the delivery equipment is 69 percent depreciated ($8,320 ÷ $12,000) at the end of the second year. Under the straight-line method it would be depreciated 40 percent ($4,800 ÷ $12,000) at that time. Because the declining-balance method produces higher depreciation expense in the early years than in the later years, it is considered an **accelerated-depreciation method**. The declining-balance method is compatible with the matching principle. The higher depreciation expense in early years is matched with the higher benefits received in these years. On the other hand, lower depreciation expense is recognized in later years when the asset's contribution to revenue is less. Also, some assets lose usefulness rapidly because of obsolescence. In these cases, the declining-balance method provides a more appropriate depreciation amount.

HELPFUL HINT

The method to be used for an asset that is expected to be more productive in the first half of its useful life is the declining-balance method.

When an asset is purchased during the year, the first year's declining-balance depreciation must be prorated on a time basis. For example, if Barb's Florists had purchased the truck on April 1, 2004, depreciation for 2004 would become $3,900 ($13,000 × 40% × 9/12). The book value at the beginning of 2005 is then $9,100

(\$13,000 − \$3,900), and the 2005 depreciation is \$3,640 (\$9,100 × 40%). Subsequent computations would follow from those amounts.

Sum-of-Years'-Digits

Similar to the straight-line method, in the **sum-of-years'-digits method**, it is necessary to determine the salvage value and the depreciable cost. Once these are determined, the digits of the years of the asset's expected useful life will be added to be used as the denominator of the calculation, while the years' digits are used in reverse order as the numerator for depreciation. Using this method, depreciation expense will be highest during the first year of usage and will decline as time passes, giving the business the most depreciation write-off at the beginning of the asset's useful life. The computation of depreciation expense for Barb's Florists is shown below.

With a five-year useful life, the denominator for the calculation will be, as the name of this method suggests, the sum of the digits: $1 + 2 + 3 + 4 + 5 = 15$. In case the life of an asset runs up to some higher figures, this formula may come in handy:

$$\text{Sum of years' digits} = n\ (n + 1)\ /\ 2$$

Since 5 is the number of years of useful life, then the sum of years' digits will be:

$$(5 \times 6) \div 2 = 15$$

Illustration 12-15 shows the depreciation schedule for the sum-of-years'-digits method for Barb's Florists.

Illustration 12-15

Sum-of-years'-digits depreciation schedule

BARB'S FLORISTS

	Computation						End of Year	
Year	Rate		Depreciable Cost		Annual Depreciation		Accumulated Depreciation	Book Value
2004	5/15	×	\$12,000	=	\$4,000		\$ 4,000	\$9,000*
2005	4/15	×	12,000	=	3,200		7,200	5,800
2006	3/15	×	12,000	=	2,400		9,600	3,400
2007	2/15	×	12,000	=	1,600		11,200	1,800
2008	1/15	×	12,000	=	800		12,000	1,000

*(\$13,000 − \$4,000)

Comparison of Methods

A comparison of annual and total depreciation expense under each of the four methods is shown for Barb's Florists in Illustration 12-16.

Illustration 12-16

Comparison of depreciation methods

Year	Straight-Line	Units-of-Activity	Declining-Balance	Sum-of-Years'-Digits
2004	\$ 2,400	\$ 1,800	\$ 5,200	\$ 4,000
2005	2,400	3,600	3,120	3,200
2006	2,400	2,400	1,872	2,400
2007	2,400	3,000	1,123	1,600
2008	2,400	1,200	685	800
	\$12,000	\$12,000	\$12,000	\$12,000

Observe that annual depreciation varies considerably among the methods. But total depreciation is the same for the five-year period under all four methods. Each method is acceptable in accounting, because each recognizes the decline in service potential of the asset in a rational and systematic manner. The depreciation expense pattern under each method is presented graphically in Illustration 12-17.

Illustration 12-17

Patterns of depreciation

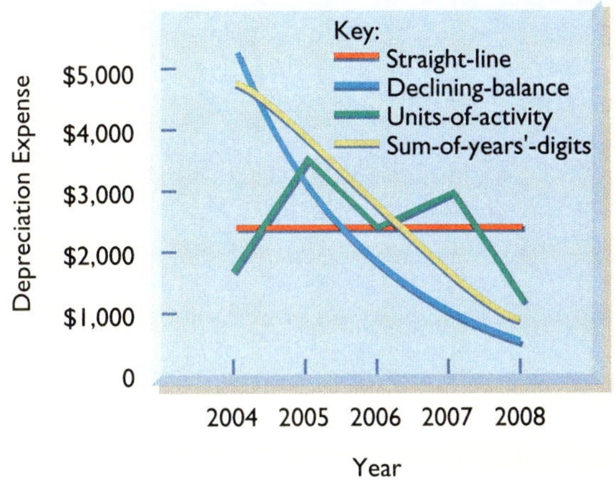

Depreciation and Income Taxes

The Internal Revenue Service (IRS) allows corporate taxpayers to deduct depreciation expense when they compute taxable income. However, the IRS does not require the taxpayer to use the same depreciation method on the tax return that is used in preparing financial statements. Many corporations use straight-line in their financial statements to maximize net income. At the same time, they use a special **accelerated-depreciation method** on their tax returns to minimize their income taxes. Taxpayers must use on their tax returns either the straight-line method or a special accelerated-depreciation method called the **Modified Accelerated Cost Recovery System (MACRS)**.

MACRS

MACRS has been in place since 1986. As its name implies, and similar to the double-declining-balance and sum-of-years'-digits method, it allows taxpayers to depreciate their assets in an accelerated rate, faster than the straight-line method. MACRS classifies property into six recovery classes of: 3-, 5-, 7-, 10-, 15-, and 20-year. For example, computers are classified as a 5-year life property, while office desks are a 10-year property. A table is normally used to assist taxpayers in determining the percentage that can be written off as depreciation for the asset depending on its class life and when in the year the asset is purchased. You will learn more about MACRS in a finance class regarding taxation implications.

TECHNOLOGY IN ACTION

Software packages to account for long-term assets exist for both large and small computer systems. Even the least sophisticated packages can maintain a control and subsidiary ledger for long-term assets and make the necessary depreciation computations and adjusting entries. Many packages also maintain separate depreciation schedules for both financial statement and income tax purposes, with reconciliations made for any differences.

REVISING PERIODIC DEPRECIATION

STUDY OBJECTIVE 4

Describe the procedure for revising periodic depreciation.

Depreciation is one example of the use of estimation in the accounting process. Annual depreciation expense should be reviewed periodically by management. If wear and tear or obsolescence indicate that annual depreciation estimates are inadequate or excessive, a change should be made.

When a change in an estimate is required, the change is made in *current and future years*. It is not made retroactively *to prior periods*. Thus, there is no correction of previously recorded depreciation expense. Instead, depreciation expense for current and future years is revised. The rationale is that continual restatement of prior periods would adversely affect confidence in financial statements.

To determine the new annual depreciation expense, we first compute the asset's depreciable cost at the time of the revision. We then allocate the revised depreciable cost to the remaining useful life. To illustrate, assume that Barb's Florists decides on January 1, 2007, to extend the useful life of the truck one year because of its excellent condition. The company has used the straight-line method to depreciate the asset to date, and book value is $5,800 ($13,000 – $7,200). The new annual depreciation is $1,600, computed in Illustration 12-18.

Illustration 12-18

Revised depreciation computation

Book value, 1/1/07	$5,800	
Less: Salvage value	1,000	
Depreciable cost	$4,800	
Remaining useful life	3 years	(2007–2010)
Revised annual depreciation ($4,800 ÷ 3)	**$1,600**	

HELPFUL HINT

Use a step-by-step approach: (1) determine new depreciable cost; (2) divide by remaining useful life.

Barb's Florists makes no entry for the change in estimate. On December 31, 2007, during the preparation of adjusting entries, it would record depreciation expense of $1,600. Significant changes in estimates must be described in the financial statements.

BEFORE YOU GO ON...

REVIEW IT

1. What is the relationship, if any, of depreciation to (a) cost allocation, (b) asset valuation, and (c) cash accumulation?
2. Explain the factors that affect the computation of depreciation.
3. What are the formulas for computing annual depreciation under each of the depreciation methods?
4. How do the methods differ in terms of their effects on annual depreciation over the useful life of the asset?
5. Are revisions of periodic depreciation made to prior periods? Explain.

DO IT

On January 1, 2004, Iron Mountain Ski Corporation purchased a new snow-grooming machine for $50,000. The machine is estimated to have a 10-year life with a $2,000 salvage value. What journal entry would Iron Mountain Ski Corporation make at December 31, 2004, if it uses the straight-line method of depreciation?

ACTION PLAN

- Calculate depreciable cost (Cost – Salvage value).
- Divide the depreciable cost by the estimated useful life.

SOLUTION

$$\text{Depreciation expense} = \frac{\text{Cost} - \text{Salvage value}}{\text{Useful life}} = \frac{\$50{,}000 - \$2{,}000}{10} = \$4{,}800$$

The entry to record the first year's depreciation would be:

Dec. 31	Depreciation Expense	4,800	
	Accumulated Depreciation		4,800
	(To record annual depreciation on snow-grooming machine)		

Related exercise material: 12-2 and 12-6.

THE NAVIGATOR

EXPENDITURES DURING USEFUL LIFE

STUDY OBJECTIVE 5

Distinguish between revenue and capital expenditures, and explain the entries for these expenditures.

During the useful life of a plant asset a company may incur costs for ordinary repairs, additions, or improvements. **Ordinary repairs** are expenditures to maintain the operating efficiency and productive life of the unit. They usually are fairly small amounts that occur frequently. Motor tune-ups and oil changes, the painting of buildings, and the replacing of worn-out gears on machinery are examples. Such repairs are debited to Repair (or Maintenance) Expense as they are incurred. Because they are immediately charged as an expense against revenues, these costs are often referred to as **revenue expenditures**.

Additions and improvements are costs incurred to increase the operating efficiency, productive capacity, or useful life of a long-term asset. They are usually material in amount and occur infrequently. Additions and improvements increase the company's investment in productive facilities and are generally debited to the long-term asset affected. They are often referred to as **capital expenditures**. Most major U.S. corporations disclose annual capital expenditures. The **Venetian** in Las Vegas spent over $275 million in an expansion project in 2003, while **Coca Cola** reported capital expenditures of $851 million in 2002.

LONG-TERM ASSET DISPOSALS

STUDY OBJECTIVE 6

Explain how to account for the disposal of a long-term asset through retirement, sale, or exchange.

Long-term assets may be disposed of in three ways—retirement, sale, or exchange—as shown in Illustration 12-19. Whatever the method, at the time of disposal it is necessary to determine the book value of the long-term asset. As noted earlier, book value is the difference between the cost of a long-term asset and the accumulated depreciation to date.

Illustration 12-19

Methods of long-term asset disposal

At the time of disposal, depreciation for the fraction of the year to the date of disposal must be recorded. The book value is then eliminated by debiting (decreasing) Accumulated Depreciation for the total depreciation to date and crediting (decreasing) the asset account for the cost of the asset. In this section we will examine the accounting for each of the three methods of long-term asset disposal.

Retirement of Long-Term Assets

To illustrate the retirement of long-term assets, assume that Hobart Country Club retires its computer printers, which cost $32,000. The accumulated depreciation on these printers is $32,000. The equipment, therefore, is fully depreciated (zero book value). The entry to record this retirement is as follows.

A	=	L	+	SE
+32,000				
−32,000				

Accumulated Depreciation—Printing Equipment	32,000	
Printing Equipment		32,000
(To record retirement of fully depreciated equipment)		

HELPFUL HINT

When a long-term asset is disposed of, all amounts related to the asset must be removed from the accounts. This includes the original cost in the asset account and the total depreciation to date in the accumulated depreciation account.

What happens if a fully depreciated long-term asset is still useful to the company? In this case, the asset and its accumulated depreciation continue to be reported on the balance sheet without further depreciation adjustment until the asset is retired. Reporting the asset and related accumulated depreciation on the balance sheet informs the financial statement reader that the asset is still in use. However, once an asset is fully depreciated, even if it is still being used, no additional depreciation should be taken. In no situation can the accumulated depreciation on a long-term asset exceed its cost.

If a long-term asset is retired before it is fully depreciated, and no scrap or salvage value is received, a loss on disposal occurs. For example, assume that Sunset Catering discards delivery equipment that cost $18,000 and has accumulated depreciation of $14,000. The entry is as follows.

A	=	L	+	SE
+14,000				−4,000
−18,000				

Accumulated Depreciation—Delivery Equipment	14,000	
Loss on Disposal	4,000	
Delivery Equipment		18,000
(To record retirement of delivery equipment at a loss)		

The loss on disposal is reported in the "other expenses and losses" section of the income statement.

Sale of Long-Term Assets

In a disposal by sale, the book value of the asset is compared with the proceeds received from the sale. **If the proceeds of the sale exceed the book value of the long-term asset, a gain on disposal occurs. If the proceeds of the sale are less than the book value of the long-term asset sold, a loss on disposal occurs.**

Only by coincidence will the book value and the fair market value of the asset be the same when the asset is sold. Gains and losses on sales of plant assets are therefore quite common. For example, **Delta Airlines** reported a $94,343,000 gain on the sale of five **Boeing** B-727-200 aircraft and five **Lockheed** L-1011-1 aircraft.

GAIN ON DISPOSAL. To illustrate a gain, assume that on July 1, 2004, Wright Hotels sells some of its hotel furniture for $16,000 cash. The furniture originally cost $60,000. As of January 1, 2004, it had accumulated depreciation of $41,000. Depreciation for the first 6 months of 2004 is $8,000. The entry to record depreciation expense and update accumulated depreciation to July 1 is as follows.

A	=	L	+	SE
−8,000				−8,000

July 1	Depreciation Expense	8,000	
	Accumulated Depreciation—Furniture		8,000
	(To record depreciation expense for the first 6 months of 2004)		

After the accumulated depreciation balance is updated, a gain on disposal of $5,000 is computed, as shown in Illustration 12-20:

Cost of furniture	$60,000
Less: Accumulated depreciation ($41,000 + $8,000)	49,000
Book value at date of disposal	11,000
Proceeds from sale	16,000
Gain on disposal	**$ 5,000**

Illustration 12-20

Computation of gain on disposal

The entry to record the sale and the gain on disposal is as follows.

July 1	Cash	16,000	
	Accumulated Depreciation—Furniture	49,000	
	Furniture		60,000
	Gain on Disposal		5,000
	(To record sale of furniture at a gain)		

A	=	L	+	SE
+16,000				+5,000
+49,000				
−60,000				

The gain on disposal is reported in the "other revenues and gains" section of the income statement.

LOSS ON DISPOSAL. Assume that instead of selling the furniture for $16,000, Wright sells it for $9,000. In this case, a loss of $2,000 is computed:

Cost of furniture	$60,000
Less: Accumulated depreciation	49,000
Book value at date of disposal	11,000
Proceeds from sale	9,000
Loss on disposal	**$ 2,000**

Illustration 12-21

Computation of loss on disposal

The entry to record the sale and the loss on disposal is as follows.

July 1	Cash	9,000	
	Accumulated Depreciation—Furniture	49,000	
	Loss on Disposal	2,000	
	Furniture		60,000
	(To record sale of furniture at a loss)		

A	=	L	+	SE
+9,000				−2,000
+49,000				
−60,000				

The loss on disposal is reported in the "other expenses and losses" section of the income statement.

Exchange of Long-Term Assets

Long-term assets may also be disposed of through exchange. Exchanges can be for either similar or dissimilar assets. Because exchanges of similar assets are more common, they are discussed here. An exchange of similar assets occurs, for example, when old office furniture is exchanged for new office furniture. In an exchange of similar assets, the new asset performs the *same function* as the old asset.

HELPFUL HINT
A building costing $200,000 was destroyed by fire. At the date of the fire, accumulated depreciation was $150,000. Insurance proceeds were $325,000. Prepare the entry to record the insurance proceeds and disposition of building. Answer: Debit Cash $325,000; debit Accumulated Depreciation $150,000; credit Building $200,000; and credit Gain on Disposal $275,000.

In exchanges of similar long-term assets, it is necessary to determine two things: (1) the cost of the asset acquired, and (2) the gain or loss on the asset given up. Because a noncash asset is given up in the exchange, cost is the **cash equivalent price** paid. That is, cost is the fair market value of the asset given up plus the cash paid. **The gain or loss on disposal is the difference between the fair market value and the book value of the asset given up.** These determinations are explained and illustrated below.

LOSS TREATMENT. A loss on the exchange of similar assets is recognized immediately. To illustrate, assume that Roland Foods exchanged old kitchen equipment for new kitchen equipment. The book value of the old equipment is $26,000 (cost $70,000 less accumulated depreciation $44,000). Its fair market value is $10,000, and cash of $81,000 is paid. Illustration 12-22 shows the cost of the new equipment, $91,000:

Illustration 12-22
Computation of cost of new office equipment

Fair market value of old kitchen equipment	$10,000
Cash	81,000
Cost of new kitchen equipment	**$91,000**

A loss on disposal of $16,000 on this exchange is incurred. The reason is that the book value is greater than the fair market value of the asset given up. The computation is shown in Illustration 12-23.

Illustration 12-23
Computation of loss on disposal

Book value of old kitchen equipment ($70,000 − $44,000)	$26,000
Fair market value of old kitchen equipment	10,000
Loss on disposal	**$16,000**

In recording an exchange at a loss, three steps are required: (1) Eliminate the book value of the asset given up, (2) record the cost of the asset acquired, and (3) recognize the loss on disposal. The entry for Roland Foods is as follows.

A	=	L	+	SE
+91,000				−16,000
+44,000				
−70,000				
−81,000				

Kitchen Equipment (new)	91,000	
Accumulated Depreciation—Kitchen Equipment (old)	44,000	
Loss on Disposal	16,000	
Kitchen Equipment (old)		70,000
Cash		81,000
(To record exchange of old kitchen equipment for similar new equipment)		

GAIN TREATMENT. A gain on the exchange of similar assets is not recognized immediately but, instead, is deferred. This is done by reducing the cost basis of the new asset. In determining the cost of the new asset, compute the *cost before deferral of the gain* and then the *cost after deferral of the gain.*

HELPFUL HINT
Why aren't gains on the exchange of similar assets recognized? Because the earnings process is not considered completed. To be conservative, however, losses are recognized.

To illustrate, assume that Mark's Express Catering decides to exchange its old delivery equipment plus cash of $3,000 for new delivery equipment. The book value of the old delivery equipment is $12,000 (cost $40,000 less accumulated depreciation $28,000). The fair market value of the old delivery equipment is $19,000.

The cost of the new asset (before deferral of the gain) **is the fair market value of the old asset exchanged plus any cash (or other consideration given up).** The cost of the new delivery equipment (before deferral of the gain) is $22,000, computed in Illustration 12-24:

Illustration 12-24

Cost of new equipment (before deferral of gain)

Fair market value of old delivery equipment	$19,000
Cash	3,000
Cost of new delivery equipment (before deferral of gain)	**$22,000**

A gain results when the fair market value is greater than the book value of the asset given up. Illustration 12-25 shows that for Mark's Express, there is a gain of $7,000 on the disposal.

Illustration 12-25

Computation of gain on disposal

Fair market value of old delivery equipment	$19,000
Book value of old delivery equipment ($40,000 − $28,000)	12,000
Gain on disposal	**$ 7,000**

The $7,000 gain on disposal is then offset against the $22,000 cost of the new delivery equipment. The result is a $15,000 cost of the new delivery equipment, after deferral of the gain, as shown in Illustration 12-26.

Illustration 12-26

Cost of new equipment (after deferral of gain)

Cost of new delivery equipment (before deferral of gain)	$22,000
Less: Gain on disposal	7,000
Cost of new delivery equipment (after deferral of gain)	**$15,000**

The entry to record the exchange is as follows.

Delivery Equipment (new)	15,000	
Accumulated Depreciation—Delivery Equipment (old)	28,000	
Delivery Equipment (old)		40,000
Cash		3,000
(To record exchange of old delivery equipment for similar new delivery equipment)		

A	=	L	+	SE
+15,000				
+28,000				
−40,000				
−3,000				

This entry does not eliminate the gain; it just postpones or defers it to future periods. The deferred gain of $7,000 reduces the $22,000 cost to $15,000. As a result, net income in future periods increases because depreciation expense on the newly acquired delivery equipment is less by $7,000.

Illustration 12-27 summarizes the rules for accounting for exchanges of similar assets:

Illustration 12-27

Accounting rules for plant asset exchanges

Type of Event	Recognition
Loss	Recognize immediately by debiting Loss on Disposal
Gain	Defer and reduce cost of new asset

BEFORE YOU GO ON...

REVIEW IT

1. How does a capital expenditure differ from a revenue expenditure?
2. What is the proper accounting for the retirement and sale of plant assets?
3. What is the proper accounting for the exchange of similar plant assets?

DO IT

Overland Catering has an old truck that cost $30,000. The truck has accumulated depreciation of $16,000 and a fair value of $17,000. Overland has a choice of either selling the truck for $17,000 cash or exchanging the old truck and $3,000 cash for a new truck. What is the entry that Overland Trucking would record under each option?

ACTION PLAN

- Compare the asset's book value and fair value to determine whether a gain or loss has occurred.
- Defer gains on the exchange of similar assets by reducing the recorded value of the new asset.

SOLUTION

Sale of truck for cash:

Cash	17,000	
Accumulated Depreciation—Truck (old)	16,000	
Truck (old)		30,000
Gain on Disposal [$17,000 – ($30,000 – $16,000)]		3,000
(To record sale of truck at a gain)		

Exchange of old truck and cash for new truck:

Truck (new)	17,000*	
Accumulated Depreciation—Truck (old)	16,000	
Truck (old)		30,000
Cash		3,000
(To record exchange of old truck for similar new truck)		
*($20,000 – $3,000)		

If the old truck is exchanged for the new truck, the $3,000 gain is deferred, and the recorded cost of the new truck is reduced by $3,000.

Related exercise material: 12-4 and 12-7.

THE NAVIGATOR

INTANGIBLE ASSETS

Intangible assets are rights, privileges, and competitive advantages that result from the ownership of assets that do not possess physical substance. Evidence of intangibles may exist in the form of contracts or licenses. Intangibles may arise from any of the following:

- Government grants, such as patents, copyrights, and trademarks
- Acquisition of another business, in which the purchase price includes a payment for the company's favorable attributes (called goodwill)
- Private monopolistic arrangements arising from contractual agreements, such as franchises and leases

Some widely known intangibles are the franchises of **McDonald's** and the trade name of Col. Sanders's **Kentucky Fried Chicken**.

Intangible assets are recorded at cost. The cost of an intangible asset should be allocated over its useful life, assuming the useful life is limited. If the life of the intangible is indefinite, the cost of the intangible should not be allocated. Indefinite means that no legal, regulatory, contractual, competitive, economic, or other factors limit the intangible's useful life. At disposal, the book value of the intangible asset is eliminated, and a gain or loss, if any, is recorded.

STUDY OBJECTIVE 7

Contrast the accounting for intangible assets with the accounting for long-term assets.

There are several differences between accounting for intangible assets and accounting for long-term assets. First, assuming an intangible asset has a limited life, the term used to describe the allocation of the cost of an intangible asset to expense is **amortization**, rather than depreciation. Also, to record amortization of an intangible, an amortization expense is debited and the specific intangible asset is credited (rather than crediting a contra account). An alternative is to credit an accumulated amortization account, similar to accumulated depreciation.

There is also a difference in determining cost. For long-term assets, cost includes both the purchase price of the asset and the costs incurred in designing and constructing the asset. In contrast, cost for an intangible asset includes only the purchase price. Any costs incurred in developing an intangible asset are expensed as incurred.

The method of amortizing an intangible asset with a limited life should reflect the pattern in which the asset's economic benefits are used. If such a pattern cannot be reliably determined, a straight-line method of amortization should be used. For homework purposes, use the straight-line method, unless otherwise indicated.

An indefinite-life intangible asset should not be amortized until its life is determined to be limited. At that time, the intangible asset should be amortized.

PATENTS

A **patent** is an exclusive right issued by the U.S. Patent Office that enables the recipient to manufacture, sell, or otherwise control an invention for a period of 20 years from the date of the grant. A patent is nonrenewable. But the legal life of a patent may be extended by obtaining new patents for improvements or other changes in the basic design.

The initial cost of a patent is the cash or cash equivalent price paid to acquire the patent. The saying, "A patent is only as good as the money you're prepared to spend defending it" is very true. Many patents are subject to some type of litigation. Legal costs an owner incurs in successfully defending a patent in an infringement suit are considered necessary to establish the validity of the patent. They are added to the Patent account and amortized over the remaining life of the patent.

The cost of a patent should be amortized over its 20-year legal life or its useful life, whichever is shorter. Obsolescence and inadequacy should be considered in determining useful life. These factors may cause a patent to become economically ineffective before the end of its legal life.

To illustrate the computation of patent expense, assume that National Labs purchases a patent at a cost of \$60,000. If the useful life of the patent is 8 years, the annual amortization expense is \$7,500 (\$60,000 ÷ 8). The entry to record the annual amortization looks like this:

Dec. 31	Amortization Expense—Patents	7,500	
	Patents		7,500
	(To record patent amortization)		

A	=	L	+	SE
−7,500				−7,500

Amortization Expense—Patents is classified as an **operating expense** in the income statement.

COPYRIGHTS

Copyrights are grants from the federal government giving the owner the exclusive right to reproduce and sell an artistic or published work. Copyrights extend for the life of the creator plus 70 years. The cost of a copyright is the **cost of acquiring and defending it.** The cost may be only the $10 fee paid to the U.S. Copyright Office. Or it may amount to a great deal more if a copyright infringement suit is involved. Because copyrights have an indefinite life, their cost is not amortized.

TRADEMARKS AND TRADE NAMES

A **trademark** or **trade name** is a word, phrase, jingle, or symbol that identifies a particular enterprise or product. Trade names like Wheaties, Hilton, Sunkist, Marriott, Coca-Cola, Big Mac, and Jeep create immediate product identification. They also generally enhance the sale of the product. The creator or original user may obtain exclusive legal right to the trademark or trade name by registering it with the U.S. Patent Office. Such registration provides 20 years' protection. The registration may be renewed indefinitely as long as the trademark or trade name is in use.

If the trademark or trade name is *purchased* by the company that will sell the product, its cost is the purchase price. If the trademark or trade name is *developed* by the company itself, the cost includes attorney's fees, registration fees, design costs, successful legal defense costs, and other expenditures directly related to securing it.

Because trademarks and trade names have indefinite lives, they are not amortized.

FRANCHISES AND LICENSES

When you drive down the street in your RAV4 purchased from a **Toyota** dealer, fill up your tank at the corner **Shell** station, or eat lunch at **Taco Bell**, you are dealing with franchises. A **franchise** is a contractual arrangement under which the franchisor grants the franchisee the right to sell certain products, render specific services, or use certain trademarks or trade names. The franchise is usually restricted to a designated geographical area.

Another type of franchise is that entered into between a governmental body (commonly municipalities) and a business enterprise. This franchise permits the enterprise to use public property in performing its services. Examples are the use of city streets for a bus line or taxi service, use of public land for telephone and electric lines, and the use of airwaves for radio or TV broadcasting. Such operating rights are referred to as **licenses**.

When costs can be identified with the acquisition of a franchise or license, an intangible asset should be recognized. Franchises and licenses may be granted for a period of time, limited or indefinite. The cost of a limited-life franchise (or license) should be amortized over the useful life. If the life is indefinite, its cost is not amortized. Annual payments made under a franchise agreement are recorded as **operating expenses** in the period in which they are incurred.

ETHICS NOTE

A pharmaceutical company was growing rapidly by buying unwanted drug licensing rights. These licensing rights, reported as intangible assets, represented over 70 percent of the company's total assets. The company experienced a 50 percent drop in value when the market realized the rights were being amortized over 40 years. If a more reasonable life had been used to amortize the rights, the company's reported profits would, instead, have been huge losses.

ACCOUNTING IN ACTION *Business Insight*

Best Western International is "THE WORLD'S LARGEST HOTEL CHAIN®" with over 4,000 hotels in 80 countries. Best Western does not own any of them but is in fact a membership organization of hotel owners and operators of Best Western properties. In fiscal 2001, Best Western posted revenues of over $157 million by providing marketing, reservations, and operational support to its members.

GOODWILL

Usually, the largest intangible asset that appears on a company's balance sheet is goodwill. **Goodwill** is the value of all favorable attributes that relate to a business enterprise. These include exceptional management, skilled employees, high-quality products, and harmonious relations with labor unions. Goodwill is unusual: Unlike other assets such as investments, long-term assets, or patents, which can be sold individually in the marketplace, goodwill can be identified only with the business as a whole.

If goodwill can be identified only with the business as a whole, how can it be determined? One could try to put a dollar value on the factors listed above (exceptional management, desirable location, and so on), but the results would be very subjective. Such subjective valuations would not contribute to the reliability of financial statements. **Therefore, goodwill is recorded only when there is a transaction that involves the purchase of an entire business. In that case, goodwill is the excess of cost over the fair market value of the net assets (assets less liabilities) acquired.**

In recording the purchase of a business, the net assets are debited at their fair market values, cash is credited for the purchase price, and goodwill is debited for the difference. Goodwill is not amortized because it is considered to have an indefinite life, but it must be written down if its value is determined to have declined (been permanently impaired). Goodwill is reported in the balance sheet under intangible assets.

HELPFUL HINT
Goodwill is recorded only when it has been purchased along with tangible and identifiable intangible assets of a business.

ACCOUNTING IN ACTION *International Insight*

Until recently, U.S. companies were required to amortize goodwill. Many people argued that this created a disadvantage for U.S. companies. British companies did not have to amortize goodwill against earnings. Rather, they bypassed the income statement completely and charged goodwill directly to stockholders' equity. For example, **Pillsbury** was purchased by **Grand Met**, a British firm. Many complained that U.S. companies were reluctant to bid for Pillsbury because it would mean that they would have to record a large amount of goodwill, which would substantially depress income in the future.

What can or should be done when accounting practices are different among countries and perhaps give one country a competitive edge?

DEMONSTRATION PROBLEM 1

DuPage Restaurant purchases an ice machine at a cost of $18,000 on January 1, 2004. The machine is expected to have a salvage value of $2,000 at the end of its four-year useful life.

During its useful life, the machine is expected to be used 160,000 hours. Actual annual hourly use was: 2004, 40,000; 2005, 60,000; 2006, 35,000; and 2007, 25,000.

Instructions

Prepare depreciation schedules for the following methods: (a) the straight-line, (b) units-of-activity, (c) declining-balance using double the straight-line rate, and (d) sum-of-years'-digits.

ACTION PLAN

- Under the straight-line method, apply the depreciation rate to depreciable cost.
- Under the units-of-activity method, compute the depreciation cost per unit by dividing depreciable cost by total units of activity.
- Under the declining-balance method, apply the depreciation rate to **book value** at the beginning of the year.
- Under the sum-of-years'-digits method, apply the depreciation rate to depreciable cost.

SOLUTION TO DEMONSTRATION PROBLEM 1

(a) **Straight-Line Method**

	Computation					End of Year	
Year	Depreciable Cost	×	Depreciation Rate	=	Annual Depreciation Expense	Accumulated Depreciation	Book Value
2004	$16,000		25%		$4,000	$ 4,000	$14,000*
2005	16,000		25%		4,000	8,000	10,000
2006	16,000		25%		4,000	12,000	6,000
2007	16,000		25%		4,000	16,000	2,000

*$18,000 − $4,000.

(b)

Units-of-Activity Method

	Computation					End of Year	
Year	Units of Activity	×	Depreciation Cost/Unit	=	Annual Depreciation Expense	Accumulated Depreciation	Book Value
2004	40,000		$0.10		$4,000	$ 4,000	$14,000
2005	60,000		0.10		6,000	10,000	8,000
2006	35,000		0.10		3,500	13,500	4,500
2007	25,000		0.10		2,500	16,000	2,000

(c)

Declining-Balance Method

	Computation					End of Year	
Year	Book Value Beginning of Year	×	Depreciation Rate	=	Annual Depreciation Expense	Accumulated Depreciation	Book Value
2004	$18,000		50%		$9,000	$ 9,000	$9,000
2005	9,000		50%		4,500	13,500	4,500
2006	4,500		50%		2,250	15,750	2,250
2007	2,250		50%		250*	16,000	2,000

*Adjusted to $250 because ending book value should not be less than expected salvage value.

(d)

Sum-of-Years'-Digits Method

	Computation					End of Year	
Year	Depreciation Cost	×	Depreciation Rate	=	Annual Depreciation	Accumulated Depreciation	Book Value
2004	4/10		$16,000		$6,400	$ 6,400	$11,600*
2005	3/10		16,000		4,800	11,200	6,800
2006	2/10		16,000		3,200	14,400	3,600
2007	1/10		16,000		1,600	16,000	2,000

*$18,000 − $6,400.

THE NAVIGATOR

DEMONSTRATION PROBLEM 2

On January 1, 2002, Skyline Hotel Co. purchased a passenger van for transporting guests to and from airports and nearby shopping areas at an acquisition cost of $28,000. The vehicle has been depreciated by the straight-line method using a four-year service life and a $4,000 salvage value. The company's fiscal year ends on December 31.

Instructions

Prepare the journal entry or entries to record the disposal of the van assuming that it was:

(a) Retired and scrapped with no salvage value on January 1, 2006.

(b) Sold for $5,000 on July 1, 2005.

(c) Traded in on a new van on January 1, 2005. The fair market value of the old vehicle was $9,000, and $22,000 was paid in cash.

(d) Traded in on a new van on January 1, 2005. The fair market value of the old vehicle was $11,000, and $22,000 was paid in cash.

SOLUTION TO DEMONSTRATION PROBLEM 2

	Date	Account	Debit	Credit
(a)	1/1/06	Accumulated Depreciation—Van	24,000	
		Loss on Disposal	4,000	
		Van		28,000
		(To record retirement of van)		
(b)	7/1/05	Depreciation Expense	3,000	
		Accumulated Depreciation—Van		3,000
		(To record depreciation to date of disposal)		
		Cash	5,000	
		Accumulated Depreciation—Van	21,000	
		Loss on Disposal	2,000	
		Van		28,000
		(To record sale of van)		
(c)	1/1/05	Van (new)	31,000	
		Accumulated Depreciation—Van (old)	18,000	
		Loss on Disposal	1,000	
		Van (old)		28,000
		Cash		22,000
		(To record exchange of limousines)		
(d)	1/1/035	Van (new)*	32,000	
		Accumulated Depreciation—Van (old)	18,000	
		Van (old)		28,000
		Cash		22,000
		(To record exchange of vans)		
		*($11,000 + $22,000 − $1,000)		

ACTION PLAN

- At the time of disposal, determine the book value of the asset.
- Recognize any gain or loss from disposal of the asset.
- Remove the book value of the asset from the records by debiting Accumulated Depreciation for the total depreciation to date of disposal and crediting the asset account for the cost of the asset.

THE NAVIGATOR

SUMMARY OF STUDY OBJECTIVES

1. *Describe the application of the cost principle to long-term assets.* The cost of long-term assets includes all expenditures necessary to acquire the asset and make it ready for its intended use. Cost is measured by the cash or cash equivalent price paid.

2. *Explain the concept of depreciation.* Depreciation is the allocation of the cost of a long-term asset to expense over its useful (service) life in a rational and systematic manner. Depreciation is not a process of valuation. Nor is it a process that results in an accumulation of cash. Depreciation is caused by wear and tear or by obsolescence.

3. *Compute periodic depreciation using different methods.* There are four depreciation methods:

Method	Effect on Annual Depreciation	Formula
Straight-line	Constant amount	Depreciable cost ÷ Useful life (in years)
Units-of-activity	Varying amount	Depreciation cost per unit × Units of activity during the year
Declining-balance	Decreasing amount	Book value at beginning of year × Declining-balance rate
Sum-of-years'-digits	Decreasing amount	Depreciable cost × Rate*

$$\text{*rate} = \frac{\text{Depreciable year}}{\text{Sum of digits of asset's useful life}}$$

4. *Describe the procedure for revising periodic depreciation.* Revisions of periodic depreciation are made in present and future periods, not retroactively. The new annual depreciation is found by dividing the depreciable cost at the time of the revision by the remaining useful life.

5. *Distinguish between revenue and capital expenditures, and explain the entries for these expenditures.* Revenue expenditures are incurred to maintain the operating efficiency and expected productive life of the asset. These expenditures are debited to Repair Expense as incurred. Capital expenditures increase the operating efficiency, productive capacity, or expected useful life of the asset. These expenditures are generally debited to the long-term asset affected.

6. *Explain how to account for the disposal of a long-term asset through retirement, sale, or exchange.* The accounting for disposal of a long-term asset through retirement or sale is as follows:

(a) Eliminate the book value of the long-term asset at the date of disposal.
(b) Record cash proceeds, if any.
(c) Account for the difference between the book value and the cash proceeds as a gain or loss on disposal.

In accounting for exchanges of similar assets:

(a) Eliminate the book value of the old asset at the date of the exchange.
(b) Record the acquisition cost of the new asset.
(c) Account for the loss or gain, if any, on the old asset:
  (1) If a loss, recognize it immediately.

(2) If a gain, defer and reduce the cost of the new asset.

7. *Contrast the accounting for intangible assets with the accounting for long-term assets.* The accounting for intangible assets and long-term assets is much the same. One difference is that the term used to describe the write-off of an intangible asset is amortization, rather than depreciation. The straight-line method is normally used for amortizing intangible assets.

THE NAVIGATOR

GLOSSARY

Accelerated-depreciation method Depreciation method that produces higher depreciation expense in the early years than in the later years (p. 393).

Additions and improvements Costs incurred to increase the operating efficiency, productive capacity, or useful life of a long-term asset (p. 397).

Amortization The allocation of the cost of a limited-life intangible asset to expense over its useful life in a systematic and rational manner (p. 403).

Capital expenditures Expenditures that increase the company's investment in productive facilities (p. 397).

Copyright Exclusive grant from the federal government that allows the owner to reproduce and sell an artistic or published work (p. 404).

Declining-balance method Depreciation method that applies a constant rate to the declining book value of the asset and produces a decreasing annual depreciation expense over the useful life of the asset (p. 392).

Depreciable cost The cost of a long-term asset less its salvage value (p. 390).

Franchise (license) A contractual arrangement under which the franchisor grants the franchisee the right to sell certain products, render specific services, or use certain trademarks or trade names, usually within a designated geographical area (p. 404).

Goodwill The value of all favorable attributes that relate to a business enterprise (p. 405).

Intangible assets Rights, privileges, and competitive advantages that result from the ownership of long-lived assets that do not possess physical substance (p. 402).

Licenses Operating rights to use public property, granted to a business enterprise by a governmental agency (p. 404).

Long-term assets Tangible resources that are used in the operations of the business and are not intended for sale to customers (p. 384).

Modified Accelerated Cost Recovery System (MACRS) Depreciation method where assets are classified into recovery classes and are depreciated at an accelerated rate (p. 395).

Ordinary repairs Expenditures to maintain the operating efficiency and productive life of the unit (p. 397).

Patent An exclusive right issued by the U.S. Patent Office that enables the recipient to manufacture, sell, or otherwise control an invention for a period of 20 years from the date of the grant (p. 403).

Revenue expenditures Expenditures that are immediately charged against revenues as an expense (p. 397).

Salvage value An estimate of an asset's value at the end of its useful life (p. 389).

Straight-line method Depreciation method in which periodic depreciation is the same for each year of the asset's useful life (p. 390).

Sum-of-years'-digits method Depreciation method in which the digits of the years of the asset's expected useful life are totaled as the denominator of the calculation and the years' digits are used in reverse order as the numerator for depreciation (p. 394).

Trademark (trade name) A word, phrase, jingle, or symbol that identifies a particular enterprise or product (p. 404).

Units-of-activity method Depreciation method in which useful life is expressed in terms of the total units of production or use expected from an asset (p. 391).

Useful life An estimate of the expected productive life, also called service life, of an asset (p. 389).

EXERCISES

Determine the cost of land. (SO 1)

12-1 The following expenditures were incurred by Shumway Hotel in purchasing land: cash price $50,000, accrued taxes $3,000, attorneys' fees $2,500, real estate broker's commission $2,000, and clearing and grading $3,500. What is the cost of the land?

Compute straight-line depreciation. (SO 3)

12-2 Mabasa Foods Company acquires a delivery truck at a cost of $30,000. The truck is expected to have a salvage value of $2,000 at the end of its four-year useful life. Compute annual depreciation for the first and second years using the straight-line method.

Compute revised depreciation. (SO 4)

12-3 On January 1, 2004, the Villaluz Mexican Foods ledger shows Equipment $32,000 and Accumulated Depreciation $9,000. The depreciation resulted from using the straight-line method with a useful life of 10 years and salvage value of $2,000. On this date, the company concludes that the equipment has a remaining useful life of only five years with the same salvage value. Compute the revised annual depreciation.

Prepare entries for disposal by retirement. (SO 6)

12-4 Prepare journal entries to record the following.

(a) Ruiz Company retires its delivery equipment, which cost $41,000. Accumulated depreciation is also $41,000 on this delivery equipment. No salvage value is received.

(b) Assume the same information as (a), except that accumulated depreciation for Ruiz Company is $39,000, instead of $41,000.

12-5 The following expenditures relating to long-term assets were made by Kosinski Sandwiches during the first two months of 2004.

Determine cost of plant acquisitions.
(SO 1)

1. Paid $5,000 of accrued taxes at time his restaurant site was acquired.
2. Paid $200 insurance to cover possible accident loss on new kitchen equipment while the equipment was in transit.
3. Paid $850 sales taxes on new delivery truck.
4. Paid $17,500 for parking lots and driveways on new plant site.
5. Paid $250 to have company name and advertising slogan painted on new delivery truck.
6. Paid $8,000 for installation of new factory machinery.
7. Paid $900 for one-year accident insurance policy on new delivery truck.
8. Paid $75 motor vehicle license fee on the new truck.

Instructions

(a) Explain the application of the cost principle in determining the acquisition cost of plant assets.
(b) List the numbers of the foregoing transactions, and opposite each indicate the account title to which each expenditure should be debited.

12-6 Always-Late Bus Lines uses the units-of-activity method in depreciating its buses. One bus was purchased on January 1, 2004, at a cost of $128,000. Over its four-year useful life, the bus is expected to be driven 100,000 miles. Salvage value is expected to be $8,000.

Compute depreciation under units-of-activity method.
(SO 3)

Instructions

(a) Compute the depreciation cost per unit.
(b) Prepare a depreciation schedule assuming actual mileage was: 2004, 26,000; 2005, 32,000; 2006, 25,000; and 2007, 17,000.

12-7 Presented below are selected transactions at Beck's Company for 2004.

Journalize entries for disposal of plant assets.
(SO 6)

Jan. 1	Retired a piece of kitchen equipment that was purchased on January 1, 1994. The machine cost $62,000 on that date. It had a useful life of 10 years with no salvage value.
June 30	Sold a computer that was purchased on January 1, 2001. The computer cost $35,000. It had a useful life of seven years with no salvage value. The computer was sold for $22,000.
Dec. 31	Discarded a delivery truck that was purchased on January 1, 2000. The truck cost $30,000. It was depreciated based on a six-year useful life with a $3,000 salvage value.

Instructions

Journalize all entries required on the above dates, including entries to update depreciation, where applicable, on assets disposed of. Beck's Company uses straight-line depreciation. (Assume depreciation is up to date as of December 31, 2003.)

12-8 Mendoza Company was organized on January 1. During the first year of operations, the following long-term asset expenditures and receipts were recorded in random order.

Determine acquisition costs of land and building.
(SO 1)

Debits	
1. Cost of filling and grading the land	$ 4,000
2. Full payment to building contractor	700,000
3. Real estate taxes on land paid for the current year	5,000
4. Cost of real estate purchased as a plant site (land $100,000 and building $45,000)	145,000
5. Excavation costs for new building	20,000
6. Architect's fees on building plans	10,000
7. Accrued real estate taxes paid at time of purchase of real estate	2,000
8. Cost of parking lots and driveways	14,000
9. Cost of demolishing building to make land suitable for construction of new building	15,000
	$915,000
Credits	
10. Proceeds from salvage of demolished building	$ 3,500

Instructions
Analyze the foregoing transactions using the following column headings. Insert the number of each transaction in the Item space, and insert the amounts in the appropriate columns. For amounts entered in the Other Accounts column, also indicate the account titles.

Item	Land	Building	Other Accounts

Compute depreciation under different methods. (SO 3)

12-9 In recent years, Waterfront Tours purchased three used buses. Because of frequent turnover in the accounting department, a different accountant selected the depreciation method for each bus, and various methods were selected. Information concerning the buses is summarized below.

Bus	Acquired	Cost	Salvage Value	Useful Life in Years	Depreciation Method
1	1/1/00	$ 86,000	$ 6,000	4	Straight-line
2	1/1/00	140,000	10,000	5	Declining-balance
3	1/1/01	80,000	8,000	5	Units-of-activity
4	1/1/01	100,000	10,000	5	Sum-of-years'-digits

For the declining-balance method, the company uses the double-declining rate. For the units-of-activity method, total miles are expected to be 120,000. Actual miles of use in the first three years were: 2003, 24,000; 2004, 34,000; and 2005, 30,000.

Instructions
(a) Compute the amount of accumulated depreciation on each bus at December 31, 2004.
(b) If bus no. 2 was purchased on April 1 instead of January 1, what is the depreciation expense for this bus in (1) 2002 and (2) 2003?

Calculate revisions to depreciation expense. (SO 3, 4)

12-10 At the beginning of 2002, Duncan Company acquired kitchen equipment costing $60,000. It was estimated that this equipment would have a useful life of six years and a residual value of $6,000 at that time. The straight-line method of depreciation was considered the most appropriate to use with this type of equipment. Depreciation is to be recorded at the end of each year.

During 2004 (the third year of the equipment's life), the company's engineers reconsidered their expectations, and estimated that the equipment's useful life would probably be seven years (in total) instead of six years. The estimated residual value was not changed at that time. However, during 2007 the estimated residual value was reduced to $4,400.

Instructions
Indicate how much depreciation expense should be recorded each year for this equipment, by completing the following table.

Year	Depreciation Expense	Accumulated Depreciation
2002		
2003		
2004		
2005		
2006		
2007		
2008		

EXPLORING THE WEB

12-11 A company's annual report identifies the amount of its plant assets and the depreciation method used.

Address: **www.reportgallery.com**

Steps
1. From Report Gallery homepage, choose **Library of Annual Reports**.
2. Select a particular company.

3. Choose **Annual Report**.
4. Follow instructions below.

Instructions

Answer the following questions.

(a) What is the name of the company?
(b) At fiscal year-end, what is the net amount of its long-term assets?
(c) What is the accumulated depreciation?
(d) Which method of depreciation does the company use?

Answer to Hilton Review It Question 2, p. 387

Hilton reports the following categories and amounts under the heading "Property, plant and equipment, net": $3,911 million.

Remember to go back to the Navigator box on the chapter-opening page and check off your completed work.

THE NAVIGATOR ✓

- Understand *Concepts for Review* ❑
- Read *Feature Story* ❑
- Scan *Study Objectives* ❑
- Read *Preview* ❑
- Read text and answer *Before You Go On*
  p. 428 ❑ *p.* 431 ❑ *p.* 434 ❑ *p.* 438 ❑
  p. 446 ❑ *p.* 450 ❑
- Work *Demonstration Problem* ❑
- Review *Summary of Study Objectives* ❑
- Complete *Assignments* ❑

CONCEPTS FOR REVIEW

Before studying this chapter, you should know or, if necessary, review:

a. The content of the stockholders' equity section of a balance sheet. (Ch. 5, pp. 164–165)

b. How to prepare closing entries for a corporation. (Ch. 5, pp. 150–154)

c. The difference between paid-in capital and retained earnings. (Ch. 1, p. 12)

THE NAVIGATOR

FEATURE STORY

"Two All Beef Patties, Special Sauce, Lettuce, Cheese, Pickles, Onions on a Sesame Seed Bun"

Many people know this saying too well, and can even say it with a rhythm. It all started with a true salesman, Raymond Albert Kroc. Ray Kroc's entrepreneurial zeal, combined with an almost evangelical ability to motivate nearly everyone he touched, enabled him to build the largest and most successful restaurant franchise company in the world. Ray didn't promise franchisees success. Instead, he offered the opportunity to achieve it. Ray's fair and balanced franchise partnership is said to be his greatest legacy. To underscore his own commitment to "taking the hamburger business more seriously than anyone else," he established Hamburger University. By so doing, he confirmed his willingness to invest in the training and education of McDonald's people and thereby accentuated his franchising commitment.

As a corporation, **McDonald's** went to Wall Street in 1965, selling stocks in round lots of 100 shares at $2,250, or $22.50 per share. If one calculates all the stock splits and dividends, the 100 shares in 1965 had grown to 74,360 shares in 1998, with a value of over $2.8 million. In 1985, McDonald's was added to one of the 30 companies whose share prices make up the formula to derive the Dow Jones Industrial Average. Ray's operating credo of "Quality, Service, Cleanliness and Value" became the mantra for all McDonald's owners, established a permanent benchmark for the entire foodservice and food processing industries, and, by extension, all service industry components. His exacting mandates for uniformity and product consistency made it possible for a customer to get a Big Mac and french fries in Houston, Texas, or in Moscow, Russia. In fact, the Golden Arches are said to be the second most widely recognized trademark in the world. Ray's company changed the dining lifestyle of an entire society in less than one generation. Consequently, 96 percent of all Americans have eaten at a McDonald's restaurant on at least one occasion.

Sources: www.mcdonalds.com/corporate/info/history and www.hrm.uh.edu/?PageID=191

THE NAVIGATOR

STUDY OBJECTIVES

After studying this chapter, you should be able to

1. Identify the major characteristics of a sole proprietorship.
2. Identify the major characteristics of a partnership.
3. Explain the accounting entries for the formation of a partnership.
4. Identify the bases for dividing net income or net loss.
5. Identify the major characteristics of a corporation.
6. Record the issuance of common stock.
7. Explain the accounting for treasury stock.
8. Differentiate preferred stock from common stock.
9. Prepare the entries for cash dividends and stock dividends.
10. Identify the items that are reported in a retained earnings statement.

THE NAVIGATOR

PREVIEW OF CHAPTER 13

At some time in your hospitality career, you might want to open up your own restaurant, build your own bed and breakfast, or purchase a franchise hotel. How should you structure or organize your business? Small businesses mostly start as sole proprietorships. Others will get together with friends or business partners and will pull resources together to form a partnership. In contrast, corporations like **Hilton, Disney,** and **Marriott** have substantial resources. In fact, the corporation is the dominant form of business organization in the United States in terms of dollar volume of sales and earnings, and number of employees. All of the 500 largest companies in the United States are corporations. In this chapter, we will explain the essential features of a proprietorship, a partnership, and a corporation, and will look at the accounting for both forms of business organizations.

The content and organization of Chapter 13 are as follows.

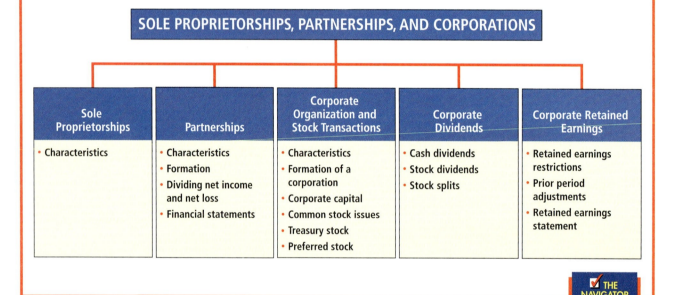

SOLE PROPRIETORSHIPS, PARTNERSHIPS, AND CORPORATIONS

Sole Proprietorships
- Characteristics

Partnerships
- Characteristics
- Formation
- Dividing net income and net loss
- Financial statements

Corporate Organization and Stock Transactions
- Characteristics
- Formation of a corporation
- Corporate capital
- Common stock issues
- Treasury stock
- Preferred stock

Corporate Dividends
- Cash dividends
- Stock dividends
- Stock splits

Corporate Retained Earnings
- Retained earnings restrictions
- Prior period adjustments
- Retained earnings statement

THE NAVIGATOR

SOLE PROPRIETORSHIPS

STUDY OBJECTIVE 1

Identify the major characteristics of a sole proprietorship.

The simplest form of business organization is **sole proprietorship**. For entrepreneurs in the hospitality business who want to own their own business, this is the easiest way to begin. A sole proprietorship is formed by a single individual and owned by this same person. This individual will register as "do business as" with the proper authority and can begin. Thus, one of characteristics of a sole proprietorship is the ease of formation. In addition, since it is owned by one person, the decision-making process is less complex, affording the business with flexibility. Moreover, when profits are reaped, the single owner will retain all the money.

However, a sole proprietorship also has some risky characteristics. Since it is owned by one person, should there be a loss in the business, this one person will have to absorb all the loss. Legally, there is also unlimited liability. Thus, the creditors can seize the owner's personal belongings to pay the bills. Another negative characteristic is that it is often difficult to raise funds through one person's collateral. Therefore, many hospitality businesses are formed as partnerships or, more often, corporations.

PARTNERSHIPS

The Uniform Partnership Act provides the basic rules for the formation and operation of partnerships in more than 90 percent of the states. This act defines a **partnership** as "an association of two or more persons to carry on as co-owners of a business for profit." The partnership form of business organization is not restricted to any particular type of business, but it is most often used in relatively small companies and in professional fields, as mentioned above.

Illustration 13-1 shows principal characteristics of the partnership form of business organization.

STUDY OBJECTIVE 2

Identify the major characteristics of a partnership.

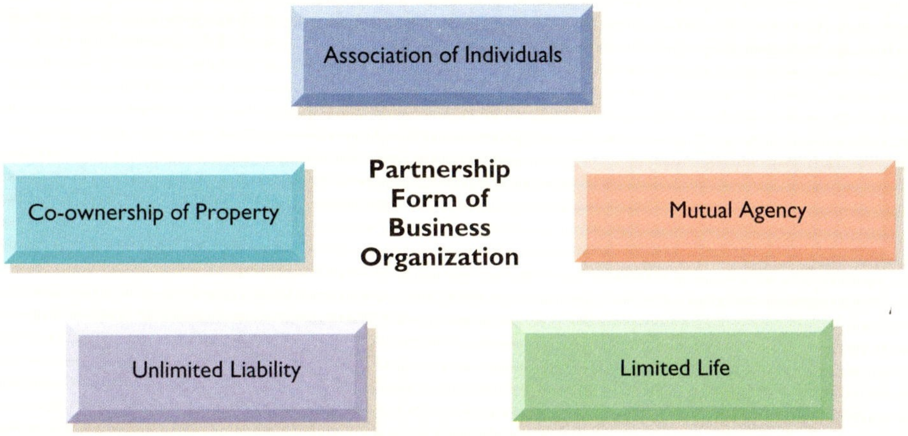

Illustration 13-1

Partnership characteristics

ASSOCIATION OF INDIVIDUALS

A partnership is a voluntary association of two or more individuals based on a legally binding contract, which may be written, oral, or implied. Under the Uniform Partnership Act, a partnership is considered a legal entity for certain purposes. For instance, property (land, buildings, equipment) can be owned in the name of the partnership, and the firm can sue or be sued. **A partnership also represents an accounting entity for financial reporting purposes.** Thus, the purely personal assets, liabilities, and personal transactions of the partners are excluded from the accounting records of the partnership, just as they are in a proprietorship. In addition, the net income of a partnership is not taxed as a separate entity. However, a partnership is required to file an information tax return showing partnership net income and each partner's share of the net income. Each partner's share is taxable, regardless of the amount of net income withdrawn from the business during the year.

MUTUAL AGENCY

Each partner acts on behalf of the partnership when engaging in partnership business. The act of any partner is binding on all other partners, even when partners act beyond the scope of their authority, as long as the act appears to be appropriate for the partnership. For example, a partner of a catering company who purchases a delivery truck creates a binding contract in the name of the partnership, even if the partnership agreement denies this authority. In contrast, if a partner in a catering company purchased a snowmobile for the partnership, such an act would not be binding on the partnership, because it is clearly outside the scope of partnership business.

LIMITED LIFE

A partnership does not have unlimited life. Its continuance as a going concern rests in the partnership contract. As long as existing partners are willing to be bound by the contract, the maximum life of a partnership is equal to the life of any one of its partners. A partnership may be ended voluntarily at any time through the acceptance of a new partner into the firm or the withdrawal of a partner. A partnership may be ended involuntarily by the death or incapacity of a partner. In short, any change in the number of partners, regardless of the cause, effects the **dissolution** of the partnership. Thus, the life of a partnership is unpredictable.

UNLIMITED LIABILITY

Each partner is personally and individually liable for all partnership liabilities. Creditors' claims attach first to partnership assets and then to the personal resources of any partner, irrespective of that partner's capital equity in the company. To illustrate, assume that: (1) the Rowe-Sanchez partnership is terminated when the claims of company creditors exceed partnership assets by $30,000, and (2) L. Rowe's personal assets total $40,000 but B. Sanchez has no personal assets. Creditors can collect their total claims from Rowe regardless of Rowe's capital balance in the firm, even though Sanchez and Rowe may be equal partners. Rowe, in turn, has a legal claim on Sanchez, but this would be worthless under the conditions described. Some states allow **limited partnerships** in which the liability of a partner is limited to the partner's capital equity. However, there must always be at least one partner with unlimited ability, often referred to as the **general partner.**

CO-OWNERSHIP OF PROPERTY

Partnership assets are co-owned by the partners. Once assets have been invested in the partnership, they are owned jointly by all the partners. Moreover, if the partnership is terminated, the assets do not legally revert to the original contributor. Each partner has a claim on total assets equal to the balance in his or her respective capital account, but this claim does not attach to specific assets that an individual partner may have contributed to the firm.

Similarly, if a partner invests a building in the partnership valued at $100,000, and the building is sold later at a gain of $20,000, that partner does not personally receive the entire gain. Partnership net income (or net loss) is also co-owned; if the partnership agreement does not specify to the contrary, all net income or net loss is shared equally by the partners. As you will see later, however, the partnership agreement may provide for unequal sharing of net income or net loss.

ADVANTAGES AND DISADVANTAGES OF A PARTNERSHIP

What are the major advantages and disadvantages of a partnership? One major advantage is that the **skills and resources of two or more individuals** can be combined. For example, a large public accounting firm such as PricewaterhouseCoopers must have combined expertise in auditing, taxation, and management consulting, not to mention specialists within each of these areas. In addition, a partnership does not have to contend with the "red tape" that a corporation must face; that is, a partnership is easily formed and is relatively free from governmental regulations and restrictions. Decisions can be made quickly on substantive matters affecting the firm, whereas in a corporation, formal meetings with the board of directors are often needed.

On the other hand, the major disadvantages of a partnership are mutual agency, limited life, and unlimited liability. Unlimited liability is particularly troublesome to many individuals, because they may lose not only their initial investment but also their personal assets, if they are needed to pay partnership creditors. As a result, it is often difficult to obtain large amounts of investment capital in a partnership. That is one reason why the largest business enterprises in the United States are corporations, not partnerships.

The advantages and disadvantages of the partnership form of business organization are summarized in Illustration 13-2.

Illustration 13-2
Advantages and disadvantages of a partnership

Advantages	Diasadvantages
Combining skills and resources of two or more individuals	Mutual agency
Ease of formation	Limited life
Freedom from government regulations and restrictions	Unlimited liability
Ease of decision making	

THE PARTNERSHIP AGREEMENT

A partnership is created by a contract expressing the voluntary agreement of two or more individuals. The written partnership agreement, often referred to as the partnership agreement or **articles of co-partnership**, contains such basic information as the name and principal location of the firm, the purpose of the business, and date of inception. In addition, different relationships that will exist among the partners, such as the following, should be specified:

- Names and capital contributions of partners
- Rights and duties of partners
- Basis for sharing net income or net loss
- Provision for withdrawals of income
- Procedures for submitting disputes to arbitration
- Procedures for the withdrawal or addition of a partner
- Rights and duties of surviving partners in the event of a partner's death

The importance of a written contract cannot be overemphasized. The agreement should be drawn with care and should attempt to anticipate all possible situations, contingencies, and disagreements. The help of a lawyer is highly desirable in preparing the agreement. A poorly drawn contract may create friction among the partners and eventually cause the termination of the partnership.

FORMATION OF A PARTNERSHIP

STUDY OBJECTIVE 3
Explain the accounting entries for the formation of a partnership.

Each partner's initial investment in a partnership should be recorded at the fair market value of the assets at the date of their transfer to the partnership. The values assigned must be agreed to by all of the partners.

To illustrate, assume that A. Rolfe and T. Shea combine their proprietorships to start a partnership named U.S. Pizza. Rolfe and Shea invest in the partnership as follows:

Illustration 13-3
Book and market value of assets invested

	Book Value		Market Value	
	A. Rolfe	T. Shea	A. Rolfe	T. Shea
Cash	$ 8,000	$ 9,000	$ 8,000	$ 9,000
Equipment	5,000		4,000	
Accumulated depreciation	(2,000)			
Accounts receivable		4,000		4,000
Allowance for doubtful accounts		(700)		(1,000)
	$11,000	$12,300	$12,000	$12,000

The entries to record the investments are:

Investment of A. Rolfe		
Cash	8,000	
Equipment	4,000	
A. Rolfe, Capital		12,000
(To record investment of Rolfe)		

Investment of T. Shea		
Cash	9,000	
Accounts Receivable	4,000	
Allowance for Doubtful Accounts		1,000
T. Shea, Capital		12,000
(To record investment of Shea)		

Note that neither the original cost of the equipment ($5,000) nor its book value ($5,000 − $2,000) is recorded by the partnership. The equipment has not been used by the partnership, so there can be no accumulated depreciation. In contrast, the gross claims on customers ($4,000) are carried forward to the partnership, and the allowance for doubtful accounts is adjusted to $1,000 to arrive at a cash (net) realizable value of $3,000. A partnership may start with an Allowance for Doubtful Accounts account, because this balance pertains to existing accounts receivable that are expected to be uncollectible in the future. In addition, this procedure maintains the control and subsidiary relationship between accounts receivable and the customers' ledger.

After the partnership has been formed, the accounting for its transactions is similar to accounting for transactions of any other type of business organization. For example, all transactions with outside parties, such as the purchase or sale of merchandise inventory and the payment or receipt of cash, should be recorded in the same manner for a partnership as for a proprietorship.

DIVISION OF NET INCOME OR NET LOSS

STUDY OBJECTIVE 4

Identify the bases for dividing net income or net loss.

Partnership net income or net loss is shared equally unless the partnership contract specifically indicates the manner in which net income and net loss are to be divided. The same basis of division usually applies to both net income and net loss. As a result, it is customary to refer to the basis as the **income ratio**, the **income and loss ratio,** or the **profit and loss ratio.** Because of its wide acceptance, we will use the term **income ratio** to identify the basis for dividing both net income and net loss. A partner's share of net income or net loss is recognized in the accounts through closing entries.

Closing Entries

You may recall from Chapter 5 that four closing entries are needed during the closing process. The first two entries close revenues and expenses to Income Summary; the last two entries transfer the balance in Income Summary to the partners' capital accounts and close their drawing accounts to their capital accounts.

To refresh your memory concerning the closing entries for a partnership, assume that L. Arbor and D. Barnett share net income and net loss equally. After closing all revenue and expense accounts, there is a credit balance in Income Summary of $32,000, which is the net income for the period. The entry to close this balance to the respective capital accounts is as follows:

Income Summary	32,000	
L. Arbor, Capital		16,000
D. Barnett, Capital		16,000
(To close net income to partners' capitals)		

If Arbor and Barnett have balances in their drawing accounts of $8,000 and $6,000, respectively, the entry to close these accounts looks like this:

L. Arbor, Capital	8,000	
D. Barnett, Capital	6,000	
L. Arbor, Drawing		8,000
D. Barnett, Drawing		6,000
(To close partners' drawings)		

Assuming the beginning capital balance is $47,000 for Arbor and $36,000 for Barnett, the following capital and drawing accounts (Illustration 13-4) will appear in the general ledger.

Illustration 13-4

Ledger balances after closing

L. Arbor, Capital

Drawing	8,000	Beg. Bal.	47,000
		Net income	16,000
		End Bal.	55,000

D. Barnett, Capital

Drawing	6,000	Beg. Bal.	36,000
		Net income	16,000
		End Bal.	46,000

L. Arbor, Drawing

End Bal.	8,000	To Capital	8,000

D. Barnett, Drawing

End Bal.	6,000	To Capital	6,000

The capital accounts indicate each partner's "permanent" investment, while the partners' drawing accounts are temporary owners' equity accounts. Normally, the capital accounts will have credit balances, whereas the drawing accounts will have debit balances. The drawing account is commonly debited in situations where cash or other assets are withdrawn by the partner for personal use. For example, the partnership contract may permit each partner to withdraw cash monthly for personal living expenses.

Income Ratios

As indicated earlier, the partnership agreement should specify the basis for sharing net income or net loss. The following are typical of the ratios that may be used.

- A fixed ratio, expressed as a proportion (6:4), a percentage (70% and 30%), or a fraction (2/3 and 1/3)
- A ratio based either on capital balances at the beginning of the year or on average capital balances during the year
- Salaries to partners and the remainder on a fixed ratio
- Interest on partners' capitals and the remainder on a fixed ratio
- Salaries to partners, interest on partners' capitals, and the remainder on a fixed ratio

The objective is to reach agreement on a basis that will equitably reflect the differences among partners in terms of their capital investment and service to the partnership.

A fixed ratio is easy to apply, and it may be an equitable basis in some circumstances. Assume, for example, that Hughes and Lane are partners. Each contributes the same amount of capital, but Hughes expects to work full-time in the partnership and Lane expects to work only half-time. Accordingly, the partners agree to a fixed ratio of 2/3 to Hughes and 1/3 to Lane.

A ratio based on capital balances may be appropriate when the funds invested in the partnership are considered the critical factor. This might be true when the partners expect to give equal service to the partnership. Capital balances may also be equitable when a manager is hired to run the business and the partners do not plan to take an active role in daily operations.

The three remaining ratios give specific recognition to differences that may exist among partners by providing salary allowances for time worked and interest allowances for capital invested. Then, any remaining net income or net loss is allocated on a fixed ratio. Some caution needs to be exercised in working with these types of income ratios. These ratios pertain exclusively to the computations that are required in dividing net income or net loss. **Salaries to partners and interest on partners' capitals are not expenses of the partnership.** Therefore, these items do not enter into the matching of expenses with revenues and the determination of net income or net loss. For a partnership, as well as for other entities, salaries expense pertains to the cost of services performed by employees, and interest expense relates to the cost of borrowing money from creditors. Partners in their ownership capacity are not considered either employees or creditors. When the income ratio includes a salary allowance for partners, some partnership agreements permit the partner to make monthly withdrawals of cash based on their "salary." In such cases, the withdrawals are debited to the partner's drawing account.

Salaries, Interest, and Remainder on a Fixed Ratio

Under this income ratio the provisions for salaries and interest must be applied before the remainder is allocated on the specified fixed ratio. This is true even if the provisions exceed net income or the partnership has suffered a net loss for the year. Detailed information concerning the division of net income or net loss should be shown at the bottom of the income statement.

To illustrate this income ratio, we will assume that Sara King and Ray Lee are co-partners in Kingslee Pizza. The partnership agreement provides for (1) salary allowances of $8,400 to King and $6,000 to Lee, (2) interest allowances of 10 percent on capital balances at the beginning of the year, and (3) the remainder equally. Capital balances on January 1 were King, $28,000, and Lee, $24,000. In 2004, partnership net income was $22,000. The division of net income is as shown in Illustration 13-5.

Illustration 13-5

Income statement with division of net income

KINGSLEE PIZZA
Income Statement
For the Year Ended December 31, 2004

Sales			$200,000
Net income			$ 22,000
	Division of Net Income		
	Sara King	Ray Lee	Total
Salary allowance	$ 8,400	$6,000	$14,400
Interest allowance			
Sara King ($28,000 × 10%)	2,800		
Ray Lee ($24,000 × 10%)		2,400	
Total interest			5,200
Total salaries and interest	11,200	8,400	19,600
Remaining income, $2,400			
Sara King ($2,400 × 50%)	1,200		
Ray Lee ($2,400 × 50%)		1,200	
Total remainder			2,400
Total division	$12,400	$9,600	$22,000

The entry to record the division of net income looks like this:

Dec. 31	Income Summary	22,000	
	Sara King, Capital		12,400
	Ray Lee, Capital		9,600
	(To close net income to partners' capitals)		

To illustrate a situation in which the salary and interest allowances exceed net income, we will assume that net income in Kingslee Pizza was only $18,000. In this case, the allowances will create a deficiency of $1,600 ($19,600 − $18,000). Since the computations of the salary and interest allowances are the same as those above, we will begin the division of net income with total salaries and interest as shown in Illustration 13-6.

Illustration 13-6

Division of net income—income deficiency

	Sara King	Ray Lee	Total
Total salaries and interest	$11,200	$8,400	$19,600
Remaining deficiency ($1,600)			
Sara King ($1,600 × 50%)	(800)		
Ray Lee ($1,600 × 50%)		(800)	
Total remainder			(1,600)
Total division	$10,400	$7,600	$18,000

PARTNERSHIP FINANCIAL STATEMENTS

The financial statements of a partnership are similar to those of a proprietorship. The differences are generally related to the fact that a number of owners are involved in a partnership. In a balance sheet, for instance, each partner's capital balance is reported. The income statement for a partnership is identical to the income statement for a proprietorship, except for the division of net income, as shown earlier.

The owner's equity statement for a partnership is called **partners' capital statement**. Its function is to explain the changes in each partner's capital account and in total partnership capital during the year. As in a proprietorship, changes in capital may result from three causes: additional capital investment, drawings, and net income or net loss.

The partners' capital statement for Kingslee Pizza shown in Illustration 13-7 is based on the division of $22,000 of net income. The statement includes assumed data for the additional investment and for drawings.

Illustration 13-7

Partners' capital statement

KINGSLEE PIZZA
Partners' Capital Statement
For the Year Ended December 31, 2004

	Sara King	Ray Lee	Total
Capital, January 1	$28,000	$24,000	$52,000
Add: Additional investment	2,000		2,000
Net income	12,400	9,600	22,000
	42,400	33,600	76,000
Less Drawings	7,000	5,000	12,000
Capital, December 31	$35,400	$28,600	$64,000

The capital statement is prepared from the income statement and the partners' capital and drawing accounts.

THE CORPORATE FORM OF ORGANIZATION AND STOCK TRANSACTIONS

In 1819, Chief Justice John Marshall defined a **corporation** as "an artificial being, invisible, intangible, and existing only in contemplation of law." This definition is the foundation for the prevailing legal interpretation that a corporation is an entity separate and distinct from its owners.

A corporation is created by law, and its continued existence depends on the statutes of the state in which it is incorporated. As a legal entity, a corporation has most of the rights and privileges of a person. The major exceptions relate to privileges that only a living person can exercise, such as the right to vote or to hold public office. A corporation is subject to the same duties and responsibilities as a person. For example, it must abide by the laws and it must pay taxes.

Corporations may be classified in a variety of ways. Two common bases are by purpose and by ownership. A corporation may be organized for the purpose of making a **profit,** or it may be **nonprofit.** Corporations for profit include such well-known companies as **McDonald's**, **Darden**, **Landry's**, **Hilton**, **Starwood**, and **Marriott**. Nonprofit corporations are organized for charitable, medical, or educational purposes. Examples are the **Salvation Army**, the **American Cancer Society**, the **Hilton Foundation**, and the **Forte Foundation**.

Classification by *ownership* distinguishes between publicly held and privately held corporations. A **publicly held corporation** may have thousands of stockholders. Its stock is regularly traded on a national securities exchange such as the New York Stock Exchange. Most of the largest U.S. corporations are publicly held. Examples of publicly held hospitality corporations are **Starwood**, **Hilton**, **Marriott**, **Disney**, **Darden**, and **Landry's**. In contrast, a **privately held corporation**, often referred to as a closely held corporation, usually has only a few stockholders, and does not offer its stock for sale to the general public. Privately held companies are generally much smaller than publicly held companies, although some notable exceptions exist. **Hyatt Hotels** is one of the most well known hotel companies in the United States that is privately held.

CHARACTERISTICS OF A CORPORATION

STUDY OBJECTIVE 5

Identify the major characteristics of a corporation.

A number of characteristics distinguish a corporation from proprietorships and partnerships. The most important of these characteristics are explained below.

Separate Legal Existence

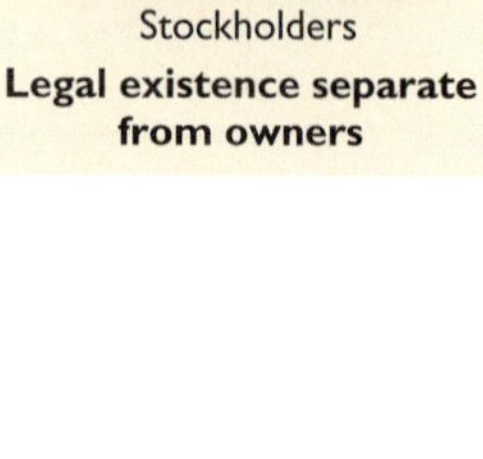

Legal existence separate from owners

As an entity separate and distinct from its owners, the corporation acts under its own name rather than in the name of its stockholders. **Disney** may buy, own, and sell property. It may borrow money, and may enter into legally binding contracts in its own name. It may also sue or be sued, and it pays its own taxes.

In contrast to a partnership, in which acts of the owners (partners) bind the partnership, the acts of its owners (stockholders) do not bind the corporation unless such owners are duly appointed agents of the corporation. For example, if you owned shares of Disney stock, you would not have the right to purchase a theme park for the company unless you were appointed as an agent of the corporation.

Limited Liability of Stockholders

Since a corporation is a separate legal entity, creditors have recourse only to corporate assets to satisfy their claims. The liability of stockholders is normally limited to their investment in the corporation. Creditors have no legal claim on the personal assets of the owners unless fraud has occurred. Even in the event of bankruptcy, stockholders' losses are generally limited to their capital investment in the corporation.

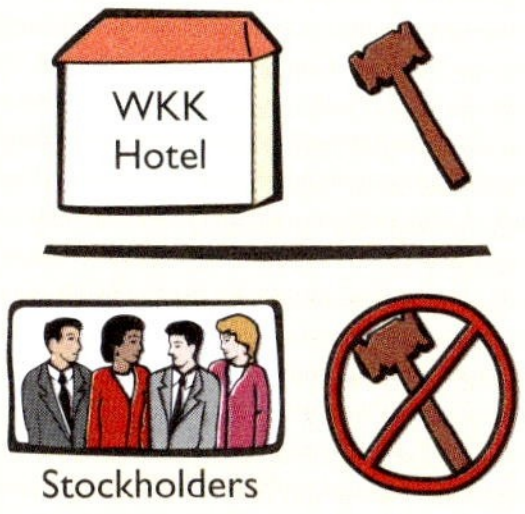

Limited liability of stockholders

Transferable Ownership Rights

Ownership of a corporation is held in shares of capital stock. These are transferable units. Stockholders may dispose of part or all of their interest in a corporation simply by selling their stock. The transfer of an ownership interest in a partnership requires the consent of each owner. In contrast, the transfer of stock is entirely at the discretion of the stockholder. It does not require the approval of either the corporation or other stockholders.

The transfer of ownership rights between stockholders normally has no effect on the operating activities of the corporation. Nor does it affect the corporation's assets, liabilities, and total ownership equity. The transfer of these ownership rights is a transaction between individual owners. The enterprise does not participate in such transfers after it issues the capital stock.

Transferable ownership rights

Ability to Acquire Capital

It is relatively easy for a corporation to obtain capital through the issuance of stock. Buying stock in a corporation is often attractive to an investor because a stockholder has limited liability and shares of stock are readily transferable. Also, numerous individuals can become stockholders by investing small amounts of money. In sum, the ability of a successful corporation to obtain capital is virtually unlimited.

Ability to acquire capital

Continuous Life

The life of a corporation is stated in its charter. The life may be perpetual or it may be limited to a specific number of years. If it is limited, the life can be extended through renewal of the charter. Since a corporation is a separate legal entity, its continuance as a going concern is not affected by the withdrawal, death, or incapacity of a stockholder, employee, or officer. As a result, a successful enterprise can have a continuous and perpetual life.

Continuous life

Corporation Management

As in **Marriott**, stockholders legally own the corporation. But they manage the corporation indirectly through a board of directors they elect. The board, in turn, formulates the operating policies for the company. The board also selects officers, such as a president and one or more vice presidents, to execute policy and to perform daily management functions.

A typical organization chart showing the delegation of responsibility is shown in Illustration 13-8.

The **president** is the chief executive officer. This individual has direct responsibility for managing the business. As the organization chart shows, the president delegates responsibility to other officers. The chief accounting officer is the **controller**. The controller's responsibilities include (1) maintaining the accounting records, (2) maintaining an adequate system of internal control, and (3) preparing financial statements, tax returns, and internal reports. The **treasurer** has cus-

Illustration 13-8

Corporation organization chart

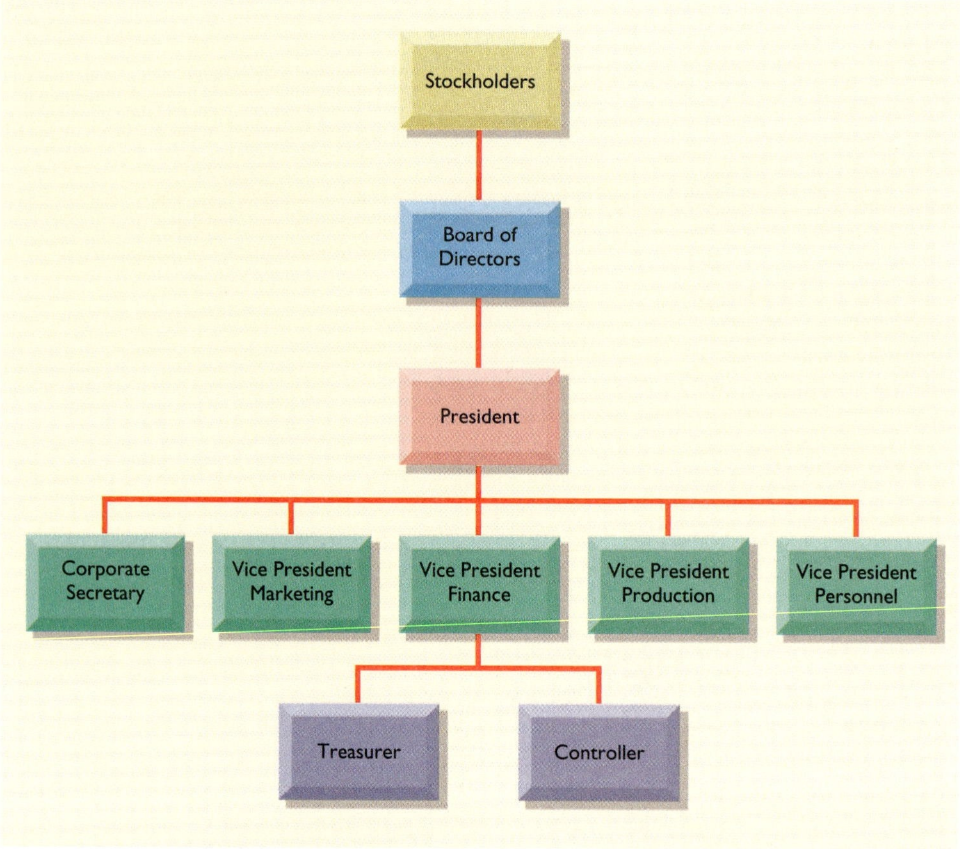

ETHICS NOTE

Managers who are not owners are often compensated based on the performance of the firm. They thus may be tempted to exaggerate firm performance by inflating income figures.

tody of the corporation's funds and is responsible for maintaining the company's cash position.

On one hand, the organizational structure of a corporation enables a company to hire professional managers to run the business. On the other hand, the separation of ownership and management prevents owners from having an active role in managing the company, which some owners like to have.

ACCOUNTING IN ACTION e Business Insight

When a group of investors in a company is unhappy with a company's performance, it sometimes tries to elect new members to the board of directors at the company's annual stockholder meeting. This is referred to as a proxy fight. Usually these efforts fail because it has been very expensive to get in contact with all of the company's shareholders to try to convince them to vote for your group of nominees.

But the Internet has changed that, says James Heard, chief executive of **Proxy Monitor**, a New York firm that consults institutional shareholders on how to vote on corporate governance issues. "Increasingly the Internet is being used as a tool of communication among shareholders to pressure managements," he said. One recent case involved an effort by a shareholder at **Luby's** to get four new people elected to that company's board of directors. He attracted considerable support from other Luby's shareholders by posting messages on a **Yahoo!** message board.

SOURCE: Aaron Elstein, "Online Grousing Over Luby's Escalates to Proxy Solicitation," *Wall Street Journal* (October 25, 2000).

Government Regulations

A corporation is subject to numerous state and federal regulations. State laws usually prescribe the requirements for issuing stock, the distributions of earnings permitted to stockholders, and the effects of retiring stock. Federal securities laws govern the sale of capital stock to the general public. Also, most publicly held corporations are required to make extensive disclosure of their financial affairs to the Securities and Exchange Commission through quarterly and annual reports. In addition, when a corporate stock is traded on organized securities exchanges, the corporation must comply with the reporting requirements of these exchanges. Government regulations are designed to protect the owners of the corporation. Such protection is needed because most stockholders do not participate in the day-to-day management of the company.

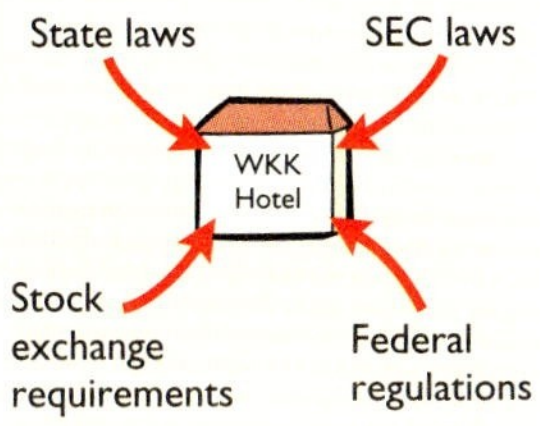

Goverment regulations

Additional Taxes

Neither proprietorships nor partnerships pay income taxes. The owner's share of earnings from these organizations is reported on his or her personal income tax return. Taxes are then paid by the individual on this amount. Corporations, on the other hand, must pay federal and state income taxes as a separate legal entity. These taxes are substantial: They can amount to more than 40 percent of taxable income.

Additional taxes

In addition, stockholders are required to pay taxes on cash dividends (pro rata distributions of net income). Thus, many argue that corporate income is **taxed twice (double taxation)**, once at the corporate level, and again at the individual level.

From the foregoing, we can identify the following advantages and disadvantages of a corporation compared to a proprietorship and partnership (Illustration 13-9).

Illustration 13-9

Advantages and disadvantages of a corporation

Advantages	Disadvantages
Separate legal existence	Corporation management—separation of ownership and management
Limited liability of stockholders	Government regulations
Transferable ownership rights	Additional taxes
Ability to acquire capital	
Continuous life	
Corporation management—professional managers	

S-Corporation

As you can see, while the characteristics of a regular corporation provide more liability protection for the investors, it is not practical for small, individual entrepreneurs to really take the advantage of forming a corporation. In order to encourage business development, the government does allow a category of corporation known as the sub-chapter S corporation under the Internal Revenue Services Code, more widely known as S-corp, for smaller investors. The one characteristic of an S-corp that is similar to that of a regular corporation is limited liability. However, there is no double-taxation. The earnings or losses are passed directly to the owners and are taxed at the owners' individual tax rates.

If S-corp has these good characteristics, why do all corporations not become S-corp? As I mentioned, the aim of the government is to encourage small businesses to still form as businesses but not to bear some of the disadvantages of a sole proprietorship. To become an S-corp, a corporation must have fewer than 35 shareholders, be a domestic corporation, and have only one class of stocks. These are all set up to provide protection and encouragement for domestic small businesses.

FORMING A CORPORATION

ALTERNATIVE TERMINOLOGY The charter is often referred to as the *articles of incorporation.*

The initial step in forming a corporation is to file an application with the secretary of state in the state in which incorporation is desired. The application contains such information as: (1) the name and purpose of the proposed corporation; (2) amounts, kinds, and number of shares of capital stock to be authorized; (3) the names of the incorporators; and (4) the shares of stock to which each has subscribed.

After the application is approved, a **charter** is granted. The charter may be an approved copy of the application form or it may be a separate document containing the same basic data. The issuance of the charter creates the corporation. Upon receipt of the charter, the corporation develops its bylaws. The **bylaws** establish the internal rules and procedures for conducting the affairs of the corporation. They also indicate the powers of the stockholders, directors, and officers of the enterprise.[1]

INTERNATIONAL NOTE

U.S. corporations are identified by *Inc.*, which stands for Incorporated. In Italy the letters used are *SpA* (Societa per Azioni); in Sweden *AB* (Aktiebolag); in France *SA* (Sociedad Anonima); and in the Netherlands *NV* (Naamloze Vennootschap).

In the United Kingdom public limited corporations are identified by *PLC*, and private corporations are denoted by *LTD*. The parallel designations in Germany are *AG* for public corporations and *GmbH* for private corporations.

Regardless of the number of states in which a corporation has operating divisions, it is incorporated in only one state. It is to the company's advantage to incorporate in a state whose laws are favorable to the corporate form of business organization.

Corporations engaged in interstate commerce must also obtain a license from each state in which they do business. The license subjects the corporation's operating activities to the corporation laws of the state.

Costs incurred in the formation of a corporation are called **organization costs**. These costs include legal and state fees, and promotional expenditures involved in the organization of the business. **Organization costs are expensed as incurred.** To determine the amount and timing of future benefits is so difficult that a conservative approach of expensing these costs immediately is followed.

ACCOUNTING IN ACTION *Business Insight*

It is not necessary for a corporation to have an office in the state in which it incorporates. In fact, more than 50 percent of the Fortune 500 corporations are incorporated in Delaware. A primary reason is the Delaware courts' longstanding "business judgment rule." The rule provides that as long as directors exercise "due care" in the interests of stockholders, their actions will not be second-guessed by the courts. The rule has enabled directors to reject hostile takeover offers and to spurn takeovers simply because they did not want to sell the company. However, new interpretations are emerging. In a recent case, the state court ruled for a company that made a hostile takeover bid. On appeal, the Delaware Supreme Court ruled for the directors but gave the following guideline to the state courts: "Was the board's response reasonable in the light of the threat posed?"

CORPORATE CAPITAL

Owners' equity in a corporation is identified as **stockholders' equity, shareholders' equity,** or **corporate capital**. The stockholders' equity section of a corporation's balance sheet consists of (1) paid-in (contributed) capital, and (2) retained earnings (earned capital). The distinction between paid-in capital and retained earnings is important from both a legal and a financial point of view. Legally, distributions of earnings (dividends) can be declared out of retained

[1]Following approval by two-thirds of the stockholders, the bylaws become binding upon all stockholders, directors, and officers. Legally, a corporation is regulated first by the laws of the state, second by its charter, and third by its bylaws. Care must be exercised to ensure that the provisions of the bylaws are not in conflict with either state laws or the charter.

earnings in all states, but in many states dividends cannot be declared out of paid-in capital. Financially, management, stockholders, and others look to earnings for the continued existence and growth of the corporation.

Ownership Rights of Stockholders

When chartered, the corporation may begin selling ownership rights in the form of shares of stock. When a corporation has only one class of stock, it is identified as **common stock**. Each share of common stock gives the stockholder the ownership rights pictured in Illustration 13-10. The ownership rights of a share of stock are stated in the articles of incorporation or in the bylaws.

Illustration 13-10

Ownership rights of stockholders

Stockholders have the right to:

1. Vote in the election of board of directors at annual meeting. To vote on actions that require stockholder approval.

2. Share the corporate earnings through receipt of dividends.

3. Keep same percentage ownership when new shares of stock are issued (**preemptive right**[2]).

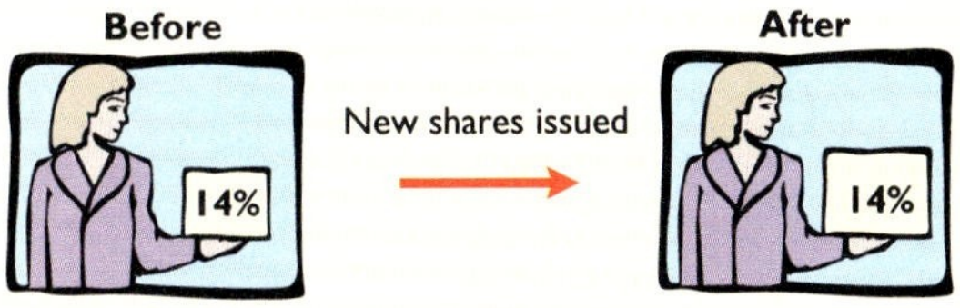

4. Share in assets upon liquidation, in proportion to their holdings. Called a **residual claim** because owners are paid with assets remaining after all claims have been paid.

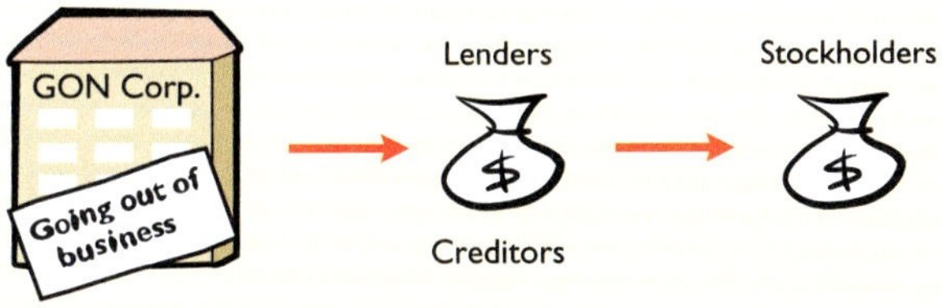

ACCOUNTING IN ACTION *International Insight*

In Japan, stockholders are considered to be far less important to a corporation than employees, customers, and suppliers. There, stockholders are rarely asked to vote on an issue, and the notion of bending corporate policy to favor stockholders borders on the heretical. This attitude toward stockholders appears to be slowly changing, however, as influential Japanese are advocating listening to investors, raising the extremely low dividends paid by Japanese corporations, and improving disclosure of financial information.

[2]A number of companies have eliminated the preemptive right, because they believe it makes an unnecessary and cumbersome demand on management. For example, by stockholder approval, IBM has dropped its preemptive right for stockholders.

Proof of stock ownership is evidenced by a form known as a **stock certificate**. As shown in Illustration 13-11, the face of the certificate shows the name of the corporation, the stockholder's name, the class and special features of the stock, the number of shares owned, and the signatures of duly authorized corporate officials. Certificates are prenumbered to facilitate accountability. They may be issued for any quantity of shares.

Illustration 13-11

A stock certificate

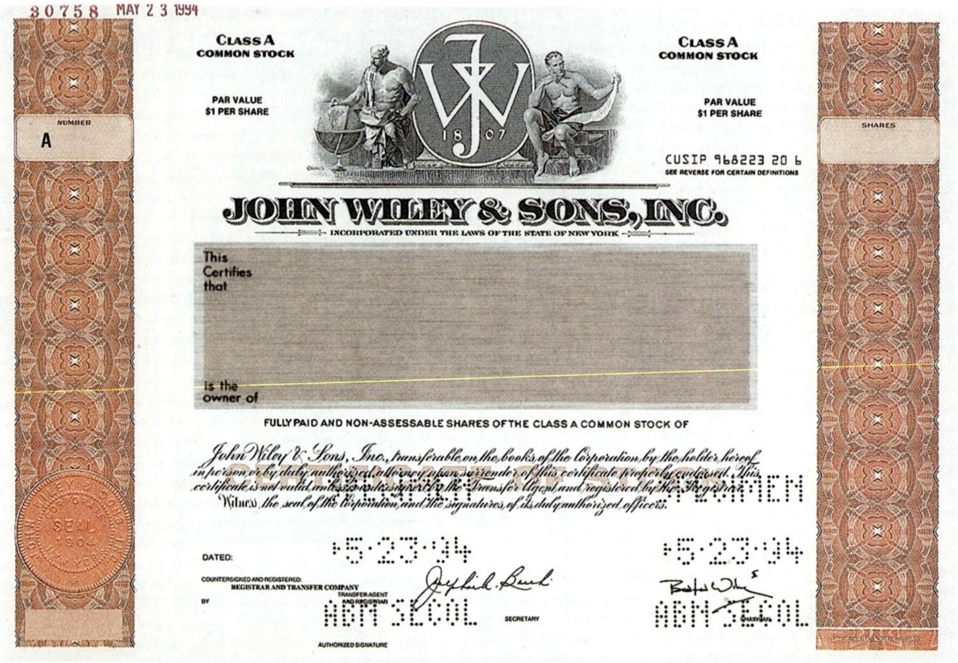

BEFORE YOU GO ON...

REVIEW IT

1. What are the advantages and disadvantages of a corporation compared to a proprietorship and a partnership?
2. Identify the principal steps in forming a corporation.
3. What rights are inherent in owning a share of stock in a corporation?

THE NAVIGATOR

Stock Issue Considerations

INTERNATIONAL NOTE

U.S. and U.K. corporations raise most of their capital through millions of outside shareholders and bondholders. In contrast, companies in Germany, France, and Japan acquire financing from large banks or other institutions. In the latter environment, shareholders are less important, and external reporting and auditing receive less emphasis.

In considering the issuance of stock, a corporation must resolve a number of basic questions: How many shares should be authorized for sale? How should the stock be issued? At what price should the shares be issued? What value should be assigned to the stock? These questions are answered in the following sections.

AUTHORIZED STOCK. The amount of stock that a corporation is *authorized* to sell is indicated in its charter. The total amount of **authorized stock** at the time of incorporation normally anticipates both initial and subsequent capital needs. As a result, the number of shares authorized generally exceeds the number initially sold. If all authorized stock is sold, a corporation must obtain consent of the state to amend its charter before it can issue additional shares.

The authorization of capital stock does not result in a formal accounting entry. This event has no immediate effect on either corporate assets or stockhold-

ers' equity. But, disclosure of the number of authorized shares is often reported in the stockholders' equity section. It is then simple to determine the number of unissued shares that can be issued without amending the charter: subtract the total shares issued from the total authorized. For example, if Micro Hotel was authorized to sell 100,000 shares of common stock and issued 80,000 shares, 20,000 shares would remain unissued.

Indirect Issuance

ISSUANCE OF STOCK. A corporation can issue common stock directly to investors. Or it can issue the stock indirectly through an investment banking firm (brokerage house) that specializes in bringing securities to the attention of prospective investors. Direct issue is typical in closely held companies. Indirect issue is customary for a publicly held corporation.

In an indirect issue, the investment banking firm may agree to **underwrite** the entire stock issue. In this arrangement, the investment banker buys the stock from the corporation at a stipulated price and resells the shares to investors. The corporation thus avoids any risk of being unable to sell the shares. Also, it obtains immediate use of the cash received from the underwriter. The investment banking firm, in turn, assumes the risk of reselling the shares in return for an underwriting fee.[3] For example, Bahama Resorts, used an underwriter to help it issue common stock to the public. The underwriter charged a 6.6 percent underwriting fee on Bahama's approximately $20 million public offering.

How does a corporation set the price for a new issue of stock? Among the factors to be considered are (1) the company's anticipated future earnings, (2) its expected dividend rate per share, (3) its current financial position, (4) the current state of the economy, and (5) the current state of the securities market. The calculation can be complex and is properly the subject of a finance course.

MARKET VALUE OF STOCK. The stock of publicly held companies is traded on organized exchanges. The dollar prices per share are established by the interaction between buyers and sellers. In general, the prices set by the marketplace tend to follow the trend of a company's earnings and dividends. But factors beyond a company's control, such as international turmoil, changes in interest rates, and the outcome of a presidential election, may cause day-to-day fluctuations in market prices.

ACCOUNTING IN ACTION *Business Insight*

The volume of trading on national and international exchanges is heavy. Shares in excess of 800 million are often traded daily on the New York Stock Exchange alone. For each listed stock, the financial press reports the total volume of stock traded for a given day, the high and low price for the day (now in decimals), the closing market price, and the net change for the day. A recent listing for **Disney** is shown below.

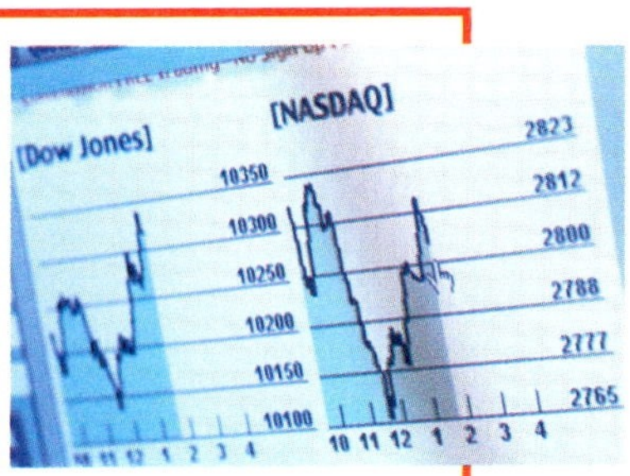

Stock	Volume	High	Low	Close	Net Change
Disney	4,700,600	18.46	18.00	18.18	−0.13

These numbers indicate that Disney's trading volume was 4,700,600 shares. The high, low, and closing prices for that date were $18.46, $18.00, and $18.18, respectively. The net change for the day was a decrease of $0.13 per share.

[3]Alternatively, the investment banking firm may agree only to enter into a **best efforts** contract with the corporation. In such cases, the banker agrees to sell as many shares as possible at a specified price. The corporation bears the risk of unsold stock. Under a best efforts arrangement, the banking firm is paid a fee or commission for its services.

The trading of capital stock on securities exchanges involves the transfer of **already issued shares** from an existing stockholder to another investor. These transactions have no impact on a corporation's stockholders' equity.

TECHNOLOGY IN ACTION

Giant, publicly held corporations could not exist without the organized stock markets, and the stock markets could not exist without massive computerization. Not too many years ago, the NYSE "ticker" would run behind, or trading would even be halted, when sales exceeded 30 million shares or so. Now, with sales sometimes in excess of 800 million shares, the NYSE and its companion exchanges throughout the country operate efficiently with computer technology. Technology has also made possible extended trading hours. An investor in New York can trade electronically at 3:30 A.M., which is the time in New York when the London Stock Exchange opens. Some predict that 24-hour trading is not far off.

PAR AND NO-PAR VALUE STOCKS. **Par value stock** is capital stock that has been assigned a value per share in the corporate charter. The par value may be any amount selected by the corporation. Generally, the par value is quite low, because states often levy a tax on the corporation based on par value. For example, **Starwood** has a par of $0.01. **Hilton's** common stock carries a par value of $2.50 per share while its preferred stock has a par value of $1.00 per share.

Par value does not indicate the worth or market value of the stock. **Disney**, like **Starwood**, also carries stocks with a par value $0.01, but its recent market price was $18.18 per share. **Par value** has legal significance. It represents the **legal capital** per share that must be retained in the business for the protection of corporate creditors. That amount is not available for withdrawal by stockholders. Thus, most states require the corporation to sell its shares at par or above.

No-par value stock is capital stock that has not been assigned a value in the corporate charter. It is often issued because some confusion still exists concerning par value and fair market value. If shares are not assigned a par value, the questionable use of par value as a basis for fair market value never arises. The major disadvantage of no-par value stock is that some states levy a high tax on such shares.

No-par value stock is quite common today. For example, **Marriott's** preferred stock has no par value. In many states the board of directors is permitted to assign a **stated value** to the no-par shares. This value becomes the legal capital per share. The stated value of no-par stock may be changed at any time by action of the directors. Stated value, like par value, does not indicate the market value of the stock. When there is no assigned stated value, the entire proceeds received upon issuance of the stock is considered to be legal capital.

The relationship of par and no-par value to legal capital is shown in Illustration 13-12.

Illustration 13-12

Relationship of par and no-par value stock to legal capital

Stock		Legal Capital per Share
Par value	→	Par value
No-par value with stated value	→	Stated value
No-par value without stated value	→	Entire proceeds

BEFORE YOU GO ON...

REVIEW IT

1. Of what significance to a corporation is the amount of authorized stock?
2. What alternative approaches may a corporation use in issuing stock?
3. Distinguish between par value and fair market value.

DO IT

At the end of its first year of operation, Doral Restaurants, Inc. has $750,000 of common stock and net income of $122,000. Prepare (a) the closing entry for net income (as shown in Illustration 5-7, page 153), and (b) the stockholders' equity section at year-end (as shown in Illustration 5-26, page 166).

ACTION PLAN

- Record net income in Retained Earnings by a closing entry in which Income Summary is debited and Retained Earnings is credited.
- In the stockholders' equity section, show (1) paid-in capital and (2) retained earnings.

SOLUTION

(a) Income Summary	122,000	
Retained Earnings		122,000
(To close income summary and transfer net income to retained earnings)		

(b) Stockholders' equity		
Paid-in capital		
Common stock	$750,000	
Retained earnings	122,000	
Total stockholders' equity		$872,000

THE NAVIGATOR

ACCOUNTING FOR COMMON STOCK ISSUES

STUDY OBJECTIVE 6

Record the issuance of common stock.

Let's now look at how to account for issues of common stock. The primary objectives in accounting for the issuance of common stock are (1) to identify the specific sources of paid-in capital and (2) to maintain the distinction between paid-in capital and retained earnings. **The issuance of common stock affects only paid-in capital accounts.**

Issuing Par Value Common Stock for Cash

As discussed earlier, par value does not indicate a stock's market value. Therefore, the cash proceeds from issuing par value stock may be equal to, greater than, or less than par value. When the issuance of common stock for cash is recorded, the par value of the shares is credited to Common Stock. The portion of the proceeds that is above or below par value is recorded in a separate paid-in capital account.

To illustrate, assume that Hydro-SlideTheme Park issues 1,000 shares of $1 par value common stock at par for cash. The entry to record this transaction is:

Cash	1,000	
Common Stock		1,000
(To record issuance of 1,000 shares of $1 par common stock at par)		

A	=	L	+	SE
+1,000				+1,000

ALTERNATIVE TERMINOLOGY
Paid-in Capital in Excess of Par is also called *Premium on Stock.*

If Hydro-Slide issues an additional 1,000 shares of the $1 par value common stock for cash at $5 per share, the entry is:

A	=	L	+	SE
+5,000				+1,000
				+4,000

Cash	5,000	
Common Stock		1,000
Paid-in Capital in Excess of Par Value		4,000
(To record issuance of 1,000 shares of common stock in excess of par)		

The total paid-in capital from these two transactions is $6,000, and the legal capital is $2,000. If Hydro-Slide has retained earnings of $27,000, the stockholders' equity section is shown in Illustration 13-13.

Illustration 13-13
Stockholders' equity—paid-in capital in excess of par value

HYDRO-SLIDE THEME PARK
Balance Sheet (partial)

Stockholders' equity	
Paid-in-capital	
Common stock	$ 2,000
Paid-in capital in excess of par value	**4,000**
Total paid-in capital	6,000
Retained earnings	27,000
Total stockholders' equity	$33,000

When stock is issued for less than par value, the account Paid-in Capital in Excess of Par Value is debited, if a credit balance exists in this account. If a credit balance does not exist, then the amount less than par is debited to Retained Earnings. This situation occurs only rarely: The sale of common stock below par value is not permitted in most states, because stockholders may be held personally liable for the difference between the price paid upon original sale and par value.

Issuing No-Par Common Stock for Cash

When no-par common stock has a stated value, the entries are similar to those illustrated for par value stock. The stated value represents legal capital. Therefore, it is credited to Common Stock. Also, when the selling price of no-par stock exceeds stated value, the excess is credited to Paid-in Capital in Excess of Stated Value. For example, assume that instead of $1 par value stock, Hydro-Slide Theme Park has $5 stated value no-par stock and the company issues 5,000 shares at $8 per share for cash. The entry looks like this:

A	=	L	+	SE
+40,000				+25,000
				+15,000

Cash	40,000	
Common Stock		25,000
Paid-in Capital in Excess of Stated Value		15,000
(To record issue of 5,000 shares of $5 stated value no-par stock)		

Paid-in Capital in Excess of Stated Value is reported as part of paid-in capital in the stockholders' equity section.

What happens when no-par stock does not have a stated value? In that case, the entire proceeds from the issue become legal capital and are credited to Common Stock. Thus, if Hydro-Slide does not assign a stated value to its no-par stock, the issuance of the 5,000 shares at $8 per share for cash is recorded as follows.

Cash	40,000	
Common Stock		40,000
(To record issue of 5,000 shares of no-par stock)		

A	=	L	+	SE
+40,000				+40,000

The amount of legal capital for Hydro-Slide stock with a $5 stated value is $25,000. Without a stated value, it is $40,000.

Issuing Common Stock for Services or Noncash Assets

Stock may also be issued for services (compensation to attorneys or consultants) or for noncash assets (land, buildings, and equipment). In such cases, what cost should be recognized in the exchange transaction? To comply with the **cost principle**, in a noncash transaction **cost is the cash equivalent price**. Thus, **cost is either the fair market value of the consideration given up, or the fair market value of the consideration received, whichever is more clearly determinable.**

To illustrate, assume that attorneys have helped Jordan Sports Spa incorporate. They have billed the company $5,000 for their services. They agree to accept 4,000 shares of $1 par value common stock in payment of their bill. At the time of the exchange, there is no established market price for the stock. In this case, the market value of the consideration received, $5,000, is more clearly evident. Accordingly, the entry is:

Organization Expense	5,000	
Common Stock		4,000
Paid-in Capital in Excess of Par Value		1,000
(To record issuance of 4,000 shares of $1 par value stock to attorneys)		

A	=	L	+	SE
				−5,000
				+4,000
				+1,000

As explained on page 426, organization costs are expensed as incurred.

In contrast, assume that Athletic Rock Climbing Camp is an existing publicly held corporation. Its $5 par value stock is actively traded at $8 per share. The company issues 10,000 shares of stock to acquire land recently advertised for sale at $90,000. The most clearly evident value in this noncash transaction is the market price of the consideration given, $80,000. The transaction is recorded as follows.

Land	80,000	
Common Stock		50,000
Paid-in Capital in Excess of Par Value		30,000
(To record issuance of 10,000 shares of $5 par value stock for land)		

A	=	L	+	SE
+80,000				+50,000
				+30,000

As illustrated in these examples, **the par value of the stock is never a factor in determining the cost of the assets received**. This is also true of the stated value of no-par stock.

BEFORE YOU GO ON...

REVIEW IT

1. Explain the accounting for par and no-par common stock issued for cash.
2. Explain the accounting for the issuance of stock for services or noncash assets.

DO IT

Cayman Resorts begins operations on March 1 by issuing 100,000 shares of $10 par value common stock for cash at $12 per share. On March 15 it issues 5,000 shares of common stock to attorneys in settlement of their bill of $50,000 for organization costs. Journalize the issuance of the shares, assuming the stock is not publicly traded.

ACTION PLAN

- In issuing shares for cash, credit Common Stock for par value per share.
- Credit any additional proceeds in excess of par value to a separate paid-in capital account.
- When stock is issued for services, use the cash equivalent price.
- For the cash equivalent price use either the fair market value of what is given up or the fair market value of what is received, whichever is more clearly determinable.

SOLUTION

Mar. 1	Cash	1,200,000	
	Common Stock		1,000,000
	Paid-in Capital in Excess of Par Value		200,000
	(To record issuance of 100,000 shares at $12 per share)		
Mar. 15	Organization Expense	50,000	
	Common Stock		50,000
	(To record issuance of 5,000 shares for attorneys' fees)		

Related exercise material: 13-5 and 13-6.

THE NAVIGATOR

ACCOUNTING FOR TREASURY STOCK

STUDY OBJECTIVE 7

Explain the accounting for treasury stock.

Treasury stock is a corporation's own stock that has been issued, fully paid for, and reacquired by the corporation but not retired. A corporation may acquire treasury stock for various reasons:

1. To reissue the shares to officers and employees under bonus and stock compensation plans.
2. To increase trading of the company's stock in the securities market in the hopes of enhancing its market value.
3. To have additional shares available for use in the acquisition of other companies.
4. To reduce the number of shares outstanding and thereby increase earnings per share.
5. To rid the company of disgruntled investors, perhaps to avoid a takeover.

HELPFUL HINT
Treasury stock is so named because the company often holds the shares in its treasury for safekeeping.

HELPFUL HINT
Treasury shares do not have dividend rights or voting rights.

Many corporations have treasury stock. One survey of 600 companies in the United States found that 66 percent have treasury stock.[4] Specifically, **The Coca-Cola Company** recently reported as of December 31, 2002 $14,389 million and **United Airlines** $1,472 million in treasury stock.

[4] *Accounting Trends & Techniques 2000* (New York: American Institute of Certified Public Accountants).

ACCOUNTING IN ACTION *Business Insight*

Why would a company use its own cash or, worse yet, borrow money to buy back its own shares? Wouldn't a company want the public to buy its shares so that it can raise funds for future projects? Stock repurchase is a really interesting phenomenon. In 2000, more than a dozen lodging companies initiated repurchase programs. These include **Cendant Corporation**, **Choice Hotels International**, **Marriott International**, **Park Place Entertainment**, and **Sun International**, among others. Some companies believe their stocks are undervalued and, therefore, a stock repurchase program can maximize their returns. Such is the case with **John Q. Hammons Hotels**; it realized a 63 percent gain on its repurchase move.

Restaurants also use this tactic. **Landry's** repurchased its own shares in 1999, 2000, and 2001, totaling more than $89 million. In 2002, **Starbucks Corporation** also announced the repurchase of 3.5 million of its common stock at a value of more than $50 million. Its board has also approved up to a 10-million-share repurchase.

SOURCES: M. Whitford, "Stock Buybacks Spur Demand," *Hotel and Motel Management*, 215(16) (2000), 44.

"Starbucks Perks Up Stock Buyback Plan," *Nation's Restaurant News*, 36(26) (2002), 12.

Purchase of Treasury Stock

Treasury stock is generally accounted for by the cost method. This method uses the cost of the shares purchased to value the treasury stock. **Under the cost method, Treasury Stock is debited for the price paid to reacquire the shares.**

The same amount is credited to Treasury Stock when the shares are disposed of. To illustrate, assume that on January 1, 2004, the stockholders' equity section of Mead Foods Inc. has 100,000 shares of $5 par value common stock outstanding (all issued at par value) and Retained Earnings of $200,000. The stockholders' equity section before purchase of treasury stock is shown in Illustration 13-14.

Illustration 13-14
Stockholders' equity with no treasury stock

MEAD FOODS INC. Balance Sheet (partial)	
Stockholders' equity	
Paid-in capital	
Common stock, $5 par value, 100,000 shares issued and outstanding	$500,000
Retained earnings	200,000
Total stockholders' equity	$700,000

On February 1, 2004, Mead acquires 4,000 shares of its stock at $8 per share:

Feb. 1	Treasury Stock	32,000	
	Cash		32,000
	(To record purchase of 4,000 shares of treasury stock at $8 per share)		

A	=	L	+	SE
−32,000				−32,000

Note that Treasury Stock is debited for the cost of the shares purchased. Is the original paid-in capital account, Common Stock, affected? No, because the number of issued shares does not change. In the stockholders' equity section of the balance sheet, treasury stock is deducted from total paid-in capital and retained earnings. Treasury Stock is a contra stockholders' equity account.

The stockholders' equity section of Mead Foods after purchase of treasury stock is shown in Illustration 13-15.

Illustration 13-15

Stockholders' equity with treasury stock

MEAD FOODS INC.
Balance Sheet (partial)

Stockholders' equity	
Paid-in capital	
Common stock, $5 par value, 100,000 shares issued and 96,000 shares outstanding	$500,000
Retained earnings	200,000
Total paid-in capital and retained earnings	700,000
Less: **Treasury stock (4,000 shares)**	**32,000**
Total stockholders' equity	$668,000

Thus, the acquisition of treasury stock reduces stockholders' equity.

In the balance sheet, both the number of shares issued (100,000) and the number in the treasury (4,000) are disclosed. The difference between these two amounts is the number of shares of stock outstanding (96,000). The term **outstanding stock** means the number of shares of issued stock that are being held by stockholders.

Some maintain that treasury stock should be reported as an asset because it can be sold for cash. Under this reasoning, unissued stock should also be shown as an asset, clearly an erroneous conclusion. Rather than being an asset, treasury stock reduces stockholder claims on corporate assets. This effect is correctly shown by reporting treasury stock as a deduction from total paid-in capital and retained earnings.

Disposal of Treasury Stock

Treasury stock is usually sold or retired. The accounting for its sale is different when treasury stock is sold above cost than when it is sold below cost.

HELPFUL HINT

Treasury stock transactions are classified as capital stock transactions. As in the case when stock is issued, the income statement is not involved.

SALE OF TREASURY STOCK ABOVE COST. If the selling price of the treasury shares is equal to cost, the sale of the shares is recorded by a debit to Cash and a credit to Treasury Stock. When the selling price of the shares is greater than cost, the difference is credited to Paid-in Capital from Treasury Stock.

To illustrate, assume that 1,000 shares of treasury stock of Mead Foods Inc., previously acquired at $8 per share, are sold at $10 per share on July 1. The entry is as follows.

A	=	L	+	SE
+10,000				+8,000
				+2,000

July 1	Cash	10,000	
	Treasury Stock		8,000
	Paid-in Capital from Treasury Stock		2,000
	(To record sale of 1,000 shares of treasury stock above cost)		

The $2,000 credit in the entry would not be considered a gain on sale of treasury stock for two reasons: (1) Gains on sales occur when **assets** are sold, and treasury stock is not an asset. (2) A corporation does not realize a gain or suffer a loss from stock transactions with its own stockholders. Thus, paid-in capital arising from the sale of treasury stock should not be included in the measurement of net income. Paid-in Capital from Treasury Stock is listed separately on the balance sheet as a part of paid-in capital.

SALE OF TREASURY STOCK BELOW COST. When treasury stock is sold below its cost, the excess of cost over selling price is usually debited to Paid-in Capital from Treasury Stock. Thus, if Mead Foods Inc. sells an additional 800 shares of treasury stock on October 1 at $7 per share, the entry is as follows.

Oct. 1	Cash	5,600	
	Paid-in Capital from Treasury Stock	800	
	Treasury Stock		6,400
	(To record sale of 800 shares of treasury stock below cost)		

A	=	L	+	SE
+5,600				−800
				+6,400

Observe the following from the two sales entries: (1) Treasury Stock is credited at cost in each entry. (2) Paid-in Capital from Treasury Stock is used for the difference between cost and the resale price of the shares. And (3) the original paid-in capital account, Common Stock, is not affected. **The sale of treasury stock increases both total assets and total stockholders' equity.**

After posting the foregoing entries, the treasury stock accounts will show the following balances on October 1 (Illustration 13-16).

Illustration 13-16

Treasury stock accounts

Treasury Stock

Feb. 1	32,000	July 1	8,000
		Oct. 1	6,400
Oct. 1 Bal.	17,600		

Paid-in Capital from Treasury Stock

Oct. 1	800	July 1	2,000
		Oct. 1 Bal.	1,200

When the credit balance in Paid-in Capital from Treasury Stock is eliminated, any additional excess of cost over selling price is debited to Retained Earnings. To illustrate, assume that Mead Foods, Inc. sells its remaining 2,200 shares at $7 per share on December 1. The excess of cost over selling price is $2,200 [$2{,}200 \times (\$8 - \$7)$]. In this case, $1,200 of the excess is debited to Paid-in Capital from Treasury Stock. The remainder is debited to Retained Earnings. The entry follows:

Dec. 1	Cash	15,400	
	Paid-in Capital from Treasury Stock	1,200	
	Retained Earnings	1,000	
	Treasury Stock		17,600
	(To record sale of 2,200 shares of treasury stock at $7 per share)		

A	=	L	+	SE
+15,400				−1,200
				−1,000
				+17,600

BEFORE YOU GO ON...

REVIEW IT

1. What is treasury stock, and why do companies acquire it?
2. How is treasury stock recorded?
3. Where is treasury stock reported in the financial statements? Does a company record gains and losses on treasury stock transactions? Explain.

DO IT

Santa Anita Resorts Inc. purchases 3,000 shares of its $50 par value common stock for $180,000 cash on July 1. The shares are to be held in the treasury until resold. On November 1, the corporation sells 1,000 shares of treasury stock for cash at $70 per share. Journalize the treasury stock transactions.

ACTION PLAN

- Record the purchase of treasury stock at cost.
- When treasury stock is sold above its cost, credit the excess of the selling price over cost to Paid-in Capital from Treasury Stock.
- When treasury stock is sold below its cost, debit the excess of cost over selling price to Paid-in Capital from Treasury Stock.

SOLUTION

July 1	Treasury Stock	180,000	
	Cash		180,000
	(To record the purchase of 3,000 shares at $60 per share)		
Nov. 1	Cash	70,000	
	Treasury Stock		60,000
	Paid-in Capital from Treasury Stock		10,000
	(To record the sale of 1,000 shares at $70 per share)		

Related exercise material: 13-6 and 13-7.

THE NAVIGATOR

PREFERRED STOCK

STUDY OBJECTIVE 8

Differentiate preferred stock from common stock.

To appeal to more potential investors, a corporation may issue an additional class of stock, called preferred stock. **Preferred stock** has contractual provisions that give it a preference or priority over common stock in certain areas. Typically, preferred stockholders have a priority as to (1) distributions of earnings (dividends) and (2) assets in the event of liquidation. However, they generally do not have voting rights.

Like common stock, preferred stock may be issued for cash or for noncash assets. The entries for these transactions are similar to the entries for common stock. When a corporation has more than one class of stock, each paid-in capital account title should identify the stock to which it relates. For example, a company might have the following accounts: Preferred Stock, Common Stock, Paid-in Capital in Excess of Par Value—Preferred Stock, and Paid-in Capital in Excess of Par Value—Common Stock. Assume that Stine Hotel Corporation issues 10,000 shares of $10 par value preferred stock for $12 cash per share. The entry to record the issuance follows:

A	=	L	+	SE
+120,000				+100,000
				+20,000

Cash	120,000	
Preferred Stock		100,000
Paid-in Capital in Excess of Par Value–Preferred Stock		20,000
(To record the issuance of 10,000 shares of $10 par value preferred stock)		

Preferred stock may have either a par value or no-par value. In the stockholders' equity section of the balance sheet, preferred stock is shown first because of its dividend and liquidation preferences over common stock.

Various features associated with the issuance of preferred stock, including dividend preferences, liquidation preferences, convertibility, and callability, are discussed on the following pages.

Dividend Preferences

As noted earlier, **preferred stockholders have the right to share in the distribution of corporate income before common stockholders.** For example, if the dividend rate on preferred stock is $5 per share, common shareholders will not receive any dividends in the current year until preferred stockholders have received $5 per share. The first claim to dividends does not, however, guarantee the payment of dividends. Dividends depend on many factors, such as adequate retained earnings and availability of cash.

The per share dividend amount is stated as a percentage of the preferred stock's par value or as a specified amount. For example, Crane Resorts specifies a 3¾ percent dividend on its $100 par value preferred ($100 × 3¾% = $3.75 per share).

I hope there is some money left when it's my turn.
Preferred stockholders
Common stockholders

Dividend Preference

Cumulative Dividend

Preferred stock often contains a **cumulative dividend** feature. This means that preferred stockholders must be paid both current-year dividends and any unpaid prior-year dividends before common stockholders receive dividends. When preferred stock is cumulative, preferred dividends not declared in a given period are called **dividends in arrears**.

HELPFUL HINT
The cumulative dividend feature is often critical in investors' acceptance of a preferred stock issue. Investors are much less interested in a noncumulative preferred stock because a dividend passed in any year is lost forever.

To illustrate, assume that Sun Resorts and Spas has 5,000 shares of 7 percent, $100 par value, cumulative preferred stock outstanding. The annual dividend is $35,000 (5,000 × $7 per share), but dividends are two years in arrears. In this case preferred stockholders are entitled to receive the following dividends in the current year.

Illustration 13-17
Computation of total dividends to preferred stock

Dividends in arrears ($35,000 × 2)	$ 70,000
Current-year dividends	35,000
Total preferred dividends	**$105,000**

No distribution can be made to common stockholders until this entire preferred dividend is paid. In other words, dividends cannot be paid to common stockholders while any preferred stock is in arrears.

Dividends in arrears are not considered a liability. No payment obligation exists until a dividend is declared by the board of directors. However, the amount of dividends in arrears should be disclosed in the notes to the financial statements. Doing so enables investors to assess the potential impact of this commitment on the corporation's financial position.

Companies that are unable to meet their dividend obligations are not looked upon favorably by the investment community. As a financial officer noted in discussing one company's failure to pay its cumulative preferred dividend for a period of time, "Not meeting your obligations on something like that is a major black mark on your record." The accounting entries for preferred stock dividends are explained in the following section.

DIVIDENDS

STUDY OBJECTIVE 9

Prepare the entries for cash dividends and stock dividends.

A **dividend** is a distribution by a corporation to its stockholders on a pro rata (proportional) basis. Potential buyers and sellers of stock are very interested in a company's dividend policies and practices. Dividends can take four forms: cash, property, scrip (a promissory note to pay cash), or stock. Cash dividends predominate in practice. Also, stock dividends are declared with some frequency. These two forms of dividends will be the focus of discussion in this chapter.

Dividends may be expressed in two ways: (1) as a percentage of the par or stated value of the stock, or (2) as a dollar amount per share. In the financial press, dividends are generally reported **quarterly** as a **dollar amount per share**.

CASH DIVIDENDS

A **cash dividend** is a pro rata distribution of cash to stockholders. For a corporation to pay a cash dividend, it must have three things:

1. **Retained earnings.** The legality of a cash dividend depends on the laws of the state in which the company is incorporated. Payment of cash dividends from retained earnings is legal in all states. In general, cash dividend distributions based only on common stock (legal capital) are illegal. Statutes vary considerably with respect to cash dividends based on paid-in capital in excess of par or stated value. Many states permit such dividends. A dividend declared out of paid-in capital is termed a **liquidating dividend**. The amount originally paid in by stockholders is being reduced or "liquidated" by such a dividend.
2. **Adequate cash.** The legality of a dividend and the ability to pay a dividend are two different things. For example, Best Hotels, with retained earnings of \$3 million, could legally declare a dividend of \$3 million. But Best's cash balance is only \$250,000. In order to pay a \$3 million dividend, Best would need to raise additional cash through the sale of other assets or through additional financing.

   Before declaring a cash dividend, a company's board of directors must carefully consider both current and future demands on the company's cash resources. In some cases, current liabilities may make a cash dividend inappropriate. In other cases, a major plant expansion program may warrant only a relatively small dividend. **Hilton** declared a \$0.02 per share dividend per quarter in 2002. For the same period, **Landry's** declared a \$0.03 per share dividend, while **Marriott** paid \$0.06 to \$0.07 per share.
3. **A declaration of dividends.** A company does not pay dividends unless its board of directors decides to do so, at which point the board "declares" the dividend. The board of directors has full authority to determine the amount of income to be distributed in the form of a dividend and the amount to be retained in the business. Dividends do not accrue like interest on a note payable, and they are not a liability until declared.

The amount and timing of a dividend are important issues. The payment of a large cash dividend could lead to liquidity problems for the enterprise. On the other hand, a small dividend or a missed dividend may cause unhappiness among stockholders. Many of them expect to receive a reasonable cash payment from the company on a periodic basis. Many companies declare and pay cash dividends quarterly.

Entries for Cash Dividends

Three dates are important in connection with dividends: (1) the declaration date, (2) the record date, and (3) the payment date. Normally, there are two to four

ACCOUNTING IN ACTION *Business Insight*

In order to remain in business, companies must honor their interest payments to creditors, bankers, and bondholders. The payment of dividends to stockholders is another matter. Many companies can survive, even thrive, without such payouts. In fact, some managements consider dividend payments unnecessary, or even harmful. Pay your creditors, by all means. But, fork over perfectly good cash to stockholders? "Why give money to those strangers?" is the response of one company president.

Investors must keep an eye on the company's dividend policy and understand what it may signal. For most companies, regular boosts in the face of irregular earnings can be a warning signal of financial trouble. Companies with high dividends and rising debt may be borrowing money to pay shareholders. Low dividends sometimes indicate an expectation by management of low future earnings. Or, they may indicate a policy of retaining earnings for corporate expansion that will result in a higher stock price in the future.

weeks between each date. Accounting entries are required on two of the dates—the declaration date and the payment date.

On the **declaration date**, the board of directors formally declares (authorizes) the cash dividend and announces it to stockholders. Declaration of a cash dividend **commits the corporation to a legal obligation**. The obligation is binding and cannot be rescinded. An entry is required to recognize the decrease in retained earnings and the increase in the liability Dividends Payable. To illustrate, assume that on December 1, 2004, the directors of Heavenly Resorts declare a 50¢ per share cash dividend on 100,000 shares of $10 par value common stock. The dividend is $50,000 (100,000 × 50¢). The entry to record the declaration is:

HELPFUL HINT
What is the effect of the *declaration* of a cash dividend on (1) total stockholders' equity, (2) total liabilities, (3) total assets? Answer: (1) decrease, (2) increase, (3) no effect.

Declaration Date

Dec. 1	Retained Earnings	50,000	
	Dividends Payable		50,000
	(To record declaration of cash dividend)		

A	=	L	+	SE
		+50,000		−50,000

Dividends Payable is a current liability: it will normally be paid within the next several weeks.

Instead of debiting Retained Earnings, the account Dividends may be debited. This account provides additional information in the ledger. Also, a company may have separate dividend accounts for each class of stock. When a dividend account is used, its balance is transferred to Retained Earnings at the end of the year by a closing entry. Whichever account is used for the dividend declaration, the effect is the same: retained earnings is decreased and a current liability is increased. For homework problems, you should use the Retained Earnings account for recording dividend declarations.

At the **record date**, ownership of the outstanding shares is determined for dividend purposes. The records maintained by the corporation supply this information. In the interval between the declaration date and the record date, the corporation updates its stock ownership records. For Heavenly Resorts, the record date is December 22. No entry is required on this date because the corporation's liability recognized on the declaration date is unchanged.

HELPFUL HINT
Between the declaration date and record date, the number of shares outstanding should remain the same. The purpose of the record date is to identify the persons or entities that will receive the dividend, not to determine the amount of the dividend liability.

Record Date

Dec. 22	No entry necessary		

A	=	L	+	SE
−50,000		−50,000		

On the **payment date**, dividend checks are mailed to the stockholders and the payment of the dividend is recorded. Assuming that the payment date is January 20 for Heavenly Resorts, the entry on that date follows:

Payment Date

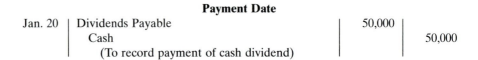

Jan. 20	Dividends Payable	50,000	
	Cash		50,000
	(To record payment of cash dividend)		

Note that payment of the dividend reduces both current assets and current liabilities. It has no effect on stockholders' equity. The **cumulative effect** of the **declaration and payment** of a cash dividend is to **decrease both stockholders' equity and total assets**. Illustration 13-18 summarizes the three important dates associated with dividends.

Illustration 13-18
Key dividend dates

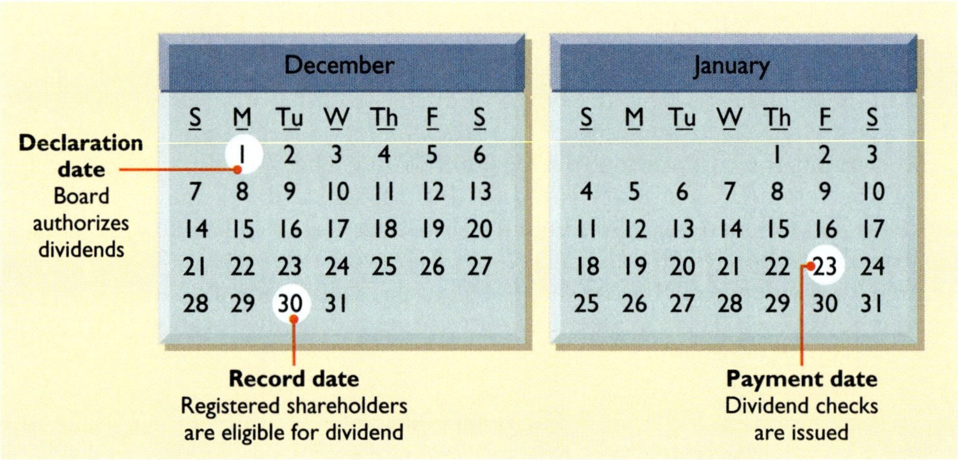

Allocating Cash Dividends between Preferred and Common Stock

As explained earlier in this chapter, preferred stock has priority over common stock in regard to dividends. Preferred stockholders must be paid any unpaid prior-year dividends before common stockholders receive dividends.

To illustrate, assume that at December 31, 2004, IBR Hotels Inc. has 1,000 shares of 8%, $100 par value cumulative preferred stock. It also has 50,000 shares of $10 par value common stock outstanding. The dividend per share for preferred stock is $8 ($100 par value × 8%). The required annual dividend for preferred stock is therefore $8,000 (1,000 × $8). At December 31, 2004, the directors declare a $6,000 cash dividend. In this case, the entire dividend amount goes to preferred stockholders because of their dividend preference. The entry to record the declaration of the dividend looks like this:

A	=	L	+	SE
		+6,000		−6,000

Dec. 31	Retained Earnings	6,000	
	Dividends Payable		6,000
	(To record $6 per share cash dividend to preferred stockholders)		

Because of the cumulative feature, dividends of $2 per share are in arrears on preferred stock for 2004. These dividends must be paid to preferred stockholders before any future dividends can be paid to common stockholders. Dividends in arrears should be disclosed in the financial statements.

At December 31, 2005, IBR declares a $50,000 cash dividend. Illustration 13-19 shows the allocation of the dividend to the two classes of stock.

Total dividend		$50,000
Allocated to preferred stock		
Dividends in arrears, 2004 (1,000 × $2)	**$2,000**	
2005 dividend (1,000 × $8)	**8,000**	10,000
Remainder allocated to common stock		$40,000

Illustration 13-19

Allocating dividends to preferred and common stock

The entry to record the declaration of the dividend looks like this:

Dec. 31	Retained Earnings	50,000	
	Dividends Payable		50,000
	(To record declaration of cash dividends of $10,000 to preferred stock and $40,000 to common stock)		

A	=	L	+	SE
		+50,000		−50,000

What if IBR's preferred stock were not cumulative? In that case, preferred stockholders would have received only $8,000 in dividends in 2005. Common stockholders would have received $42,000.

STOCK DIVIDENDS

A **stock dividend** is a pro rata distribution to stockholders of the corporation's own stock. Whereas a cash dividend is paid in cash, a stock dividend is paid in stock. **A stock dividend results in a decrease in retained earnings and an increase in paid-in capital.** Unlike a cash dividend, a stock dividend does not decrease total stockholders' equity or total assets.

To illustrate, assume that you have a 2 percent ownership interest in Cetus Restaurant Inc.; you own 20 of its 1,000 shares of common stock. If Cetus declares a 10 percent stock dividend, it would issue 100 shares (1,000 × 10%) of stock. You would receive 2 shares (2% × 100). Would your ownership interest change? No, it would remain at 2% (22 ÷ 1,100). **You now own more shares of stock, but your ownership interest has not changed.** Illustration 13-20 shows the effect of a stock dividend for stockholders.

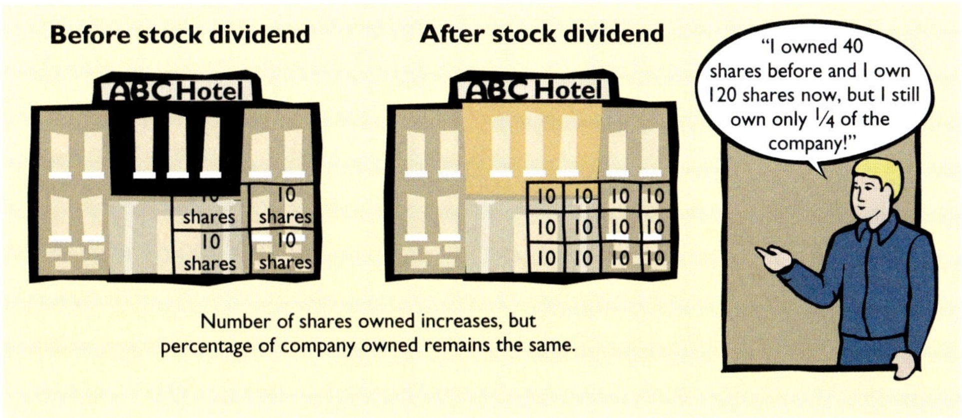

Illustration 13-20

Effect of stock dividend for stockholders

From the company's point of view, no cash has been disbursed, and no liabilities have been assumed by the corporation. What are the purposes and benefits of a stock dividend? Corporations issue stock dividends generally for one or more of the following reasons.

1. To satisfy stockholders' dividend expectations without spending cash.
2. To increase the marketability of the corporation's stock. When the number of shares outstanding increases, the market price per share decreases. Decreasing the market price of the stock makes it easier for smaller investors to purchase the shares.
3. To emphasize that a portion of stockholders' equity has been permanently reinvested in the business (and is unavailable for cash dividends).

The size of the stock dividend and the value to be assigned to each dividend share are determined by the board of directors when the dividend is declared. The per share amount must be at least equal to the par or stated value in order to meet legal requirements.

The accounting profession distinguishes between a **small stock dividend** (less than 20–25% of the corporation's issued stock) and a **large stock dividend** (greater than 20–25%). For small stock dividends, it recommends that the directors assign the **fair market value per share**. This treatment is based on the assumption that a small stock dividend will have little effect on the market price of the outstanding shares. Many stockholders consider small stock dividends to be distributions of earnings equal to the fair market value of the shares distributed. The amount to be assigned for a large stock dividend is not specified by the accounting profession. **Par or stated value per share** is normally assigned. Small stock dividends predominate in practice. Thus, we will illustrate only the entries for small stock dividends.

ENTRIES FOR STOCK DIVIDENDS

To illustrate the accounting for small stock dividends, assume that Medland Restaurants Corporation has a balance of $300,000 in retained earnings. It declares a 10% stock dividend on its 50,000 shares of $10 par value common stock. The current fair market value of its stock is $15 per share. The number of shares to be issued is 5,000 (10% × 50,000). Therefore the total amount to be debited to Retained Earnings is $75,000 (5,000 × $15). The entry to record the declaration of the stock dividend is as follows.

A	=	L	+	SE
				−75,000
				+50,000
				+25,000

Retained Earnings	75,000	
Common Stock Dividends Distributable		50,000
Paid-in Capital in Excess of Par Value		25,000
(To record declaration of 10% stock dividend)		

Note that Retained Earnings is debited for the fair market value of the stock issued ($15 × 5,000). Common Stock Dividends Distributable is credited for the par value of the dividend shares ($10 × 5,000), and the excess over par ($5 × 5,000) is credited to Paid-in Capital in Excess of Par Value.

Common Stock Dividends Distributable is a **stockholders' equity account**. It is not a liability because assets will not be used to pay the dividend. If a balance sheet is prepared before the dividend shares are issued, the distributable account is reported under Paid-in capital, as an addition to common stock issued. This is shown in Illustration 13-21.

Illustration 13-21

Statement presentation of common stock dividends distributable

Paid-in capital		
Common stock	$500,000	
Common stock dividends distributable	**50,000**	$550,000

When the dividend shares are issued, Common Stock Dividends Distributable is debited, and Common Stock is credited as follows.

Common Stock Dividends Distributable	50,000	
Common Stock		50,000
(To record issuance of 5,000 shares in a stock dividend)		

A	=	L	+	SE
				−50,000
				+50,000

EFFECTS OF STOCK DIVIDENDS

How do stock dividends affect stockholders' equity? They change the composition of stockholders' equity, because a portion of retained earnings is transferred to paid-in capital. However, **total stockholders' equity remains the same.** Stock dividends also have no effect on the par or stated value per share. But the number of shares outstanding increases. These effects are shown for Medland Corporation in Illustration 13-22.

Illustration 13-22

Stock dividend effects

	Before Dividend	After Dividend
Stockholders' equity		
Paid-in capital		
Common stock, $10 par	$ 500,000	$ 550,000
Paid-in capital in excess of par value	–0–	25,000
Total paid-in capital	500,000	575,000
Retained earnings	300,000	225,000
Total stockholders' equity	**$ 800,000**	**$ 800,000**
Outstanding shares	**50,000**	**55,000**

In this example, total paid-in capital is increased by $75,000, and retained earnings is decreased by the same amount. Note also that total stockholders' equity remains unchanged at $800,000.

STOCK SPLITS

A **stock split**, like a stock dividend, involves the issuance of additional shares to stockholders according to their percentage ownership. **A stock split results in a reduction in the par or stated value per share.** The purpose of a stock split is to increase the marketability of the stock by lowering its market value per share. A lower market value also makes it easier for the corporation to issue additional stock.

The effect of a split on market value is generally inversely proportional to the size of the split. For example, after a 2-for-1 stock split, the market value of a stock will fall. The lower market value stimulates market activity.

In a stock split, the number of shares is increased in the same proportion that par or stated value per share is decreased. For example, in a 2-for-1 split, one share

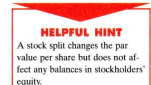

HELPFUL HINT
A stock split changes the par value per share but does not affect any balances in stockholders' equity.

of $10 par value stock is exchanged for two shares of $5 par value stock. **A stock split does not have any effect on total paid-in capital, retained earnings, or total stockholders' equity.** But the number of shares outstanding increases. These effects are shown in Illustration 13-23 for Medland Restaurants, assuming that it splits its 50,000 shares of common stock on a 2-for-1 basis.

Illustration 13-23

Stock split effects

	Before Stock Split	After Stock Split
Stockholders' equity		
Paid-in capital		
Common stock	$500,000	$500,000
Paid-in capital in excess of par value	–0–	–0–
Total paid-in capital	500,000	500,000
Retained earnings	300,000	300,000
Total stockholders' equity	**$800,000**	**$800,000**
Outstanding shares	**50,000**	**100,000**

Sysco Corporation is well known for splitting its stocks. In the past 25 years, it has had eight splits. The earlier splits were 3-for-2 and the latter were 2-for-1. If you owned two shares of Sysco in 1979, you will have 288 shares today! A stock split does not affect the balances in any stockholders' equity accounts. Therefore, **it is not necessary to journalize a stock split.** However, a memorandum entry explaining the effect of the split is typically made.

The significant differences between stock splits and stock dividends are shown in Illustration 13-24.

Illustration 13-24

Differences between the effects of stock splits and stock dividends

Item	Stock Split	Stock Dividend
Total paid-in capital	No change	Increase
Total retained earnings	No change	Decrease
Total par value (common stock)	No change	Increase
Par value per share	Decrease	No change

ACCOUNTING IN ACTION *Business Insight*

A handful of U.S. companies have no intention of keeping their stock trading in a range accessible to mere mortals. These companies never split their stock, no matter how high their stock price gets. The king is investment company **Berkshire Hathaway's** Class A stock, which sells for a pricey $70,000—per share! The company's Class B stock is a relative bargain at roughly $2,333 per share. Other "premium" stocks are **A. D. Makepeace** at $9,000 and **Mechanics Bank** of Richmond, California, at $11,000.

BEFORE YOU GO ON...

REVIEW IT

1. What entries are made for cash dividends on (a) the declaration date, (b) the record date, and (c) the payment date?

2. Distinguish between a small and large stock dividend, and indicate the basis for valuing each kind of dividend.
3. Contrast the effects of a small stock dividend and a 2-for-1 stock split on (a) stockholders' equity and (b) outstanding shares.

DO IT

Sing Resort Company has had 5 years of record earnings. Due to this success, the market price of its 500,000 shares of $2 par value common stock has tripled from $15 per share to $45. During this period, paid-in capital remained the same at $2,000,000. Retained earnings increased from $1,500,000 to $10,000,000. President Jan Ellis is considering either (1) a 10% stock dividend or (2) a 2-for-1 stock split. She asks you to show the before-and-after effects of each option on (a) retained earnings and (b) total stockholders' equity and the total shares outstanding.

ACTION PLAN

- Calculate the stock dividend's effect on retained earnings by multiplying the number of new shares times the market price of the stock (or par value for a large stock dividend).
- Recall that a stock dividend increases the number of shares without affecting total equity.
- Recall that a stock split only increases the number of shares outstanding and decreases the par value per share.

SOLUTION

(a) **(1)** The stock dividend amount is $2,250,000 [(500,000 × 10%) × $45]. The new balance in retained earnings is $7,750,000 ($10,000,000 − $2,250,000).

(2) The retained earnings balance after the stock split would be the same as it was before the split: $10,000,000.

(b) The effects on total stockholders' equity and total shares outstanding are:

	Original Balances	After Dividend	After Split
Paid-in capital	$ 2,000,000	$ 4,250,000	$ 2,000,000
Retained earnings	10,000,000	7,750,000	10,000,000
Total stockholders' equity	$12,000,000	$12,000,000	$12,000,000
Shares outstanding	500,000	550,000	1,000,000

Related exercise material: 13-8 and 13-9.

THE NAVIGATOR

RETAINED EARNINGS

STUDY OBJECTIVE 10

Identify the items that are reported in a retained earnings statement.

Retained earnings is net income that is retained in the business. The balance in retained earnings is part of the stockholders' claim on the total assets of the corporation. It does not, though, represent a claim on any specific asset. Nor can the amount of retained earnings be associated with the balance of any asset account. For example, a $100,000 balance in retained earnings does not mean that there should be $100,000 in cash. The reason is that the cash resulting from the excess of revenues over expenses may have been used to purchase buildings, equipment, and other assets. To illustrate that retained earnings and cash may be quite different, Illustration 13-25 shows recent amounts of retained earnings and cash in selected companies.

Illustration 13-25

Retained earnings and cash balances

	(in millions)	
Company	Retained Earnings	Cash
Walt Disney Co.	$12,281	$414
Sears, Roebuck and Co.	5,952	729
The Home Depot	7,941	168
Amazon.com	(882)	117

HELPFUL HINT
Remember that Retained Earnings is a stockholders' equity account, whose normal balance is a credit.

Remember that when a company has net profit, the net income that is retained in the business is recorded in retained earnings by means of a closing entry. This entry debits Income Summary and credits Retained Earnings.

However, when expenses exceed revenues, a **net loss** results. A net loss is debited to Retained Earnings in a closing entry. This is done even if it results in a debit balance in Retained Earnings. **Net losses are not debited to paid-in capital accounts.** To do so would destroy the distinction between paid-in and earned capital. A debit balance in Retained Earnings is identified as a **deficit**. It is reported as a deduction in the stockholders' equity section, as shown in Illustration 13-26.

Illustration 13-26

Stockholders' equity with deficit

Balance Sheet (partial)

Stockholders' equity	
Paid-in capital	
Common stock	$800,000
Retained earnings (deficit)	(50,000)
Total stockholders' equity	$750,000

RETAINED EARNINGS RESTRICTIONS

The balance in retained earnings is generally available for dividend declarations. Some companies state this fact.

In some cases, there may be **retained earnings restrictions**. These make a portion of the retained earnings balance currently unavailable for dividends. Restrictions result from one or more of the following causes: legal, contractual, or voluntary.

1. **Legal restrictions.** Many states require a corporation to restrict retained earnings for the cost of treasury stock purchased. The restriction keeps intact the corporation's legal capital that is being temporarily held as treasury stock. When the treasury stock is sold, the restriction is lifted.
2. **Contractual restrictions.** Long-term debt contracts may restrict retained earnings as a condition for the loan. The restriction limits the use of corporate assets for payment of dividends. Thus, it increases the likelihood that the corporation will be able to meet required loan payments.
3. **Voluntary restrictions.** The board of directors may voluntarily create retained earnings restrictions for specific purposes. For example, the board may authorize a restriction for future plant expansion. By reducing the amount of retained earnings available for dividends, more cash may be available for the planned expansion.

Retained earnings restrictions are generally disclosed in the notes to the financial statements.

PRIOR PERIOD ADJUSTMENTS

Suppose that a corporation's books have been closed and the financial statements have been issued. The corporation then discovers that a material error has been made in reporting net income of a prior year. How should this situation be recorded in the accounts and reported in the financial statements?

The correction of an error in previously issued financial statements is known as a **prior period adjustment**. The correction is made directly to Retained Earnings because the effect of the error is now in this account: The net income for the prior period has been recorded in retained earnings through the journalizing and posting of closing entries.

To illustrate, assume that General Microtels discovers in 2004 that it understated depreciation expense in 2001 by $300,000 due to computational errors. These errors overstated both net income for 2001 and the current balance in retained earnings. The entry for the prior period adjustment, assuming all tax effects are ignored, is as follows.

Retained Earnings	300,000	
Accumulated Depreciation		300,000
(To adjust for understatement of depreciation in a prior period)		

A	=	L	+	SE
−300,000				−300,000

A debit to an income statement account in 2004 would be incorrect because the error pertains to a prior year.

Prior period adjustments are reported in the retained earnings statement.[5] They are added (or deducted, as the case may be) from the beginning retained earnings balance. This results in an adjusted beginning balance. Assuming General Microtels has a beginning balance of $800,000 in retained earnings, the prior period adjustment is reported in Illustration 13-27.

Illustration 13-27

Statement presentation of prior period adjustments

GENERAL MICROTELS Retained Earnings Statement (partial)	
Balance, January 1, as reported	$800,000
Correction for overstatement of net income in prior period (depreciation error)	**(300,000)**
Balance, January 1, as adjusted	$500,000

Again, reporting the correction in the current year's income statement would be incorrect because it applies to a prior year's income statement.

RETAINED EARNINGS STATEMENT

The **retained earnings statement** shows the changes in retained earnings during the year. The statement is prepared from the Retained Earnings account. Transactions and events that affect retained earnings are tabulated in account form as shown in Illustration 13-28.

[5] A complete retained earnings statement is shown in Illustration 13-29.

Illustration 13-28

Debits and credits to retained earnings

Retained Earnings	
1. Net loss 2. Prior period adjustments for overstatement of net income 3. Cash dividends and stock dividends 4. Some disposals of treasury stock	1. Net income 2. Prior period adjustments for understatement of net income

As indicated, net income increases retained earnings, and a net loss decreases retained earnings. Prior period adjustments may either increase or decrease retained earnings. Both cash dividends and stock dividends decrease retained earnings. The circumstances under which treasury stock transactions decrease retained earnings were explained earlier, on pages 435–437.

Illustration 13-29 shows a complete retained earnings statement for Graber Hotels Inc., based on assumed data.

Illustration 13-29

Retained earnings statement

GRABER HOTELS INC.
Retained Earnings Statement
For the Year Ended December 31, 2004

Balance, January 1, as reported		$1,050,000
Correction for understatement of net income in prior period (inventory error)		50,000
Balance, January 1, as adjusted		1,100,000
Add: Net income		360,000
		1,460,000
Less: Cash dividends	$100,000	
Stock dividends	200,000	300,000
Balance, December 31		$1,160,000

BEFORE YOU GO ON...

REVIEW IT

1. How are retained earnings restrictions generally reported?
2. What is a prior period adjustment, and how is it reported?
3. What are the principal sources of debits and credits to Retained Earnings?

DO IT

Vega Casino Corporation has retained earnings of $5,130,000 on January 1, 2004. During the year, Vega earns $2,000,000 of net income. It declares and pays a $250,000 cash dividend. In 2004, Vega records an adjustment of $180,000 due to the understatement of 2003 depreciation expense from a mathematical error. Prepare a retained earnings statement for 2004.

ACTION PLAN

- Recall that a retained earnings statement begins with retained earnings, as reported at the end of the previous year.
- Add or subtract any prior period adjustments to arrive at the adjusted beginning figure.
- Add net income and subtract dividends declared to arrive at the ending balance in retained earnings.

SOLUTION

VEGA CASINO CORPORATION **Retained Earnings Statement** **For the Year Ended December 31, 2004**	
Balance, January 1, as reported	$5,130,000
Correction for overstatement of net income in prior period (depreciation error)	(180,000)
Balance, January 1, as adjusted	4,950,000
Add: Net income	2,000,000
	6,950,000
Less: Cash dividends	250,000
Balance, December 31	$6,700,000

Related exercise material: 13-9.

THE NAVIGATOR

DEMONSTRATION PROBLEM

The Rolman Hotel Corporation is authorized to issue 1,000,000 shares of $5 par value common stock. In its first year, 2004, the company has the following stock transactions.

Jan. 10 Issued 400,000 shares of stock at $8 per share.

July 1 Issued 100,000 shares of stock for land. The land had an asking price of $900,000. The stock is currently selling on a national exchange at $8.25 per share.

Sept. 1 Purchased 10,000 shares of common stock for the treasury at $9 per share.

Dec. 1 Sold 4,000 shares of the treasury stock at $10 per share.

Instructions

(a) Journalize the transactions.

(b) Prepare the stockholders' equity section assuming the company had retained earnings of $200,000 at December 31, 2004.

SOLUTION TO DEMONSTRATION PROBLEM

(a) Jan. 10	Cash	3,200,000	
	Common Stock		2,000,000
	Paid-in Capital in Excess of Par Value		1,200,000
	(To record issuance of 400,000 shares of $5 par value stock)		
July 1	Land	825,000	
	Common Stock		500,000
	Paid-in Capital in Excess of Par Value		325,000
	(To record issuance of 100,000 shares of $5 par value stock for land)		
Sept. 1	Treasury Stock	90,000	
	Cash		90,000
	(To record purchase of 10,000 shares of treasury stock at cost)		

ACTION PLAN

- When common stock has a par value, credit Common Stock for par value.
- Use fair market value in a noncash transaction.
- Debit and credit the Treasury Stock account at cost.
- Record differences between the cost and selling price of treasury stock in stockholders' equity accounts, not as gains or losses.

Dec. 1	Cash	40,000	
	Treasury Stock		36,000
	Paid-in Capital from Treasury Stock		4,000
	(To record sale of 4,000 shares of treasury stock above cost)		

(b)

ROLMAN HOTEL CORPORATION
Balance Sheet (partial)
December 31, 2004

Stockholders' equity		
Paid-in capital		
Capital stock		
Common stock, $5 par value, 1,000,000 shares authorized, 500,000 shares issued, 494,000 shares outstanding		$2,500,000
Additional paid-in capital		
In excess of par value	$1,525,000	
From treasury stock	4,000	
Total additional paid-in capital		1,529,000
Total paid-in capital		4,029,000
Retained earnings		200,000
Total paid-in capital and retained earnings		4,229,000
Less: Treasury stock (6,000 shares)		(54,000)
Total stockholders' equity		$4,175,000

THE NAVIGATOR

SUMMARY OF STUDY OBJECTIVES

1. ***Identify the major characteristics of a sole proprietorship.*** The major characteristics of a sole proprietorship are easy formation, no dilution of profits, limited life, and unlimited liability.

2. ***Identify the major characteristics of a partnership.*** The major characteristics of a partnership are association of individuals, mutual agency, limited life, unlimited liability, and co-ownership of property.

3. ***Explain the accounting entries for the formation of a partnership.*** Each partner's initial investment in a partnership should be recorded at the fair market value of the assets at the date of their transfer to the partnership. The values assigned must be agreed to by all of the partners. Cash, Equipment, or other asset accounts are debited. The same amount is credited under the partner's name in the capital account.

4. ***Identify the bases for dividing net income or net loss.*** Partnership net income or loss is shared equally unless the partnership contract specifically indicates the manner in which net income and net loss are to be divided. The same basis of division usually applies to both net income and net loss.

5. ***Identify the major characteristics of a corporation.*** The major characteristics of a corporation are separate legal existence, limited liability of stockholders, transferable ownership rights, ability to acquire capital, continuous life, corporation management, government regulations, and additional taxes.

6. ***Record the issuance of common stock.*** When the issuance of common stock for cash is recorded, the par value of the shares is credited to Common Stock; the portion of the proceeds that is above or below par value is recorded in a separate paid-in capital account. When no-par common stock has a stated value, the entries are similar to those for par value stock. When no-par does not have a stated value, the entire proceeds from the issue become legal capital and are credited to Common Stock.

7. ***Explain the accounting for treasury stock.*** The cost method is generally used in accounting for treasury stock. Under this approach, Treasury Stock is debited at the price paid to reacquire the shares. The same amount is credited to Treasury Stock when the shares are sold. The difference between the sales price and cost is recorded in stockholders' equity accounts, not in income statement accounts.

8. ***Differentiate preferred stock from common stock.*** Preferred stock has contractual provisions that give it priority over common stock in certain areas. Typically, preferred stockholders have a preference as to (1) dividends and (2) assets in the event of liquidation. They usually do not have voting rights.

9. ***Prepare the entries for cash dividends and stock dividends.*** Entries for both cash and stock dividends are required at the declaration date and at the payment date. At the declaration date the entries are: Cash dividend—debit Retained Earnings and credit Dividends Payable; small stock dividend—debit

Retained Earnings, credit Paid-in Capital in Excess of Par (or Stated) Value, and credit Common Stock Dividends Distributable. At the payment date, the entries for cash and stock dividends, respectively, are: debit Dividends Payable and credit Cash; and debit Common Stock Dividends Distributable and credit Common Stock.

10. ***Identify the items that are reported in a retained earnings statement.*** Each of the individual debits and credits to retained earnings should be reported in the retained earnings statement. Additions consist of net income and prior period adjustments to correct understatements of prior years' net income. Deductions consist of net loss, adjustments to correct overstatements of prior years' net income, cash and stock dividends, and some disposals of treasury stock.

THE NAVIGATOR

GLOSSARY

Articles of co-partnership A document detailing the organization of the partnership and include information such as name and principal location of the firm, the purpose of the business and the date of inception (p. 417).

Authorized stock The amount of stock that a corporation is authorized to sell as indicated in its charter (p. 428).

Bylaws The internal rules and procedures for conducting the affairs of a corporation (p. 426).

Cash dividend A pro rata distribution of cash to stockholders (p. 440).

Charter A document that creates a corporation (p. 426).

Corporation A business organized as a legal entity separate and distinct from its owners under state corporation law (p. 421).

Corporate capital The owners' equity in a corporation. Also called *stockholders' equity* or *shareholders' equity* (p. 426).

Cumulative dividend A feature of preferred stock entitling the stockholder to receive current and unpaid prior-year dividends before common stockholders receive any dividends (p. 439).

Declaration date The date the board of directors formally declares the dividend and announces it to stockholders (p. 441).

Deficit A debit balance in retained earnings (p. 448).

Dividend A distribution by a corporation to its stockholders on a pro rata (equal) basis (p. 440).

General partner This partner's liability is not limited to his or her capital equity in the business. There must always be at least one partner with unlimited liability in a partnership (p. 416).

Income ratio The basis for dividing both net income and net loss in a partnership (p. 418).

Legal capital The amount per share of stock that must be retained in the business for the protection of corporate creditors (p. 430).

Limited partnership This partner's liability is limited to his or her capital equity in the business (p. 416).

Liquidating dividend A dividend declared out of paid-in capital (p. 440).

No-par value stock Capital stock that has not been assigned a value in the corporate charter (p. 430).

Organization costs Costs incurred in the formation of a corporation (p. 426).

Outstanding stock Capital stock that has been issued and is being held by stockholders (p. 436).

Partnership An asssociation of two or more persons to carry on as co-owners of a business for profit (p. 415).

Partners' capital statement The owners' equity statement for a partnership (p. 423).

Par value stock Capital stock that has been assigned a value per share in the corporate charter (p. 430).

Payment date The date dividend checks are mailed to stockholders (p. 442).

Preferred stock Capital stock that has contractual preferences over common stock in certain areas (p. 438).

Prior period adjustment The correction of an error in previously issued financial statements (p. 449).

Privately held corporation A corporation that has only a few stockholders and whose stock is not available for sale to the general public (p. 421).

Publicly held corporation A corporation that may have thousands of stockholders and whose stock is regularly traded on a national securities market (p. 421).

Record date The date when ownership of outstanding shares is determined for dividend purposes (p. 441).

Retained earnings Net income that is retained in the business (p. 447).

Retained earnings restrictions Circumstances that make a portion of retained earnings currently unavailable for dividends (p. 448).

Retained earnings statement A financial statement that shows the changes in retained earnings during the year (p. 449).

Sole proprietorship A business owned by one individual (p. 414).

Stated value The amount per share assigned by the board of directors to no-par stock that becomes legal capital per share (p. 430).

Stock dividend A pro rata distribution of the corporation's own stock to stockholders (p. 443).

Stock split The issuance of additional shares of stock to stockholders accompanied by a reduction in the par or stated value per share (p. 445).

Stockholders' equity account A statement that shows the changes in each stockholders' equity account and in total stockholders' equity during the year (p. 444).

Treasury stock A corporation's own stock that has been issued, fully paid for, and reacquired by the corporation but not retired (p. 434).

EXERCISES

Prepare entries for the formation of a partnership. (SO 3)

13-1 Jane Moreno and Javier Sanchez combine their resources and open a Latin American tapas restaurant. Moreno puts in $15,000 cash and kitchen equipment with a book value of $6,000, accumulated depreciation of $3,000, and a market value of $4,500. Sanchez contributes his share all in cash form for a total of $25,000. Please provide the entries to record the investments.

13-2 Sarah and Allison have been partners for more than 10 years in their bakery. They invested equal amounts to open up the business. After all these years, they would like to close the books. If the total amount in the Income Summary is $50,000, prepare the entries needed for Sarah and Allison to close the Income Summary account and also their capital accounts.

Journalize the division of income of a partnership. (SO 4)

13-3 Todd and Carlo became partners on January 1, 2005, in their joint venture ToLo Sports Bar. Todd put in $50,000, while Carlo's share was $75,000. The net income for the year is $12,000. If the income is divided according to their capital, how should the income be divided?

13-4 Referring back to 13-3, prepare the partner's capital statement for the year ended December 2005 for ToLo Sports Bar if both Todd and Carlo withdraw $1,000 from their partnership.

Journalize issuance of common stock. (SO 6)

13-5 During its first year of operations, Evanston Motel Corporation had the following transactions pertaining to its common stock.

Jan. 10	Issued 80,000 shares for cash at $5 per share.
July 1	Issued 30,000 shares for cash at $7 per share.

Instructions

(a) Journalize the transactions, assuming that the common stock has a par value of $5 per share.

(b) Journalize the transactions, assuming that the common stock is no-par with a stated value of $1 per share.

Prepare entries for issuance of common and preferred stock and purchase of treasury stock. (SO 6,7,8)

13-6 Phoenix Hotels and Clubs had the following transactions during the current period.

Mar. 2	Issued 5,000 shares of $1 par value common stock to attorneys in payment of a bill for $27,000 for services rendered in helping the company to incorporate.
June 12	Issued 60,000 shares of $1 par value common stock for cash of $375,000.
July 11	Issued 1,000 shares of $100 par value preferred stock for cash at $105 per share.
Nov. 28	Purchased 2,000 shares of treasury stock for $80,000.

Journalize treasury stock transactions. (SO 7)

13-7 On January 1, 2004, the stockholders' equity section of Parge Hotels Corporation shows: common stock ($5 par value) $1,500,000; paid-in capital in excess of par value $1,000,000; and retained earnings $1,200,000. During the year, the following treasury stock transactions occurred.

Mar. 1	Purchased 50,000 shares for cash at $14 per share.
July 1	Sold 10,000 treasury shares for cash at $16 per share.
Sept. 1	Sold 8,000 treasury shares for cash at $13 per share.

Instructions

(a) Journalize the treasury stock transactions.

(b) Restate the entry for September 1, assuming the treasury shares were sold at $11 per share.

Journalize cash dividends; indicate statement presentation. (SO 9)

13-8 On January 1, Moyer Hotel Corporation had 75,000 shares of no-par common stock issued and outstanding. The stock has a stated value of $5 per share. During the year, the following occurred.

Apr. 1	Issued 5,000 additional shares of common stock.
June 15	Declared a cash dividend of $1 per share to stockholders of record on June 30.
July 10	Paid the $1 cash dividend.
Dec. 1	Issued 2,000 additional shares of common stock.
15	Declared a cash dividend on outstanding shares of $1.20 per share to stockholders of record on December 31.

Instructions

(a) Prepare the entries, if any, on each of the three dividend dates.

(b) How are dividends and dividends payable reported in the financial statements prepared at December 31?

13-9 On January 1, 2004, Yorkville Hotels Corporation had Retained Earnings of $580,000. During the year, Yorkville had the following selected transactions.

Prepare a retained earnings statement.
(SO 10)

1. Declared cash dividends $120,000.
2. Corrected overstatement of 2003 net income because of depreciation error $20,000.
3. Earned net income $310,000.
4. Declared stock dividends $60,000.

Instructions
Prepare a retained earnings statement for the year.

13-10 A June 1999 issue of *Money* magazine includes an article by David Futrelle entitled "Stock Splits: How the Dumb Get Rich."

Instructions
Read the article and answer the following questions.

(a) What is a stock split?
(b) How do anxious traders and investors obtain timely information about stock splits?
(c) What are the statistics relative to market price reactions for stocks of companies that have split their stocks?
(d) Is there a downside to buying the stock of companies that announce stock splits?

EXPLORING THE WEB

13-11 SEC filings of publicly traded companies are available to view online.

Address: **http//biz.yahoo.com/i**

Steps
1. Pick a company and type in the company's name.
2. Choose **Quote**.

Instructions
Answer the following questions.

(a) What company did you select?
(b) What is its stock symbol?
(c) What was the stock's trading range today?
(d) What was the stock's trading range for the year?

Remember to go back to the Navigator box on the chapter-opening page and check off your completed work.

APPENDIX

SPECIMEN FINANCIAL STATEMENTS: Hilton Hotels Corporation

Consolidated Statements of Income

(in millions, except per share amounts)	Year ended December 31, 1999	2000	2001
Revenue			
Owned hotels	$1,813	2,429	2,122
Leased hotels	26	398	168
Management and franchise fees	120	350	342
Other fees and income	191	274	418
	2,150	3,451	3,050
Expenses			
Owned hotels	1,196	1,571	1,468
Leased hotels	26	365	152
Depreciation and amortization	187	382	391
Other operating expenses	173	241	336
Corporate expense, net	73	62	71
	1,655	2,621	2,418
Operating Income	495	830	632
Interest and dividend income	57	86	64
Interest expense	(237)	(453)	(385)
Interest expense, net, from unconsolidated affiliates	(2)	(16)	(17)
Net gain (loss) on asset dispositions	-	32	(44)
Income Before Income Taxes and Minority Interest	313	479	250
Provision for income taxes	(130)	(200)	(77)
Minority interest, net	(7)	(7)	(7)
Income Before Cumulative Effect of Accounting Change	176	272	166
Cumulative effect of accounting change, net of tax benefit of $1 in 1999	(2)	-	-
Net Income	**$ 174**	**272**	**166**
Basic Earnings Per Share			
Income before cumulative effect of accounting change	$ .66	.74	.45
Cumulative effect of accounting change	(.01)	-	-
Net Income Per Share	**$ .65**	**.74**	**.45**
Diluted Earnings Per Share			
Income before cumulative effect of accounting change	$ .66	.73	.45
Cumulative effect of accounting change	(.01)	-	-
Net Income Per Share	**$ .65**	**.73**	**.45**

See notes to consolidated financial statements

Consolidated Balance Sheets

(in millions)	December 31, 2000	December 31, 2001
Assets		
Current Assets		
Cash and equivalents	$ 47	35
Accounts receivable, net	403	291
Inventories	137	148
Deferred income taxes	44	61
Current portion of notes receivable, net	32	40
Current portion of long-term receivable	-	300
Assets held for sale	73	-
Other current assets	104	121
Total current assets	840	996
Investments, Property and Other Assets		
Investments and notes receivable, net	570	580
Long-term receivable	625	325
Property and equipment, net	3,986	3,911
Management and franchise contracts, net	528	487
Leases, net	147	122
Brands, net	1,022	971
Goodwill, net	1,307	1,273
Other assets	115	120
Total investments, property and other assets	8,300	7,789
Total Assets	**$9,140**	**8,785**
Liabilities and Stockholders' Equity		
Current Liabilities		
Accounts payable and accrued expenses	$ 618	533
Current maturities of long-term debt	23	365
Income taxes payable	5	4
Total current liabilities	646	902
Long-term debt	5,693	4,950
Deferred income taxes	902	871
Insurance reserves and other	257	279
Total liabilities	7,498	7,002
Commitments and Contingencies		
Stockholders' Equity		
Common Stock, 369 million shares outstanding at the end of each year	947	948
Additional paid-in capital	861	873
Retained earnings	35	168
Accumulated other comprehensive income (loss)	6	(5)
	1,849	1,984
Less treasury stock, at cost	(207)	(201)
Total stockholders' equity	1,642	1,783
Total Liabilities and Stockholders' Equity	**$9,140**	**8,785**

See notes to consolidated financial statements

Consolidated Statements of Cash Flow

(in millions)	Year ended December 31, 1999	2000	2001
Operating Activities			
Net income	$ 174	272	166
Adjustments to reconcile net income to net cash provided by operating activities:			
Cumulative effect of accounting change	2	-	-
Depreciation and amortization	187	382	391
Amortization of loan costs	3	8	10
Net (gain) loss on asset dispositions	-	(32)	44
Change in working capital components:			
Inventories	(30)	(26)	(19)
Accounts receivable	(58)	(6)	111
Other current assets	15	(18)	(32)
Accounts payable and accrued expenses	16	(48)	(48)
Income taxes payable	(29)	-	(1)
Change in deferred income taxes	(5)	13	(41)
Change in other liabilities	4	30	-
Unconsolidated affiliates' distributions (less than) in excess of earnings	(7)	40	19
Other	7	(26)	(15)
Net cash provided by operating activities	279	589	585
Investing Activities			
Capital expenditures	(254)	(458)	(370)
Additional investments	(102)	(140)	(139)
Proceeds from asset dispositions	-	165	230
Payments on notes and other	78	190	125
Acquisitions, net of cash acquired	(2,036)	-	-
Net cash used in investing activities	(2,314)	(243)	(154)
Financing Activities			
Change in commercial paper borrowings and revolving loans	2,264	(918)	(1,387)
Long-term borrowings	-	655	992
Reduction of long-term debt	(64)	(115)	(24)
Issuance of common stock	5	4	6
Purchase of common stock	(90)	-	-
Cash dividends	(23)	(29)	(30)
Net cash provided by (used in) financing activities	2,092	(403)	(443)
Increase (Decrease) in Cash and Equivalents	57	(57)	(12)
Cash and Equivalents at Beginning of Year	47	104	47
Cash and Equivalents at End of Year	**$ 104**	**47**	**35**

See notes to consolidated financial statements

Consolidated Statements of Stockholders' Equity

(in millions, except per share amounts)	Common Stock	Additional Paid-In Capital	Retained Earnings (Deficit)	Accumulated Comprehensive Income (Loss)	Treasury Stock	Total
Balance at December 31, 1998	$663	-	(347)	-	(129)	187
Net Income	-	-	174	-	-	174
Other comprehensive income:						
Cumulative translation adjustment, net of deferred tax	-	-	-	(1)	-	(1)
Change in unrealized gain/loss on marketable securities, net of deferred tax	-	-	-	25	-	25
Comprehensive income for 1999	-	-	174	24	-	198
Issuance of common stock	283	843	-	-	-	1,126
Exercise of stock options	-	-	(5)	-	8	3
Treasury stock acquired	-	-	-	-	(90)	(90)
Deferred compensation	-	10	-	-	-	10
Common dividends ($.08 per share)	-	-	(23)	-	-	(23)
Adjustment to spin-off of Park Place Entertainment Corporation	-	-	4	-	-	4
Balance at December 31, 1999	946	853	(197)	24	(211)	1,415
Net Income	-	-	272	-	-	272
Other comprehensive income:						
Cumulative translation adjustment, net of deferred tax	-	-	-	(1)	-	(1)
Change in unrealized gain/loss on marketable securities, net of deferred tax	-	-	-	(17)	-	(17)
Comprehensive income (loss) for 2000	-	-	272	(18)	-	254
Issuance of common stock	1	2	-	-	-	3
Exercise of stock options	-	-	(3)	-	4	1
Deferred compensation	-	6	-	-	-	6
Common dividends ($.08 per share)	-	-	(29)	-	-	(29)
Adjustment to spin-off of Park Place Entertainment Corporation	-	-	(8)	-	-	(8)
Balance at December 31, 2000	947	861	35	6	(207)	1,642
Net Income	-	-	166	-	-	166
Other comprehensive income:						
Cash flow hedge adjustment, net of deferred tax	-	-	-	(2)	-	(2)
Change in unrealized gain/loss on marketable securities, net of deferred tax	-	-	-	(9)	-	(9)
Comprehensive income (loss) for 2001	-	-	166	(11)	-	155
Issuance of common stock	1	2	-	-	-	3
Exercise of stock options	-	-	(3)	-	6	3
Deferred compensation	-	10	-	-	-	10
Common dividends ($.08 per share)	-	-	(30)	-	-	(30)
Balance at December 31, 2001	**$948**	**873**	**168**	**(5)**	**(201)**	**1,783**

See notes to consolidated financial statements

Notes to Consolidated Financial Statements
December 31, 2001

BASIS OF PRESENTATION AND ORGANIZATION

Hilton Hotels Corporation is primarily engaged in the ownership, management and development of hotels, resorts and timeshare properties and the franchising of lodging properties. We operate in select markets throughout the world, predominately in the United States. Revenue and income are derived from three reportable segments: Hotel Ownership, Managing and Franchising, and Timeshare.

On November 30, 1999, we acquired Promus Hotel Corporation in a business combination accounted for as a purchase. Accordingly, our consolidated financial results include the results of Promus and its subsidiaries from the date of acquisition.

EFFECTS OF THE SEPTEMBER 11, 2001 TERRORIST ATTACKS

Our operating results for the year ended December 31, 2001 have been negatively affected by the September 11th terrorist attacks, which resulted in severe declines in occupancy and room rates at most of our owned hotels in urban markets in the weeks following the attacks. Our 2001 results include a $7 million fourth quarter charge related to certain notes receivable that, as a result of the economic impact of the events of September 11th, are unlikely to be collected.

SUMMARY OF SIGNIFICANT ACCOUNTING POLICIES

Principles of Consolidation

The consolidated financial statements include the accounts of Hilton Hotels Corporation and its majority owned and controlled subsidiaries. All material intercompany transactions are eliminated and net earnings are reduced by the portion of the earnings of affiliates applicable to other ownership interests.

Cash and Equivalents

Cash and equivalents include investments with initial maturities of three months or less. Cash and equivalents includes cash related to certain consolidated hotels, the use of which is restricted for hotel purposes under the terms of collateralized borrowings, totaling approximately $17 million and $19 million at December 31, 2000 and 2001, respectively.

Accounts Receivable

Accounts receivable are reflected net of allowance for uncollectable accounts of $15 million and $16 million as of December 31, 2000 and 2001, respectively.

Investments

We maintain investments in unconsolidated affiliates, including hotel joint ventures as well as other entities that support the operations of our hotel properties. Investments are accounted for using the equity method when we exercise significant influence, which is generally when we have a 20% to 50% ownership interest. When we control the investment, which is generally when our ownership interest exceeds 50%, the balance sheet and results of operations are consolidated. All other investments are generally accounted for under the cost method.

Currency Translation

Assets and liabilities denominated in most foreign currencies are translated into U.S. dollars at year-end exchange rates and related gains and losses, net of applicable deferred income taxes, are reflected in stockholders' equity. Gains and losses from foreign currency transactions are included in earnings.

Valuation of Long-Lived Assets

The carrying value of our long-lived assets are reviewed when events or changes in circumstances indicate that the carrying amount of an asset may not be recoverable. If it is determined that an impairment loss has occurred based on the lowest level of identifiable expected future cash flow, then a loss is recognized in the income statement using a fair value based model.

Property and Equipment

Property and equipment are stated at cost less accumulated depreciation. Interest incurred during construction of facilities is capitalized and amortized over the life of the asset. Costs of improvements are capitalized. These capitalized costs may include structural costs, equipment, fixtures and floor and wall coverings. Costs of normal repairs and maintenance are charged to expense as incurred. Upon the sale or retirement of property and equipment, the cost and related accumulated depreciation are removed from the respective accounts, and the resulting gain or loss, if any, is included in income.

Depreciation is provided on a straight-line basis over the estimated useful life of the assets. Leasehold improvements are amortized over the shorter of the asset life or lease term. The service lives of assets are generally 40 years for buildings and three to eight years for building improvements and furniture and equipment.

Pre-Opening Costs

In April 1998, the American Institute of Certified Public Accountants issued Statement of Position (SOP) 98-5, "Reporting on the Costs of Start-Up Activities." This SOP requires that all nongovernmental entities expense the costs of start-up activities (pre-opening, pre-operating and organizational costs) as those costs are incurred and required the write-off of any unamortized balances upon implementation. Our adoption of SOP 98-5 resulted in a cumulative effect of accounting change of $2 million, net of a tax benefit of $1 million, in the first quarter of 1999.

Management and Franchise Contracts

Management and franchise contracts acquired in acquisitions that were accounted for as purchases are recorded at the estimated present value of net cash flow expected to be received over the lives of the contracts. This value is amortized using the straight-line method over the remaining contract lives. Costs incurred to acquire individual management and franchise contracts are amortized using the straight-line method over the life of the respective contract. Accumulated amortization of management and franchise contracts totaled $52 million and $105 million at December 31, 2000 and 2001, respectively.

Leases

Leases acquired in acquisitions that were accounted for as purchases are recorded at the estimated present value of net cash flow expected to be received over the lives of the lease agreements. This value is amortized using the straight-line method over the remaining lease terms. Accumulated amortization of leases totaled $5 million and $7 million at December 31, 2000 and 2001, respectively.

Goodwill and Brands

Goodwill arising in connection with purchase acquisitions is amortized using the straight-line method over 40 years. Accumulated amortization of goodwill totaled $39 million and $72 million at December 31, 2000 and 2001, respectively. The brand names of hotels acquired in acquisitions are assigned a fair market value. To arrive at a value for each brand name, an estimation is made of the amount of royalty income that could be generated from the brand name if it was licensed to an independent third-party owner. The resulting cash flow is discounted back using the estimated weighted average cost of capital for each respective brand name. Brand values are amortized on a straight-line basis over 40 years. Accumulated amortization of brands totaled $28 million and $53 million at December 31, 2000 and 2001, respectively. Effective January 1, 2002, we will account for goodwill and brands in accordance with Statement of Financial Accounting Standard (FAS) 142. The new rules require that intangible assets with indefinite lives are not amortized, but are reviewed annually for impairment. We expect to receive future benefits from previously acquired goodwill and brands over an indefinite period of time, and accordingly we will not amortize them.

Derivative Instruments

We have an outstanding swap agreement which qualifies for hedge accounting as a cash flow hedge of a foreign currency denominated liability. The gain or loss on the change in fair value of the derivative is included in earnings to the extent it offsets the earnings impact of changes in fair value of the hedged obligation. Any difference is deferred in accumulated comprehensive income, a component of stockholders' equity.

We also have two interest rate swaps on floating rate mortgages of two majority owned hotels which qualify as cash flow hedges. These derivatives impact earnings to the extent of increasing or decreasing actual interest expense on the hedged mortgages to simulate a fixed interest rate, with any incremental fair value changes deferred in accumulated comprehensive income.

There were no amounts recognized or reclassified into earnings for the years ended December 31, 1999, 2000 or 2001 due to hedge ineffectiveness or due to excluding from the assessment of effectiveness any component of the derivatives. We assess on a quarterly basis the effectiveness of our hedges in offsetting the variability in the cash flow of hedged obligations.

Unamortized Loan Costs

Debt discount and issuance costs incurred in connection with the placement of long-term debt are capitalized and amortized to interest expense over the lives of the related debt.

Self-Insurance

We are self-insured for various levels of general liability, workers' compensation and employee medical and dental insurance coverage. Insurance reserves include the present values of projected settlements for claims.

Revenue Recognition

Revenue is generally recognized as services are performed. Owned and leased hotel revenue represents primarily room rentals and food and beverage sales from owned, majority owned and leased hotels.

Management fees represent fees earned on hotels managed by us, usually under long-term contracts with the hotel owner. Management fees include a base fee, which is generally a percentage of hotel revenue, and an incentive fee, which is generally based on the hotel's profitability. We recognize base fees as revenue when earned in accordance with the terms of the contract. In interim periods we recognize incentive fees that would be due if the contract were terminated at the end of the interim period.

Franchise fees represent fees received in connection with the franchise of our brand names, usually under long-term contracts with the hotel owner. Depending on the brand, we charge franchise royalty fees of up to five percent of rooms revenue. We recognize fee revenue as earned, in accordance with FAS 45, "Accounting for Franchise Fee Revenue."

Other fees and income primarily consist of earnings from timeshare operations and equity income from unconsolidated affiliates. Timeshare revenue is generated primarily from the sale of timeshare intervals, financing consumer purchases of timeshare intervals and operating timeshare resorts. We recognize revenue from timeshare sales in accordance with FAS 66, "Accounting for Real Estate Sales." Sales are included in revenue when a minimum of a 10 percent down payment has been received and certain minimum sales thresholds have been attained.

Earnings Per Share (EPS)

Basic EPS is computed by dividing net income available to common stockholders by the weighted average number of common shares outstanding for the period. The weighted average number of common shares outstanding for 1999, 2000 and 2001 were 266 million, 368 million and 369 million, respectively. Diluted EPS reflects the potential dilution that could occur if securities or other contracts to issue common stock were exercised or converted. The dilutive effect of the assumed exercise of stock options and convertible securities increased the weighted average number of common shares by 24 million in 1999 and 2000, and 25 million in 2001. In addition, the increase to net income resulting from interest on convertible securities assumed to have not been paid was approximately $15 million per year for 1999, 2000 and 2001.

Use of Estimates

The preparation of financial statements in conformity with accounting principles generally accepted in the United States requires us to make estimates and assumptions that affect the reported amounts of assets and liabilities and disclosure of contingent assets and liabilities at the date of the financial statements and the reported amounts of revenue and expenses during the reporting period. Actual results could differ from our estimates and assumptions.

New Accounting Standards

In January 2001, we adopted FAS 133, "Accounting for Derivative Instruments and Hedging Activities," as amended. This statement requires that all derivative instruments be recorded on the balance sheet at fair value. Adoption of the statement did not have a material impact on our consolidated financial statements.

In June 2001, the Financial Accounting Standards Board (FASB) issued FAS 142, "Goodwill and Other Intangible Assets." The effective date for implementation of this new standard is January 1, 2002. The new rules require that goodwill and other intangible assets with indefinite lives are not amortized, but are reviewed annually for impairment. We expect to receive future benefits from previously acquired goodwill and brands over an indefinite period of time, and accordingly we will not amortize them. We estimate that the adoption of FAS 142 will result in an annual increase to net income of approximately $50 million.

In response to a recent FASB staff announcement, we are in the process of reviewing the reporting of reimbursable costs incurred on behalf of managed hotel properties and franchisees. We plan to record the reimbursements received as revenue and the costs incurred on behalf of managed properties and franchisees as expenses, commencing in the first quarter of 2002. These costs relate primarily to payroll costs at managed properties where we are the employer. Although we are in the process of summarizing such amounts, we estimate that reporting in accordance with this staff announcement would have increased revenues and expenses between $.9 billion and $1.1 billion in 2001, between $.8 billion and $1.0 billion in 2000 and between $.1 billion and $.3 billion in 1999. Upon application of this staff announcement, comparative financial statements for prior periods will be reclassified to conform with the presentation in the 2002 financial statements. Since the reimbursements are made based upon the costs incurred with no added margin, the adoption of this guidance will have no effect on our operating income, total or per share net income, cash flow or financial position.

ACQUISITIONS AND DISPOSITIONS

Acquisition of Promus Hotel Corporation

On November 30, 1999, we completed the acquisition of Promus pursuant to an agreement dated September 3, 1999. Aggregate consideration consisted of approximately $1.7 billion in cash in exchange for 55 percent of the outstanding shares of Promus common stock and approximately 113 million shares of our common stock in exchange for the remaining 45 percent of Promus stock for a combined equity value of approximately $2.8 billion, transaction costs of $175 million, and the assumption of Promus and Promus subsidiary debt totaling $750 million.

The acquisition was accounted for using the purchase method of accounting, and accordingly, the acquisition cost was allocated to the assets acquired and liabilities assumed based on estimates of their fair value. A total of $1.27 billion, representing the excess of acquisition cost over the final determination of the fair value of Promus' tangible and identifiable intangible net assets, was allocated to goodwill.

Our consolidated results of operations incorporate Promus' activity from the date of the acquisition. The following unaudited pro forma information has been prepared assuming that this acquisition had taken place at the beginning of the year. This pro forma information does not purport to be indicative of what would have occurred had the acquisition been made as of that date.

(in millions, except per share amounts) (unaudited)	1999
Revenue	$3,161
Operating income	703
Income before cumulative effect of accounting change	216
Net income	214
Basic earnings per share	.58
Diluted earnings per share	.58

Asset Dispositions

In January 2000, we entered into an agreement with RFS Hotel Investors, Inc., which gave RFS the option to terminate 52 operating leases and four management contracts on hotels owned by RFS. In November 2000, RFS notified us of its intention to exercise the option to terminate these agreements. In January 2001, RFS paid us approximately $60 million in cash as consideration for terminating the leases and management contracts. We also sold 973,684 shares of RFS preferred stock to RFS for $13 million in cash. The values of these leases, management contracts and shares of preferred stock are reflected as assets held for sale in our December 31, 2000 consolidated balance sheet.

In January 2001, we sold the Red Lion Houston for approximately $20 million. In April 2001, we completed the sale of the Homewood Suites by Hilton in Washington D.C. for approximately $23 million under the terms of an agreement announced in December 2000. In June 2001, we completed the sale of two Homewood Suites by Hilton properties in Chesterfield, Missouri and Portland, Oregon for approximately $22 million. We have retained franchise agreements and will manage the three Homewood Suites by Hilton properties.

In September 2001, we entered into a partnership agreement with CNL Hospitality Corp. The partnership owns four hotel properties: the 500-room Hilton Miami Airport in Florida; the 276-room Embassy Suites Portland in Oregon; the 484-room Hilton Costa Mesa in California, and the 224-room Hilton Suites Auburn Hills in Michigan. We contributed the Embassy Suites Portland and the Hilton Suites Auburn Hills while CNL contributed the Hilton Miami Airport and the Hilton Costa Mesa to the partnership. CNL purchased the Hilton Costa Mesa from us in September 2001 for approximately $58 million, prior to the formation of the partnership. The gain resulting from the sale and contribution of these hotels has been deferred and will be recognized over the life of the long-term management contracts we retained on each of the properties. In October 2001, the partnership mortgaged these four hotels, and used a portion of the loan proceeds to distribute $43 million to Hilton. Following this distribution, we have a 30 percent ownership interest in the partnership.

On December 31, 2001, we sold the Red Lion hotel chain to WestCoast Hospitality Corporation through a sale of the capital stock of Red Lion Hotels, Inc. The Red Lion portfolio consisted of 41 Red Lion hotels (8 owned, 11 leased and 22 franchised) and two Doubletree hotels (one owned and one leased) with a total of approximately 6,500 rooms. Total consideration of approximately $51 million included approximately $21 million of cash and approximately $30 million in redeemable preferred stock of WestCoast. The preferred stock is in two $15 million series, which pay preferred dividends of 7% and 10% annually. The preferred stock is accounted for as a cost basis investment in our consolidated financial statements.

Our total pre-tax loss on asset dispositions was $44 million in 2001, $42 million of which was attributable to the Red Lion sale. As the Red Lion sale also resulted in a large capital loss for tax purposes, we were able to carryback a portion of this loss to offset capital gains recorded in prior years. The transaction, including the impact of the tax loss carrybacks, resulted in a $47 million book tax benefit. Thus, on an after-tax basis, the sale of the Red Lion Hotels, Inc. capital stock resulted in a gain of approximately $5 million.

We realized a pre-tax gain on asset dispositions of $32 million in 2000 from the sale of marketable securities.

INVENTORIES

Included in inventories at December 31, 2000 and 2001 are unsold intervals at our timeshare properties of $111 million and $132 million, respectively. Inventories are valued at the lower of cost or estimated net realizable value.

INVESTMENTS AND NOTES RECEIVABLE

Investments and notes receivable at December 31, 2000 and 2001 are as follows:

(in millions)	2000	2001
Equity investments		
Hotels	$236	259
Other	34	32
Timeshare notes receivable, with an average rate of 14.9%, due 2002 to 2011	147	177
Other notes receivable, with an average rate of 8.8%, due 2002 to 2015	141	88
Marketable securities	44	29
Other investments	-	35
	602	620
Less current portion of notes receivable	(32)	(40)
Total	$570	580

Notes receivable are reflected net of allowances for uncollectable amounts of $11 million and $17 million as of December 31, 2000 and 2001, respectively.

Our investment in unconsolidated affiliates accounted for under the equity method totaled $270 million and $291 million at December 31, 2000 and 2001, respectively, representing three percent of total assets at the end of each period. At December 31, 2001, our unconsolidated affiliates accounted for under the equity method had total assets of approximately $1.9 billion and total debt of approximately $945 million. Of the $945 million of total debt, $913 million is secured solely by the affiliate's assets or is guaranteed by other partners without recourse to us.

PROPERTY AND EQUIPMENT

Property and equipment at December 31, 2000 and 2001 are as follows:

(in millions)	2000	2001
Land	$ 569	568
Buildings and leasehold improvements	3,258	3,474
Furniture and equipment	912	876
Property held for sale or development	45	43
Construction in progress	200	104
	4,984	5,065
Less accumulated depreciation	(998)	(1,154)
Total	$3,986	3,911

ACCOUNTS PAYABLE AND ACCRUED EXPENSES

Accounts payable and accrued expenses at December 31, 2000 and 2001 are as follows:

(in millions)	2000	2001
Accounts and notes payable	$146	129
Accrued compensation and benefits	149	125
Deposits	38	19
Deferred timeshare sales	34	-
Accrued property tax	32	33
Accrued interest	29	49
Other accrued expenses	190	178
Total	$618	533

LONG-TERM DEBT

Long-term debt at December 31, 2000 and 2001 is as follows:

(in millions)	2000	2001
Industrial development revenue bonds at adjustable rates, due 2015	$ 82	82
Senior notes, with an average rate of 7.8%, due 2002 to 2031	1,052	1,935
Senior notes, with an average rate of 7.2%, due 2002 to 2004[(1)]	625	625
Mortgage notes, 6.0% to 8.6%, due 2002 to 2022	353	357
7.95% Collateralized borrowings, due 2010	499	493
7.43% Chilean inflation-indexed notes, due 2009	-	105
5% Convertible subordinated notes due 2006	495	496
Commercial paper	235	-
Revolving loans	2,372	1,220
Other	3	2
	5,716	5,315
Less current maturities	(23)	(365)
Net long-term debt	$5,693	4,950

[(1)] *Represents balances assumed by Park Place in connection with the December 31, 1998 spin-off of our gaming business.*

Interest paid, net of amounts capitalized, was $187 million, $402 million and $324 million in 1999, 2000 and 2001, respectively. Capitalized interest totaled $7 million, $9 million and $10 million in 1999, 2000 and 2001, respectively.

Debt maturities are as follows:

(in millions)	
2002	$ 365
2003	400
2004	1,433
2005	12
2006	514
Thereafter	2,591
Total	$5,315

In October 1996, we entered into a $1.75 billion five-year revolving credit facility. In August 2001, this facility was repaid and the commitment was extinguished. We currently have two revolving credit facilities. In June 1998, we entered into a five-year $500 million revolving credit facility to acquire the remaining 50% interest in the Hilton Hawaiian Village Beach Resort & Spa. In August 2001, we reduced the commitment under the $500 million revolver to $425 million. As of December 31, 2001, approximately $390 million of borrowings were outstanding under the $425 million revolver, which bears interest at the London Interbank Offered Rate (LIBOR) plus a spread based on our public debt rating or leverage ratio. The all-in borrowing cost under this facility was approximately LIBOR plus 87.5 basis points as of December 31, 2001. In November 1999, we entered into a $1.8 billion revolving credit facility consisting of a $1.4 billion revolver which expires in 2004 and a $400 million 364-day revolver. In November 2001, we extended the 364-day revolver through November 2002 and reduced the commitment to $150 million. As of December 31, 2001, $830 million of borrowings were outstanding under the $1.4 billion revolver. The 364-day revolver was undrawn at December 31, 2001. Borrowings under this facility bear interest at LIBOR plus a spread based on our public debt rating or leverage ratio. The all-in borrowing cost under this facility was approximately LIBOR plus 125 basis points at December 31, 2001. Total revolving debt capacity of approximately $730 million was available to us at December 31, 2001.

In October 1997, we filed a shelf registration statement with the Securities and Exchange Commission registering up to $2.5 billion in debt or equity securities. In February 2001, we issued $300 million of 8.25% Senior Notes due 2011. In May 2001, we issued $400 million of 7.625% Senior Notes due 2008. In August 2001, we issued $200 million of 8% Quarterly Interest Bonds due 2031. The net proceeds from these issuances were used to pay down outstanding amounts and to reduce the commitment under the 1996 revolving credit facility. At December 31, 2001, available financing under the shelf totaled $1.2 billion. The terms of any additional securities offered under the shelf will be determined by market conditions at the time of issuance.

In August 2001, we issued $100 million of 7.43% bonds due 2009 denominated in Chilean Pesos. Payments of principal and interest on the bonds are to be adjusted for movements of the Unidad de Fomento (the Chilean inflation index) published monthly by the Central Bank of Chile. We have swapped out the Chilean currency exchange rate and inflation risk of these bonds by entering into a derivative contract which swaps the principal payment to a fixed U.S. dollar amount of $100 million and fixed interest payments at 7.65% of that amount. The net proceeds from this issuance were used to extinguish the 1996 revolving credit facility and to pay down outstanding amounts under the 1999 revolving credit facility.

On December 31, 1998, we completed a spin-off that split our operations into two independent public corporations, one for conducting our hotel business and one for conducting our gaming business. We retained ownership of the hotel business and transferred the gaming business to a new corporation named Park Place Entertainment Corporation. Pursuant to a debt assumption agreement entered into at the time of the spin-off, Park Place assumed and agreed to pay 100% of the amount of each payment required to be made by us under the terms of the indentures governing our $300 million 7.375% Senior Notes due 2002 and our $325 million 7% Senior Notes due 2004. These notes remain in our debt balance and a receivable from Park Place in an equal amount is included in our 2000 and 2001 consolidated balance sheets. As of December 31, 2001, the $300 million 7.375% Senior Notes due June 2002 are classified in the accompanying balance sheet as current maturities of long-term debt with the offsetting receivable classified in current assets. In the event of an increase in the interest rate on these notes as a result of certain actions taken by us or in certain other limited circumstances, we will be required to reimburse Park Place for such increase. We are obligated to make any payment Park Place fails to make. In this event, Park Place would be obligated to pay to us the amount of this payment together with interest, at the rate per annum borne by the applicable notes plus two percent, to the date of reimbursement.

The 5% convertible subordinated notes due 2006 are convertible at any time into our common stock at a conversion price of $22.17 per share. However, the market price of our common stock was substantially below the conversion price as of December 31, 2001.

As of December 31, 2001, approximately 28% of our long-term debt (excluding the Park Place allocated debt) was floating rate debt.

Provisions under various loan agreements require us to comply with certain covenants which include limiting the amount of outstanding indebtedness. Our revolving credit facilities contain two significant financial covenants: a leverage ratio and a debt service coverage ratio. In November 2001, we amended these two covenants to provide greater flexibility. We are in compliance with our loan covenants as of December 31, 2001.

FINANCIAL INSTRUMENTS

The estimated fair values of our financial instruments at December 31, 2000 and 2001 are as follows:

	2000		2001	
(in millions)	Carrying Amount	Fair Value	Carrying Amount	Fair Value
Cash and equivalents and long-term marketable securities	$ 91	91	64	64
Long-term debt (including current maturities)	5,716	5,481	5,315	5,196
Derivative instruments	-	-	2	2

Cash Equivalents and Long-Term Marketable Securities

The fair value of cash equivalents and long-term marketable securities is estimated based on the quoted market price of the investments.

Long-Term Debt

The estimated fair value of long-term debt is based on the quoted market prices for the same or similar issues or on the current rates offered to us for debt of the same remaining maturities.

Derivative Instruments

In August 2001, we issued $100 million of 7.43% bonds due 2009 denominated in Chilean Pesos. We have swapped out the Chilean currency exchange rate and inflation risk of these bonds by entering into a derivative contract. The estimated fair value of this derivative instrument is based on the present value of future estimated cash flow using foreign currency forward exchange rates. We also have two outstanding interest rate swaps used to hedge the cash flow on floating rate mortgages of two majority owned hotels with a combined notional balance of $47 million as of December 31, 2001. The fair value of these derivatives is based on the present value of future estimated cash flow.

INCOME TAXES

The provisions for income taxes for the three years ended December 31 are as follows:

(in millions)	1999	2000	2001
Current			
Federal	$ 98	169	83
State, foreign and local	34	33	34
	132	202	117
Deferred	(2)	(2)	(40)
Total	**$130**	**200**	**77**

During 1999, 2000 and 2001, we paid income taxes of $141 million, $138 million and $150 million, respectively.

The income tax effects of temporary differences between financial and income tax reporting that gave rise to deferred income tax assets and liabilities at December 31, 2000 and 2001 are as follows:

(in millions)	2000	2001
Deferred tax assets		
Compensation	$ 77	88
Deferred income	15	30
Insurance	19	34
Business combination expense	11	5
Foreign taxes	5	2
Franchise system funds	4	4
Reserves	3	7
NOL carry forwards, expiring 2005 to 2008	2	2
Capital loss carry forward, expiring 2006	-	47
Other	10	-
	146	219
Valuation allowance	(3)	(51)
	143	168
Deferred tax liabilities		
Basis difference	(299)	(243)
Property	(169)	(213)
Investments	(118)	(123)
Brand value	(415)	(390)
Other	-	(9)
	(1,001)	(978)
Net deferred tax liability	**$ (858)**	**(810)**

The reconciliations of the Federal income tax rate to our effective tax rate for the three years ended December 31 are as follows:

	1999	2000	2001
Federal income tax rate	35.0%	35.0	35.0
Increase (reduction) in taxes			
State and local income taxes, net of Federal tax benefits	4.7	4.2	3.9
Foreign taxes, net	3.7	2.3	3.1
Goodwill	.3	2.4	4.7
Federal income tax credits	(3.4)	(2.7)	(4.4)
Disposition of Red Lion Hotels, Inc. stock	-	-	(13.4)
Other	1.2	.6	1.9
Effective tax rate	41.5%	41.8	30.8

Our tax provision, deferred taxes and effective rate in 2001 were impacted by the sale of the Red Lion Hotels, Inc. capital stock on December 31, 2001. The sale resulted in a large capital loss for tax purposes. A portion of the capital loss was carried back to offset capital gains recorded in prior years, resulting in a reduction of the tax provision and effective tax rate in 2001. Excluding the impact of the Red Lion sale, our effective tax rate in 2001 was 42.5 percent. The portion of the tax loss available to offset future capital gains is recorded as a deferred tax asset and has been fully reserved. The increase in the deferred tax asset valuation allowance at December 31, 2001 reflects this reserve.

STOCKHOLDERS' EQUITY

Five hundred million shares of common stock with a par value of $2.50 per share are authorized, of which 379 million were issued at December 31, 2000 and 2001, including treasury shares of ten million in 2000 and 2001. We have 25 million shares of preferred stock with a par value of $1.00 per share authorized for issuance. No preferred shares were issued or outstanding at December 31, 2000 and 2001.

To reflect the spin-off of Park Place, the book value of net assets of our discontinued gaming operations as of December 31, 1998 was charged against our retained earnings and additional paid-in capital. During 1999 and 2000, spin-off adjustments totaling $4 million and $8 million, respectively, were recorded through retained earnings.

Our Board of Directors has approved the repurchase of up to 20 million shares of our common stock pursuant to a stock repurchase program. The timing of stock purchases are made at the discretion of management. There were no shares repurchased during 2000 and 2001. As of December 31, 2001, 9.3 million shares are authorized for repurchase.

We have a Preferred Share Purchase Rights Plan under which a right is attached to each share of our common stock. The rights may only become exercisable under certain circumstances involving actual or potential acquisitions of 20% or more of our common stock by certain people or groups. Depending on the circumstances, if the rights become exercisable, the holder may be entitled to purchase units of our junior participating preferred stock, shares of our common stock or shares of common stock of the acquiror. The rights remain in existence until November 2009 unless they are terminated, exercised or redeemed.

STOCK PLANS

At December 31, 2001, 57 million shares of common stock were reserved for the exercise of options under our stock incentive plans. Options may be granted to salaried officers, directors and other key employees to purchase our common stock at not less than the fair market value at the date of grant. Generally, options may be exercised in installments commencing one year after the date of grant. The stock incentive plans also permit the granting of Stock Appreciation Rights (SARs). No SARs have been granted as of December 31, 2001.

A summary of the status of our stock option plans as of December 31, 1999, 2000 and 2001, and changes during the years ending on those dates is presented below:

	Options Price Range (per share)	Weighted Average Price (per share)	Options Outstanding	Available for Grant
Balance at December 31, 1998	$ 4.68 – 27.53	$15.25	20,693,770	12,416,446
Granted	10.84 – 15.31	14.84	3,157,400	(3,157,400)
Exercised	4.72 – 16.59	9.35	(270,276)	-
Cancelled	10.48 – 21.30	16.39	(823,152)	823,152
Balance at December 31, 1999	4.68 – 27.53	15.22	22,757,742	10,082,198
Authorized			-	25,000,000
Granted	6.66 – 15.28	9.20	7,765,000	(7,765,000)
Exercised	4.68 – 10.48	5.29	(207,400)	-
Cancelled	7.78 – 20.66	14.92	(2,032,325)	1,738,259
Balance at December 31, 2000	4.68 – 27.53	13.66	28,283,017	29,055,457
Granted	10.64 – 12.22	12.20	5,986,300	(5,986,300)
Exercised	4.68 – 11.08	9.52	(335,206)	-
Cancelled	6.66 – 20.56	13.66	(1,402,975)	1,218,437
Balance at December 31, 2001	$ 6.66 – 27.53	$13.44	32,531,136	24,287,594

The following table summarizes information about stock options outstanding at December 31, 2001:

	Options Outstanding			Options Exercisable	
Exercise Price	Number Outstanding	Weighted Average Remaining Contractual Life	Weighted Average Exercise Price	Number Exercisable	Weighted Average Exercise Price
$ 6.66 – 11.63	8,097,276	7.1	$ 9.37	3,062,376	$ 9.64
11.88 – 12.22	11,640,800	6.2	12.05	6,000,000	11.88
12.51 – 16.59	8,758,922	6.3	14.53	6,657,584	14.62
16.65 – 27.53	4,034,138	6.4	23.26	1,648,731	18.93
$ 6.66 – 27.53	32,531,136	6.5	$13.44	17,368,691	$13.20

We apply Accounting Principles Board Opinion No. 25 and related interpretations in accounting for our stock-based compensation plans. Accordingly, compensation expense recognized was different than what would have otherwise been recognized under the fair value based method defined in FAS 123, "Accounting for Stock-Based Compensation." Had compensation expense for our stock-based compensation plans been determined based on the fair value at the grant dates for awards under those plans consistent with the method of FAS 123, our net income and net income per share would have been reduced to the pro forma amounts indicated below:

(in millions, except per share amounts)	1999	2000	2001
Income before cumulative effect of accounting change	$169	255	150
Cumulative effect of accounting change	(2)	-	-
Net income	$167	255	150
Basic EPS			
Income before cumulative effect of accounting change	$.63	.69	.41
Cumulative effect of accounting change	(.01)	-	-
Net income	$ .62	.69	.41
Diluted EPS			
Income before cumulative effect of accounting change	$ .63	.69	.41
Cumulative effect of accounting change	(.01)	-	-
Net income	$ .62	.69	.41

The fair value of each option grant is estimated on the date of grant using the Black-Scholes option-pricing model with the following weighted-average assumptions used for grants in 1999, 2000 and 2001, respectively: dividend yield of one percent for each of the three years; expected volatility of 31, 40 and 48 percent; risk-free interest rates of 4.8, 6.0 and 5.2 percent and expected lives of seven years for 1999 and 2000, and six years for 2001.

We also have an Employee Stock Purchase Plan by which we are authorized to issue up to two million shares of common stock to our full-time employees. Under the terms of the Plan, employees can elect to have a percentage of their earnings withheld to purchase our common stock.

EMPLOYEE BENEFIT PLANS

We have various employee investment plans whereby we contribute certain percentages of employee contributions. The aggregate expense under these plans totaled $6 million, $10 million and $10 million in 1999, 2000 and 2001, respectively.

We have provided supplemental retirement benefits to eligible senior executives in the form of fixed stock units that settle for shares of our common stock on a one-for-one basis. The compensation expense associated with the benefits is expensed over a four year vesting period. The aggregate expense under these plans totaled $6 million and $8 million in 2000 and 2001, respectively; no such benefits were provided in 1999.

A significant number of our employees are covered by union sponsored, collectively bargained multi-employer pension plans. We contributed and charged to expense $13 million, $14 million and $18 million in 1999, 2000 and 2001, respectively, for such plans. Information from the plans' administrators is not sufficient to permit us to determine our share, if any, of unfunded vested benefits.

We apply Accounting Principles Board Opinion No. 25 and related interpretations in accounting for our stock-based compensation plans. Accordingly, compensation expense recognized was different than what would have otherwise been recognized under the fair value based method defined in FAS 123, "Accounting for Stock-Based Compensation." Had compensation expense for our stock-based compensation plans been determined based on the fair value at the grant dates for awards under those plans consistent with the method of FAS 123, our net income and net income per share would have been reduced to the pro forma amounts indicated below:

(in millions, except per share amounts)	1999	2000	2001
Income before cumulative effect of accounting change	$169	255	150
Cumulative effect of accounting change	(2)	-	-
Net income	$167	255	150
Basic EPS			
Income before cumulative effect of accounting change	$.63	.69	.41
Cumulative effect of accounting change	(.01)	-	-
Net income	$ .62	.69	.41
Diluted EPS			
Income before cumulative effect of accounting change	$ .63	.69	.41
Cumulative effect of accounting change	(.01)	-	-
Net income	$ .62	.69	.41

The fair value of each option grant is estimated on the date of grant using the Black-Scholes option-pricing model with the following weighted-average assumptions used for grants in 1999, 2000 and 2001, respectively: dividend yield of one percent for each of the three years; expected volatility of 31, 40 and 48 percent; risk-free interest rates of 4.8, 6.0 and 5.2 percent and expected lives of seven years for 1999 and 2000, and six years for 2001.

We also have an Employee Stock Purchase Plan by which we are authorized to issue up to two million shares of common stock to our full-time employees. Under the terms of the Plan, employees can elect to have a percentage of their earnings withheld to purchase our common stock.

EMPLOYEE BENEFIT PLANS

We have various employee investment plans whereby we contribute certain percentages of employee contributions. The aggregate expense under these plans totaled $6 million, $10 million and $10 million in 1999, 2000 and 2001, respectively.

We have provided supplemental retirement benefits to eligible senior executives in the form of fixed stock units that settle for shares of our common stock on a one-for-one basis. The compensation expense associated with the benefits is expensed over a four year vesting period. The aggregate expense under these plans totaled $6 million and $8 million in 2000 and 2001, respectively; no such benefits were provided in 1999.

A significant number of our employees are covered by union sponsored, collectively bargained multi-employer pension plans. We contributed and charged to expense $13 million, $14 million and $18 million in 1999, 2000 and 2001, respectively, for such plans. Information from the plans' administrators is not sufficient to permit us to determine our share, if any, of unfunded vested benefits.

Segment results for the three years ended December 31 are as follows:

(in millions)	1999	2000	2001
Revenue			
Hotel Ownership	$1,886	2,930	2,388
Managing and Franchising	120	350	342
Timeshare	144	171	320
Total revenue	$2,150	3,451	3,050
Operating Income			
Hotel Ownership	$ 474	716	470
Managing and Franchising	113	302	290
Timeshare	22	30	86
Corporate and other unallocated expenses	(114)	(218)	(214)
Total operating income	$ 495	830	632

Segment assets as of December 31 are as follows:

(in millions)	2000	2001
Assets		
Hotel Ownership	$4,925	4,542
Managing and Franchising	680	668
Timeshare	315	333
Corporate and other	3,220	3,242
Total assets	$9,140	8,785

COMMITMENTS AND CONTINGENCIES

We have established franchise financing programs with third party lenders to support the growth of our Hilton Garden Inn, Homewood Suites by Hilton, Hampton and Embassy Suites hotels. As of December 31, 2001, we have provided guarantees of $48 million on loans outstanding under the programs. As part of an agreement made by a Promus subsidiary prior to our acquisition of Promus, we provide credit support for a loan facility utilized by Candlewood Hotel Company to provide construction and permanent financing to Candlewood and its franchisees. At December 31, 2001, we have guaranteed $18 million of such financing, which represents our maximum exposure under the credit support agreement. In addition, we have guaranteed $66 million of debt and other obligations of unconsolidated affiliates and third parties, bringing our total guarantees to $132 million. We also have commitments under letters of credit totaling $25 million as of December 31, 2001. We believe it is unlikely that significant payments will be required under these agreements.

In addition, we remain a guarantor on the 12 operating leases sold to WestCoast Hospitality Corporation as part of the Red Lion sale on December 31, 2001. However, we have entered into an indemnification and reimbursement agreement with WestCoast, which requires WestCoast to reimburse us for any costs and expenses incurred in connection with the guarantee. The minimum lease commitment under these 12 operating leases totals approximately $5 million annually through 2020.

Under limited circumstances, we may be obligated to provide additional guarantees or letters of credit totaling $61 million.

At December 31, 2001, we had contractual commitments for construction and renovation projects of approximately $49 million.

Various lawsuits are pending against us. In our opinion, resolution of these lawsuits is not expected to have a material effect on our financial position or results of operations.

Report of Independent Public Accountants

TO THE BOARD OF DIRECTORS AND STOCKHOLDERS OF HILTON HOTELS CORPORATION:

We have audited the accompanying consolidated balance sheets of Hilton Hotels Corporation (a Delaware corporation) and subsidiaries as of December 31, 2000 and 2001, and the related consolidated statements of income, stockholders' equity and cash flow for each of the three years in the period ended December 31, 2001. These financial statements are the responsibility of the Company's management. Our responsibility is to express an opinion on these financial statements based on our audits.

We conducted our audits in accordance with auditing standards generally accepted in the United States. Those standards require that we plan and perform the audit to obtain reasonable assurance about whether the financial statements are free of material misstatement. An audit includes examining, on a test basis, evidence supporting the amounts and disclosures in the financial statements. An audit also includes assessing the accounting principles used and significant estimates made by management, as well as evaluating the overall financial statement presentation. We believe that our audits provide a reasonable basis for our opinion.

In our opinion, the financial statements referred to above present fairly, in all material respects, the financial position of Hilton Hotels Corporation and subsidiaries as of December 31, 2000 and 2001 and the results of their operations and their cash flow for each of the three years in the period ended December 31, 2001, in conformity with accounting principles generally accepted in the United States.

Arthur Andersen LLP

Arthur Andersen LLP
Los Angeles, California
January 29, 2002

PHOTO CREDITS

Chapter 1
Opener: Courtesy Hospitality Archives, Conrad N. Hilton Collection, University of Houston. Page 5: Photo courtesy Morgan Geddie. Page 6: Photo by Michael Scott, Michael Scott Studios www.michaelscottstudios.com. Pages 7, 10, and 23: Courtesy PhotoDisc, Inc. Page 13: Courtesy the Hilton Hotels Corporation.

Chapter 2
Opener and page 44: Photo by Michael Scott, Michael Scott Studios www.michaelscottstudios.com. Pages 37 and 43: Courtesy Corbis Digital Stock. Page 53: Courtesy Hospitality Archives, Conrad N. Hilton Collection, University of Houston. Page 55: Courtesy PhotoDisc, Inc.

Chapter 3
Opener: Courtesy the Hilton Hotels Corporation. Pages 80 and 95: Courtesy Corbis Digital Stock. Page 83: Courtesy Imagestate. Page 86: Courtesy Artville/Getty Images. Page 88: Courtesy PhotoDisc, Inc.

Chapter 4
Opener: Courtesy PhotoDisc, Inc. Pages 122 and 127: Photo by Michael Scott, Michael Scott Studios www.michaelscottstudios.com.

Chapter 5
Opener and page 154: Courtesy PhotoDisc, Inc. Page 147: Photo by Michael Scott, Michael Scott Studios www.michaelscottstudios.com.

Chapter 6
Opener: Photo by Michael Scott, Michael Scott Studios www.michaelscottstudios.com. Page 178: Courtesy Corbis Digital Stock.

Chapter 7
Opener: Courtesy Artville, Inc. Page 202: Courtesy Corbis Digital Stock.

Chapter 8
Opener and page 236: Courtesy PhotoDisc, Inc.

Chapter 9
Opener: Photo by Michael Scott, Michael Scott Studios www.michaelscottstudios.com. Page 275: Courtesy Corbis Digital Stock.

Chapter 10
Opener and pages 302, 326, and 336: Photo by Michael Scott, Michael Scott Studios www.michaelscottstudios.com. Page 318: The Quaker name and logo are registered trademarks of The Quaker Oats Company; used with permission. Page 323: Courtesy Artville/Getty Images. Page 338: Courtesy Corbis Digital Stock.

Chapter 11
Opener and pages 354 and 359: Photo by Michael Scott, Michael Scott Studios www.michaelscottstudios.com. Page 370: Courtesy Artville/Getty Images.

Chapter 12
Opener: Courtesy PhotoDisc, Inc. Page 389: Photo by Michael Scott, Michael Scott Studios www.michaelscottstudios.com. Page 405: Courtesy Grand Met.

Chapter 13
Opener: Courtesy PhotoDisc, Inc. Page 424: Photo by Michael Scott, Michael Scott Studios www.michaelscottstudios.com. Page 427: Courtesy IMS Communications Ltd. Page 429: Courtesy Corbis Digital Stock.

INDEX